STRANGERS IN PARADISE

POCKET BOOK COLLECTION

art and story by

TERRY MOORE

6

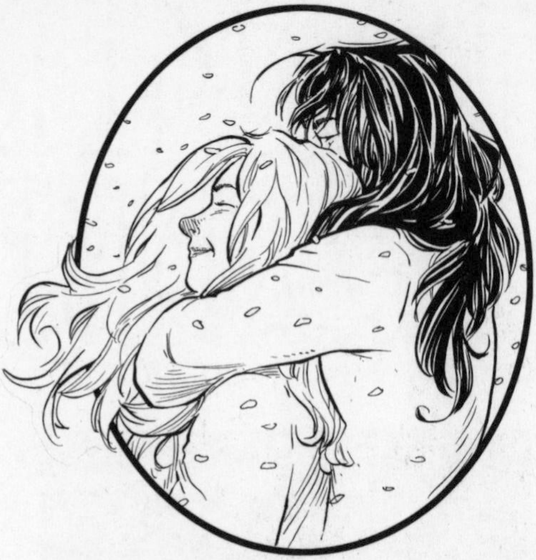

This book collects the complete works of
Strangers in Paradise Volume III, issues #77-90

publisher • Robyn Moore

colorist • Brian Miller

www.strangersinparadise.com

Published by
Abstract Studio, Inc.
P. O. Box 271487
Houston, TX 77277

ISBN: 978-1-892597-39-7

Second Printing.

Printed in Canada

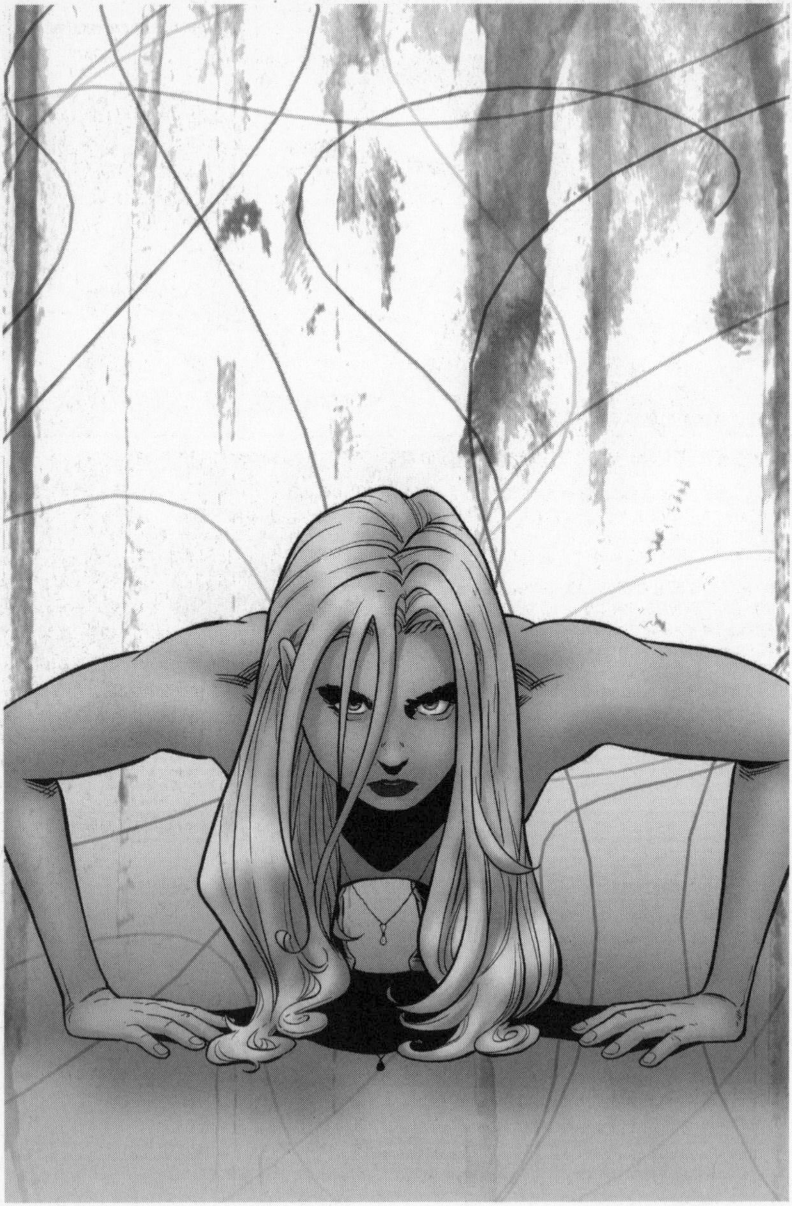

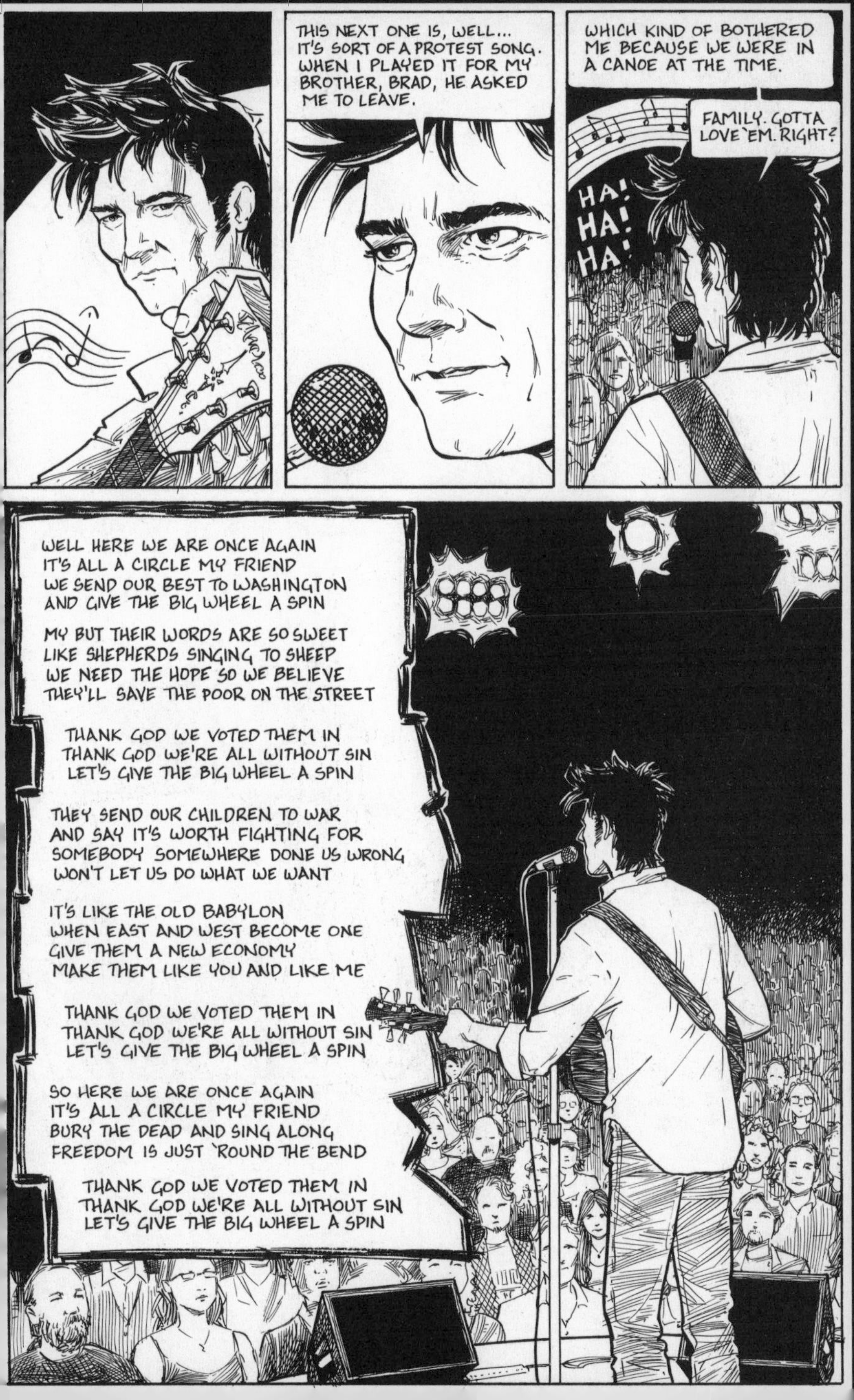
THIS NEXT ONE IS, WELL... IT'S SORT OF A PROTEST SONG. WHEN I PLAYED IT FOR MY BROTHER, BRAD, HE ASKED ME TO LEAVE.
WHICH KIND OF BOTHERED ME BECAUSE WE WERE IN A CANOE AT THE TIME.
FAMILY. GOTTA LOVE 'EM. RIGHT?
HA! HA! HA!
WELL HERE WE ARE ONCE AGAIN
IT'S ALL A CIRCLE MY FRIEND
WE SEND OUR BEST TO WASHINGTON
AND GIVE THE BIG WHEEL A SPIN
MY BUT THEIR WORDS ARE SO SWEET
LIKE SHEPHERDS SINGING TO SHEEP
WE NEED THE HOPE SO WE BELIEVE
THEY'LL SAVE THE POOR ON THE STREET
THANK GOD WE VOTED THEM IN
THANK GOD WE'RE ALL WITHOUT SIN
LET'S GIVE THE BIG WHEEL A SPIN
THEY SEND OUR CHILDREN TO WAR
AND SAY IT'S WORTH FIGHTING FOR
SOMEBODY SOMEWHERE DONE US WRONG
WON'T LET US DO WHAT WE WANT
IT'S LIKE THE OLD BABYLON
WHEN EAST AND WEST BECOME ONE
GIVE THEM A NEW ECONOMY
MAKE THEM LIKE YOU AND LIKE ME
THANK GOD WE VOTED THEM IN
THANK GOD WE'RE ALL WITHOUT SIN
LET'S GIVE THE BIG WHEEL A SPIN
SO HERE WE ARE ONCE AGAIN
IT'S ALL A CIRCLE MY FRIEND
BURY THE DEAD AND SING ALONG
FREEDOM IS JUST 'ROUND THE BEND
THANK GOD WE VOTED THEM IN
THANK GOD WE'RE ALL WITHOUT SIN
LET'S GIVE THE BIG WHEEL A SPIN

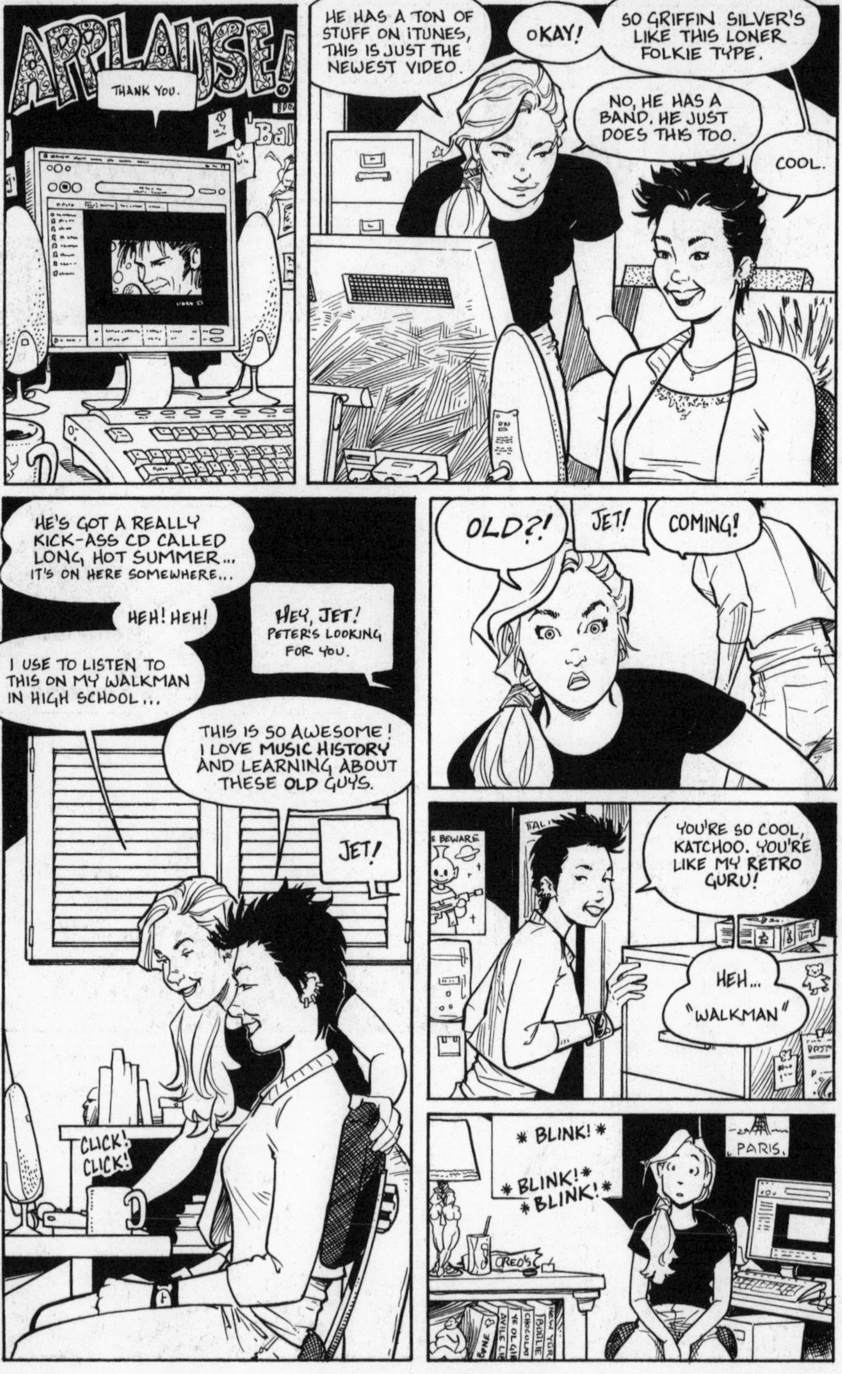
APPLAUSE!
THANK YOU.
HE HAS A TON OF STUFF ON iTUNES, THIS IS JUST THE NEWEST VIDEO.
OKAY!
SO GRIFFIN SILVER'S LIKE THIS LONER FOLKIE TYPE.
NO, HE HAS A BAND. HE JUST DOES THIS TOO.
COOL.
HE'S GOT A REALLY KICK-ASS CD CALLED LONG HOT SUMMER... IT'S ON HERE SOMEWHERE...
HEH! HEH!
I USE TO LISTEN TO THIS ON MY WALKMAN IN HIGH SCHOOL...
HEY, JET! PETER'S LOOKING FOR YOU.
THIS IS SO AWESOME! I LOVE MUSIC HISTORY AND LEARNING ABOUT THESE OLD GUYS.
JET!
CLICK! CLICK!
OLD?!
JET!
COMING!
YOU'RE SO COOL, KATCHOO. YOU'RE LIKE MY RETRO GURU!
HEH... "WALKMAN"
* BLINK! *
* BLINK! *
* BLINK! *
PARIS.

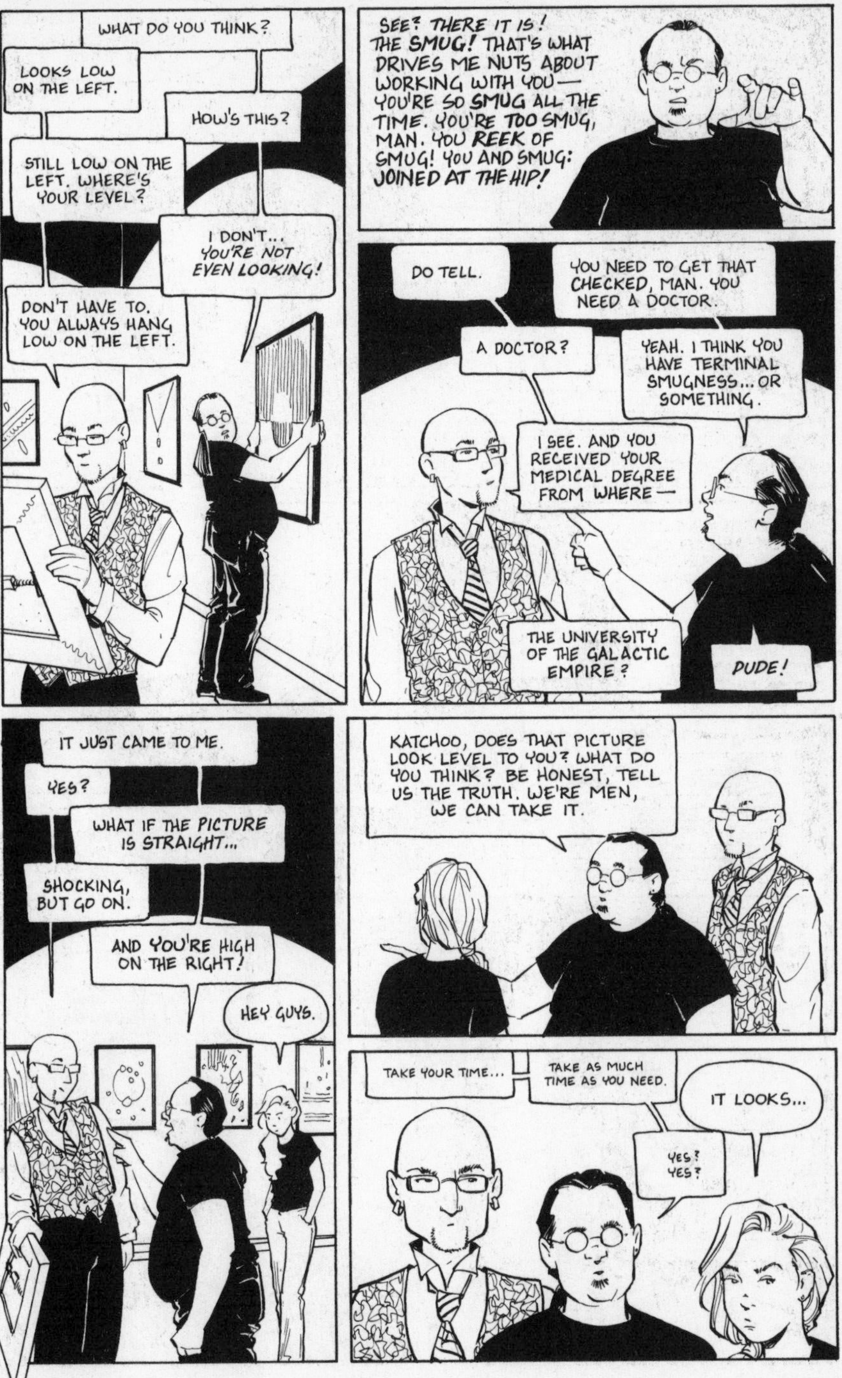
WHAT DO YOU THINK?
LOOKS LOW ON THE LEFT.
HOW'S THIS?
STILL LOW ON THE LEFT. WHERE'S YOUR LEVEL?
I DON'T... YOU'RE NOT EVEN LOOKING!
DON'T HAVE TO. YOU ALWAYS HANG LOW ON THE LEFT.
SEE? THERE IT IS! THE SMUG! THAT'S WHAT DRIVES ME NUTS ABOUT WORKING WITH YOU— YOU'RE SO SMUG ALL THE TIME. YOU'RE TOO SMUG, MAN. YOU REEK OF SMUG! YOU AND SMUG: JOINED AT THE HIP!
DO TELL.
YOU NEED TO GET THAT CHECKED, MAN. YOU NEED A DOCTOR.
A DOCTOR?
YEAH. I THINK YOU HAVE TERMINAL SMUGNESS... OR SOMETHING.
I SEE. AND YOU RECEIVED YOUR MEDICAL DEGREE FROM WHERE—
THE UNIVERSITY OF THE GALACTIC EMPIRE?
DUDE!
IT JUST CAME TO ME.
YES?
WHAT IF THE PICTURE IS STRAIGHT...
SHOCKING, BUT GO ON.
AND YOU'RE HIGH ON THE RIGHT!
HEY GUYS.
KATCHOO, DOES THAT PICTURE LOOK LEVEL TO YOU? WHAT DO YOU THINK? BE HONEST, TELL US THE TRUTH. WE'RE MEN, WE CAN TAKE IT.
TAKE YOUR TIME...
TAKE AS MUCH TIME AS YOU NEED.
IT LOOKS...
YES? YES?

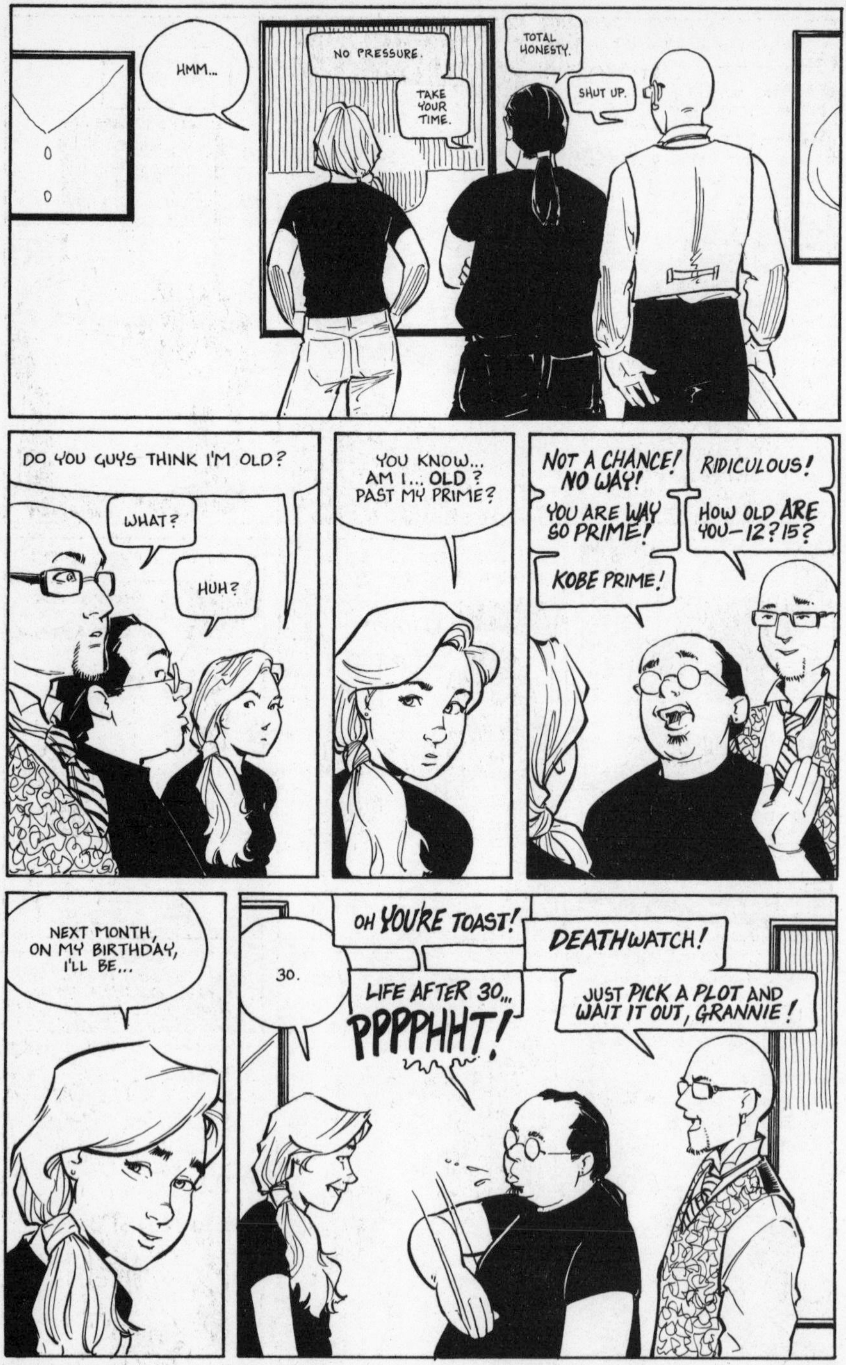
HMM...
NO PRESSURE.
TAKE YOUR TIME.
TOTAL HONESTY.
SHUT UP.
DO YOU GUYS THINK I'M OLD?
WHAT?
HUH?
YOU KNOW... AM I... OLD? PAST MY PRIME?
NOT A CHANCE! NO WAY!
YOU ARE WAY SO PRIME!
KOBE PRIME!
RIDICULOUS!
HOW OLD ARE YOU—12? 15?
NEXT MONTH, ON MY BIRTHDAY, I'LL BE...
30.
OH YOU'RE TOAST!
DEATHWATCH!
LIFE AFTER 30... PPPPHHT!
JUST PICK A PLOT AND WAIT IT OUT, GRANNIE!

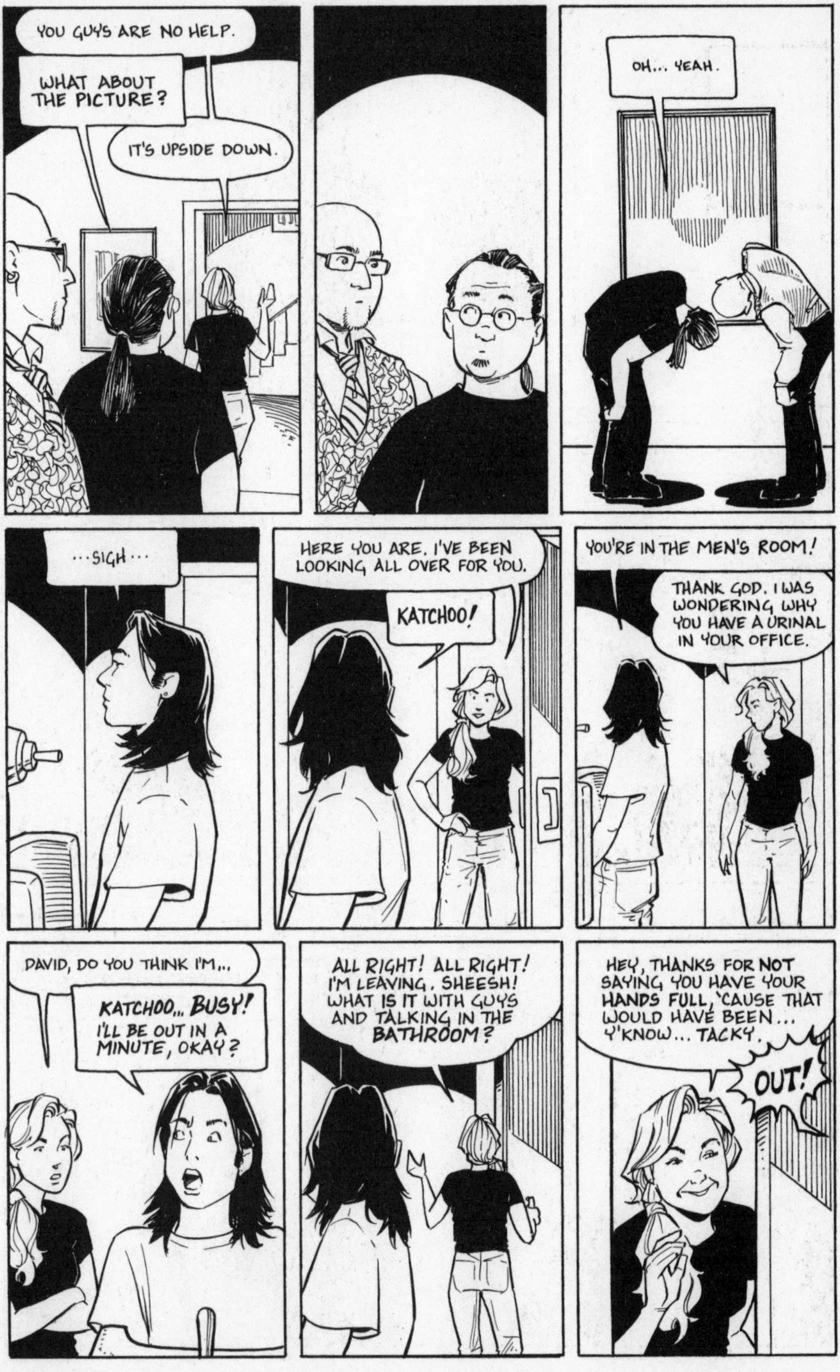
YOU GUYS ARE NO HELP.
WHAT ABOUT THE PICTURE?
IT'S UPSIDE DOWN.
OH... YEAH.
...SIGH...
HERE YOU ARE. I'VE BEEN LOOKING ALL OVER FOR YOU.
KATCHOO!
YOU'RE IN THE MEN'S ROOM!
THANK GOD. I WAS WONDERING WHY YOU HAVE A URINAL IN YOUR OFFICE.
DAVID, DO YOU THINK I'M...
KATCHOO... BUSY! I'LL BE OUT IN A MINUTE, OKAY?
ALL RIGHT! ALL RIGHT! I'M LEAVING. SHEESH! WHAT IS IT WITH GUYS AND TALKING IN THE BATHROOM?
HEY, THANKS FOR NOT SAYING YOU HAVE YOUR HANDS FULL, 'CAUSE THAT WOULD HAVE BEEN... Y'KNOW... TACKY.
OUT!

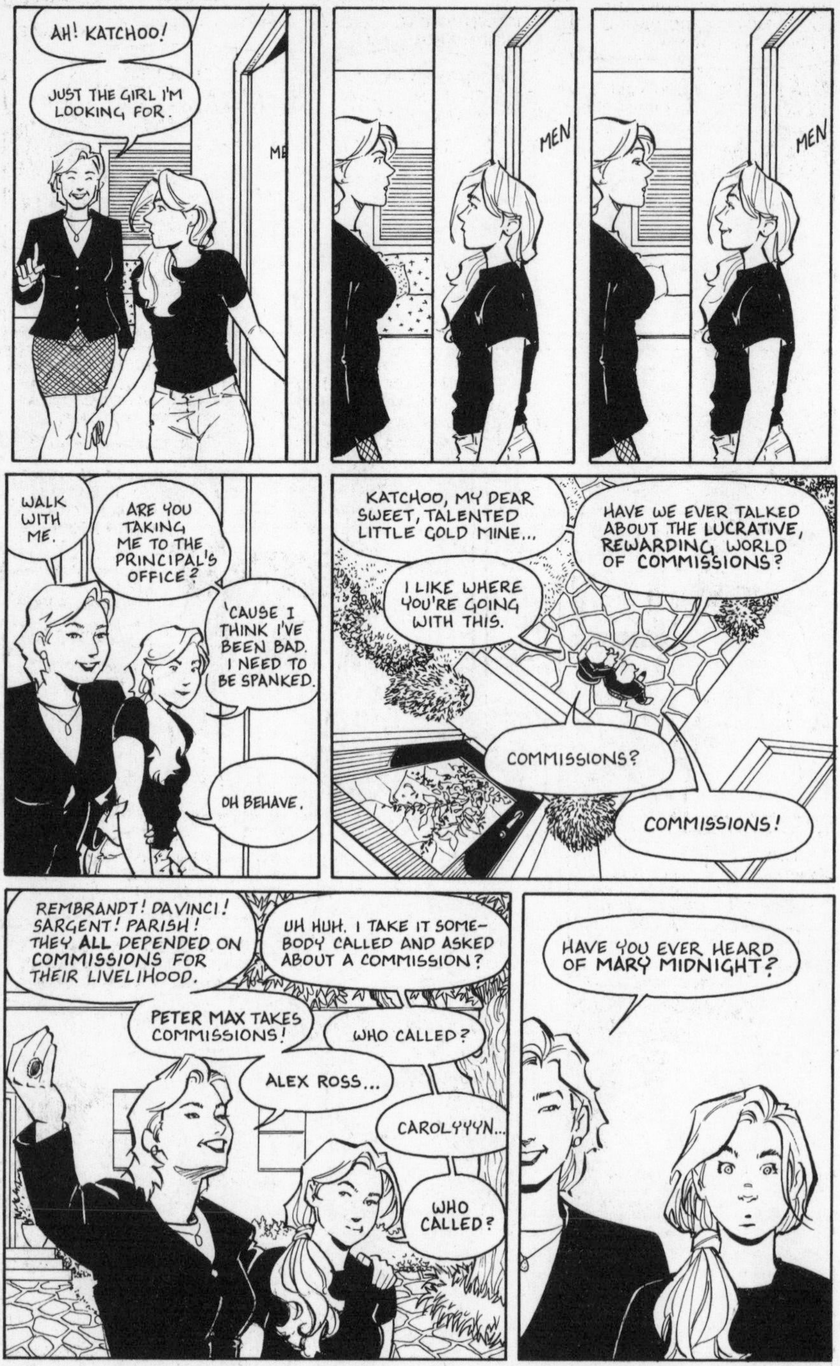
AH! KATCHOO!
JUST THE GIRL I'M LOOKING FOR.
MEN
MEN
WALK WITH ME.
ARE YOU TAKING ME TO THE PRINCIPAL'S OFFICE?
'CAUSE I THINK I'VE BEEN BAD. I NEED TO BE SPANKED.
OH BEHAVE.
KATCHOO, MY DEAR SWEET, TALENTED LITTLE GOLD MINE...
HAVE WE EVER TALKED ABOUT THE LUCRATIVE, REWARDING WORLD OF COMMISSIONS?
I LIKE WHERE YOU'RE GOING WITH THIS.
COMMISSIONS?
COMMISSIONS!
REMBRANDT! DAVINCI! SARGENT! PARISH! THEY ALL DEPENDED ON COMMISSIONS FOR THEIR LIVELIHOOD.
UH HUH. I TAKE IT SOMEBODY CALLED AND ASKED ABOUT A COMMISSION?
PETER MAX TAKES COMMISSIONS!
WHO CALLED?
ALEX ROSS...
CAROLYYYN...
WHO CALLED?
HAVE YOU EVER HEARD OF MARY MIDNIGHT?

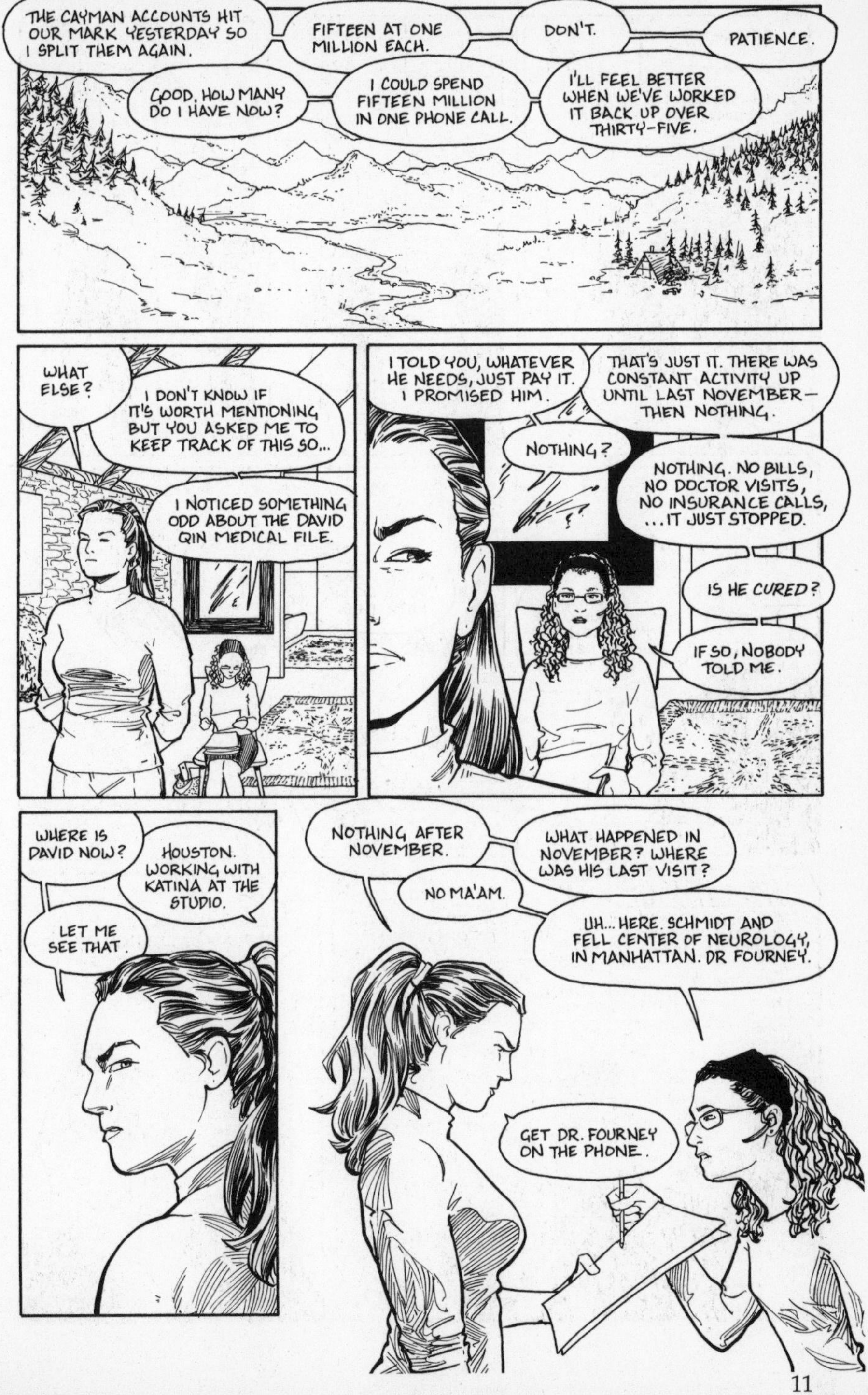
THE CAYMAN ACCOUNTS HIT OUR MARK YESTERDAY SO I SPLIT THEM AGAIN.
GOOD, HOW MANY DO I HAVE NOW?
FIFTEEN AT ONE MILLION EACH.
I COULD SPEND FIFTEEN MILLION IN ONE PHONE CALL.
DON'T.
I'LL FEEL BETTER WHEN WE'VE WORKED IT BACK UP OVER THIRTY-FIVE.
PATIENCE.
WHAT ELSE?
I DON'T KNOW IF IT'S WORTH MENTIONING BUT YOU ASKED ME TO KEEP TRACK OF THIS SO...
I NOTICED SOMETHING ODD ABOUT THE DAVID QIN MEDICAL FILE.
I TOLD YOU, WHATEVER HE NEEDS, JUST PAY IT. I PROMISED HIM.
THAT'S JUST IT. THERE WAS CONSTANT ACTIVITY UP UNTIL LAST NOVEMBER— THEN NOTHING.
NOTHING?
NOTHING. NO BILLS, NO DOCTOR VISITS, NO INSURANCE CALLS, ...IT JUST STOPPED.
IS HE CURED?
IF SO, NOBODY TOLD ME.
WHERE IS DAVID NOW?
HOUSTON. WORKING WITH KATINA AT THE STUDIO.
LET ME SEE THAT.
NOTHING AFTER NOVEMBER.
NO MA'AM.
WHAT HAPPENED IN NOVEMBER? WHERE WAS HIS LAST VISIT?
UH... HERE. SCHMIDT AND FELL CENTER OF NEUROLOGY, IN MANHATTAN. DR FOURNEY.
GET DR. FOURNEY ON THE PHONE.

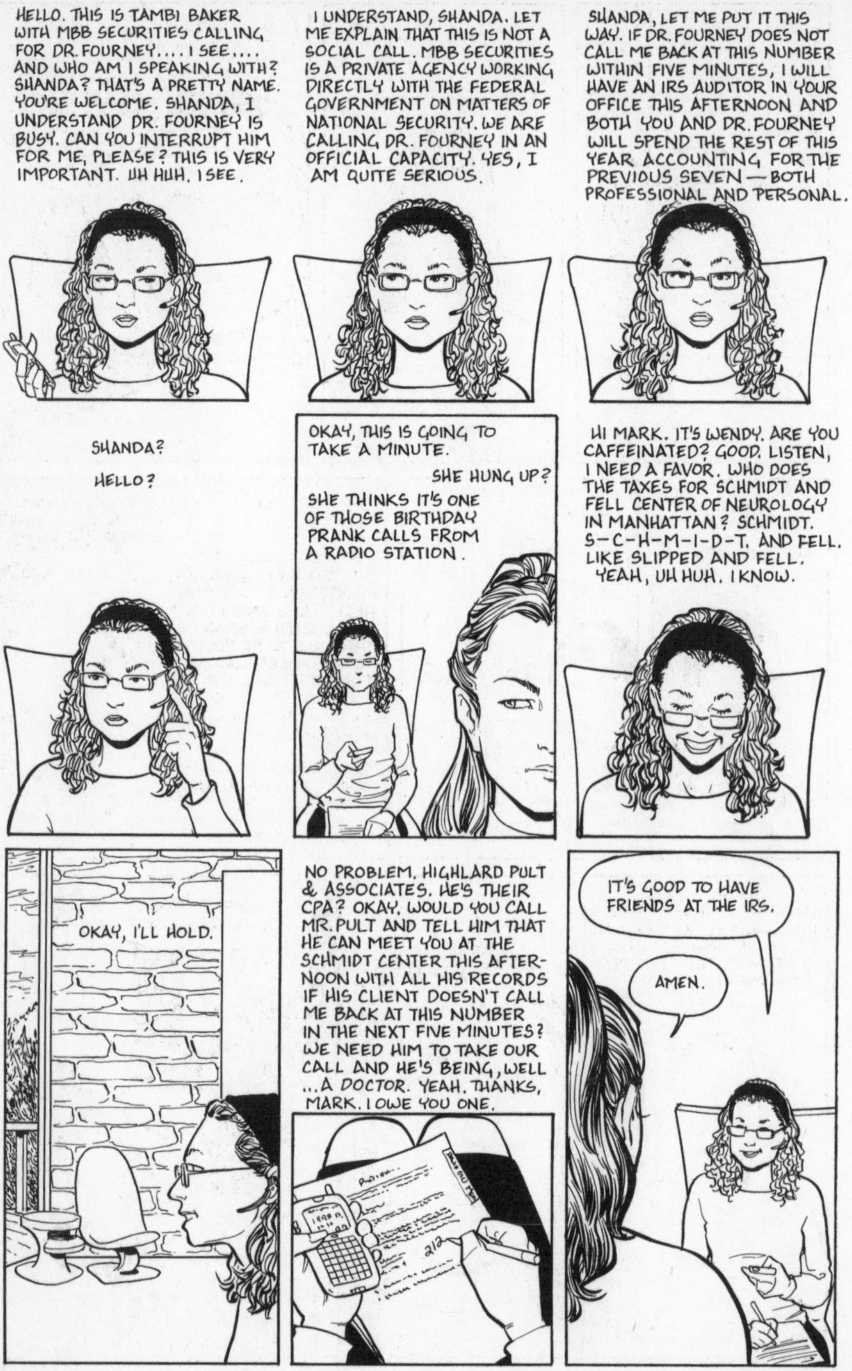
HELLO. THIS IS TAMBI BAKER WITH MBB SECURITIES CALLING FOR DR. FOURNEY.... I SEE.... AND WHO AM I SPEAKING WITH? SHANDA? THAT'S A PRETTY NAME. YOU'RE WELCOME. SHANDA, I UNDERSTAND DR. FOURNEY IS BUSY. CAN YOU INTERRUPT HIM FOR ME, PLEASE? THIS IS VERY IMPORTANT. UH HUH. I SEE.
I UNDERSTAND, SHANDA. LET ME EXPLAIN THAT THIS IS NOT A SOCIAL CALL. MBB SECURITIES IS A PRIVATE AGENCY WORKING DIRECTLY WITH THE FEDERAL GOVERNMENT ON MATTERS OF NATIONAL SECURITY. WE ARE CALLING DR. FOURNEY IN AN OFFICIAL CAPACITY. YES, I AM QUITE SERIOUS.
SHANDA, LET ME PUT IT THIS WAY. IF DR. FOURNEY DOES NOT CALL ME BACK AT THIS NUMBER WITHIN FIVE MINUTES, I WILL HAVE AN IRS AUDITOR IN YOUR OFFICE THIS AFTERNOON AND BOTH YOU AND DR. FOURNEY WILL SPEND THE REST OF THIS YEAR ACCOUNTING FOR THE PREVIOUS SEVEN — BOTH PROFESSIONAL AND PERSONAL.
SHANDA?
HELLO?
OKAY, THIS IS GOING TO TAKE A MINUTE.
SHE HUNG UP?
SHE THINKS IT'S ONE OF THOSE BIRTHDAY PRANK CALLS FROM A RADIO STATION.
HI MARK. IT'S WENDY. ARE YOU CAFFEINATED? GOOD. LISTEN, I NEED A FAVOR. WHO DOES THE TAXES FOR SCHMIDT AND FELL CENTER OF NEUROLOGY IN MANHATTAN? SCHMIDT. S-C-H-M-I-D-T. AND FELL. LIKE SLIPPED AND FELL. YEAH, UH HUH. I KNOW.
OKAY, I'LL HOLD.
NO PROBLEM. HIGHLARD PULT & ASSOCIATES. HE'S THEIR CPA? OKAY. WOULD YOU CALL MR. PULT AND TELL HIM THAT HE CAN MEET YOU AT THE SCHMIDT CENTER THIS AFTERNOON WITH ALL HIS RECORDS IF HIS CLIENT DOESN'T CALL ME BACK AT THIS NUMBER IN THE NEXT FIVE MINUTES? WE NEED HIM TO TAKE OUR CALL AND HE'S BEING, WELL ...A *DOCTOR*. YEAH. THANKS, MARK. I OWE YOU ONE.
212
IT'S GOOD TO HAVE FRIENDS AT THE IRS.
AMEN.

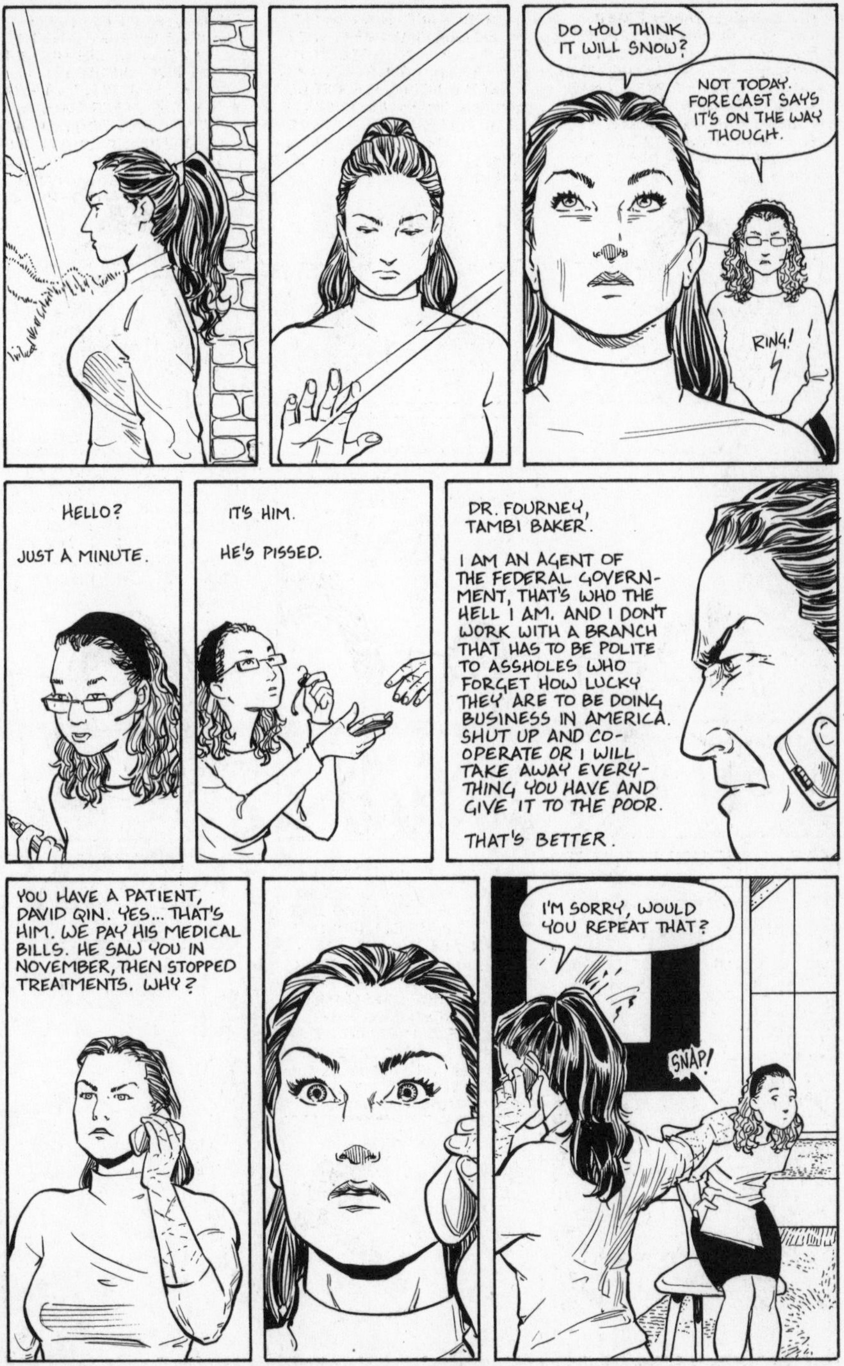
DO YOU THINK IT WILL SNOW?
NOT TODAY. FORECAST SAYS IT'S ON THE WAY THOUGH.
RING!
HELLO?
JUST A MINUTE.
IT'S HIM.
HE'S PISSED.
DR. FOURNEY, TAMBI BAKER.
I AM AN AGENT OF THE FEDERAL GOVERNMENT, THAT'S WHO THE HELL I AM. AND I DON'T WORK WITH A BRANCH THAT HAS TO BE POLITE TO ASSHOLES WHO FORGET HOW LUCKY THEY ARE TO BE DOING BUSINESS IN AMERICA. SHUT UP AND CO-OPERATE OR I WILL TAKE AWAY EVERYTHING YOU HAVE AND GIVE IT TO THE POOR.
THAT'S BETTER.
YOU HAVE A PATIENT, DAVID QIN. YES... THAT'S HIM. WE PAY HIS MEDICAL BILLS. HE SAW YOU IN NOVEMBER, THEN STOPPED TREATMENTS. WHY?
I'M SORRY, WOULD YOU REPEAT THAT?
SNAP!

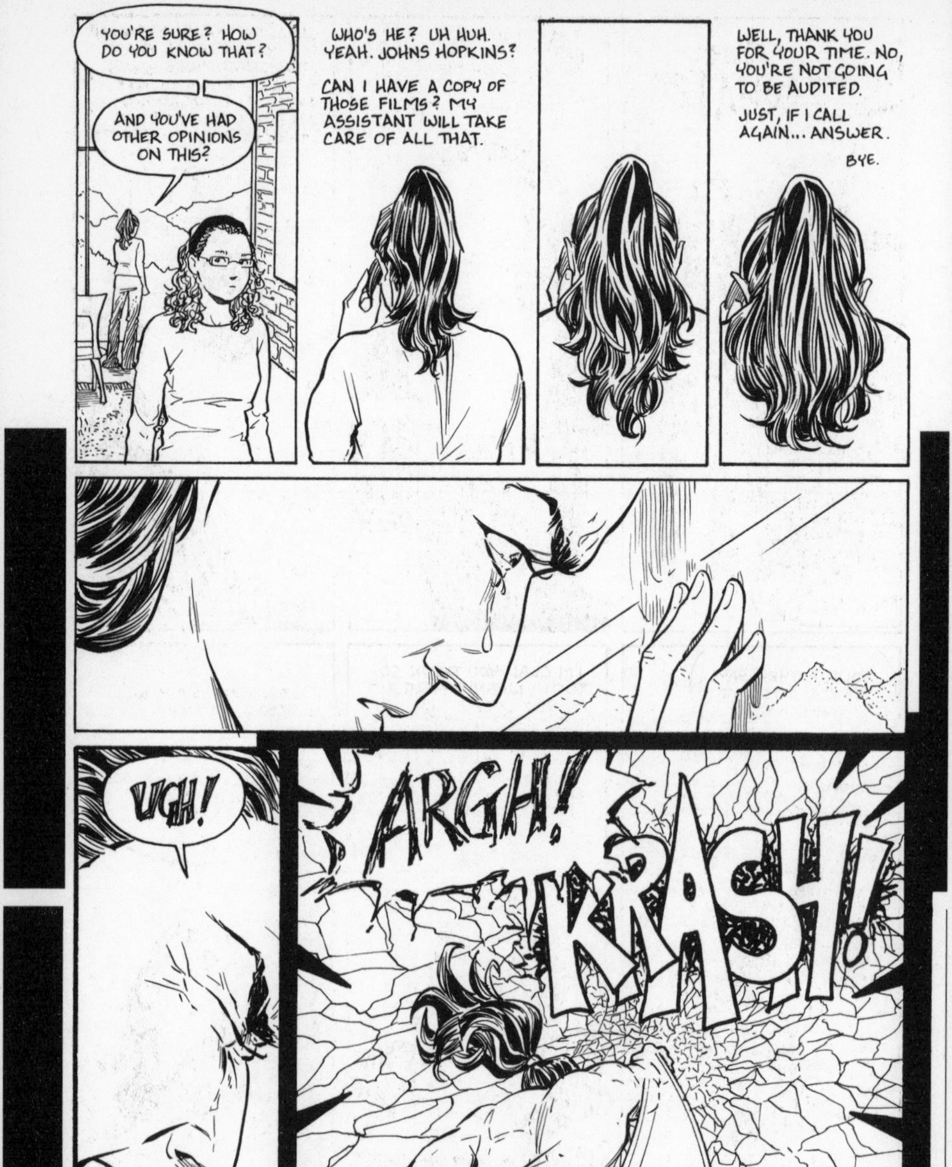
YOU'RE SURE? HOW DO YOU KNOW THAT?
AND YOU'VE HAD OTHER OPINIONS ON THIS?
WHO'S HE? UH HUH. YEAH. JOHNS HOPKINS?
CAN I HAVE A COPY OF THOSE FILMS? MY ASSISTANT WILL TAKE CARE OF ALL THAT.
WELL, THANK YOU FOR YOUR TIME. NO, YOU'RE NOT GOING TO BE AUDITED.
JUST, IF I CALL AGAIN... ANSWER.
BYE.
UGH!
ARGH!
KRASH!

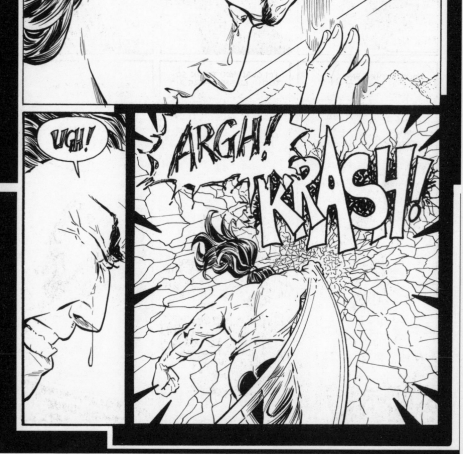

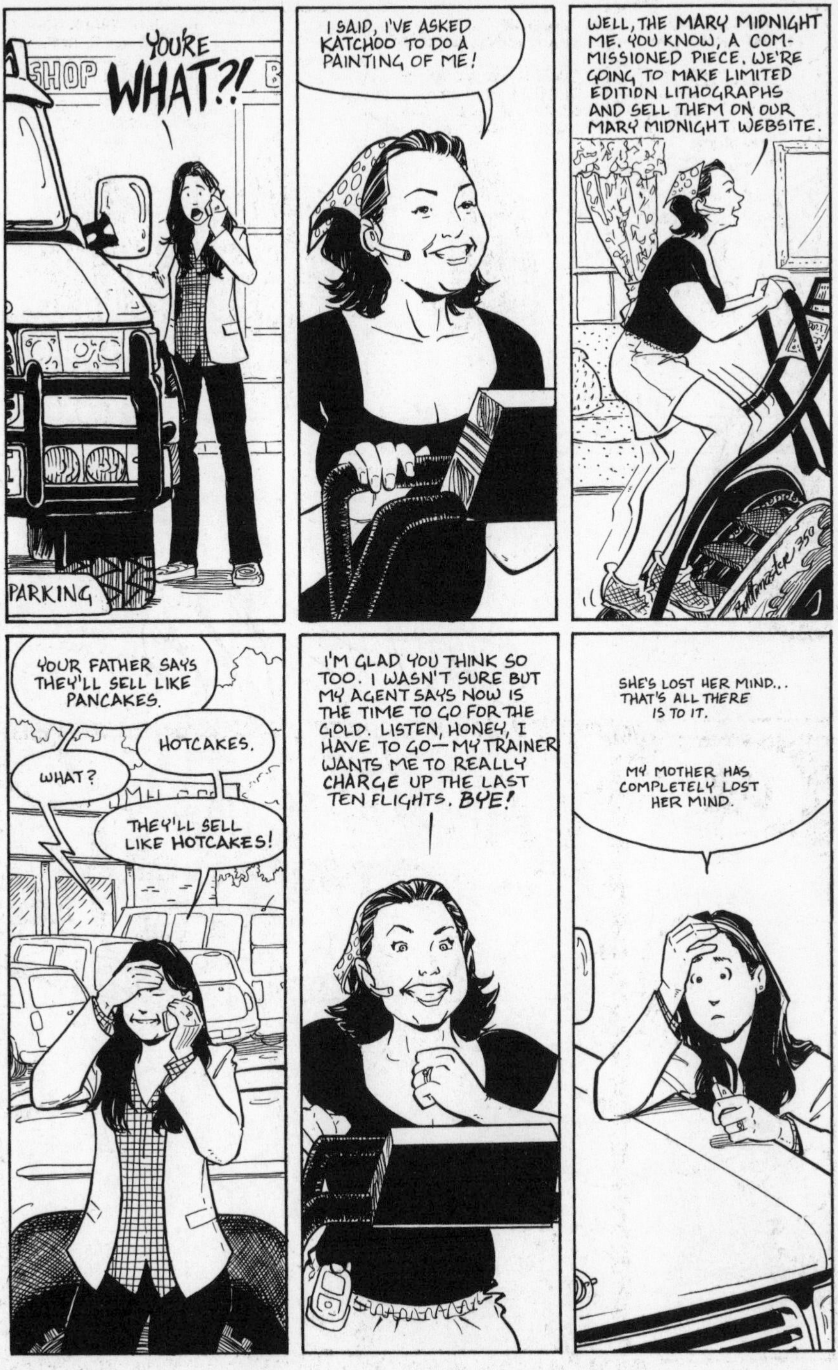
SHOP
YOU'RE WHAT?!
PARKING
I SAID, I'VE ASKED KATCHOO TO DO A PAINTING OF ME!
WELL, THE MARY MIDNIGHT ME. YOU KNOW, A COMMISSIONED PIECE. WE'RE GOING TO MAKE LIMITED EDITION LITHOGRAPHS AND SELL THEM ON OUR MARY MIDNIGHT WEBSITE.
YOUR FATHER SAYS THEY'LL SELL LIKE PANCAKES.
HOTCAKES.
WHAT?
THEY'LL SELL LIKE HOTCAKES!
I'M GLAD YOU THINK SO TOO. I WASN'T SURE BUT MY AGENT SAYS NOW IS THE TIME TO GO FOR THE GOLD. LISTEN, HONEY, I HAVE TO GO— MY TRAINER WANTS ME TO REALLY CHARGE UP THE LAST TEN FLIGHTS. BYE!
SHE'S LOST HER MIND... THAT'S ALL THERE IS TO IT.
MY MOTHER HAS COMPLETELY LOST HER MIND.

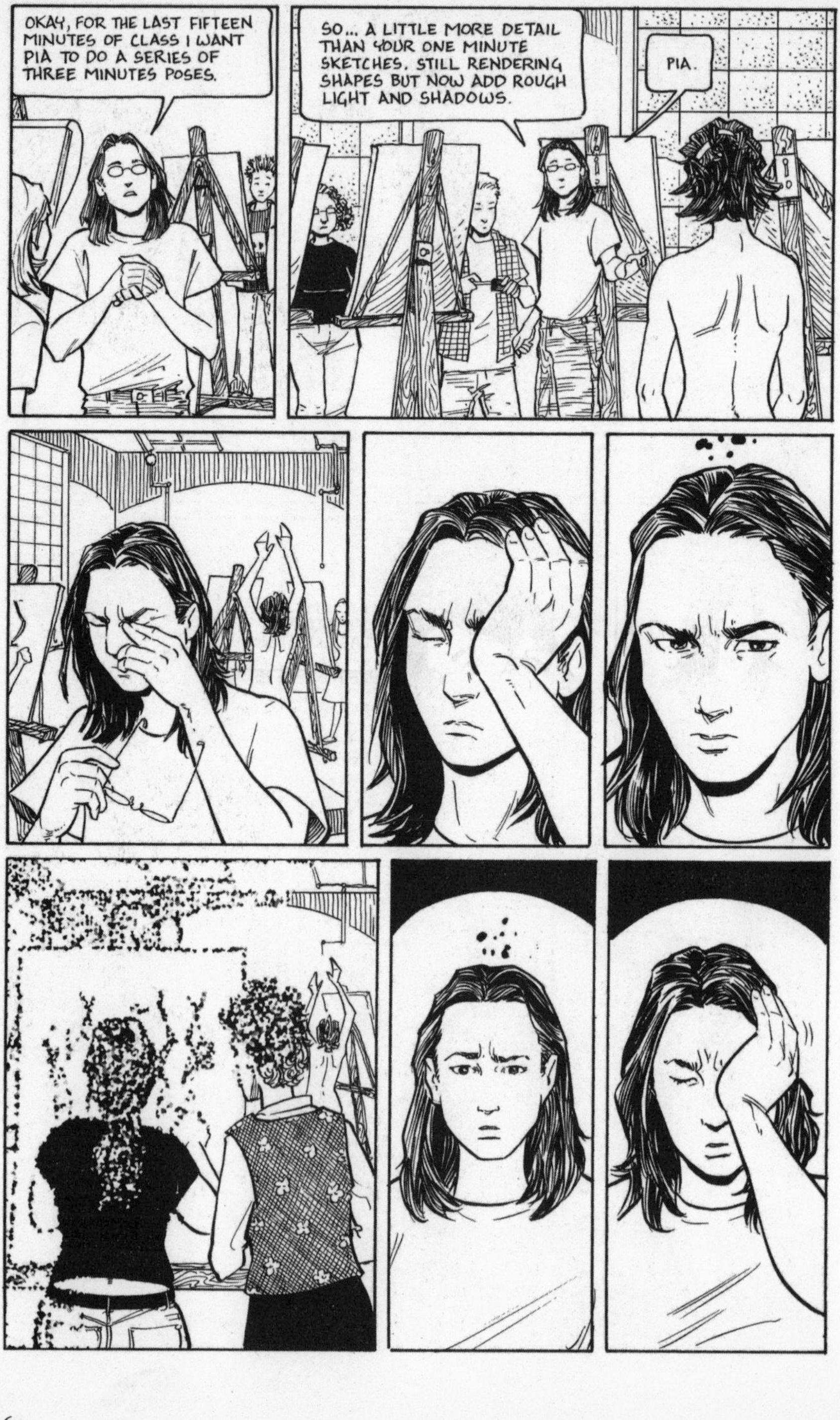
OKAY, FOR THE LAST FIFTEEN MINUTES OF CLASS I WANT PIA TO DO A SERIES OF THREE MINUTES POSES.
SO... A LITTLE MORE DETAIL THAN YOUR ONE MINUTE SKETCHES. STILL RENDERING SHAPES BUT NOW ADD ROUGH LIGHT AND SHADOWS.
PIA.

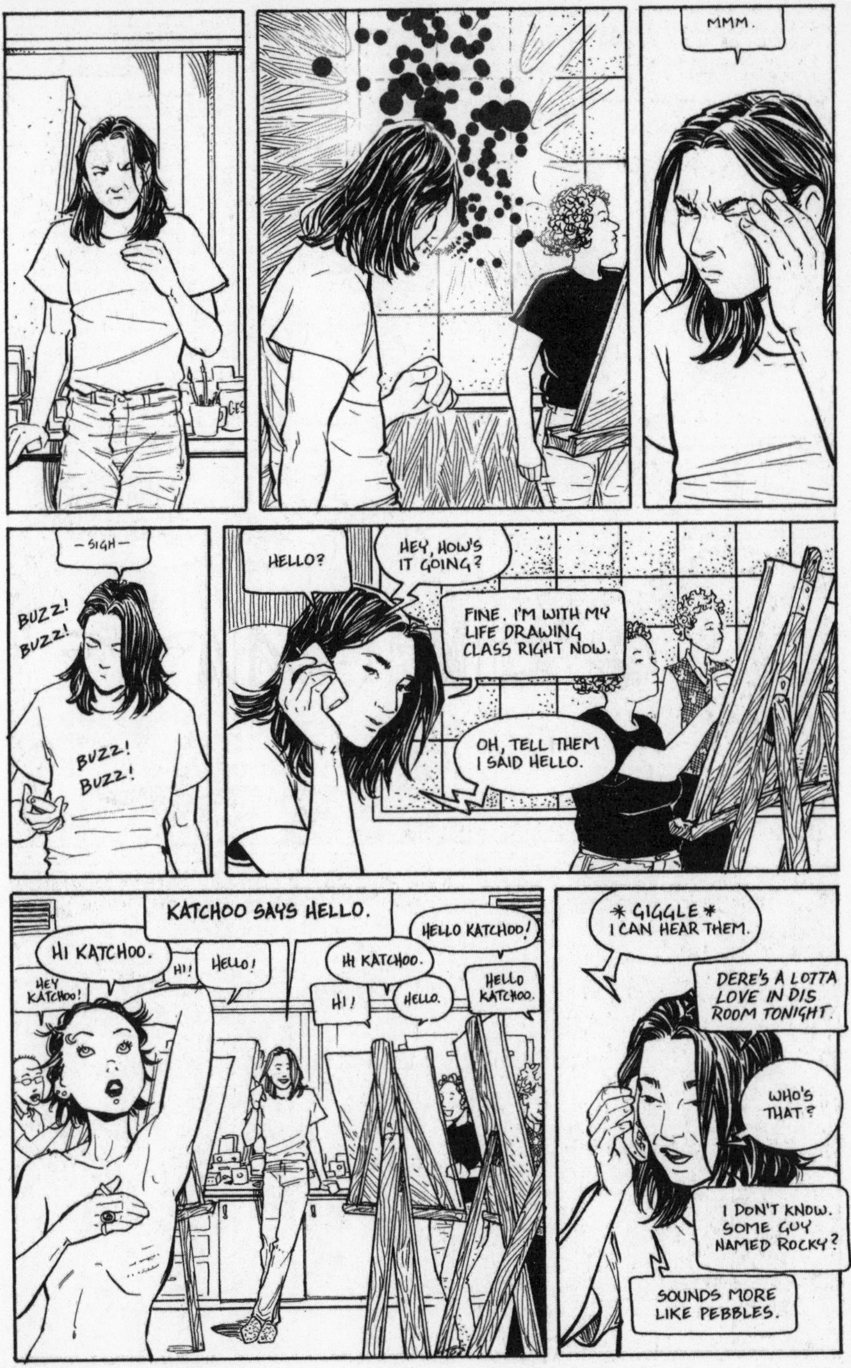
MMM.
— SIGH —
BUZZ! BUZZ!
BUZZ! BUZZ!
HELLO?
HEY, HOW'S IT GOING?
FINE. I'M WITH MY LIFE DRAWING CLASS RIGHT NOW.
OH, TELL THEM I SAID HELLO.
KATCHOO SAYS HELLO.
HI KATCHOO.
HEY KATCHOO!
HI!
HELLO!
HI KATCHOO.
HELLO KATCHOO!
HI!
HELLO.
HELLO KATCHOO.
* GIGGLE * I CAN HEAR THEM.
DERE'S A LOTTA LOVE IN DIS ROOM TONIGHT.
WHO'S THAT?
I DON'T KNOW. SOME GUY NAMED ROCKY?
SOUNDS MORE LIKE PEBBLES.

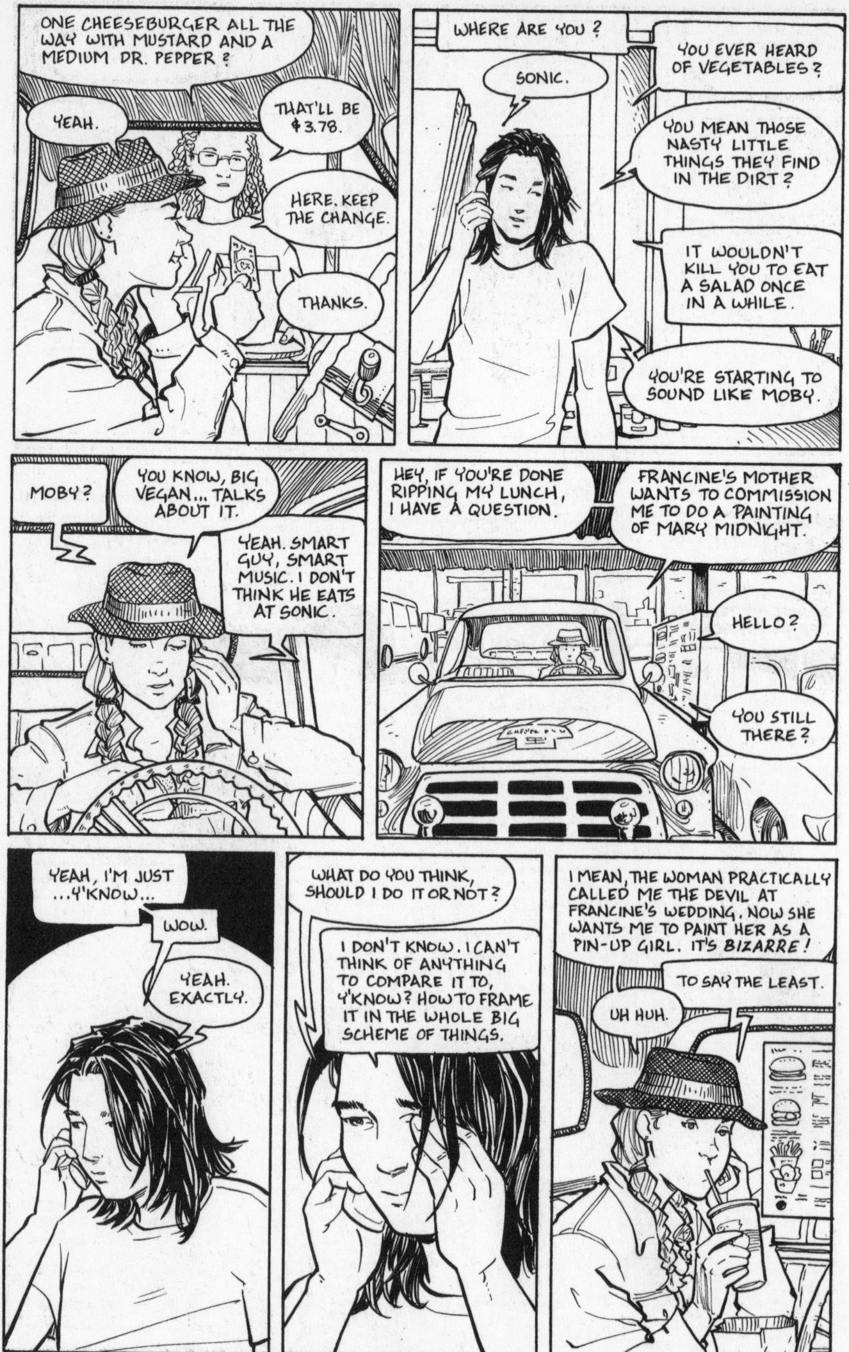
ONE CHEESEBURGER ALL THE WAY WITH MUSTARD AND A MEDIUM DR. PEPPER ?
YEAH.
THAT'LL BE $3.78.
HERE. KEEP THE CHANGE.
THANKS.
WHERE ARE YOU ?
SONIC.
YOU EVER HEARD OF VEGETABLES ?
YOU MEAN THOSE NASTY LITTLE THINGS THEY FIND IN THE DIRT ?
IT WOULDN'T KILL YOU TO EAT A SALAD ONCE IN A WHILE.
YOU'RE STARTING TO SOUND LIKE MOBY.
MOBY ?
YOU KNOW, BIG VEGAN... TALKS ABOUT IT.
YEAH. SMART GUY, SMART MUSIC. I DON'T THINK HE EATS AT SONIC.
HEY, IF YOU'RE DONE RIPPING MY LUNCH, I HAVE A QUESTION.
FRANCINE'S MOTHER WANTS TO COMMISSION ME TO DO A PAINTING OF MARY MIDNIGHT.
HELLO ?
YOU STILL THERE ?
YEAH, I'M JUST ...Y'KNOW...
WOW.
YEAH. EXACTLY.
WHAT DO YOU THINK, SHOULD I DO IT OR NOT ?
I DON'T KNOW. I CAN'T THINK OF ANYTHING TO COMPARE IT TO, Y'KNOW? HOW TO FRAME IT IN THE WHOLE BIG SCHEME OF THINGS.
I MEAN, THE WOMAN PRACTICALLY CALLED ME THE DEVIL AT FRANCINE'S WEDDING. NOW SHE WANTS ME TO PAINT HER AS A PIN-UP GIRL. IT'S *BIZARRE* !
TO SAY THE LEAST.
UH HUH.

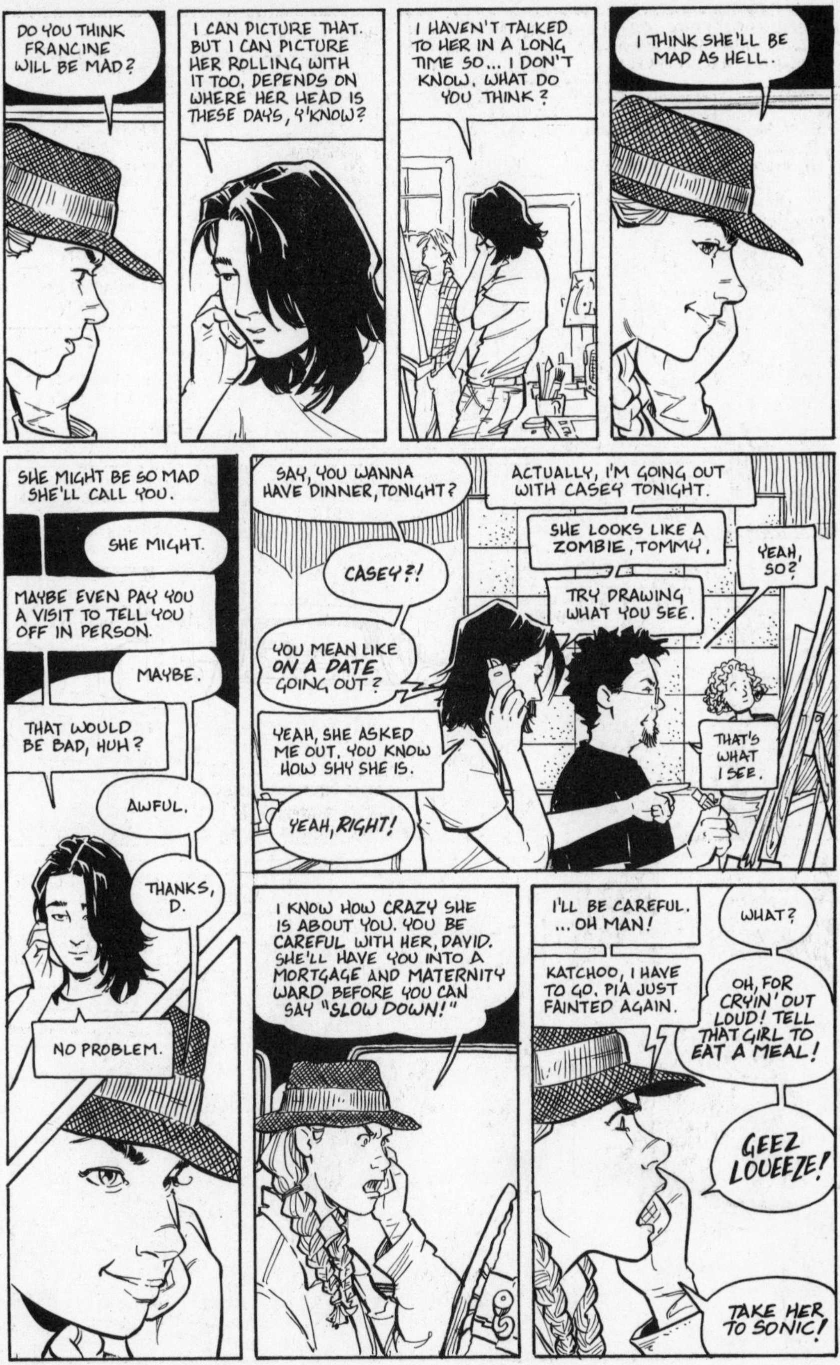
DO YOU THINK FRANCINE WILL BE MAD?
I CAN PICTURE THAT. BUT I CAN PICTURE HER ROLLING WITH IT TOO, DEPENDS ON WHERE HER HEAD IS THESE DAYS, Y'KNOW?
I HAVEN'T TALKED TO HER IN A LONG TIME SO... I DON'T KNOW. WHAT DO YOU THINK?
I THINK SHE'LL BE MAD AS HELL.
SHE MIGHT BE SO MAD SHE'LL CALL YOU.
SHE MIGHT.
MAYBE EVEN PAY YOU A VISIT TO TELL YOU OFF IN PERSON.
MAYBE.
THAT WOULD BE BAD, HUH?
AWFUL.
THANKS, D.
NO PROBLEM.
SAY, YOU WANNA HAVE DINNER, TONIGHT?
ACTUALLY, I'M GOING OUT WITH CASEY TONIGHT.
CASEY?!
SHE LOOKS LIKE A ZOMBIE, TOMMY.
YEAH, SO?
TRY DRAWING WHAT YOU SEE.
YOU MEAN LIKE ON A DATE GOING OUT?
YEAH, SHE ASKED ME OUT. YOU KNOW HOW SHY SHE IS.
THAT'S WHAT I SEE.
YEAH, RIGHT!
I KNOW HOW CRAZY SHE IS ABOUT YOU. YOU BE CAREFUL WITH HER, DAVID. SHE'LL HAVE YOU INTO A MORTGAGE AND MATERNITY WARD BEFORE YOU CAN SAY "SLOW DOWN!"
I'LL BE CAREFUL. ...OH MAN!
WHAT?
KATCHOO, I HAVE TO GO. PIA JUST FAINTED AGAIN.
OH, FOR CRYIN' OUT LOUD! TELL THAT GIRL TO EAT A MEAL!
GEEZ LOUEEZE!
TAKE HER TO SONIC!

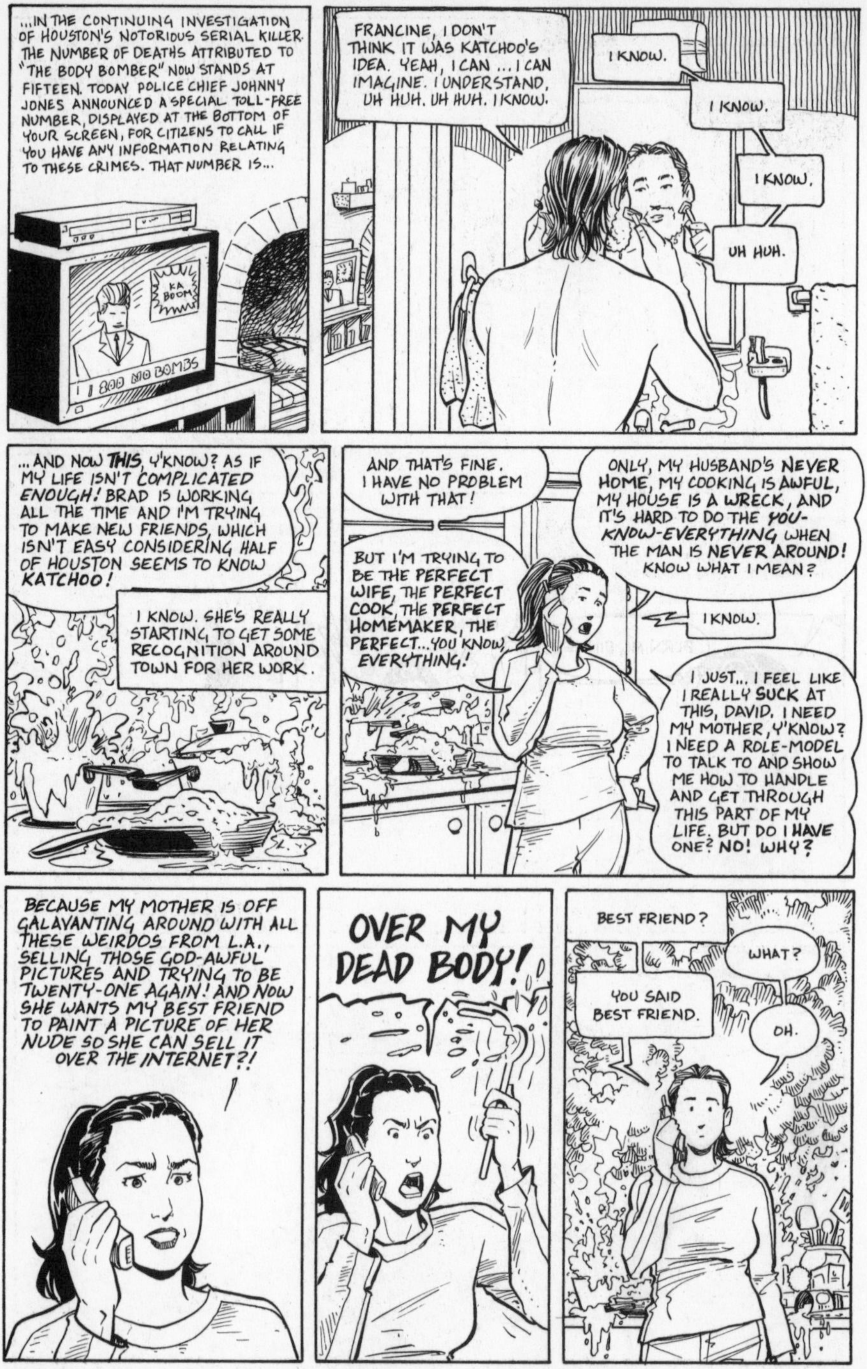
...IN THE CONTINUING INVESTIGATION OF HOUSTON'S NOTORIOUS SERIAL KILLER. THE NUMBER OF DEATHS ATTRIBUTED TO "THE BODY BOMBER" NOW STANDS AT FIFTEEN. TODAY POLICE CHIEF JOHNNY JONES ANNOUNCED A SPECIAL TOLL-FREE NUMBER, DISPLAYED AT THE BOTTOM OF YOUR SCREEN, FOR CITIZENS TO CALL IF YOU HAVE ANY INFORMATION RELATING TO THESE CRIMES. THAT NUMBER IS...
KA BOOM
1 800 NO BOMBS
FRANCINE, I DON'T THINK IT WAS KATCHOO'S IDEA. YEAH, I CAN ... I CAN IMAGINE. I UNDERSTAND. UH HUH. UH HUH. I KNOW.
I KNOW.
I KNOW.
I KNOW.
UH HUH.
...AND NOW THIS, Y'KNOW? AS IF MY LIFE ISN'T COMPLICATED ENOUGH! BRAD IS WORKING ALL THE TIME AND I'M TRYING TO MAKE NEW FRIENDS, WHICH ISN'T EASY CONSIDERING HALF OF HOUSTON SEEMS TO KNOW KATCHOO!
I KNOW. SHE'S REALLY STARTING TO GET SOME RECOGNITION AROUND TOWN FOR HER WORK.
AND THAT'S FINE. I HAVE NO PROBLEM WITH THAT!
BUT I'M TRYING TO BE THE PERFECT WIFE, THE PERFECT COOK, THE PERFECT HOMEMAKER, THE PERFECT...YOU KNOW, EVERYTHING!
ONLY, MY HUSBAND'S NEVER HOME, MY COOKING IS AWFUL, MY HOUSE IS A WRECK, AND IT'S HARD TO DO THE YOU-KNOW-EVERYTHING WHEN THE MAN IS NEVER AROUND! KNOW WHAT I MEAN?
I KNOW.
I JUST... I FEEL LIKE I REALLY SUCK AT THIS, DAVID. I NEED MY MOTHER, Y'KNOW? I NEED A ROLE-MODEL TO TALK TO AND SHOW ME HOW TO HANDLE AND GET THROUGH THIS PART OF MY LIFE. BUT DO I HAVE ONE? NO! WHY?
BECAUSE MY MOTHER IS OFF GALAVANTING AROUND WITH ALL THESE WEIRDOS FROM L.A., SELLING THOSE GOD-AWFUL PICTURES AND TRYING TO BE TWENTY-ONE AGAIN! AND NOW SHE WANTS MY BEST FRIEND TO PAINT A PICTURE OF HER NUDE SO SHE CAN SELL IT OVER THE INTERNET?!
OVER MY DEAD BODY!
BEST FRIEND?
WHAT?
YOU SAID BEST FRIEND.
OH.

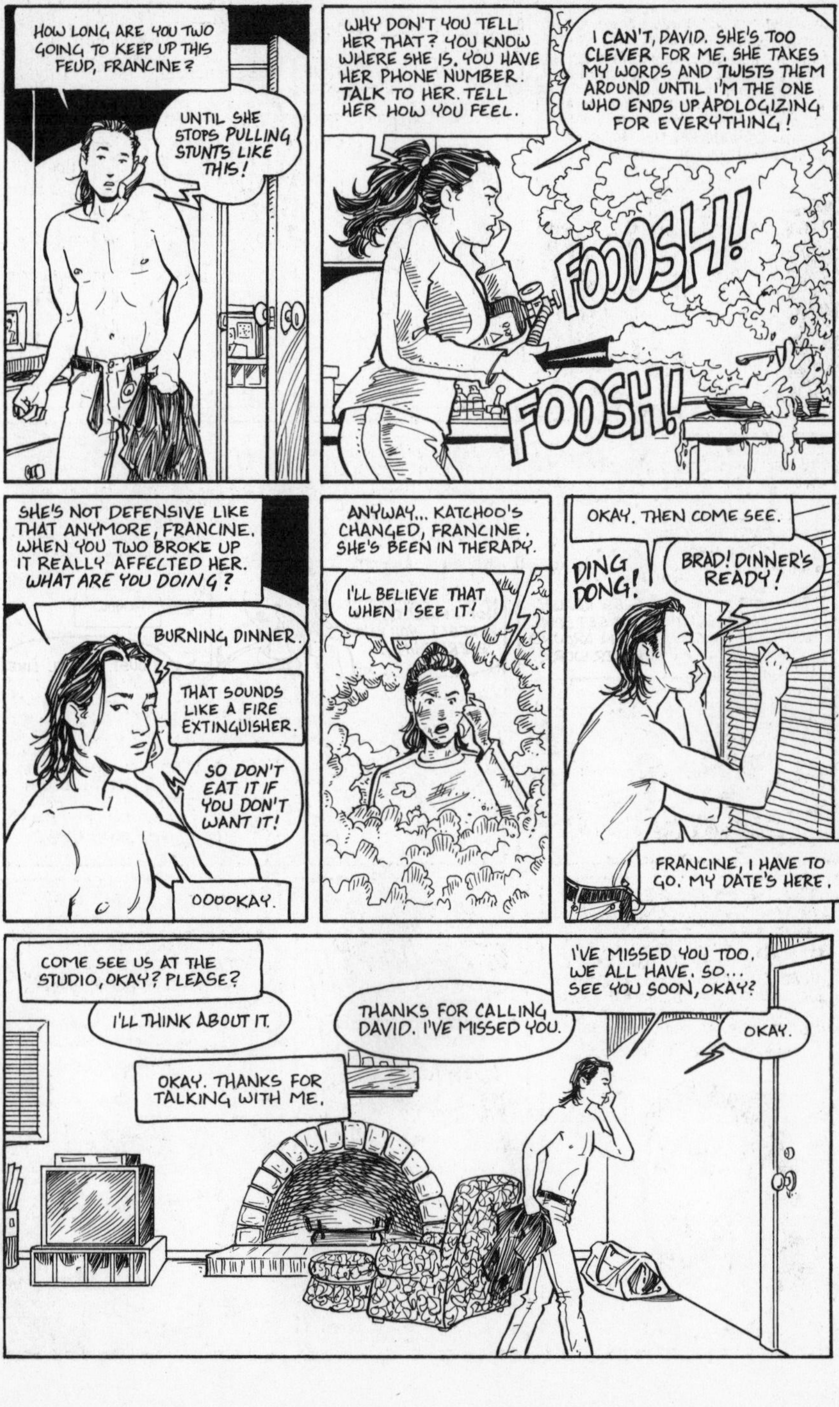
HOW LONG ARE YOU TWO GOING TO KEEP UP THIS FEUD, FRANCINE?
UNTIL SHE STOPS PULLING STUNTS LIKE THIS!
WHY DON'T YOU TELL HER THAT? YOU KNOW WHERE SHE IS. YOU HAVE HER PHONE NUMBER. TALK TO HER. TELL HER HOW YOU FEEL.
I CAN'T, DAVID. SHE'S TOO CLEVER FOR ME. SHE TAKES MY WORDS AND TWISTS THEM AROUND UNTIL I'M THE ONE WHO ENDS UP APOLOGIZING FOR EVERYTHING!
FOOOSH!
FOOSH!
SHE'S NOT DEFENSIVE LIKE THAT ANYMORE, FRANCINE. WHEN YOU TWO BROKE UP IT REALLY AFFECTED HER. WHAT ARE YOU DOING?
BURNING DINNER.
THAT SOUNDS LIKE A FIRE EXTINGUISHER.
SO DON'T EAT IT IF YOU DON'T WANT IT!
OOOOKAY.
ANYWAY... KATCHOO'S CHANGED, FRANCINE. SHE'S BEEN IN THERAPY.
I'LL BELIEVE THAT WHEN I SEE IT!
OKAY. THEN COME SEE.
DING DONG!
BRAD! DINNER'S READY!
FRANCINE, I HAVE TO GO. MY DATE'S HERE.
COME SEE US AT THE STUDIO, OKAY? PLEASE?
I'LL THINK ABOUT IT.
THANKS FOR CALLING DAVID. I'VE MISSED YOU.
I'VE MISSED YOU TOO. WE ALL HAVE. SO... SEE YOU SOON, OKAY?
OKAY.
OKAY. THANKS FOR TALKING WITH ME.

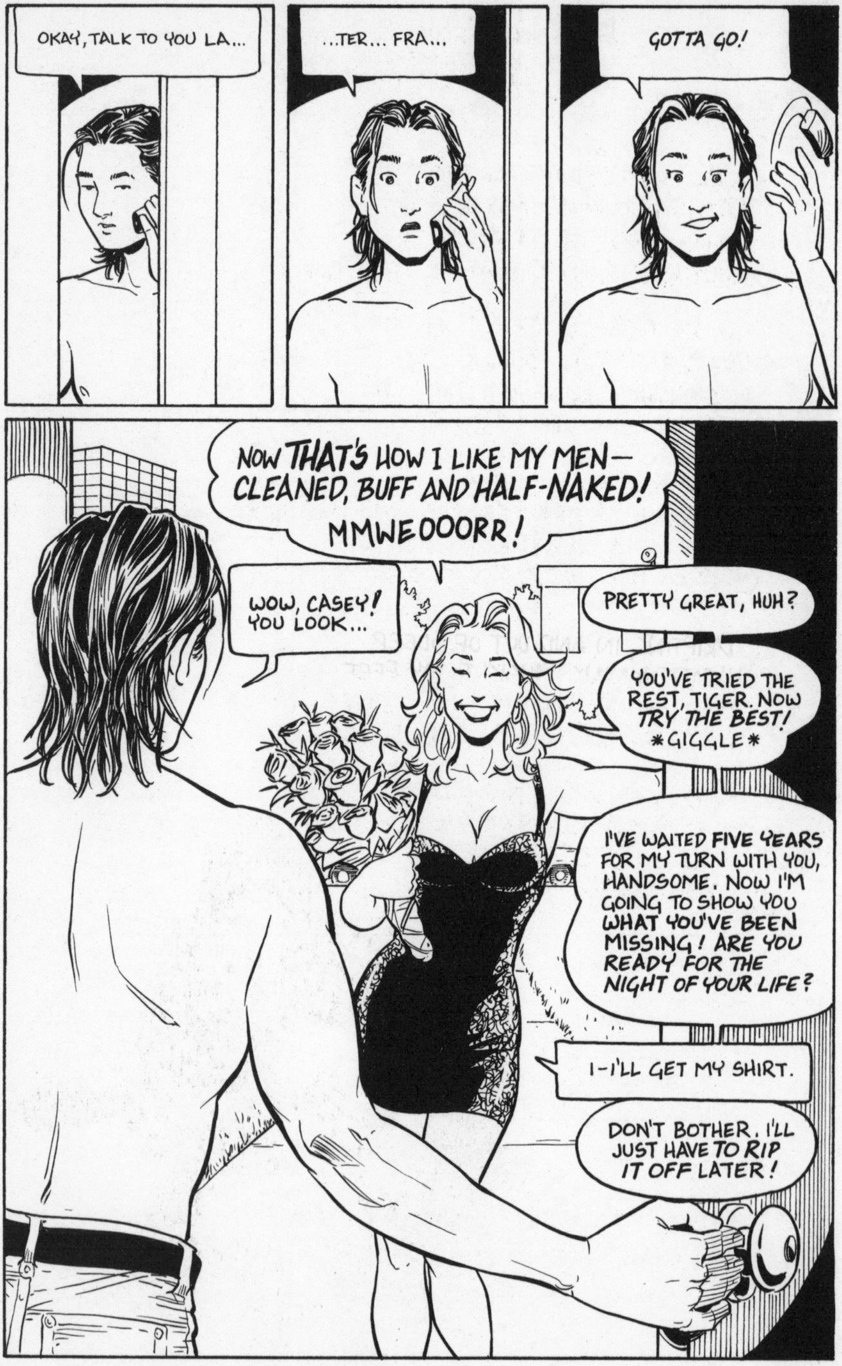
OKAY, TALK TO YOU LA...
...TER... FRA...
GOTTA GO!
NOW THAT'S HOW I LIKE MY MEN— CLEANED, BUFF AND HALF-NAKED!
MMWEOOORR!
WOW, CASEY! YOU LOOK...
PRETTY GREAT, HUH?
YOU'VE TRIED THE REST, TIGER. NOW TRY THE BEST! *GIGGLE*
I'VE WAITED FIVE YEARS FOR MY TURN WITH YOU, HANDSOME. NOW I'M GOING TO SHOW YOU WHAT YOU'VE BEEN MISSING! ARE YOU READY FOR THE NIGHT OF YOUR LIFE?
I-I'LL GET MY SHIRT.
DON'T BOTHER. I'LL JUST HAVE TO RIP IT OFF LATER!

NIGHT FLIGHT
GRIFFIN SILVER

RIDING ON THE PLANE ALL NIGHT
LETTING THE HOURS PASS IN FLIGHT
WAITING WITH HALF A BREATH ALONE
WAITING FOR ENGLAND'S COUNTRY HOME

NO ONE THERE TO SEE ME OFF
NO ONE IS UP AT FOUR O'CLOCK
NO WONDER I LIVE THE WAY I DO
NO ONE WILL STAY WITH ME BUT YOU

Chorus {
NOW, HERE WE'RE BOTH ALONE
SOMEWHERE BETWEEN THE STARS AND HOME
HERE WE'RE SO FAR FROM VIEW
I ONLY BELIEVE IN NOW AND YOU

DRIFTING IN AND OUT OF SLEEP
HEADPHONING MUSIC TO MY FEET
FEELING VIBRATIONS IN MY BONES
LETTING THE MUSIC TAKE ME HOME

Chorus {
NOW, HERE WE'RE BOTH ALONE
SOMEWHERE BETWEEN THE STARS AND HOME
HERE WE'RE SO FAR FROM VIEW
I ONLY BELIEVE IN NOW AND YOU

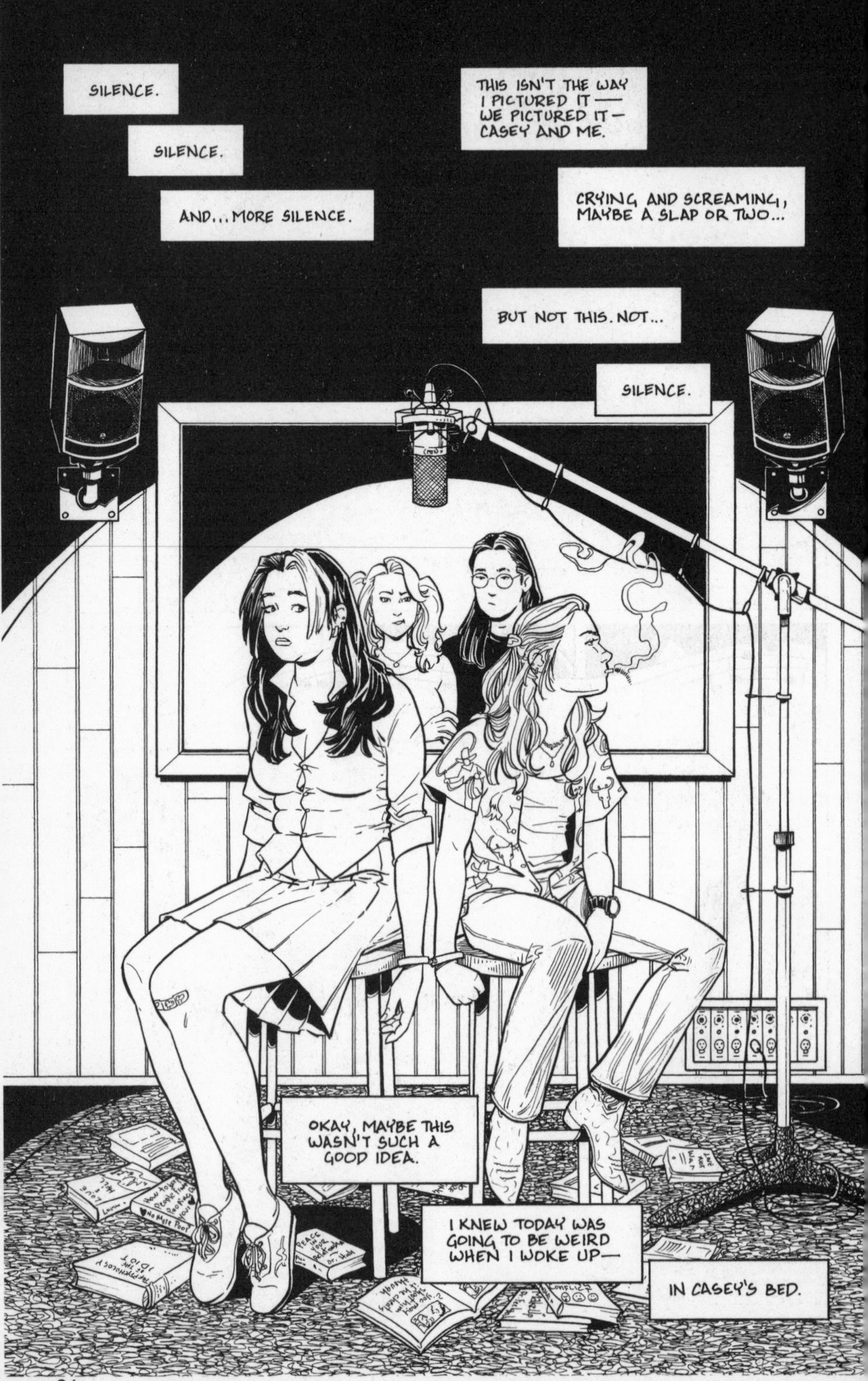
SILENCE.
SILENCE.
AND... MORE SILENCE.
THIS ISN'T THE WAY I PICTURED IT — WE PICTURED IT — CASEY AND ME.
CRYING AND SCREAMING, MAYBE A SLAP OR TWO...
BUT NOT THIS. NOT...
SILENCE.
OKAY, MAYBE THIS WASN'T SUCH A GOOD IDEA.
I KNEW TODAY WAS GOING TO BE WEIRD WHEN I WOKE UP—
IN CASEY'S BED.

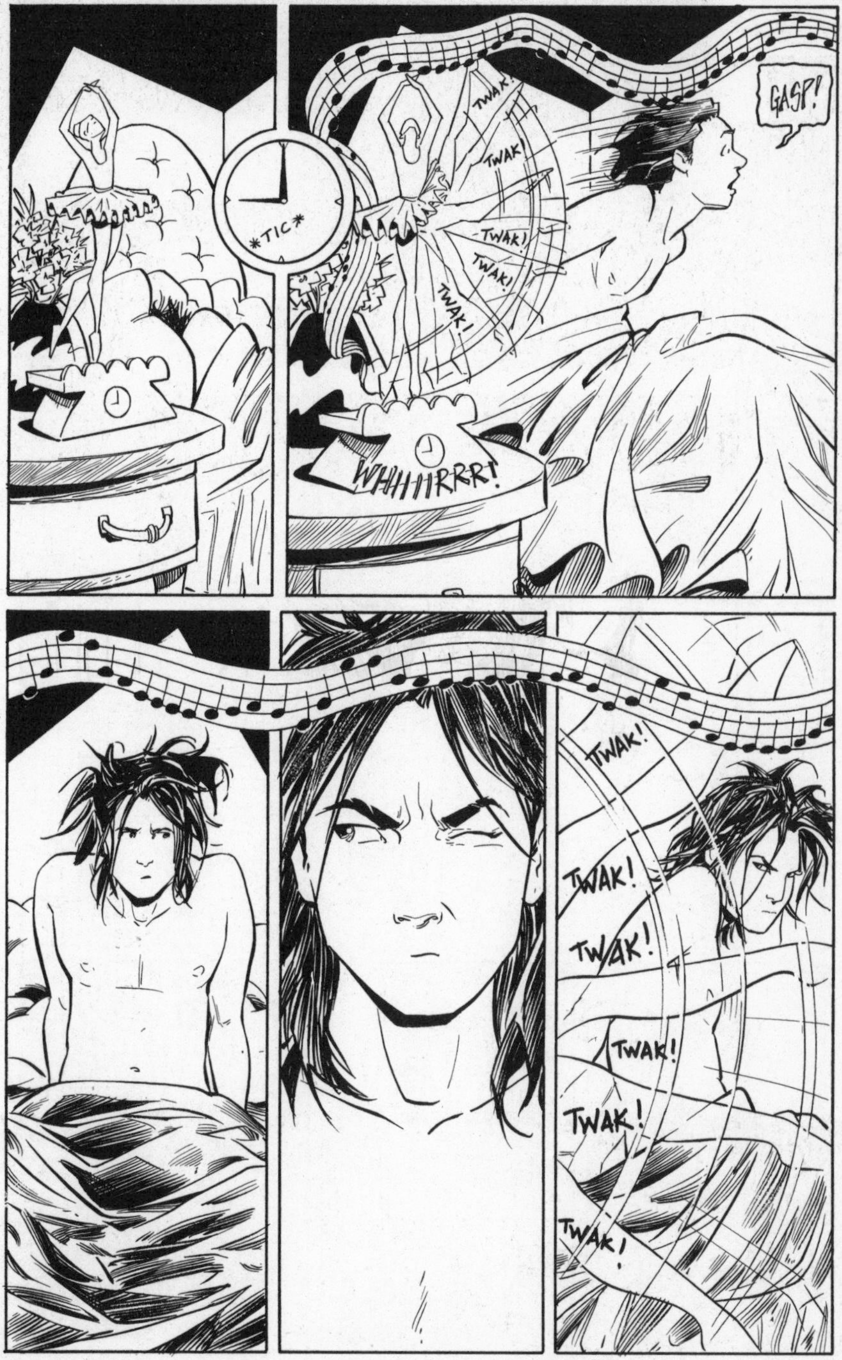
TIC
TWAK!
TWAK!
TWAK!
TWAK!
TWAK!
WHIIIIRRR!
GASP!
TWAK!
TWAK!
TWAK!
TWAK!
TWAK!
TWAK!

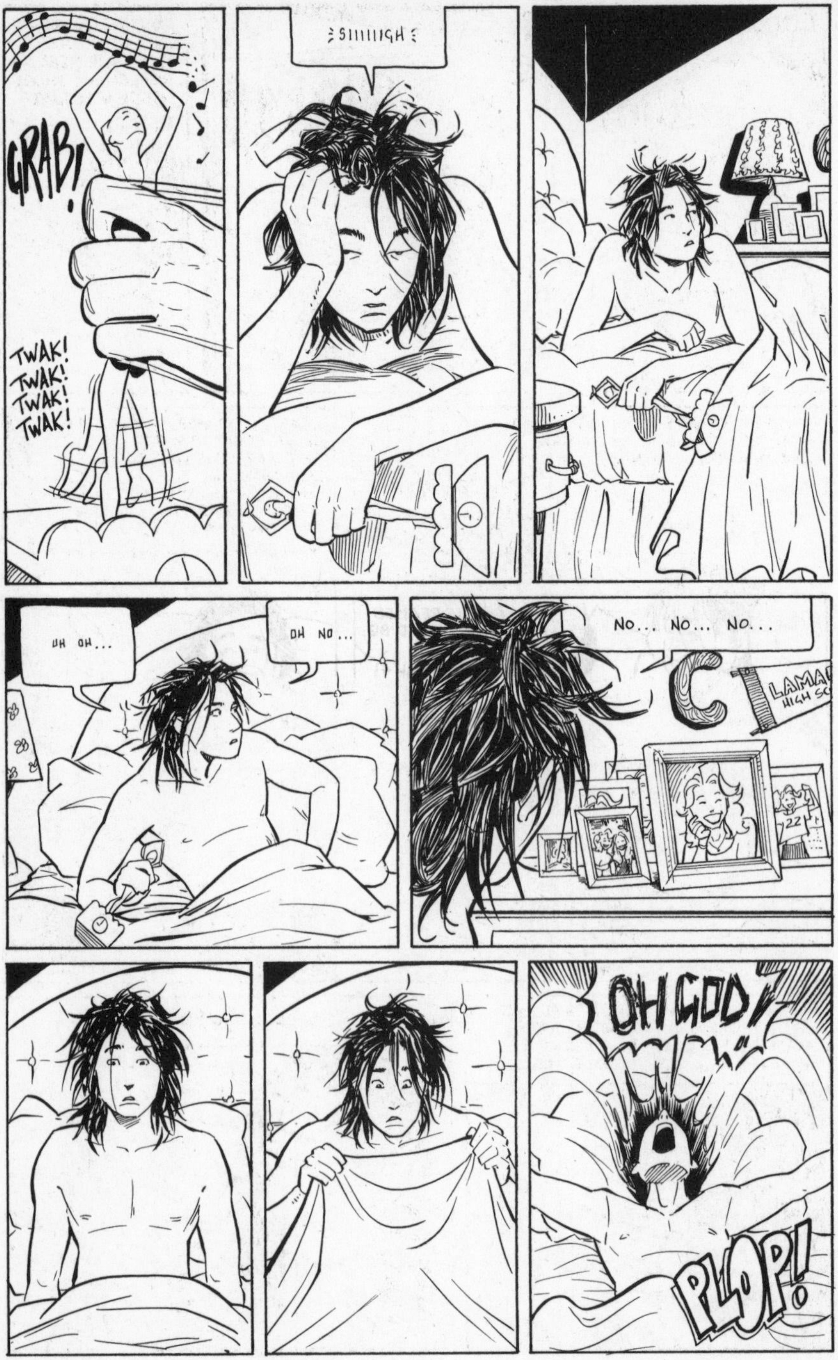
GRAB!
TWAK! TWAK! TWAK! TWAK!
SIIIIIGH
UH OH...
OH NO...
NO... NO... NO...
OH GOD!
PLOP!

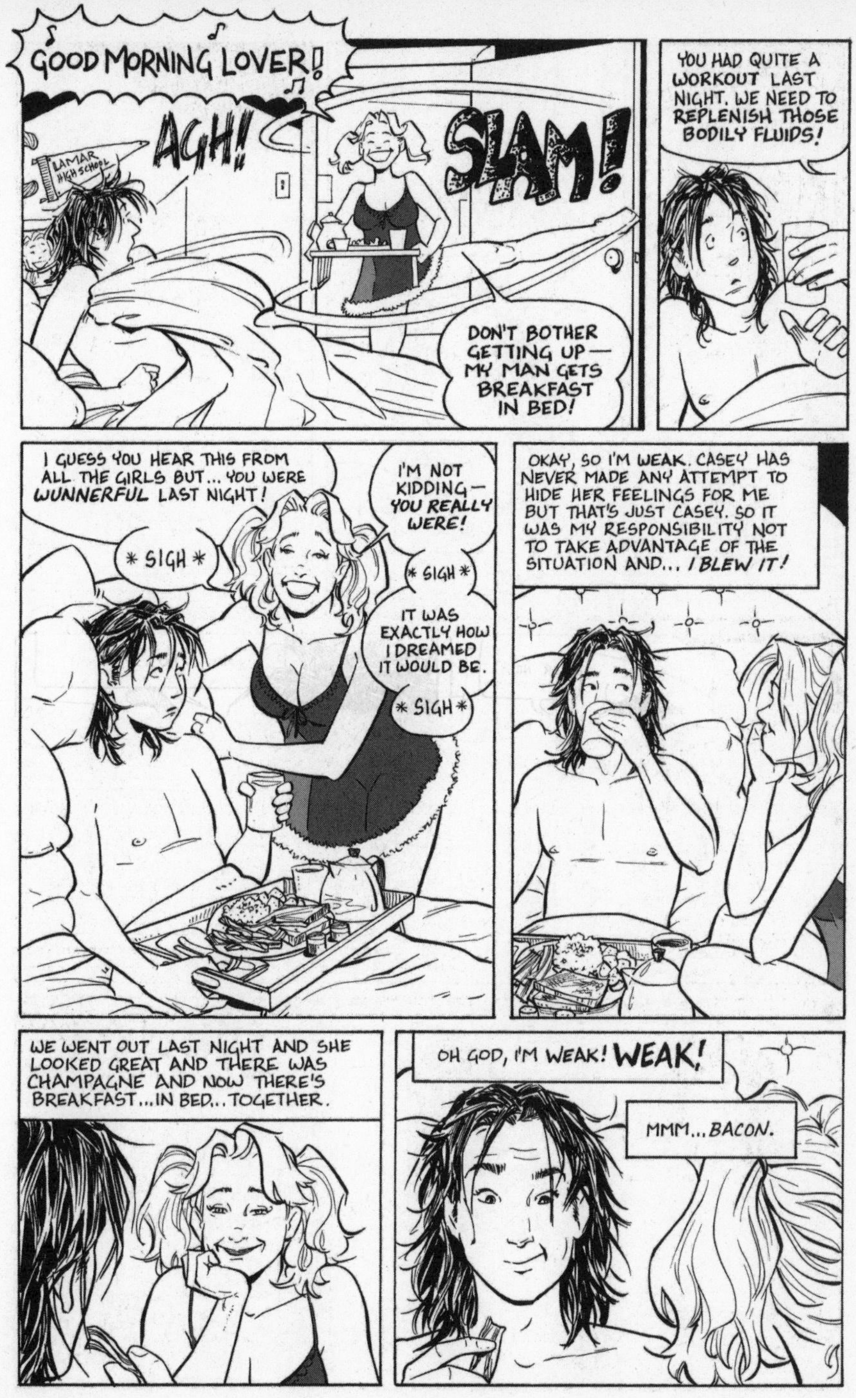
GOOD MORNING LOVER!
AGH!
LAMAR HIGH SCHOOL
SLAM!
DON'T BOTHER GETTING UP— MY MAN GETS BREAKFAST IN BED!
YOU HAD QUITE A WORKOUT LAST NIGHT. WE NEED TO REPLENISH THOSE BODILY FLUIDS!
I GUESS YOU HEAR THIS FROM ALL THE GIRLS BUT... YOU WERE WUNNERFUL LAST NIGHT!
* SIGH *
I'M NOT KIDDING— YOU REALLY WERE!
* SIGH *
IT WAS EXACTLY HOW I DREAMED IT WOULD BE.
* SIGH *
OKAY, SO I'M WEAK. CASEY HAS NEVER MADE ANY ATTEMPT TO HIDE HER FEELINGS FOR ME BUT THAT'S JUST CASEY. SO IT WAS MY RESPONSIBILITY NOT TO TAKE ADVANTAGE OF THE SITUATION AND... I BLEW IT!
WE WENT OUT LAST NIGHT AND SHE LOOKED GREAT AND THERE WAS CHAMPAGNE AND NOW THERE'S BREAKFAST...IN BED...TOGETHER.
OH GOD, I'M WEAK! WEAK!
MMM...BACON.

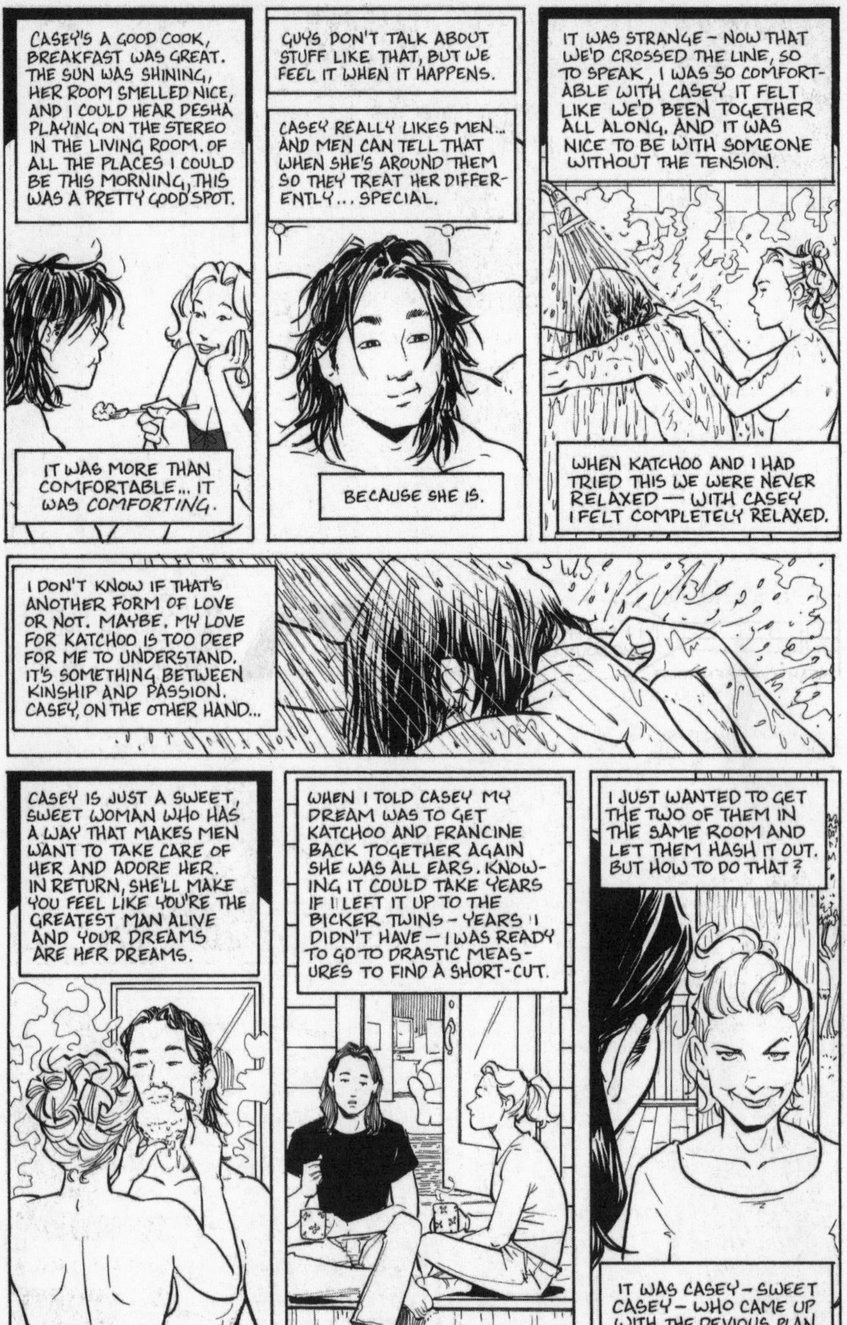
CASEY'S A GOOD COOK, BREAKFAST WAS GREAT. THE SUN WAS SHINING, HER ROOM SMELLED NICE, AND I COULD HEAR DESHA PLAYING ON THE STEREO IN THE LIVING ROOM. OF ALL THE PLACES I COULD BE THIS MORNING, THIS WAS A PRETTY GOOD SPOT.
IT WAS MORE THAN COMFORTABLE... IT WAS COMFORTING.
GUYS DON'T TALK ABOUT STUFF LIKE THAT, BUT WE FEEL IT WHEN IT HAPPENS.
CASEY REALLY LIKES MEN... AND MEN CAN TELL THAT WHEN SHE'S AROUND THEM SO THEY TREAT HER DIFFERENTLY... SPECIAL.
BECAUSE SHE IS.
IT WAS STRANGE — NOW THAT WE'D CROSSED THE LINE, SO TO SPEAK, I WAS SO COMFORTABLE WITH CASEY IT FELT LIKE WE'D BEEN TOGETHER ALL ALONG. AND IT WAS NICE TO BE WITH SOMEONE WITHOUT THE TENSION.
WHEN KATCHOO AND I HAD TRIED THIS WE WERE NEVER RELAXED — WITH CASEY I FELT COMPLETELY RELAXED.
I DON'T KNOW IF THAT'S ANOTHER FORM OF LOVE OR NOT. MAYBE. MY LOVE FOR KATCHOO IS TOO DEEP FOR ME TO UNDERSTAND. IT'S SOMETHING BETWEEN KINSHIP AND PASSION. CASEY, ON THE OTHER HAND...
CASEY IS JUST A SWEET, SWEET WOMAN WHO HAS A WAY THAT MAKES MEN WANT TO TAKE CARE OF HER AND ADORE HER. IN RETURN, SHE'LL MAKE YOU FEEL LIKE YOU'RE THE GREATEST MAN ALIVE AND YOUR DREAMS ARE HER DREAMS.
WHEN I TOLD CASEY MY DREAM WAS TO GET KATCHOO AND FRANCINE BACK TOGETHER AGAIN SHE WAS ALL EARS. KNOWING IT COULD TAKE YEARS IF I LEFT IT UP TO THE BICKER TWINS — YEARS I DIDN'T HAVE — I WAS READY TO GO TO DRASTIC MEASURES TO FIND A SHORT-CUT.
I JUST WANTED TO GET THE TWO OF THEM IN THE SAME ROOM AND LET THEM HASH IT OUT. BUT HOW TO DO THAT?
IT WAS CASEY — SWEET CASEY — WHO CAME UP WITH THE DEVIOUS PLAN.

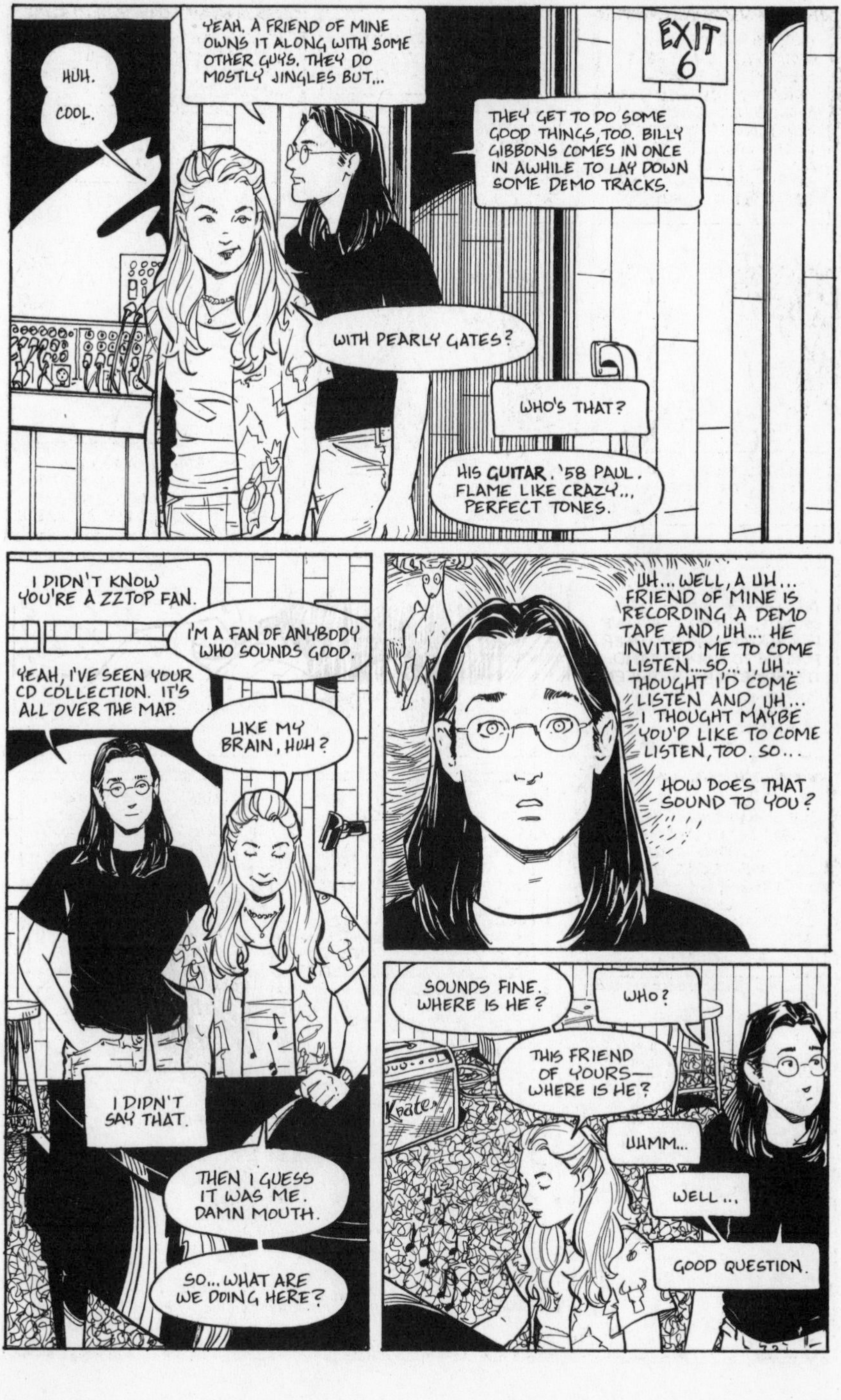
HUH.
COOL.
YEAH. A FRIEND OF MINE OWNS IT ALONG WITH SOME OTHER GUYS. THEY DO MOSTLY JINGLES BUT...
EXIT 6
THEY GET TO DO SOME GOOD THINGS, TOO. BILLY GIBBONS COMES IN ONCE IN AWHILE TO LAY DOWN SOME DEMO TRACKS.
WITH PEARLY GATES?
WHO'S THAT?
HIS GUITAR. '58 PAUL. FLAME LIKE CRAZY... PERFECT TONES.
I DIDN'T KNOW YOU'RE A ZZTOP FAN.
I'M A FAN OF ANYBODY WHO SOUNDS GOOD.
YEAH, I'VE SEEN YOUR CD COLLECTION. IT'S ALL OVER THE MAP.
LIKE MY BRAIN, HUH?
I DIDN'T SAY THAT.
THEN I GUESS IT WAS ME. DAMN MOUTH.
SO... WHAT ARE WE DOING HERE?
UH... WELL, A UH... FRIEND OF MINE IS RECORDING A DEMO TAPE AND, UH... HE INVITED ME TO COME LISTEN...SO... I, UH... THOUGHT I'D COME LISTEN AND, UH... I THOUGHT MAYBE YOU'D LIKE TO COME LISTEN, TOO. SO...
HOW DOES THAT SOUND TO YOU?
SOUNDS FINE. WHERE IS HE?
WHO?
THIS FRIEND OF YOURS— WHERE IS HE?
UHMM...
WELL...
GOOD QUESTION.

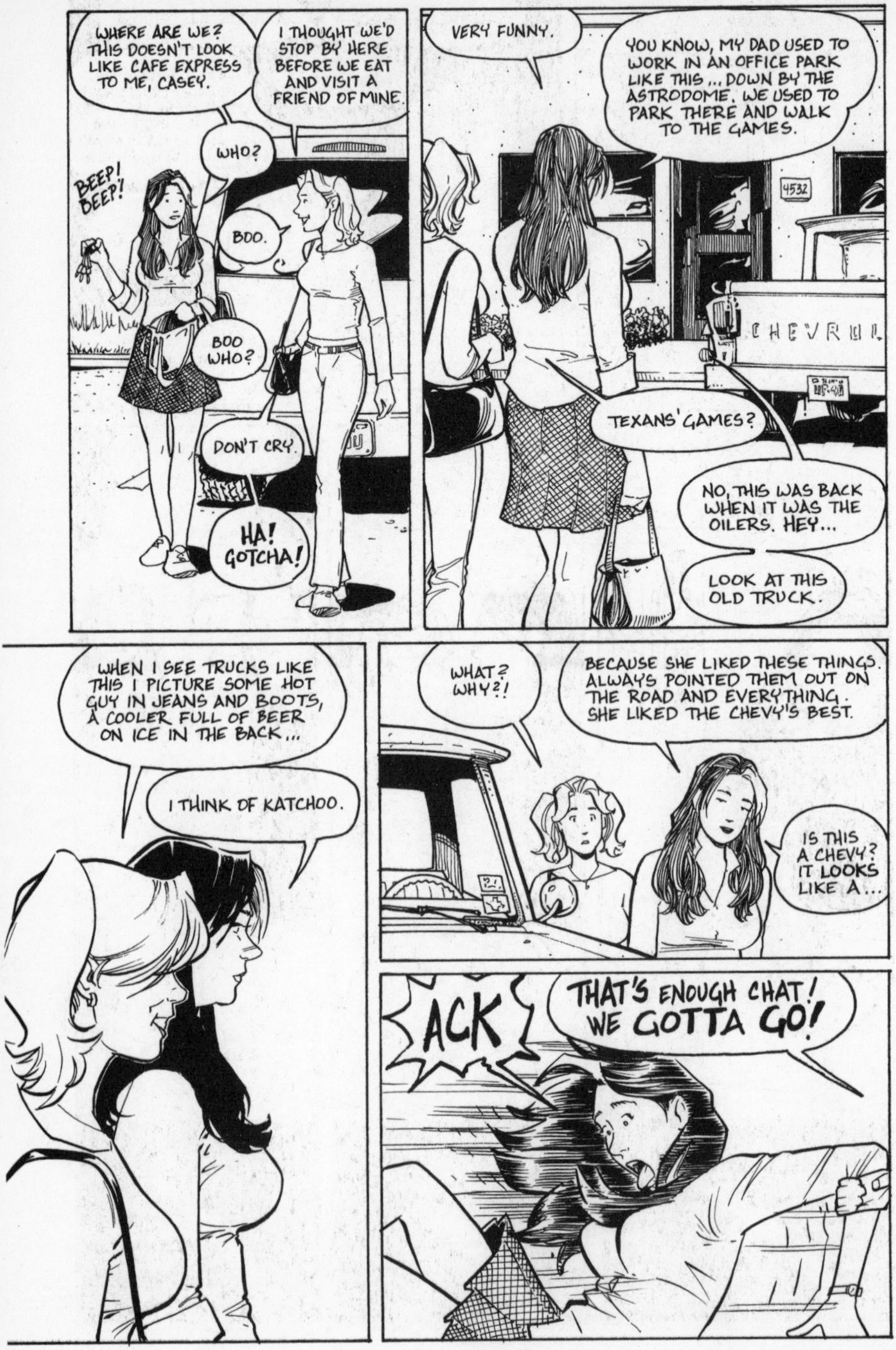
WHERE ARE WE? THIS DOESN'T LOOK LIKE CAFE EXPRESS TO ME, CASEY.
I THOUGHT WE'D STOP BY HERE BEFORE WE EAT AND VISIT A FRIEND OF MINE.
WHO?
BEEP! BEEP!
BOO.
BOO WHO?
DON'T CRY.
HA! GOTCHA!
VERY FUNNY.
YOU KNOW, MY DAD USED TO WORK IN AN OFFICE PARK LIKE THIS ... DOWN BY THE ASTRODOME. WE USED TO PARK THERE AND WALK TO THE GAMES.
4532
CHEVROLET
TEXANS' GAMES?
NO, THIS WAS BACK WHEN IT WAS THE OILERS. HEY...
LOOK AT THIS OLD TRUCK.
WHEN I SEE TRUCKS LIKE THIS I PICTURE SOME HOT GUY IN JEANS AND BOOTS, A COOLER FULL OF BEER ON ICE IN THE BACK...
I THINK OF KATCHOO.
WHAT? WHY?!
BECAUSE SHE LIKED THESE THINGS. ALWAYS POINTED THEM OUT ON THE ROAD AND EVERYTHING. SHE LIKED THE CHEVY'S BEST.
IS THIS A CHEVY? IT LOOKS LIKE A...
ACK
THAT'S ENOUGH CHAT! WE GOTTA GO!

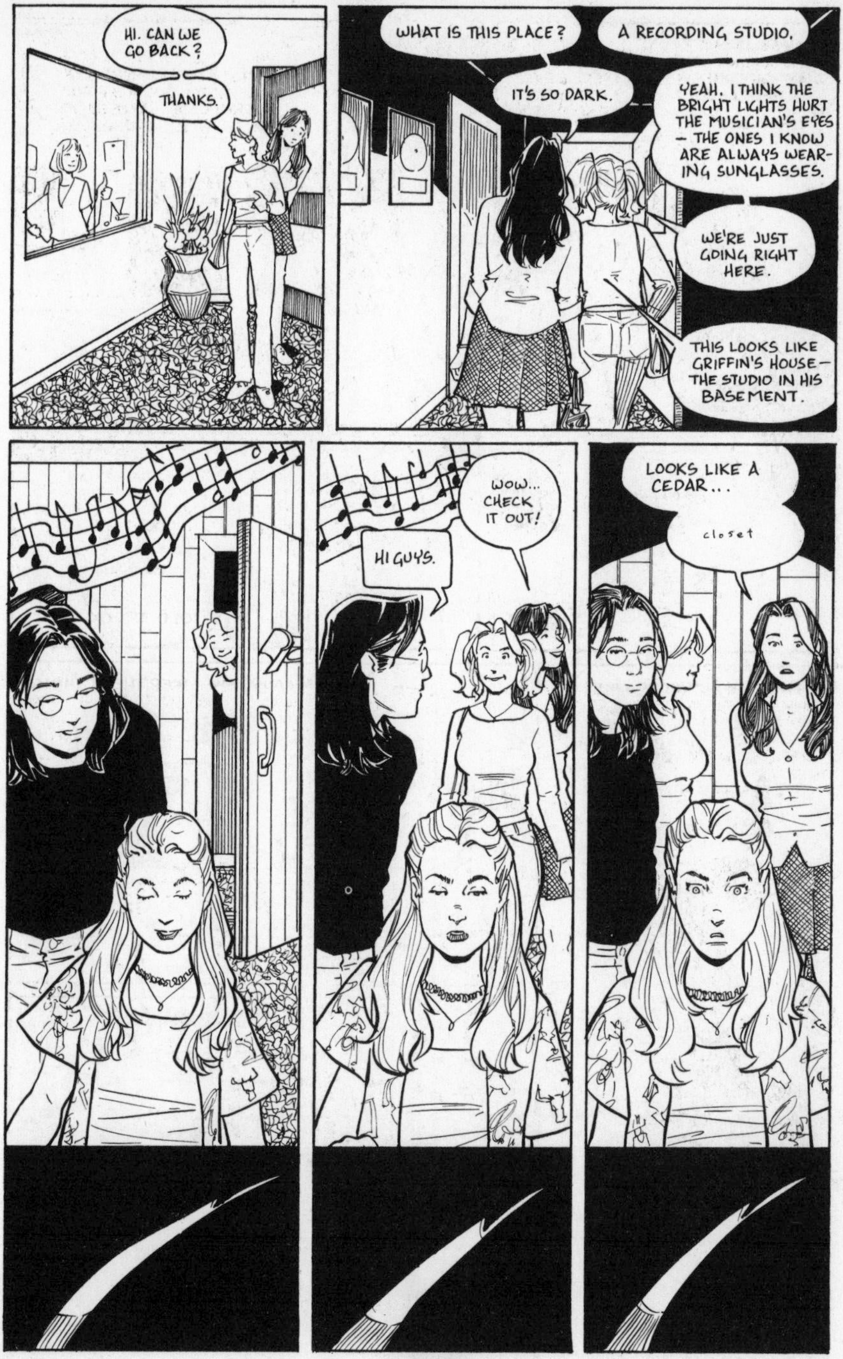
HI. CAN WE GO BACK?
THANKS.
WHAT IS THIS PLACE?
A RECORDING STUDIO.
IT'S SO DARK.
YEAH. I THINK THE BRIGHT LIGHTS HURT THE MUSICIAN'S EYES — THE ONES I KNOW ARE ALWAYS WEARING SUNGLASSES.
WE'RE JUST GOING RIGHT HERE.
THIS LOOKS LIKE GRIFFIN'S HOUSE— THE STUDIO IN HIS BASEMENT.
HI GUYS.
WOW... CHECK IT OUT!
LOOKS LIKE A CEDAR...
closet

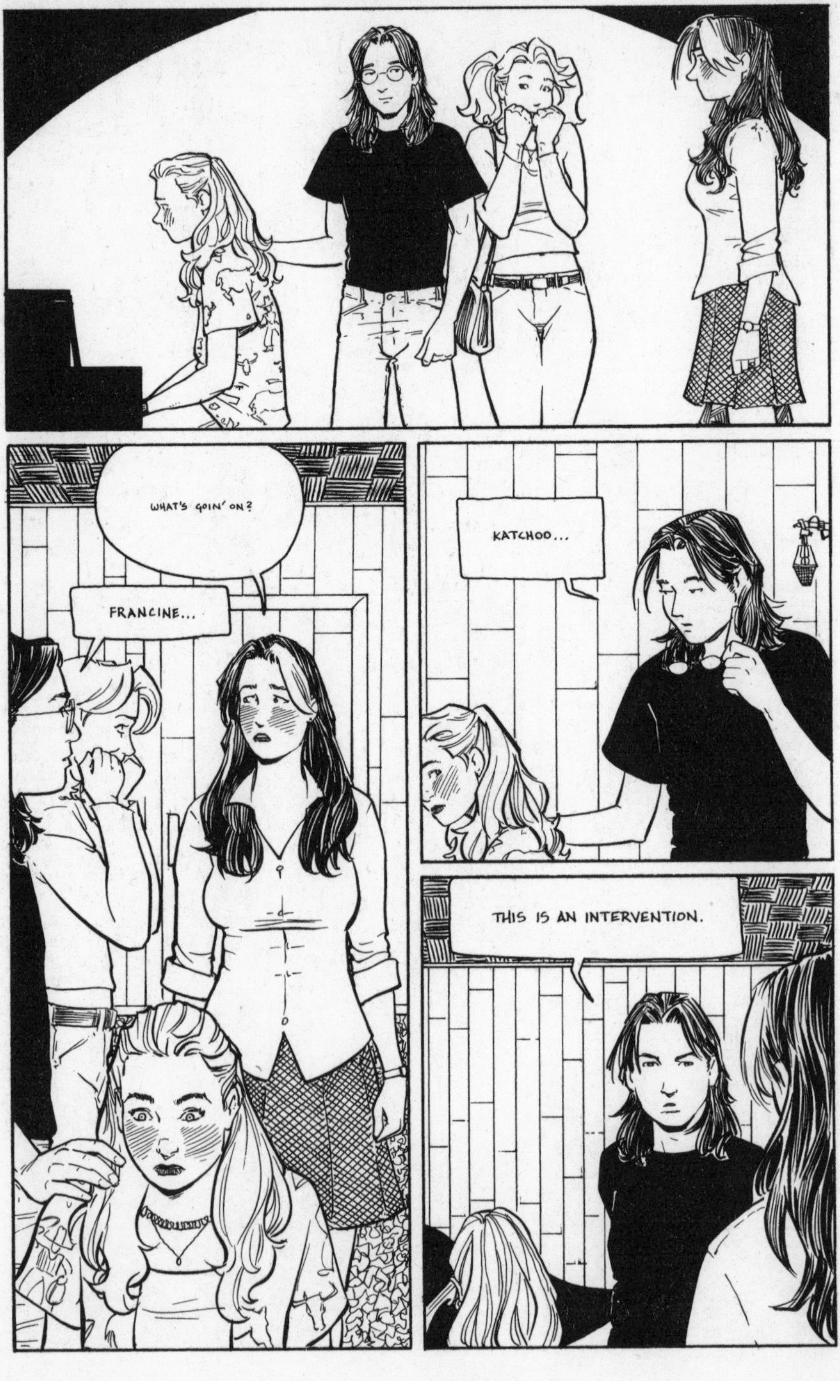
WHAT'S GOIN' ON?
FRANCINE...
KATCHOO...
THIS IS AN INTERVENTION.

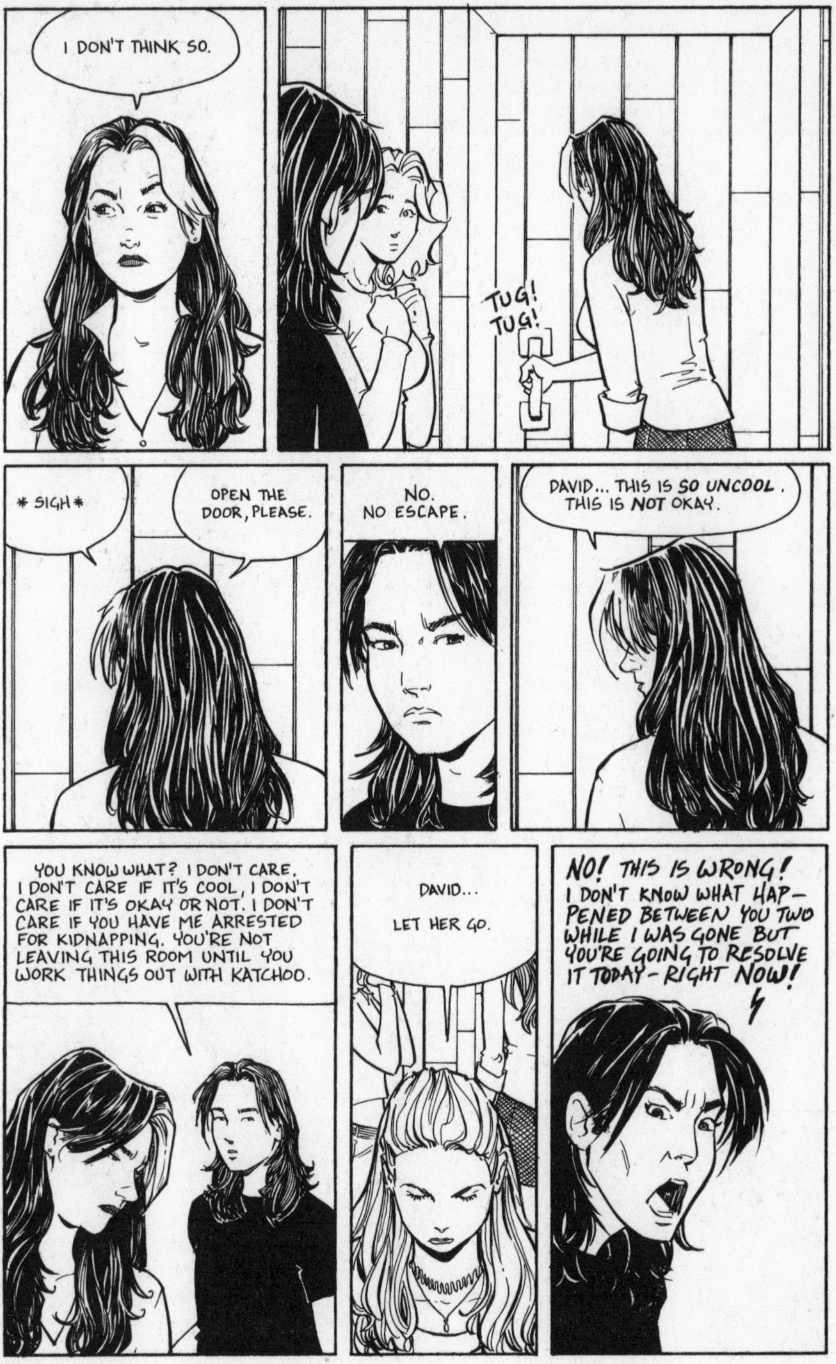
I DON'T THINK SO.
TUG! TUG!
* SIGH *
OPEN THE DOOR, PLEASE.
NO. NO ESCAPE.
DAVID... THIS IS SO UNCOOL. THIS IS NOT OKAY.
YOU KNOW WHAT? I DON'T CARE. I DON'T CARE IF IT'S COOL, I DON'T CARE IF IT'S OKAY OR NOT. I DON'T CARE IF YOU HAVE ME ARRESTED FOR KIDNAPPING. YOU'RE NOT LEAVING THIS ROOM UNTIL YOU WORK THINGS OUT WITH KATCHOO.
DAVID... LET HER GO.
NO! THIS IS WRONG! I DON'T KNOW WHAT HAPPENED BETWEEN YOU TWO WHILE I WAS GONE BUT YOU'RE GOING TO RESOLVE IT TODAY - RIGHT NOW!

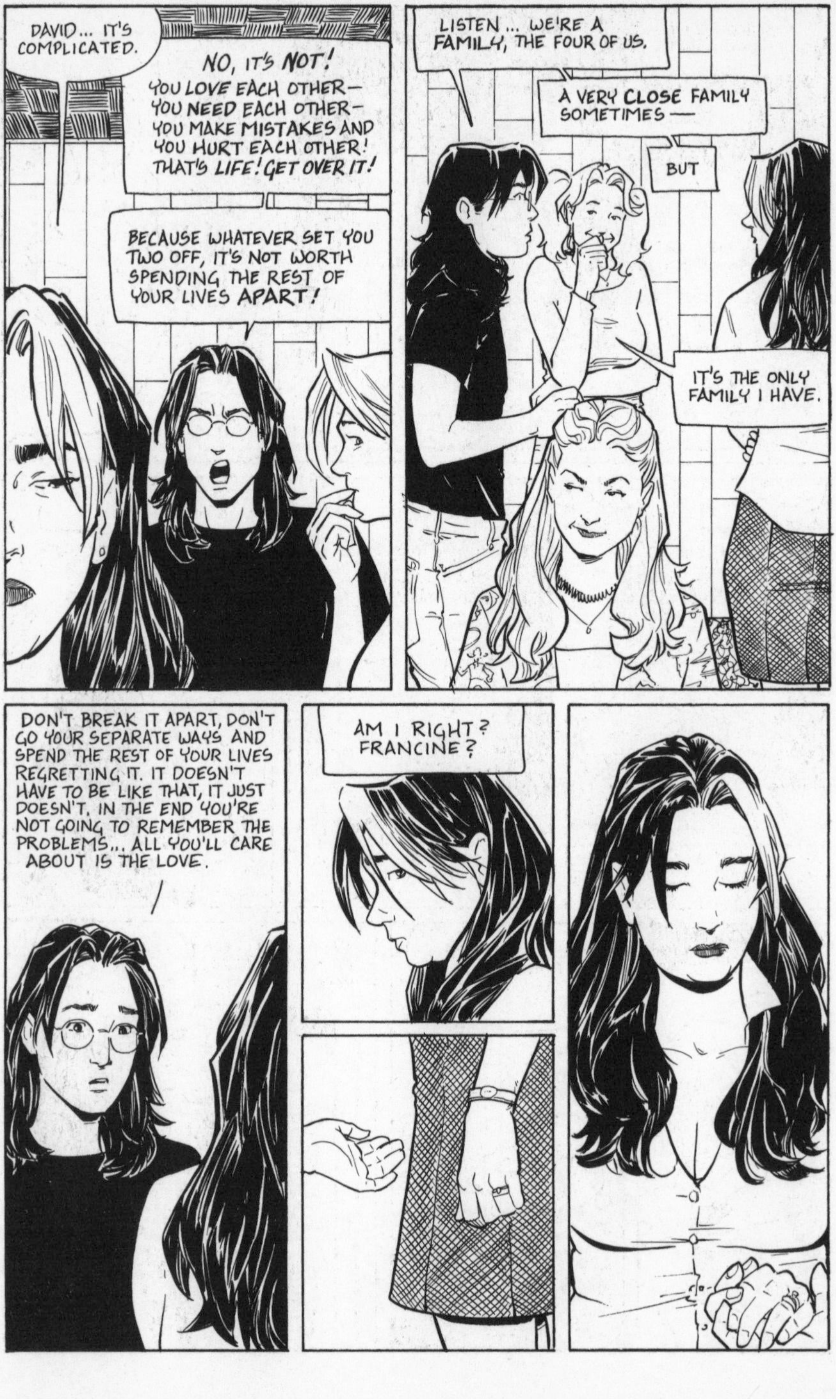
DAVID... IT'S COMPLICATED.
NO, IT'S NOT! YOU LOVE EACH OTHER— YOU NEED EACH OTHER— YOU MAKE MISTAKES AND YOU HURT EACH OTHER! THAT'S LIFE! GET OVER IT!
BECAUSE WHATEVER SET YOU TWO OFF, IT'S NOT WORTH SPENDING THE REST OF YOUR LIVES APART!
LISTEN... WE'RE A FAMILY, THE FOUR OF US.
A VERY CLOSE FAMILY SOMETIMES—
BUT
IT'S THE ONLY FAMILY I HAVE.
DON'T BREAK IT APART, DON'T GO YOUR SEPARATE WAYS AND SPEND THE REST OF YOUR LIVES REGRETTING IT. IT DOESN'T HAVE TO BE LIKE THAT, IT JUST DOESN'T. IN THE END YOU'RE NOT GOING TO REMEMBER THE PROBLEMS... ALL YOU'LL CARE ABOUT IS THE LOVE.
AM I RIGHT? FRANCINE?

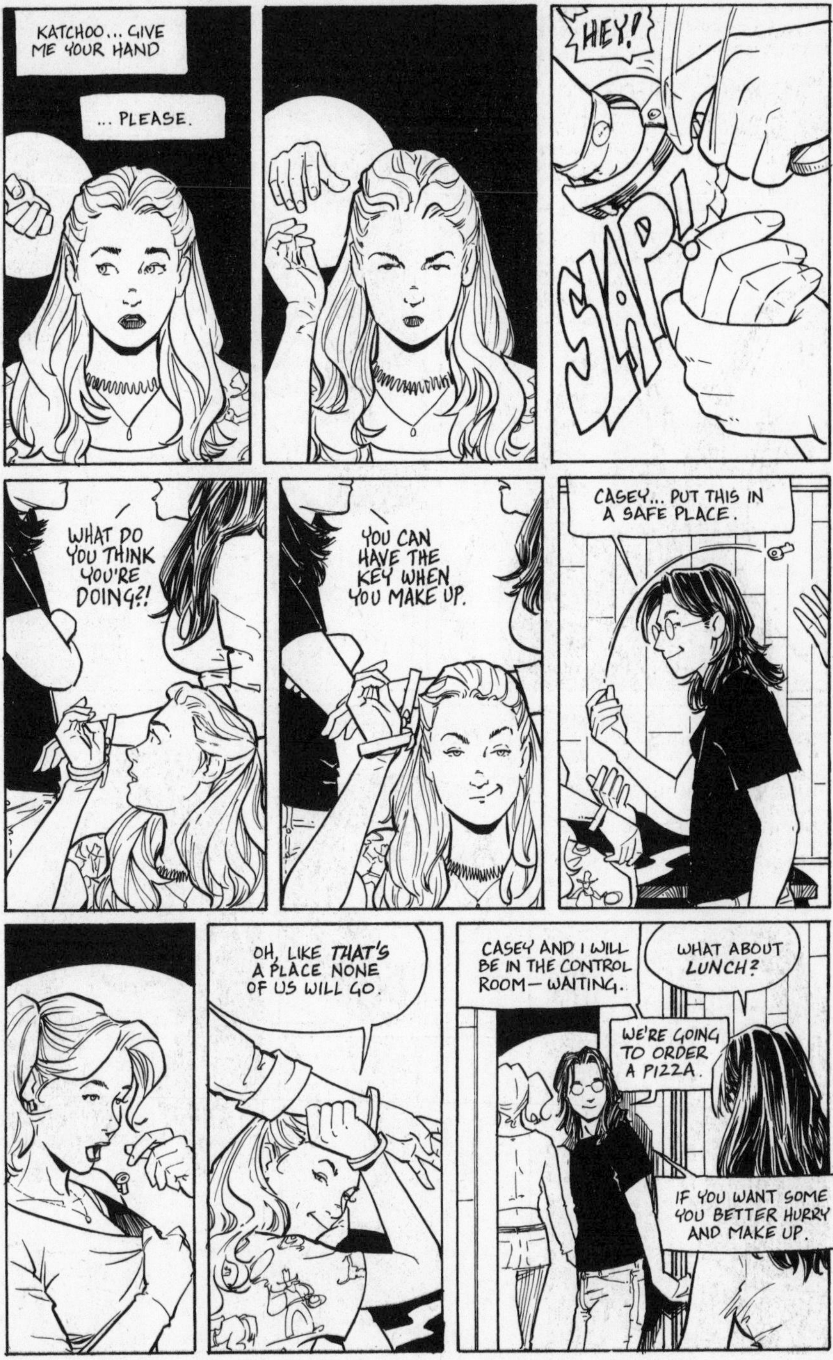
KATCHOO... GIVE ME YOUR HAND
... PLEASE.
HEY!
SNAP!
WHAT DO YOU THINK YOU'RE DOING?!
YOU CAN HAVE THE KEY WHEN YOU MAKE UP.
CASEY... PUT THIS IN A SAFE PLACE.
OH, LIKE THAT'S A PLACE NONE OF US WILL GO.
CASEY AND I WILL BE IN THE CONTROL ROOM— WAITING.
WHAT ABOUT LUNCH?
WE'RE GOING TO ORDER A PIZZA.
IF YOU WANT SOME YOU BETTER HURRY AND MAKE UP.

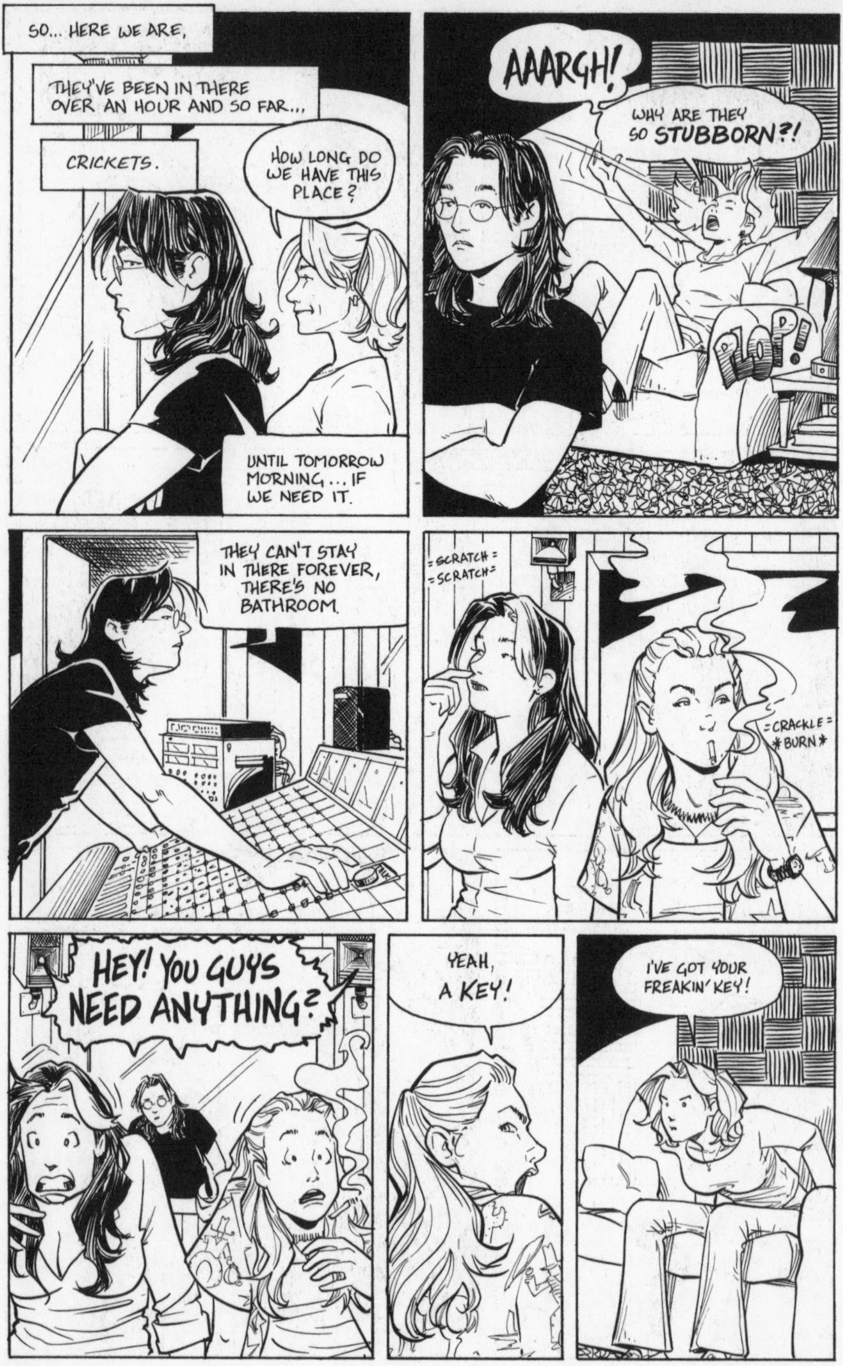
SO... HERE WE ARE,
THEY'VE BEEN IN THERE OVER AN HOUR AND SO FAR...,
CRICKETS.
HOW LONG DO WE HAVE THIS PLACE?
UNTIL TOMORROW MORNING... IF WE NEED IT.
AAARGH!
WHY ARE THEY SO STUBBORN?!
PLOP!
THEY CAN'T STAY IN THERE FOREVER, THERE'S NO BATHROOM.
=SCRATCH=
=SCRATCH=
=CRACKLE=
BURN
HEY! YOU GUYS NEED ANYTHING?
YEAH, A KEY!
I'VE GOT YOUR FREAKIN' KEY!

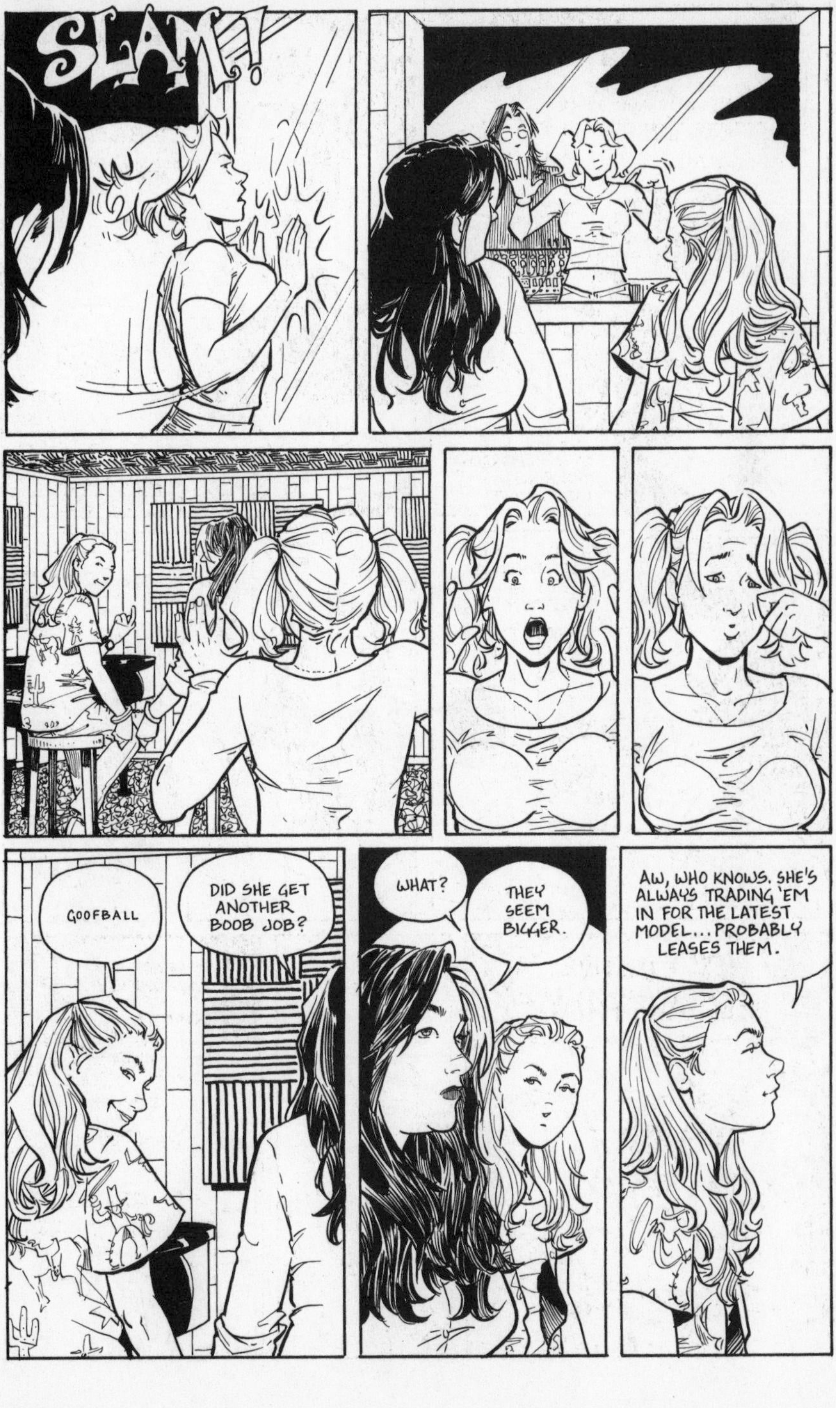
SLAM!
GOOFBALL
DID SHE GET ANOTHER BOOB JOB?
WHAT?
THEY SEEM BIGGER.
AW, WHO KNOWS. SHE'S ALWAYS TRADING 'EM IN FOR THE LATEST MODEL... PROBABLY LEASES THEM.

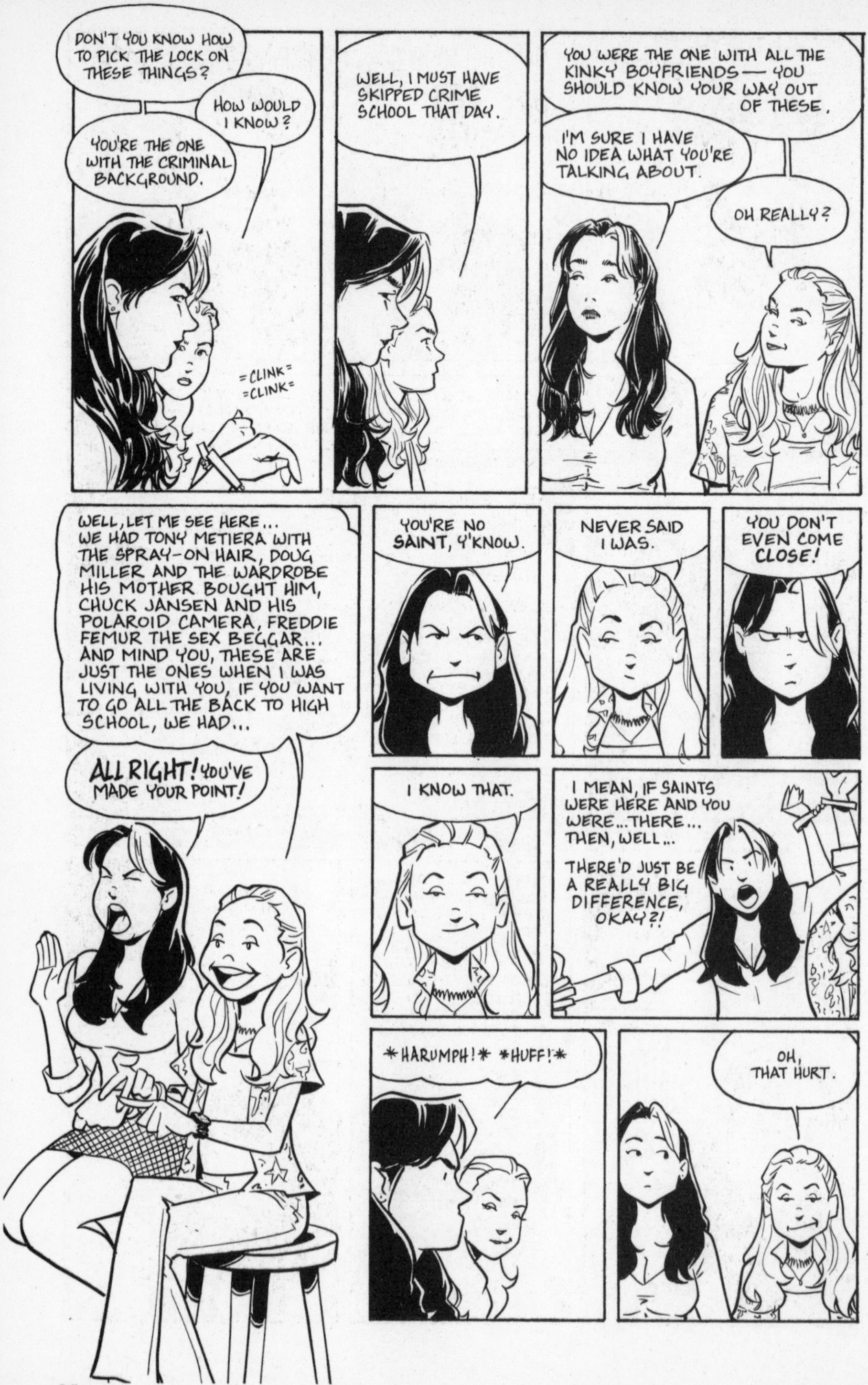
DON'T YOU KNOW HOW TO PICK THE LOCK ON THESE THINGS?
HOW WOULD I KNOW?
YOU'RE THE ONE WITH THE CRIMINAL BACKGROUND.
=CLINK= =CLINK=
WELL, I MUST HAVE SKIPPED CRIME SCHOOL THAT DAY.
YOU WERE THE ONE WITH ALL THE KINKY BOYFRIENDS— YOU SHOULD KNOW YOUR WAY OUT OF THESE.
I'M SURE I HAVE NO IDEA WHAT YOU'RE TALKING ABOUT.
OH REALLY?
WELL, LET ME SEE HERE... WE HAD TONY METIERA WITH THE SPRAY-ON HAIR, DOUG MILLER AND THE WARDROBE HIS MOTHER BOUGHT HIM, CHUCK JANSEN AND HIS POLAROID CAMERA, FREDDIE FEMUR THE SEX BEGGAR... AND MIND YOU, THESE ARE JUST THE ONES WHEN I WAS LIVING WITH YOU, IF YOU WANT TO GO ALL THE BACK TO HIGH SCHOOL, WE HAD...
ALL RIGHT! YOU'VE MADE YOUR POINT!
YOU'RE NO SAINT, Y'KNOW.
NEVER SAID I WAS.
YOU DON'T EVEN COME CLOSE!
I KNOW THAT.
I MEAN, IF SAINTS WERE HERE AND YOU WERE...THERE... THEN, WELL...
THERE'D JUST BE A REALLY BIG DIFFERENCE, OKAY?!
HARUMPH! *HUFF!*
OH, THAT HURT.

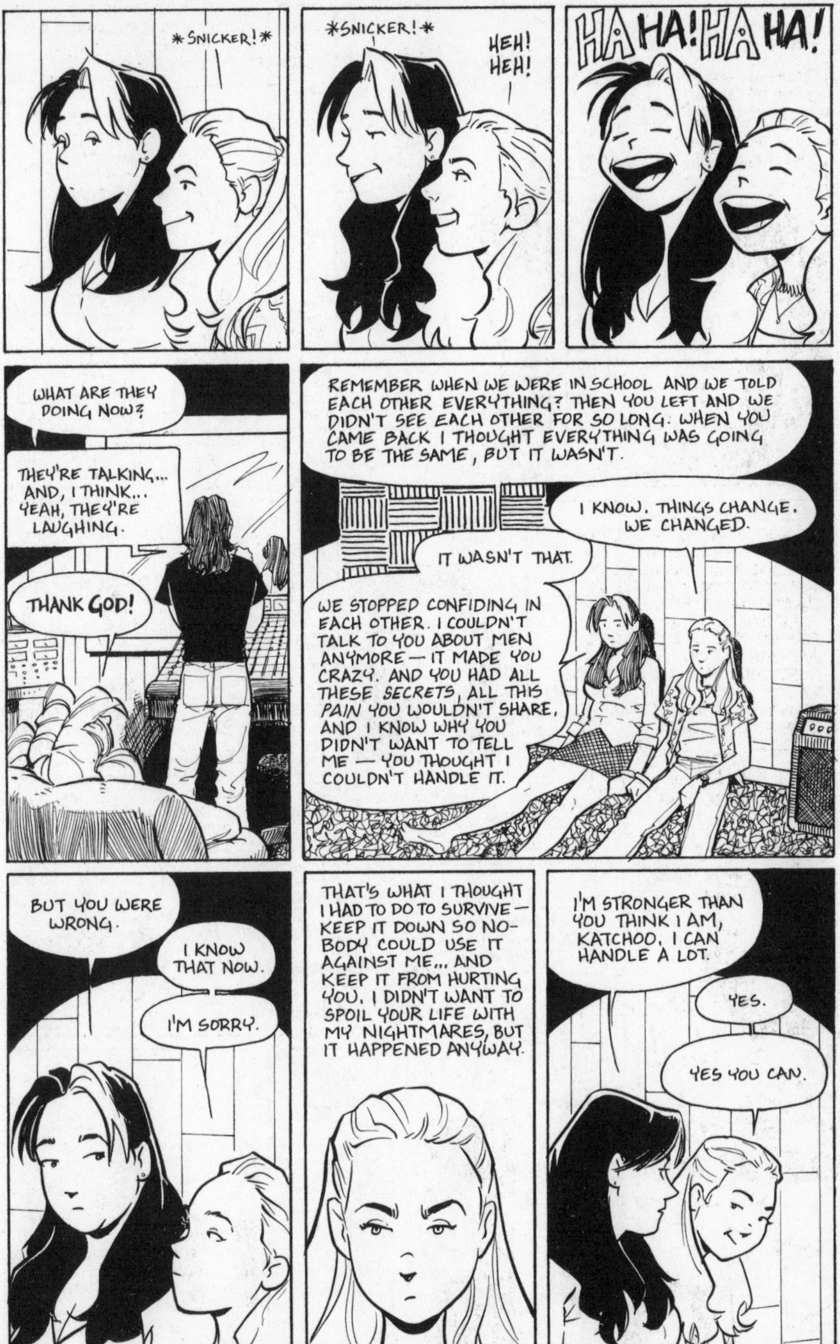
SNICKER!
SNICKER!
HEH! HEH!
HAHA!HAHA HA!
WHAT ARE THEY DOING NOW?
THEY'RE TALKING... AND, I THINK... YEAH, THEY'RE LAUGHING.
THANK GOD!
REMEMBER WHEN WE WERE IN SCHOOL AND WE TOLD EACH OTHER EVERYTHING? THEN YOU LEFT AND WE DIDN'T SEE EACH OTHER FOR SO LONG. WHEN YOU CAME BACK I THOUGHT EVERYTHING WAS GOING TO BE THE SAME, BUT IT WASN'T.
I KNOW. THINGS CHANGE. WE CHANGED.
IT WASN'T THAT.
WE STOPPED CONFIDING IN EACH OTHER. I COULDN'T TALK TO YOU ABOUT MEN ANYMORE — IT MADE YOU CRAZY. AND YOU HAD ALL THESE *SECRETS*, ALL THIS *PAIN* YOU WOULDN'T SHARE, AND I KNOW WHY YOU DIDN'T WANT TO TELL ME — YOU THOUGHT I COULDN'T HANDLE IT.
BUT YOU WERE WRONG.
I KNOW THAT NOW.
I'M SORRY.
THAT'S WHAT I THOUGHT I HAD TO DO TO SURVIVE — KEEP IT DOWN SO NOBODY COULD USE IT AGAINST ME... AND KEEP IT FROM HURTING YOU. I DIDN'T WANT TO SPOIL YOUR LIFE WITH MY NIGHTMARES, BUT IT HAPPENED ANYWAY.
I'M STRONGER THAN YOU THINK I AM, KATCHOO. I CAN HANDLE A LOT.
YES.
YES YOU CAN.

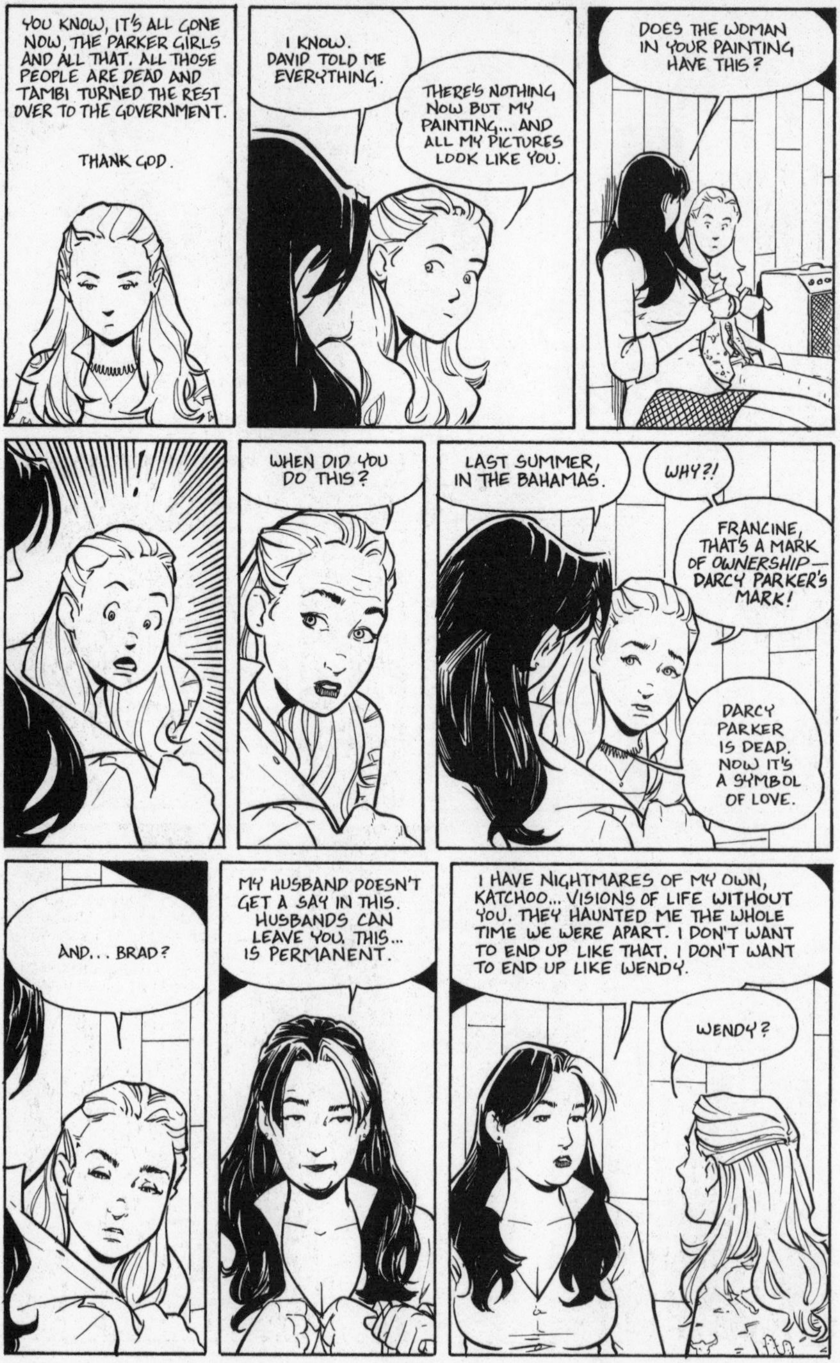
YOU KNOW, IT'S ALL GONE NOW, THE PARKER GIRLS AND ALL THAT. ALL THOSE PEOPLE ARE DEAD AND TAMBI TURNED THE REST OVER TO THE GOVERNMENT.
THANK GOD.
I KNOW. DAVID TOLD ME EVERYTHING.
THERE'S NOTHING NOW BUT MY PAINTING... AND ALL MY PICTURES LOOK LIKE YOU.
DOES THE WOMAN IN YOUR PAINTING HAVE THIS?
!
WHEN DID YOU DO THIS?
LAST SUMMER, IN THE BAHAMAS.
WHY?!
FRANCINE, THAT'S A MARK OF OWNERSHIP— DARCY PARKER'S MARK!
DARCY PARKER IS DEAD. NOW IT'S A SYMBOL OF LOVE.
AND... BRAD?
MY HUSBAND DOESN'T GET A SAY IN THIS. HUSBANDS CAN LEAVE YOU. THIS... IS PERMANENT.
I HAVE NIGHTMARES OF MY OWN, KATCHOO... VISIONS OF LIFE WITHOUT YOU. THEY HAUNTED ME THE WHOLE TIME WE WERE APART. I DON'T WANT TO END UP LIKE THAT. I DON'T WANT TO END UP LIKE WENDY.
WENDY?

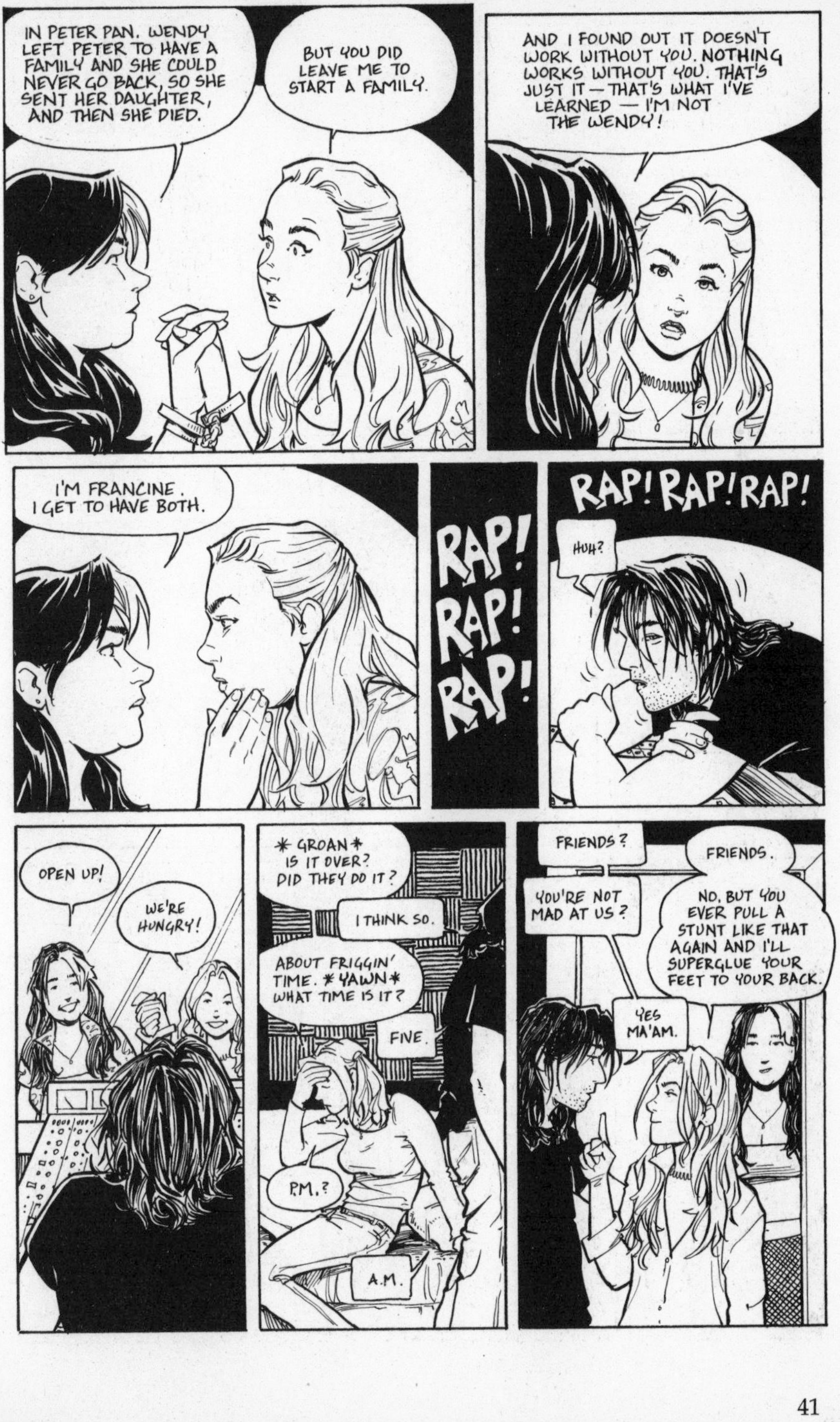
IN PETER PAN, WENDY LEFT PETER TO HAVE A FAMILY AND SHE COULD NEVER GO BACK, SO SHE SENT HER DAUGHTER, AND THEN SHE DIED.
BUT YOU DID LEAVE ME TO START A FAMILY.
AND I FOUND OUT IT DOESN'T WORK WITHOUT YOU. NOTHING WORKS WITHOUT YOU. THAT'S JUST IT — THAT'S WHAT I'VE LEARNED — I'M NOT THE WENDY!
I'M FRANCINE. I GET TO HAVE BOTH.
RAP! RAP! RAP!
RAP! RAP! RAP!
HUH?
OPEN UP!
WE'RE HUNGRY!
* GROAN * IS IT OVER? DID THEY DO IT?
I THINK SO.
ABOUT FRIGGIN' TIME. * YAWN * WHAT TIME IS IT?
FIVE.
P.M.?
A.M.
FRIENDS?
FRIENDS.
YOU'RE NOT MAD AT US?
NO, BUT YOU EVER PULL A STUNT LIKE THAT AGAIN AND I'LL SUPERGLUE YOUR FEET TO YOUR BACK.
YES MA'AM.

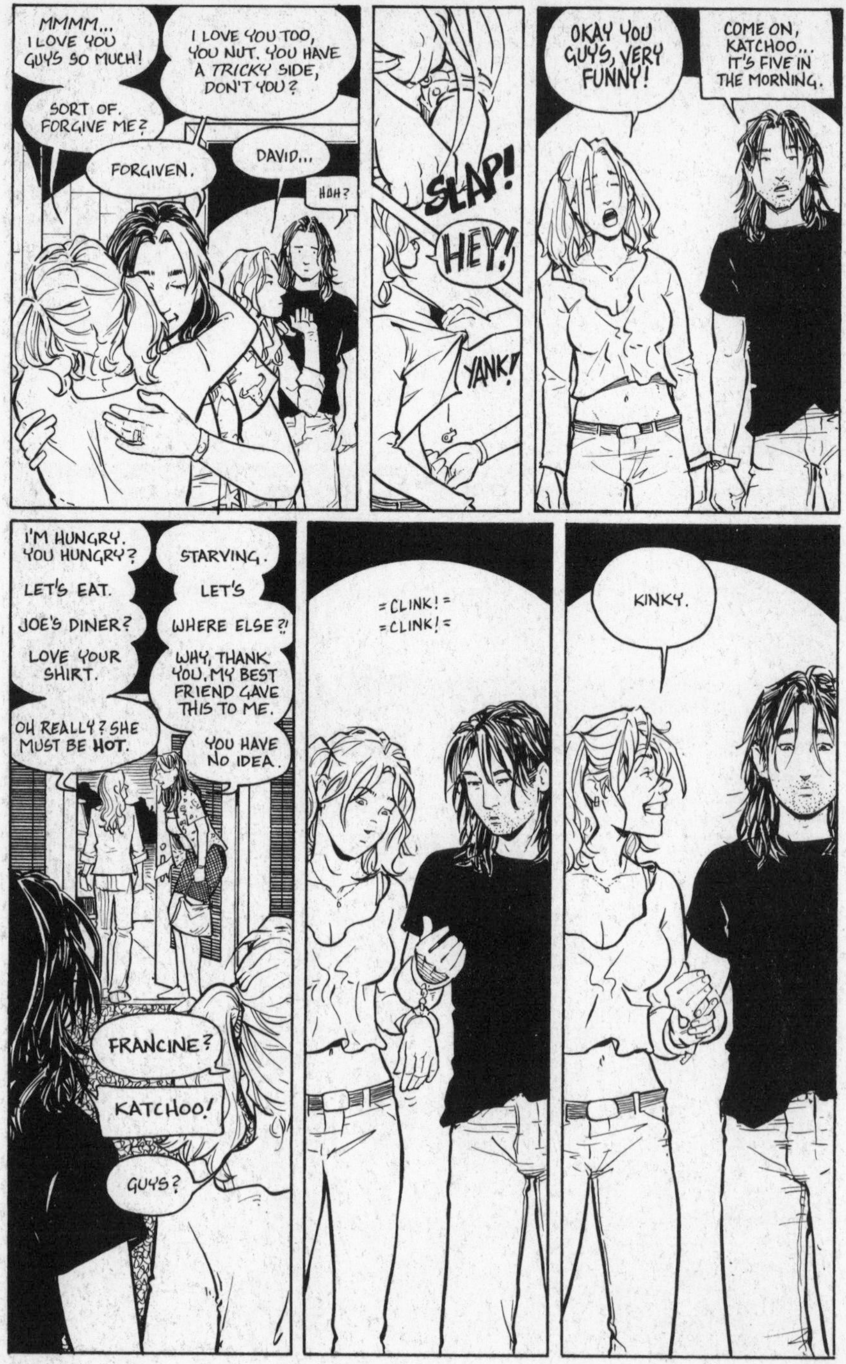
MMMM... I LOVE YOU GUYS SO MUCH!
I LOVE YOU TOO, YOU NUT. YOU HAVE A TRICKY SIDE, DON'T YOU?
SORT OF. FORGIVE ME?
FORGIVEN.
DAVID...
HUH?
SLAP!
HEY!
YANK!
OKAY YOU GUYS, VERY FUNNY!
COME ON, KATCHOO... IT'S FIVE IN THE MORNING.
I'M HUNGRY. YOU HUNGRY?
STARVING.
LET'S EAT.
LET'S
JOE'S DINER?
WHERE ELSE?!
LOVE YOUR SHIRT.
WHY, THANK YOU. MY BEST FRIEND GAVE THIS TO ME.
OH REALLY? SHE MUST BE HOT.
YOU HAVE NO IDEA.
FRANCINE?
KATCHOO!
GUYS?
=CLINK!=
=CLINK!=
KINKY.

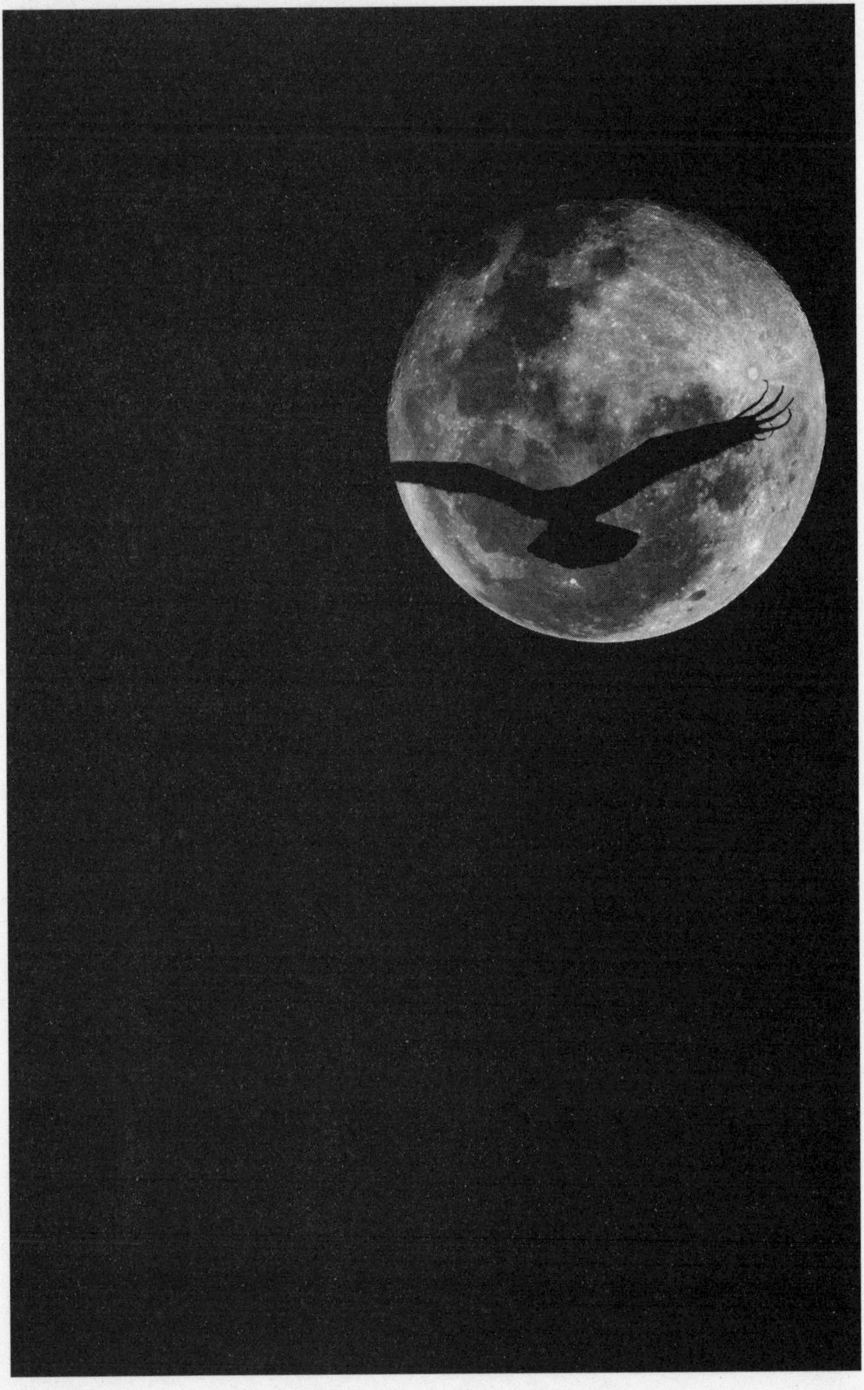

IF YOU DON'T WANT TO START WITH LILLIAN GISH, THEN IT REALLY BEGAN WITH AUDREY HEPBURN.

AUDREY WAS A SKINNY BALLET DANCER SO BEAUTIFUL THEY MADE HER INTO AN ACTRESS. IN THE MIDST OF THE POPULAR 1950'S BUXOM GIRLS, HERE WAS THIS THIN, LOVELY WAIF WITH THE GRACE OF A PRINCESS AND THE EYES OF A DOE. COMPARED TO AUDREY, ELIZABETH TAYLOR WAS A FIREPLUG AND MARILYN MONROE WALKED LIKE A DONKEY ON PERCODAN.

AUDREY MADE THIN CHIC.

AFTER THAT IT WAS TWIGGY, THEN — WITH THE NOTABLE EXCEPTION OF CHERYL TIEGS, WHO BEGAT HER OWN LINE OF BUSTY SUPERMODEL DESCENDANTS — EVERY FASHION MODEL, ACTRESS, SINGER, HEIRESS, AND ALL THE ABOVE WANNABES SINCE, UNTIL WE REPLICATED DOWN TO THE UMPTEENTH GENERATION OF ACTOR'S KIDS WHO INHERITED HOLLYWOOD FOR NO APPRECIABLE REASON WHATSOEVER.

THIS BATCH OF EINSTEINS SUBSTITUTED RICHES FOR ACCOMPLISHMENTS AND DIETING FOR TALENT UNTIL WE HAD AN ENTIRE INDUSTRY WHO BELIEVED ANY WOMAN LARGER THAN A SIZE 2 WAS AN UNDESIRABLE RHINOCEROS. I KID YOU NOT.

WHICH BRINGS US TO PIA.

PIA ALEXANDRIA PETRESCU... OR AS SHE PREFERS, "PIA PIZA... MY *STAGE NAME.*" PIA, MY STARVING YOUNG MODEL, HAS NEVER HEARD OF AUDREY HEPBURN OR TWIGGY AND SHE FIRMLY BELIEVES HOLLYWOOD HAS NOTHING TO DO WITH WHY SHE IS 30 POUNDS UNDERWEIGHT AND DESPERATE TO BE ON MTV — DOING *WHAT* EXACTLY SHE'S NOT SURE BUT, AND I QUOTE, "WHAT DIFFERENCE DOES IT MAKE? *MTV!*"

LITTLE PIA, WHOSE ONLY TALENTS ARE FAINTING AND LOOKING BETRAYED...

SHE'LL PROBABLY MAKE IT IN HOLLYWOOD, SHE'S SKINNY ENOUGH.

SO, ANYWAY, AFTER PIA'S LATEST FAINTING SPELL, JET AND I DECIDED TO HAVE A FACE TO FACE WITH THE GIRL AND TRY TO FLIP THE BREAKER IN HER HEAD THAT CLEARLY BLEW SOMEWHERE AROUND MIDDLE SCHOOL.

UNFORTUNATELY, YOU CAN LEAD A HORSE TO WATER BUT... GETTING HIM, OR HER, TO SWIG IT DOWN WITH A CARBOHYDRATE IS ANOTHER MATTER.

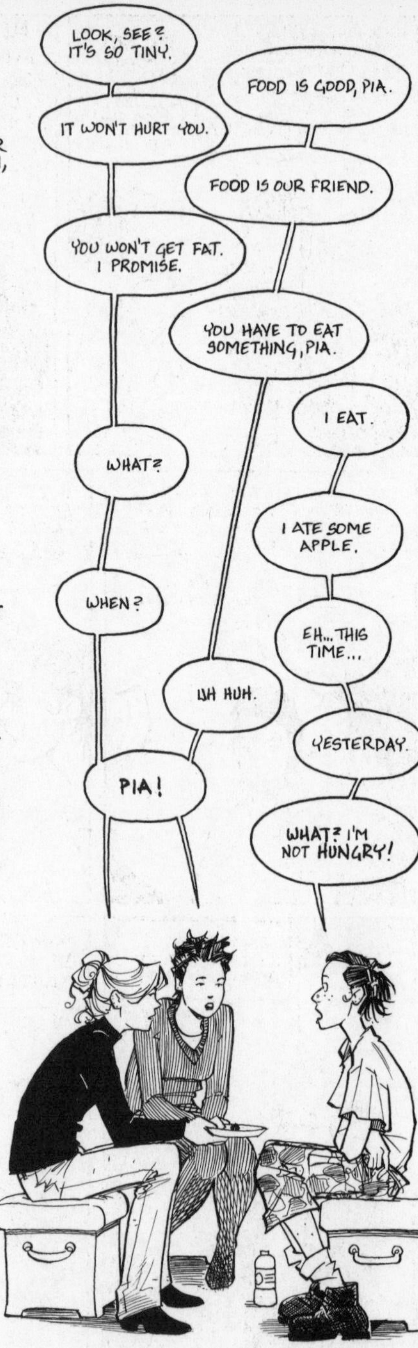
LOOK, SEE? IT'S SO TINY.
FOOD IS GOOD, PIA.
IT WON'T HURT YOU.
FOOD IS OUR FRIEND.
YOU WON'T GET FAT. I PROMISE.
YOU HAVE TO EAT SOMETHING, PIA.
I EAT.
WHAT?
I ATE SOME APPLE.
WHEN?
EH... THIS TIME...
UH HUH.
YESTERDAY.
PIA!
WHAT? I'M NOT HUNGRY!

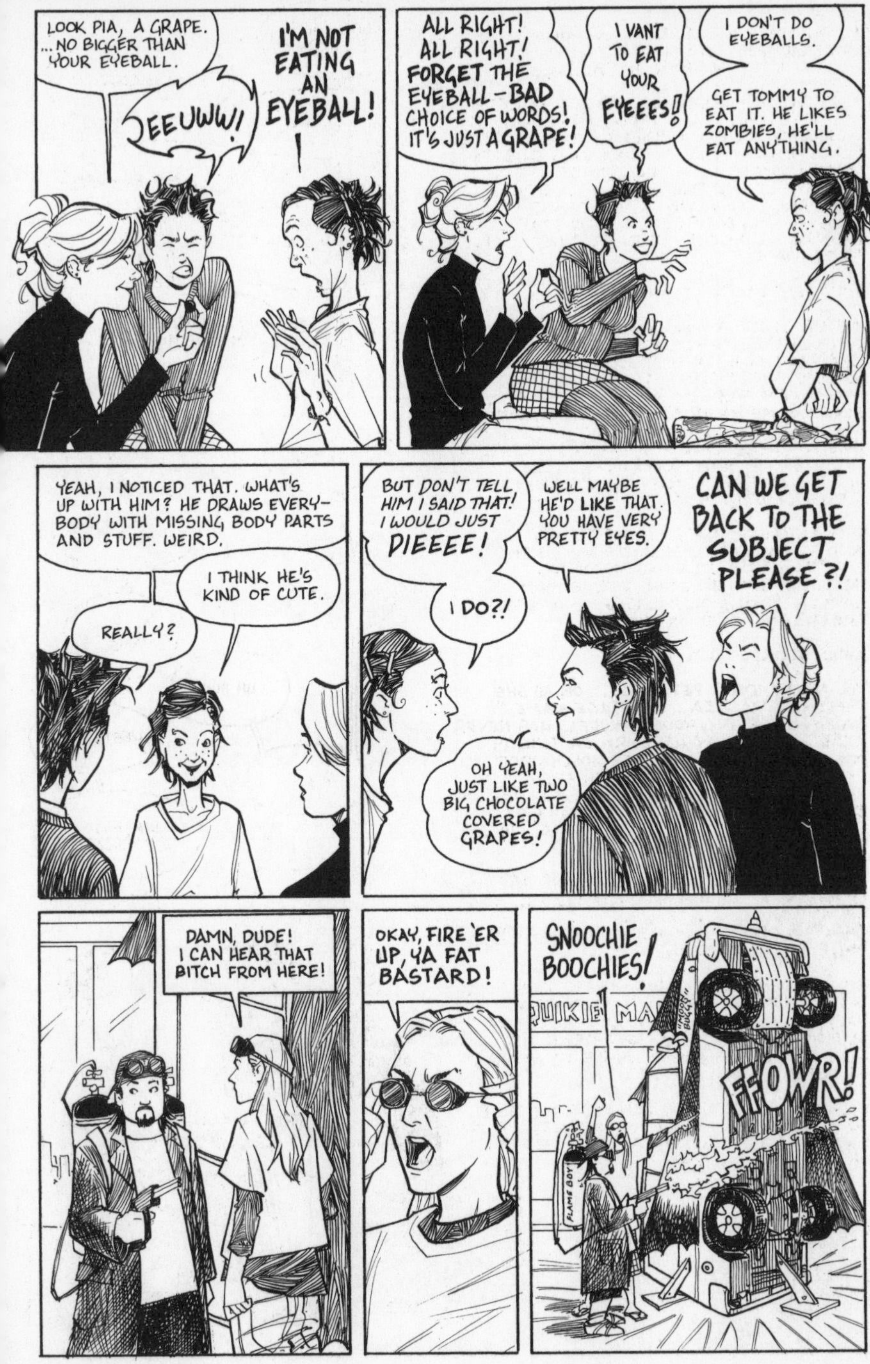
LOOK PIA, A GRAPE. ...NO BIGGER THAN YOUR EYEBALL.
EEUWW!
I'M NOT EATING AN EYEBALL!
ALL RIGHT! ALL RIGHT! FORGET THE EYEBALL—BAD CHOICE OF WORDS! IT'S JUST A GRAPE!
I VANT TO EAT YOUR EYEEES!
I DON'T DO EYEBALLS.
GET TOMMY TO EAT IT. HE LIKES ZOMBIES, HE'LL EAT ANYTHING.
YEAH, I NOTICED THAT. WHAT'S UP WITH HIM? HE DRAWS EVERY-BODY WITH MISSING BODY PARTS AND STUFF. WEIRD.
I THINK HE'S KIND OF CUTE.
REALLY?
BUT DON'T TELL HIM I SAID THAT! I WOULD JUST DIEEEE!
WELL MAYBE HE'D LIKE THAT. YOU HAVE VERY PRETTY EYES.
I DO?!
OH YEAH, JUST LIKE TWO BIG CHOCOLATE COVERED GRAPES!
CAN WE GET BACK TO THE SUBJECT PLEASE?!
DAMN, DUDE! I CAN HEAR THAT BITCH FROM HERE!
OKAY, FIRE 'ER UP, YA FAT BASTARD!
SNOOCHIE BOOCHIES!
QUIKIE MA
FLAME BOY
FFOWR!

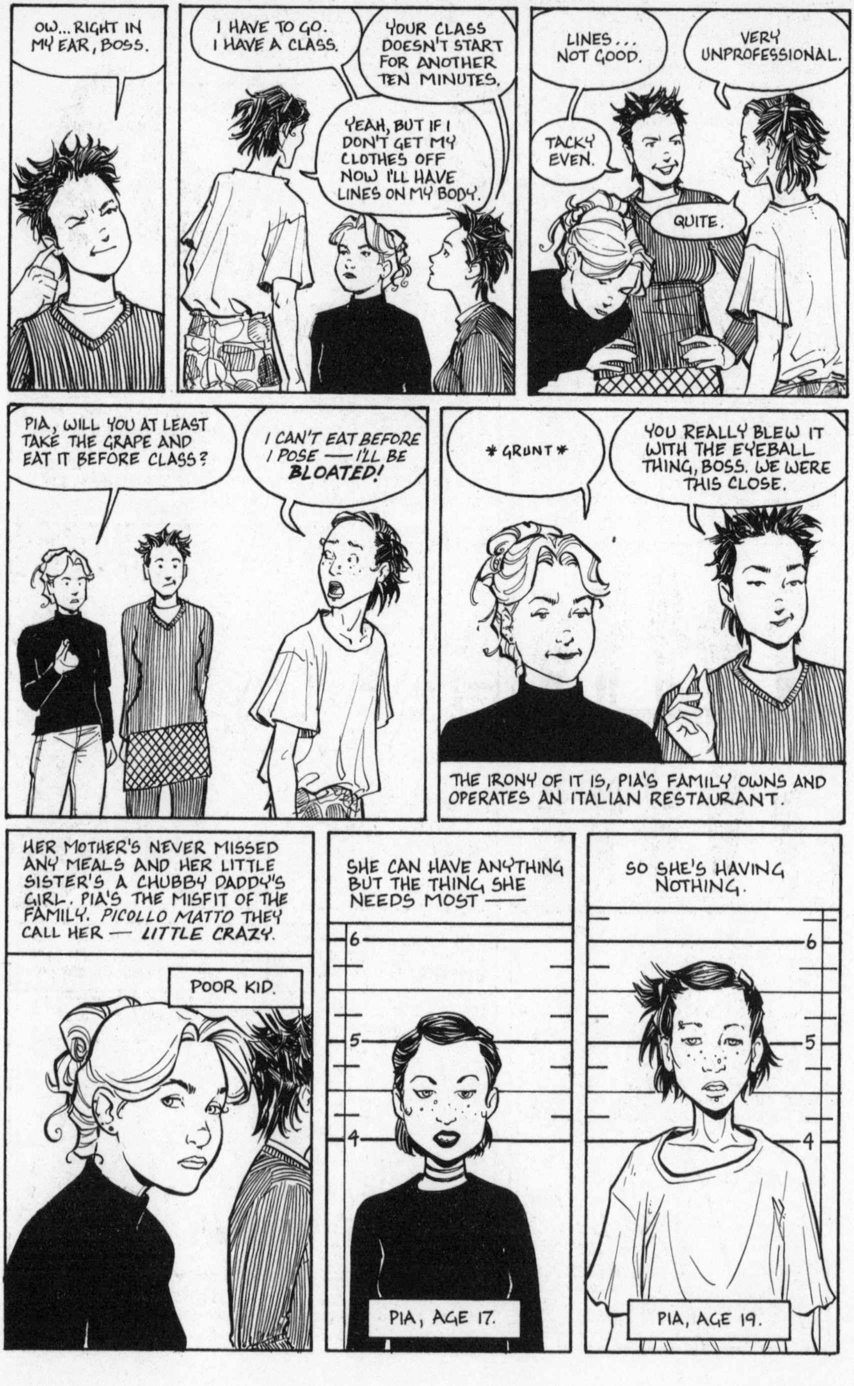
OW... RIGHT IN MY EAR, BOSS.
I HAVE TO GO. I HAVE A CLASS.
YOUR CLASS DOESN'T START FOR ANOTHER TEN MINUTES.
YEAH, BUT IF I DON'T GET MY CLOTHES OFF NOW I'LL HAVE LINES ON MY BODY.
LINES... NOT GOOD.
VERY UNPROFESSIONAL.
TACKY EVEN.
QUITE.
PIA, WILL YOU AT LEAST TAKE THE GRAPE AND EAT IT BEFORE CLASS?
I CAN'T EAT BEFORE I POSE — I'LL BE BLOATED!
GRUNT
YOU REALLY BLEW IT WITH THE EYEBALL THING, BOSS. WE WERE THIS CLOSE.
THE IRONY OF IT IS, PIA'S FAMILY OWNS AND OPERATES AN ITALIAN RESTAURANT.
HER MOTHER'S NEVER MISSED ANY MEALS AND HER LITTLE SISTER'S A CHUBBY DADDY'S GIRL. PIA'S THE MISFIT OF THE FAMILY. PICOLLO MATTO THEY CALL HER — LITTLE CRAZY.
POOR KID.
SHE CAN HAVE ANYTHING BUT THE THING SHE NEEDS MOST —
6
5
4
PIA, AGE 17.
SO SHE'S HAVING NOTHING.
6
5
4
PIA, AGE 19.

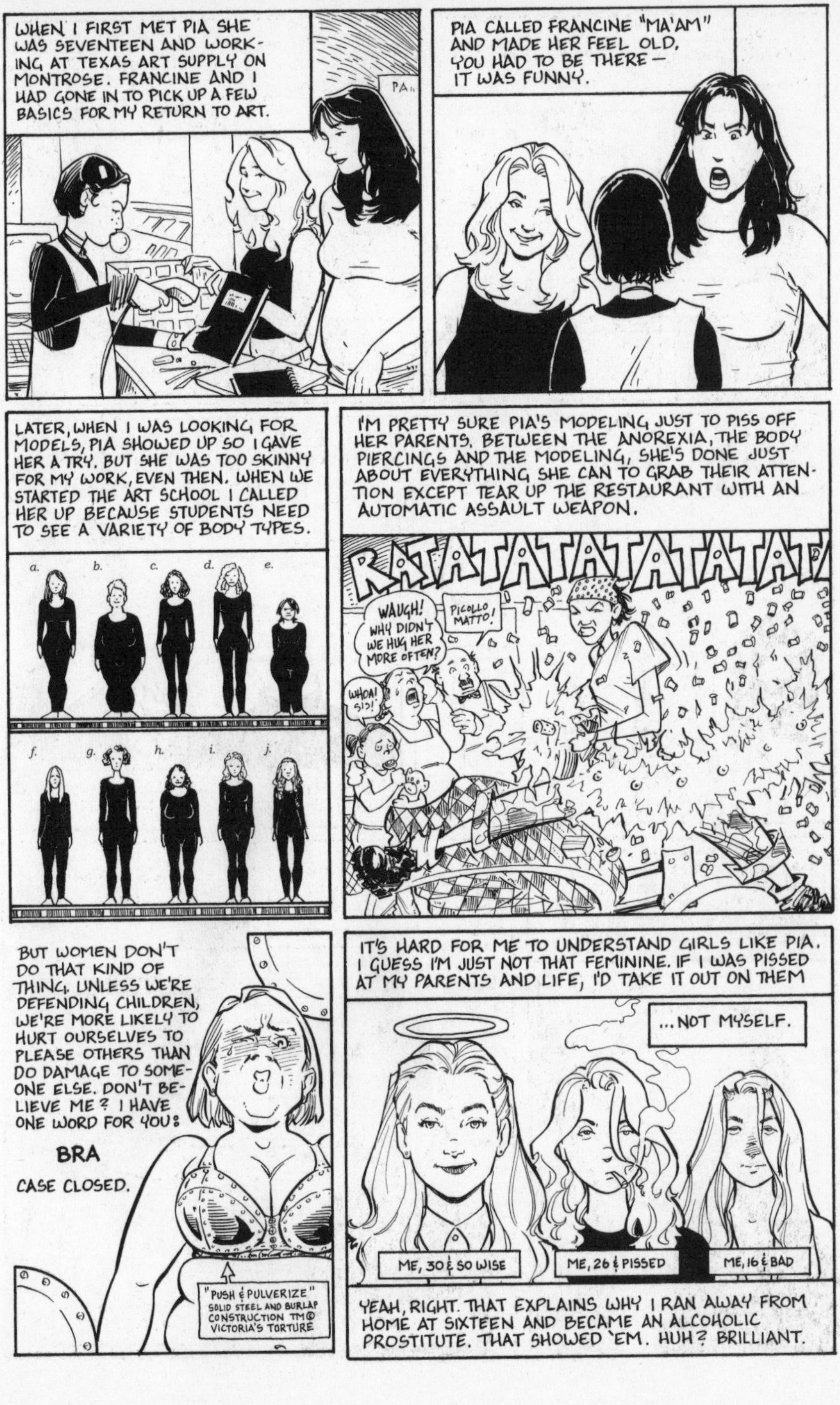

WHEN I FIRST MET PIA SHE WAS SEVENTEEN AND WORKING AT TEXAS ART SUPPLY ON MONTROSE. FRANCINE AND I HAD GONE IN TO PICK UP A FEW BASICS FOR MY RETURN TO ART.
PIA CALLED FRANCINE "MA'AM" AND MADE HER FEEL OLD. YOU HAD TO BE THERE — IT WAS FUNNY.
LATER, WHEN I WAS LOOKING FOR MODELS, PIA SHOWED UP SO I GAVE HER A TRY. BUT SHE WAS TOO SKINNY FOR MY WORK, EVEN THEN. WHEN WE STARTED THE ART SCHOOL I CALLED HER UP BECAUSE STUDENTS NEED TO SEE A VARIETY OF BODY TYPES.
a. b. c. d. e.
f. g. h. i. j.
I'M PRETTY SURE PIA'S MODELING JUST TO PISS OFF HER PARENTS. BETWEEN THE ANOREXIA, THE BODY PIERCINGS AND THE MODELING, SHE'S DONE JUST ABOUT EVERYTHING SHE CAN TO GRAB THEIR ATTENTION EXCEPT TEAR UP THE RESTAURANT WITH AN AUTOMATIC ASSAULT WEAPON.
RATATATATATATATAT
WAUGH! WHY DIDN'T WE HUG HER MORE OFTEN?
PICOLLO MATTO!
WHOA! SIS!
BUT WOMEN DON'T DO THAT KIND OF THING. UNLESS WE'RE DEFENDING CHILDREN, WE'RE MORE LIKELY TO HURT OURSELVES TO PLEASE OTHERS THAN DO DAMAGE TO SOMEONE ELSE. DON'T BELIEVE ME? I HAVE ONE WORD FOR YOU:
BRA
CASE CLOSED.
"PUSH & PULVERIZE" SOLID STEEL AND BURLAP CONSTRUCTION TM© VICTORIA'S TORTURE
IT'S HARD FOR ME TO UNDERSTAND GIRLS LIKE PIA. I GUESS I'M JUST NOT THAT FEMININE. IF I WAS PISSED AT MY PARENTS AND LIFE, I'D TAKE IT OUT ON THEM
...NOT MYSELF.
ME, 30 & SO WISE
ME, 26 & PISSED
ME, 16 & BAD
YEAH, RIGHT. THAT EXPLAINS WHY I RAN AWAY FROM HOME AT SIXTEEN AND BECAME AN ALCOHOLIC PROSTITUTE. THAT SHOWED 'EM. HUH? BRILLIANT.

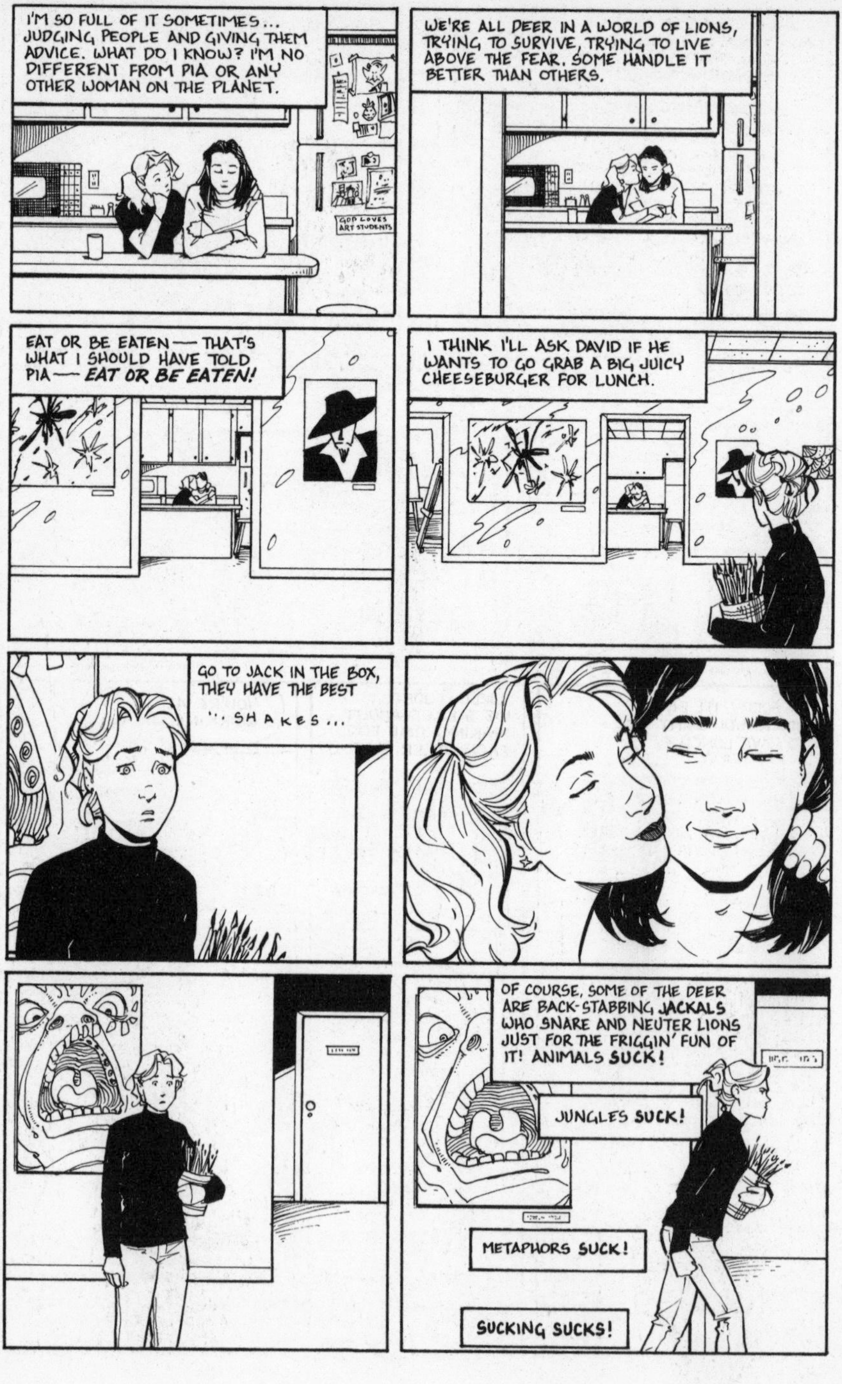
I'M SO FULL OF IT SOMETIMES... JUDGING PEOPLE AND GIVING THEM ADVICE. WHAT DO I KNOW? I'M NO DIFFERENT FROM PIA OR ANY OTHER WOMAN ON THE PLANET.
GOD LOVES ART STUDENTS
WE'RE ALL DEER IN A WORLD OF LIONS, TRYING TO SURVIVE, TRYING TO LIVE ABOVE THE FEAR. SOME HANDLE IT BETTER THAN OTHERS.
EAT OR BE EATEN — THAT'S WHAT I SHOULD HAVE TOLD PIA — EAT OR BE EATEN!
I THINK I'LL ASK DAVID IF HE WANTS TO GO GRAB A BIG JUICY CHEESEBURGER FOR LUNCH.
GO TO JACK IN THE BOX, THEY HAVE THE BEST
... SHAKES...
OF COURSE, SOME OF THE DEER ARE BACK-STABBING JACKALS WHO SNARE AND NEUTER LIONS JUST FOR THE FRIGGIN' FUN OF IT! ANIMALS SUCK!
JUNGLES SUCK!
METAPHORS SUCK!
SUCKING SUCKS!

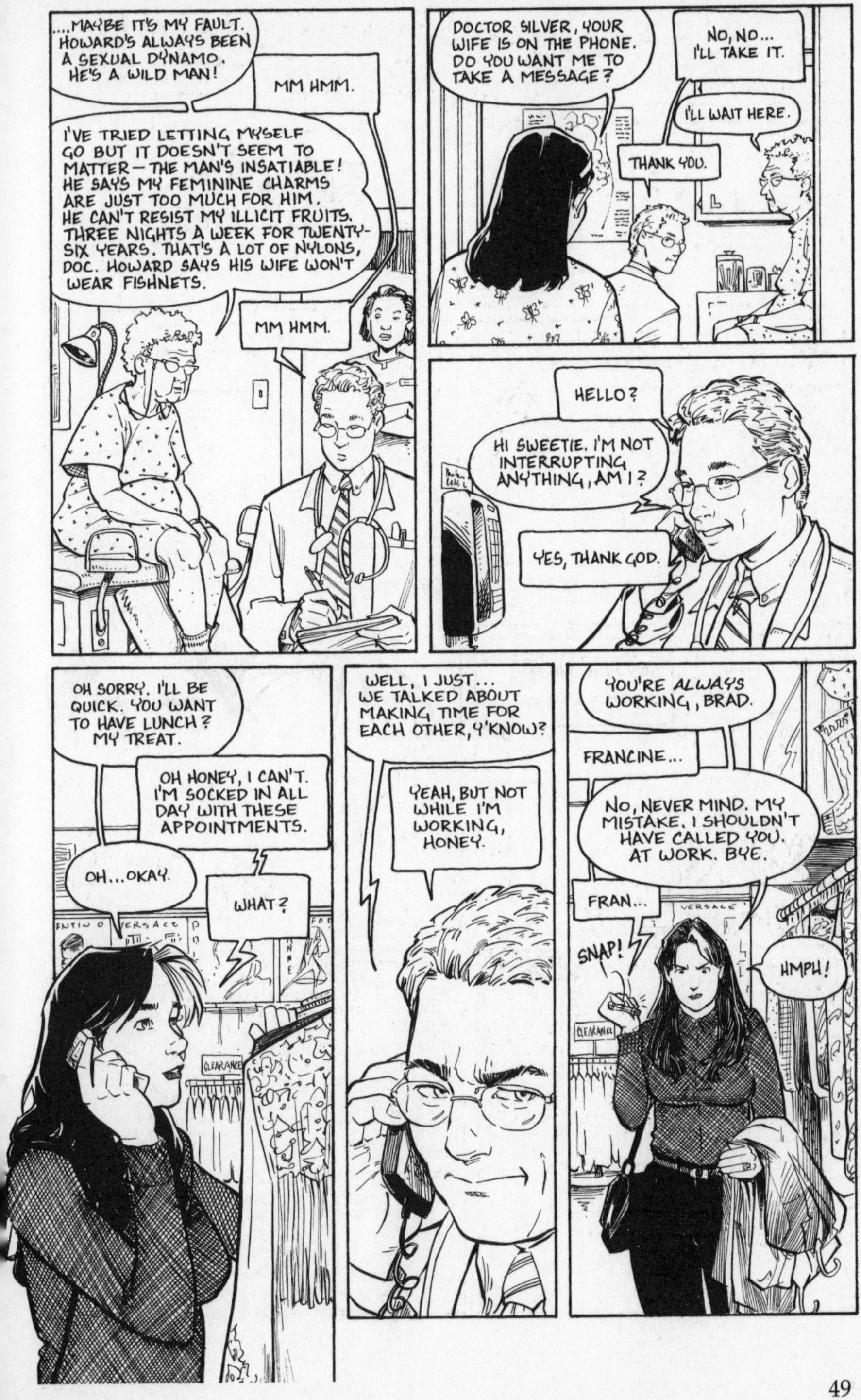
....MAYBE IT'S MY FAULT. HOWARD'S ALWAYS BEEN A SEXUAL DYNAMO. HE'S A WILD MAN!
MM HMM.
I'VE TRIED LETTING MYSELF GO BUT IT DOESN'T SEEM TO MATTER—THE MAN'S INSATIABLE! HE SAYS MY FEMININE CHARMS ARE JUST TOO MUCH FOR HIM. HE CAN'T RESIST MY ILLICIT FRUITS. THREE NIGHTS A WEEK FOR TWENTY-SIX YEARS. THAT'S A LOT OF NYLONS, DOC. HOWARD SAYS HIS WIFE WON'T WEAR FISHNETS.
MM HMM.
DOCTOR SILVER, YOUR WIFE IS ON THE PHONE. DO YOU WANT ME TO TAKE A MESSAGE?
NO, NO... I'LL TAKE IT.
I'LL WAIT HERE.
THANK YOU.
HELLO?
HI SWEETIE. I'M NOT INTERRUPTING ANYTHING, AM I?
YES, THANK GOD.
OH SORRY. I'LL BE QUICK. YOU WANT TO HAVE LUNCH? MY TREAT.
OH HONEY, I CAN'T. I'M SOCKED IN ALL DAY WITH THESE APPOINTMENTS.
OH...OKAY.
WHAT?
WELL, I JUST... WE TALKED ABOUT MAKING TIME FOR EACH OTHER, Y'KNOW?
YEAH, BUT NOT WHILE I'M WORKING, HONEY.
YOU'RE ALWAYS WORKING, BRAD.
FRANCINE...
NO, NEVER MIND. MY MISTAKE. I SHOULDN'T HAVE CALLED YOU. AT WORK. BYE.
FRAN...
SNAP!
HMPH!

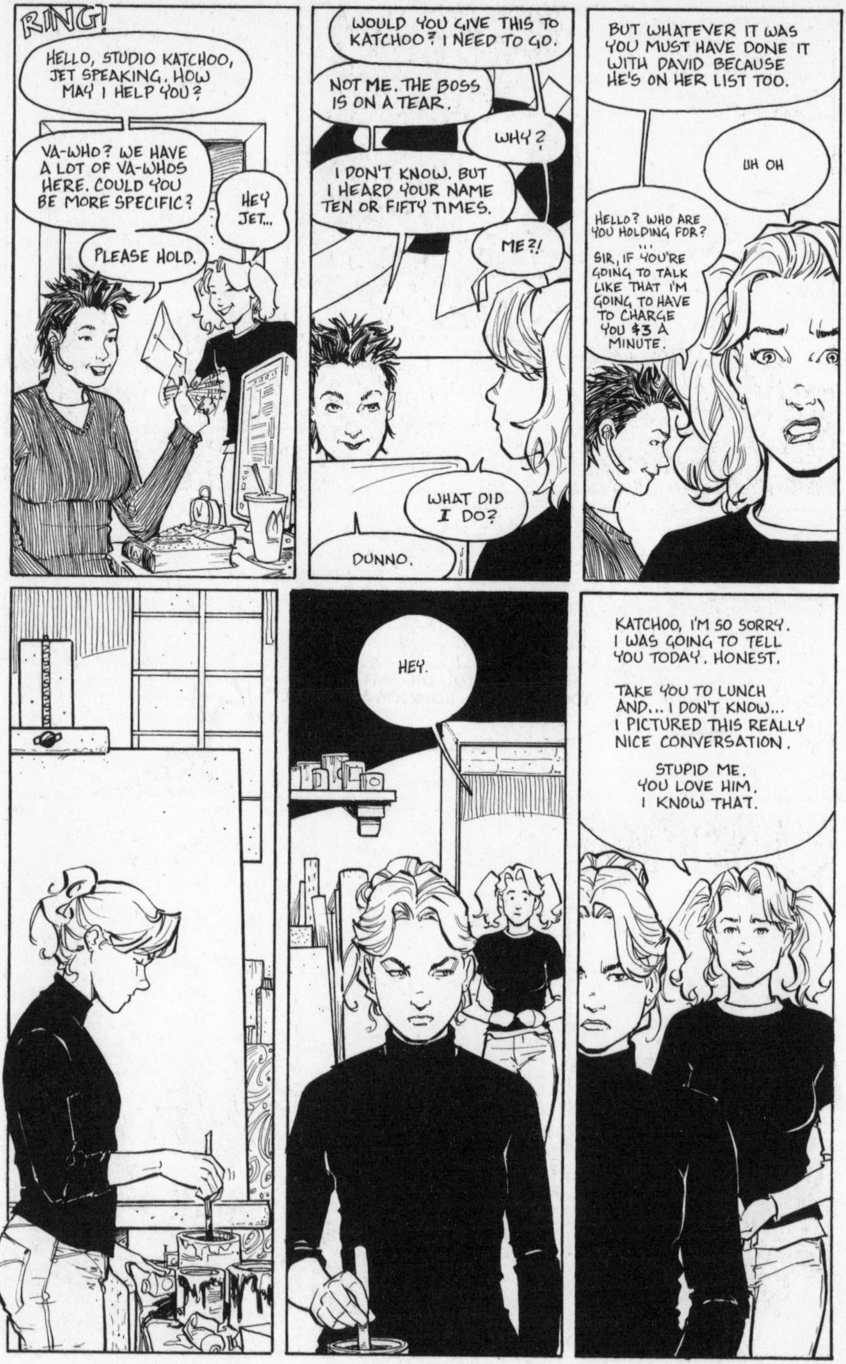
RING!
HELLO, STUDIO KATCHOO, JET SPEAKING. HOW MAY I HELP YOU?
VA-WHO? WE HAVE A LOT OF VA-WHOS HERE. COULD YOU BE MORE SPECIFIC?
HEY JET...
PLEASE HOLD.
WOULD YOU GIVE THIS TO KATCHOO? I NEED TO GO.
NOT ME. THE BOSS IS ON A TEAR.
WHY?
I DON'T KNOW. BUT I HEARD YOUR NAME TEN OR FIFTY TIMES.
ME?!
WHAT DID I DO?
DUNNO.
BUT WHATEVER IT WAS YOU MUST HAVE DONE IT WITH DAVID BECAUSE HE'S ON HER LIST TOO.
UH OH
HELLO? WHO ARE YOU HOLDING FOR? ... SIR, IF YOU'RE GOING TO TALK LIKE THAT I'M GOING TO HAVE TO CHARGE YOU $3 A MINUTE.
HEY.
KATCHOO, I'M SO SORRY. I WAS GOING TO TELL YOU TODAY. HONEST.
TAKE YOU TO LUNCH AND... I DON'T KNOW... I PICTURED THIS REALLY NICE CONVERSATION.
STUPID ME. YOU LOVE HIM. I KNOW THAT.

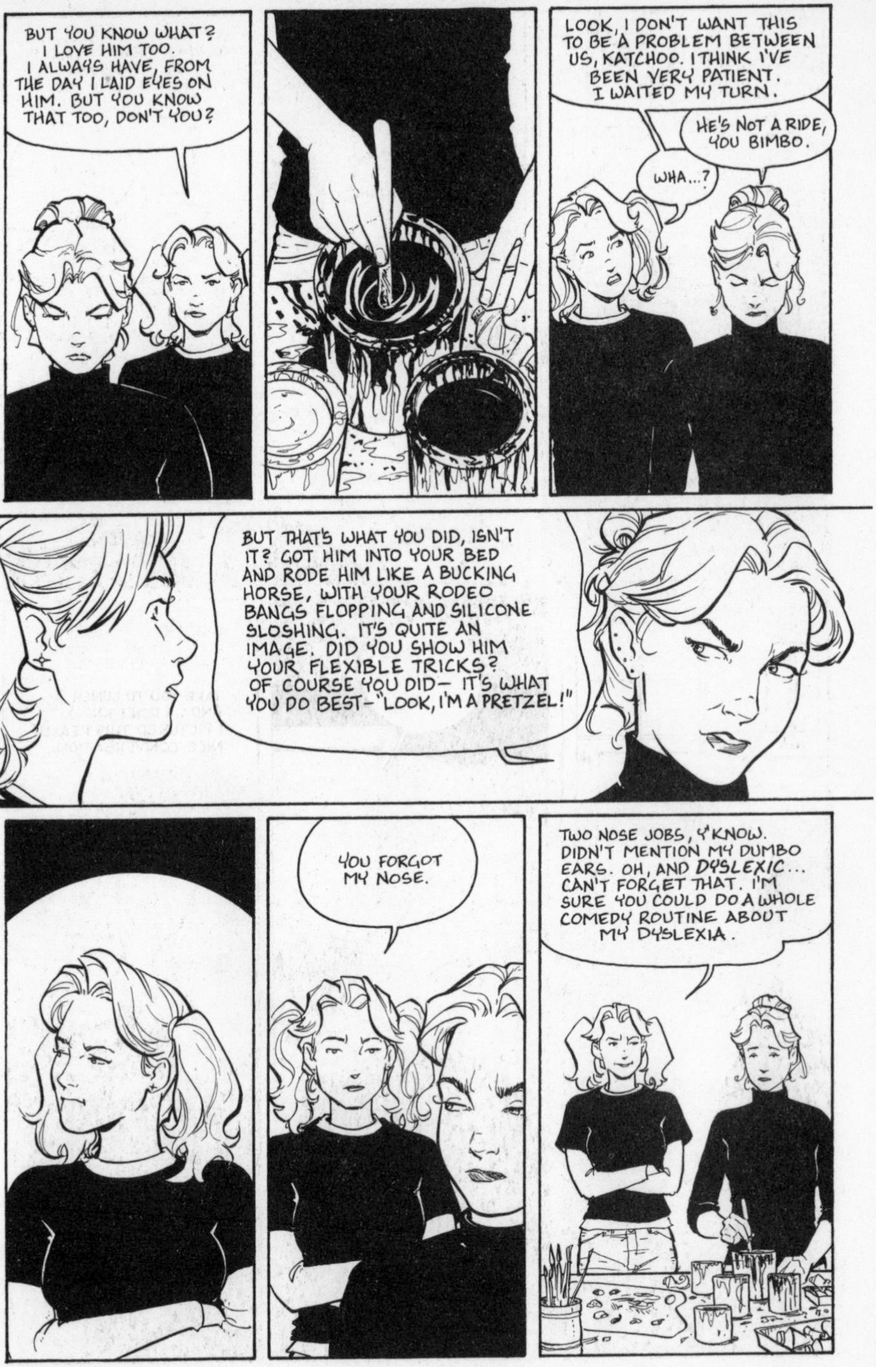
BUT YOU KNOW WHAT? I LOVE HIM TOO. I ALWAYS HAVE, FROM THE DAY I LAID EYES ON HIM. BUT YOU KNOW THAT TOO, DON'T YOU?
LOOK, I DON'T WANT THIS TO BE A PROBLEM BETWEEN US, KATCHOO. I THINK I'VE BEEN VERY PATIENT. I WAITED MY TURN.
WHA...?
HE'S NOT A RIDE, YOU BIMBO.
BUT THAT'S WHAT YOU DID, ISN'T IT? GOT HIM INTO YOUR BED AND RODE HIM LIKE A BUCKING HORSE, WITH YOUR RODEO BANGS FLOPPING AND SILICONE SLOSHING. IT'S QUITE AN IMAGE. DID YOU SHOW HIM YOUR FLEXIBLE TRICKS? OF COURSE YOU DID– IT'S WHAT YOU DO BEST– "LOOK, I'M A PRETZEL!"
YOU FORGOT MY NOSE.
TWO NOSE JOBS, Y'KNOW. DIDN'T MENTION MY DUMBO EARS. OH, AND DYSLEXIC... CAN'T FORGET THAT. I'M SURE YOU COULD DO A WHOLE COMEDY ROUTINE ABOUT MY DYSLEXIA.

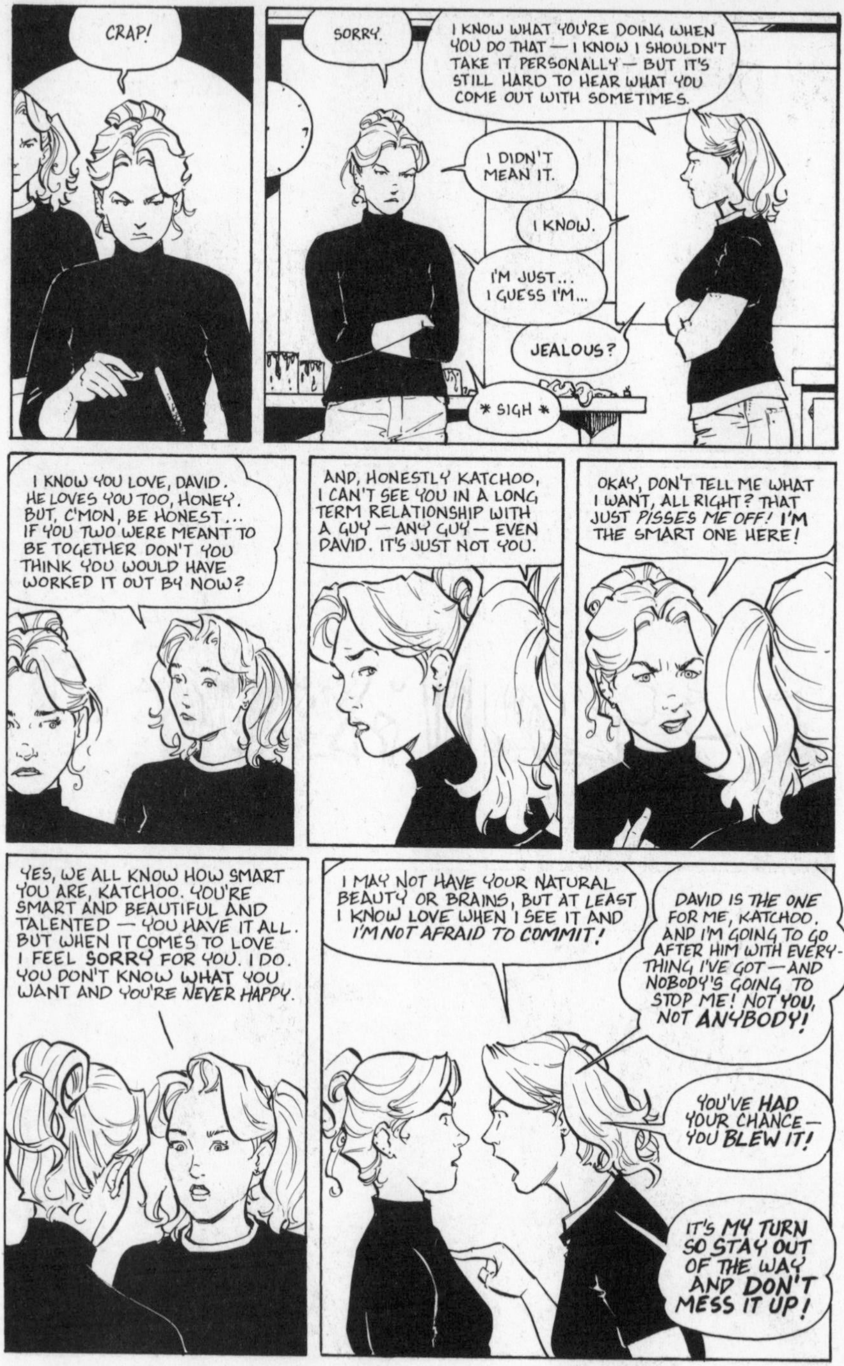
CRAP!
SORRY.
I KNOW WHAT YOU'RE DOING WHEN YOU DO THAT — I KNOW I SHOULDN'T TAKE IT PERSONALLY — BUT IT'S STILL HARD TO HEAR WHAT YOU COME OUT WITH SOMETIMES.
I DIDN'T MEAN IT.
I KNOW.
I'M JUST... I GUESS I'M...
JEALOUS?
SIGH
I KNOW YOU LOVE, DAVID. HE LOVES YOU TOO, HONEY. BUT, C'MON, BE HONEST... IF YOU TWO WERE MEANT TO BE TOGETHER DON'T YOU THINK YOU WOULD HAVE WORKED IT OUT BY NOW?
AND, HONESTLY KATCHOO, I CAN'T SEE YOU IN A LONG TERM RELATIONSHIP WITH A GUY — ANY GUY — EVEN DAVID. IT'S JUST NOT YOU.
OKAY, DON'T TELL ME WHAT I WANT, ALL RIGHT? THAT JUST *PISSES ME OFF!* **I'M THE SMART ONE HERE!**
YES, WE ALL KNOW HOW SMART YOU ARE, KATCHOO. YOU'RE SMART AND BEAUTIFUL AND TALENTED — YOU HAVE IT ALL. BUT WHEN IT COMES TO LOVE I FEEL **SORRY** FOR YOU. I DO. YOU DON'T KNOW **WHAT** YOU WANT AND YOU'RE *NEVER HAPPY*.
I MAY NOT HAVE YOUR NATURAL BEAUTY OR BRAINS, BUT AT *LEAST* I KNOW LOVE WHEN I SEE IT AND *I'M NOT AFRAID TO COMMIT!*
DAVID IS *THE ONE* FOR ME, KATCHOO. AND I'M GOING TO GO AFTER HIM WITH EVERYTHING I'VE GOT — AND NOBODY'S GOING TO STOP ME! NOT **YOU**, NOT **ANYBODY!**
YOU'VE **HAD** YOUR CHANCE — YOU **BLEW IT!**
IT'S **MY TURN SO STAY OUT OF THE WAY AND DON'T MESS IT UP!**

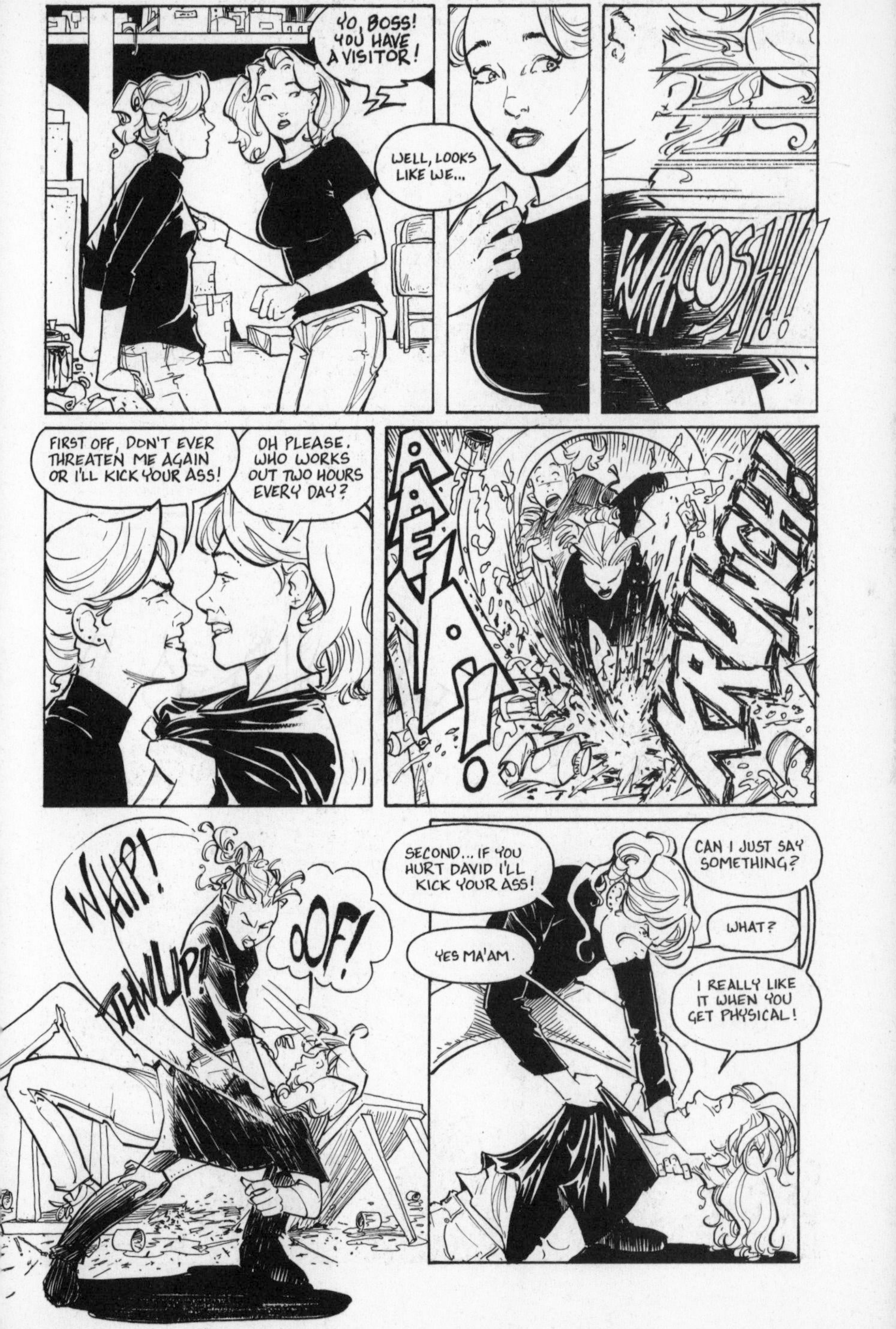

YO, BOSS! YOU HAVE A VISITOR!
WELL, LOOKS LIKE WE...
WHOOSH!!
FIRST OFF, DON'T EVER THREATEN ME AGAIN OR I'LL KICK YOUR ASS!
OH PLEASE. WHO WORKS OUT TWO HOURS EVERY DAY?
AEEA!
KRUNCH!
WHIP!
THWUP!
OOF!
SECOND... IF YOU HURT DAVID I'LL KICK YOUR ASS!
YES MA'AM.
CAN I JUST SAY SOMETHING?
WHAT?
I REALLY LIKE IT WHEN YOU GET PHYSICAL!

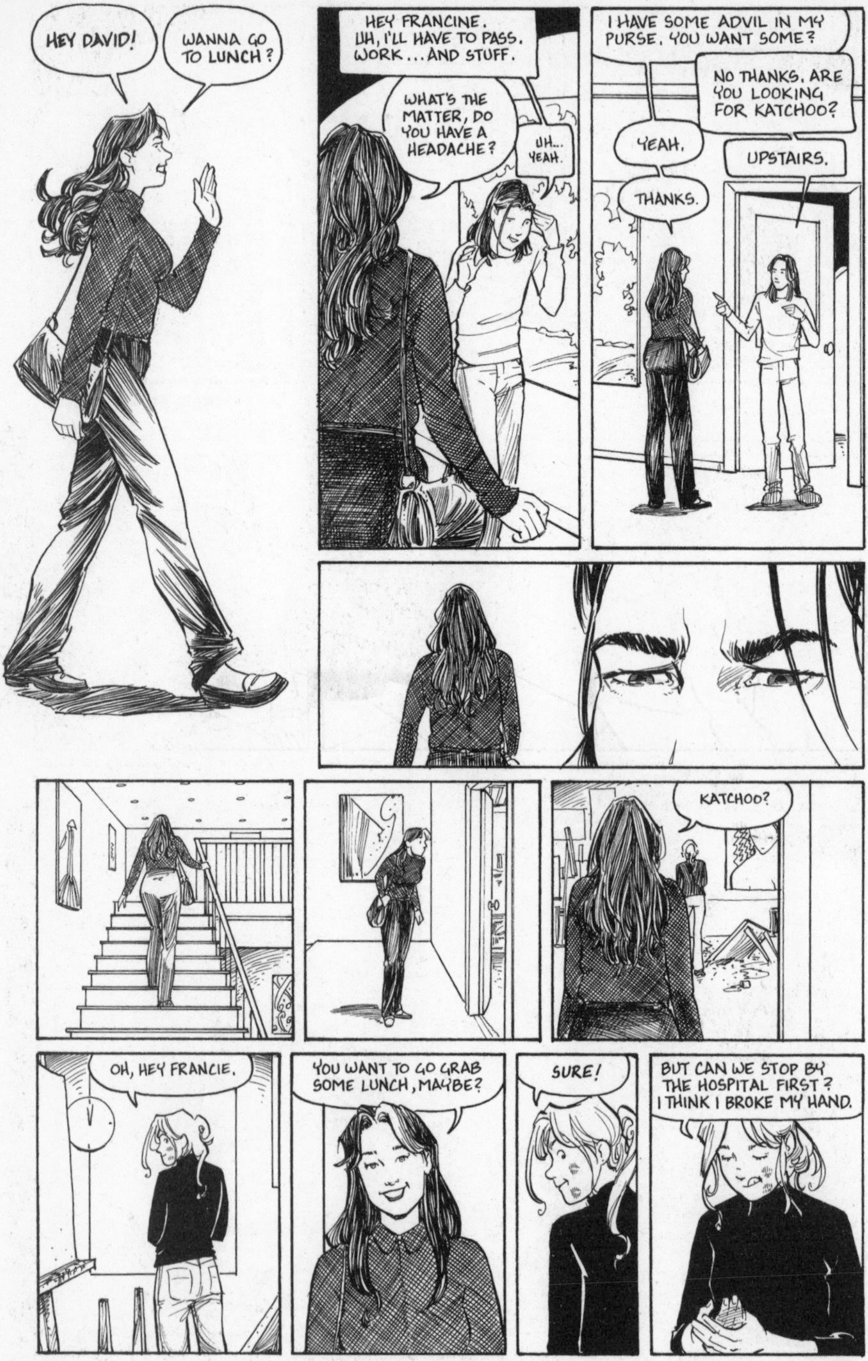
HEY DAVID!
WANNA GO TO LUNCH?
HEY FRANCINE. UH, I'LL HAVE TO PASS. WORK... AND STUFF.
WHAT'S THE MATTER, DO YOU HAVE A HEADACHE?
UH... YEAH.
I HAVE SOME ADVIL IN MY PURSE. YOU WANT SOME?
NO THANKS. ARE YOU LOOKING FOR KATCHOO?
YEAH.
UPSTAIRS.
THANKS.
KATCHOO?
OH, HEY FRANCIE.
YOU WANT TO GO GRAB SOME LUNCH, MAYBE?
SURE!
BUT CAN WE STOP BY THE HOSPITAL FIRST? I THINK I BROKE MY HAND.

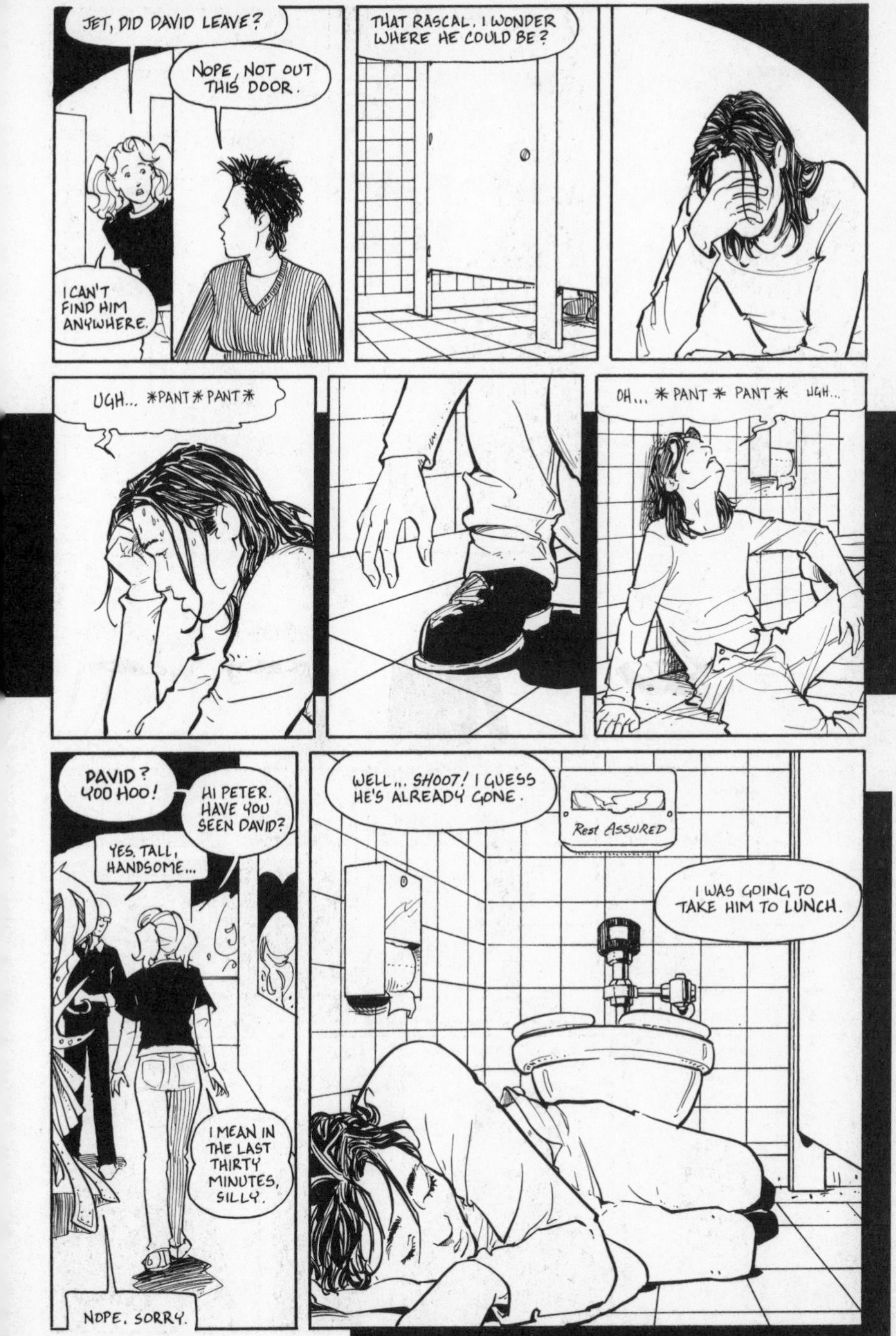
JET, DID DAVID LEAVE?
NOPE, NOT OUT THIS DOOR.
I CAN'T FIND HIM ANYWHERE.
THAT RASCAL. I WONDER WHERE HE COULD BE?
UGH... *PANT* PANT*
OH... *PANT* PANT* UGH...
DAVID? YOO HOO!
HI PETER. HAVE YOU SEEN DAVID?
YES. TALL, HANDSOME...
I MEAN IN THE LAST THIRTY MINUTES, SILLY.
NOPE. SORRY.
WELL... SHOOT! I GUESS HE'S ALREADY GONE.
Rest ASSURED
I WAS GOING TO TAKE HIM TO LUNCH.

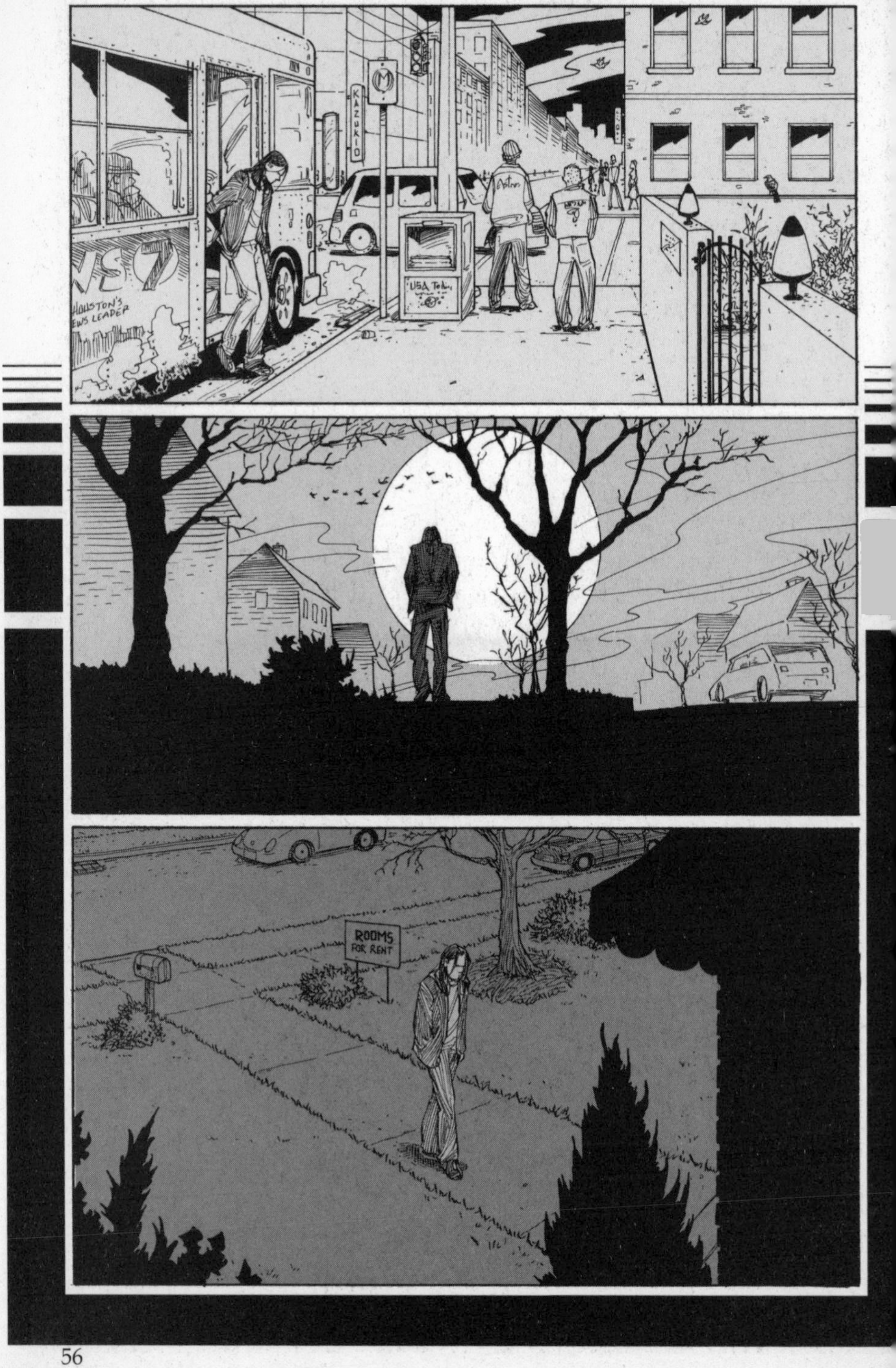
KAZUKIO
ROOMS
FOR RENT

I'VE LISTENED TO THE DEATHBIRD SING
I'VE HEARD THE BEATING OF HIS WINGS
HIS SHADOW DARKENS ALL I SEE
MURDERING ETERNITY.
MERCY PLEASE! WE ALWAYS CRY
JUST BEFORE WE HAVE TO DIE
BUT NO HOPE DRIVES THE DEATHBIRD WILD
THAT COMES UPON A GODLESS CHILD.
STILL THE STORM APPROACHES
AND THERE'S NOTHING I CAN DO
SO I WATCH AND WAIT TO FEEL HIS BREATH
AGAINST MY FACE, COOL AND GRAVE.
HIS SALT UPON MY HEART
HIS PROMISE IN MY EYES
HE MAKES HIS PRESENCE KNOWN TO ME
IN WHISPERS AND GOODBYES.
SEE THE MOON IN PITCH BLACK SKY
I KNOW WHY THE CHILDREN CRY
THE DEATHBIRD COMES
THE DEATHBIRD COMES
THERE'S NOWHERE LEFT TO HIDE.

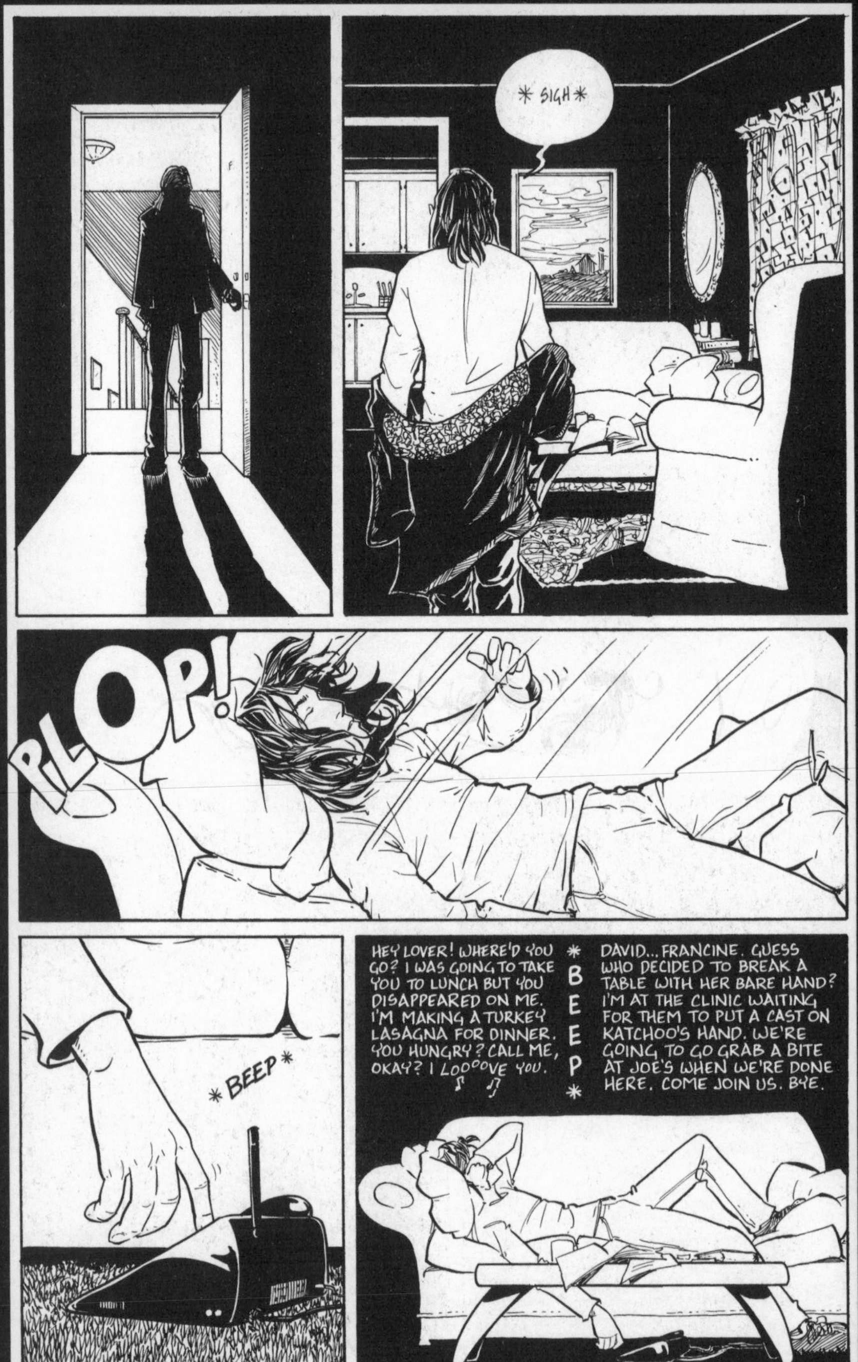
* SIGH *
PLOP!
* BEEP *
HEY LOVER! WHERE'D YOU GO? I WAS GOING TO TAKE YOU TO LUNCH BUT YOU DISAPPEARED ON ME. I'M MAKING A TURKEY LASAGNA FOR DINNER. YOU HUNGRY? CALL ME, OKAY? I LOOOOVE YOU.
* BEEP *
DAVID... FRANCINE. GUESS WHO DECIDED TO BREAK A TABLE WITH HER BARE HAND? I'M AT THE CLINIC WAITING FOR THEM TO PUT A CAST ON KATCHOO'S HAND. WE'RE GOING TO GO GRAB A BITE AT JOE'S WHEN WE'RE DONE HERE. COME JOIN US. BYE.

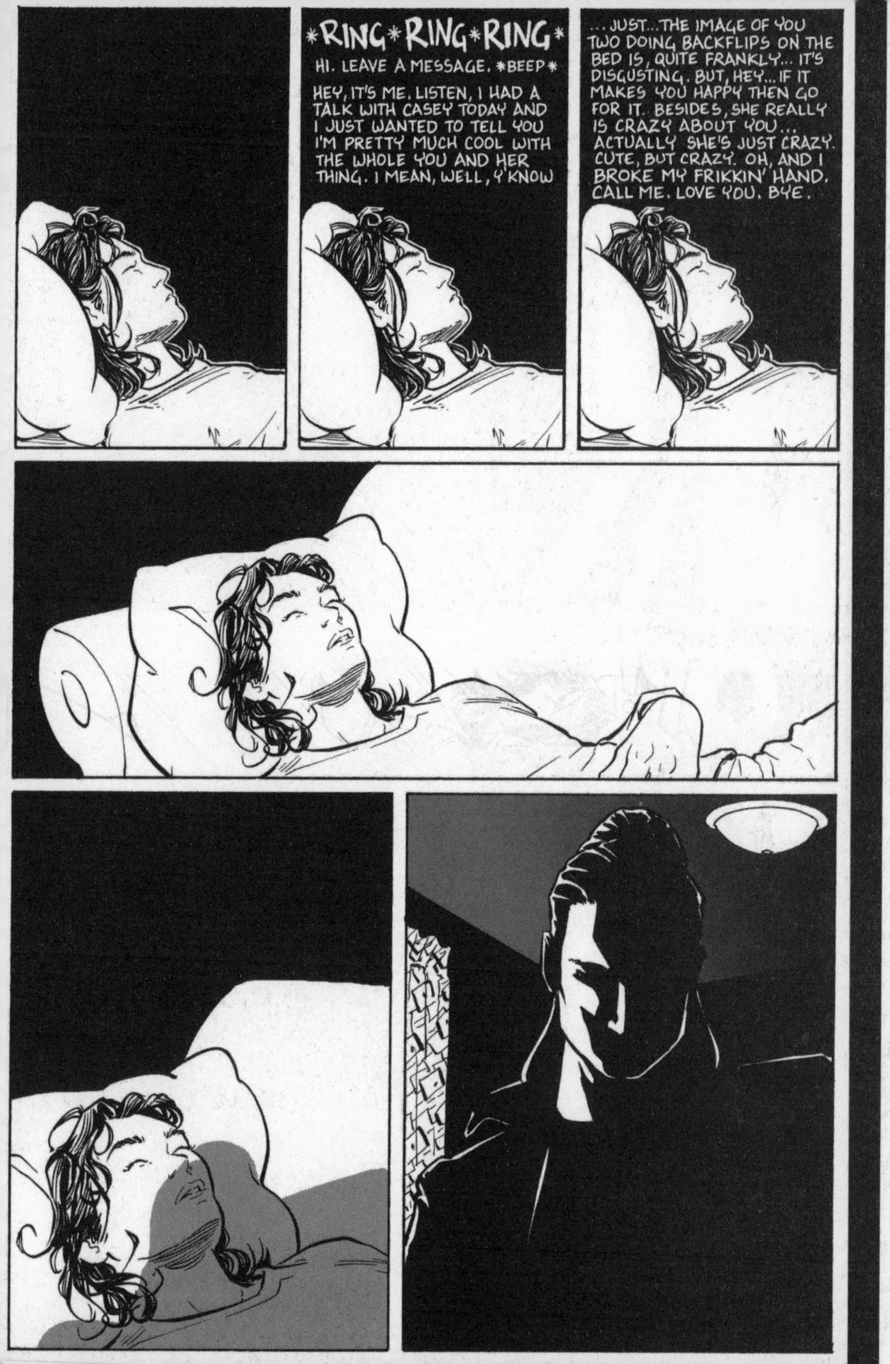
*RING*RING*RING*
HI. LEAVE A MESSAGE. *BEEP*
HEY, IT'S ME. LISTEN, I HAD A TALK WITH CASEY TODAY AND I JUST WANTED TO TELL YOU I'M PRETTY MUCH COOL WITH THE WHOLE YOU AND HER THING. I MEAN, WELL, Y'KNOW
...JUST...THE IMAGE OF YOU TWO DOING BACKFLIPS ON THE BED IS, QUITE FRANKLY... IT'S DISGUSTING. BUT, HEY...IF IT MAKES YOU HAPPY THEN GO FOR IT. BESIDES, SHE REALLY IS CRAZY ABOUT YOU... ACTUALLY SHE'S JUST CRAZY. CUTE, BUT CRAZY. OH, AND I BROKE MY FRIKKIN' HAND. CALL ME. LOVE YOU. BYE.

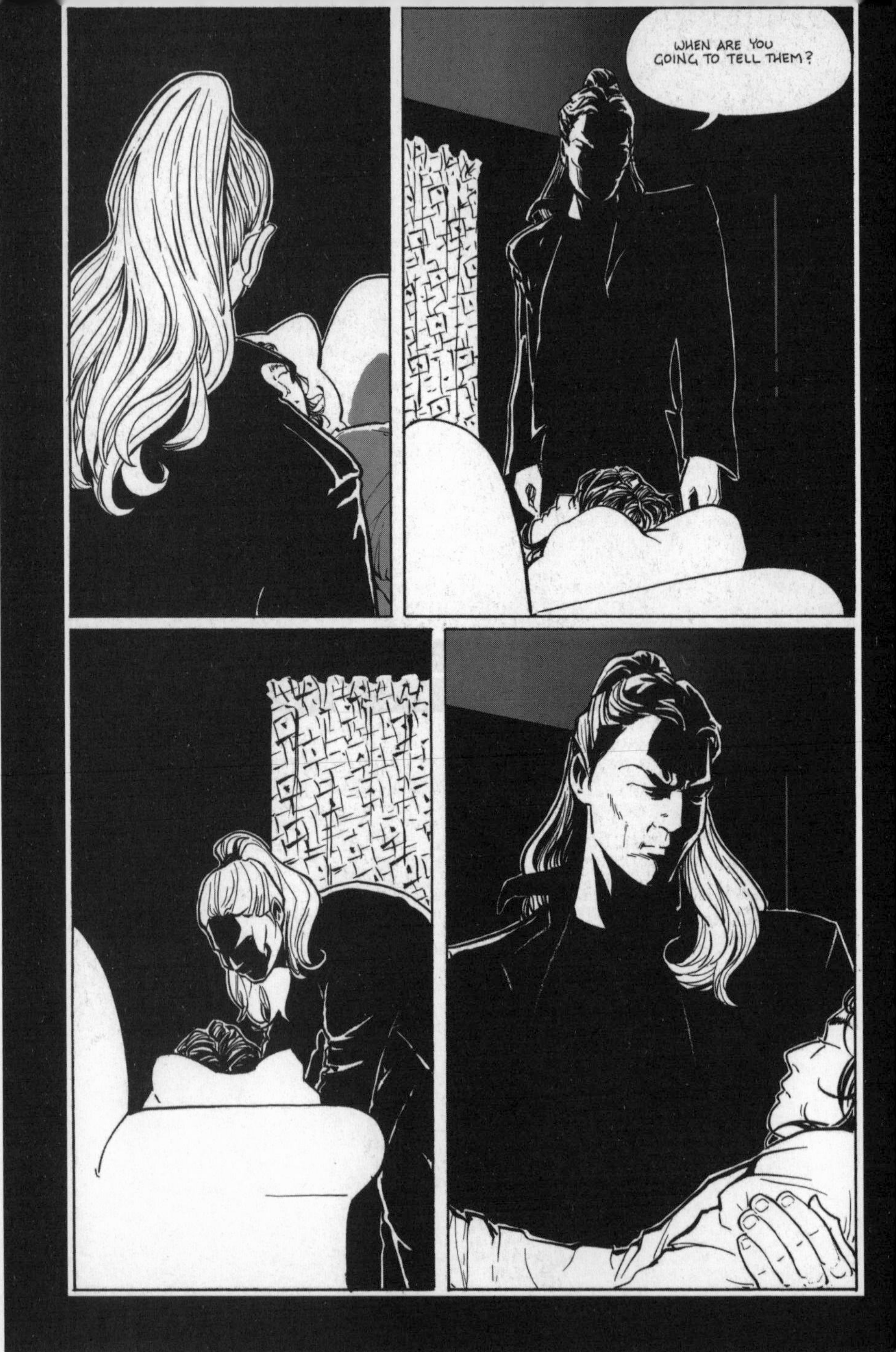
WHEN ARE YOU GOING TO TELL THEM?

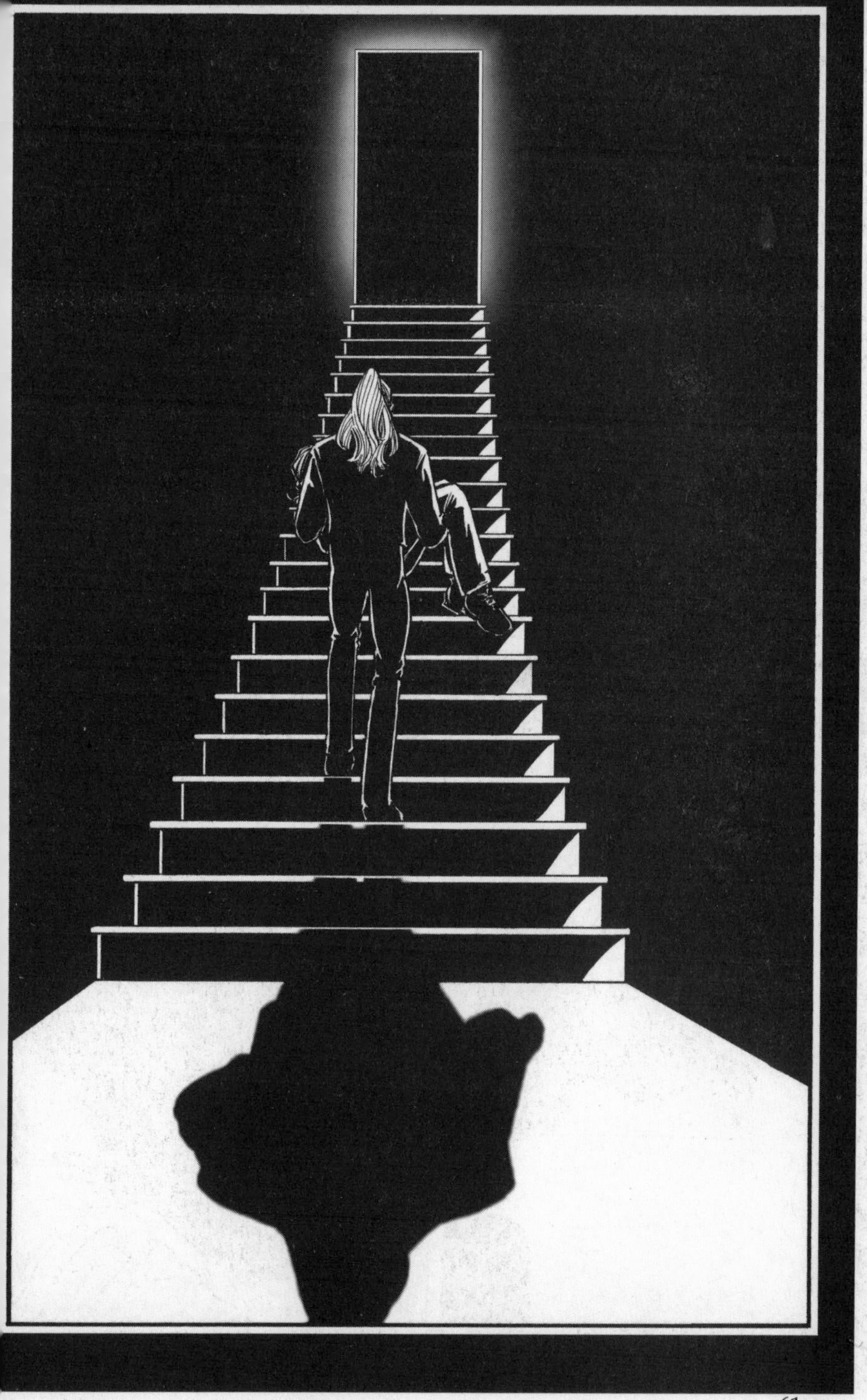

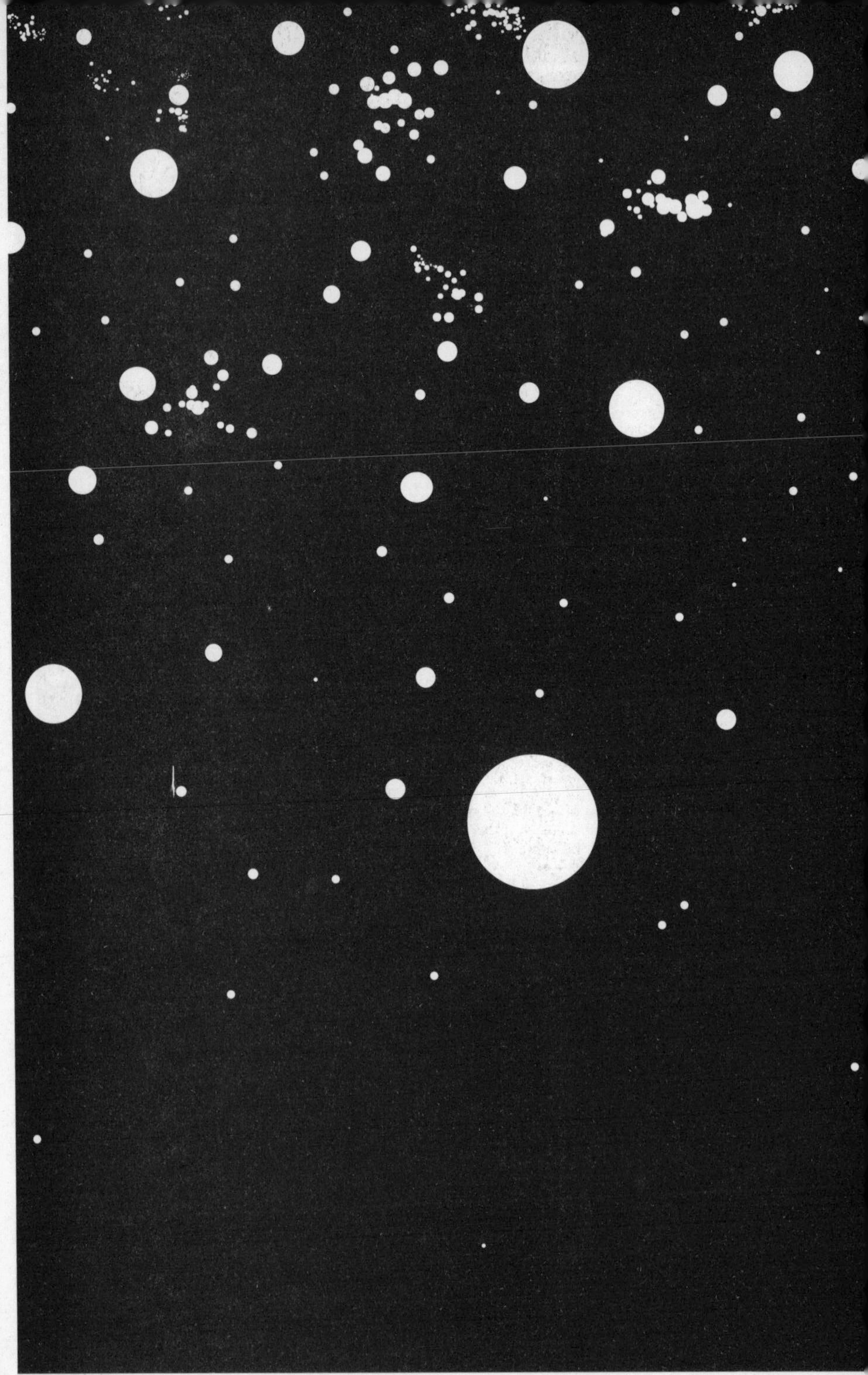

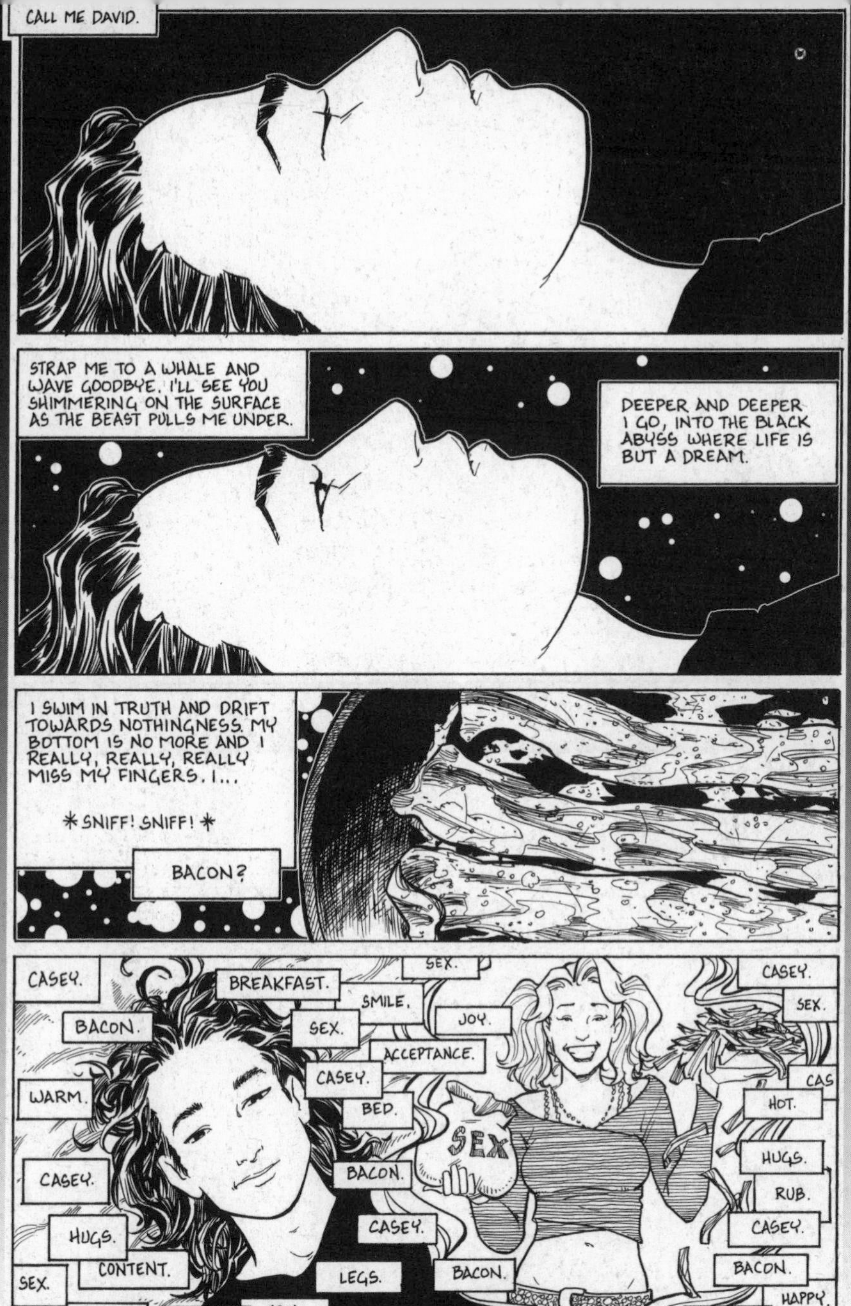
CALL ME DAVID.
STRAP ME TO A WHALE AND WAVE GOODBYE. I'LL SEE YOU SHIMMERING ON THE SURFACE AS THE BEAST PULLS ME UNDER.
DEEPER AND DEEPER I GO, INTO THE BLACK ABYSS WHERE LIFE IS BUT A DREAM.
I SWIM IN TRUTH AND DRIFT TOWARDS NOTHINGNESS. MY BOTTOM IS NO MORE AND I REALLY, REALLY, REALLY MISS MY FINGERS. I...
SNIFF! SNIFF!
BACON?
CASEY.
BREAKFAST.
SEX.
CASEY.
BACON.
SMILE.
SEX.
JOY.
SEX.
ACCEPTANCE.
CASEY.
WARM.
BED.
HOT.
SEX
HUGS.
CASEY.
BACON.
RUB.
CASEY.
CASEY.
HUGS.
CONTENT.
SEX.
LEGS.
BACON.
BACON.
HAPPY.
JOY.
PRETZEL.
CASEY.
KISS.
SEX.
LOVE.
CASEY.
NICE.

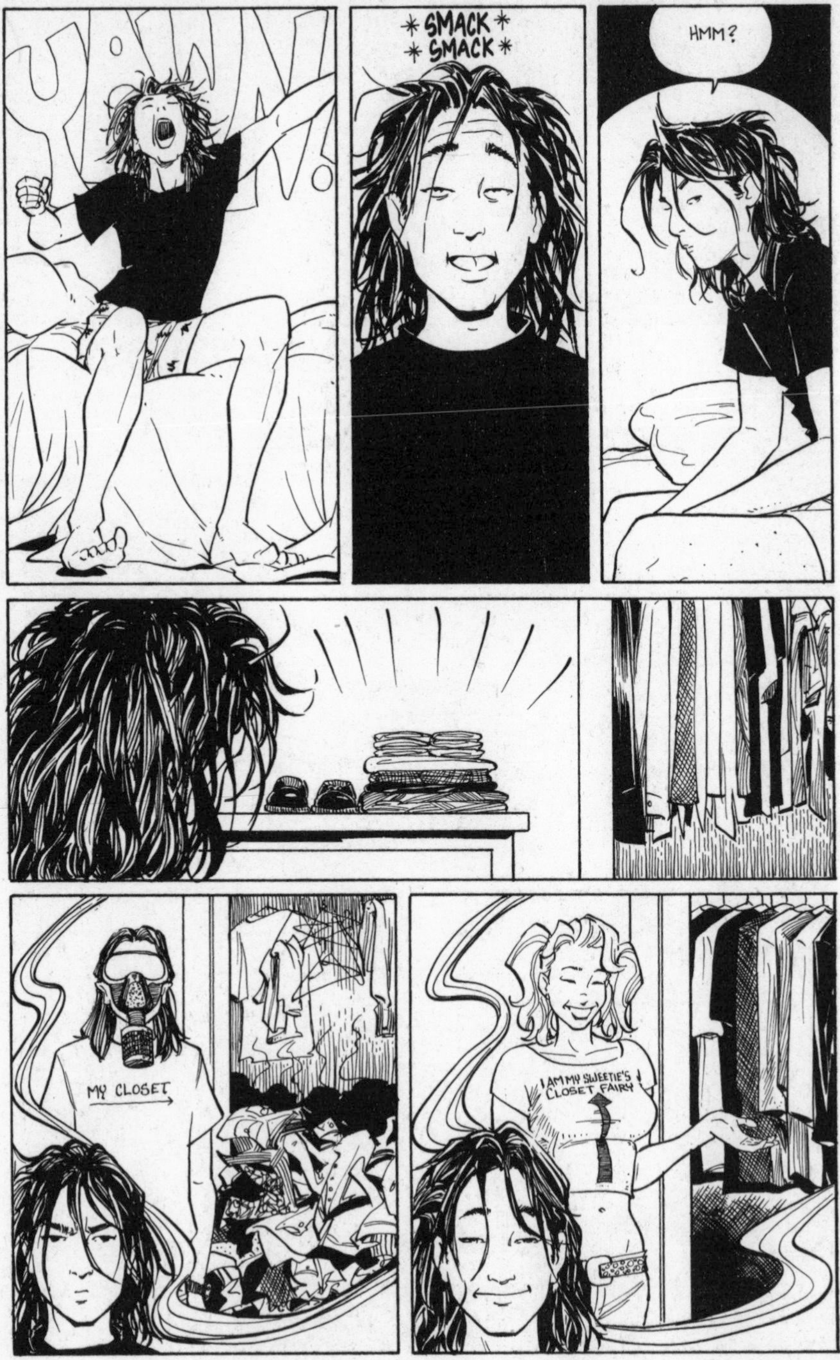
YAWN!
SMACK
SMACK
HMM?
MY CLOSET
I AM MY SWEETIE'S
CLOSET FAIRY

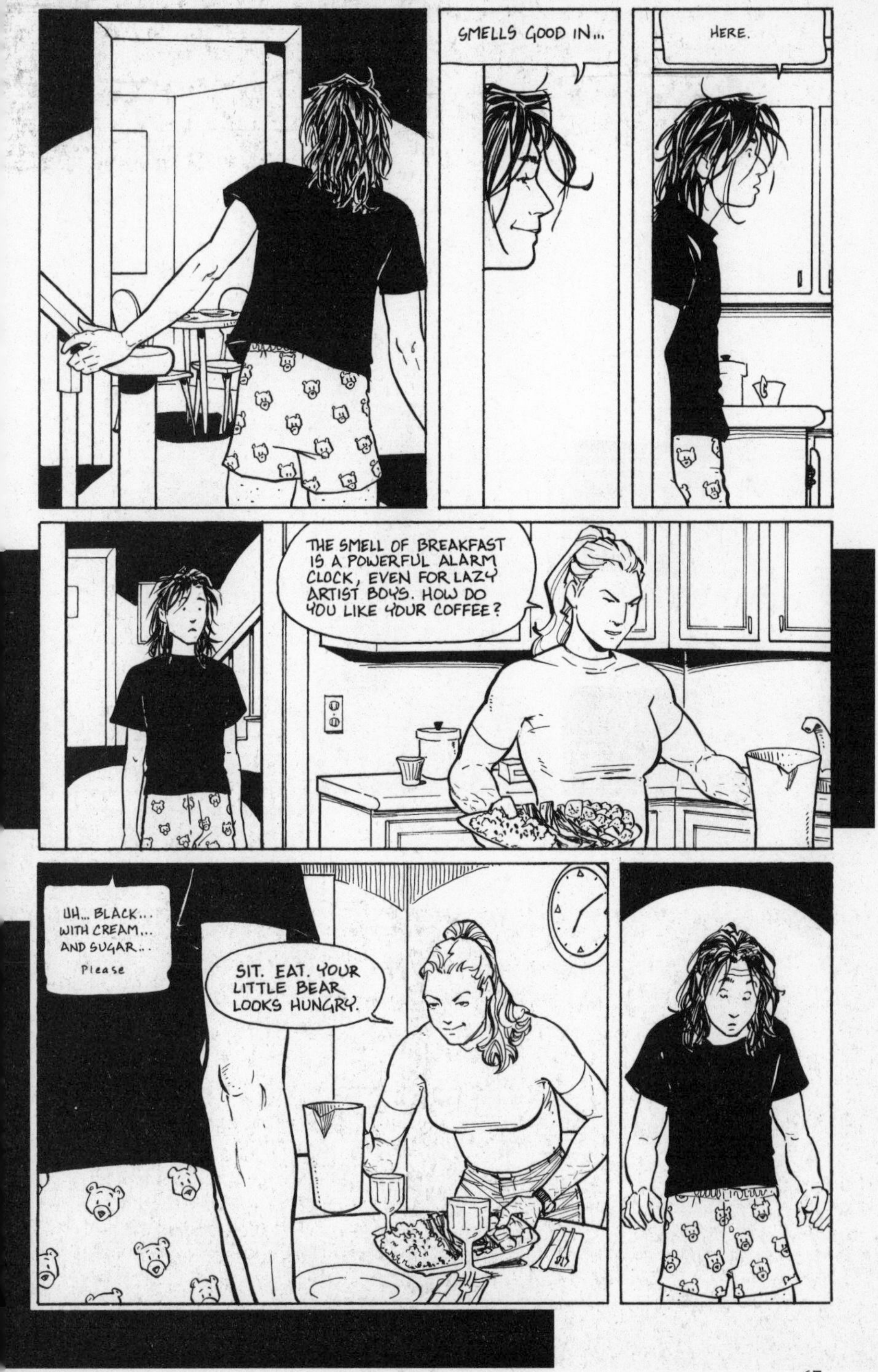
SMELLS GOOD IN...
HERE.
THE SMELL OF BREAKFAST IS A POWERFUL ALARM CLOCK, EVEN FOR LAZY ARTIST BOYS. HOW DO YOU LIKE YOUR COFFEE?
UH... BLACK... WITH CREAM... AND SUGAR... Please
SIT. EAT. YOUR LITTLE BEAR LOOKS HUNGRY.

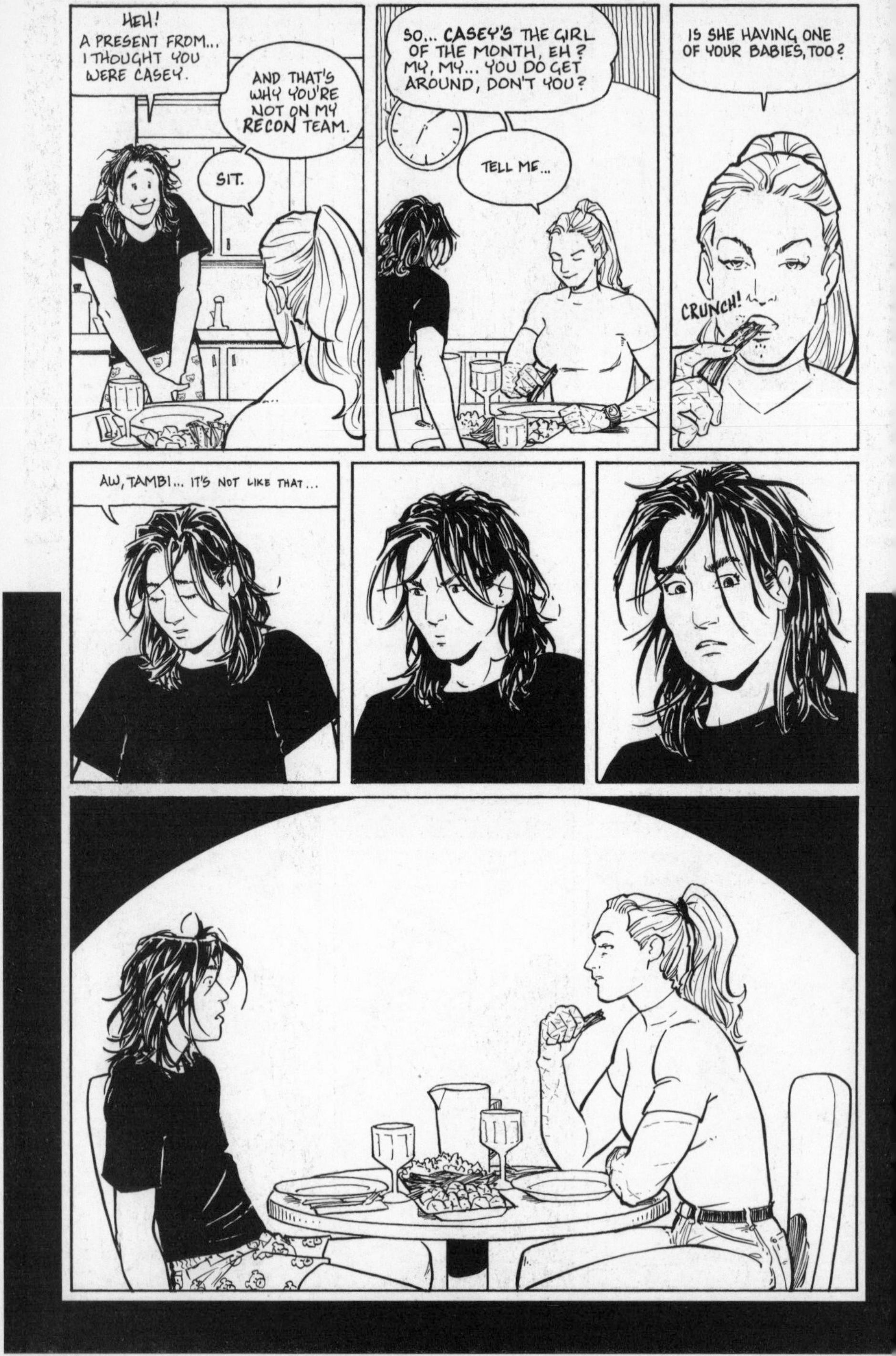

HEH!
A PRESENT FROM... I THOUGHT YOU WERE CASEY.
AND THAT'S WHY YOU'RE NOT ON MY RECON TEAM.
SIT.
SO... CASEY'S THE GIRL OF THE MONTH, EH? MY, MY... YOU DO GET AROUND, DON'T YOU?
TELL ME...
IS SHE HAVING ONE OF YOUR BABIES, TOO?
CRUNCH!
AW, TAMBI... IT'S NOT LIKE THAT...

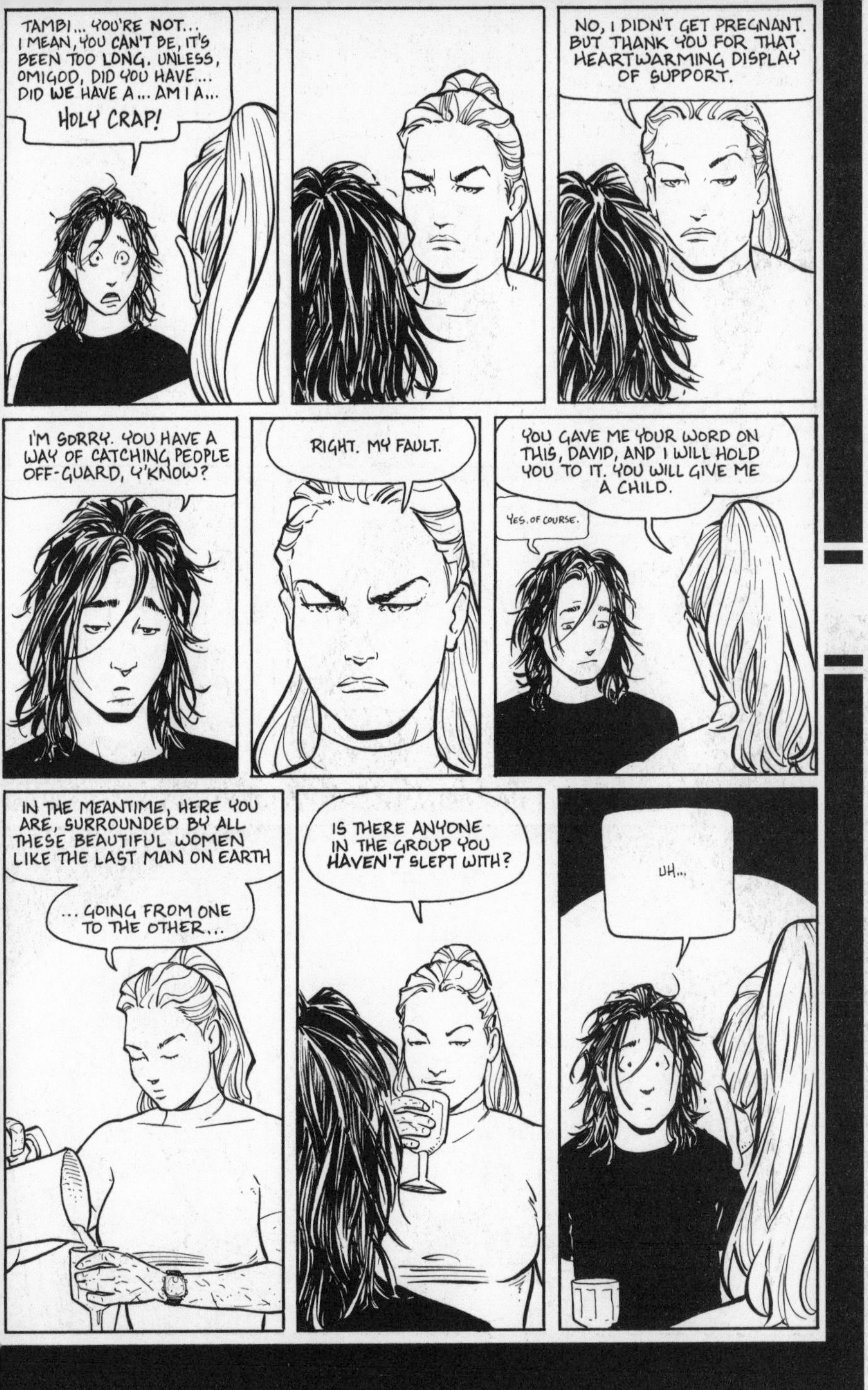
TAMBI... YOU'RE NOT... I MEAN, YOU CAN'T BE, IT'S BEEN TOO LONG. UNLESS, OMIGOD, DID YOU HAVE... DID WE HAVE A... AM I A... HOLY CRAP!
NO, I DIDN'T GET PREGNANT. BUT THANK YOU FOR THAT HEARTWARMING DISPLAY OF SUPPORT.
I'M SORRY. YOU HAVE A WAY OF CATCHING PEOPLE OFF-GUARD, Y'KNOW?
RIGHT. MY FAULT.
YOU GAVE ME YOUR WORD ON THIS, DAVID, AND I WILL HOLD YOU TO IT. YOU WILL GIVE ME A CHILD.
YES, OF COURSE.
IN THE MEANTIME, HERE YOU ARE, SURROUNDED BY ALL THESE BEAUTIFUL WOMEN LIKE THE LAST MAN ON EARTH
... GOING FROM ONE TO THE OTHER...
IS THERE ANYONE IN THE GROUP YOU HAVEN'T SLEPT WITH?
UH...

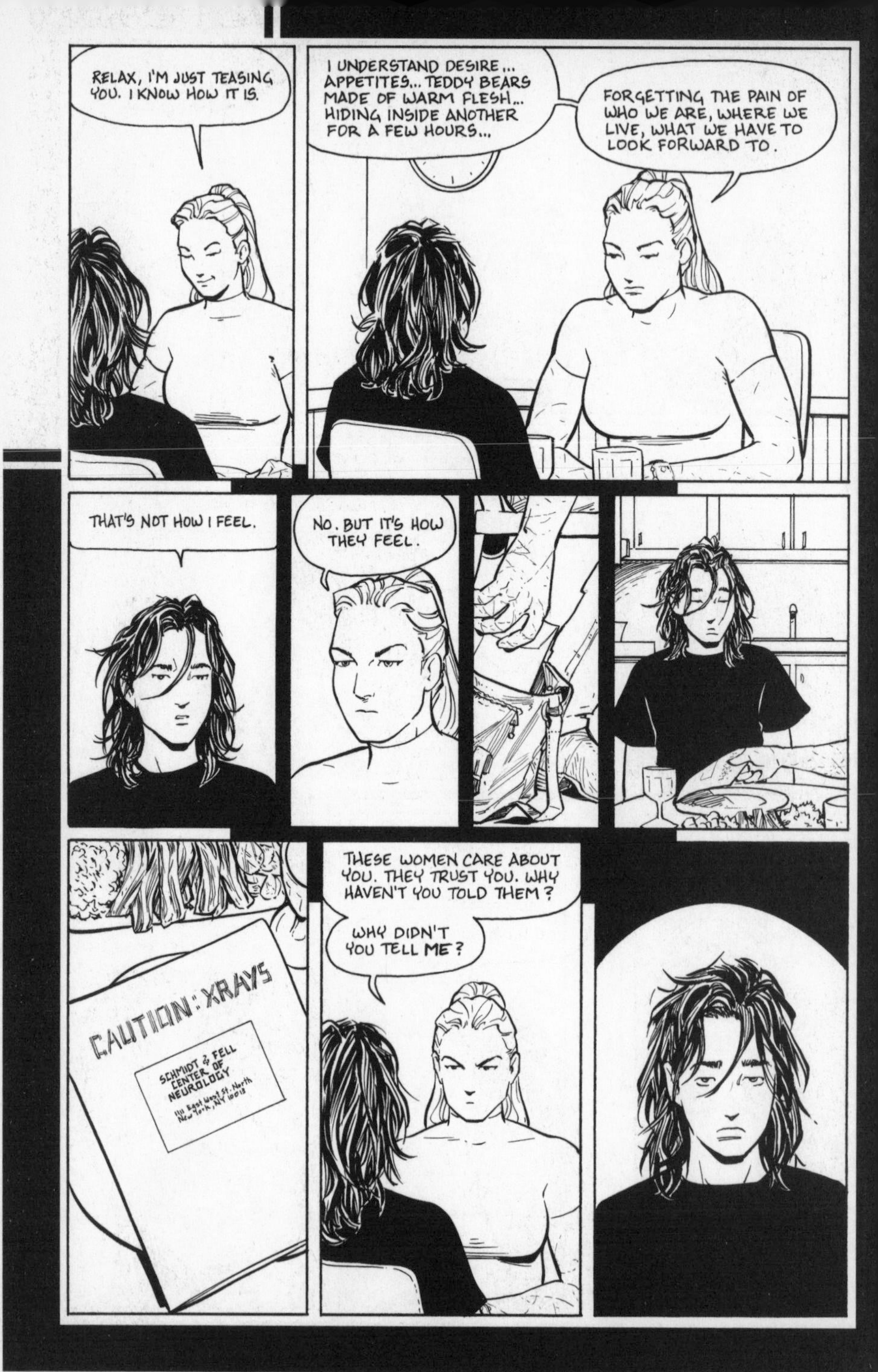
RELAX, I'M JUST TEASING YOU. I KNOW HOW IT IS.
I UNDERSTAND DESIRE... APPETITES... TEDDY BEARS MADE OF WARM FLESH... HIDING INSIDE ANOTHER FOR A FEW HOURS...
FORGETTING THE PAIN OF WHO WE ARE, WHERE WE LIVE, WHAT WE HAVE TO LOOK FORWARD TO.
THAT'S NOT HOW I FEEL.
NO. BUT IT'S HOW THEY FEEL.
CAUTION: XRAYS
SCHMIDT & FELL CENTER OF NEUROLOGY
111 East West St. North
New York, NY 10013
THESE WOMEN CARE ABOUT YOU. THEY TRUST YOU. WHY HAVEN'T YOU TOLD THEM?
WHY DIDN'T YOU TELL ME?

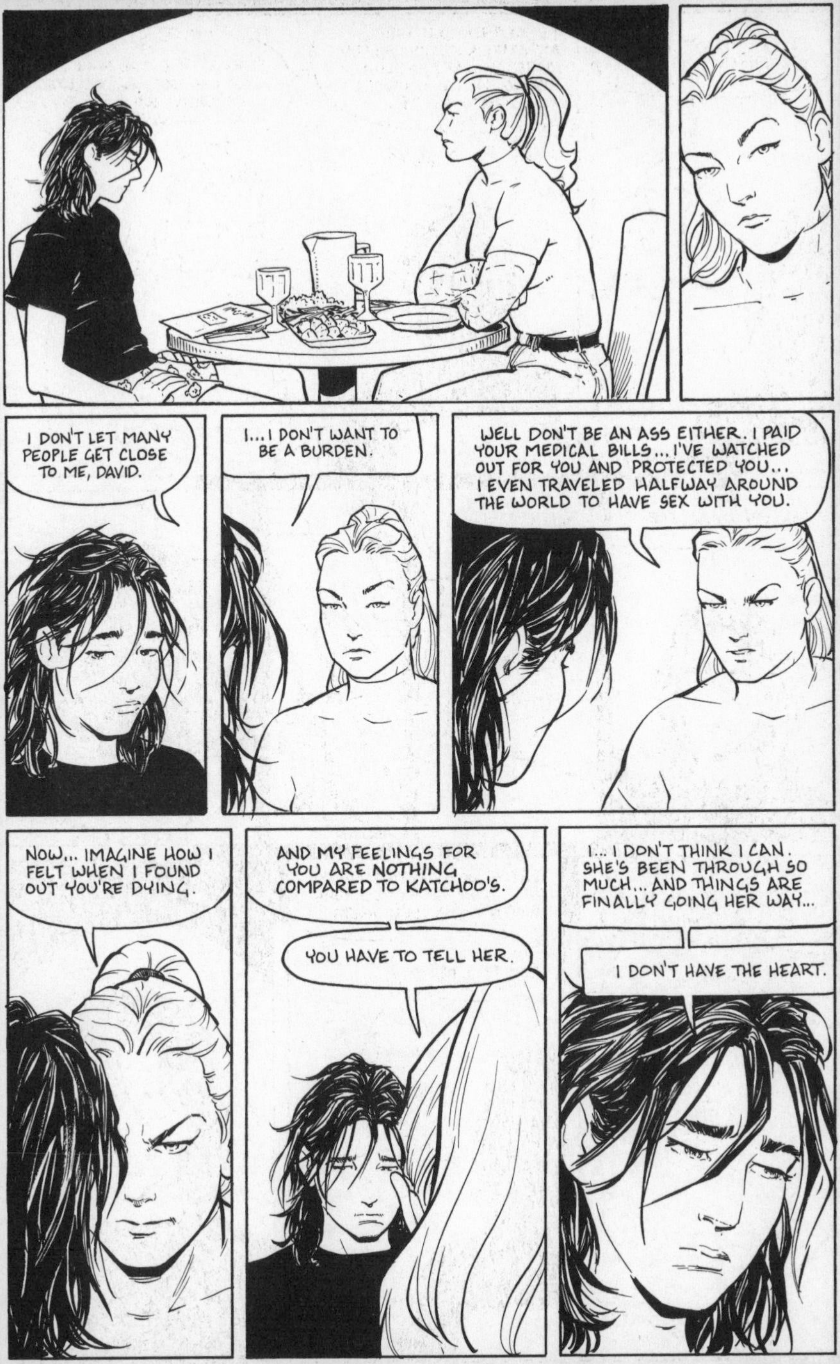
I DON'T LET MANY PEOPLE GET CLOSE TO ME, DAVID.
I... I DON'T WANT TO BE A BURDEN.
WELL DON'T BE AN ASS EITHER. I PAID YOUR MEDICAL BILLS... I'VE WATCHED OUT FOR YOU AND PROTECTED YOU... I EVEN TRAVELED HALFWAY AROUND THE WORLD TO HAVE SEX WITH YOU.
NOW... IMAGINE HOW I FELT WHEN I FOUND OUT YOU'RE DYING.
AND MY FEELINGS FOR YOU ARE NOTHING COMPARED TO KATCHOO'S.
YOU HAVE TO TELL HER.
I... I DON'T THINK I CAN. SHE'S BEEN THROUGH SO MUCH... AND THINGS ARE FINALLY GOING HER WAY...
I DON'T HAVE THE HEART.

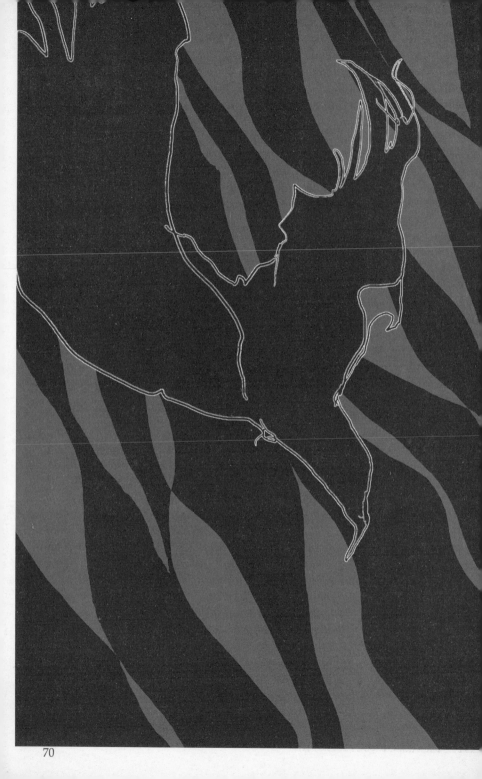

"CAROLYN HOBBS' NEW PROTEGEE IS A DIMINUITIVE ARTIST WHO OVER-COMPENSATES FOR HER ORDINARY ABILITIES BY PAINTING OVER-SIZED CANVASES SELLING SEX AND VOYEURISM AS ART."

"THE ARTIST'S NAME IS KATCHOO—AS IF THE WORLD NEEDS ANOTHER ONE-NAME CELEBRITY WANNABE. UNFORTUNATELY, KATCHOO DOES NOT POSSESS THE TALENT OR ORIGINALITY OF A PICASSO OR WARHOL ... OR EVEN CHER."

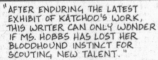

"AFTER ENDURING THE LATEST EXHIBIT OF KATCHOO'S WORK, THIS WRITER CAN ONLY WONDER IF MS. HOBBS HAS LOST HER BLOODHOUND INSTINCT FOR SCOUTING NEW TALENT."

"TO BE BLUNT, KATCHOO'S WORK CONSISTS OF LESSER ATOMS."

– WOODWARD BEINSTEIN
HOUSTON ART CRITIC

TAP!
TAP!
TAP!
TAP!
TAP!
TAP!

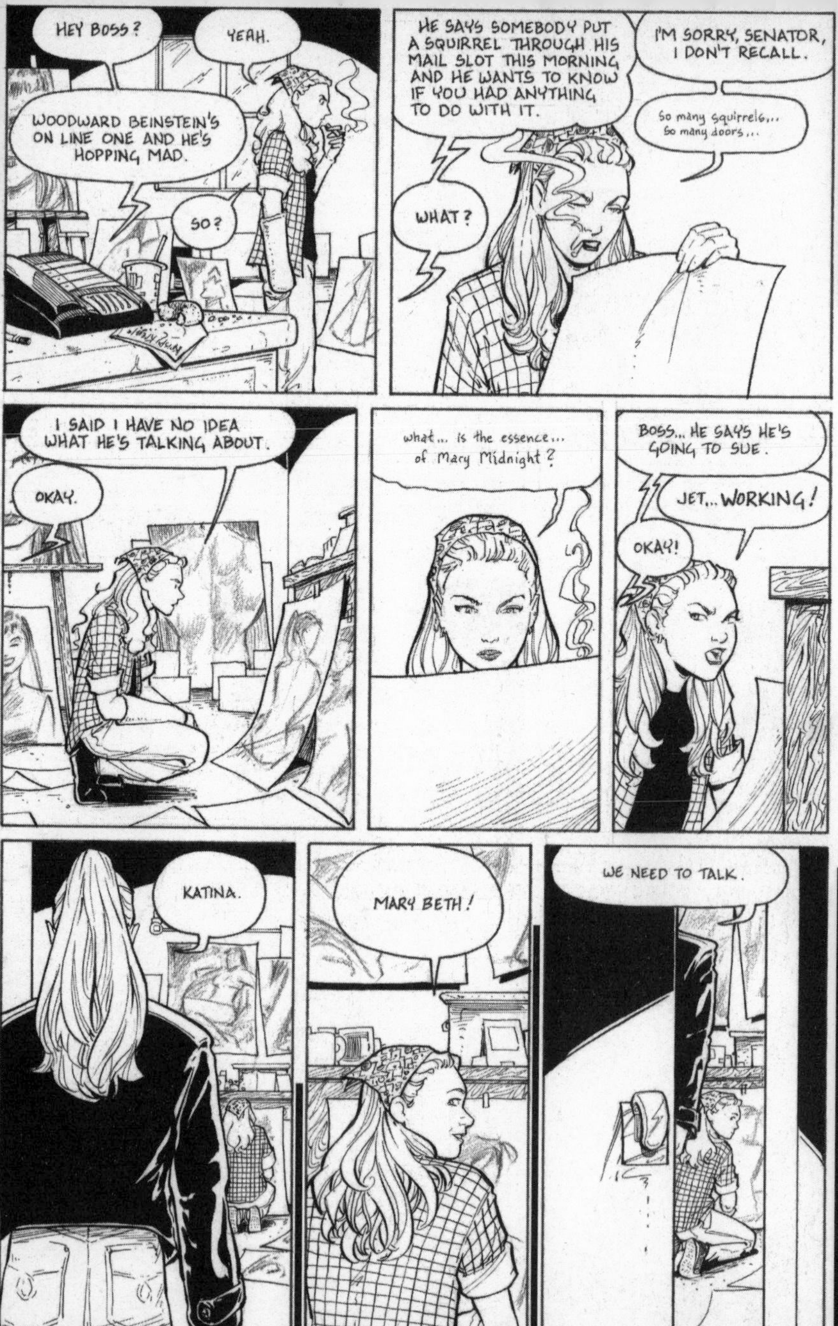
HEY BOSS?
YEAH.
WOODWARD BEINSTEIN'S ON LINE ONE AND HE'S HOPPING MAD.
SO?
HE SAYS SOMEBODY PUT A SQUIRREL THROUGH HIS MAIL SLOT THIS MORNING AND HE WANTS TO KNOW IF YOU HAD ANYTHING TO DO WITH IT.
I'M SORRY, SENATOR, I DON'T RECALL.
So many squirrels... So many doors...
WHAT?
I SAID I HAVE NO IDEA WHAT HE'S TALKING ABOUT.
OKAY.
what... is the essence... of Mary Midnight?
BOSS... HE SAYS HE'S GOING TO SUE.
JET... WORKING!
OKAY!
KATINA.
MARY BETH!
WE NEED TO TALK.

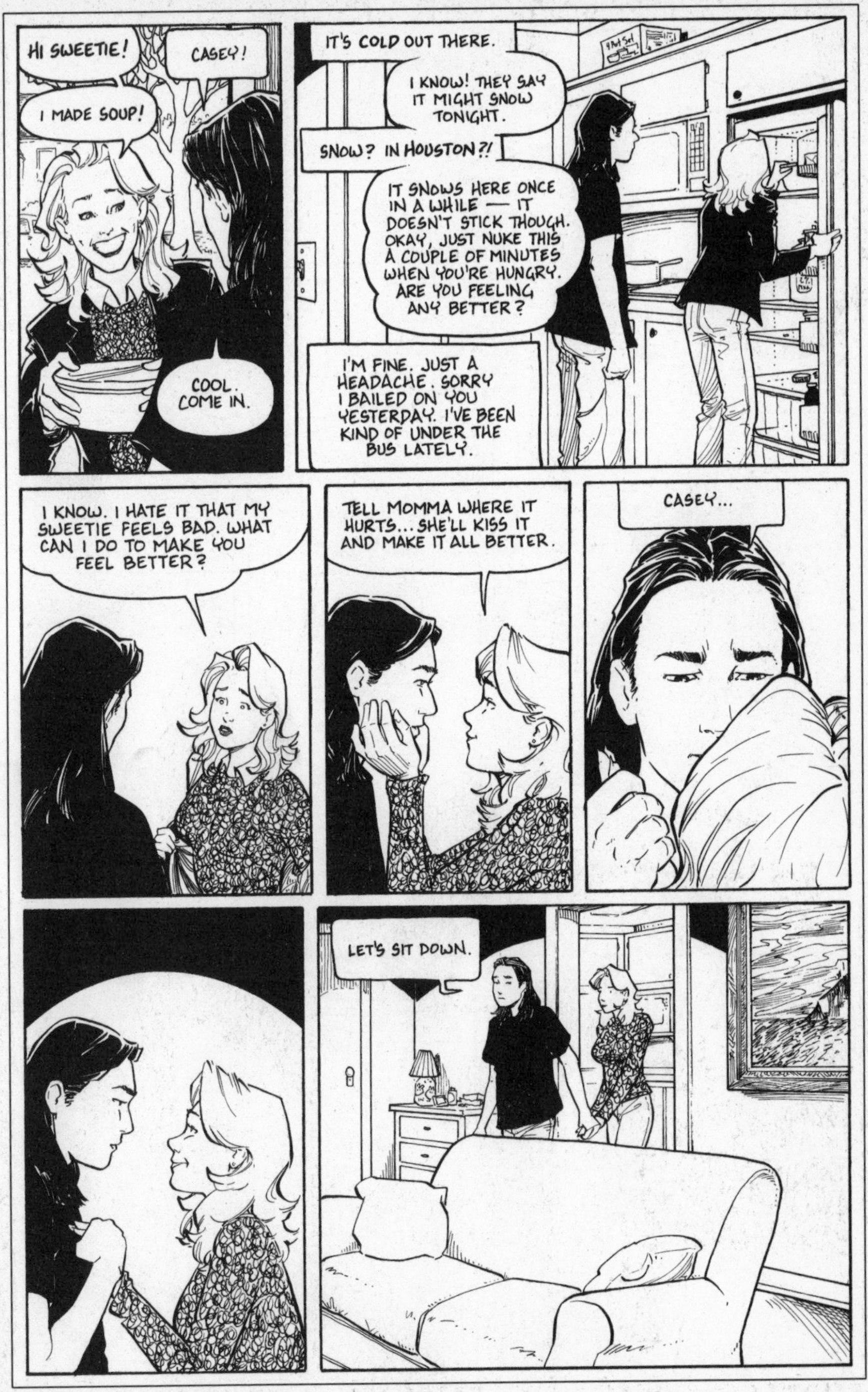
HI SWEETIE!
CASEY!
I MADE SOUP!
COOL. COME IN.
IT'S COLD OUT THERE.
I KNOW! THEY SAY IT MIGHT SNOW TONIGHT.
SNOW? IN HOUSTON?!
IT SNOWS HERE ONCE IN A WHILE — IT DOESN'T STICK THOUGH. OKAY, JUST NUKE THIS A COUPLE OF MINUTES WHEN YOU'RE HUNGRY. ARE YOU FEELING ANY BETTER?
I'M FINE. JUST A HEADACHE. SORRY I BAILED ON YOU YESTERDAY. I'VE BEEN KIND OF UNDER THE BUS LATELY.
I KNOW. I HATE IT THAT MY SWEETIE FEELS BAD. WHAT CAN I DO TO MAKE YOU FEEL BETTER?
TELL MOMMA WHERE IT HURTS... SHE'LL KISS IT AND MAKE IT ALL BETTER.
CASEY...
LET'S SIT DOWN.

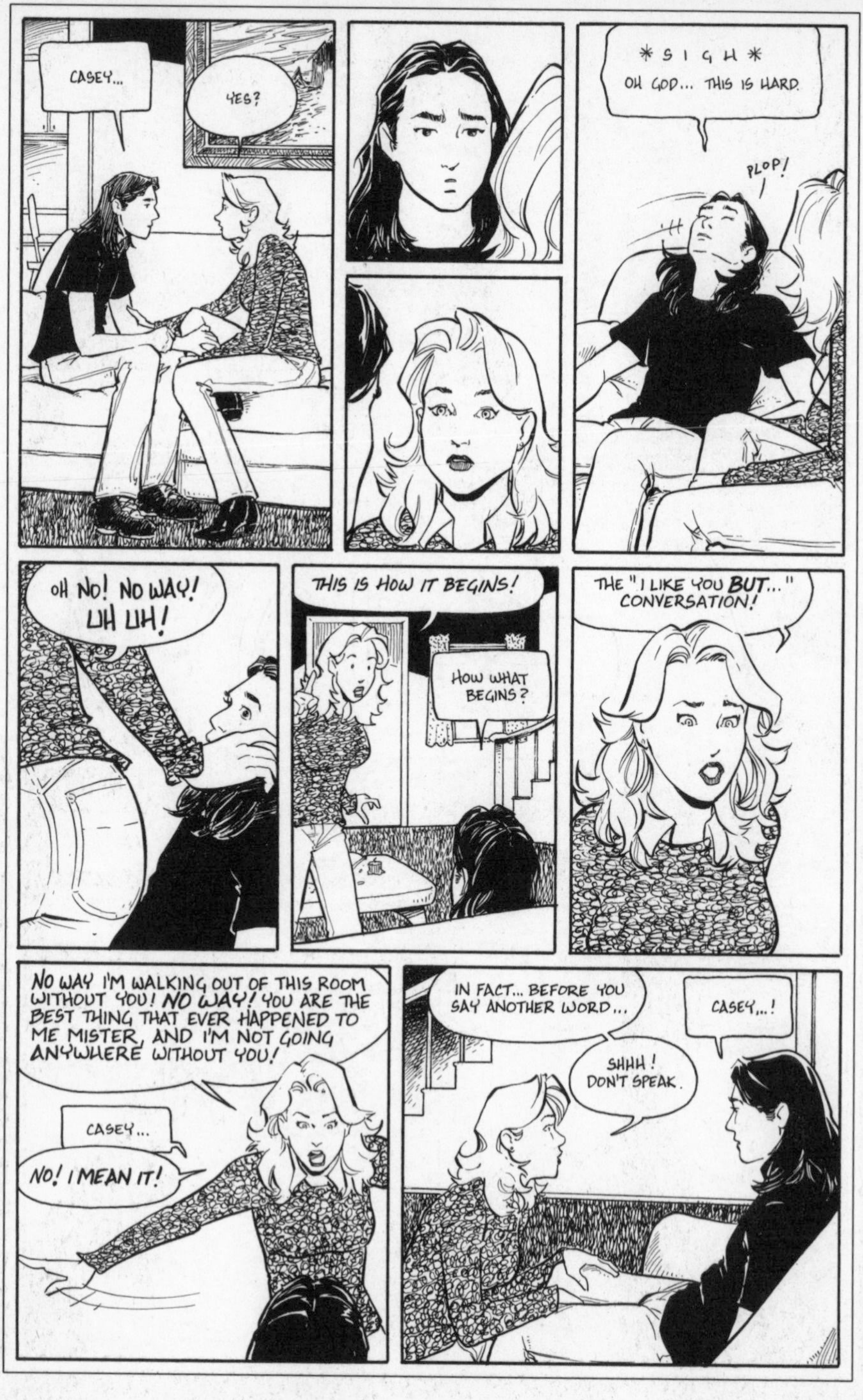

CASEY...
YES?
SIGH
OH GOD... THIS IS HARD.
PLOP!
OH NO! NO WAY! UH UH!
THIS IS HOW IT BEGINS!
HOW WHAT BEGINS?
THE "I LIKE YOU BUT..." CONVERSATION!
NO WAY I'M WALKING OUT OF THIS ROOM WITHOUT YOU! NO WAY! YOU ARE THE BEST THING THAT EVER HAPPENED TO ME MISTER, AND I'M NOT GOING ANYWHERE WITHOUT YOU!
CASEY...
NO! I MEAN IT!
IN FACT... BEFORE YOU SAY ANOTHER WORD...
CASEY...!
SHHH! DON'T SPEAK.

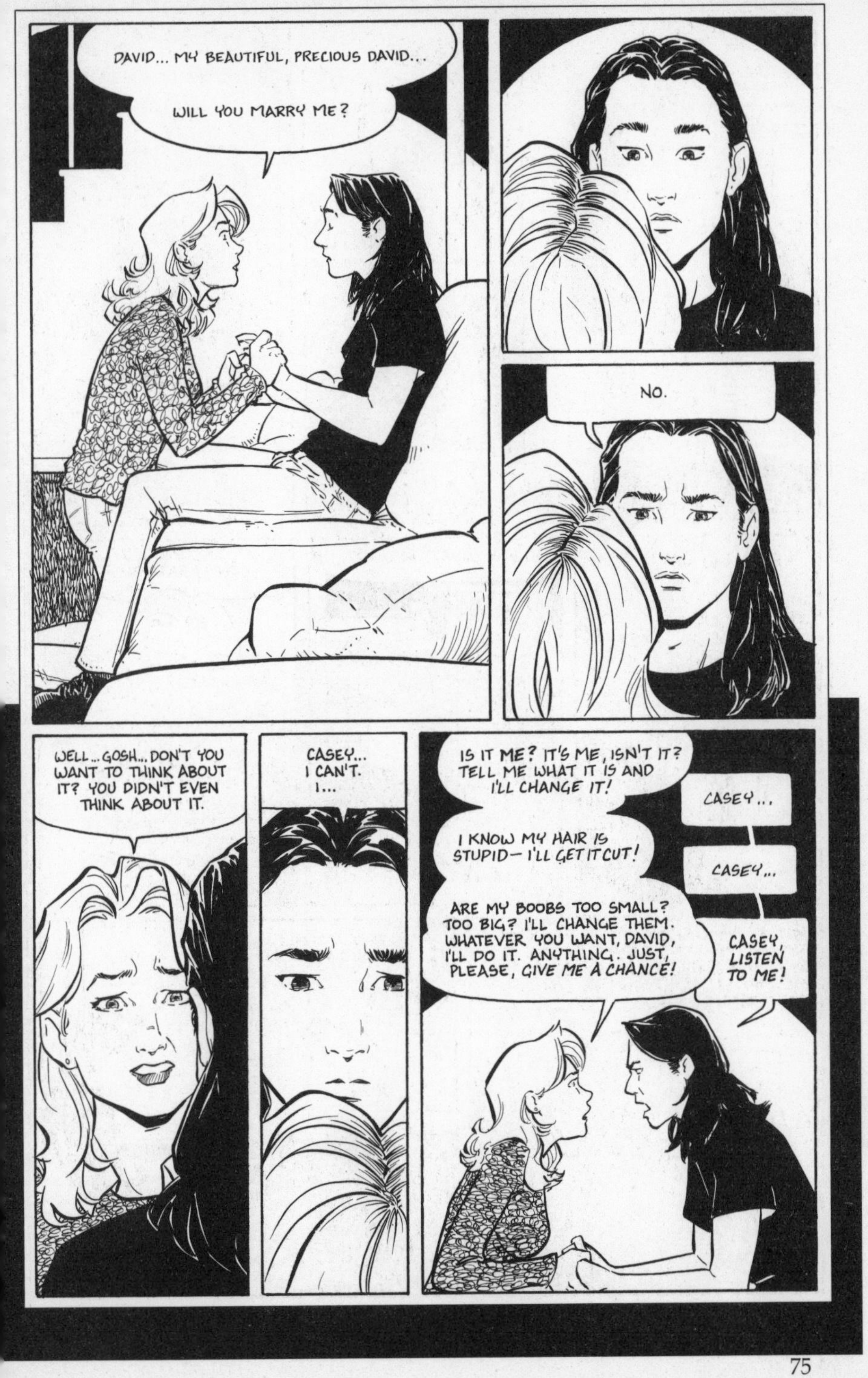
DAVID... MY BEAUTIFUL, PRECIOUS DAVID...
WILL YOU MARRY ME?
NO.
WELL... GOSH... DON'T YOU WANT TO THINK ABOUT IT? YOU DIDN'T EVEN THINK ABOUT IT.
CASEY... I CAN'T. I...
IS IT ME? IT'S ME, ISN'T IT? TELL ME WHAT IT IS AND I'LL CHANGE IT!
I KNOW MY HAIR IS STUPID— I'LL GET IT CUT!
ARE MY BOOBS TOO SMALL? TOO BIG? I'LL CHANGE THEM. WHATEVER YOU WANT, DAVID, I'LL DO IT. ANYTHING. JUST, PLEASE, GIVE ME A CHANCE!
CASEY...
CASEY...
CASEY, LISTEN TO ME!

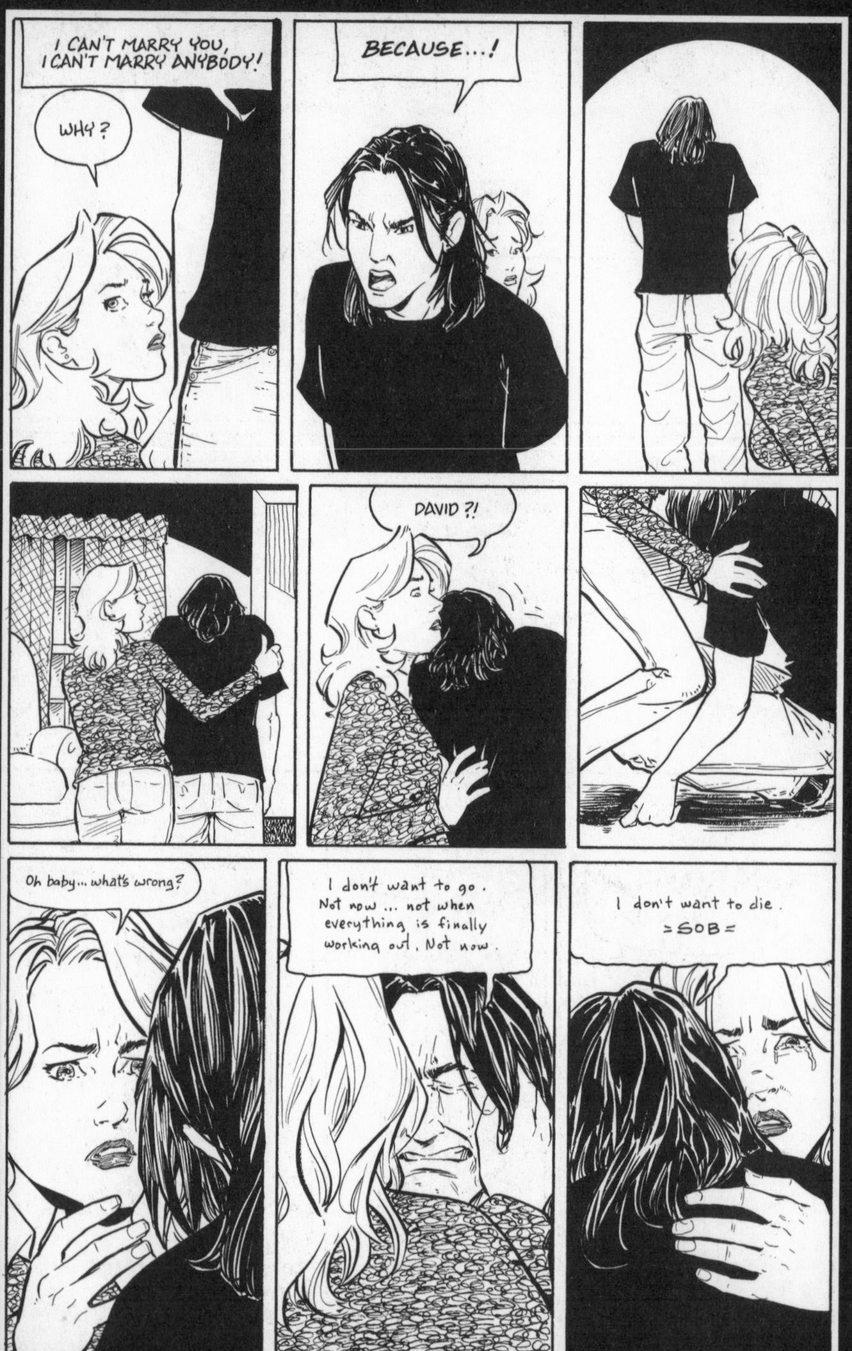
I CAN'T MARRY YOU, I CAN'T MARRY ANYBODY!
WHY?
BECAUSE...!
DAVID?!
Oh baby... what's wrong?
I don't want to go. Not now ... not when everything is finally working out. Not now.
I don't want to die.
=SOB=

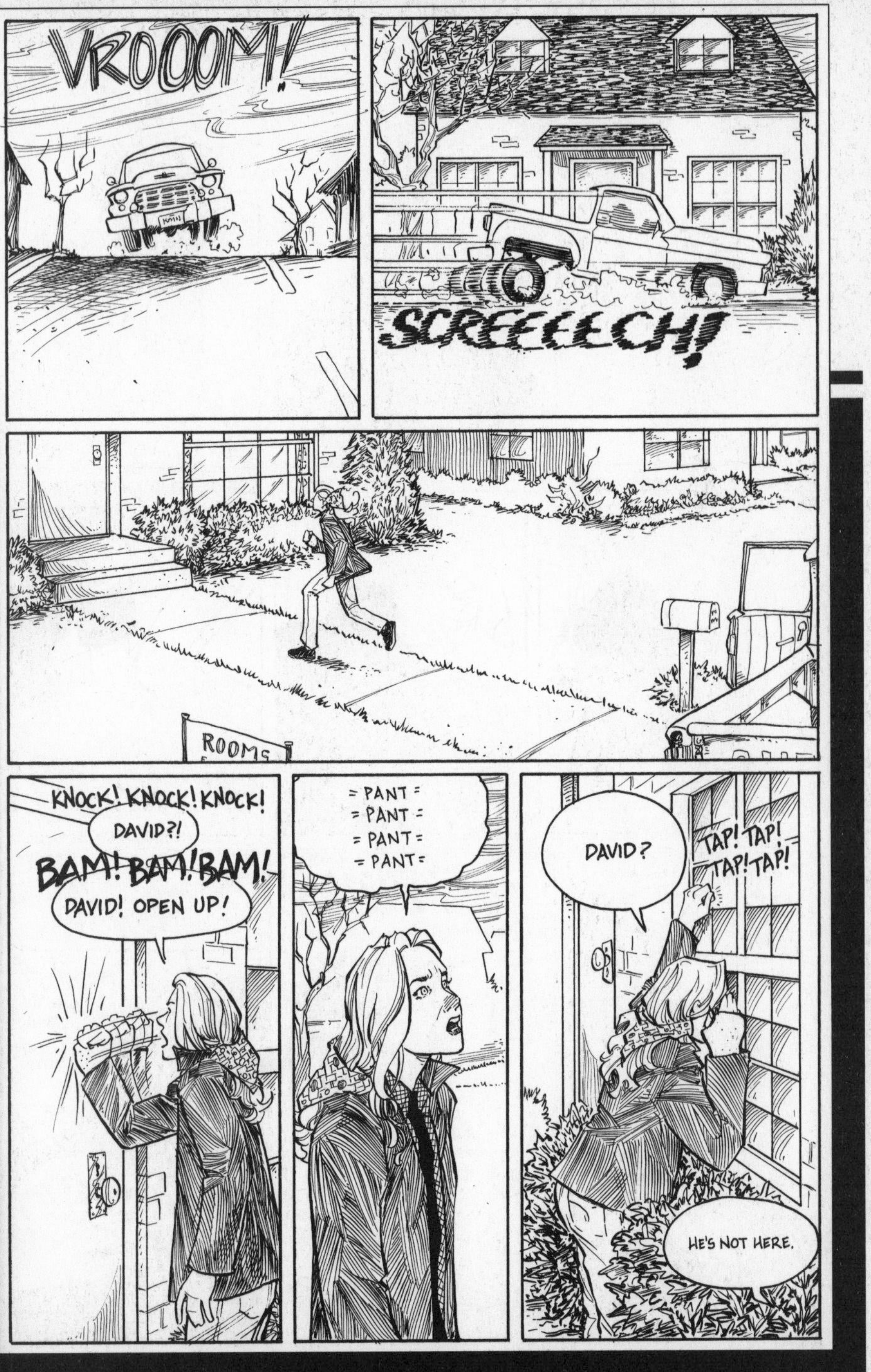
VROOOM!
SCREEEECH!
ROOMS
KNOCK! KNOCK! KNOCK!
DAVID?!
BAM! BAM! BAM!
DAVID! OPEN UP!
= PANT =
= PANT =
= PANT =
= PANT =
DAVID?
TAP! TAP!
TAP! TAP!
HE'S NOT HERE.

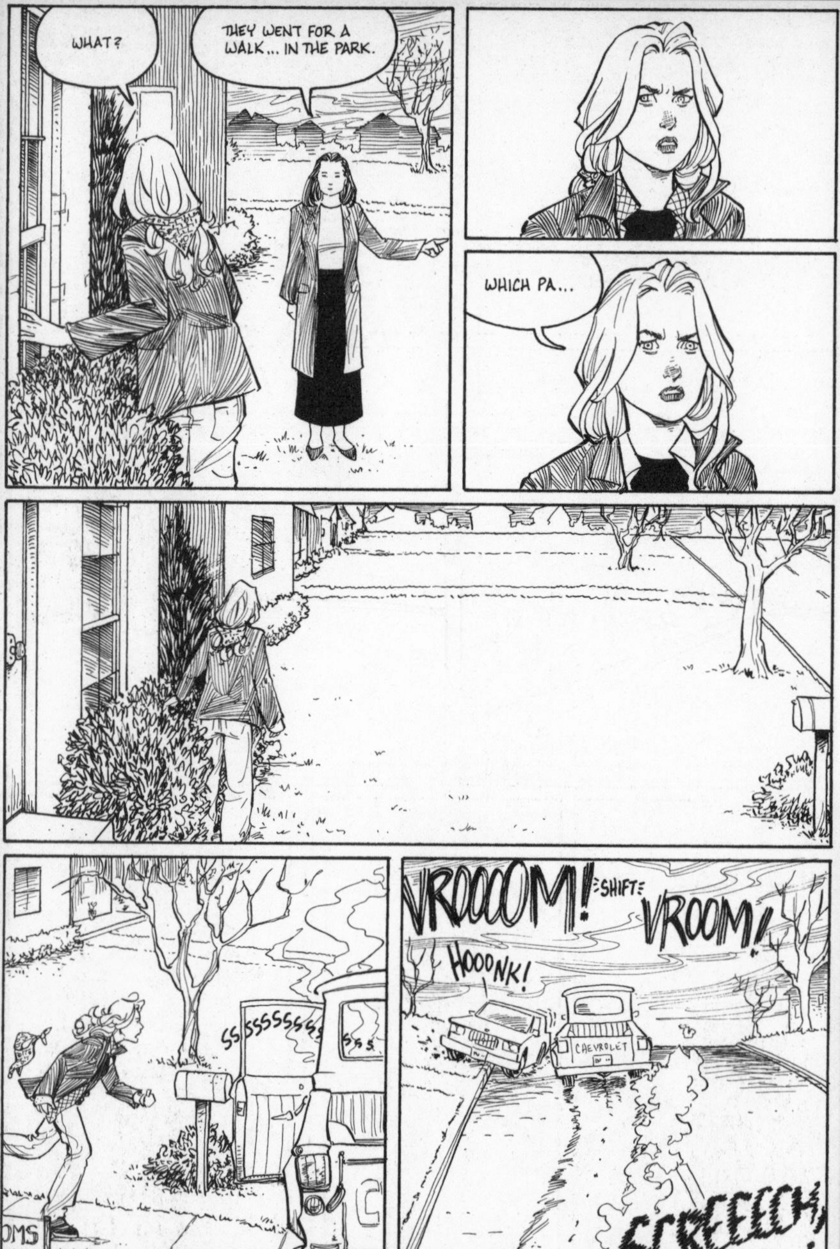
WHAT?
THEY WENT FOR A WALK... IN THE PARK.
WHICH PA...
VROOOOM!
SHIFT
VROOM!
HOOONK!
CHEVROLET
SCREEECH!

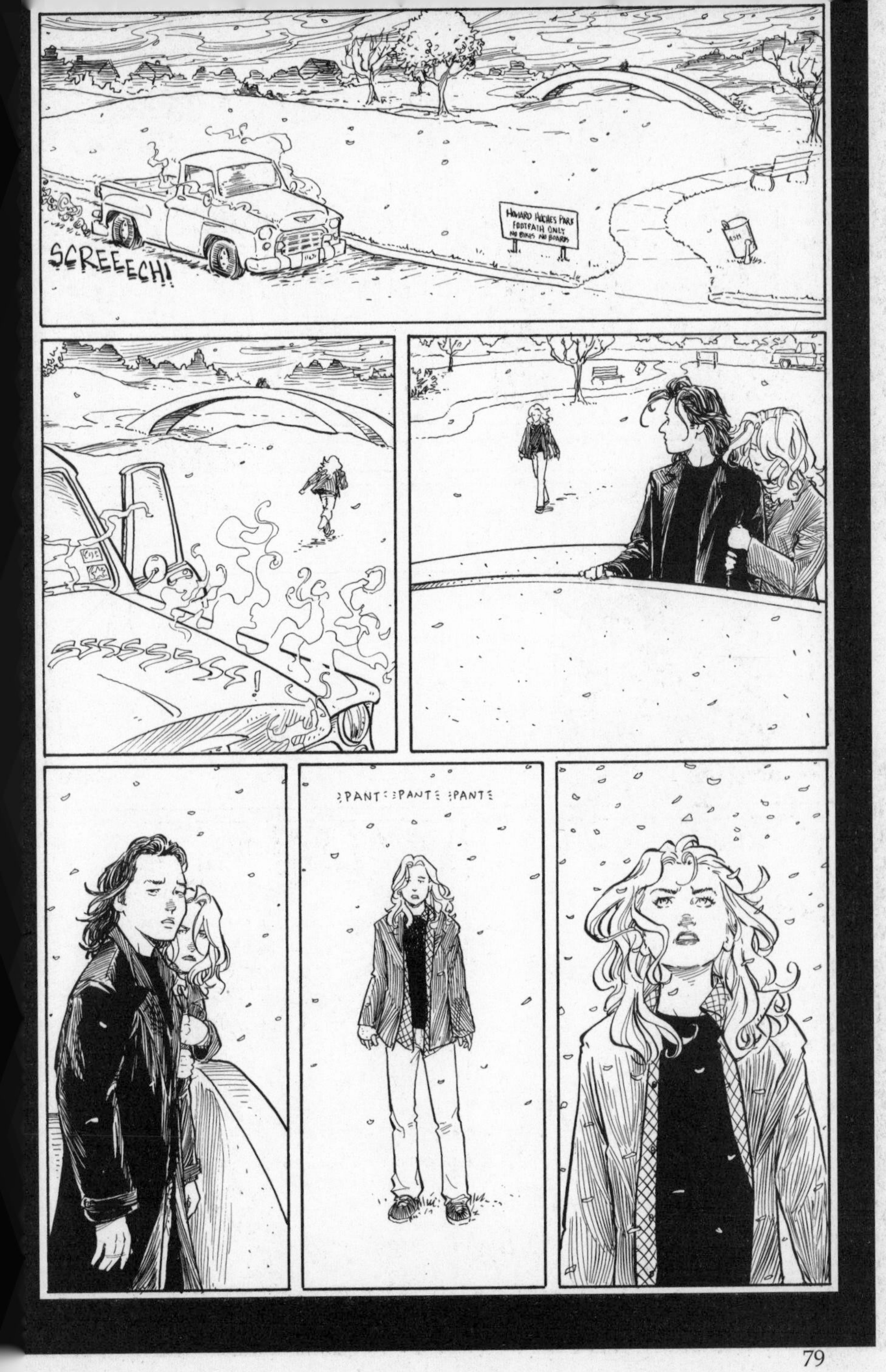
SCREEECH!
HOWARD HUGHES PARK
FOOTPATH ONLY
NO BIKES NO BOARDS
SSSSSSSSS!
PANT PANT PANT

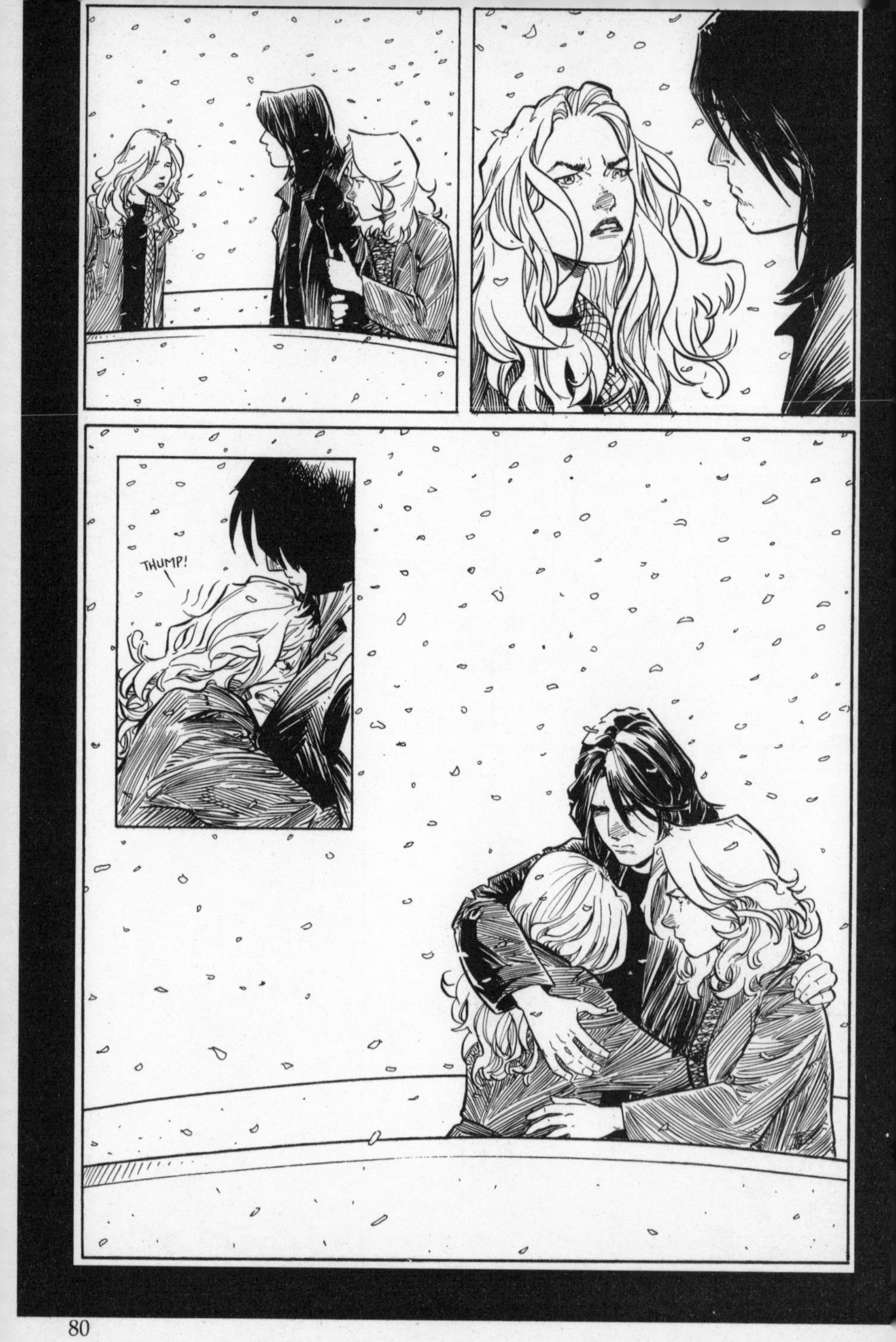
THUMP!

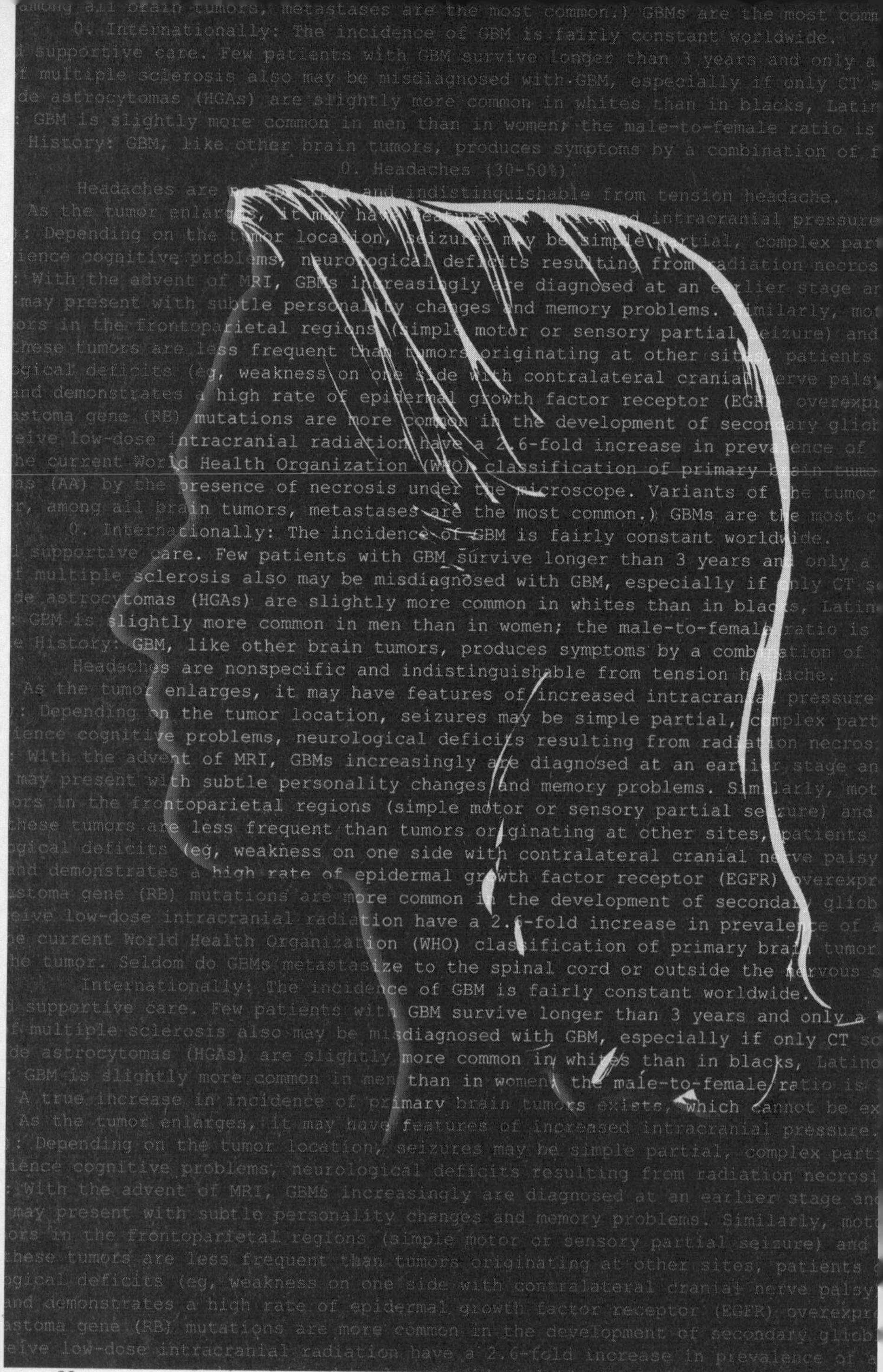

among all brain tumors, metastases are the most common.) GBMs are the most comm
O. Internationally: The incidence of GBM is fairly constant worldwide.
d supportive care. Few patients with GBM survive longer than 3 years and only a
f multiple sclerosis also may be misdiagnosed with GBM, especially if only CT s
de astrocytomas (HGAs) are slightly more common in whites than in blacks, Latin
GBM is slightly more common in men than in women; the male-to-female ratio is
History: GBM, like other brain tumors, produces symptoms by a combination of f
O. Headaches (30-50%)
Headaches are nonspecific and indistinguishable from tension headache.
As the tumor enlarges, it may have features of increased intracranial pressure
: Depending on the tumor location, seizures may be simple partial, complex part
ience cognitive problems, neurological deficits resulting from radiation necros
: With the advent of MRI, GBMs increasingly are diagnosed at an earlier stage an
may present with subtle personality changes and memory problems. Similarly, mot
ors in the frontoparietal regions (simple motor or sensory partial seizure) and
these tumors are less frequent than tumors originating at other sites, patients
ogical deficits (eg, weakness on one side with contralateral cranial nerve palsy
and demonstrates a high rate of epidermal growth factor receptor (EGFR) overexp
astoma gene (RB) mutations are more common in the development of secondary glio
eive low-dose intracranial radiation have a 2.6-fold increase in prevalence of
he current World Health Organization (WHO) classification of primary brain tumo
as (AA) by the presence of necrosis under the microscope. Variants of the tumor
r, among all brain tumors, metastases are the most common.) GBMs are the most c
O. Internationally: The incidence of GBM is fairly constant worldwide.
d supportive care. Few patients with GBM survive longer than 3 years and only a
f multiple sclerosis also may be misdiagnosed with GBM, especially if only CT s
de astrocytomas (HGAs) are slightly more common in whites than in blacks, Latin
GBM is slightly more common in men than in women; the male-to-female ratio is
History: GBM, like other brain tumors, produces symptoms by a combination of f
Headaches are nonspecific and indistinguishable from tension headache.
As the tumor enlarges, it may have features of increased intracranial pressure
: Depending on the tumor location, seizures may be simple partial, complex part
ience cognitive problems, neurological deficits resulting from radiation necros
: With the advent of MRI, GBMs increasingly are diagnosed at an earlier stage an
may present with subtle personality changes and memory problems. Similarly, mot
ors in the frontoparietal regions (simple motor or sensory partial seizure) and
these tumors are less frequent than tumors originating at other sites, patients
ogical deficits (eg, weakness on one side with contralateral cranial nerve palsy
and demonstrates a high rate of epidermal growth factor receptor (EGFR) overexp
astoma gene (RB) mutations are more common in the development of secondary glio
eive low-dose intracranial radiation have a 2.6-fold increase in prevalence of
he current World Health Organization (WHO) classification of primary brain tumor
he tumor. Seldom do GBMs metastasize to the spinal cord or outside the nervous s
Internationally: The incidence of GBM is fairly constant worldwide.
d supportive care. Few patients with GBM survive longer than 3 years and only a
f multiple sclerosis also may be misdiagnosed with GBM, especially if only CT so
de astrocytomas (HGAs) are slightly more common in whites than in blacks, Latino
GBM is slightly more common in men than in women; the male-to-female ratio is
A true increase in incidence of primary brain tumors exists, which cannot be ex
As the tumor enlarges, it may have features of increased intracranial pressure.
: Depending on the tumor location, seizures may be simple partial, complex part
ience cognitive problems, neurological deficits resulting from radiation necrosi
: With the advent of MRI, GBMs increasingly are diagnosed at an earlier stage an
may present with subtle personality changes and memory problems. Similarly, mot
ors in the frontoparietal regions (simple motor or sensory partial seizure) and
these tumors are less frequent than tumors originating at other sites, patients
ogical deficits (eg, weakness on one side with contralateral cranial nerve palsy
and demonstrates a high rate of epidermal growth factor receptor (EGFR) overexp
astoma gene (RB) mutations are more common in the development of secondary glio
eive low-dose intracranial radiation have a 2.6-fold increase in prevalence of

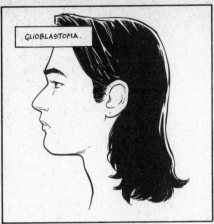

GLIOBLASTOMA.

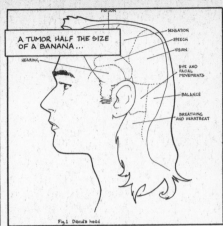

A TUMOR HALF THE SIZE OF A BANANA...

MOTION
SENSATION
SPEECH
VISION
EYE AND FACIAL MOVEMENTS
BALANCE
BREATHING AND HEARTBEAT
HEARING

Fig.1 David's head

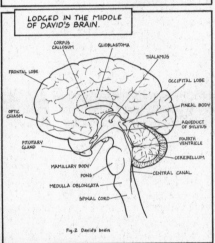

LODGED IN THE MIDDLE OF DAVID'S BRAIN.

CORPUS CALLOSUM
GLIOBLASTOMA
THALAMUS
FRONTAL LOBE
OCCIPITAL LOBE
PINEAL BODY
OPTIC CHIASM
AQUEDUCT OF SYLVIUS
FOURTH VENTRICLE
PITUITARY GLAND
CEREBELLUM
MAMILLARY BODY
CENTRAL CANAL
PONS
MEDULLA OBLONGATA
SPINAL CORD

Fig.2 David's brain

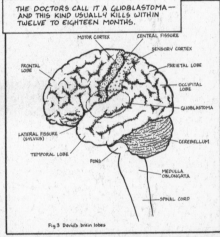

THE DOCTORS CALL IT A GLIOBLASTOMA— AND THIS KIND USUALLY KILLS WITHIN TWELVE TO EIGHTEEN MONTHS.

MOTOR CORTEX
CENTRAL FISSURE
SENSORY CORTEX
FRONTAL LOBE
PARIETAL LOBE
OCCIPITAL LOBE
GLIOBLASTOMA
LATERAL FISSURE (SYLVIUS)
CEREBELLUM
TEMPORAL LOBE
PONS
MEDULLA OBLONGATA
SPINAL CORD

Fig.3 David's brain lobes

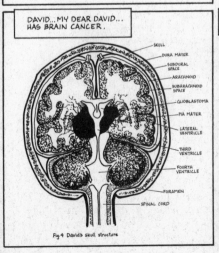

DAVID... MY DEAR DAVID... HAS BRAIN CANCER.

SKULL
DURA MATER
SUBDURAL SPACE
ARACHNOID
SUBARACHNOID SPACE
GLIOBLASTOMA
PIA MATER
LATERAL VENTRICLE
THIRD VENTRICLE
FOURTH VENTRICLE
FORAMEN
SPINAL CORD

Fig.4 David's skull structure

CASEY AND I FOUND OUT THIS AFTERNOON, DAVID FOUND OUT THREE MONTHS AGO.

THAT LEAVES NINE TO FIFTEEN MONTHS.

83

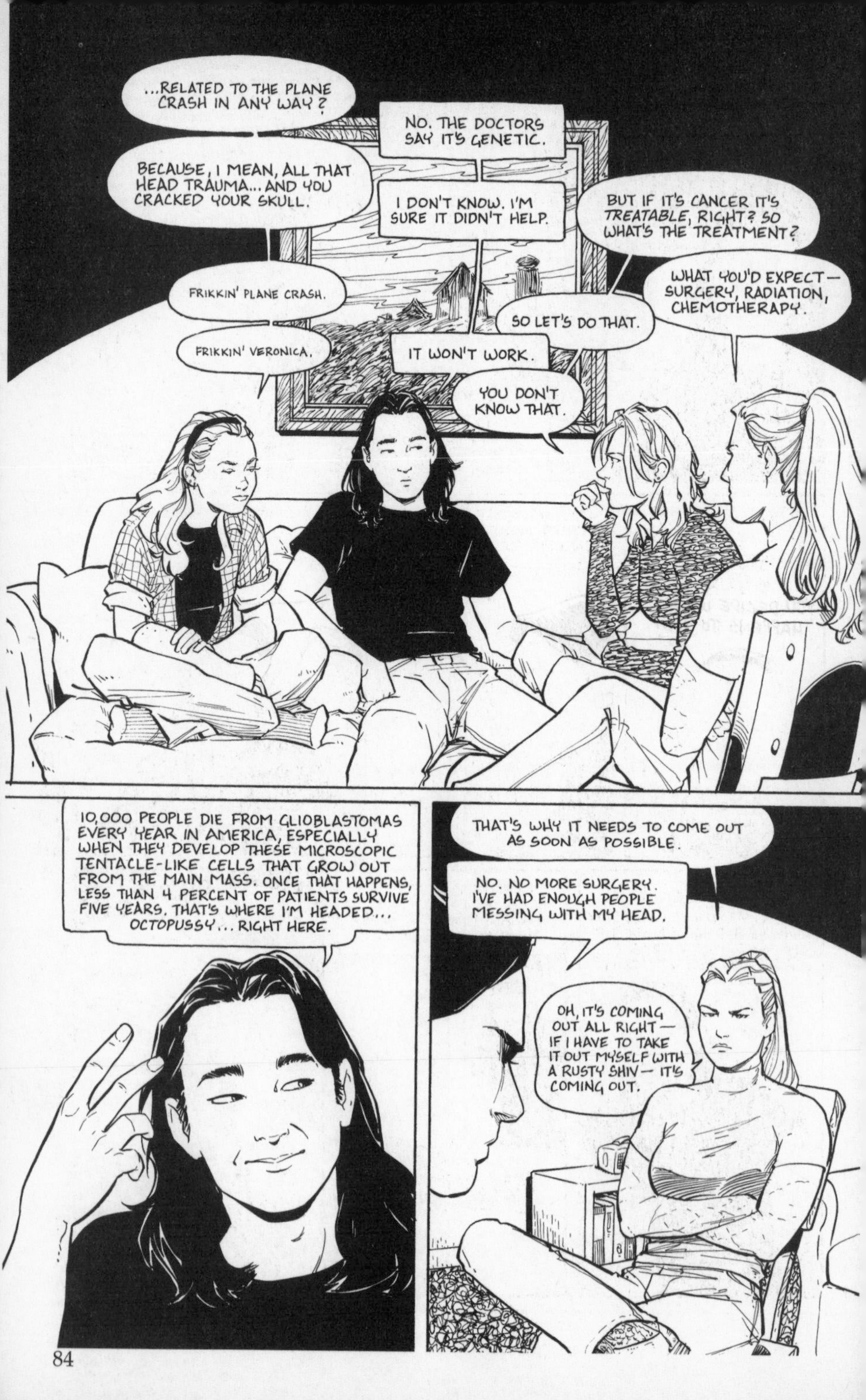

...RELATED TO THE PLANE CRASH IN ANY WAY?
BECAUSE, I MEAN, ALL THAT HEAD TRAUMA... AND YOU CRACKED YOUR SKULL.
NO. THE DOCTORS SAY IT'S GENETIC.
I DON'T KNOW. I'M SURE IT DIDN'T HELP.
FRIKKIN' PLANE CRASH.
FRIKKIN' VERONICA.
BUT IF IT'S CANCER IT'S *TREATABLE*, RIGHT? SO WHAT'S THE TREATMENT?
WHAT YOU'D EXPECT— SURGERY, RADIATION, CHEMOTHERAPY.
SO LET'S DO THAT.
IT WON'T WORK.
YOU DON'T KNOW THAT.
10,000 PEOPLE DIE FROM GLIOBLASTOMAS EVERY YEAR IN AMERICA, ESPECIALLY WHEN THEY DEVELOP THESE MICROSCOPIC TENTACLE-LIKE CELLS THAT GROW OUT FROM THE MAIN MASS. ONCE THAT HAPPENS, LESS THAN 4 PERCENT OF PATIENTS SURVIVE FIVE YEARS. THAT'S WHERE I'M HEADED... OCTOPUSSY... RIGHT HERE.
THAT'S WHY IT NEEDS TO COME OUT AS SOON AS POSSIBLE.
NO. NO MORE SURGERY. I'VE HAD ENOUGH PEOPLE MESSING WITH MY HEAD.
OH, IT'S COMING OUT ALL RIGHT— IF I HAVE TO TAKE IT OUT MYSELF WITH A RUSTY SHIV— IT'S COMING OUT.

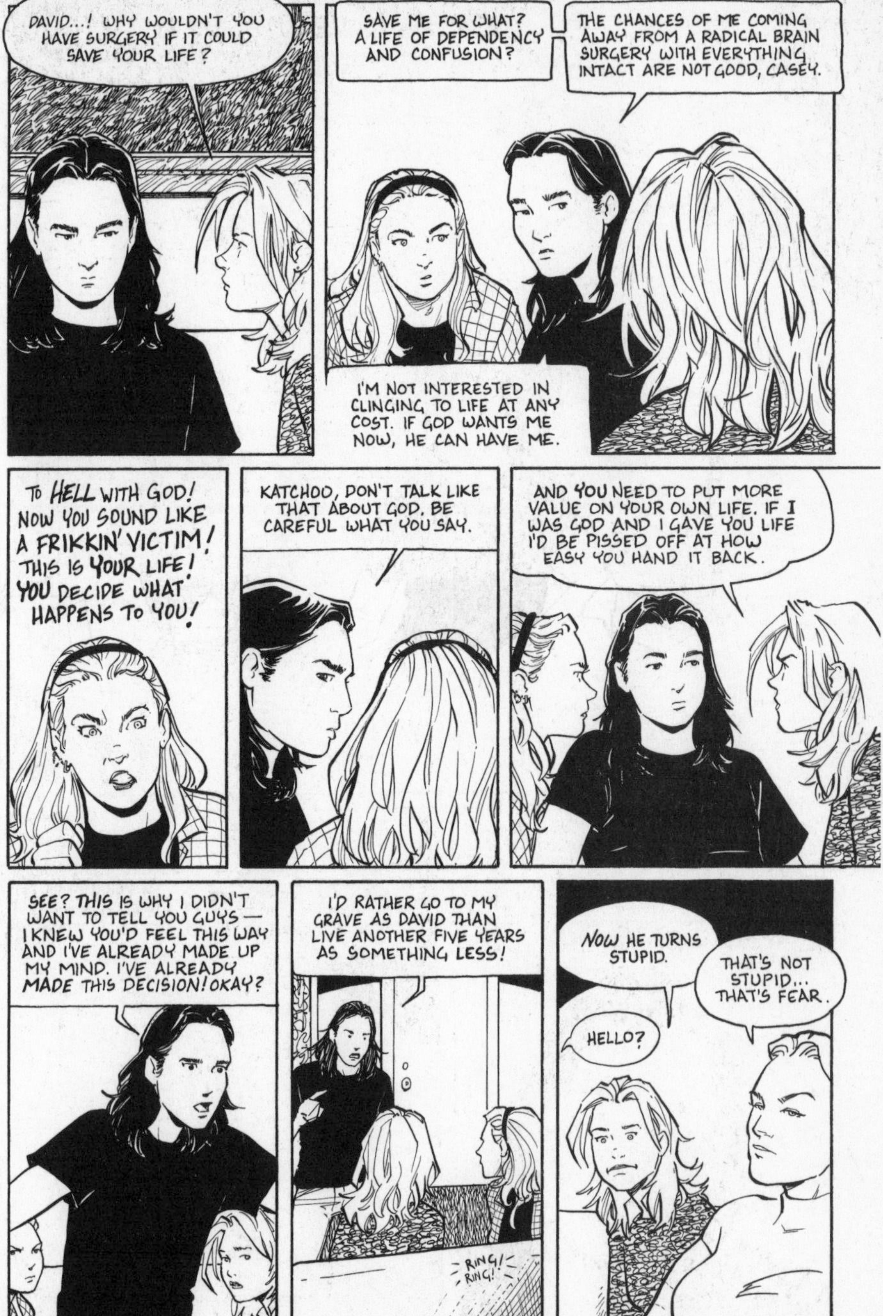
DAVID...! WHY WOULDN'T YOU HAVE SURGERY IF IT COULD SAVE YOUR LIFE?
SAVE ME FOR WHAT? A LIFE OF DEPENDENCY AND CONFUSION?
THE CHANCES OF ME COMING AWAY FROM A RADICAL BRAIN SURGERY WITH EVERYTHING INTACT ARE NOT GOOD, CASEY.
I'M NOT INTERESTED IN CLINGING TO LIFE AT ANY COST. IF GOD WANTS ME NOW, HE CAN HAVE ME.
TO HELL WITH GOD! NOW YOU SOUND LIKE A FRIKKIN' VICTIM! THIS IS YOUR LIFE! YOU DECIDE WHAT HAPPENS TO YOU!
KATCHOO, DON'T TALK LIKE THAT ABOUT GOD. BE CAREFUL WHAT YOU SAY.
AND YOU NEED TO PUT MORE VALUE ON YOUR OWN LIFE. IF I WAS GOD AND I GAVE YOU LIFE I'D BE PISSED OFF AT HOW EASY YOU HAND IT BACK.
SEE? THIS IS WHY I DIDN'T WANT TO TELL YOU GUYS— I KNEW YOU'D FEEL THIS WAY AND I'VE ALREADY MADE UP MY MIND. I'VE ALREADY MADE THIS DECISION! OKAY?
I'D RATHER GO TO MY GRAVE AS DAVID THAN LIVE ANOTHER FIVE YEARS AS SOMETHING LESS!
RING! RING!
NOW HE TURNS STUPID.
THAT'S NOT STUPID... THAT'S FEAR.
HELLO?

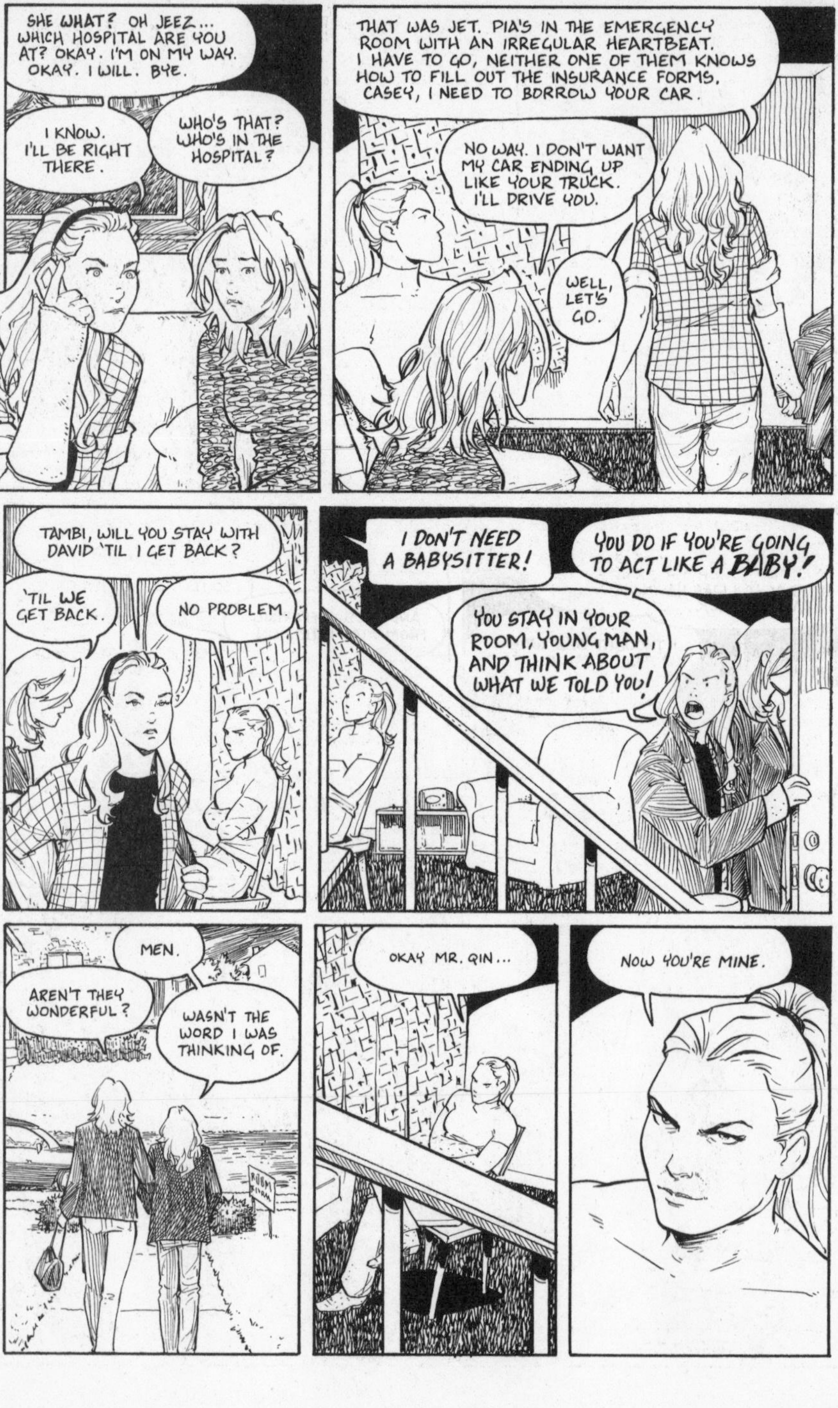
SHE WHAT? OH JEEZ... WHICH HOSPITAL ARE YOU AT? OKAY. I'M ON MY WAY. OKAY. I WILL. BYE.
WHO'S THAT? WHO'S IN THE HOSPITAL?
I KNOW. I'LL BE RIGHT THERE.
THAT WAS JET. PIA'S IN THE EMERGENCY ROOM WITH AN IRREGULAR HEARTBEAT. I HAVE TO GO, NEITHER ONE OF THEM KNOWS HOW TO FILL OUT THE INSURANCE FORMS. CASEY, I NEED TO BORROW YOUR CAR.
NO WAY. I DON'T WANT MY CAR ENDING UP LIKE YOUR TRUCK. I'LL DRIVE YOU.
WELL, LET'S GO.
TAMBI, WILL YOU STAY WITH DAVID 'TIL I GET BACK?
'TIL WE GET BACK.
NO PROBLEM.
I DON'T NEED A BABYSITTER!
YOU DO IF YOU'RE GOING TO ACT LIKE A BABY!
YOU STAY IN YOUR ROOM, YOUNG MAN, AND THINK ABOUT WHAT WE TOLD YOU!
MEN.
AREN'T THEY WONDERFUL?
WASN'T THE WORD I WAS THINKING OF.
OKAY MR. QIN...
NOW YOU'RE MINE.

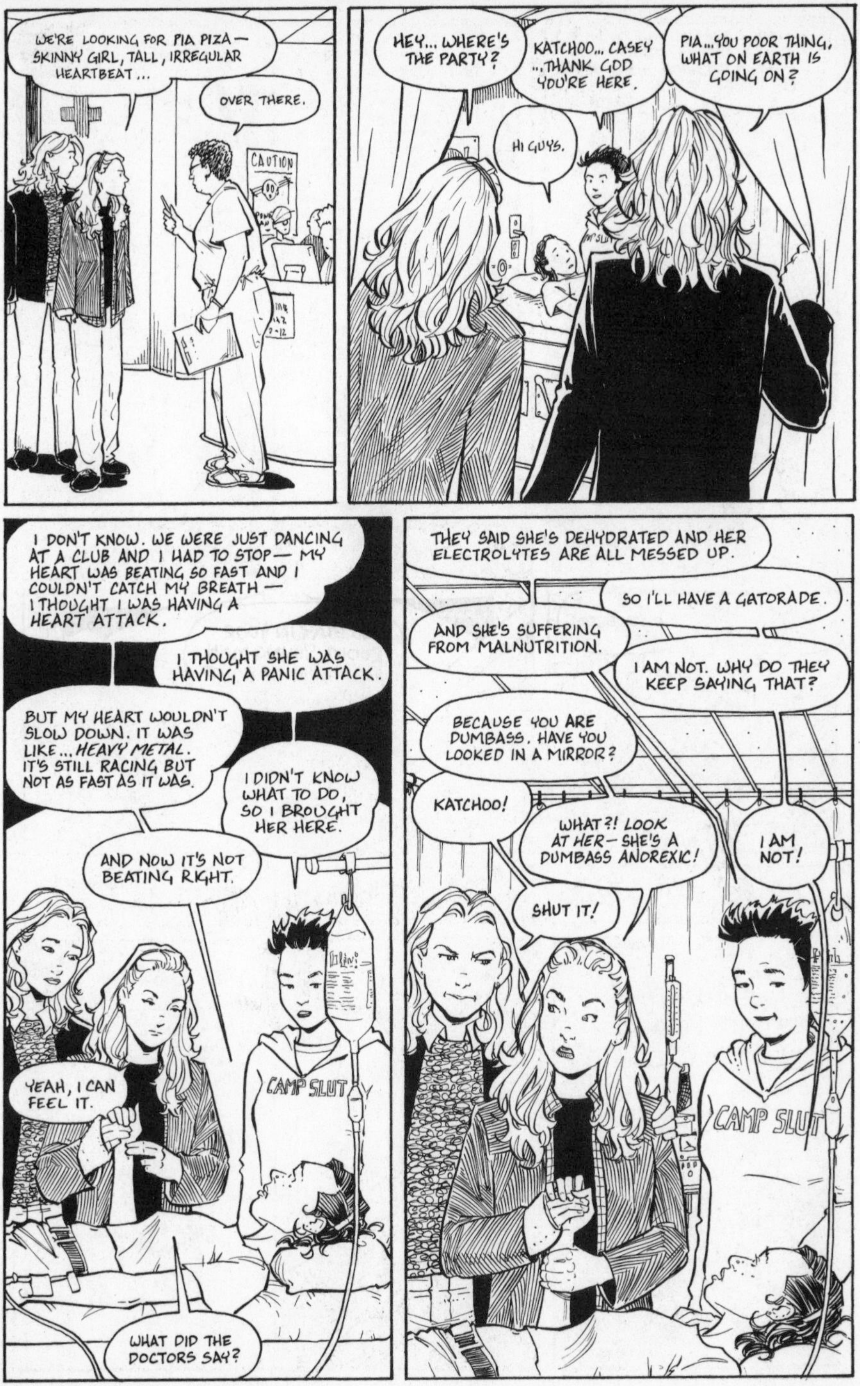
WE'RE LOOKING FOR PIA PIZA— SKINNY GIRL, TALL, IRREGULAR HEARTBEAT...
OVER THERE.
CAUTION
HEY... WHERE'S THE PARTY?
KATCHOO... CASEY ...THANK GOD YOU'RE HERE.
PIA...YOU POOR THING, WHAT ON EARTH IS GOING ON?
HI GUYS.
I DON'T KNOW. WE WERE JUST DANCING AT A CLUB AND I HAD TO STOP— MY HEART WAS BEATING SO FAST AND I COULDN'T CATCH MY BREATH— I THOUGHT I WAS HAVING A HEART ATTACK.
I THOUGHT SHE WAS HAVING A PANIC ATTACK.
BUT MY HEART WOULDN'T SLOW DOWN. IT WAS LIKE... *HEAVY METAL*. IT'S STILL RACING BUT NOT AS FAST AS IT WAS.
I DIDN'T KNOW WHAT TO DO, SO I BROUGHT HER HERE.
AND NOW IT'S NOT BEATING RIGHT.
YEAH, I CAN FEEL IT.
CAMP SLUT
WHAT DID THE DOCTORS SAY?
THEY SAID SHE'S DEHYDRATED AND HER ELECTROLYTES ARE ALL MESSED UP.
SO I'LL HAVE A GATORADE.
AND SHE'S SUFFERING FROM MALNUTRITION.
I AM NOT. WHY DO THEY KEEP SAYING THAT?
BECAUSE YOU ARE DUMBASS. HAVE YOU LOOKED IN A MIRROR?
KATCHOO!
WHAT?! LOOK AT HER— SHE'S A DUMBASS ANOREXIC!
I AM NOT!
SHUT IT!
CAMP SLUT

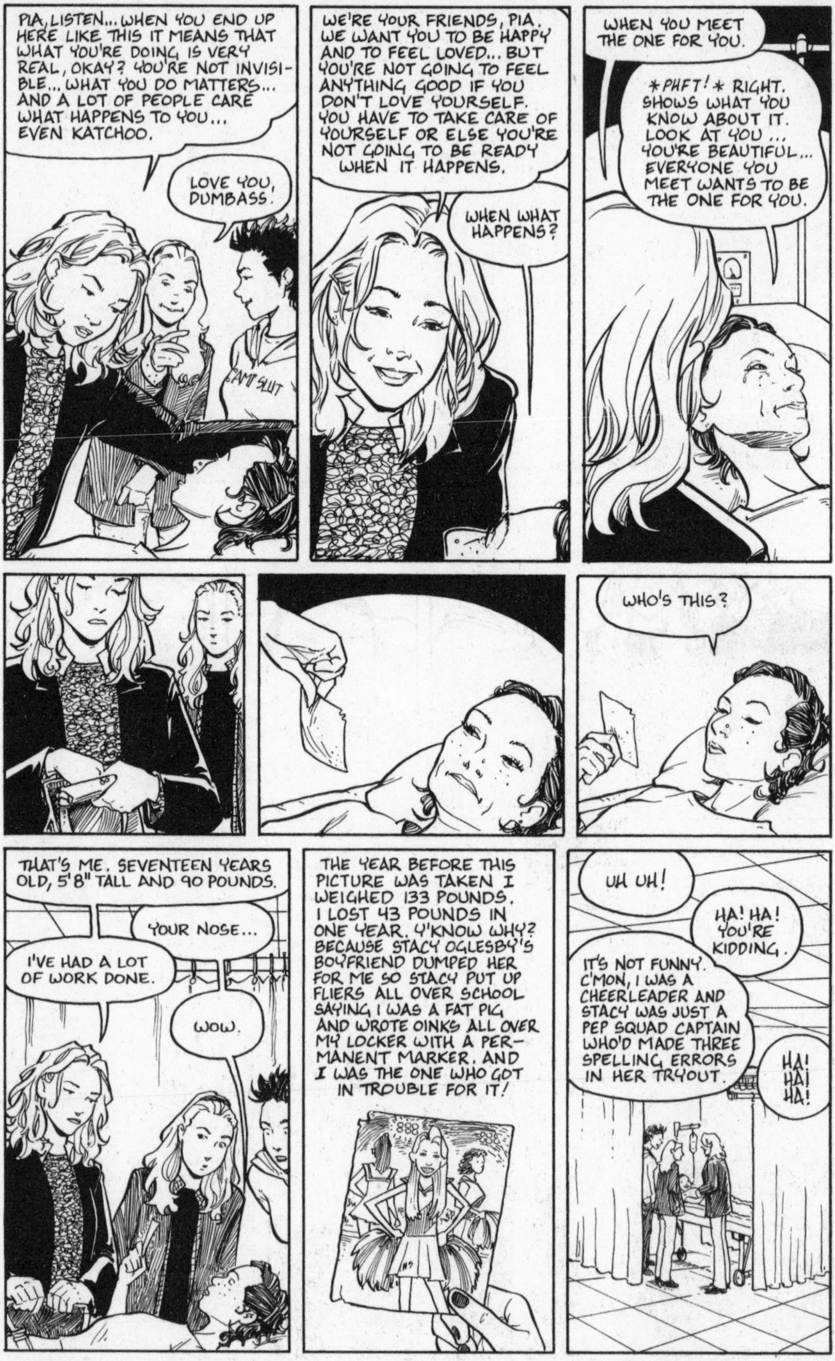
PIA, LISTEN... WHEN YOU END UP HERE LIKE THIS IT MEANS THAT WHAT YOU'RE DOING IS VERY REAL, OKAY? YOU'RE NOT INVISIBLE... WHAT YOU DO MATTERS... AND A LOT OF PEOPLE CARE WHAT HAPPENS TO YOU... EVEN KATCHOO.
LOVE YOU, DUMBASS!
WE'RE YOUR FRIENDS, PIA. WE WANT YOU TO BE HAPPY AND TO FEEL LOVED... BUT YOU'RE NOT GOING TO FEEL ANYTHING GOOD IF YOU DON'T LOVE YOURSELF. YOU HAVE TO TAKE CARE OF YOURSELF OR ELSE YOU'RE NOT GOING TO BE READY WHEN IT HAPPENS.
WHEN WHAT HAPPENS?
WHEN YOU MEET THE ONE FOR YOU.
PHFT! RIGHT. SHOWS WHAT YOU KNOW ABOUT IT. LOOK AT YOU... YOU'RE BEAUTIFUL... EVERYONE YOU MEET WANTS TO BE THE ONE FOR YOU.
WHO'S THIS?
THAT'S ME. SEVENTEEN YEARS OLD, 5'8" TALL AND 90 POUNDS.
YOUR NOSE...
I'VE HAD A LOT OF WORK DONE.
WOW.
THE YEAR BEFORE THIS PICTURE WAS TAKEN I WEIGHED 133 POUNDS. I LOST 43 POUNDS IN ONE YEAR. Y'KNOW WHY? BECAUSE STACY OGLESBY'S BOYFRIEND DUMPED HER FOR ME SO STACY PUT UP FLIERS ALL OVER SCHOOL SAYING I WAS A FAT PIG AND WROTE OINKS ALL OVER MY LOCKER WITH A PERMANENT MARKER. AND I WAS THE ONE WHO GOT IN TROUBLE FOR IT!
UH UH!
HA! HA! YOU'RE KIDDING.
IT'S NOT FUNNY. C'MON, I WAS A CHEERLEADER AND STACY WAS JUST A PEP SQUAD CAPTAIN WHO'D MADE THREE SPELLING ERRORS IN HER TRYOUT.
HA! HA! HA!

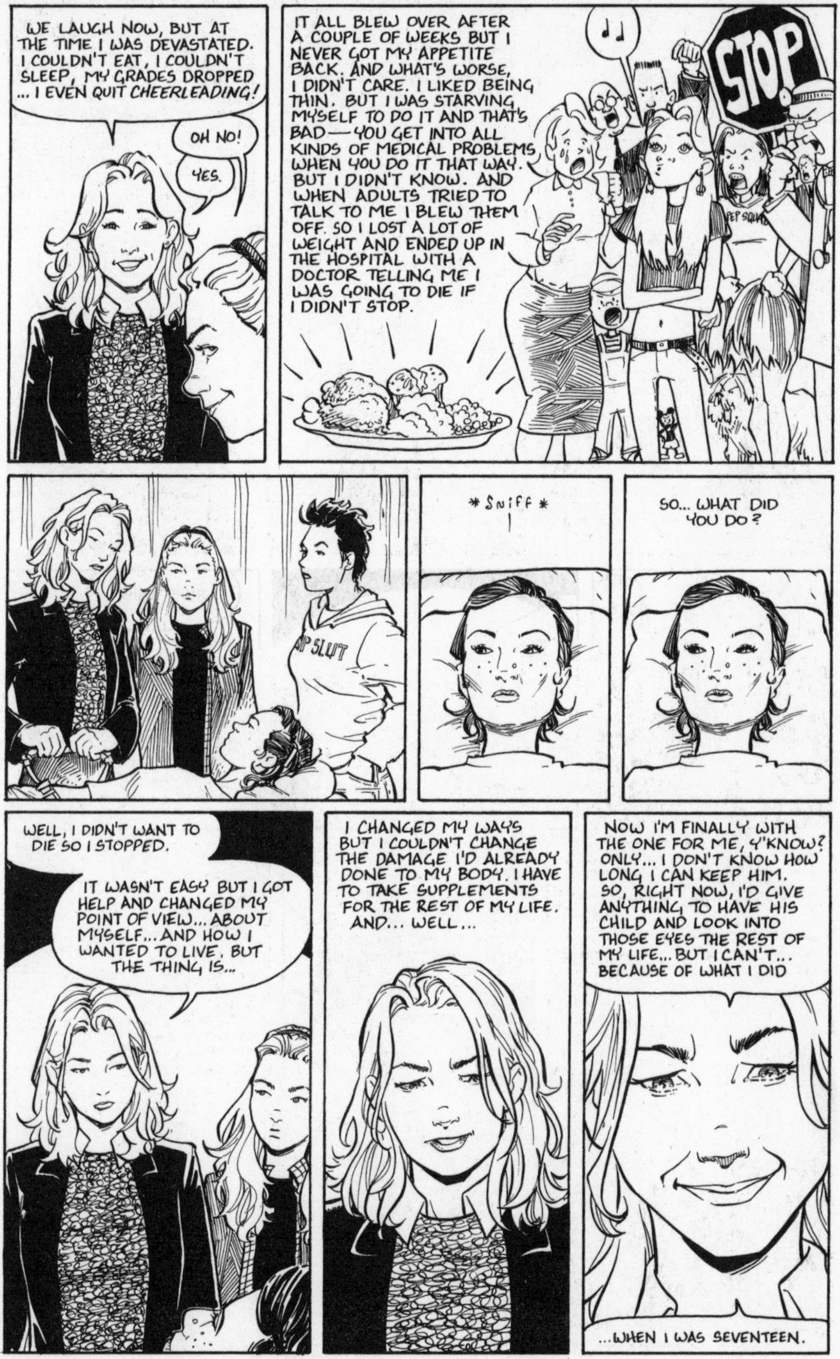
WE LAUGH NOW, BUT AT THE TIME I WAS DEVASTATED. I COULDN'T EAT, I COULDN'T SLEEP, MY GRADES DROPPED ... I EVEN QUIT CHEERLEADING!
OH NO!
YES.
IT ALL BLEW OVER AFTER A COUPLE OF WEEKS BUT I NEVER GOT MY APPETITE BACK. AND WHAT'S WORSE, I DIDN'T CARE. I LIKED BEING THIN. BUT I WAS STARVING MYSELF TO DO IT AND THAT'S BAD—YOU GET INTO ALL KINDS OF MEDICAL PROBLEMS WHEN YOU DO IT THAT WAY. BUT I DIDN'T KNOW. AND WHEN ADULTS TRIED TO TALK TO ME I BLEW THEM OFF. SO I LOST A LOT OF WEIGHT AND ENDED UP IN THE HOSPITAL WITH A DOCTOR TELLING ME I WAS GOING TO DIE IF I DIDN'T STOP.
STOP
PEP SQUAD
SNIFF
SO... WHAT DID YOU DO?
WELL, I DIDN'T WANT TO DIE SO I STOPPED.
IT WASN'T EASY BUT I GOT HELP AND CHANGED MY POINT OF VIEW... ABOUT MYSELF... AND HOW I WANTED TO LIVE. BUT THE THING IS...
I CHANGED MY WAYS BUT I COULDN'T CHANGE THE DAMAGE I'D ALREADY DONE TO MY BODY. I HAVE TO TAKE SUPPLEMENTS FOR THE REST OF MY LIFE. AND... WELL...
NOW I'M FINALLY WITH THE ONE FOR ME, Y'KNOW? ONLY... I DON'T KNOW HOW LONG I CAN KEEP HIM. SO, RIGHT NOW, I'D GIVE ANYTHING TO HAVE HIS CHILD AND LOOK INTO THOSE EYES THE REST OF MY LIFE... BUT I CAN'T... BECAUSE OF WHAT I DID
...WHEN I WAS SEVENTEEN.

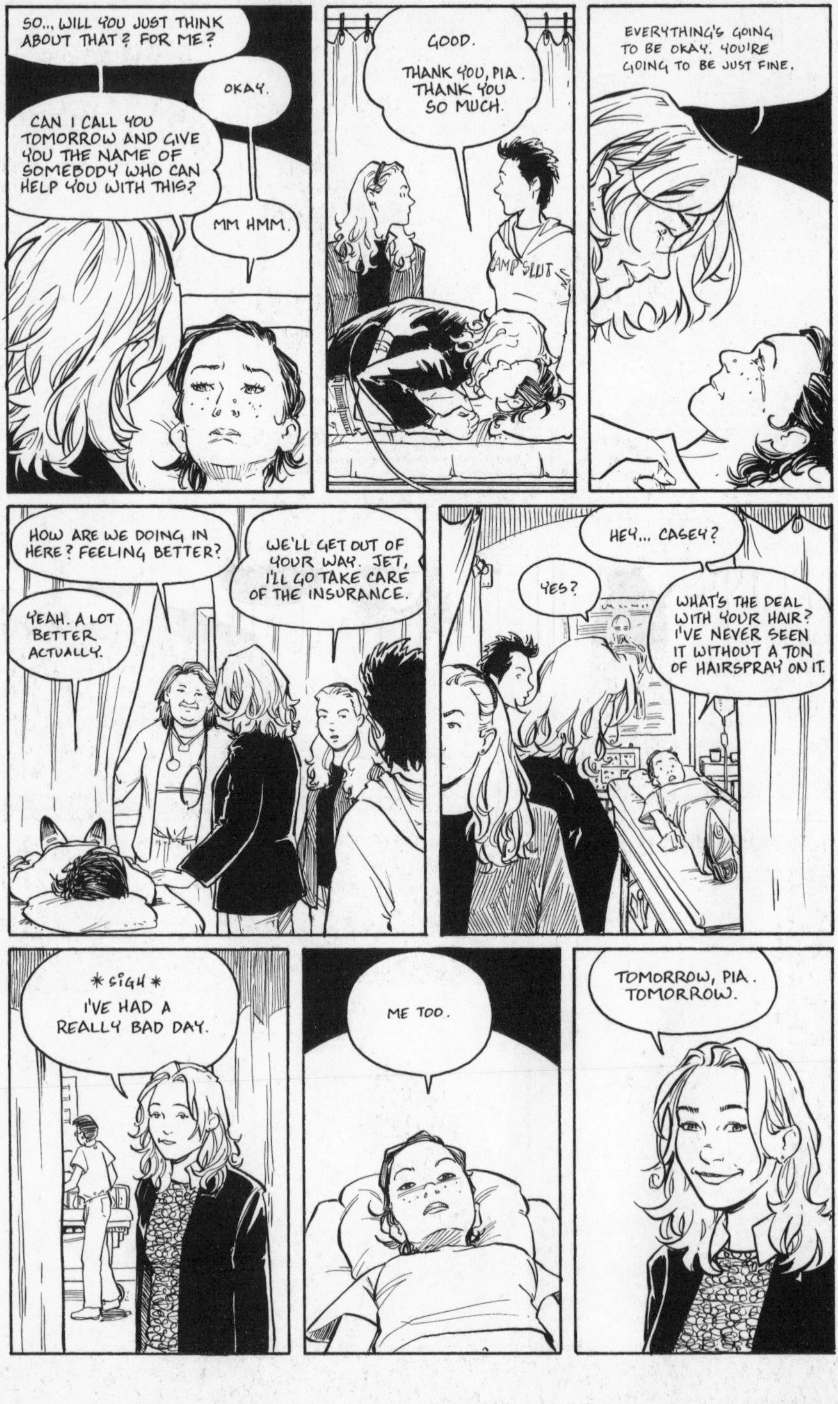
SO... WILL YOU JUST THINK ABOUT THAT? FOR ME?
OKAY.
CAN I CALL YOU TOMORROW AND GIVE YOU THE NAME OF SOMEBODY WHO CAN HELP YOU WITH THIS?
MM HMM.
GOOD.
THANK YOU, PIA. THANK YOU SO MUCH.
CAMP SLUT
EVERYTHING'S GOING TO BE OKAY. YOU'RE GOING TO BE JUST FINE.
HOW ARE WE DOING IN HERE? FEELING BETTER?
YEAH. A LOT BETTER ACTUALLY.
WE'LL GET OUT OF YOUR WAY. JET, I'LL GO TAKE CARE OF THE INSURANCE.
HEY... CASEY?
YES?
WHAT'S THE DEAL WITH YOUR HAIR? I'VE NEVER SEEN IT WITHOUT A TON OF HAIRSPRAY ON IT.
SIGH
I'VE HAD A REALLY BAD DAY.
ME TOO.
TOMORROW, PIA. TOMORROW.

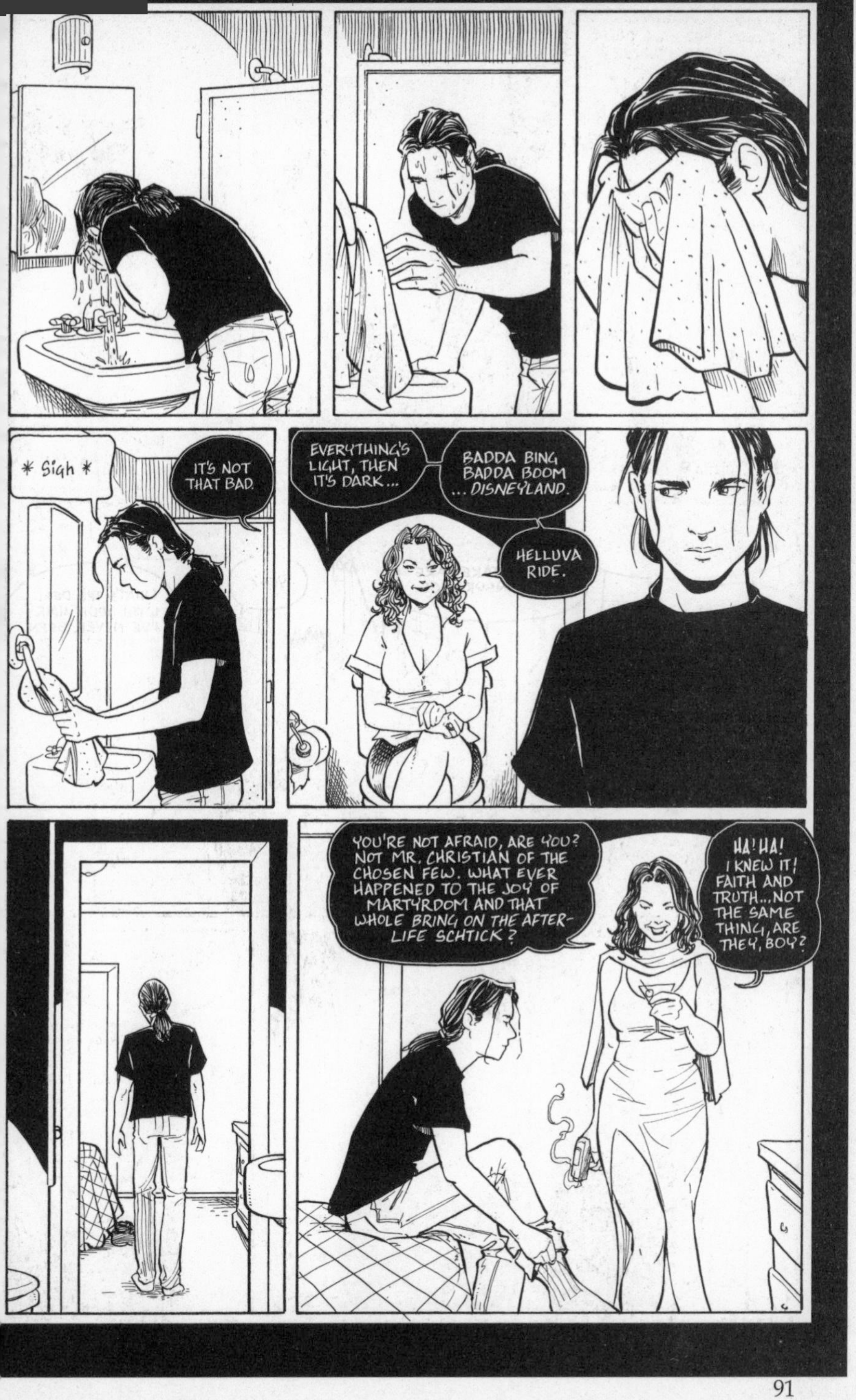
* Sigh *
IT'S NOT THAT BAD.
EVERYTHING'S LIGHT, THEN IT'S DARK...
BADDA BING BADDA BOOM ...DISNEYLAND.
HELLUVA RIDE.
YOU'RE NOT AFRAID, ARE YOU? NOT MR. CHRISTIAN OF THE CHOSEN FEW. WHAT EVER HAPPENED TO THE JOY OF MARTYRDOM AND THAT WHOLE BRING ON THE AFTER-LIFE SCHTICK?
HA! HA! I KNEW IT! FAITH AND TRUTH...NOT THE SAME THING, ARE THEY, BOY?

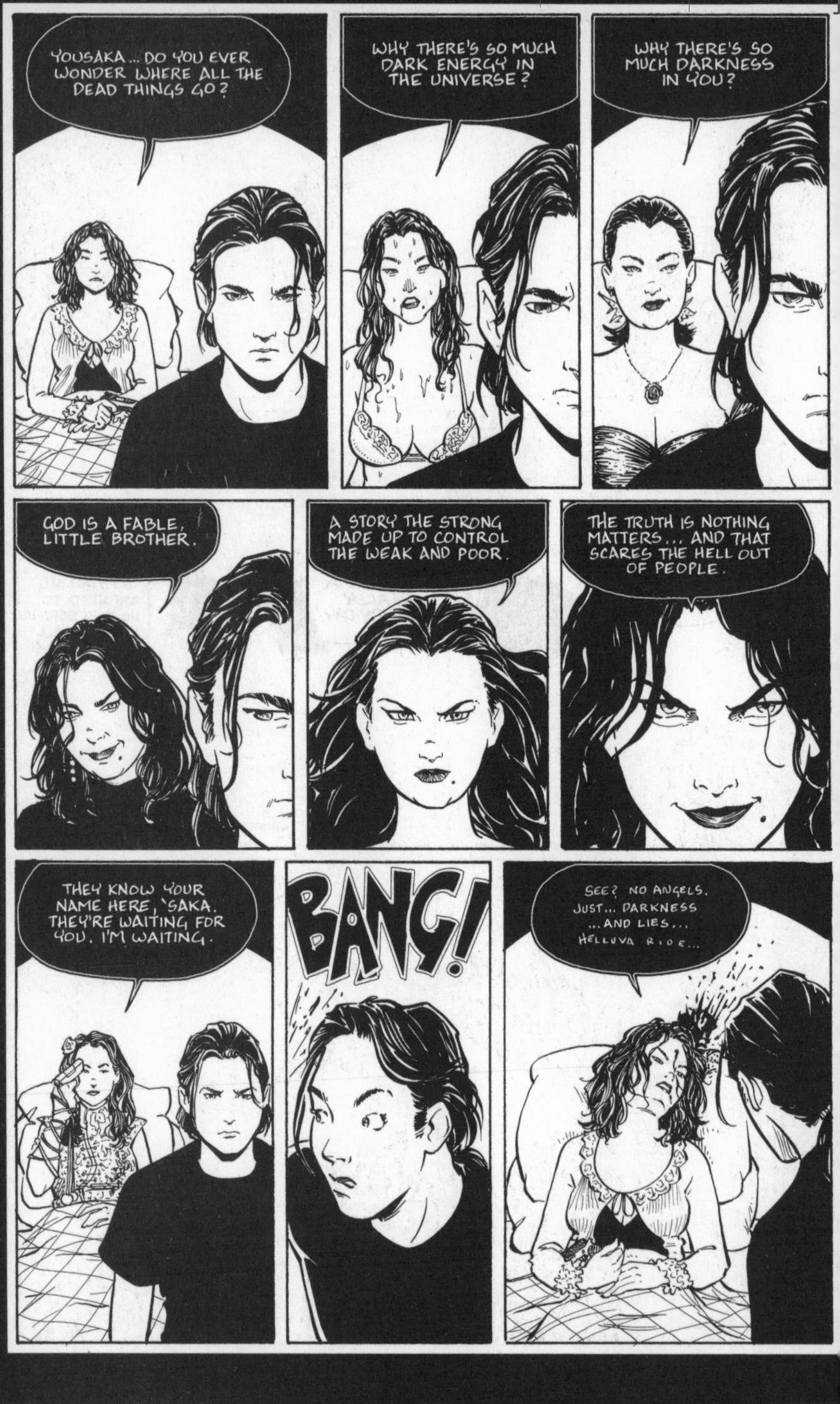
YOUSAKA... DO YOU EVER WONDER WHERE ALL THE DEAD THINGS GO?
WHY THERE'S SO MUCH DARK ENERGY IN THE UNIVERSE?
WHY THERE'S SO MUCH DARKNESS IN YOU?
GOD IS A FABLE, LITTLE BROTHER.
A STORY THE STRONG MADE UP TO CONTROL THE WEAK AND POOR.
THE TRUTH IS NOTHING MATTERS... AND THAT SCARES THE HELL OUT OF PEOPLE.
THEY KNOW YOUR NAME HERE, 'SAKA. THEY'RE WAITING FOR YOU. I'M WAITING.
BANG!
SEE? NO ANGELS. JUST... DARKNESS ...AND LIES... HELLUVA RIDE...

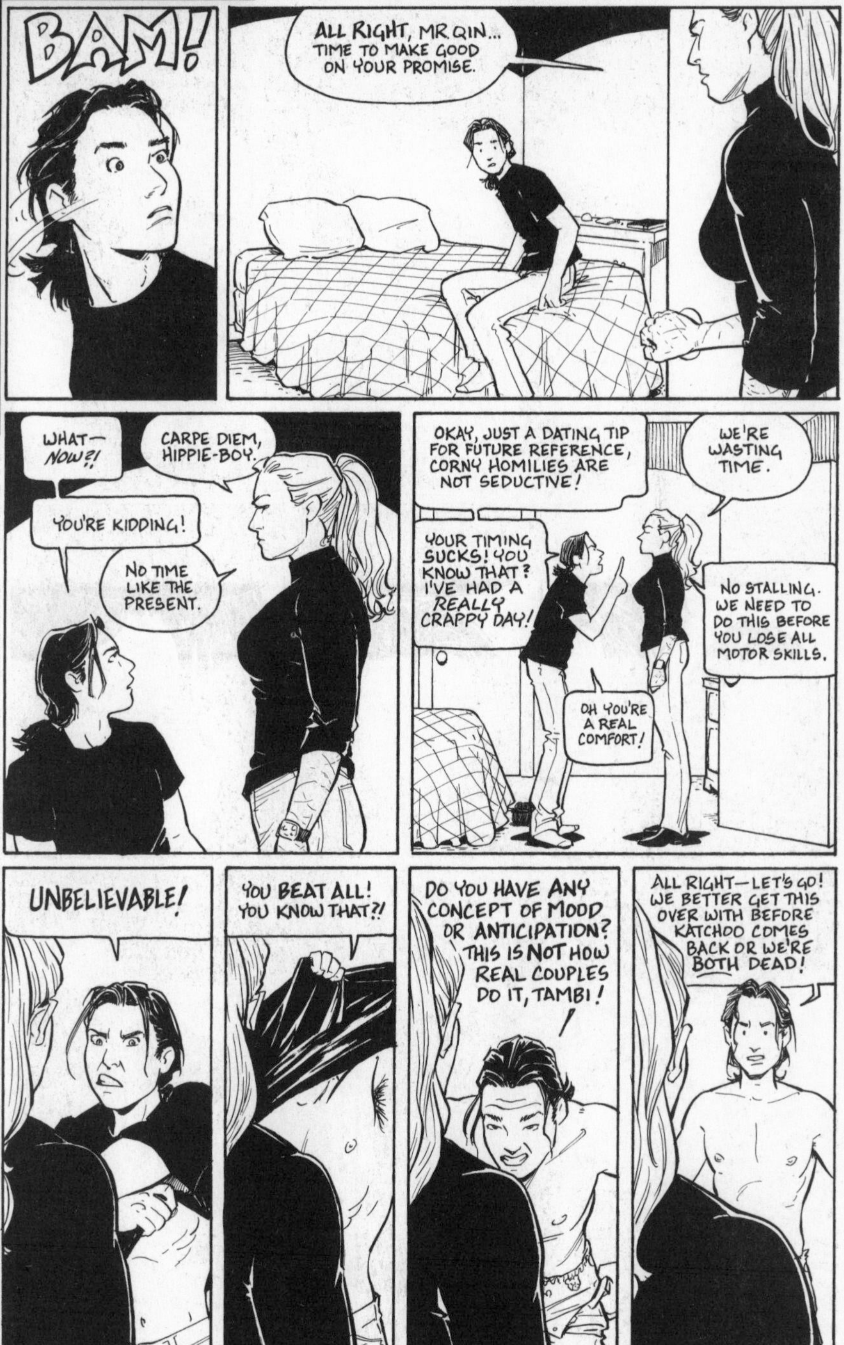
BAM!
ALL RIGHT, MR QIN... TIME TO MAKE GOOD ON YOUR PROMISE.
WHAT— NOW?!
CARPE DIEM, HIPPIE-BOY.
YOU'RE KIDDING!
NO TIME LIKE THE PRESENT.
OKAY, JUST A DATING TIP FOR FUTURE REFERENCE, CORNY HOMILIES ARE NOT SEDUCTIVE!
WE'RE WASTING TIME.
YOUR TIMING SUCKS! YOU KNOW THAT? I'VE HAD A REALLY CRAPPY DAY!
NO STALLING. WE NEED TO DO THIS BEFORE YOU LOSE ALL MOTOR SKILLS.
OH YOU'RE A REAL COMFORT!
UNBELIEVABLE!
YOU BEAT ALL! YOU KNOW THAT?!
DO YOU HAVE ANY CONCEPT OF MOOD OR ANTICIPATION? THIS IS NOT HOW REAL COUPLES DO IT, TAMBI!
ALL RIGHT— LET'S GO! WE BETTER GET THIS OVER WITH BEFORE KATCHOO COMES BACK OR WE'RE BOTH DEAD!

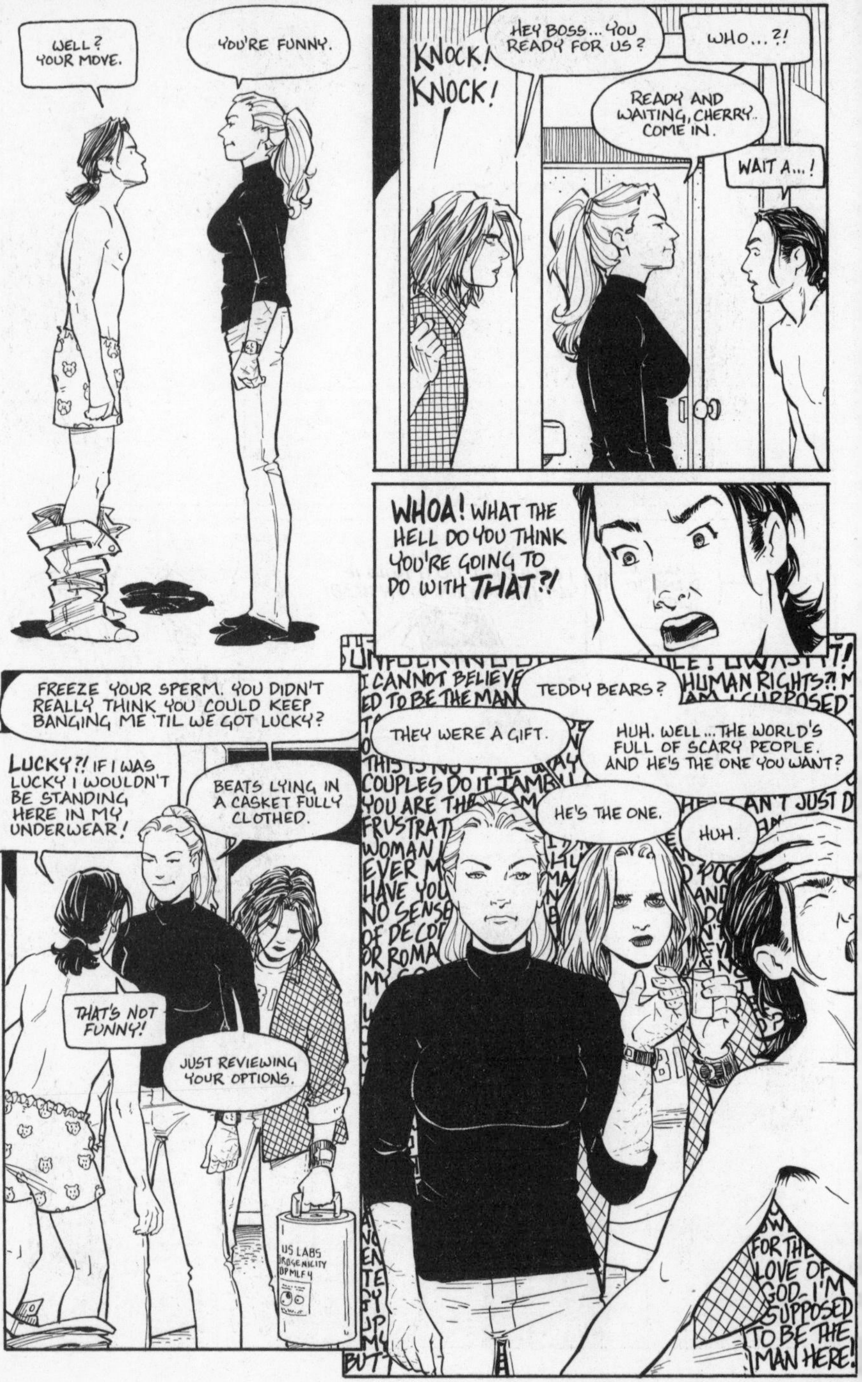

WELL? YOUR MOVE.
YOU'RE FUNNY.
KNOCK! KNOCK!
HEY BOSS... YOU READY FOR US?
WHO...?!
READY AND WAITING, CHERRY.. COME IN.
WAIT A...!
WHOA! WHAT THE HELL DO YOU THINK YOU'RE GOING TO DO WITH THAT?!
FREEZE YOUR SPERM. YOU DIDN'T REALLY THINK YOU COULD KEEP BANGING ME 'TIL WE GOT LUCKY?
LUCKY?! IF I WAS LUCKY I WOULDN'T BE STANDING HERE IN MY UNDERWEAR!
BEATS LYING IN A CASKET FULLY CLOTHED.
THAT'S NOT FUNNY!
JUST REVIEWING YOUR OPTIONS.
US LABS
TEDDY BEARS?
THEY WERE A GIFT.
HUH. WELL... THE WORLD'S FULL OF SCARY PEOPLE. AND HE'S THE ONE YOU WANT?
HE'S THE ONE.
HUH.
FOR THE LOVE OF GOD, I'M SUPPOSED TO BE THE MAN HERE!

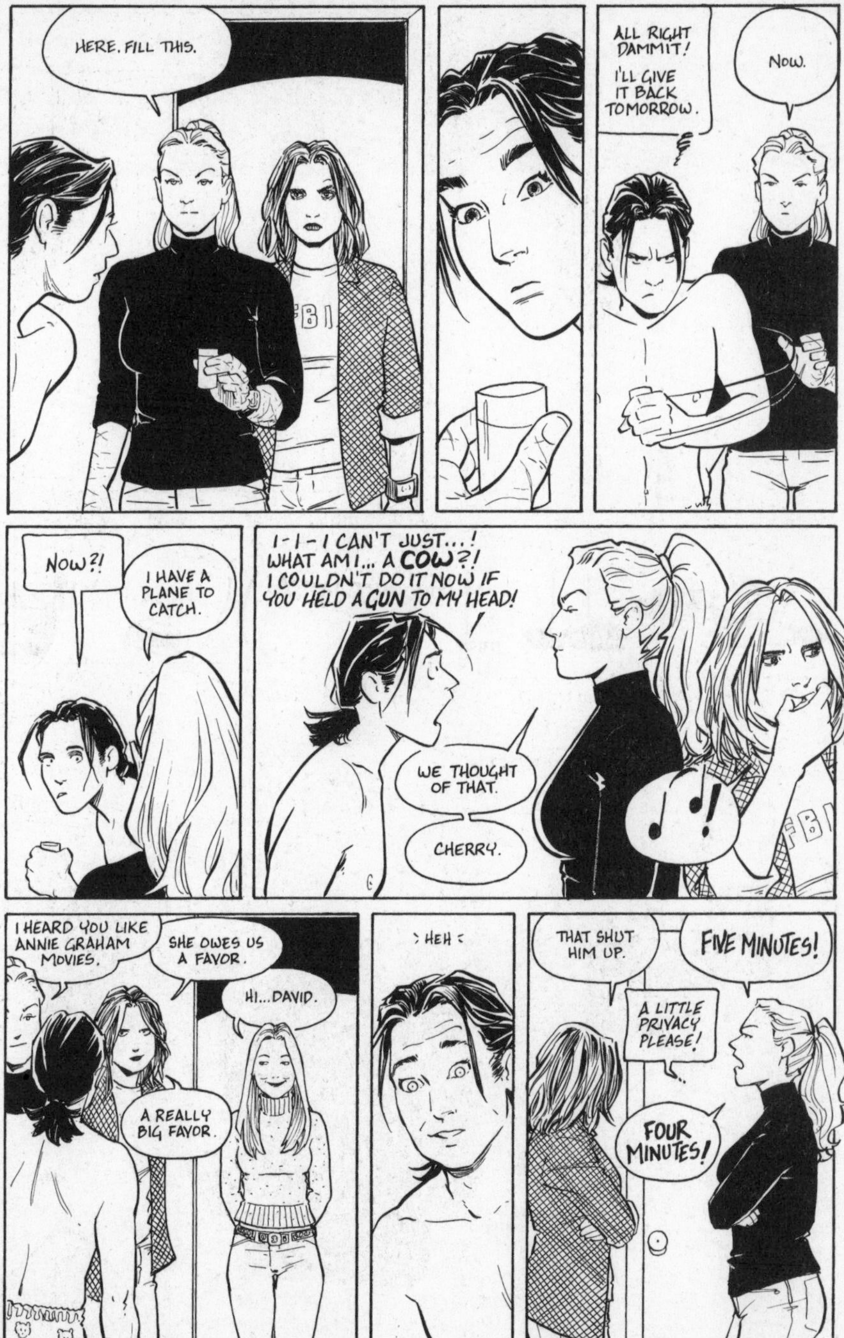
HERE. FILL THIS.
ALL RIGHT DAMMIT! I'LL GIVE IT BACK TOMORROW.
NOW.
NOW?!
I HAVE A PLANE TO CATCH.
I-I-I CAN'T JUST...! WHAT AM I... A COW?! I COULDN'T DO IT NOW IF YOU HELD A GUN TO MY HEAD!
WE THOUGHT OF THAT.
CHERRY.
FBI
I HEARD YOU LIKE ANNIE GRAHAM MOVIES.
SHE OWES US A FAVOR.
HI...DAVID.
A REALLY BIG FAVOR.
:HEH:
THAT SHUT HIM UP.
FIVE MINUTES!
A LITTLE PRIVACY PLEASE!
FOUR MINUTES!

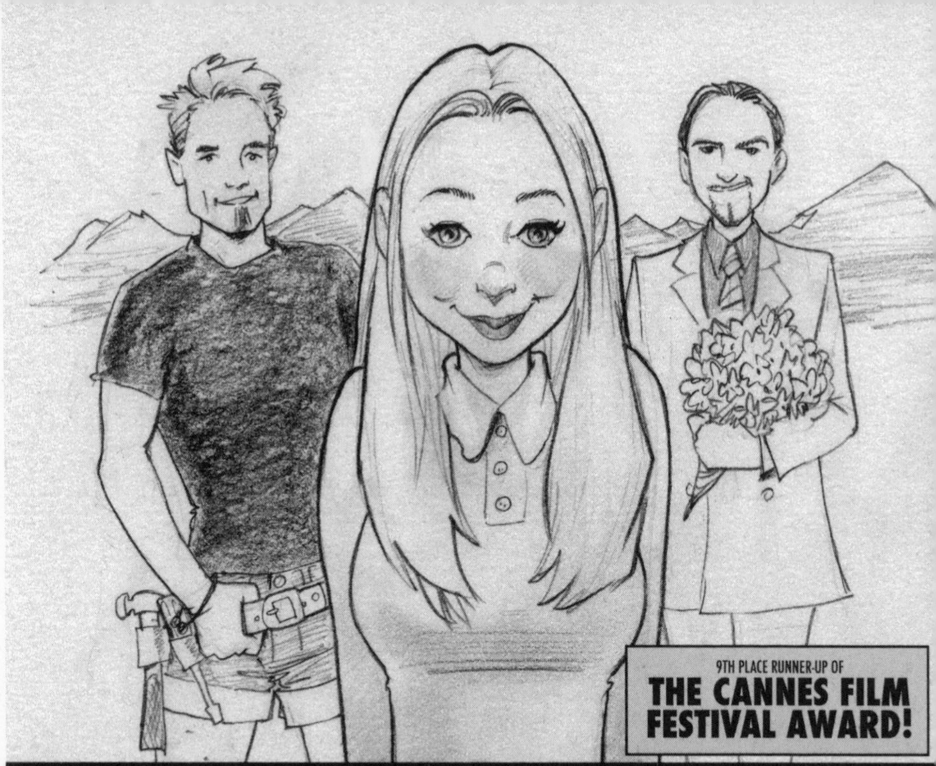
9TH PLACE RUNNER-UP OF
THE CANNES FILM FESTIVAL AWARD!

THE CRITICS LOVE THE CONSTANT VIRGIN!

"Graham's best work since Brokeback Virgin!" —*USAToday*

"America's favorite virgin puts out again!" —*New York Times*

"Not since A Virgin Runs Through It has cinema been so unshocking!" — *Rolling Stone*

A Bernie Beater Film

Starring ANNIE GRAHAM • TODD BOONIE • FRANK MESTICHIVICHE • RONSON ABBINGTON

LOUIE ATOOLE • BETH ESDA LANG • COLE WINKIE • BOB JONES

From the Graphic Novel by T. TOOTIE MOORE and KABONG SMITH • Screenplay by T. TOOTIE MOORE and ANGELA THE MIGHTY

Director MASON ANG   Producers SEAR OOFFER and BASHID RAHM   Editor HOOVER RAM   Craft Services BAGEL-BOTS

Distributed by THE MASONIC GLOBAL FILM LTD. in cooperation with the ENRON ENDOWMENT FOR THE VIRGIN ARTS

Filmed in TOOTIEVISION   DOLBY SURROUND AND POUND SOUND

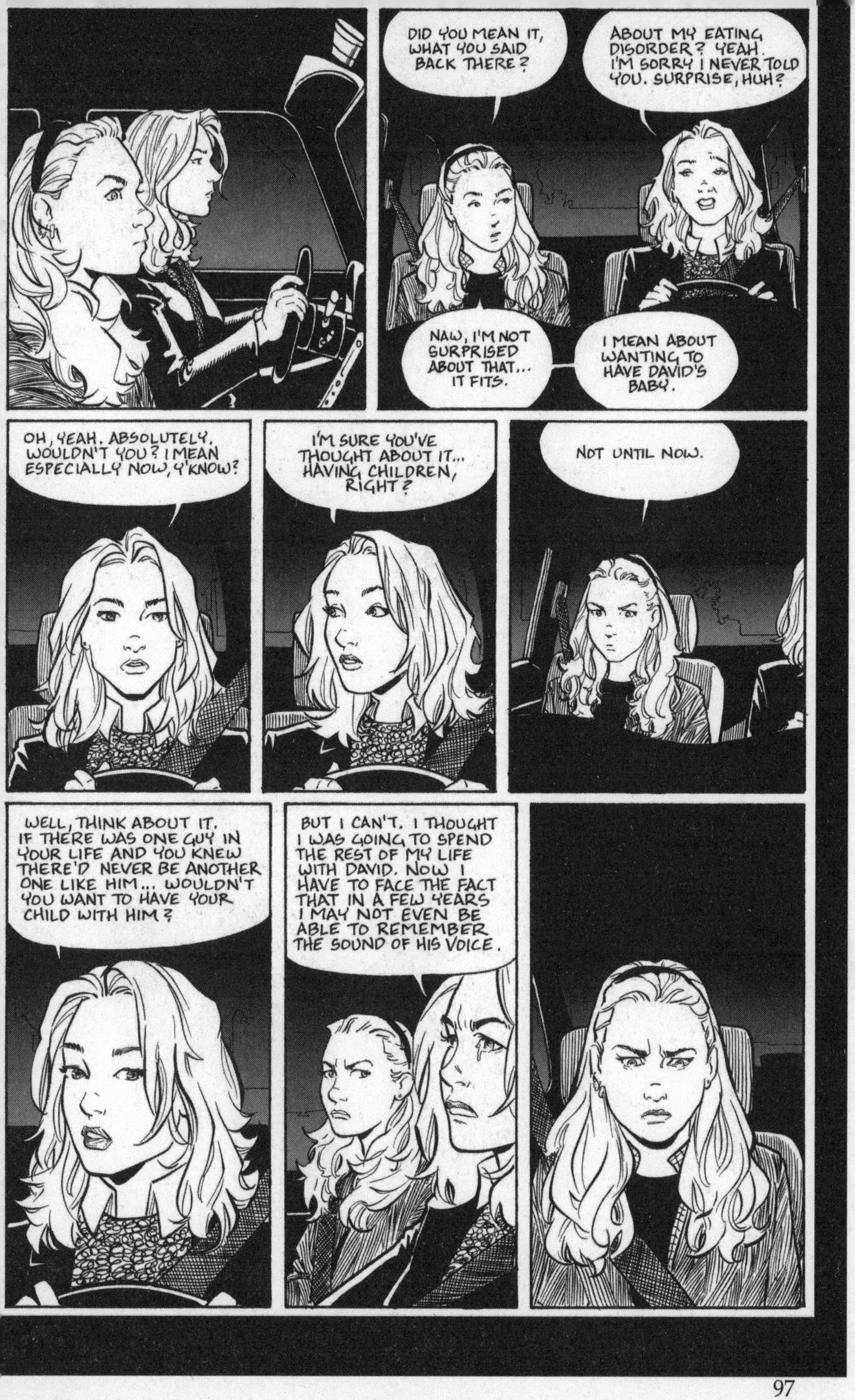
DID YOU MEAN IT, WHAT YOU SAID BACK THERE?
ABOUT MY EATING DISORDER? YEAH. I'M SORRY I NEVER TOLD YOU. SURPRISE, HUH?
NAW, I'M NOT SURPRISED ABOUT THAT... IT FITS.
I MEAN ABOUT WANTING TO HAVE DAVID'S BABY.
OH, YEAH. ABSOLUTELY. WOULDN'T YOU? I MEAN ESPECIALLY NOW, Y'KNOW?
I'M SURE YOU'VE THOUGHT ABOUT IT... HAVING CHILDREN, RIGHT?
NOT UNTIL NOW.
WELL, THINK ABOUT IT. IF THERE WAS ONE GUY IN YOUR LIFE AND YOU KNEW THERE'D NEVER BE ANOTHER ONE LIKE HIM... WOULDN'T YOU WANT TO HAVE YOUR CHILD WITH HIM?
BUT I CAN'T. I THOUGHT I WAS GOING TO SPEND THE REST OF MY LIFE WITH DAVID. NOW I HAVE TO FACE THE FACT THAT IN A FEW YEARS I MAY NOT EVEN BE ABLE TO REMEMBER THE SOUND OF HIS VOICE.

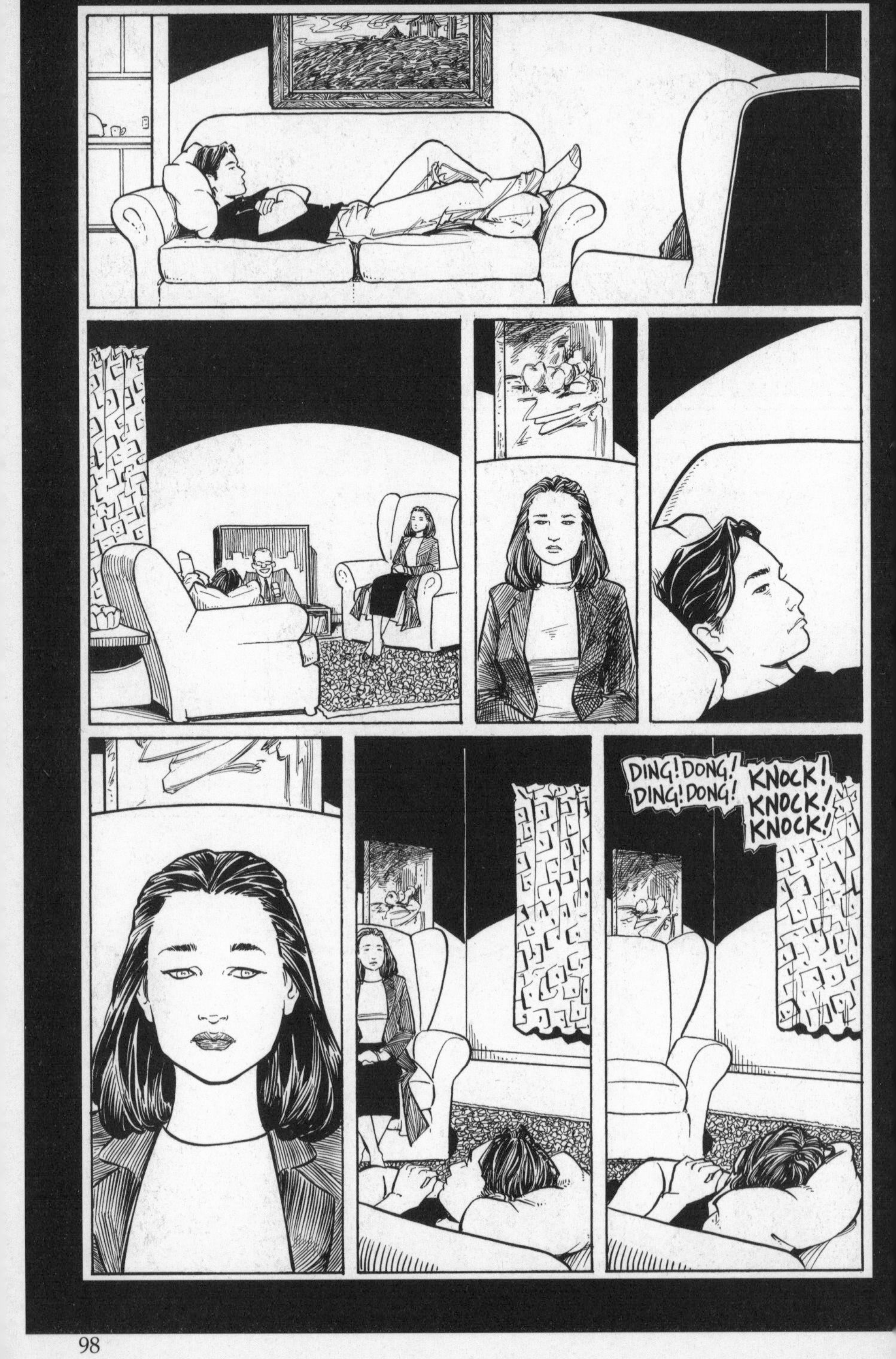
DING! DONG!
DING! DONG!
KNOCK!
KNOCK!
KNOCK!

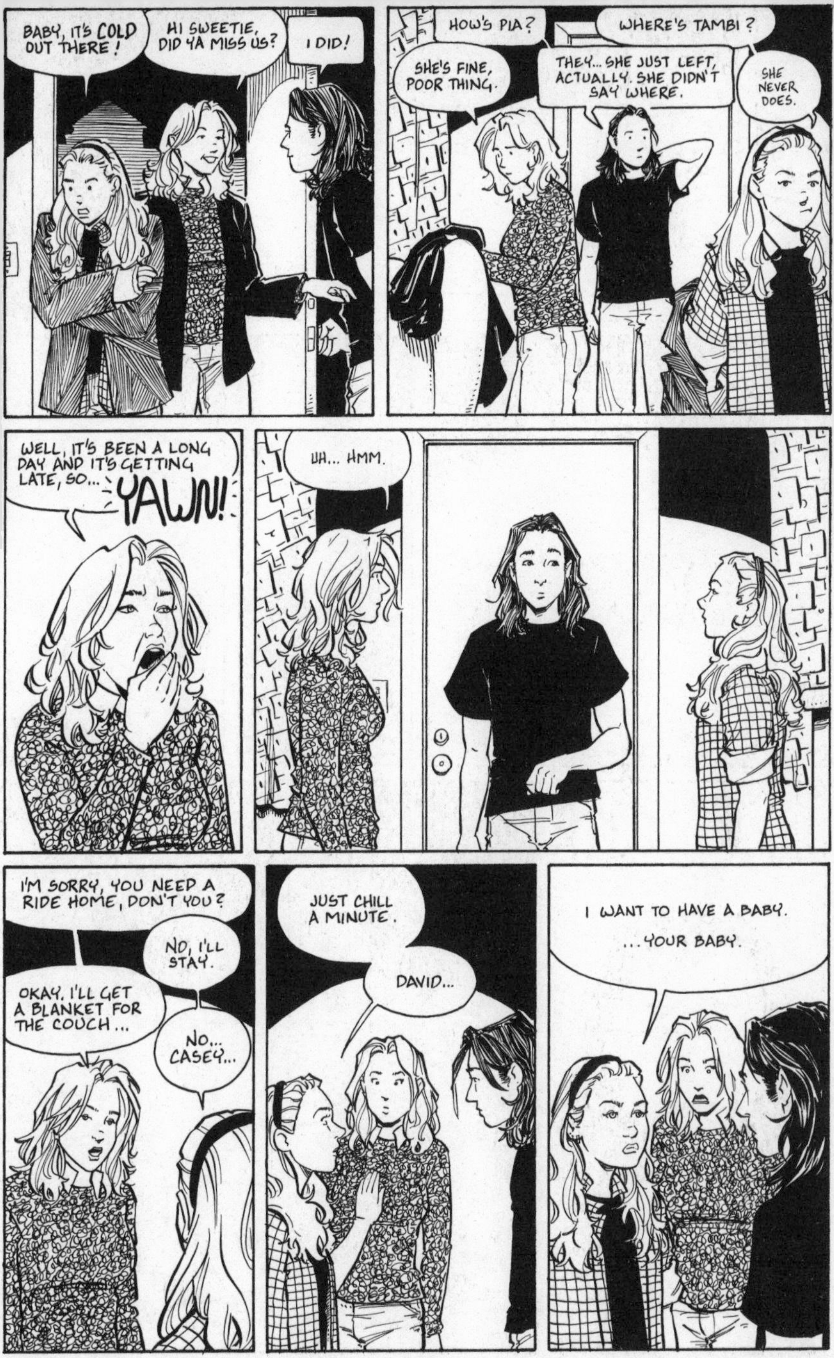
BABY, IT'S COLD OUT THERE!
HI SWEETIE, DID YA MISS US?
I DID!
HOW'S PIA?
SHE'S FINE, POOR THING.
WHERE'S TAMBI?
THEY... SHE JUST LEFT, ACTUALLY. SHE DIDN'T SAY WHERE.
SHE NEVER DOES.
WELL, IT'S BEEN A LONG DAY AND IT'S GETTING LATE, SO... YAWN!
UH... HMM.
I'M SORRY, YOU NEED A RIDE HOME, DON'T YOU?
NO, I'LL STAY.
OKAY, I'LL GET A BLANKET FOR THE COUCH...
NO... CASEY...
JUST CHILL A MINUTE.
DAVID...
I WANT TO HAVE A BABY.
...YOUR BABY.

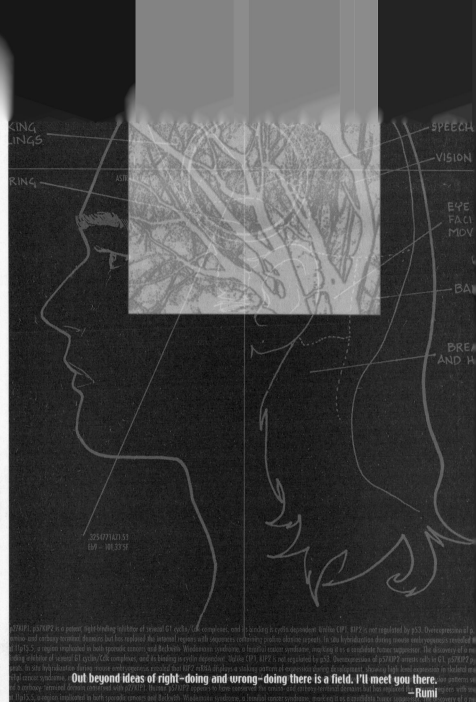

Out beyond ideas of right–doing and wrong–doing there is a field. I'll meet you there.
— Rumi

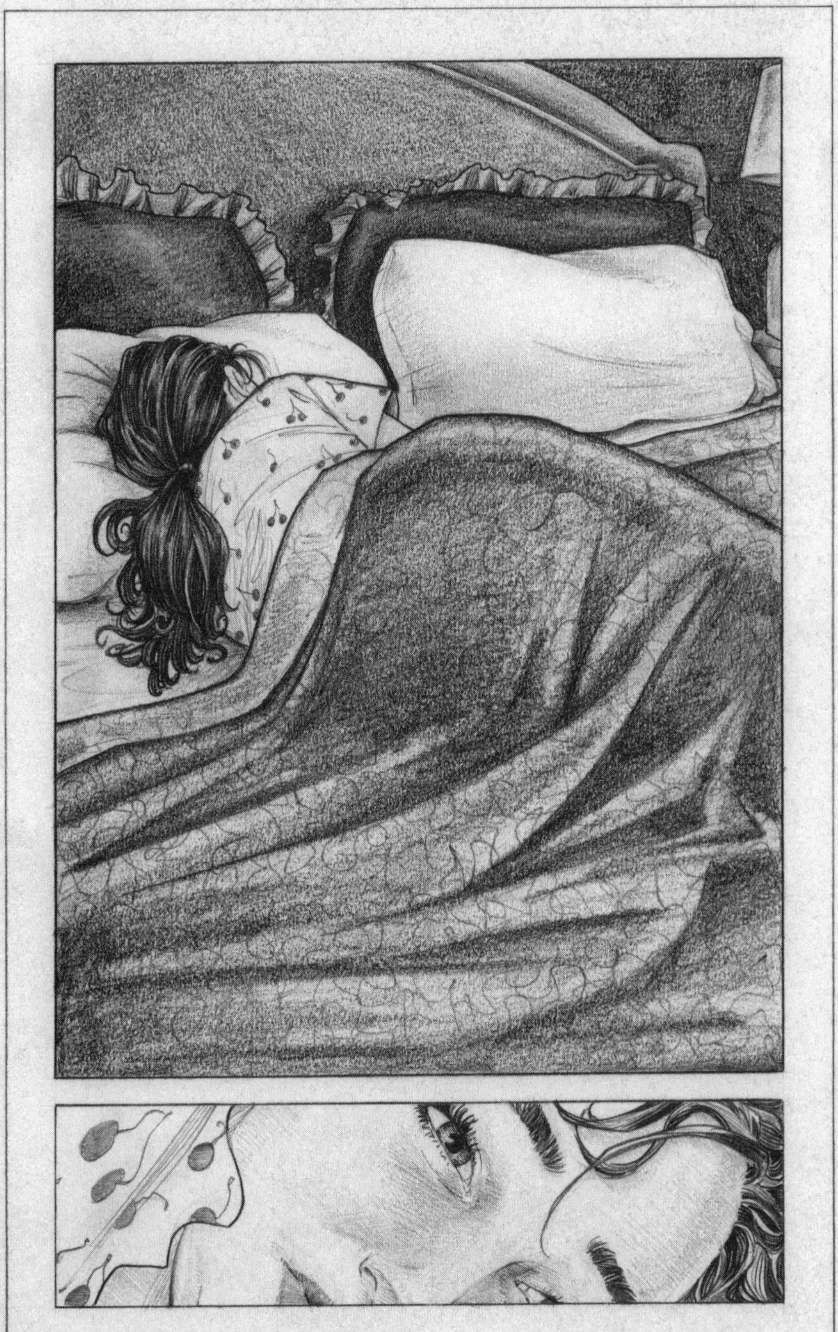

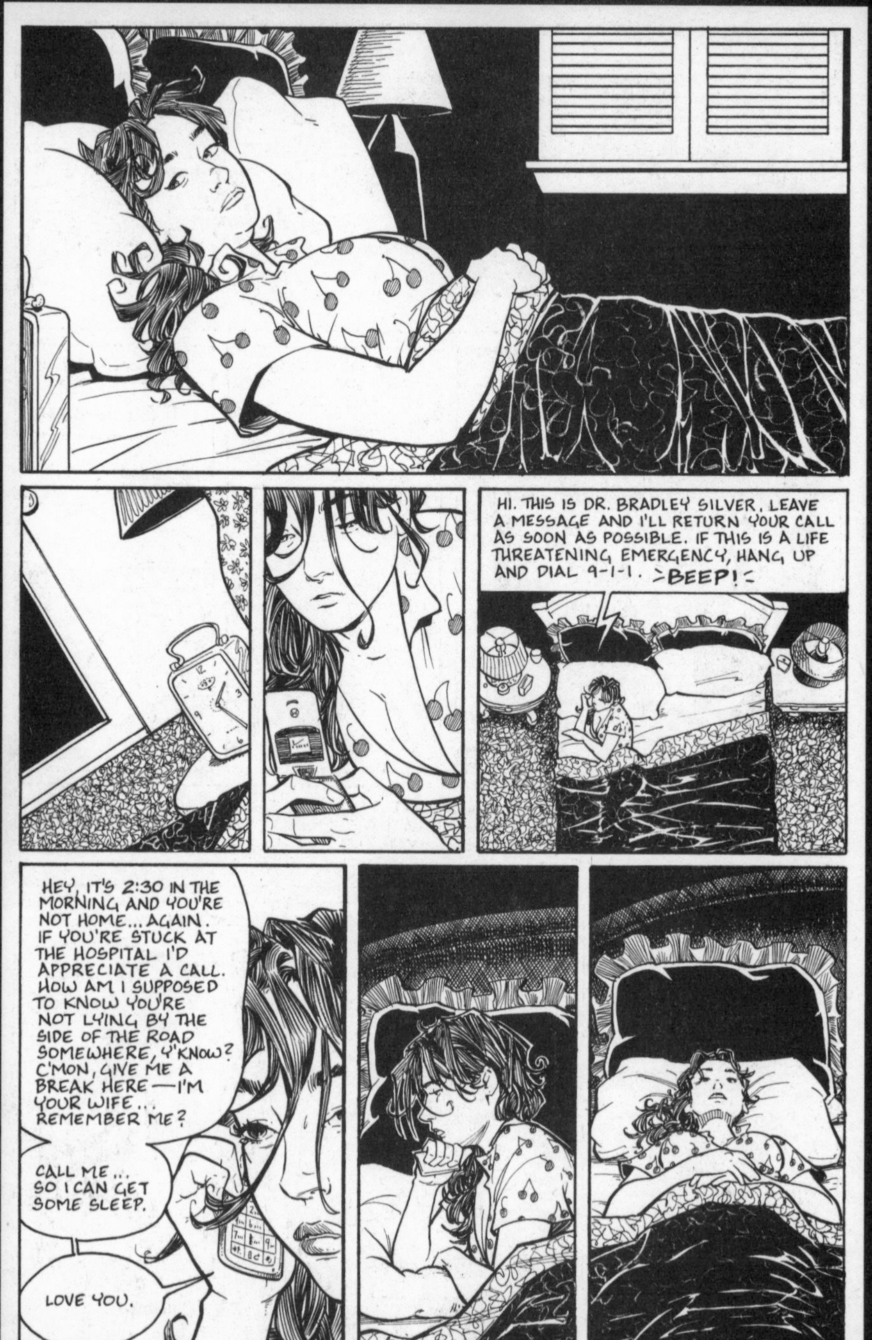
HI. THIS IS DR. BRADLEY SILVER. LEAVE A MESSAGE AND I'LL RETURN YOUR CALL AS SOON AS POSSIBLE. IF THIS IS A LIFE THREATENING EMERGENCY, HANG UP AND DIAL 9-1-1. >BEEP!<
HEY, IT'S 2:30 IN THE MORNING AND YOU'RE NOT HOME... AGAIN. IF YOU'RE STUCK AT THE HOSPITAL I'D APPRECIATE A CALL. HOW AM I SUPPOSED TO KNOW YOU'RE NOT LYING BY THE SIDE OF THE ROAD SOMEWHERE, Y'KNOW? C'MON, GIVE ME A BREAK HERE—I'M YOUR WIFE... REMEMBER ME?
CALL ME... SO I CAN GET SOME SLEEP.
LOVE YOU.

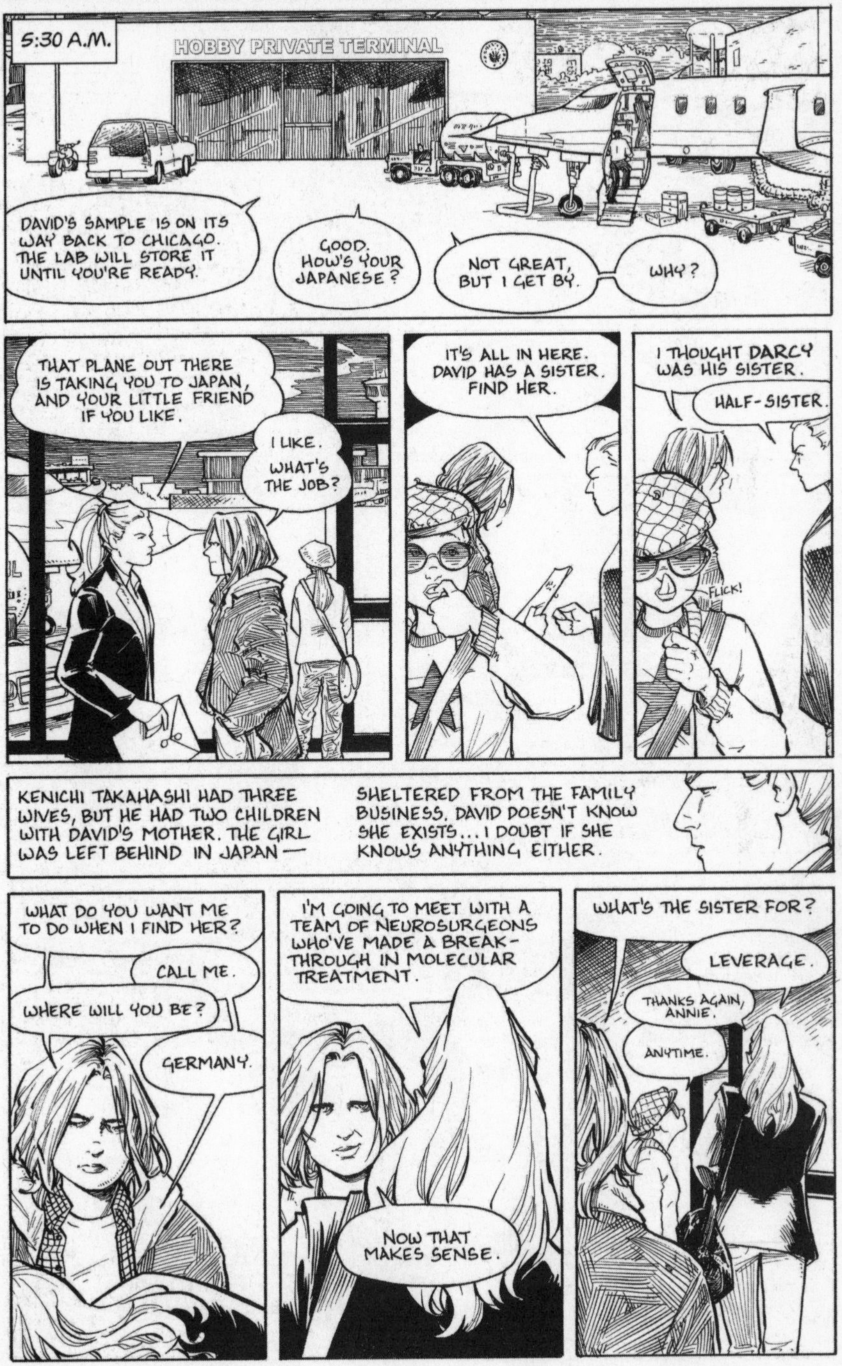
5:30 A.M.
HOBBY PRIVATE TERMINAL
DAVID'S SAMPLE IS ON ITS WAY BACK TO CHICAGO. THE LAB WILL STORE IT UNTIL YOU'RE READY.
GOOD. HOW'S YOUR JAPANESE?
NOT GREAT, BUT I GET BY.
WHY?
THAT PLANE OUT THERE IS TAKING YOU TO JAPAN, AND YOUR LITTLE FRIEND IF YOU LIKE.
I LIKE.
WHAT'S THE JOB?
IT'S ALL IN HERE. DAVID HAS A SISTER. FIND HER.
I THOUGHT DARCY WAS HIS SISTER.
HALF-SISTER.
FLICK!
KENICHI TAKAHASHI HAD THREE WIVES, BUT HE HAD TWO CHILDREN WITH DAVID'S MOTHER. THE GIRL WAS LEFT BEHIND IN JAPAN—
SHELTERED FROM THE FAMILY BUSINESS. DAVID DOESN'T KNOW SHE EXISTS... I DOUBT IF SHE KNOWS ANYTHING EITHER.
WHAT DO YOU WANT ME TO DO WHEN I FIND HER?
CALL ME.
WHERE WILL YOU BE?
GERMANY.
I'M GOING TO MEET WITH A TEAM OF NEUROSURGEONS WHO'VE MADE A BREAK-THROUGH IN MOLECULAR TREATMENT.
NOW THAT MAKES SENSE.
WHAT'S THE SISTER FOR?
LEVERAGE.
THANKS AGAIN, ANNIE.
ANYTIME.

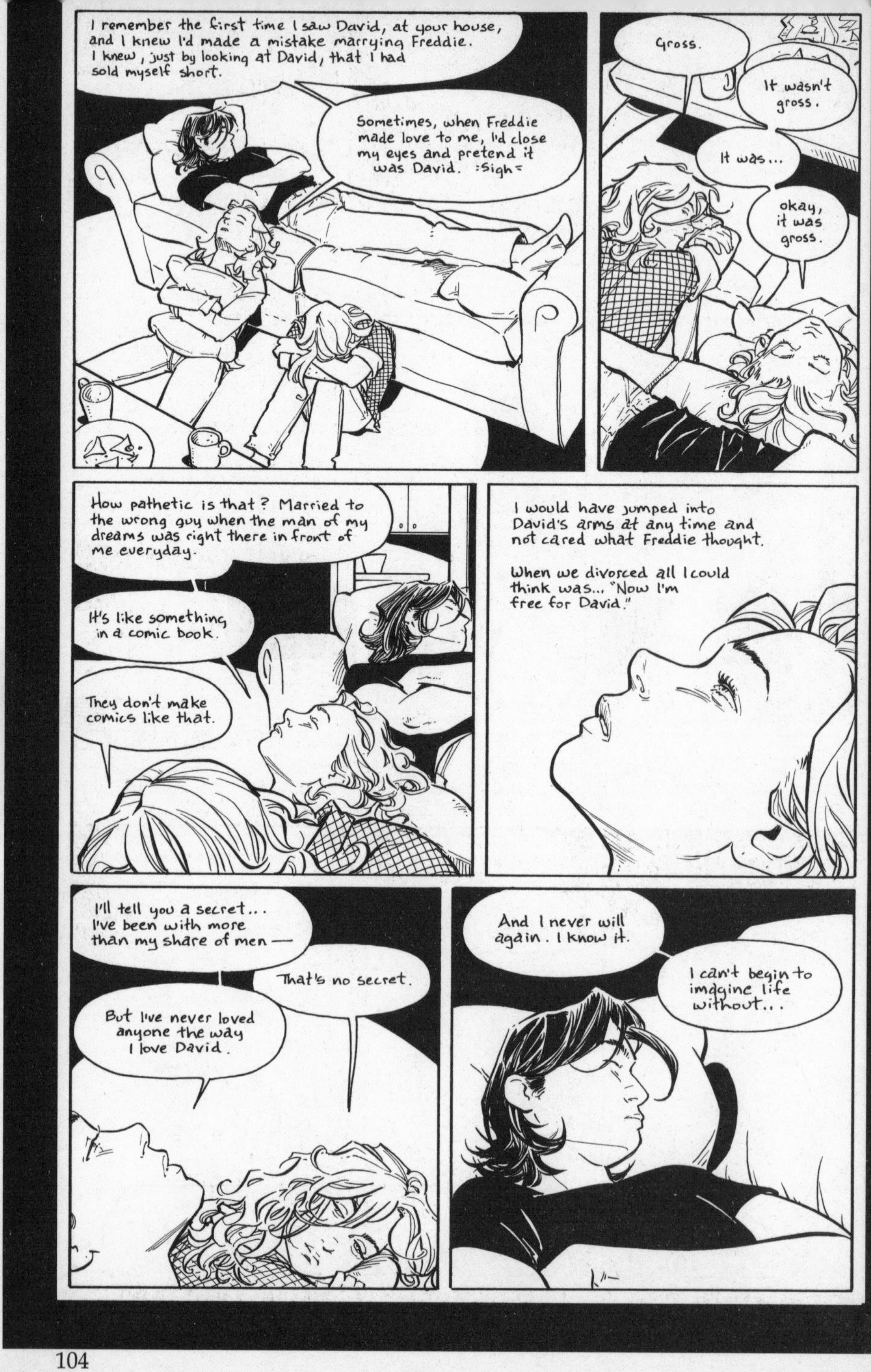
I remember the first time I saw David, at your house, and I knew I'd made a mistake marrying Freddie. I knew, just by looking at David, that I had sold myself short.
Sometimes, when Freddie made love to me, I'd close my eyes and pretend it was David. =Sigh=
Gross.
It wasn't gross.
It was...
okay, it was gross.
How pathetic is that? Married to the wrong guy when the man of my dreams was right there in front of me everyday.
It's like something in a comic book.
They don't make comics like that.
I would have jumped into David's arms at any time and not cared what Freddie thought.
When we divorced all I could think was... "Now I'm free for David."
I'll tell you a secret... I've been with more than my share of men —
That's no secret.
But I've never loved anyone the way I love David.
And I never will again. I know it.
I can't begin to imagine life without...

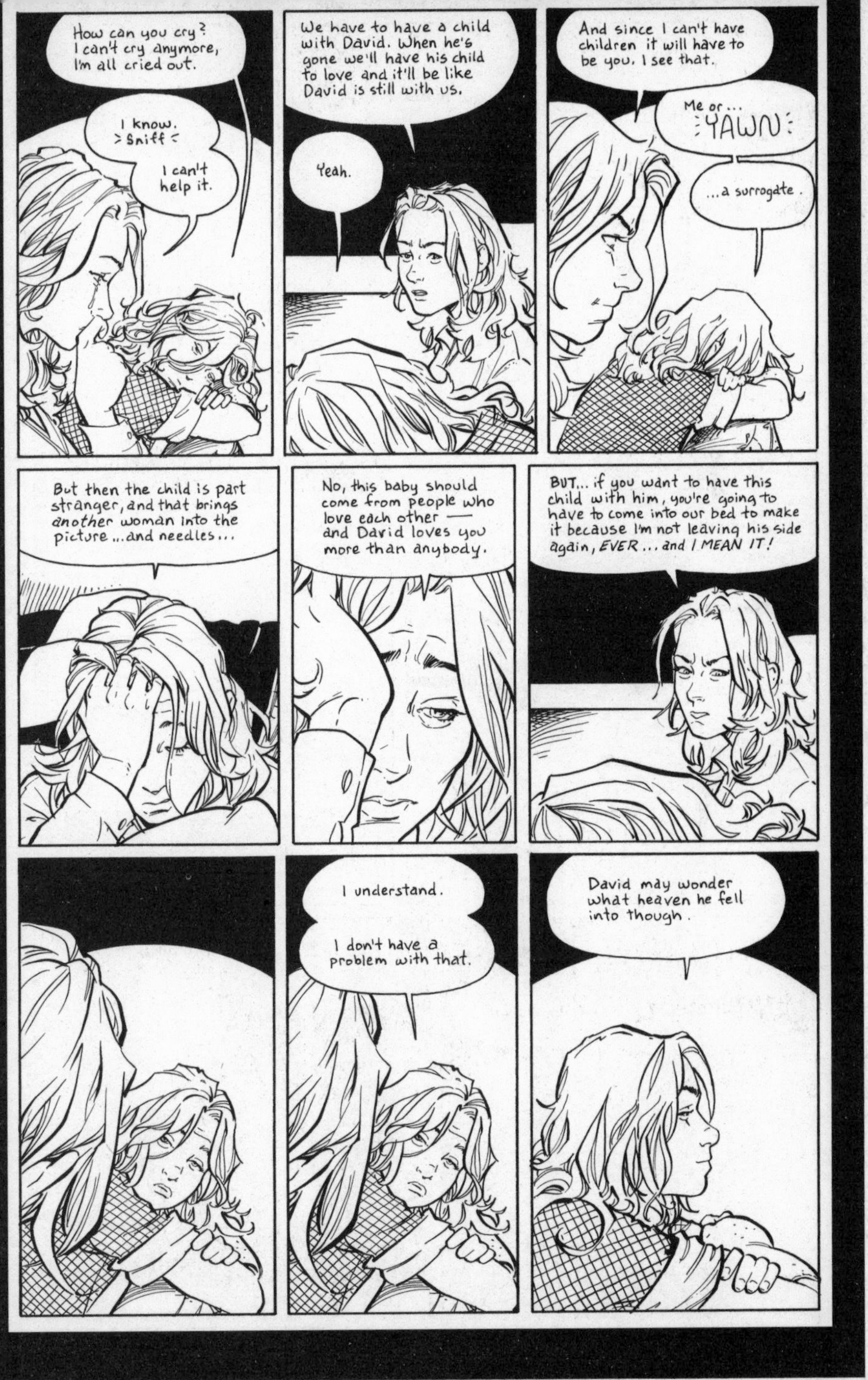
How can you cry? I can't cry anymore, I'm all cried out.
I know. Sniff
I can't help it.
We have to have a child with David. When he's gone we'll have his child to love and it'll be like David is still with us.
Yeah.
And since I can't have children it will have to be you. I see that.
Me or... YAWN
...a surrogate.
But then the child is part stranger, and that brings *another* woman into the picture... and needles...
No, this baby should come from people who love each other — and David loves you more than anybody.
BUT... if you want to have this child with him, you're going to have to come into our bed to make it because I'm not leaving his side again, *EVER*... and *I MEAN IT!*
I understand.
I don't have a problem with that.
David may wonder what heaven he fell into though.

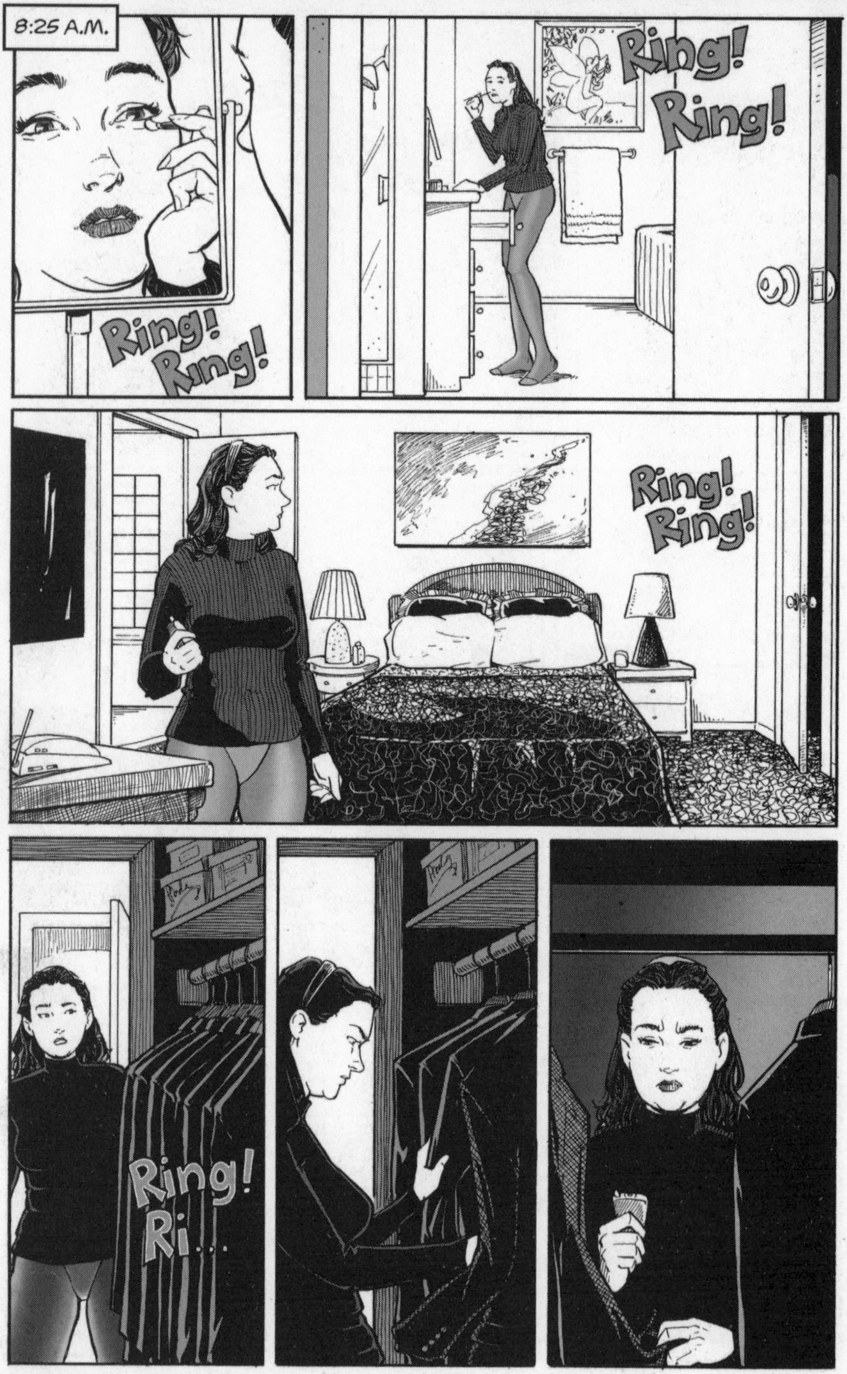
8:25 A.M.
Ring! Ring!
Ring! Ring!
Ring! Ring!
Ring! Ri....

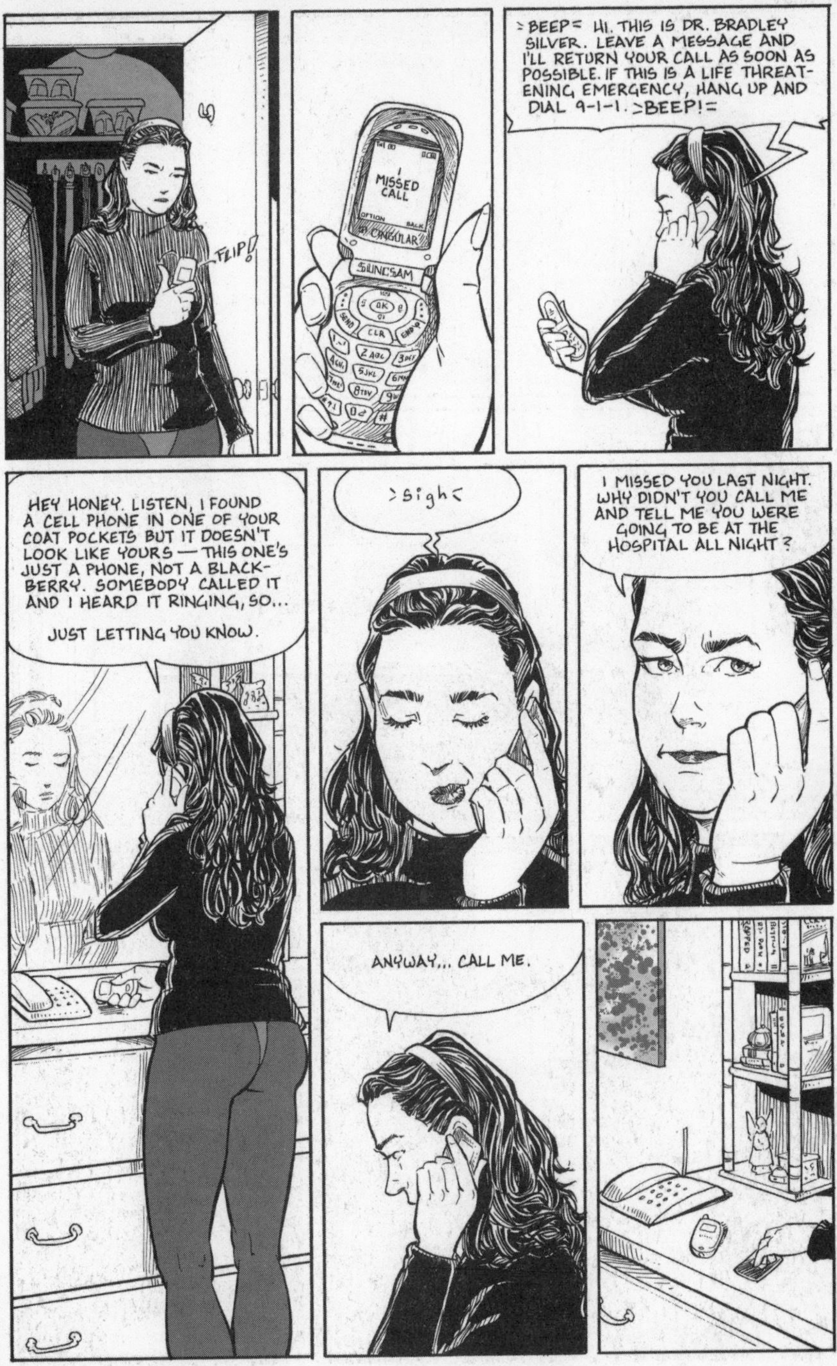
FLIP!
I MISSED CALL
OPTION BACK
CINGULAR
SUNGSAM
>BEEP< HI. THIS IS DR. BRADLEY SILVER. LEAVE A MESSAGE AND I'LL RETURN YOUR CALL AS SOON AS POSSIBLE. IF THIS IS A LIFE THREATENING EMERGENCY, HANG UP AND DIAL 9-1-1. >BEEP!<
HEY HONEY. LISTEN, I FOUND A CELL PHONE IN ONE OF YOUR COAT POCKETS BUT IT DOESN'T LOOK LIKE YOURS — THIS ONE'S JUST A PHONE, NOT A BLACKBERRY. SOMEBODY CALLED IT AND I HEARD IT RINGING, SO...
JUST LETTING YOU KNOW.
>sigh<
I MISSED YOU LAST NIGHT. WHY DIDN'T YOU CALL ME AND TELL ME YOU WERE GOING TO BE AT THE HOSPITAL ALL NIGHT?
ANYWAY... CALL ME.

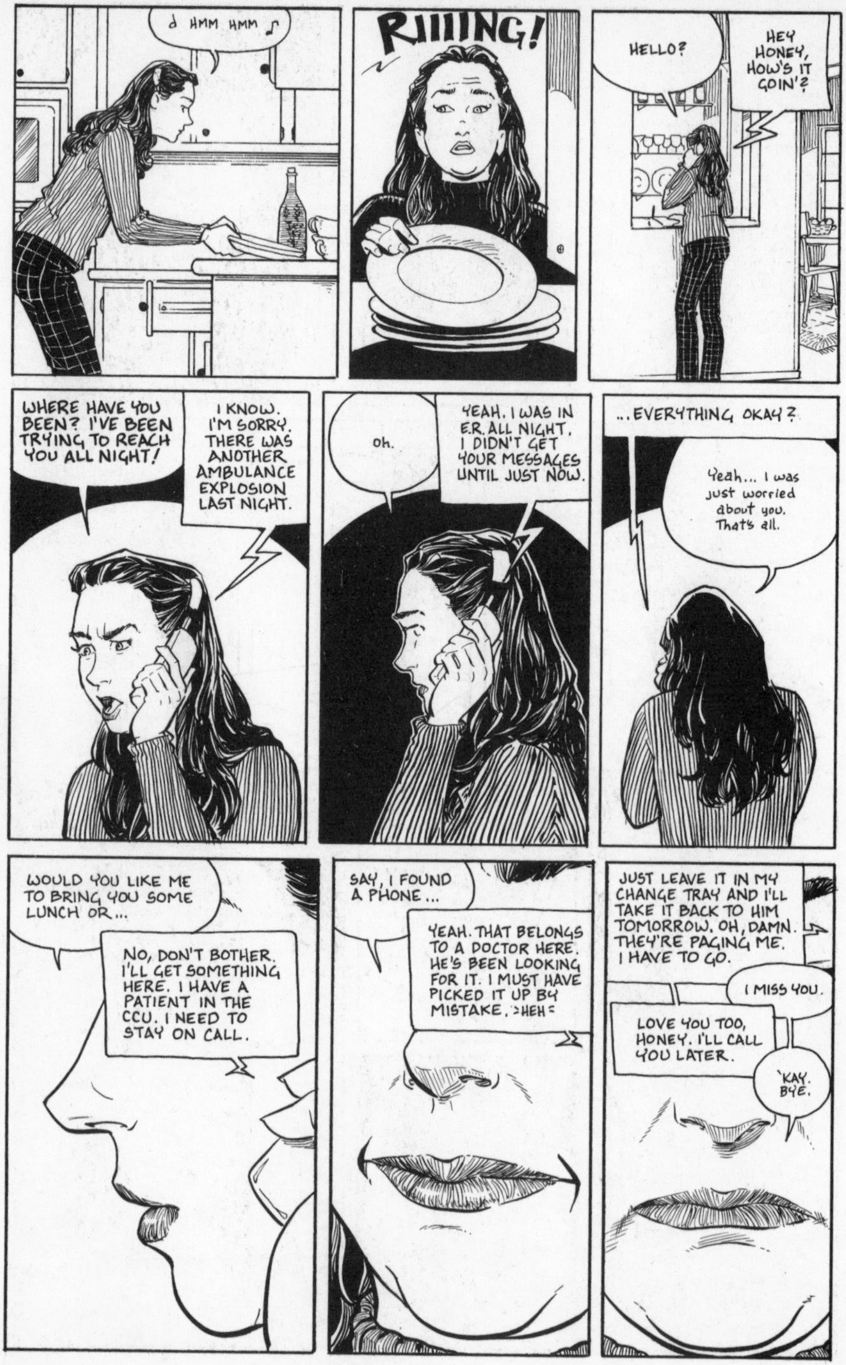
HMM HMM
RIIIING!
HELLO?
HEY HONEY, HOW'S IT GOIN'?
WHERE HAVE YOU BEEN? I'VE BEEN TRYING TO REACH YOU ALL NIGHT!
I KNOW. I'M SORRY. THERE WAS ANOTHER AMBULANCE EXPLOSION LAST NIGHT.
oh.
YEAH. I WAS IN E.R. ALL NIGHT. I DIDN'T GET YOUR MESSAGES UNTIL JUST NOW.
...EVERYTHING OKAY?
Yeah... I was just worried about you. That's all.
WOULD YOU LIKE ME TO BRING YOU SOME LUNCH OR...
NO, DON'T BOTHER. I'LL GET SOMETHING HERE. I HAVE A PATIENT IN THE CCU. I NEED TO STAY ON CALL.
SAY, I FOUND A PHONE...
YEAH. THAT BELONGS TO A DOCTOR HERE. HE'S BEEN LOOKING FOR IT. I MUST HAVE PICKED IT UP BY MISTAKE. =HEH=
JUST LEAVE IT IN MY CHANGE TRAY AND I'LL TAKE IT BACK TO HIM TOMORROW. OH, DAMN. THEY'RE PAGING ME. I HAVE TO GO.
I MISS YOU.
LOVE YOU TOO, HONEY. I'LL CALL YOU LATER.
'KAY. BYE.

TROMP! TROMP! TROMP!

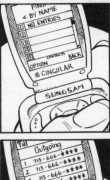

FIND
◄ BY NAME
1 NO ENTRIES
2
3
4
5
6
CONTACTS
OPTION   BACK
@ CINGULAR

SUNGSAM

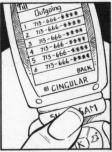

Till
Outgoing
1 713-666-*****
2 713-666-*****
3 713-666-*****
4 713-666-*****
5 713-666-*****
6 713-666-*****
BACK
@ CINGULAR

CINGULAR CUSTOMER SERVICE, THIS IS PAMELA. HOW MAY I ASSIST YOU?

HI. I NEED TO CHECK THE BALANCE ON MY ACCOUNT PLEASE. MOBILE NUMBER 713-249-****. I THINK IT MAY BE REGISTERED IN MY HUSBANDS NAME... BRADLEY SILVER.

AT 3402 SONSET?

...MA'AM?

YES.

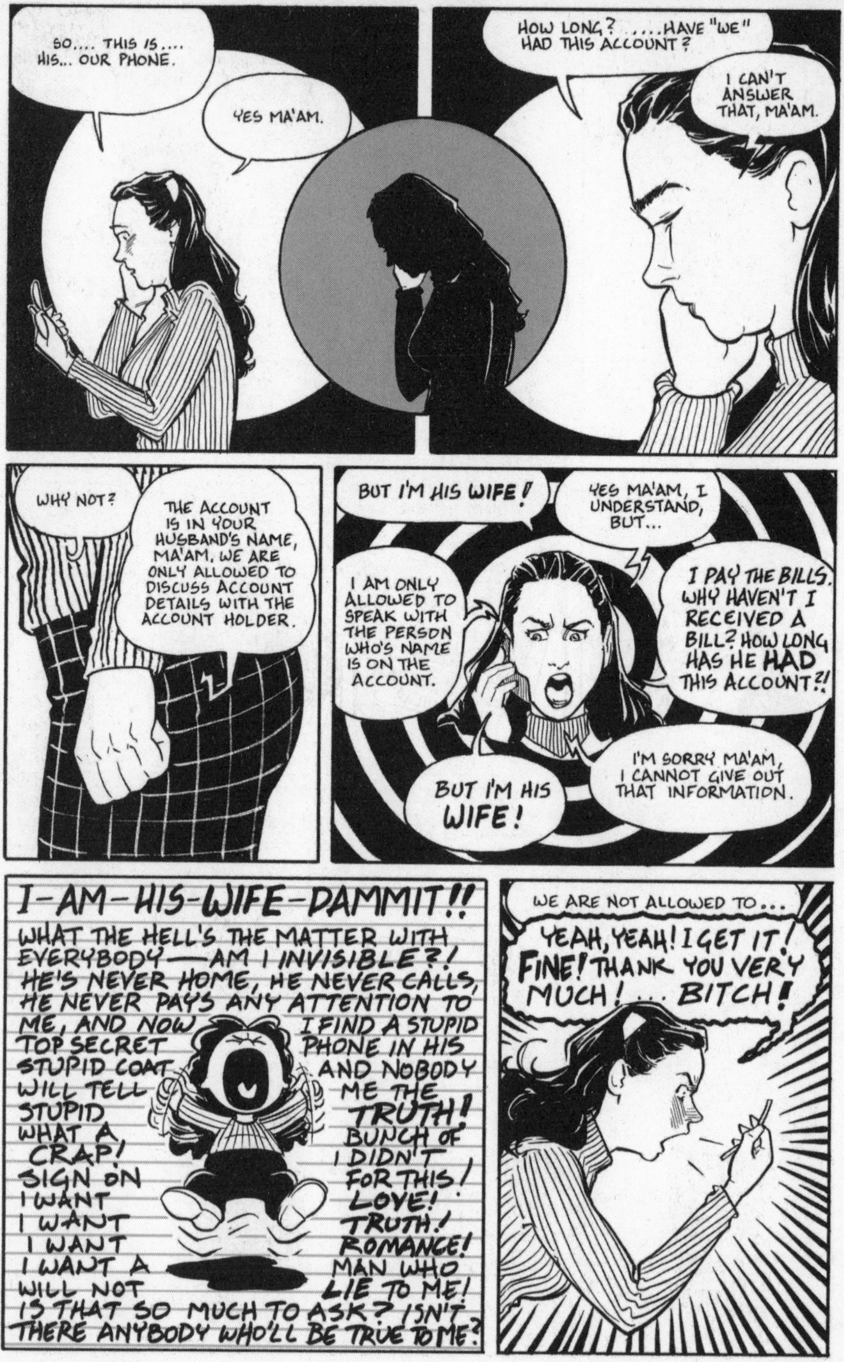
SO.... THIS IS.... HIS... OUR PHONE.
YES MA'AM.
HOW LONG? .....HAVE "WE" HAD THIS ACCOUNT?
I CAN'T ANSWER THAT, MA'AM.
WHY NOT?
THE ACCOUNT IS IN YOUR HUSBAND'S NAME, MA'AM. WE ARE ONLY ALLOWED TO DISCUSS ACCOUNT DETAILS WITH THE ACCOUNT HOLDER.
BUT I'M HIS WIFE!
YES MA'AM, I UNDERSTAND, BUT...
I AM ONLY ALLOWED TO SPEAK WITH THE PERSON WHO'S NAME IS ON THE ACCOUNT.
I PAY THE BILLS. WHY HAVEN'T I RECEIVED A BILL? HOW LONG HAS HE HAD THIS ACCOUNT?!
BUT I'M HIS WIFE!
I'M SORRY MA'AM, I CANNOT GIVE OUT THAT INFORMATION.
I-AM-HIS-WIFE-DAMMIT!!
WHAT THE HELL'S THE MATTER WITH EVERYBODY—AM I INVISIBLE?! HE'S NEVER HOME, HE NEVER CALLS, HE NEVER PAYS ANY ATTENTION TO ME, AND NOW I FIND A STUPID TOP SECRET PHONE IN HIS STUPID COAT AND NOBODY WILL TELL ME THE STUPID TRUTH! WHAT A BUNCH OF CRAP! I DIDN'T SIGN ON FOR THIS! I WANT LOVE! I WANT TRUTH! I WANT ROMANCE! I WANT A MAN WHO WILL NOT LIE TO ME! IS THAT SO MUCH TO ASK? ISN'T THERE ANYBODY WHO'LL BE TRUE TO ME?
WE ARE NOT ALLOWED TO...
YEAH, YEAH! I GET IT! FINE! THANK YOU VERY MUCH! ... BITCH!

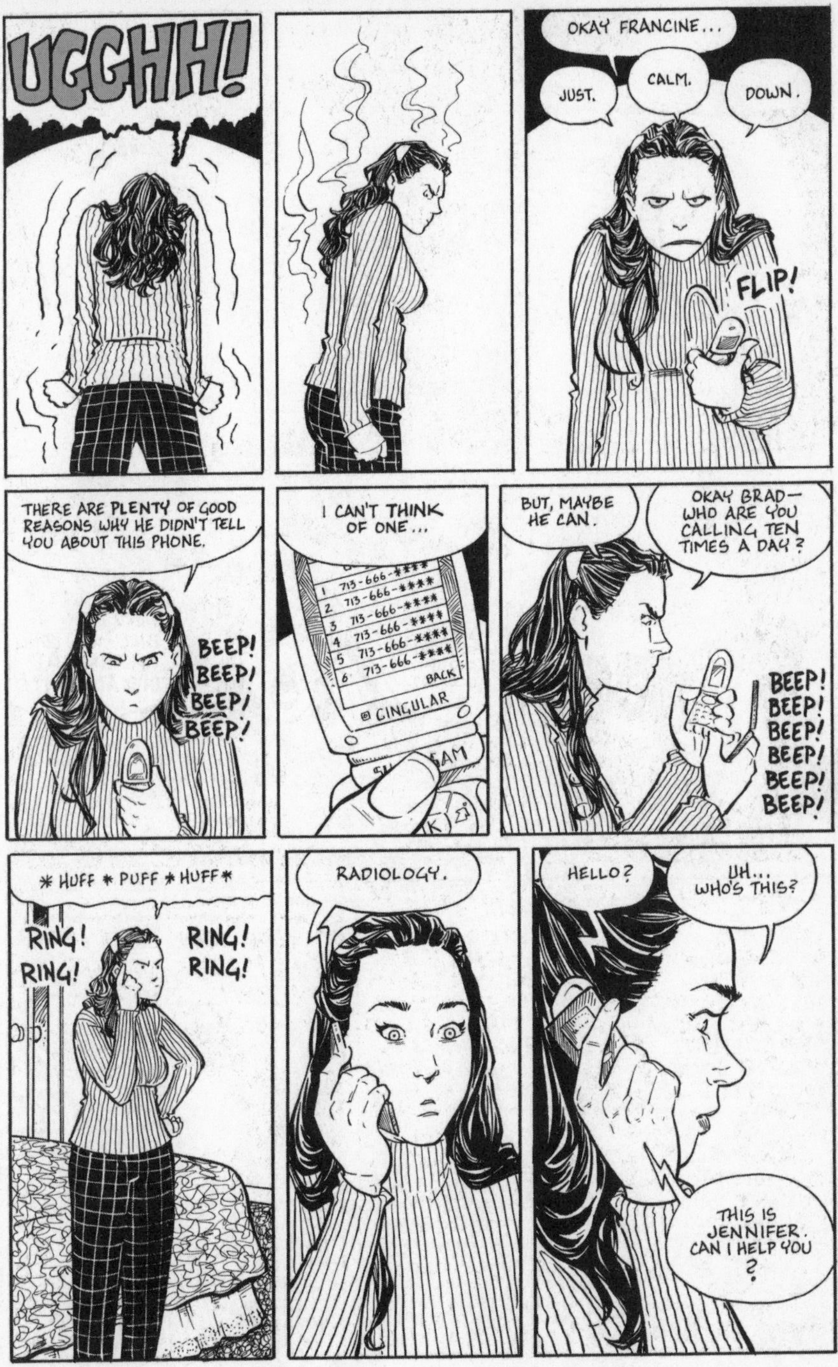
UGGHH!
OKAY FRANCINE...
JUST.
CALM.
DOWN.
FLIP!
THERE ARE PLENTY OF GOOD REASONS WHY HE DIDN'T TELL YOU ABOUT THIS PHONE.
BEEP! BEEP! BEEP! BEEP!
I CAN'T THINK OF ONE...
1 713-666-****
2 713-666-****
3 713-666-****
4 713-666-****
5 713-666-****
6 713-666-****
BACK
© CINGULAR
BUT, MAYBE HE CAN.
OKAY BRAD— WHO ARE YOU CALLING TEN TIMES A DAY?
BEEP! BEEP! BEEP! BEEP! BEEP! BEEP!
* HUFF * PUFF * HUFF *
RING! RING!
RING! RING!
RADIOLOGY.
HELLO?
UH... WHO'S THIS?
THIS IS JENNIFER. CAN I HELP YOU ?

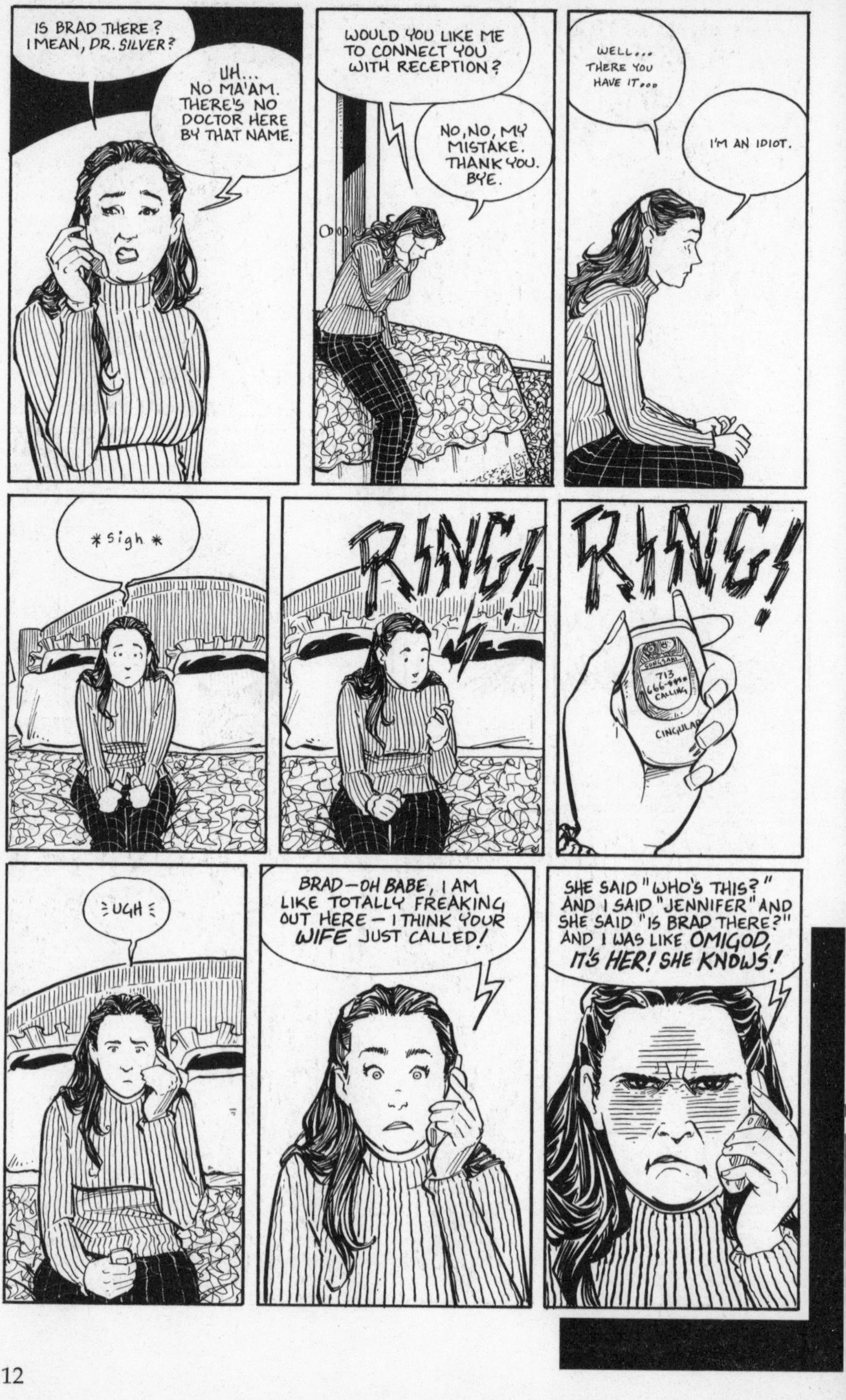
IS BRAD THERE? I MEAN, DR. SILVER?
UH... NO MA'AM. THERE'S NO DOCTOR HERE BY THAT NAME.
WOULD YOU LIKE ME TO CONNECT YOU WITH RECEPTION?
NO, NO, MY MISTAKE. THANK YOU. BYE.
WELL... THERE YOU HAVE IT...
I'M AN IDIOT.
sigh
RING!
RING!
713 666-
CALLING
CINGULAR
ƎUGHƐ
BRAD—OH BABE, I AM LIKE TOTALLY FREAKING OUT HERE—I THINK YOUR WIFE JUST CALLED!
SHE SAID "WHO'S THIS?" AND I SAID "JENNIFER" AND SHE SAID "IS BRAD THERE?" AND I WAS LIKE OMIGOD, IT'S HER! SHE KNOWS!

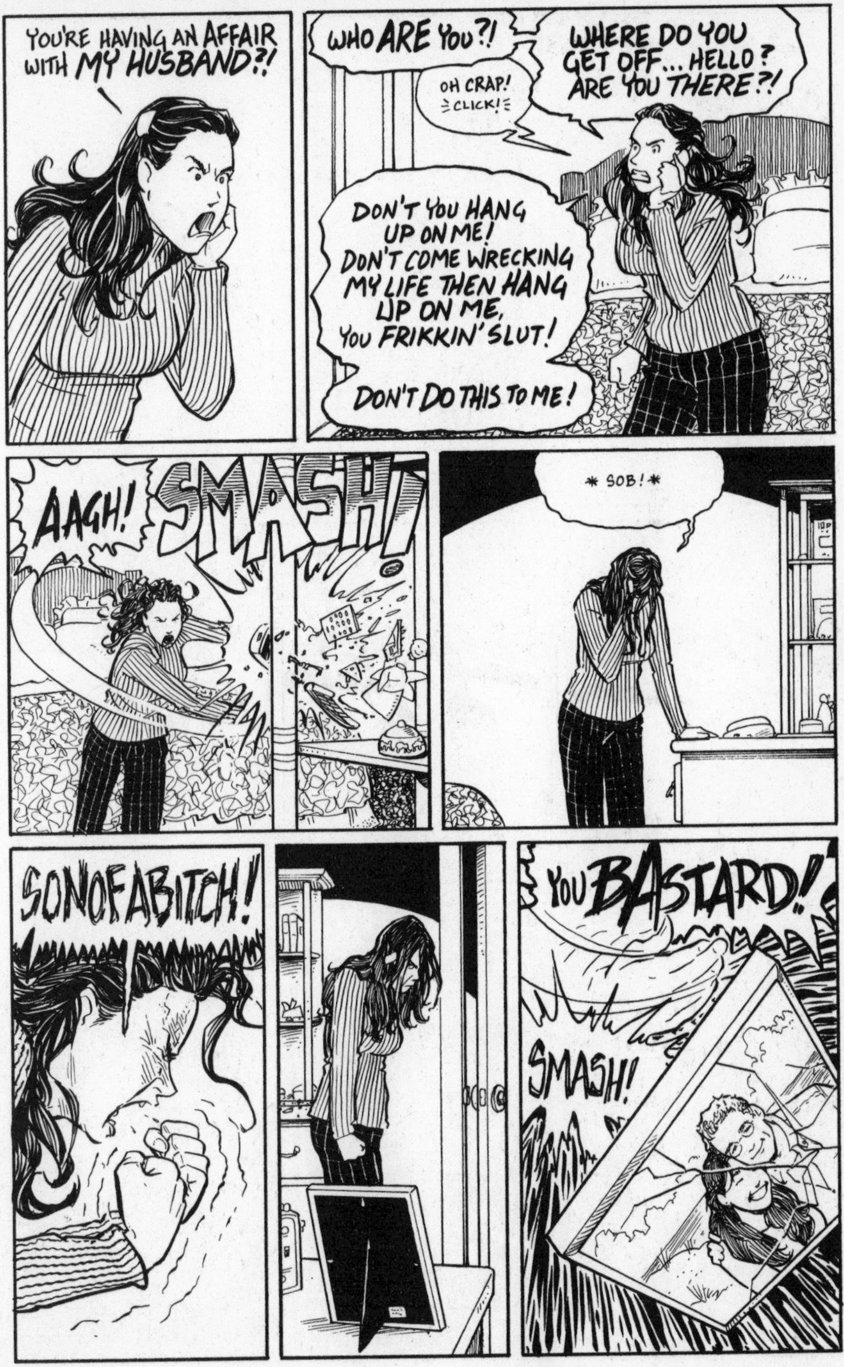
YOU'RE HAVING AN AFFAIR WITH MY HUSBAND?!
WHO ARE YOU?!
WHERE DO YOU GET OFF... HELLO? ARE YOU THERE?!
OH CRAP! CLICK!
DON'T YOU HANG UP ON ME! DON'T COME WRECKING MY LIFE THEN HANG UP ON ME, YOU FRIKKIN' SLUT!
DON'T DO THIS TO ME!
AAGH!
SMASH!
* SOB! *
SONOFABITCH!
YOU BASTARD!
SMASH!

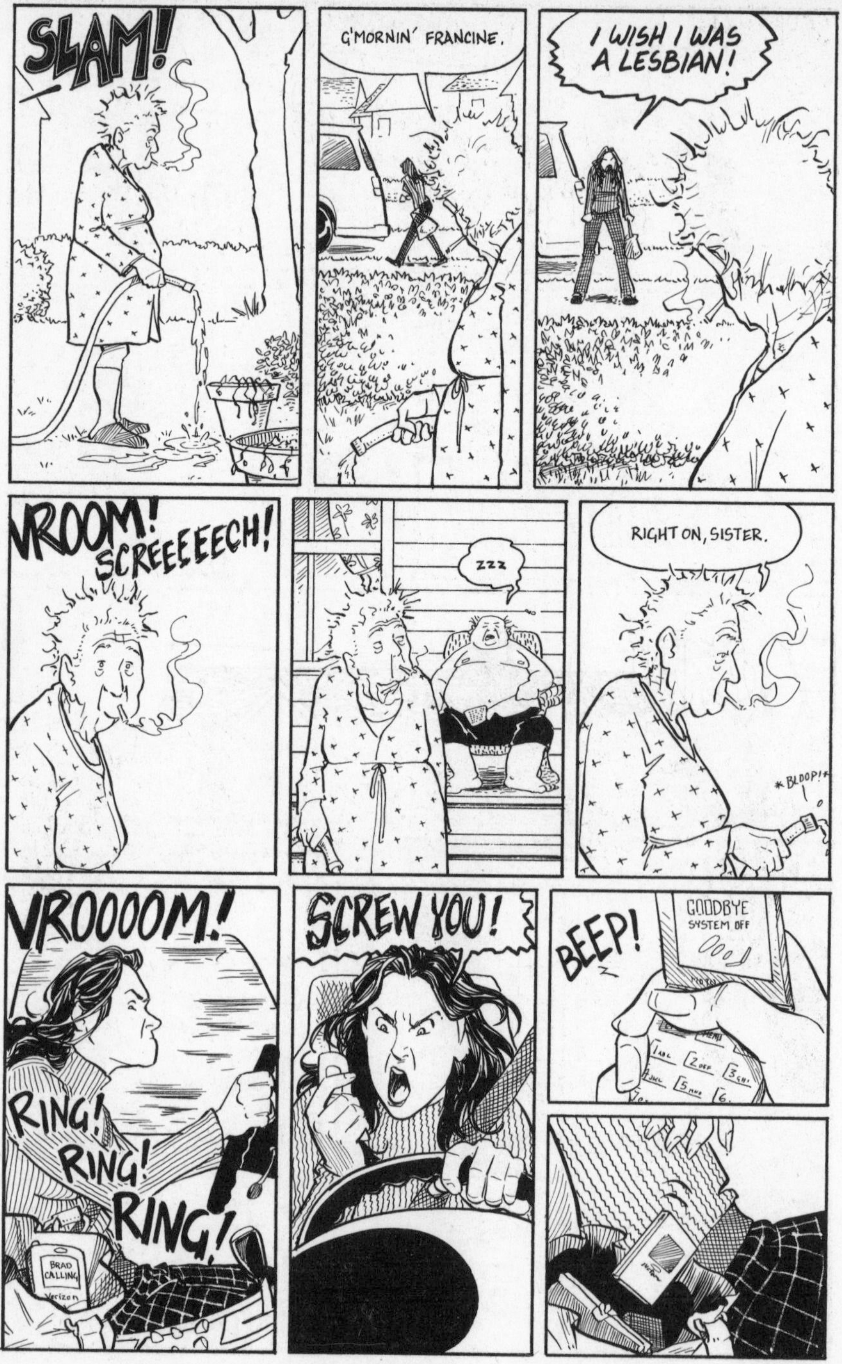
SLAM!
G'MORNIN' FRANCINE.
I WISH I WAS A LESBIAN!
VROOM!
SCREEEEECH!
ZZZ
RIGHT ON, SISTER.
BLOOP!
VROOOOM!
RING!
RING!
RING!
BRAD CALLING
Verizon
SCREW YOU!
BEEP!
GOODBYE
SYSTEM OFF

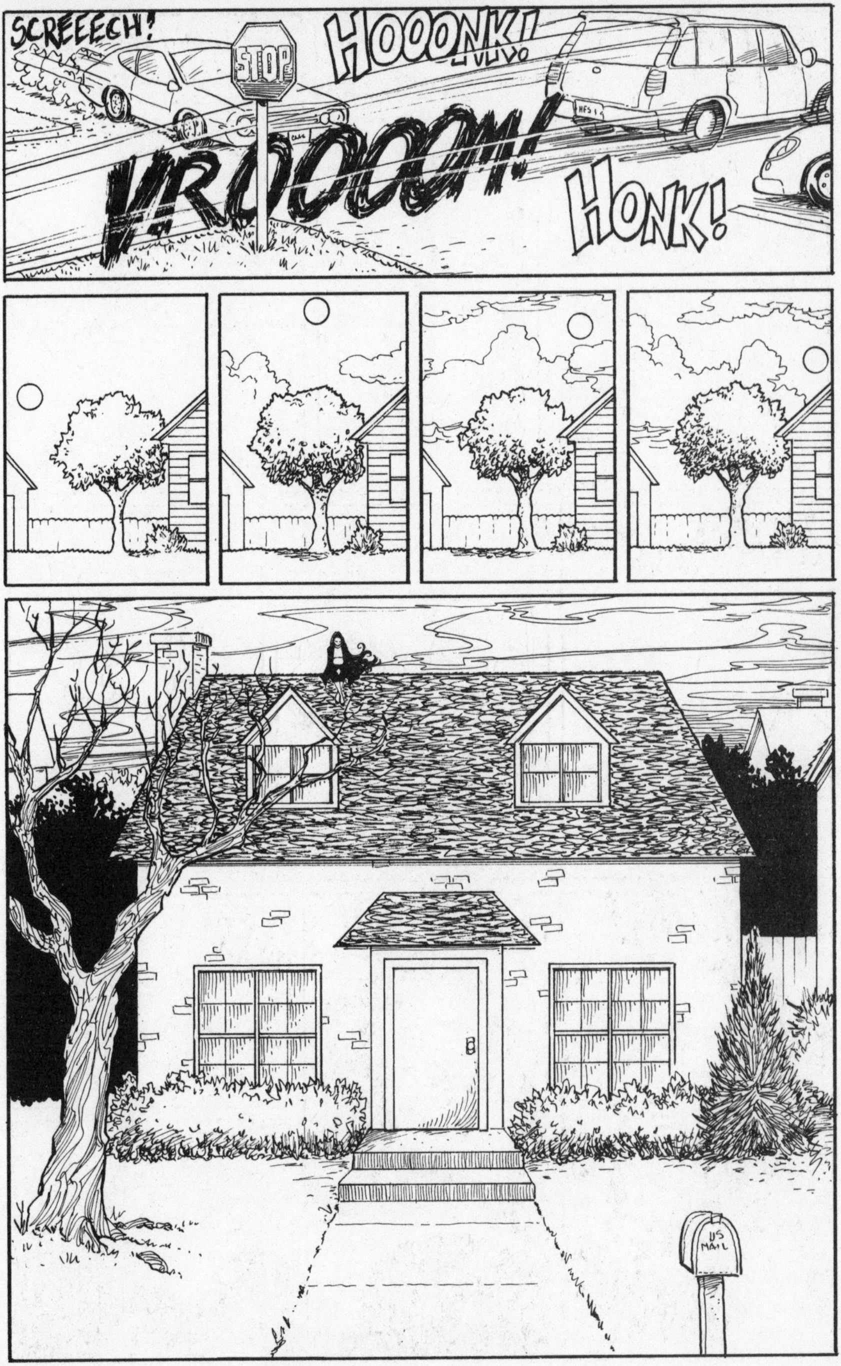

SCREEECH!
STOP
HOOONK!
VROOOOM!
HONK!
US MAIL

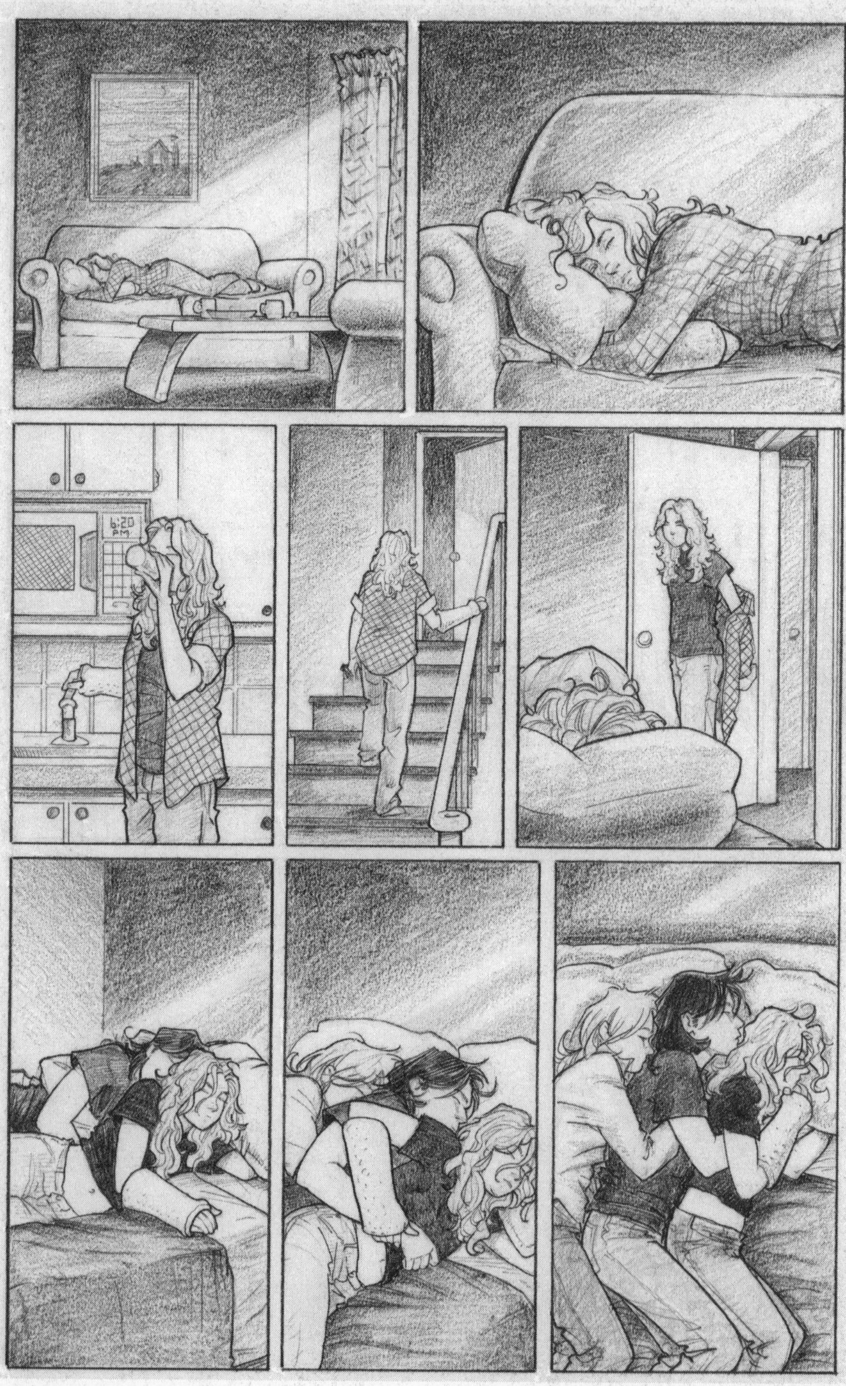
6:20
PM

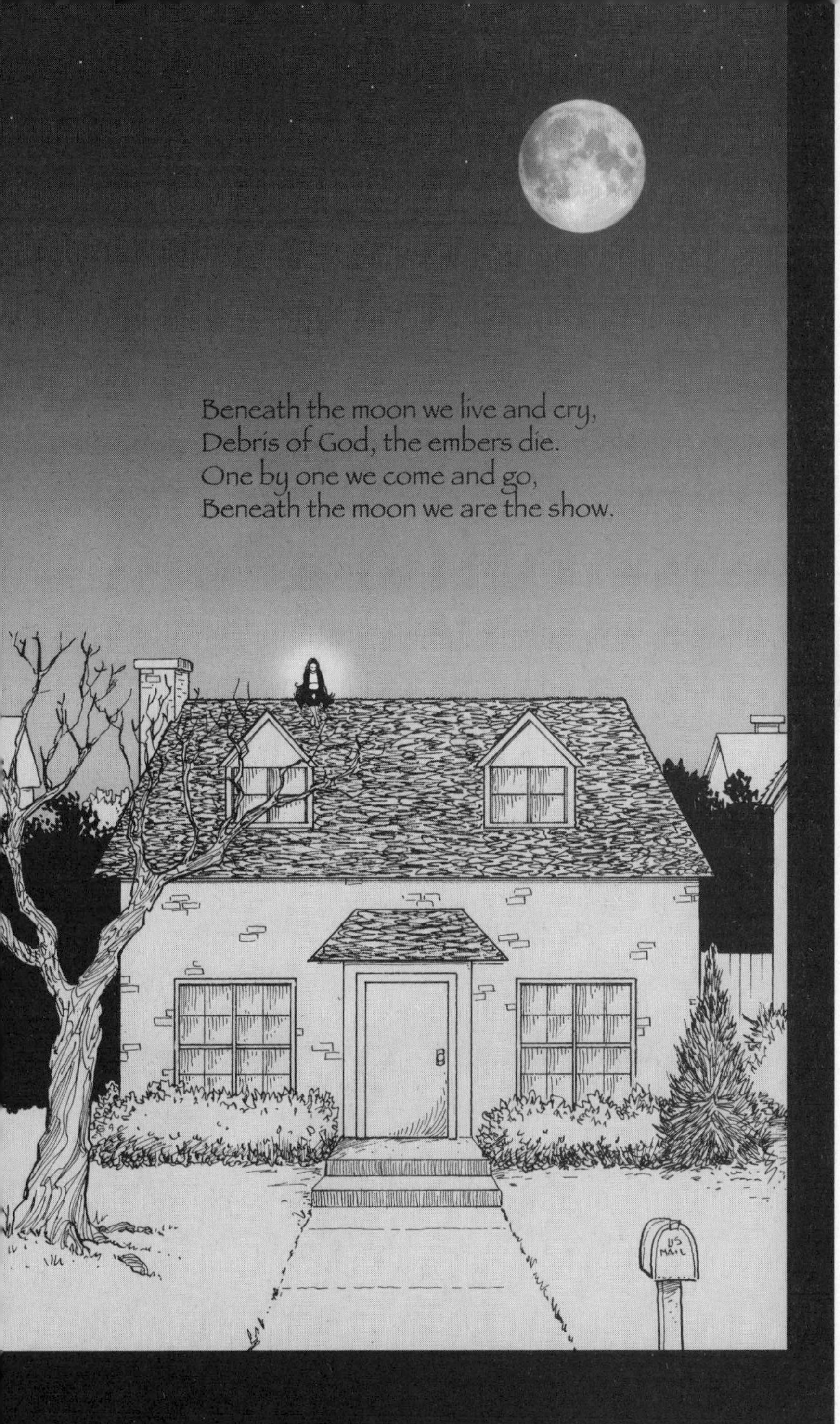
Beneath the moon we live and cry,
Debris of God, the embers die.
One by one we come and go,
Beneath the moon we are the show.
US MAIL

Welcome to
VERIZON WIRELESS

YOU HAVE
33
MESSAGES

		17 CALLS
1	BRAD	5 CALLS
2	MOTHER	4 CAL
3	KATCHOO	2 CAL
4	CASEY	2 CA
5	DAVID	1 C
6	BENJAMIN	1 C
7	MARGIE	
	(MORE)	

Motorola

Jeez Brad,
what did you do...
tell everybody we
know?

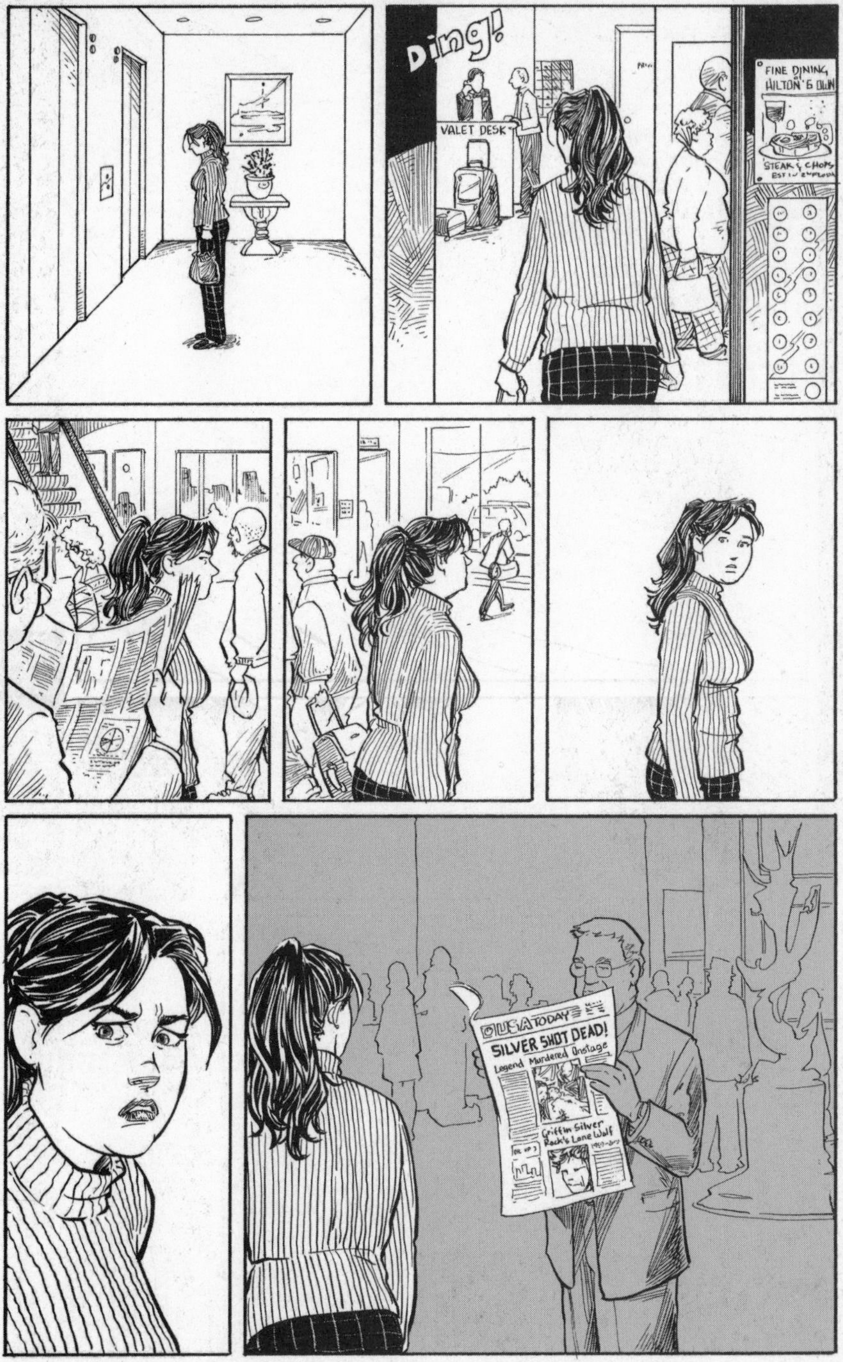
Ding!
VALET DESK
FINE DINING
HILTON'S OWN
STEAK & CHOPS
USA TODAY
SILVER SHOT DEAD!
Legend Murdered Onstage
Griffin Silver
Rock's Lone Wolf

GRIFFIN SILVER
1963 - 2006

Where were you the night Griffin Silver was shot? For years, maybe decades, people will ask each other that question and shake their heads. Like Kennedy, King, and Lennon, Griffin Silver was more than a public figure, he was an American icon. — the last rocker left from the days when bands lived or died by the strength and ingenuity of their songcraft and musicianship. No video girls or studio tricks for this guy, he was the real thing. And now he's gone, dead at the hands of a crazed fan who claimed killing Silver would make him immortal. For Silver, who never seemed comfortable with his fame, the irony is tragic.

Griffin Silver's career began at the age of 17, playing the bars of Washington D.C. with his band Silvershot. Silver's band was playing the B Lounge when David Bowie stopped by for an after-concert drink and, so the story goes, was so impressed by the young musician that he offered Silver a job on the spot. Silver declined in order to finish high school, but his reputation was made in the DC area, allowing him to record a demo that ultimately landed him a recording contract with Torrent.

Torrent released Griffin's first album, Silver Rush, to modest sales but Silver toured extensively, opening for big name

cont. pg 52

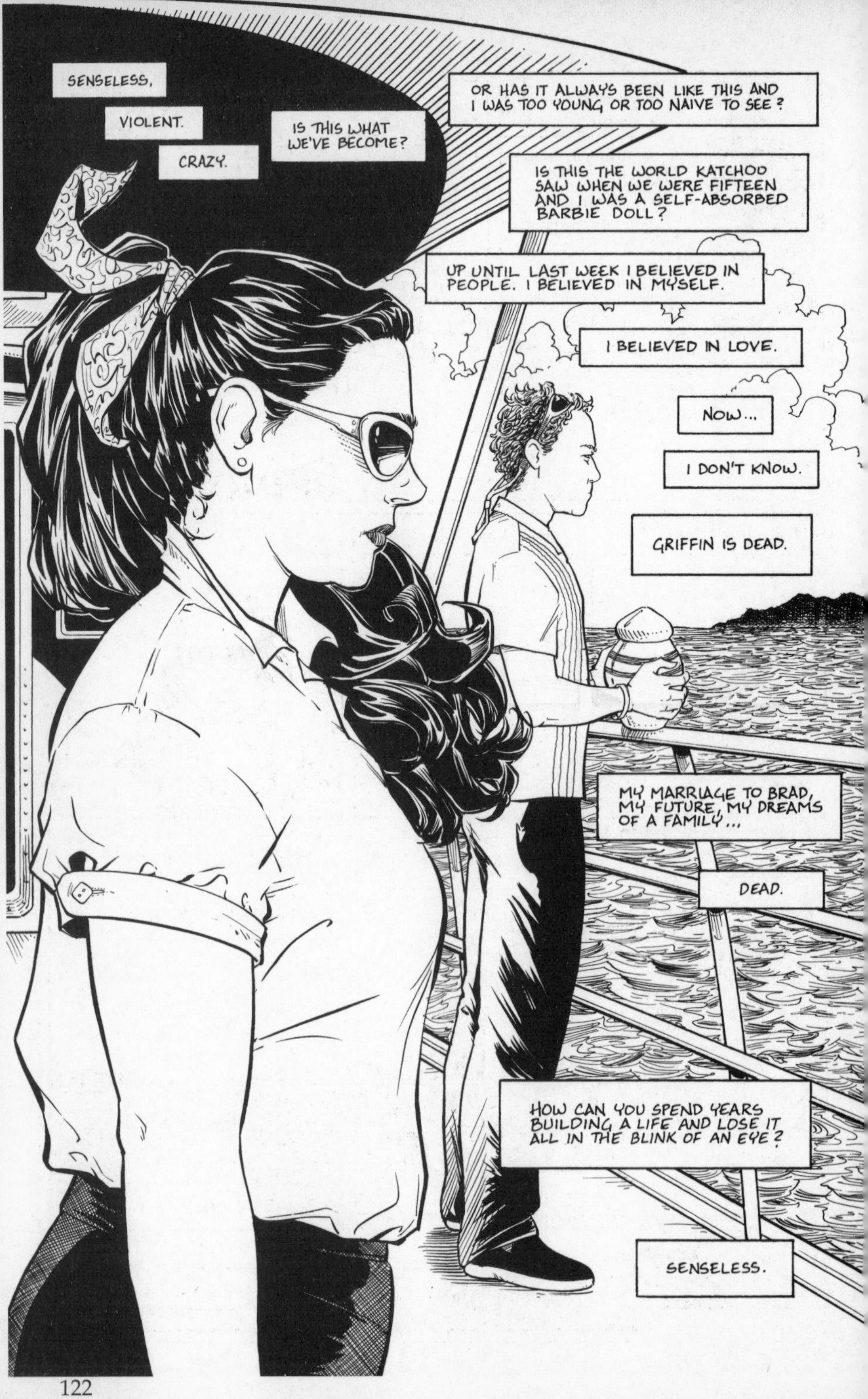
SENSELESS,
VIOLENT.
CRAZY.
IS THIS WHAT WE'VE BECOME?
OR HAS IT ALWAYS BEEN LIKE THIS AND I WAS TOO YOUNG OR TOO NAIVE TO SEE?
IS THIS THE WORLD KATCHOO SAW WHEN WE WERE FIFTEEN AND I WAS A SELF-ABSORBED BARBIE DOLL?
UP UNTIL LAST WEEK I BELIEVED IN PEOPLE. I BELIEVED IN MYSELF.
I BELIEVED IN LOVE.
NOW...
I DON'T KNOW.
GRIFFIN IS DEAD.
MY MARRIAGE TO BRAD, MY FUTURE, MY DREAMS OF A FAMILY...
DEAD.
HOW CAN YOU SPEND YEARS BUILDING A LIFE AND LOSE IT ALL IN THE BLINK OF AN EYE?
SENSELESS.

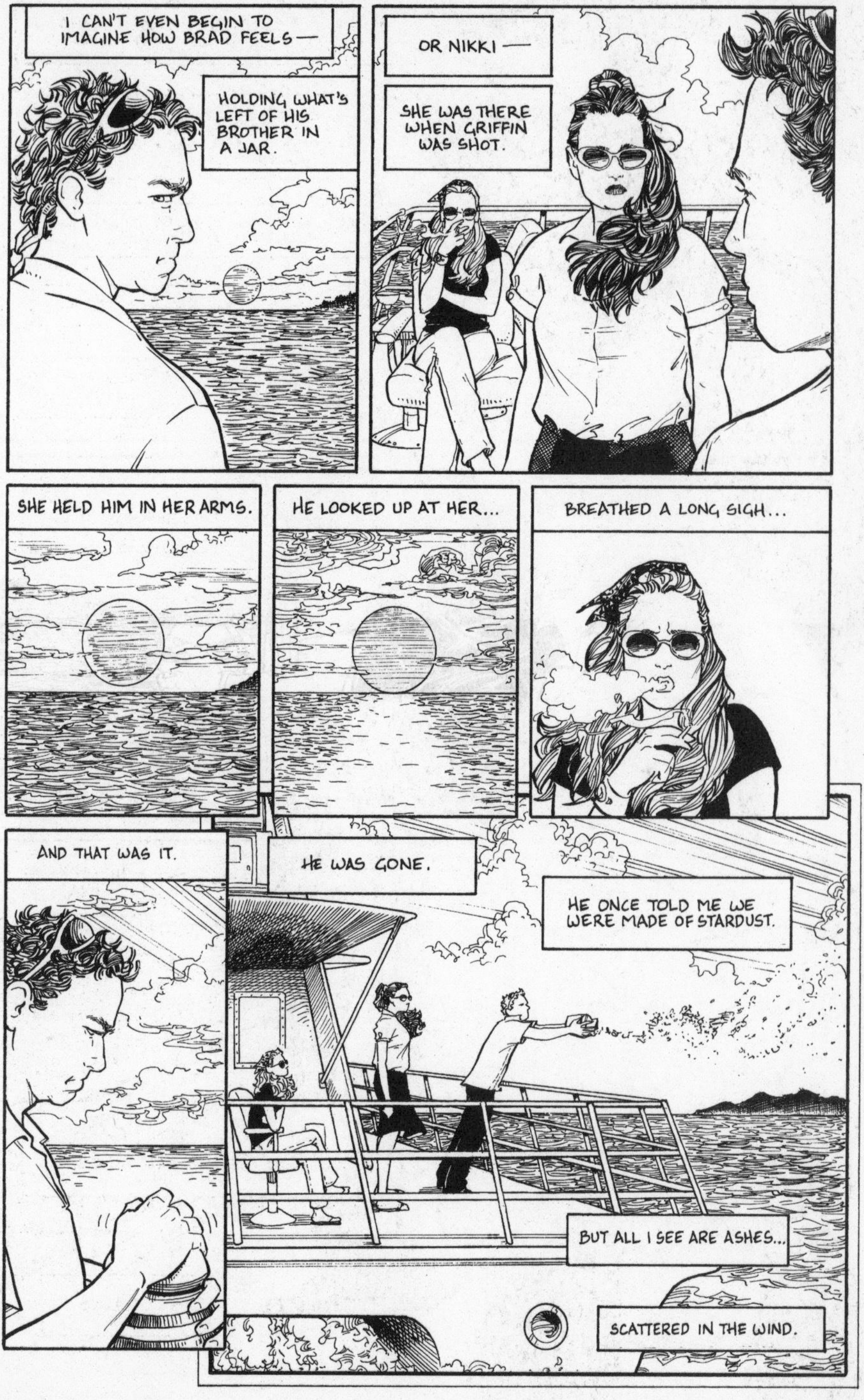
I CAN'T EVEN BEGIN TO IMAGINE HOW BRAD FEELS—
HOLDING WHAT'S LEFT OF HIS BROTHER IN A JAR.
OR NIKKI—
SHE WAS THERE WHEN GRIFFIN WAS SHOT.
SHE HELD HIM IN HER ARMS.
HE LOOKED UP AT HER...
BREATHED A LONG SIGH...
AND THAT WAS IT.
HE WAS GONE.
HE ONCE TOLD ME WE WERE MADE OF STARDUST.
BUT ALL I SEE ARE ASHES...
SCATTERED IN THE WIND.

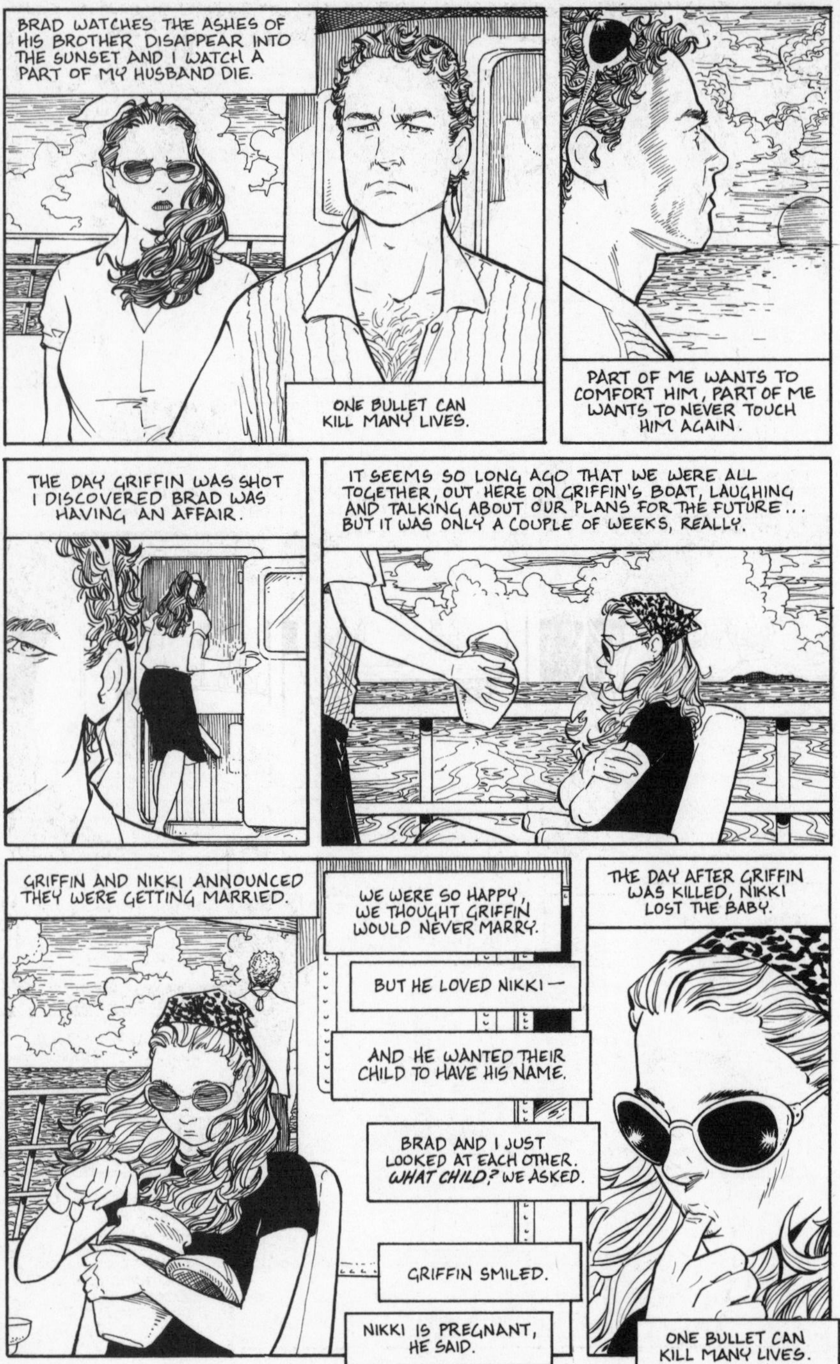
BRAD WATCHES THE ASHES OF HIS BROTHER DISAPPEAR INTO THE SUNSET AND I WATCH A PART OF MY HUSBAND DIE.
ONE BULLET CAN KILL MANY LIVES.
PART OF ME WANTS TO COMFORT HIM, PART OF ME WANTS TO NEVER TOUCH HIM AGAIN.
THE DAY GRIFFIN WAS SHOT I DISCOVERED BRAD WAS HAVING AN AFFAIR.
IT SEEMS SO LONG AGO THAT WE WERE ALL TOGETHER, OUT HERE ON GRIFFIN'S BOAT, LAUGHING AND TALKING ABOUT OUR PLANS FOR THE FUTURE... BUT IT WAS ONLY A COUPLE OF WEEKS, REALLY.
GRIFFIN AND NIKKI ANNOUNCED THEY WERE GETTING MARRIED.
WE WERE SO HAPPY, WE THOUGHT GRIFFIN WOULD NEVER MARRY.
BUT HE LOVED NIKKI—
AND HE WANTED THEIR CHILD TO HAVE HIS NAME.
BRAD AND I JUST LOOKED AT EACH OTHER. *WHAT CHILD?* WE ASKED.
GRIFFIN SMILED.
NIKKI IS PREGNANT, HE SAID.
THE DAY AFTER GRIFFIN WAS KILLED, NIKKI LOST THE BABY.
ONE BULLET CAN KILL MANY LIVES.

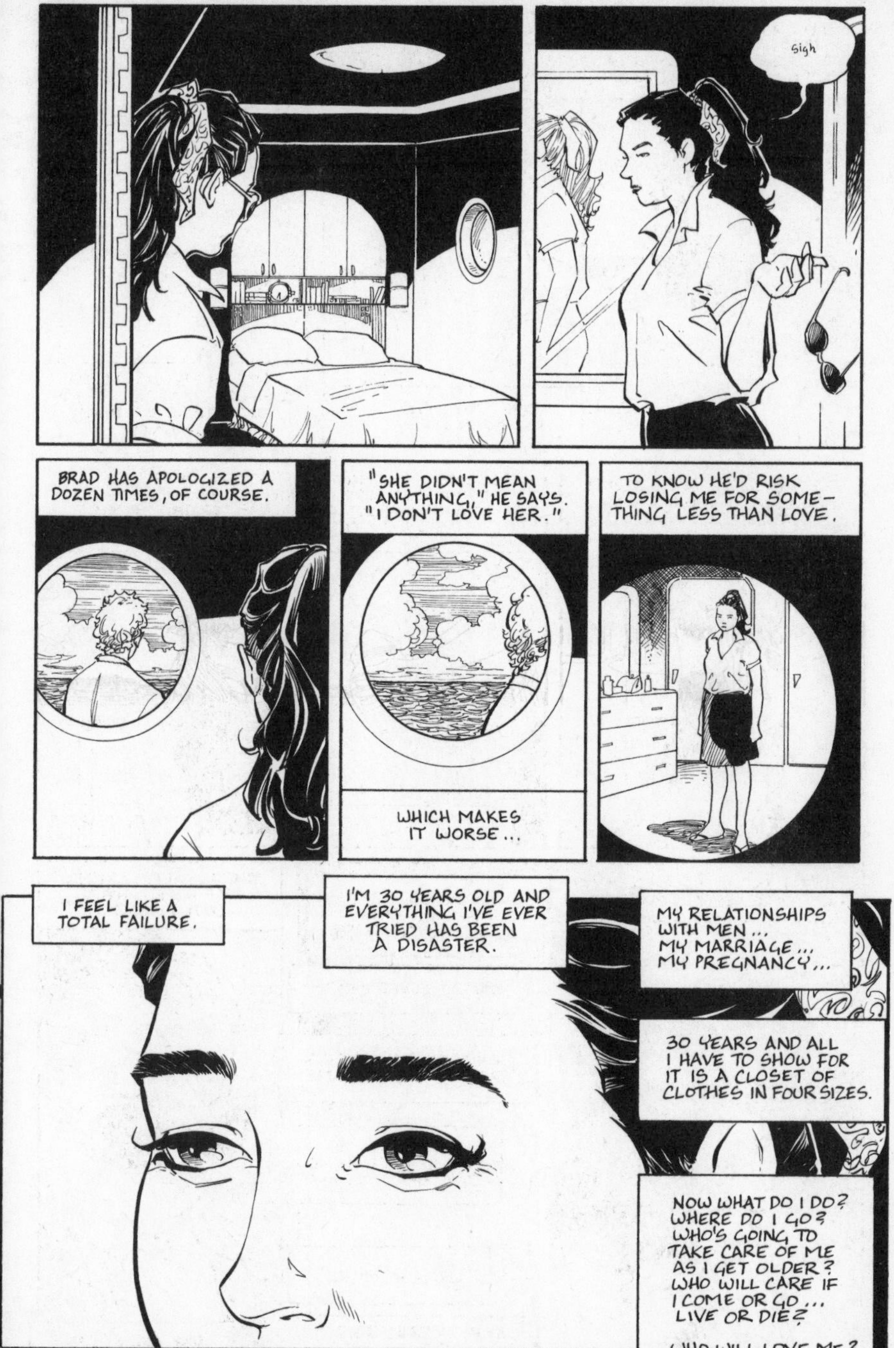
Sigh
BRAD HAS APOLOGIZED A DOZEN TIMES, OF COURSE.
"SHE DIDN'T MEAN ANYTHING," HE SAYS. "I DON'T LOVE HER."
WHICH MAKES IT WORSE...
TO KNOW HE'D RISK LOSING ME FOR SOMETHING LESS THAN LOVE.
I FEEL LIKE A TOTAL FAILURE.
I'M 30 YEARS OLD AND EVERYTHING I'VE EVER TRIED HAS BEEN A DISASTER.
MY RELATIONSHIPS WITH MEN... MY MARRIAGE... MY PREGNANCY...
30 YEARS AND ALL I HAVE TO SHOW FOR IT IS A CLOSET OF CLOTHES IN FOUR SIZES.
NOW WHAT DO I DO? WHERE DO I GO? WHO'S GOING TO TAKE CARE OF ME AS I GET OLDER? WHO WILL CARE IF I COME OR GO... LIVE OR DIE?
WHO WILL LOVE ME?

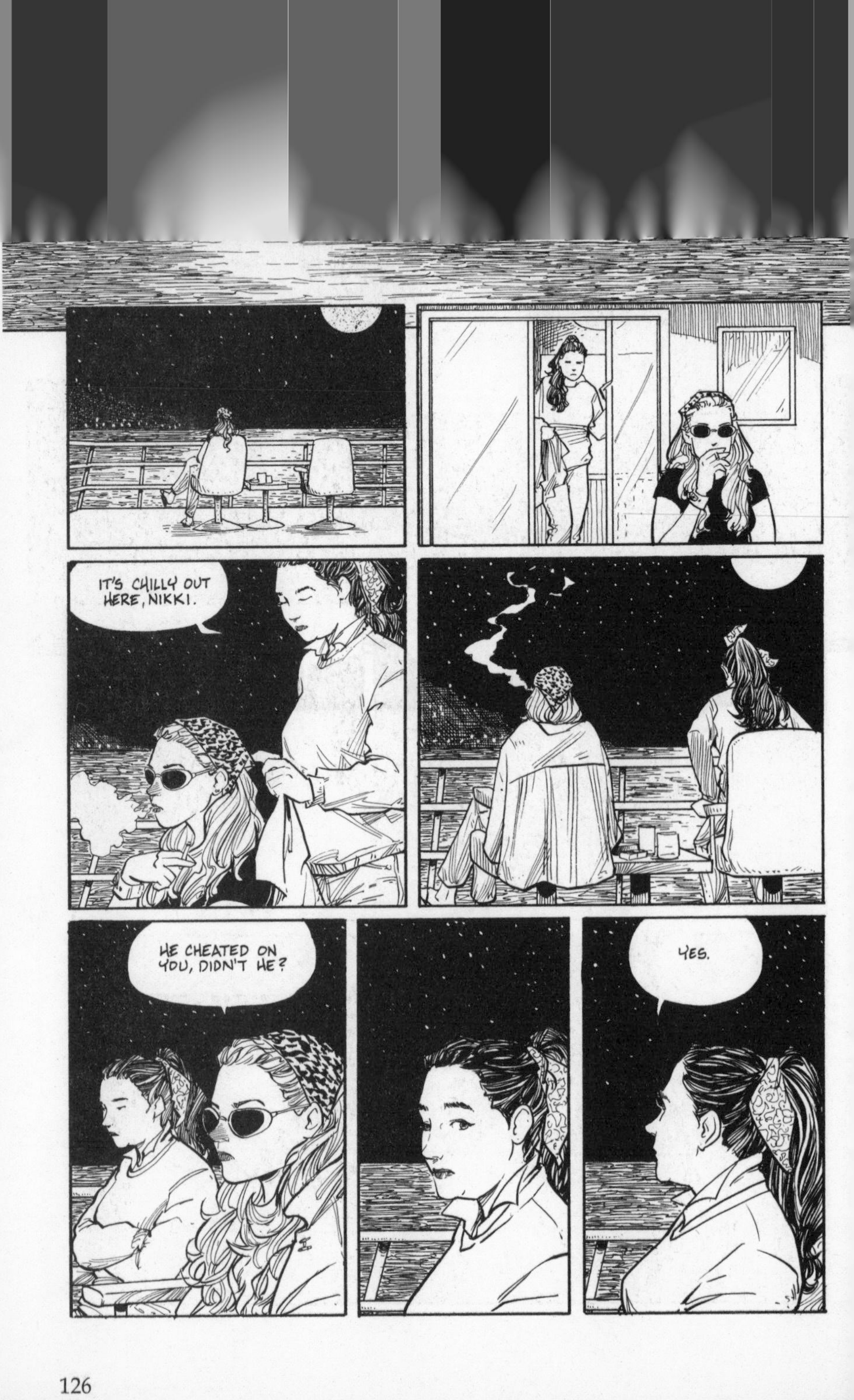
IT'S CHILLY OUT HERE, NIKKI.
HE CHEATED ON YOU, DIDN'T HE?
YES.

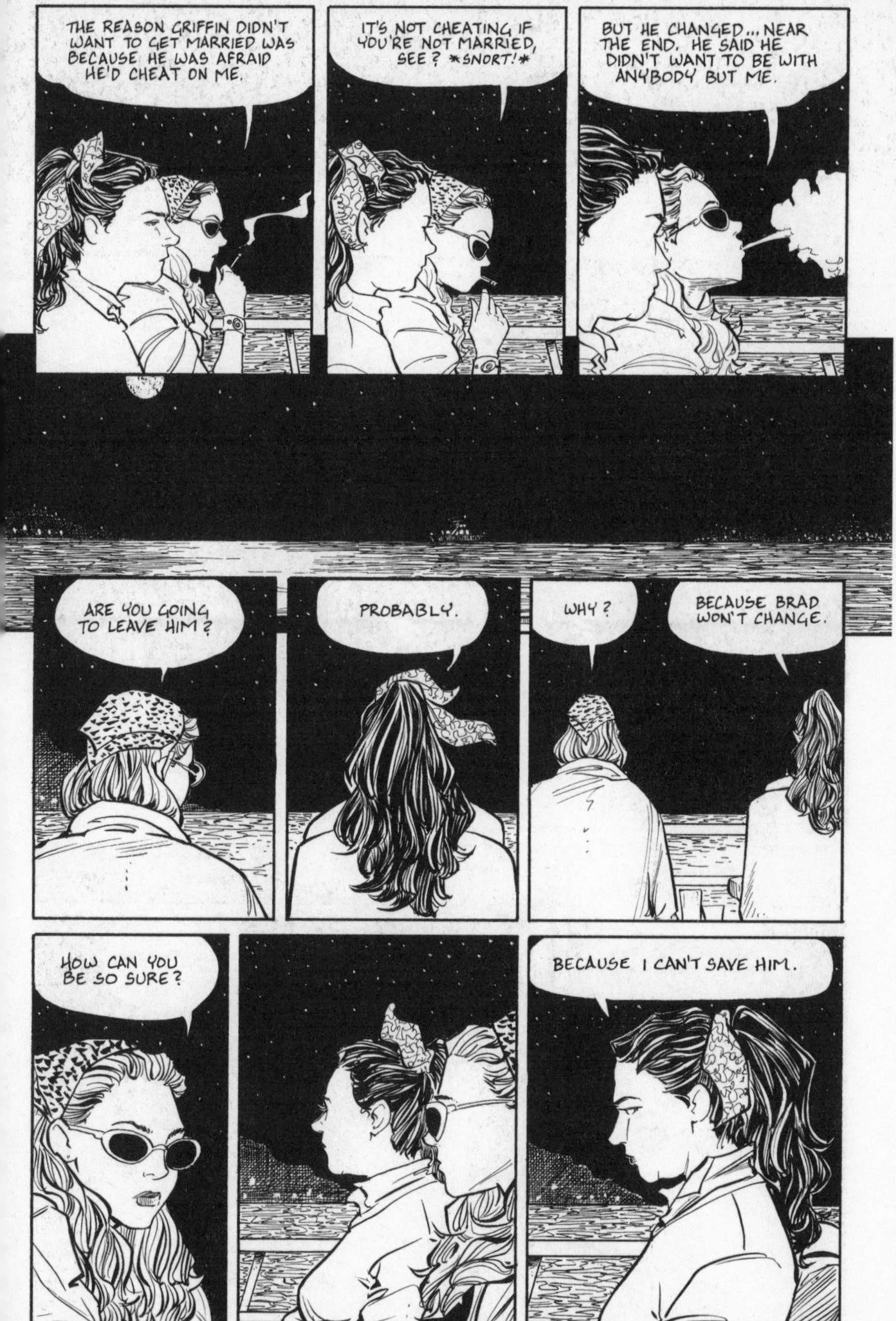

THE REASON GRIFFIN DIDN'T WANT TO GET MARRIED WAS BECAUSE HE WAS AFRAID HE'D CHEAT ON ME.
IT'S NOT CHEATING IF YOU'RE NOT MARRIED, SEE? *SNORT!*
BUT HE CHANGED... NEAR THE END. HE SAID HE DIDN'T WANT TO BE WITH ANYBODY BUT ME.
ARE YOU GOING TO LEAVE HIM?
PROBABLY.
WHY?
BECAUSE BRAD WON'T CHANGE.
HOW CAN YOU BE SO SURE?
BECAUSE I CAN'T SAVE HIM.

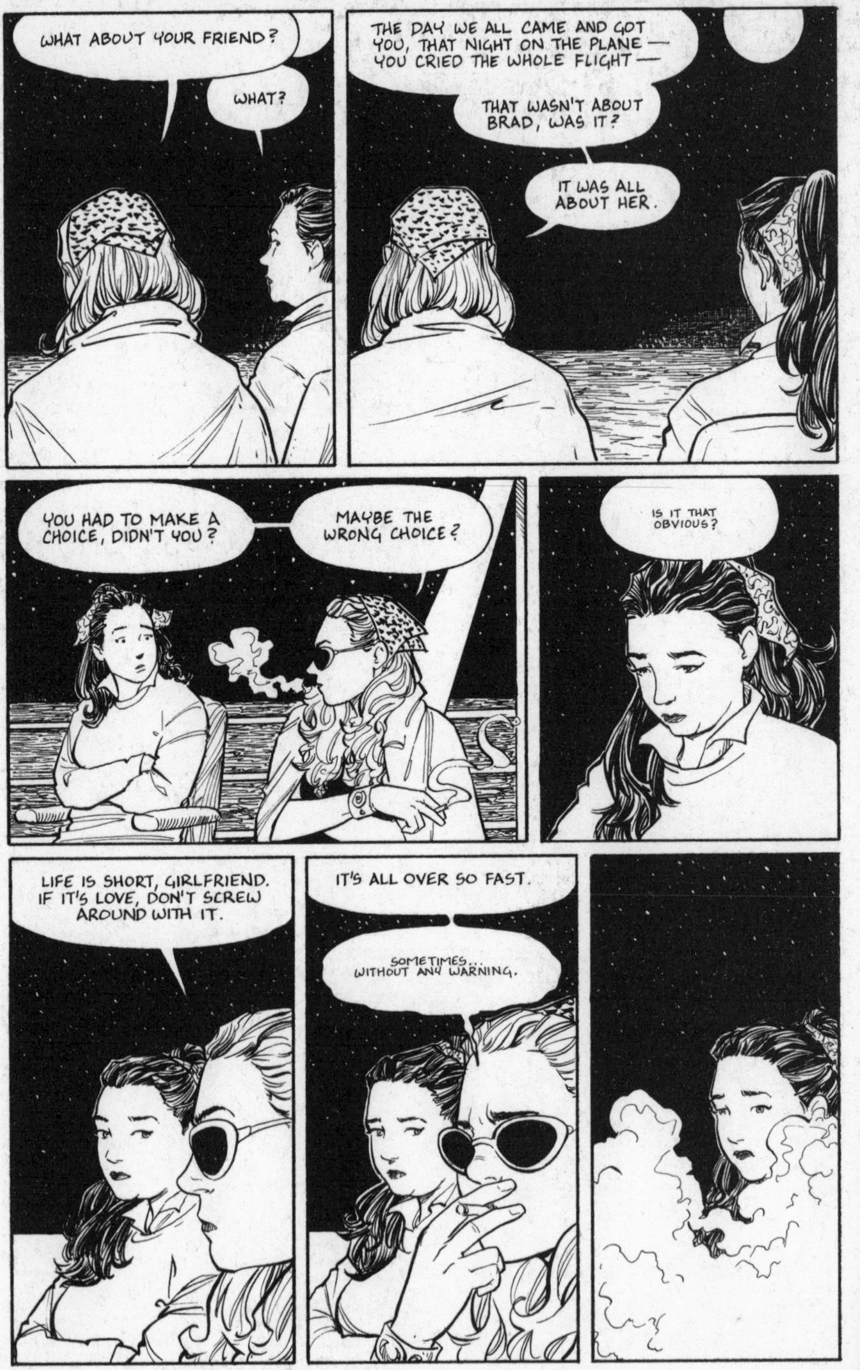
WHAT ABOUT YOUR FRIEND?
WHAT?
THE DAY WE ALL CAME AND GOT YOU, THAT NIGHT ON THE PLANE — YOU CRIED THE WHOLE FLIGHT —
THAT WASN'T ABOUT BRAD, WAS IT?
IT WAS ALL ABOUT HER.
YOU HAD TO MAKE A CHOICE, DIDN'T YOU?
MAYBE THE WRONG CHOICE?
IS IT THAT OBVIOUS?
LIFE IS SHORT, GIRLFRIEND. IF IT'S LOVE, DON'T SCREW AROUND WITH IT.
IT'S ALL OVER SO FAST.
SOMETIMES... WITHOUT ANY WARNING.

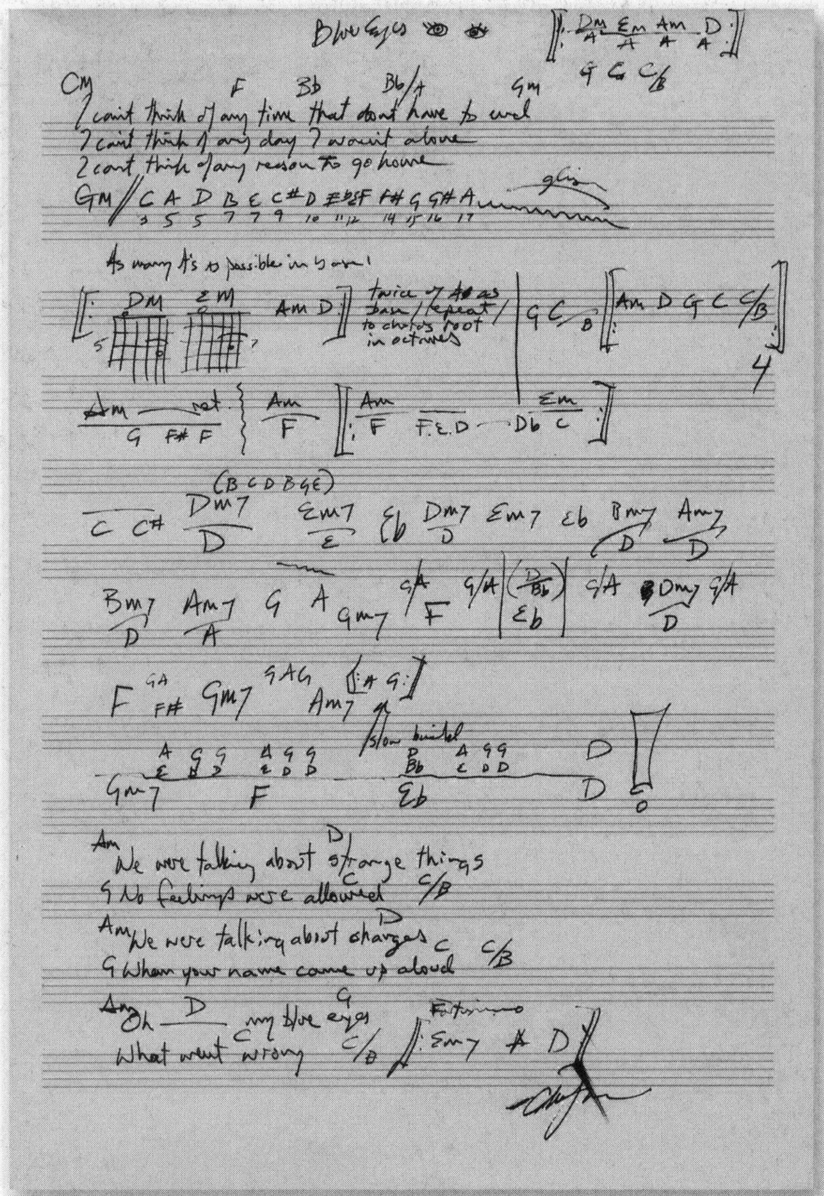
Blue Eyes
I can't think of any time that don't have to end
I can't think of any day I wasn't alone
I can't think of any reason to go home
gliss
As many A's as possible in your...
twice as bass / repeat / to chords root in octaves
slow build
We were talking about strange things
No feelings were allowed
We were talking about changes
When your name came up aloud
Oh my blue eyes
What went wrong
Fortissimo

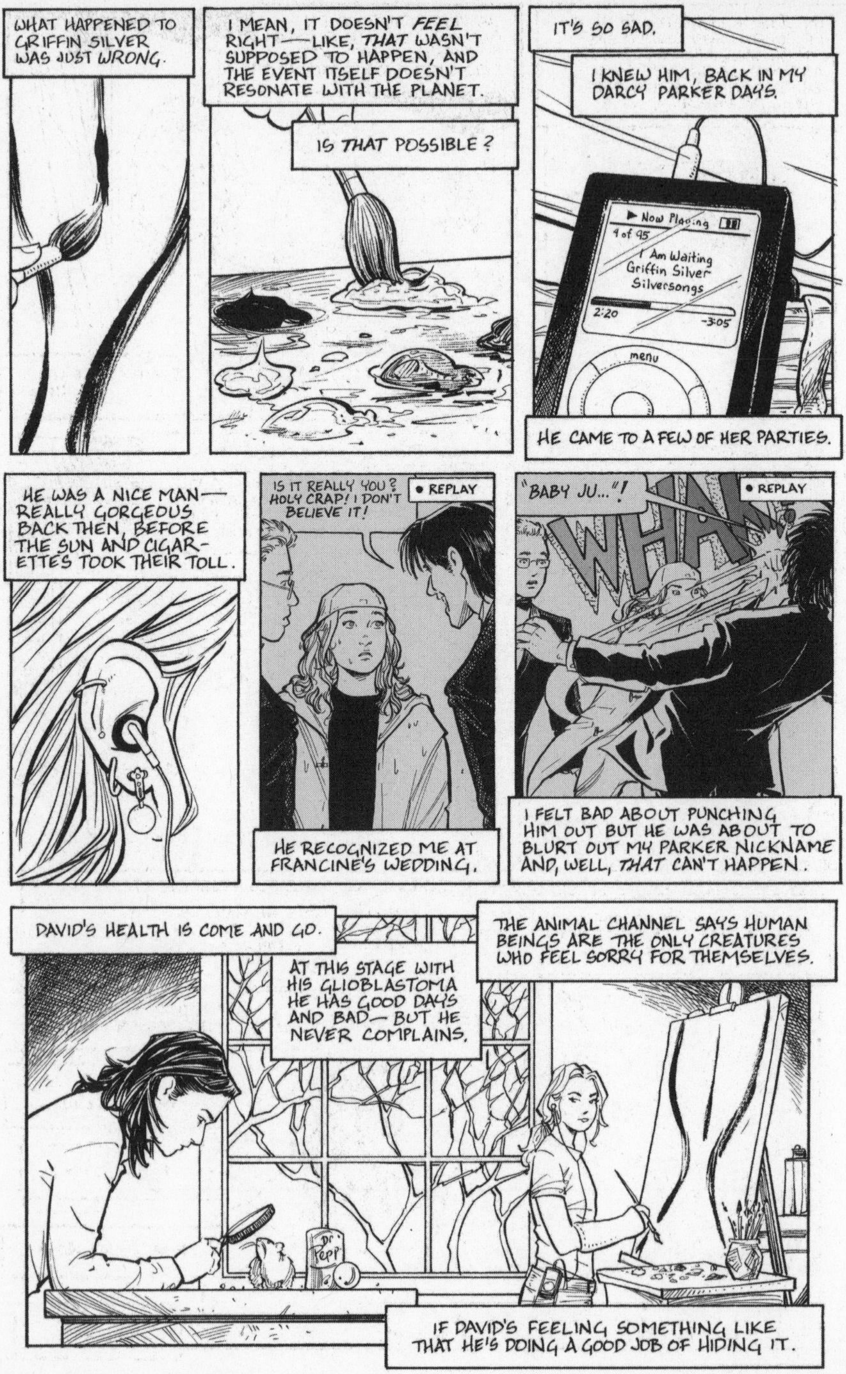
WHAT HAPPENED TO GRIFFIN SILVER WAS JUST WRONG.
I MEAN, IT DOESN'T FEEL RIGHT—LIKE, THAT WASN'T SUPPOSED TO HAPPEN, AND THE EVENT ITSELF DOESN'T RESONATE WITH THE PLANET.
IS THAT POSSIBLE?
IT'S SO SAD.
I KNEW HIM, BACK IN MY DARCY PARKER DAYS.
Now Playing
9 of 95
I Am Waiting
Griffin Silver
Silversongs
2:20
-3:05
menu
HE CAME TO A FEW OF HER PARTIES.
HE WAS A NICE MAN—REALLY GORGEOUS BACK THEN, BEFORE THE SUN AND CIGARETTES TOOK THEIR TOLL.
● REPLAY
IS IT REALLY YOU? HOLY CRAP! I DON'T BELIEVE IT!
HE RECOGNIZED ME AT FRANCINE'S WEDDING.
● REPLAY
"BABY JU..."!
WHAM
I FELT BAD ABOUT PUNCHING HIM OUT BUT HE WAS ABOUT TO BLURT OUT MY PARKER NICKNAME AND, WELL, THAT CAN'T HAPPEN.
DAVID'S HEALTH IS COME AND GO.
AT THIS STAGE WITH HIS GLIOBLASTOMA HE HAS GOOD DAYS AND BAD—BUT HE NEVER COMPLAINS.
THE ANIMAL CHANNEL SAYS HUMAN BEINGS ARE THE ONLY CREATURES WHO FEEL SORRY FOR THEMSELVES.
IF DAVID'S FEELING SOMETHING LIKE THAT HE'S DOING A GOOD JOB OF HIDING IT.

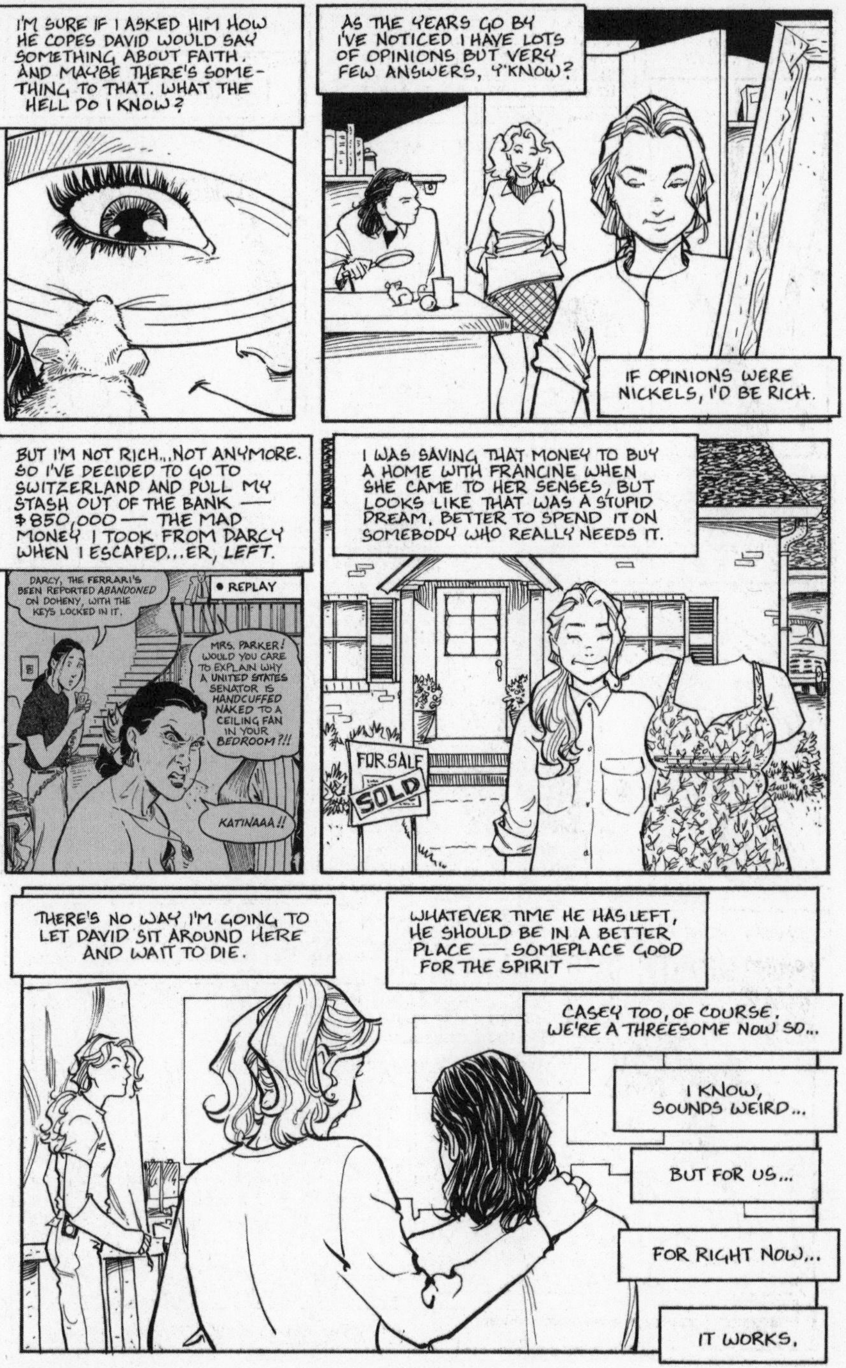

I'M SURE IF I ASKED HIM HOW HE COPES DAVID WOULD SAY SOMETHING ABOUT FAITH. AND MAYBE THERE'S SOMETHING TO THAT. WHAT THE HELL DO I KNOW?
AS THE YEARS GO BY I'VE NOTICED I HAVE LOTS OF OPINIONS BUT VERY FEW ANSWERS, Y'KNOW?
IF OPINIONS WERE NICKELS, I'D BE RICH.
BUT I'M NOT RICH...NOT ANYMORE. SO I'VE DECIDED TO GO TO SWITZERLAND AND PULL MY STASH OUT OF THE BANK — $850,000 — THE MAD MONEY I TOOK FROM DARCY WHEN I ESCAPED...ER, LEFT.
• REPLAY
DARCY, THE FERRARI'S BEEN REPORTED ABANDONED ON DOHENY, WITH THE KEYS LOCKED IN IT.
MRS. PARKER! WOULD YOU CARE TO EXPLAIN WHY A UNITED STATES SENATOR IS HANDCUFFED NAKED TO A CEILING FAN IN YOUR BEDROOM?!!
KATINAAA!!
I WAS SAVING THAT MONEY TO BUY A HOME WITH FRANCINE WHEN SHE CAME TO HER SENSES, BUT LOOKS LIKE THAT WAS A STUPID DREAM. BETTER TO SPEND IT ON SOMEBODY WHO REALLY NEEDS IT.
FOR SALE
SOLD
THERE'S NO WAY I'M GOING TO LET DAVID SIT AROUND HERE AND WAIT TO DIE.
WHATEVER TIME HE HAS LEFT, HE SHOULD BE IN A BETTER PLACE — SOMEPLACE GOOD FOR THE SPIRIT —
CASEY TOO, OF COURSE. WE'RE A THREESOME NOW SO...
I KNOW, SOUNDS WEIRD...
BUT FOR US...
FOR RIGHT NOW...
IT WORKS.

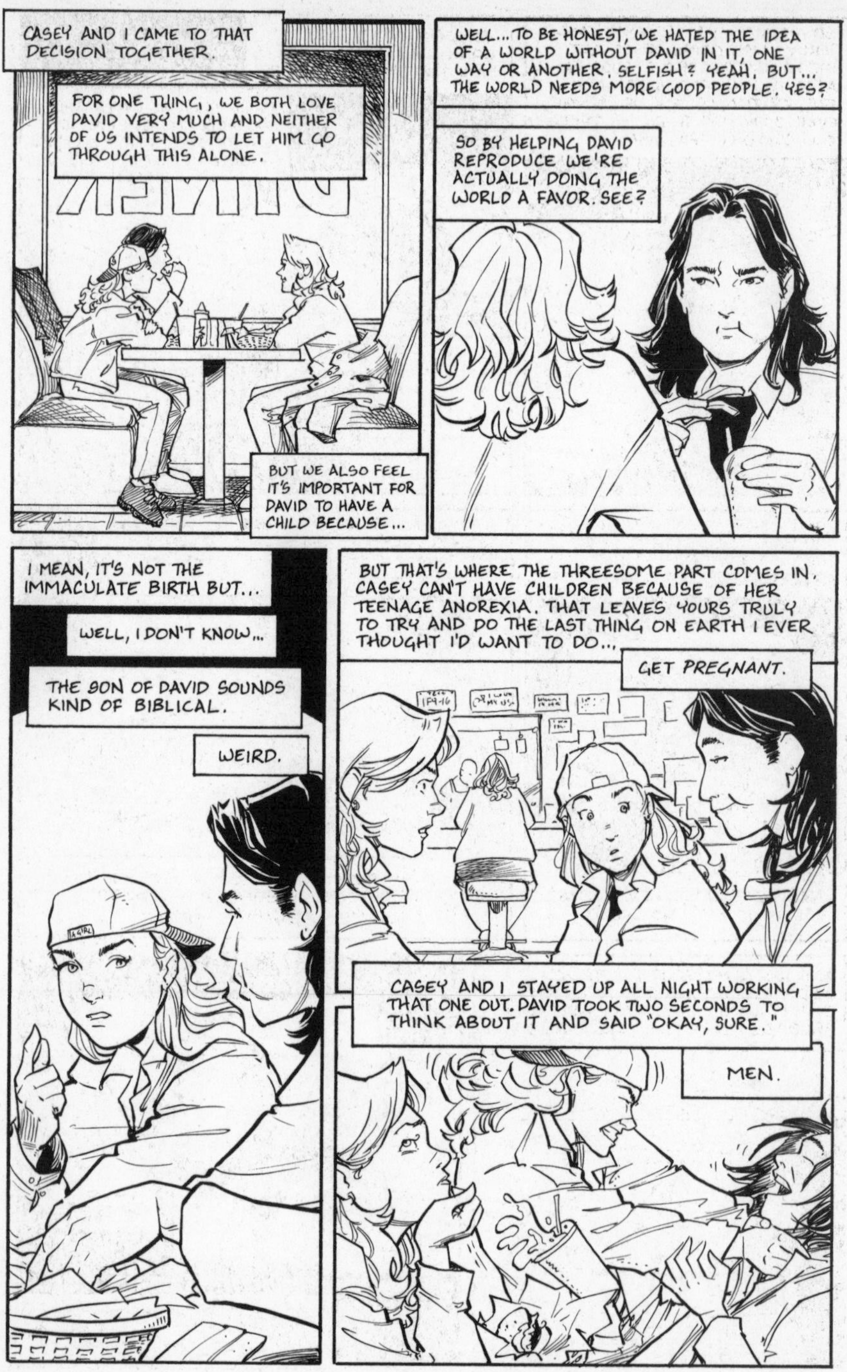
CASEY AND I CAME TO THAT DECISION TOGETHER.
FOR ONE THING, WE BOTH LOVE DAVID VERY MUCH AND NEITHER OF US INTENDS TO LET HIM GO THROUGH THIS ALONE.
BUT WE ALSO FEEL IT'S IMPORTANT FOR DAVID TO HAVE A CHILD BECAUSE...
WELL... TO BE HONEST, WE HATED THE IDEA OF A WORLD WITHOUT DAVID IN IT, ONE WAY OR ANOTHER. SELFISH? YEAH. BUT... THE WORLD NEEDS MORE GOOD PEOPLE. YES?
SO BY HELPING DAVID REPRODUCE WE'RE ACTUALLY DOING THE WORLD A FAVOR. SEE?
I MEAN, IT'S NOT THE IMMACULATE BIRTH BUT...
WELL, I DON'T KNOW...
THE SON OF DAVID SOUNDS KIND OF BIBLICAL.
WEIRD.
BUT THAT'S WHERE THE THREESOME PART COMES IN. CASEY CAN'T HAVE CHILDREN BECAUSE OF HER TEENAGE ANOREXIA. THAT LEAVES YOURS TRULY TO TRY AND DO THE LAST THING ON EARTH I EVER THOUGHT I'D WANT TO DO...
GET *PREGNANT*.
CASEY AND I STAYED UP ALL NIGHT WORKING THAT ONE OUT. DAVID TOOK TWO SECONDS TO THINK ABOUT IT AND SAID "OKAY, SURE."
MEN.

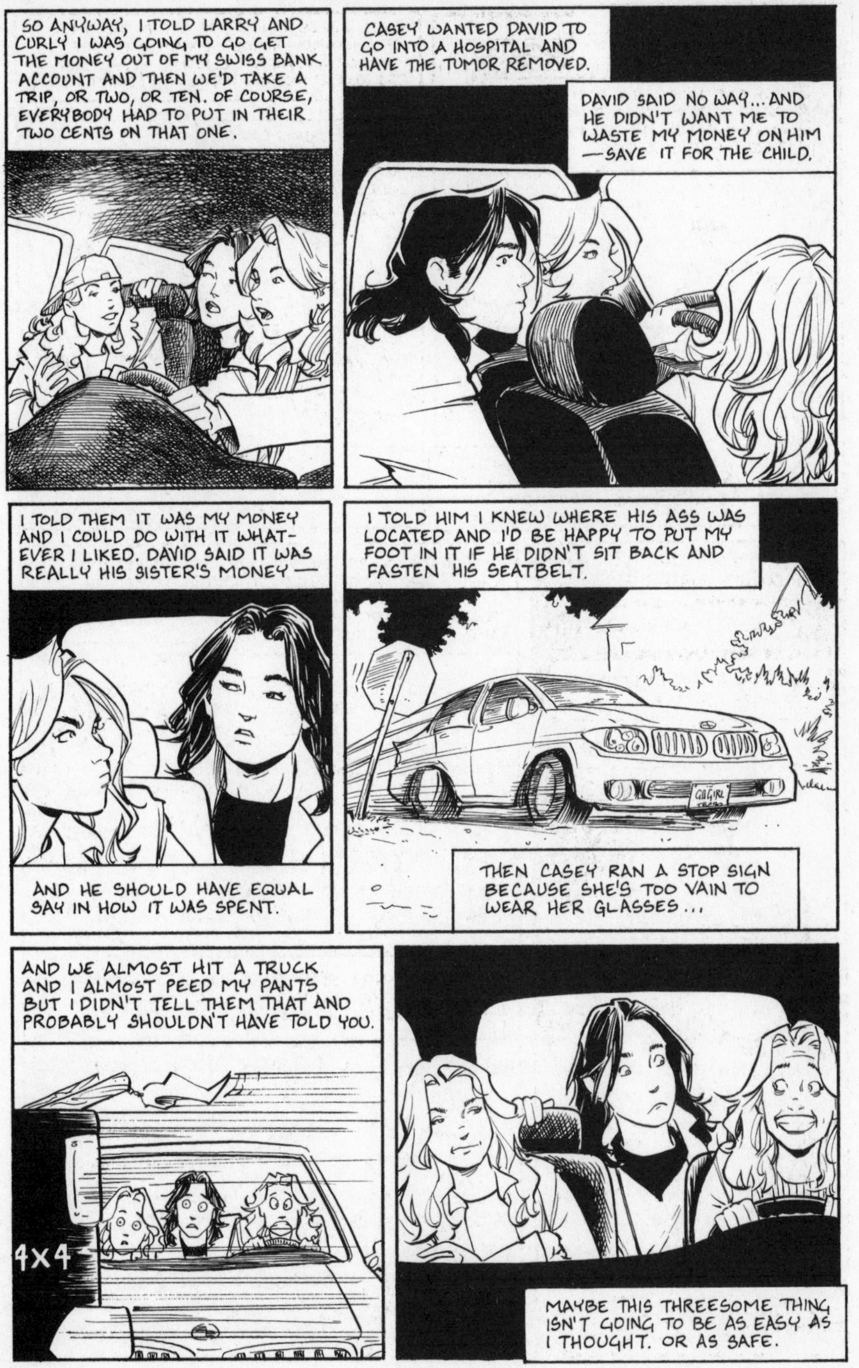
SO ANYWAY, I TOLD LARRY AND CURLY I WAS GOING TO GO GET THE MONEY OUT OF MY SWISS BANK ACCOUNT AND THEN WE'D TAKE A TRIP, OR TWO, OR TEN. OF COURSE, EVERYBODY HAD TO PUT IN THEIR TWO CENTS ON THAT ONE.
CASEY WANTED DAVID TO GO INTO A HOSPITAL AND HAVE THE TUMOR REMOVED.
DAVID SAID NO WAY... AND HE DIDN'T WANT ME TO WASTE MY MONEY ON HIM —SAVE IT FOR THE CHILD.
I TOLD THEM IT WAS MY MONEY AND I COULD DO WITH IT WHATEVER I LIKED. DAVID SAID IT WAS REALLY HIS SISTER'S MONEY —
AND HE SHOULD HAVE EQUAL SAY IN HOW IT WAS SPENT.
I TOLD HIM I KNEW WHERE HIS ASS WAS LOCATED AND I'D BE HAPPY TO PUT MY FOOT IN IT IF HE DIDN'T SIT BACK AND FASTEN HIS SEATBELT.
THEN CASEY RAN A STOP SIGN BECAUSE SHE'S TOO VAIN TO WEAR HER GLASSES...
AND WE ALMOST HIT A TRUCK AND I ALMOST PEED MY PANTS BUT I DIDN'T TELL THEM THAT AND PROBABLY SHOULDN'T HAVE TOLD YOU.
4X4
MAYBE THIS THREESOME THING ISN'T GOING TO BE AS EASY AS I THOUGHT. OR AS SAFE.

"Yes, we have found success in laboratory tests," the doctor said between puffs on his cigarette, "but our findings with the human samples have been limited, promising, but limited. The method is new. We have much testing to do. It will take years before we are ready to publish our findings."

"I don't have years," said Tambi.

They were playing a game and they both knew it. *You sniff me, I sniff you*, thought Tambi. She was asking him to do something outside the ethics of medicine; he was checking to see if she could be trusted and make the risks worth his while.

Tambi stared out the window, watching the cold gray sky of Berlin, and waited for Dr. Sturzbacher's reply. She knew he had to be careful, his aggressive theories had already cost him a respectable position at the Kaiser-Wilhelm Institute for Cerebral Research. Funding his work now meant seeking private sources, sources with personal reasons for giving him large amounts of money for a dangerous procedure that may or may not work. Tambi played the role of prospective benefactor. The doctor pretended to be torn by ethical issues. If Tambi was found to be trustworthy and determined, she would have her request granted. But she had to play the game.

"The variables are case specific. We cannot predict the outcome. The neurological consequences... the morbidity rates are uncharted."

Tambi nodded. *I understand. He may die. Let's move on.*

"Even the expense is an unknown. Each case is unique, requiring a wide range of preparations, tests, procedures..."

"My friend has a three inch glioblastoma in the middle of his brain. He has been given a year to live. We must act now."

"The procedures are taxing on the system."

"He is strong."

"We could lose much time establishing a baseline."

"I can have all his records sent to you."

"Technically I am not allowed to request his records."

"I will deliver them personally."

"You must understand… I can make no guarantees."

"I understand."

"And… the expenses…"

Finally, thought Tambi.

The doctor paused, studying his prospective client, waiting for an uncomfortable shift in the chair that did not come. He continued. "Each attempt adds to the costs as we refine the process. It is the preparation that costs so much…the labwork, the DNA…"

"How much are we talking about?" Tambi said.

"Our last patient was unable to complete the payment before she died. Now we must predict our costs before work."

"How much"

"5 million euro… cash. Before we begin."

And the mask drops, Tambi smiled to herself. "And if he dies?"

"I will be very sorry, but no refunds."

"When can you begin?"

The doctor smiled. The game was over. "You are fortunate, we have an opening in two weeks. You may reserve the opportunity with 1 million euro."

Tambi shot the doctor a look but said nothing. *And you will probably pay off your worst creditor and have enough left over to be a big shot in Monte Carlo for a few days before we begin*, she thought. Tambi reached into her left coat pocket and pulled out a thick envelope, tossing it onto the desk between them.

"1 million euro," she said.

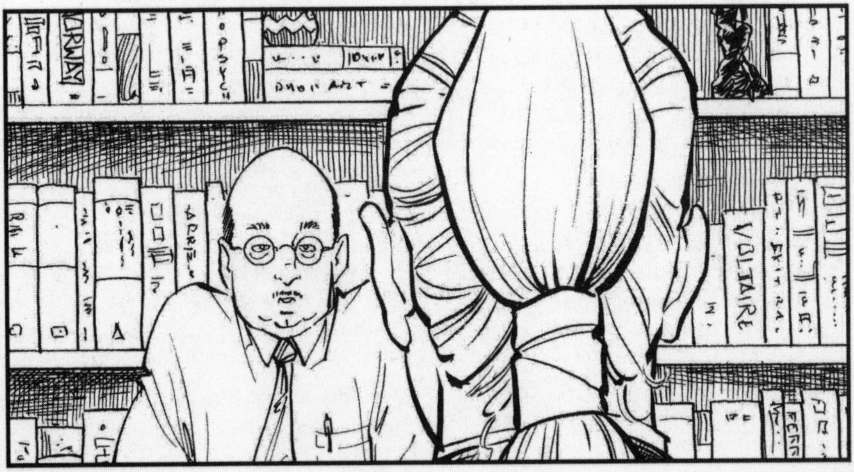
VOLTAIRE

If things had gone badly Tambi would have reached into her right hand pocket and produced a packet of photographs showing the noble doctor at a local night club, kissing a fifteen year old male prostitute. Tambi didn't like to use such cheesy tactics, but she always had a Plan B for these types of meetings. Knowing that the doctor was in the middle of a nasty divorce, the pictures might have been necessary to persuade him to work for her on her timetable. And if the meeting had been a disaster, with threats of legal action and police, there was always Plan C, known throughout the American crime community as The Baker Refund. Or, in short: Kill The Bastard.

Tambi stood from her chair. The doctor did not look at the envelope on his desk, but smiled at Tambi and offered his hand. "It will be a pleasure to work with you, Miss Baker. I will make all the necessary arrangements." He did not stand.

Tambi towered over the doctor as she leaned forward and shook his hand. His grip was weak. "Thank you. I'll be back in two weeks with my friend and his records."

"And the money."

"And the money."

Tambi turned and left. She walked out of the building into the frosty night air and stepped into a car waiting to take her back to the Hotel Kempinski. A light rain began to fall through the streetlights as the car turned onto Freidrichstraße, headed for the B2. In the dark and private sanctuary of the car, Tambi smiled. She had been prepared to pay twice the amount.

They turned west on the B2 and merged calmly into traffic. Tambi dialed two digits on her phone with the satellite card installed and waited. 5500 miles away Cherry Hammer answered the call.

"Hey boss." As always, Cherry's voice was husky and quiet, despite the crowd sounds in the background.

"Where are you?"

"Eh… I'm not sure how to pronounce it… the Omotesando café… in Tokyo. Man, this is some place, let me tell you. Futurama. They have this drink here called the Dublin Peach… pretty sure it's illegal in the states."

"That's nice. I'm glad you're having a good time and getting liquored up on my dime."

"Jealousy becomes you, boss. Before you fire me you might want to ask me why I'm here."

"Let me guess, they have an Elvis impersonator."

"Now that would be too good to be true. I did hear the Brian Setzer Orchestra is playing somewhere in town this weekend. I might check them out if there's time."

"Where's David's sister?"

"About 50 feet in front of me, at the table by the window."

Tambi paused, silently taken aback. Cherry could be trying at times, but she was the best bloodhound in the business. "Is she alone?"

"She's not a customer, boss, she's a waitress."

Tambi watched the lights of Berlin streak and flicker across her tinted window. The daughter of the most powerful Yakuza leader in recent history was a cocktail waitress. *She probably doesn't even know*, thought Tambi.

"Don't engage her," Tambi said. "Just… stay on her. Don't lose her. I'll get back to you."

"No problem"

"Cherry…"

"Yeah?"

"How… how does she look?"

"Ah… short, pretty…"

"That's not what I mean."

"Oh. She looks clean, boss. Nice kid."

Tambi breathed a sigh of relief that surprised her. "Thanks," she said, and ended the call just as the car pulled up to the entrance of the hotel.

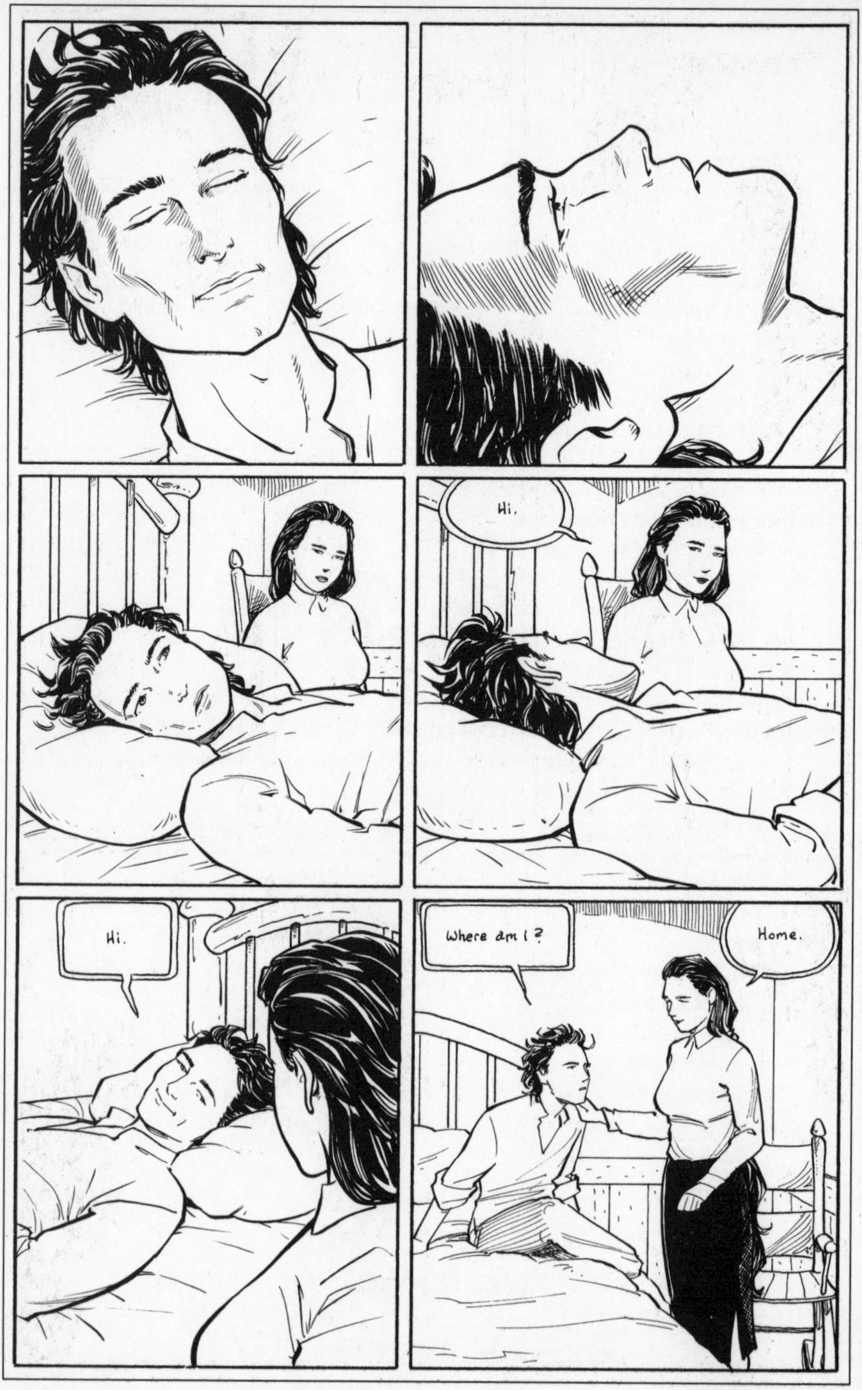
Hi.
Hi.
Where am I?
Home.

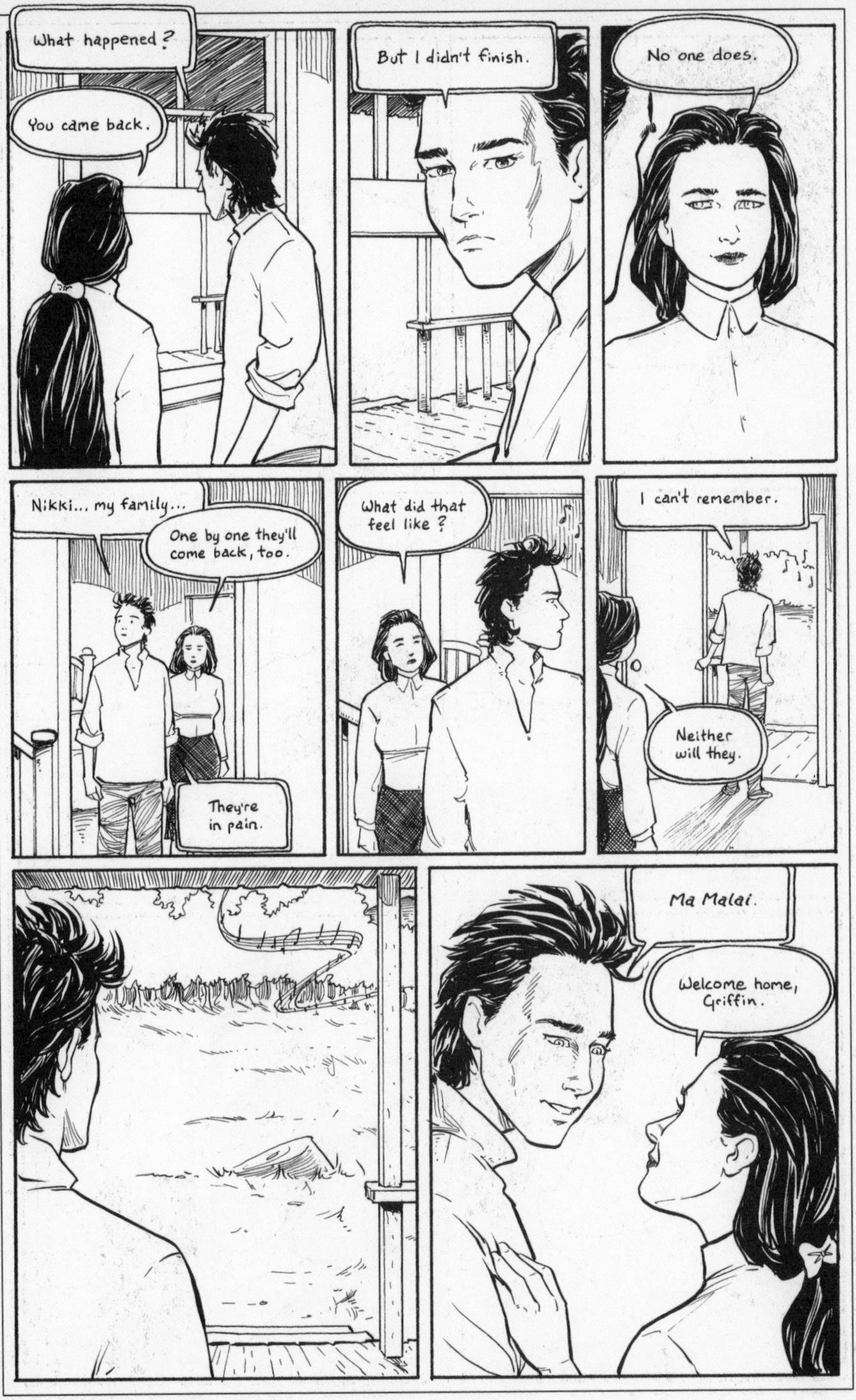
What happened?
You came back.
But I didn't finish.
No one does.
Nikki... my family...
One by one they'll come back, too.
They're in pain.
What did that feel like?
I can't remember.
Neither will they.
Ma Malai.
Welcome home, Griffin.

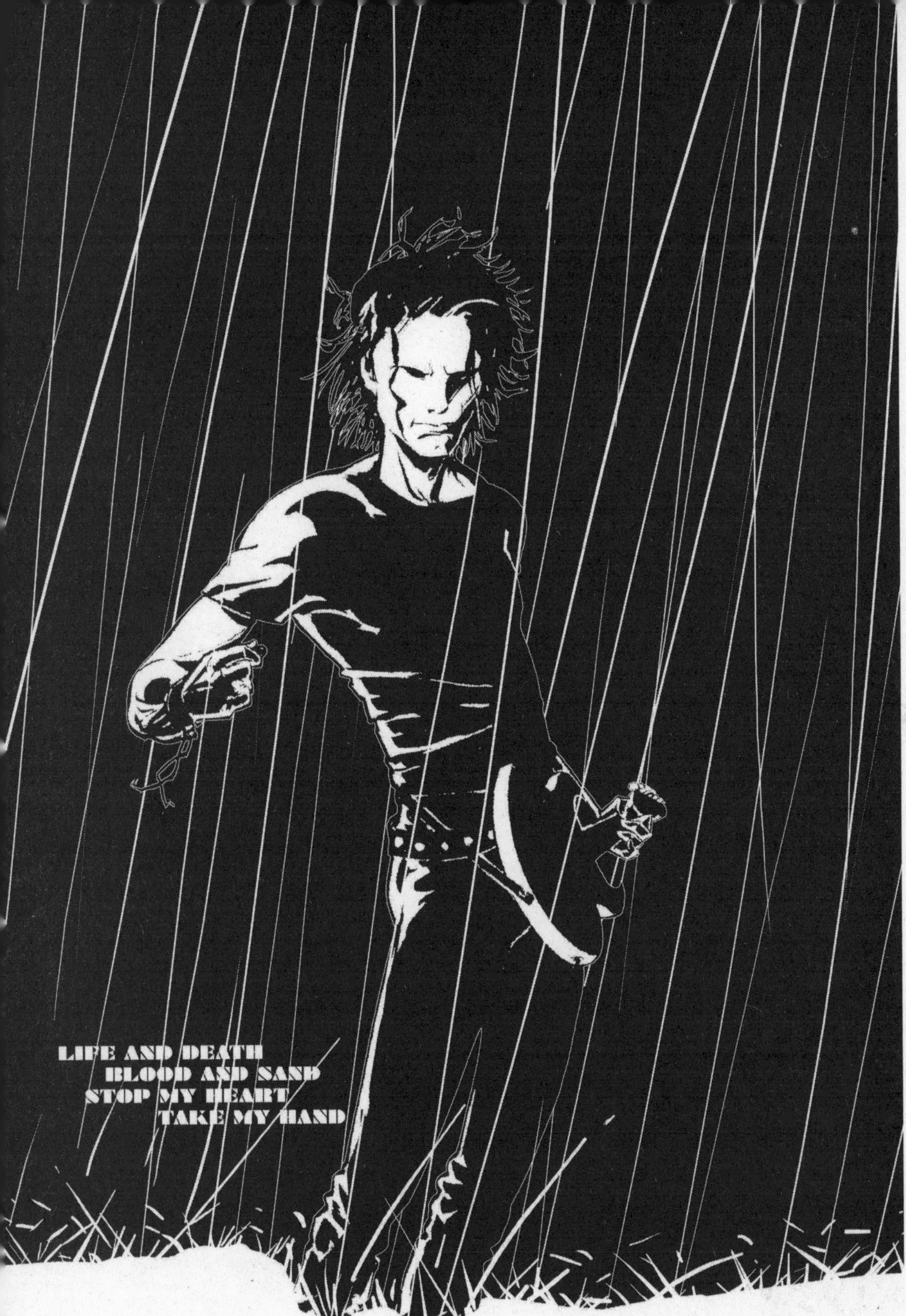
LIFE AND DEATH
BLOOD AND SAND
STOP MY HEART
TAKE MY HAND

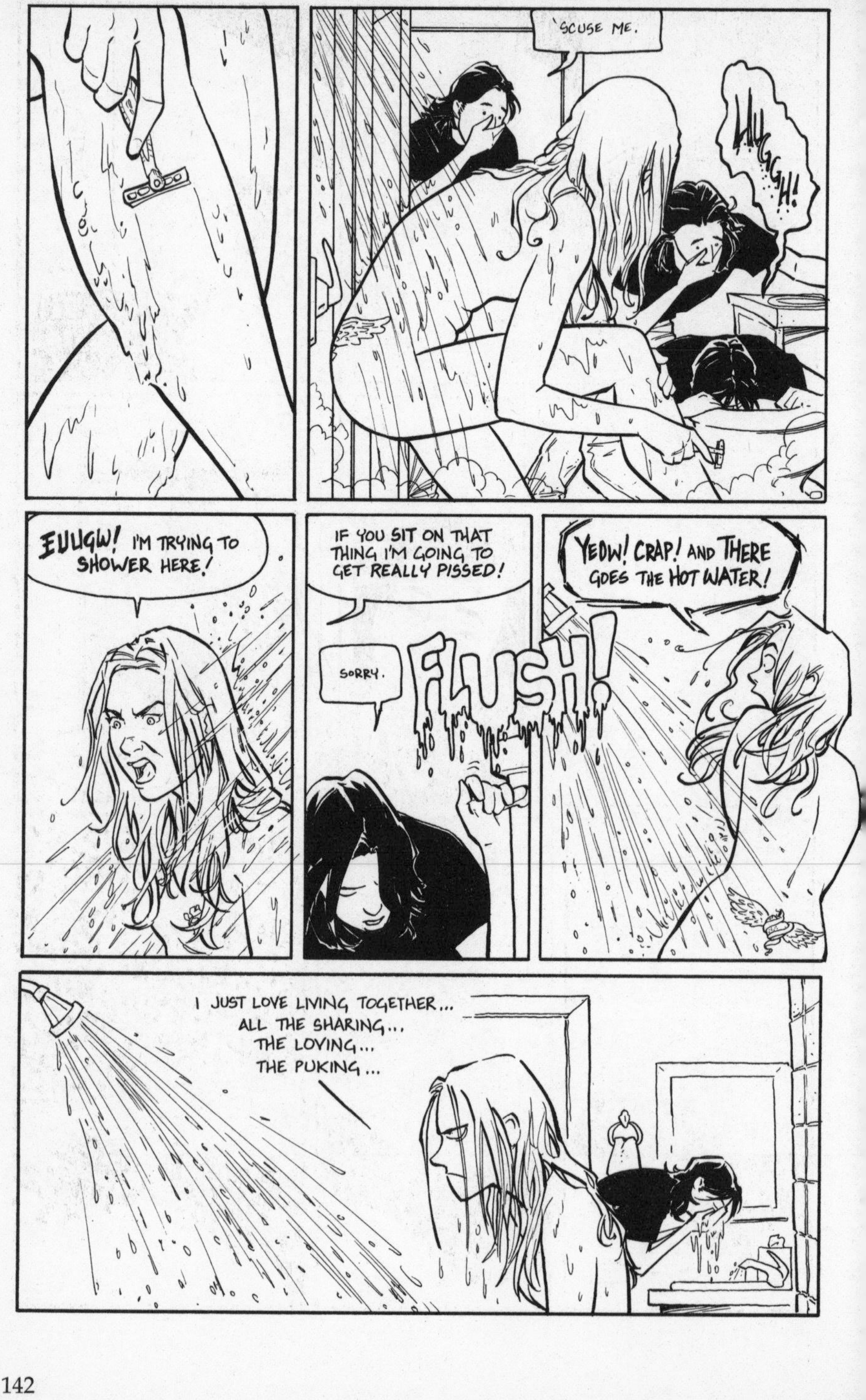
'SCUSE ME.
HUUGGH!
EUUGW! I'M TRYING TO SHOWER HERE!
IF YOU SIT ON THAT THING I'M GOING TO GET REALLY PISSED!
SORRY.
FLUSH!
YEOW! CRAP! AND THERE GOES THE HOT WATER!
I JUST LOVE LIVING TOGETHER...
ALL THE SHARING...
THE LOVING...
THE PUKING...

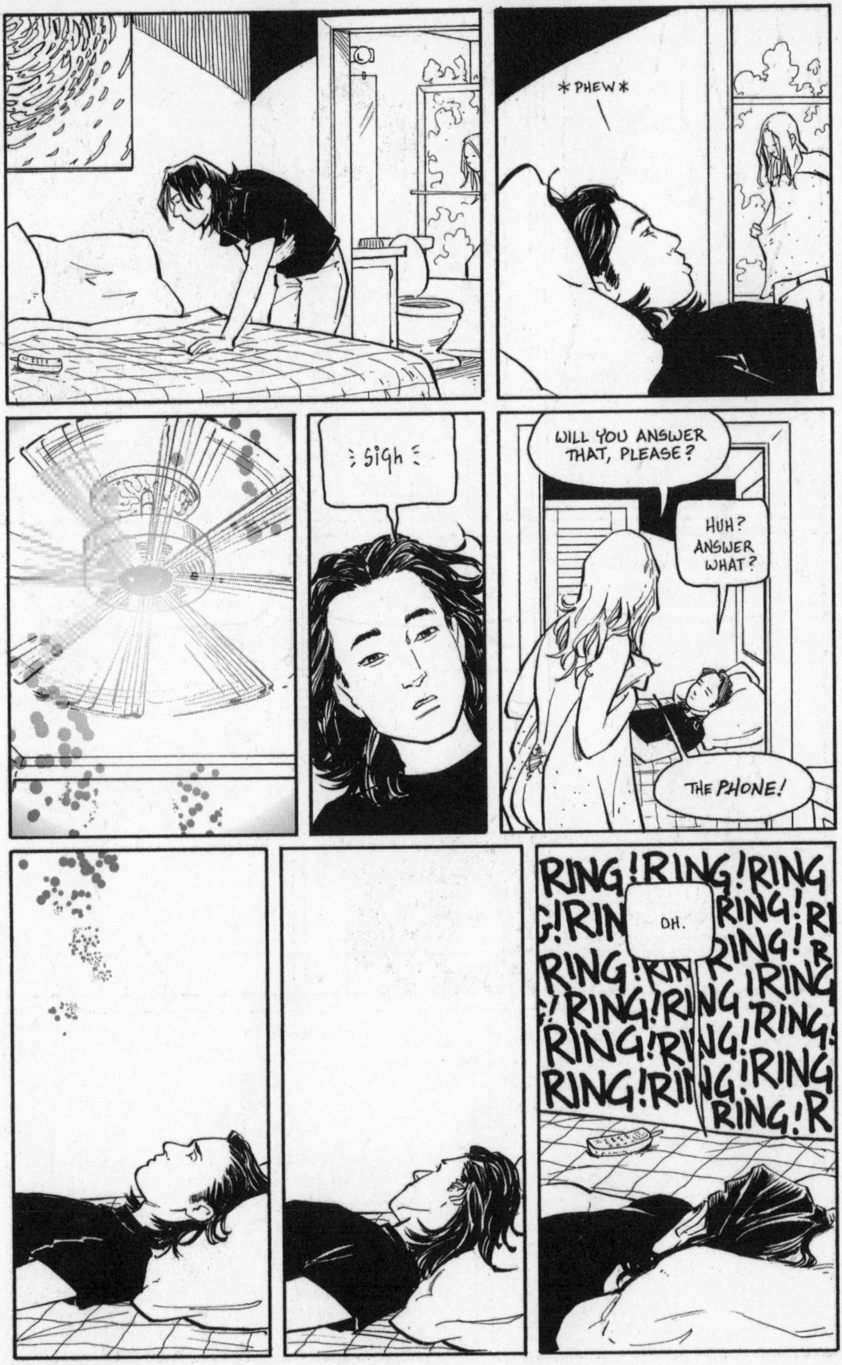
PHEW
SIGH
WILL YOU ANSWER THAT, PLEASE?
HUH? ANSWER WHAT?
THE PHONE!
RING! RING! RING! RING! RING! RING! RING! RING! RING! RING! RING! RING!
OH.

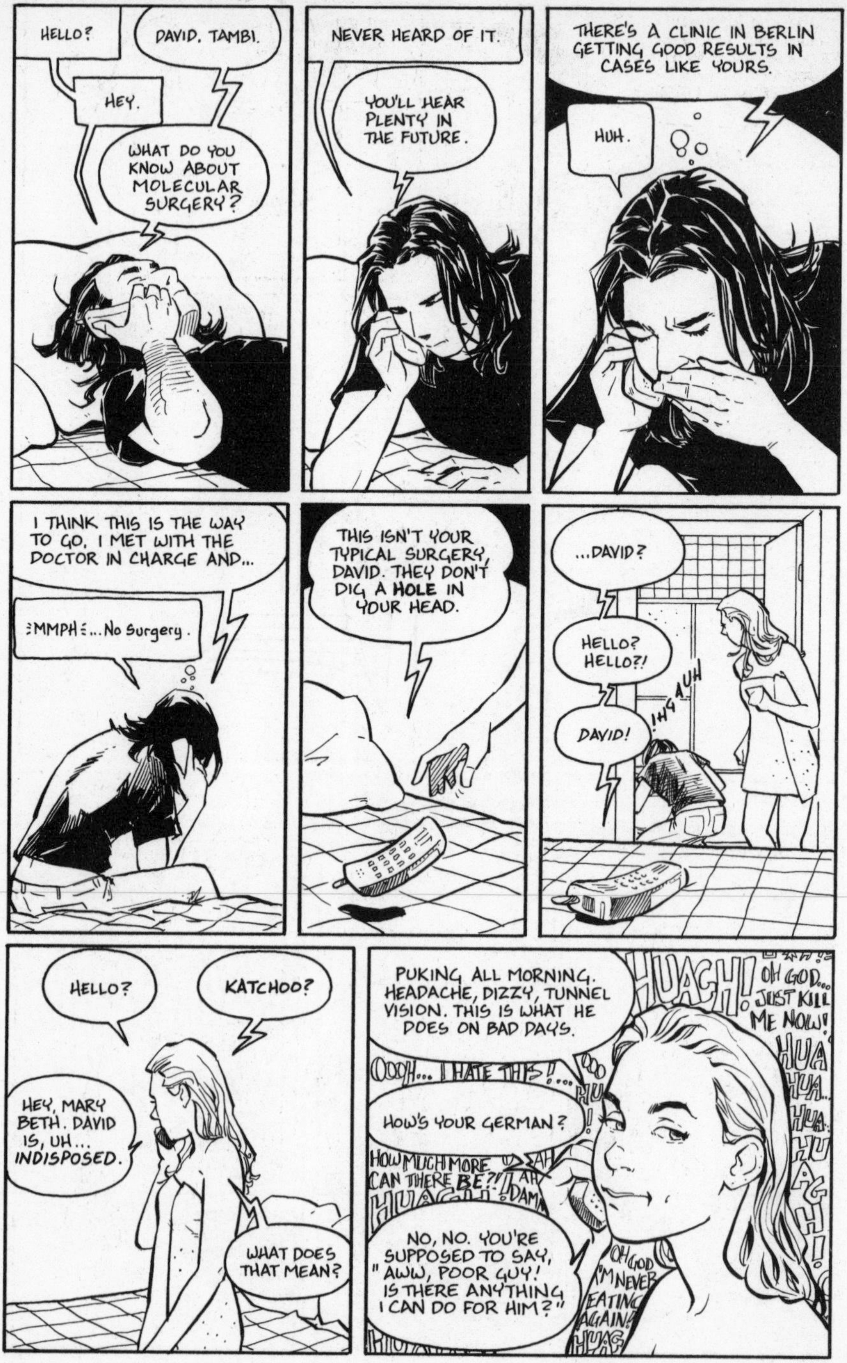

HELLO?
DAVID. TAMBI.
HEY.
WHAT DO YOU KNOW ABOUT MOLECULAR SURGERY?
NEVER HEARD OF IT.
YOU'LL HEAR PLENTY IN THE FUTURE.
THERE'S A CLINIC IN BERLIN GETTING GOOD RESULTS IN CASES LIKE YOURS.
HUH.
I THINK THIS IS THE WAY TO GO. I MET WITH THE DOCTOR IN CHARGE AND...
MMPH ... No Surgery.
THIS ISN'T YOUR TYPICAL SURGERY, DAVID. THEY DON'T DIG A HOLE IN YOUR HEAD.
...DAVID?
HELLO? HELLO?!
DAVID!
HELLO?
KATCHOO?
HEY, MARY BETH. DAVID IS, UH... INDISPOSED.
WHAT DOES THAT MEAN?
PUKING ALL MORNING. HEADACHE, DIZZY, TUNNEL VISION. THIS IS WHAT HE DOES ON BAD DAYS.
HUAGH! OH GOD... JUST KILL ME NOW!
OOOH... I HATE THIS!...
HOW'S YOUR GERMAN?
HOW MUCH MORE CAN THERE BE?!
NO, NO. YOU'RE SUPPOSED TO SAY, "AWW, POOR GUY! IS THERE ANYTHING I CAN DO FOR HIM?"
OH GOD I'M NEVER EATING AGAIN!

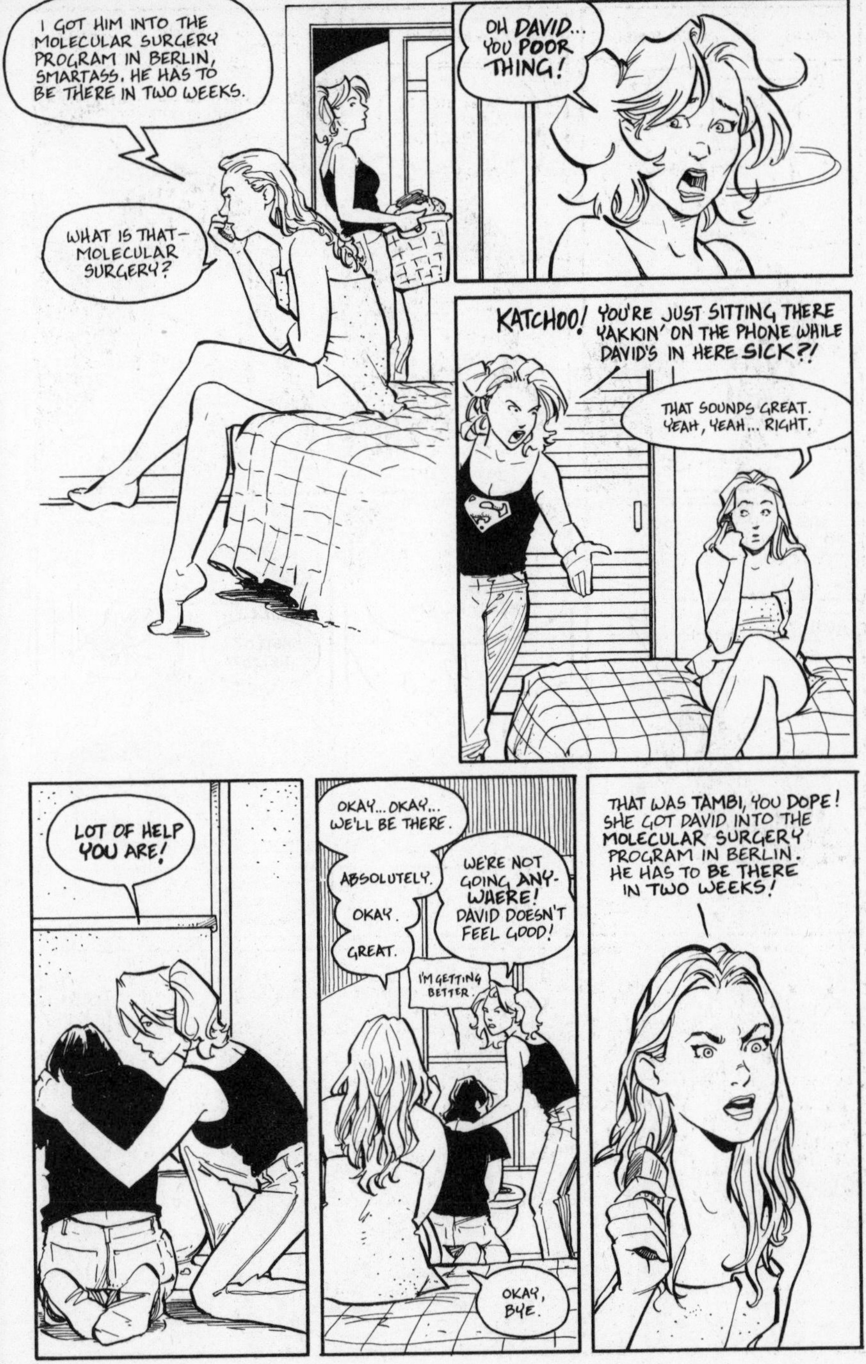
I GOT HIM INTO THE MOLECULAR SURGERY PROGRAM IN BERLIN, SMARTASS. HE HAS TO BE THERE IN TWO WEEKS.
WHAT IS THAT— MOLECULAR SURGERY?
OH DAVID... YOU POOR THING!
KATCHOO! YOU'RE JUST SITTING THERE YAKKIN' ON THE PHONE WHILE DAVID'S IN HERE SICK?!
THAT SOUNDS GREAT. YEAH, YEAH... RIGHT.
LOT OF HELP YOU ARE!
OKAY... OKAY... WE'LL BE THERE.
ABSOLUTELY.
OKAY.
GREAT.
WE'RE NOT GOING ANY-WHERE! DAVID DOESN'T FEEL GOOD!
I'M GETTING BETTER.
OKAY, BYE.
THAT WAS TAMBI, YOU DOPE! SHE GOT DAVID INTO THE MOLECULAR SURGERY PROGRAM IN BERLIN. HE HAS TO BE THERE IN TWO WEEKS!

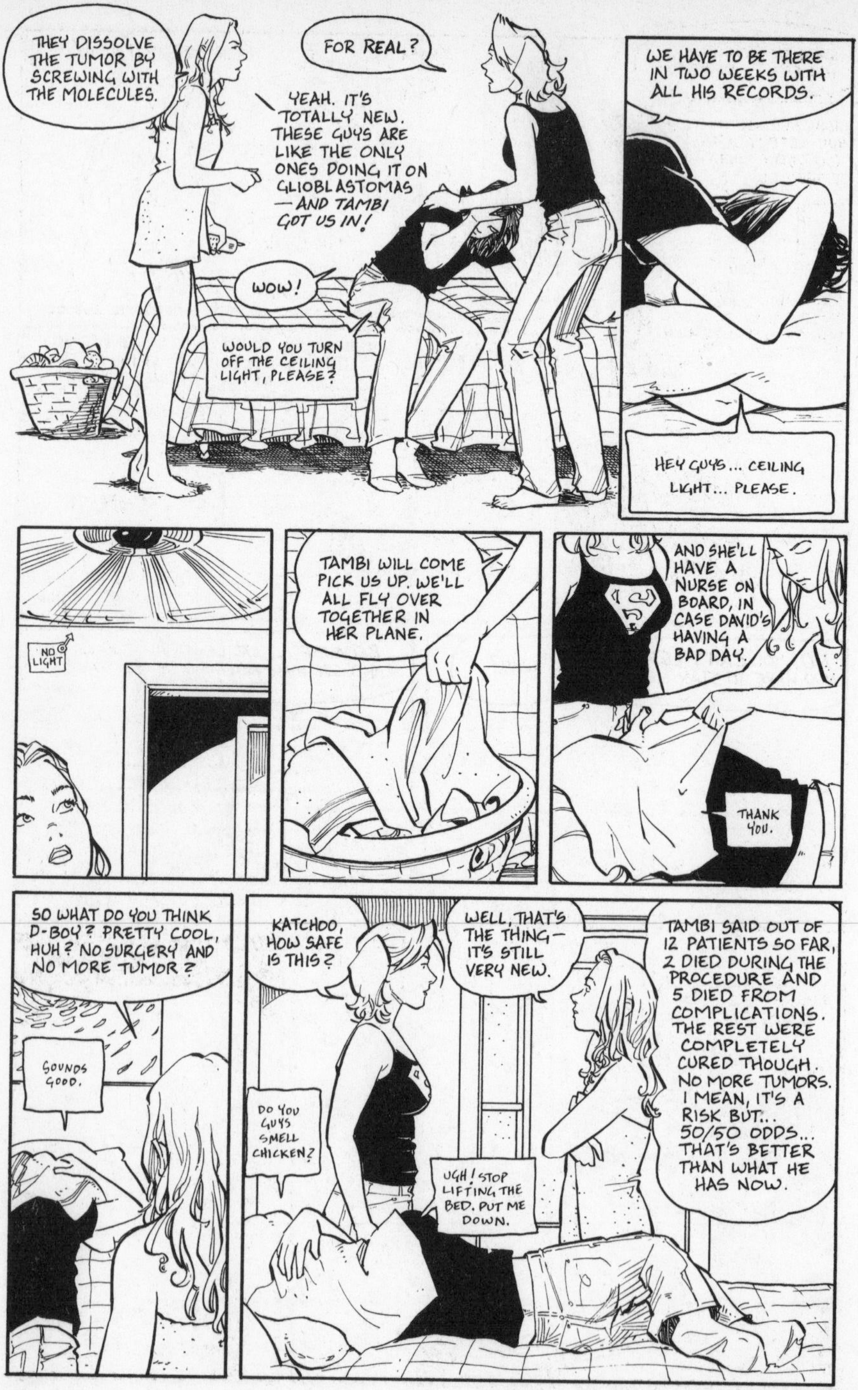
THEY DISSOLVE THE TUMOR BY SCREWING WITH THE MOLECULES.
FOR REAL?
YEAH. IT'S TOTALLY NEW. THESE GUYS ARE LIKE THE ONLY ONES DOING IT ON GLIOBLASTOMAS — AND TAMBI GOT US IN!
WOW!
WOULD YOU TURN OFF THE CEILING LIGHT, PLEASE?
WE HAVE TO BE THERE IN TWO WEEKS WITH ALL HIS RECORDS.
HEY GUYS... CEILING LIGHT... PLEASE.
NO LIGHT
TAMBI WILL COME PICK US UP. WE'LL ALL FLY OVER TOGETHER IN HER PLANE.
AND SHE'LL HAVE A NURSE ON BOARD, IN CASE DAVID'S HAVING A BAD DAY.
THANK YOU.
SO WHAT DO YOU THINK D-BOY? PRETTY COOL, HUH? NO SURGERY AND NO MORE TUMOR?
SOUNDS GOOD.
KATCHOO, HOW SAFE IS THIS?
WELL, THAT'S THE THING— IT'S STILL VERY NEW.
TAMBI SAID OUT OF 12 PATIENTS SO FAR, 2 DIED DURING THE PROCEDURE AND 5 DIED FROM COMPLICATIONS. THE REST WERE COMPLETELY CURED THOUGH. NO MORE TUMORS. I MEAN, IT'S A RISK BUT... 50/50 ODDS... THAT'S BETTER THAN WHAT HE HAS NOW.
DO YOU GUYS SMELL CHICKEN?
UGH! STOP LIFTING THE BED. PUT ME DOWN.

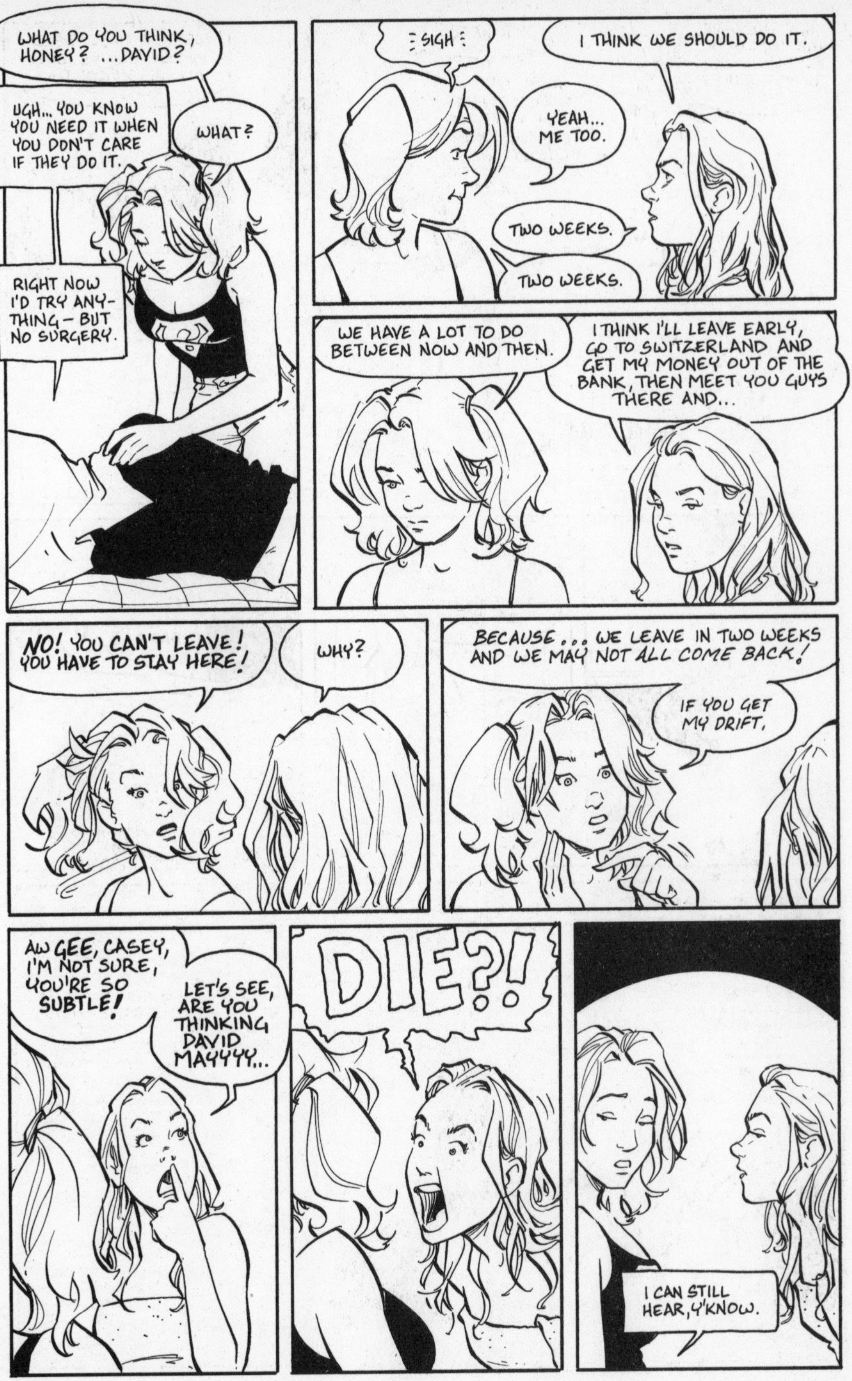

WHAT DO YOU THINK, HONEY? ...DAVID?
UGH... YOU KNOW YOU NEED IT WHEN YOU DON'T CARE IF THEY DO IT.
WHAT?
RIGHT NOW I'D TRY ANY-THING — BUT NO SURGERY.
SIGH
I THINK WE SHOULD DO IT.
YEAH... ME TOO.
TWO WEEKS.
TWO WEEKS.
WE HAVE A LOT TO DO BETWEEN NOW AND THEN.
I THINK I'LL LEAVE EARLY, GO TO SWITZERLAND AND GET MY MONEY OUT OF THE BANK, THEN MEET YOU GUYS THERE AND...
NO! YOU CAN'T LEAVE! YOU HAVE TO STAY HERE!
WHY?
BECAUSE... WE LEAVE IN TWO WEEKS AND WE MAY NOT ALL COME BACK!
IF YOU GET MY DRIFT.
AW GEE, CASEY, I'M NOT SURE, YOU'RE SO SUBTLE!
LET'S SEE, ARE YOU THINKING DAVID MAYYYY...
DIE?!
I CAN STILL HEAR, Y'KNOW.

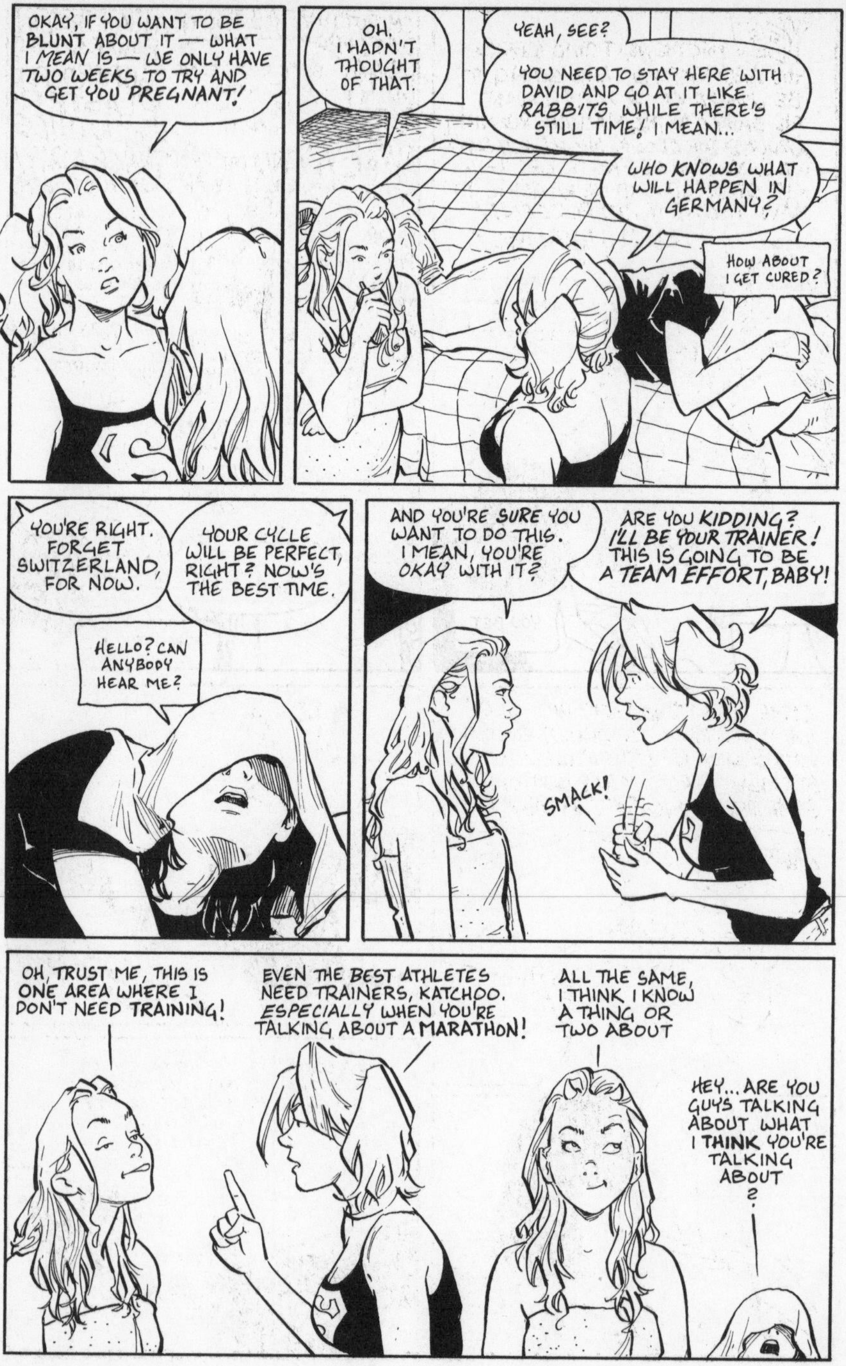
OKAY, IF YOU WANT TO BE BLUNT ABOUT IT — WHAT I MEAN IS — WE ONLY HAVE TWO WEEKS TO TRY AND GET YOU PREGNANT!
OH. I HADN'T THOUGHT OF THAT.
YEAH, SEE?
YOU NEED TO STAY HERE WITH DAVID AND GO AT IT LIKE RABBITS WHILE THERE'S STILL TIME! I MEAN...
WHO KNOWS WHAT WILL HAPPEN IN GERMANY?
HOW ABOUT I GET CURED?
YOU'RE RIGHT. FORGET SWITZERLAND, FOR NOW.
YOUR CYCLE WILL BE PERFECT, RIGHT? NOW'S THE BEST TIME.
HELLO? CAN ANYBODY HEAR ME?
AND YOU'RE SURE YOU WANT TO DO THIS. I MEAN, YOU'RE OKAY WITH IT?
ARE YOU KIDDING? I'LL BE YOUR TRAINER! THIS IS GOING TO BE A TEAM EFFORT, BABY!
SMACK!
OH, TRUST ME, THIS IS ONE AREA WHERE I DON'T NEED TRAINING!
EVEN THE BEST ATHLETES NEED TRAINERS, KATCHOO. ESPECIALLY WHEN YOU'RE TALKING ABOUT A MARATHON!
ALL THE SAME, I THINK I KNOW A THING OR TWO ABOUT
HEY... ARE YOU GUYS TALKING ABOUT WHAT I THINK YOU'RE TALKING ABOUT ?

YES! FOR THE NEXT TWO WEEKS YOU AND KATCHOO ARE GOING TO BE *JOINED AT THE HIP!* I WANT THE BABY MAKING MACHINE RUNNING *AROUND THE CLOCK, NIGHT AND DAY!* WE HAVE *TWO WEEKS* TO GET THIS KID STARTED AND WE'RE GOING TO HAVE TO GIVE IT 210 PERCENT! ARE YOU WITH ME?

MM HMM.

I SAID, ARE YOU WITH ME?!

YOU BET.

I'M PUTTING YOU TWO ON A HIGH PROTEIN DIET! FROM... MEGA... DUTY... EXTRA... VITAMIN... B1! B12 OF THE ALPHABET! HOUR OF THE DAY NO BREAKS

BETTER GET SOME REST, KIDDO... YOU'RE GONNA NEED IT.

RAW EGGS! SUPERDUPER BLASTER-SMOOTHIES TWICE A DAY! WARM BATHS EVERY

YOU GUYS AREN'T REALLY SERIOUS, ARE YOU? 'CAUSE I'M BEGINNING TO WONDER WHAT'S REAL AND...

OH YEAH... I'M REALLY GOING TO SCREW YOUR BRAINS OUT.

AND NO MORE COKES OR DIURETICS!

OYSTERS!

WHAT IF I'M NOT IN THE MOOD?

BOYS OR X-RATED VIDEOS OR LOTIONS

TWO WORDS... BABY JUNE.

OH GOD.

COME ON, KATCHOO—GET DRESSED! WE HAVE TO GO TO WHOLE FOODS AND *STOCK UP!* THEN WE'LL COME STRAIGHT BACK, MAKE OUT OUR SCHEDULE, AND *GET BUSY!*

MMWEOOR!

FWOOMP!

OH LORD... YOU MIGHT WANT TO JUST TAKE ME NOW, BECAUSE IT'S GOING TO BE A LOT HARDER TO FORGIVE ME IN TWO WEEKS.

Griffin Silver's east coast house was hidden in the middle of sixty acres of prime Long Island real estate. Billy Joel and Paul McCartney had homes nearby. After a sad trip to the Caribbean to disperse Griffin's ashes, Brad and I accompanied Nikki back to the Long Island house. Brad met with Griffin's accountants and lawyers because Griffin's will stipulated that his music catalog would be left to his brother to manage. Turns out that even though Griffin's personal career had dimmed, the popularity of his music hadn't. Funny how that works. Maybe that's why Judy Garland drank. Anyway, Griffin's company, Ma Malai Music, was worth a lot of money. With no other immediate family to share the spoils, Brad was rich. He didn't seem very happy about it, though. He and Griffin had been very close.

I didn't like staying at the house after Griffin died; it just wasn't the same. Brad spent several days in meetings and some general planning sessions that had nothing to do with me, so I wandered the grounds and poked through the library. A full time staff of four ran the house and I spent a lot of time just hanging out in the kitchen, talking to the chef, who taught me how to make gravy.

After three days I decided I didn't need to be there any longer. I hardly saw Brad, we slept in separate bedrooms, and when we did see each other we barely spoke. Nikki kept to herself, sleeping late and taking one meal a day alone on a private balcony. Griffin had left the business to Brad, but he left this house to Nikki, along with a management fund to keep it going for the rest of her days. She wasn't sure if she was going to keep it, but for now it was home and every room reminded her of Griffin and better days.

The chauffeur was putting my bags in the car to take me to the airport when Nikki came to say goodbye. She asked me to walk with her. We strolled the gardens behind the house talking about nothing in particular. The air was chilly but the sun was warm and bright. A butterfly danced above the flowers and birds chattered in the trees, resting on their way south.

At the far end of the garden, Nikki took my hand and led me into the trees and over a hill. On the other side was a small cottage, sitting peacefully in a clearing. It looked to me like something in a fairy tale. "Griffin's hideaway," Nikki smiled. I followed her to the front door.

"Griffin left me too much," she said. "I don't know what to do with it all."

"Most people would say that's a nice problem to have," I replied.

"I'd rather have Griffin."

"We need to watch the time, Nikki. I don't want to miss the plane."

"It's a private plane, Francine. He'll wait. This will only take a minute." Nikki took a key from her pocket. "Griffin liked art, you know. He bought a lot of it over the years. Matisse, Frazetta…you ever heard of Frazetta?"

"No."

"Neither had I until I met Griffin. This lock is…" She fidgeted with the door a moment before the key finally turned. "There, got it."

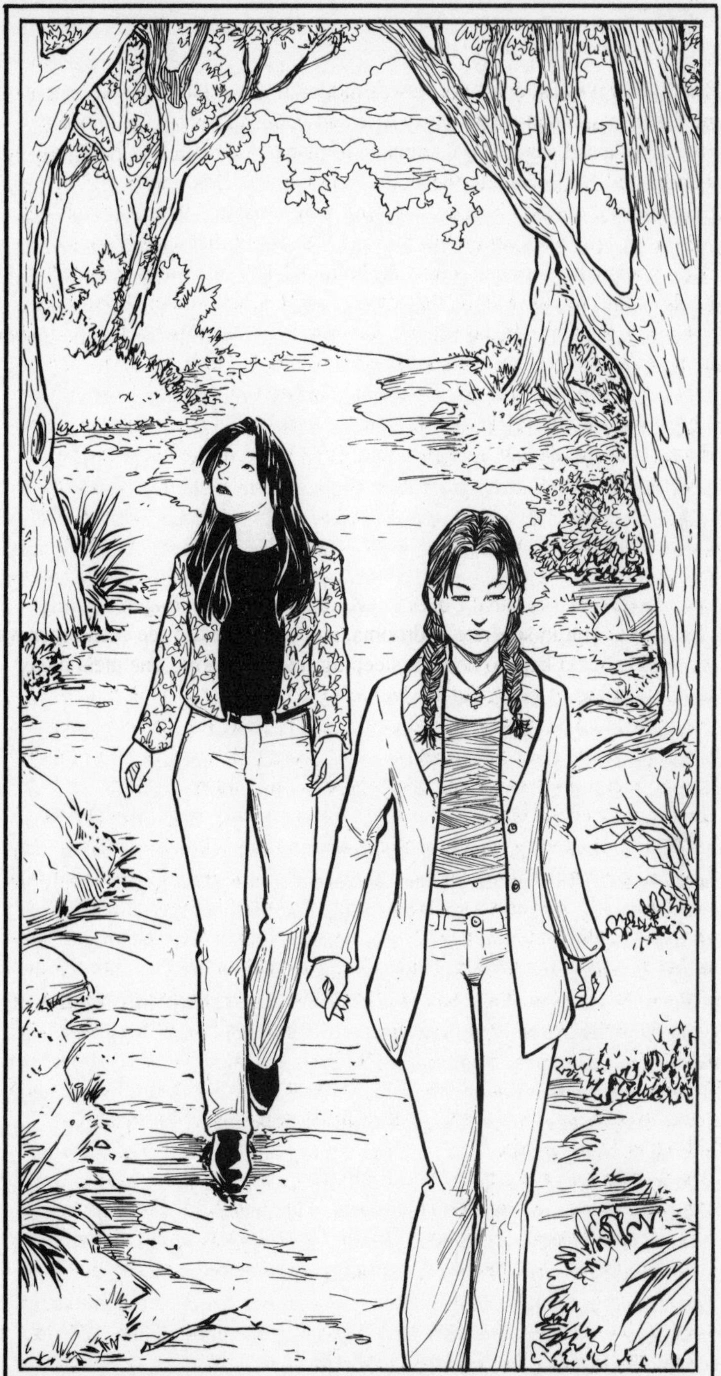

Nikki opened the door and I followed her into the room. It was dark inside, but even in the dim light I could see a massive form lurking in the shadows. Before I could recognize what I was looking at, the hair stood up on the back of my neck, as if my subconscious knew but my mind was trying to catch up.

"Griffin liked to support new artists as well," Nikki continued. She went from one window to another, opening the curtains, forcing the form to come out of the shadows. "He'd heard good things about this artist and bought this piece anonymously at her first showing. I asked him why he bought such a huge painting and he said he didn't know it was going to be so big, he just liked the title."

I stared at the giant woman who had emerged from the shadows and owned one entire wall of the room. Oh my god… it was me.

"'Portrait of Francine', by Katchoo. You've heard of her, right?"

I couldn't answer. I was speechless. I felt the arm of a chair beside me and sat down. I couldn't take my eyes from the painting. Katchoo…my god.

I was aware of Nikki watching me. "Fills the room, doesn't it?" She turned to the painting and walked up to it the way a child might approach a resting locomotive. Her hand reached out and touched the edge of the canvas. She looked tiny next to the woman, next to me, as I sat naked, legs crossed, arms folded, hair long and flowing in the breeze. I had never posed for this but Katchoo painted it anyway; she knew me so well.

"Griffin loved this painting, Francine. I think he felt something for you. Not that he would ever say anything because of Brad, and me, but I think you appealed to the Byron in him. Know what I mean?"

Nikki paused. She looked at me, waiting for my response but no words came. She smiled. "Some people would look at this painting and see a naked woman. A really big, naked woman. But Griffin saw something else. He was such a romantic." I saw Nikki's expression change; a weight pulled the joy from her face. "Griffin and I loved each other, but we never had this," she gestured to the painting. "We never had magic."

I remembered to breath. I took a deep breath and felt the tension ease from my shoulders. Nikki walked back across the room and stood beside me. In the distance, beyond the nearby birds, I heard a lawnmower. The alarm within me subsided, leaving me with a shaky sense of awe. I mean, I wasn't comfortable looking at a gigantic picture of me naked, but the sheer impact and… and… the *beauty* of the painting could not be denied. The painting revealed more about Katchoo than it did of me. For the first time I saw a side of my once dear friend that I had never seen before: genius.

Nikki's voice broke the silence. "Look," she said, in a quiet voice, "The artist loves this woman. It's not a painting, it's an embrace."

Something in Nikki's voice made me look at her. She was talking about love but her voice was hard. Her eyes met mine and didn't blink. "You're not going to find this twice in one life, Francine."

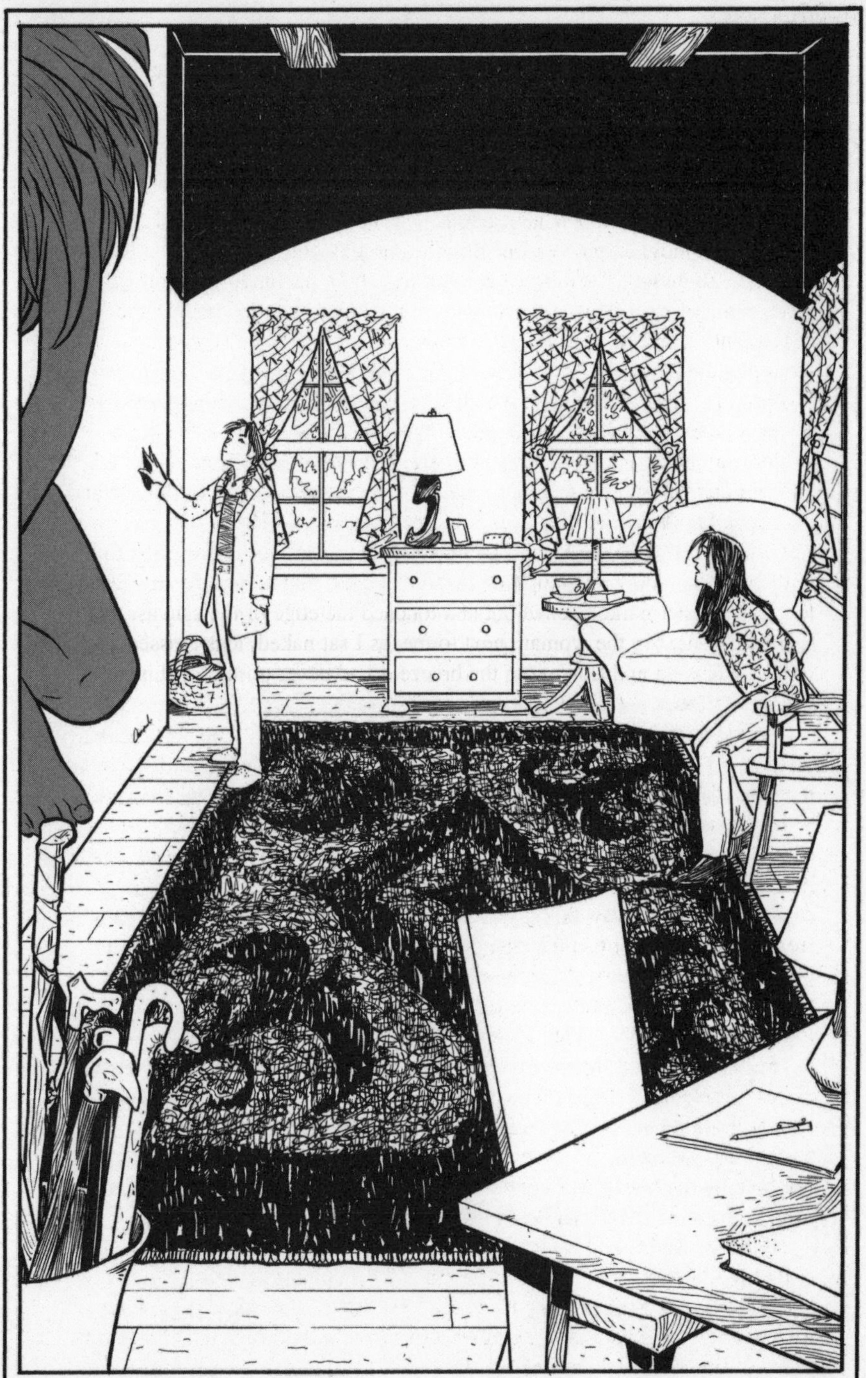

Nikki stepped back to the window and studied the painting. "Anyway, I thought you might like to have it. Griffin paid a lot of money for it, but it's yours if you want it."

"Oh Nikki, I couldn't."

"Sure you could."

"I... it's so big. I don't have room for it."

Nikki turned and looked at me like I was the slowest kid in class. "But that's the whole point of things like this, isn't it? For something like this... you *make room* in your life."

I blinked.

Something about the sight of her by the window, trying to get me to see a fact of life too big to be ignored, while the sun and shadows fought across her face... this wasn't a game anymore. We didn't have a lifetime to work things out, we had whatever was left, remnants. We were getting older. We were dying, one by one. It was possible for me to spend whatever was left of my life doing the wrong thing, or worse, nothing.

I asked Griffin once what it was like, being famous. He said most people don't lead lives, they accept them. Sitting between the towering image of Katchoo's dream girl and the disappointment on Nikki's face, I saw myself clearly for the very first time. It was as if I had been sleepwalking all these years and a spell had been broken. My life flashed before my eyes—high school, Katchoo, the school play, the college scandal, Katchoo's return to my life, Freddie, David, our little rent house above the garage, Katchoo's Parker trouble, the night we almost had sex, the arguments, the fights, running away, the plane crash, nursing David, the year at my mother's house, meeting Brad, being kidnapped, trying to get back with Katchoo and finding her with Casey, running back to Brad, our wedding day and saying goodbye to Katchoo for what I thought was the last time. All the awkwardness, the uncertainty, the indecision, the awful act of keeping Katchoo at arm's length for years while I enjoyed the attention but not the price—I saw it all as if it had been written down and shown to me in a book. Then that night in the studio when we made up... or rather, she forgave me.

I'd been a fool.

If I died today and found myself facing God tonight, He'd look at me and say, "I gave you all those chances at happiness. Why didn't you take them?" And I'd have no answer. My reasons all looked like excuses now. I had forced the love of my life to live without me. Meanwhile, I was drifting through the lives of other people, alone, unhappy, losing the inner joy that once defined me. And I had no one to blame but myself.

I'd been a fool.

I stood up.

I took my life back.

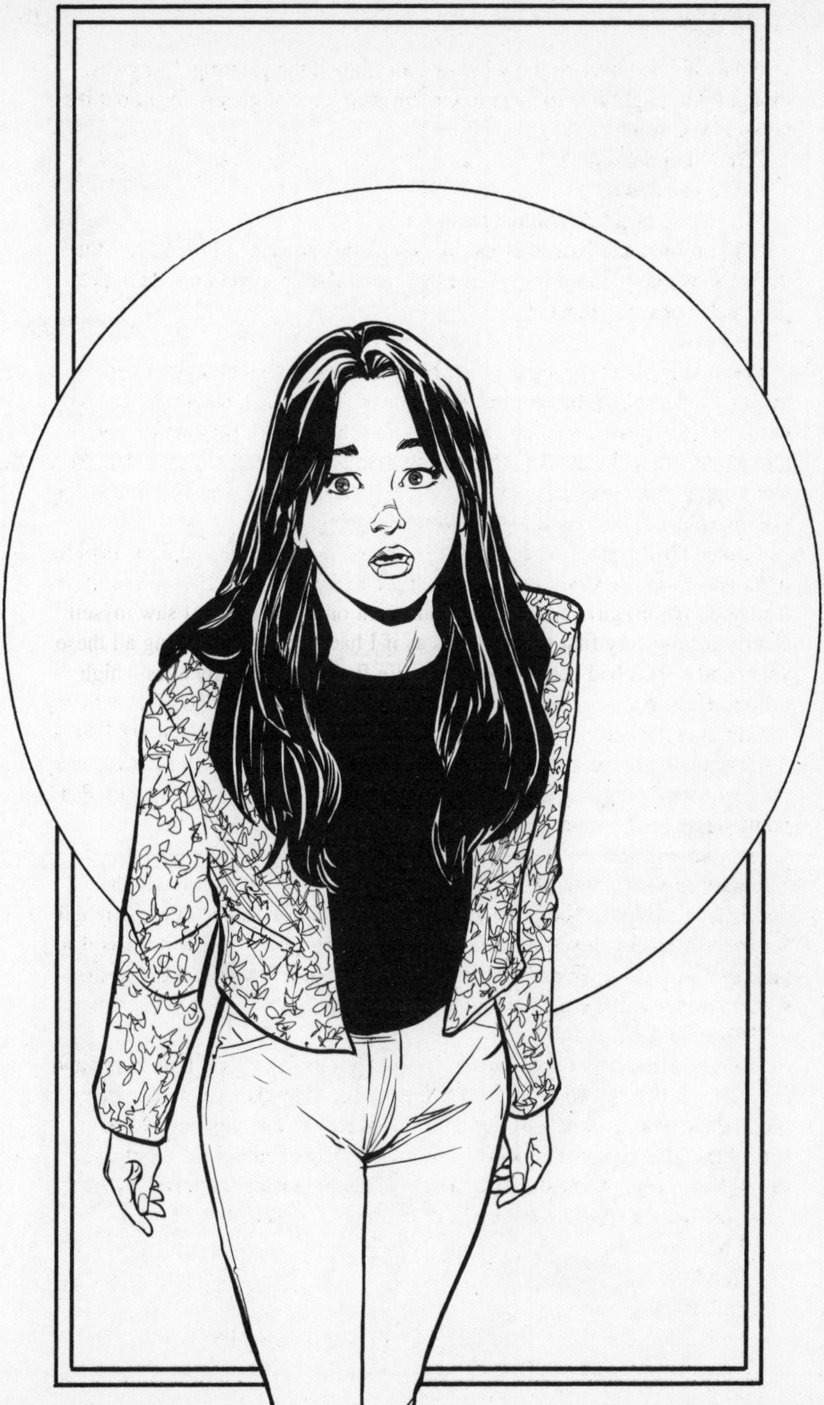

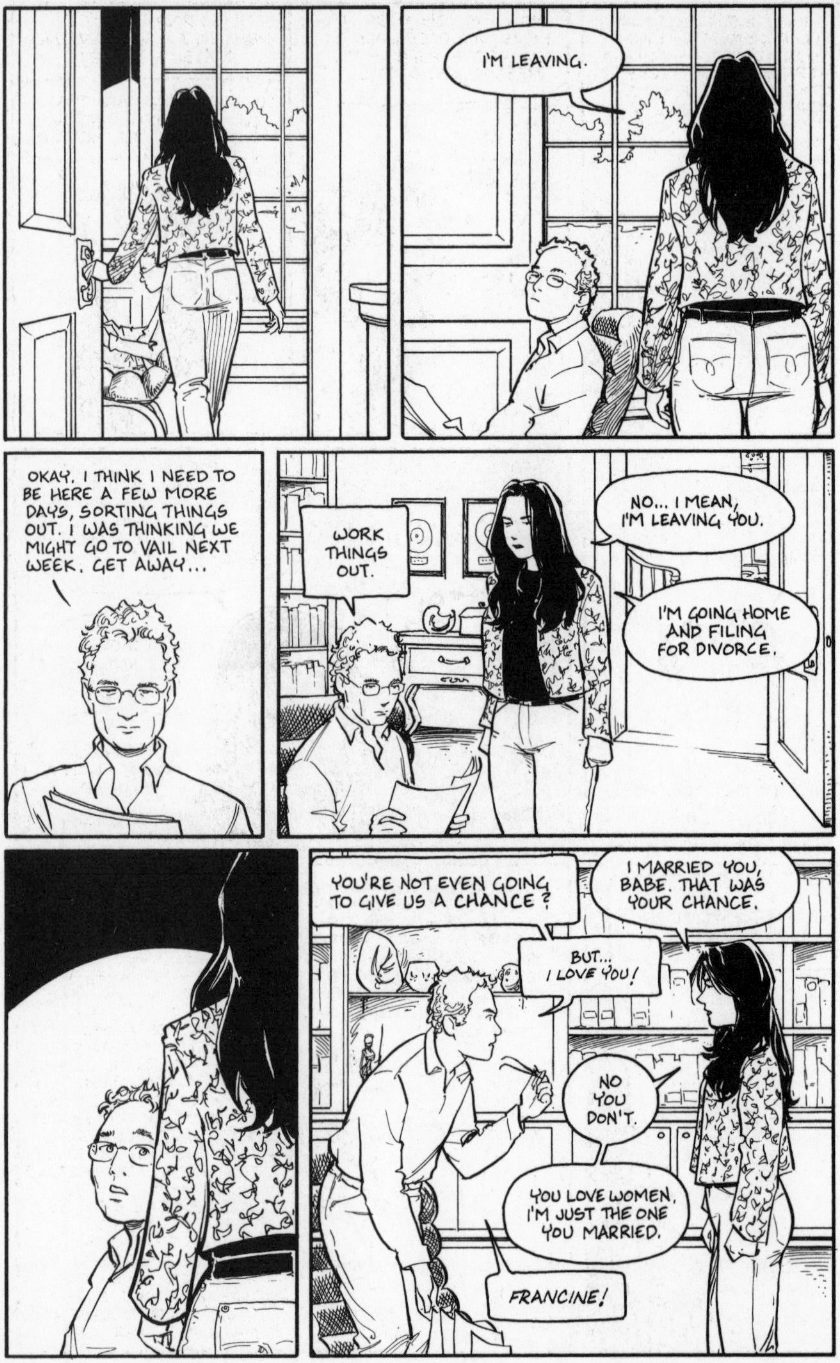
I'M LEAVING.
OKAY. I THINK I NEED TO BE HERE A FEW MORE DAYS, SORTING THINGS OUT. I WAS THINKING WE MIGHT GO TO VAIL NEXT WEEK. GET AWAY...
WORK THINGS OUT.
NO... I MEAN, I'M LEAVING YOU.
I'M GOING HOME AND FILING FOR DIVORCE.
YOU'RE NOT EVEN GOING TO GIVE US A CHANCE?
I MARRIED YOU, BABE. THAT WAS YOUR CHANCE.
BUT... I LOVE YOU!
NO YOU DON'T.
YOU LOVE WOMEN. I'M JUST THE ONE YOU MARRIED.
FRANCINE!

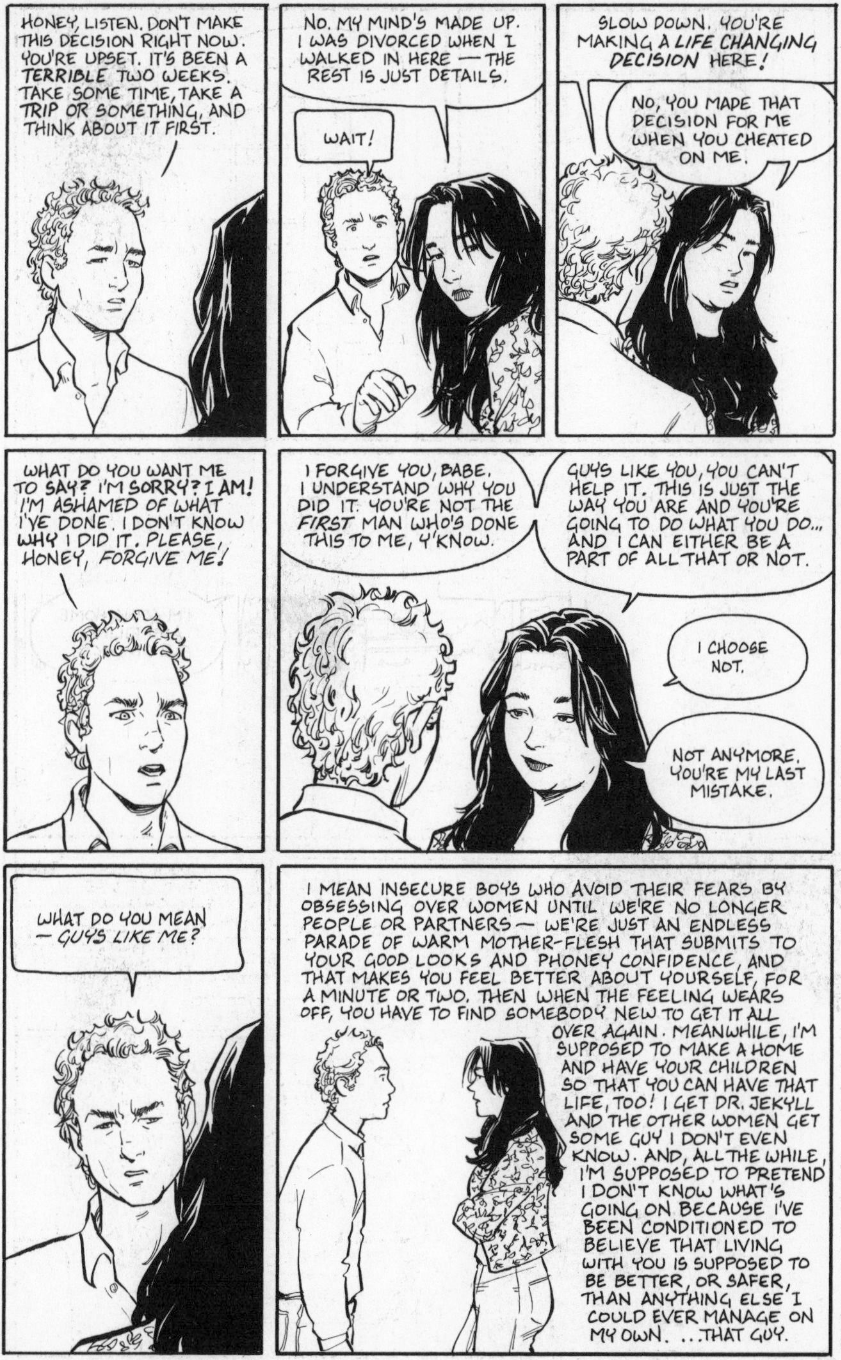
HONEY, LISTEN. DON'T MAKE THIS DECISION RIGHT NOW. YOU'RE UPSET. IT'S BEEN A TERRIBLE TWO WEEKS. TAKE SOME TIME, TAKE A TRIP OR SOMETHING, AND THINK ABOUT IT FIRST.
NO. MY MIND'S MADE UP. I WAS DIVORCED WHEN I WALKED IN HERE — THE REST IS JUST DETAILS.
WAIT!
SLOW DOWN. YOU'RE MAKING A LIFE CHANGING DECISION HERE!
NO, YOU MADE THAT DECISION FOR ME WHEN YOU CHEATED ON ME.
WHAT DO YOU WANT ME TO SAY? I'M SORRY? I AM! I'M ASHAMED OF WHAT I'VE DONE. I DON'T KNOW WHY I DID IT. PLEASE, HONEY, FORGIVE ME!
I FORGIVE YOU, BABE. I UNDERSTAND WHY YOU DID IT. YOU'RE NOT THE FIRST MAN WHO'S DONE THIS TO ME, Y'KNOW.
GUYS LIKE YOU, YOU CAN'T HELP IT. THIS IS JUST THE WAY YOU ARE AND YOU'RE GOING TO DO WHAT YOU DO... AND I CAN EITHER BE A PART OF ALL THAT OR NOT.
I CHOOSE NOT.
NOT ANYMORE. YOU'RE MY LAST MISTAKE.
WHAT DO YOU MEAN — GUYS LIKE ME?
I MEAN INSECURE BOYS WHO AVOID THEIR FEARS BY OBSESSING OVER WOMEN UNTIL WE'RE NO LONGER PEOPLE OR PARTNERS — WE'RE JUST AN ENDLESS PARADE OF WARM MOTHER-FLESH THAT SUBMITS TO YOUR GOOD LOOKS AND PHONEY CONFIDENCE, AND THAT MAKES YOU FEEL BETTER ABOUT YOURSELF, FOR A MINUTE OR TWO. THEN WHEN THE FEELING WEARS OFF, YOU HAVE TO FIND SOMEBODY NEW TO GET IT ALL OVER AGAIN. MEANWHILE, I'M SUPPOSED TO MAKE A HOME AND HAVE YOUR CHILDREN SO THAT YOU CAN HAVE THAT LIFE, TOO! I GET DR. JEKYLL AND THE OTHER WOMEN GET SOME GUY I DON'T EVEN KNOW. AND, ALL THE WHILE, I'M SUPPOSED TO PRETEND I DON'T KNOW WHAT'S GOING ON BECAUSE I'VE BEEN CONDITIONED TO BELIEVE THAT LIVING WITH YOU IS SUPPOSED TO BE BETTER, OR SAFER, THAN ANYTHING ELSE I COULD EVER MANAGE ON MY OWN. ...THAT GUY.

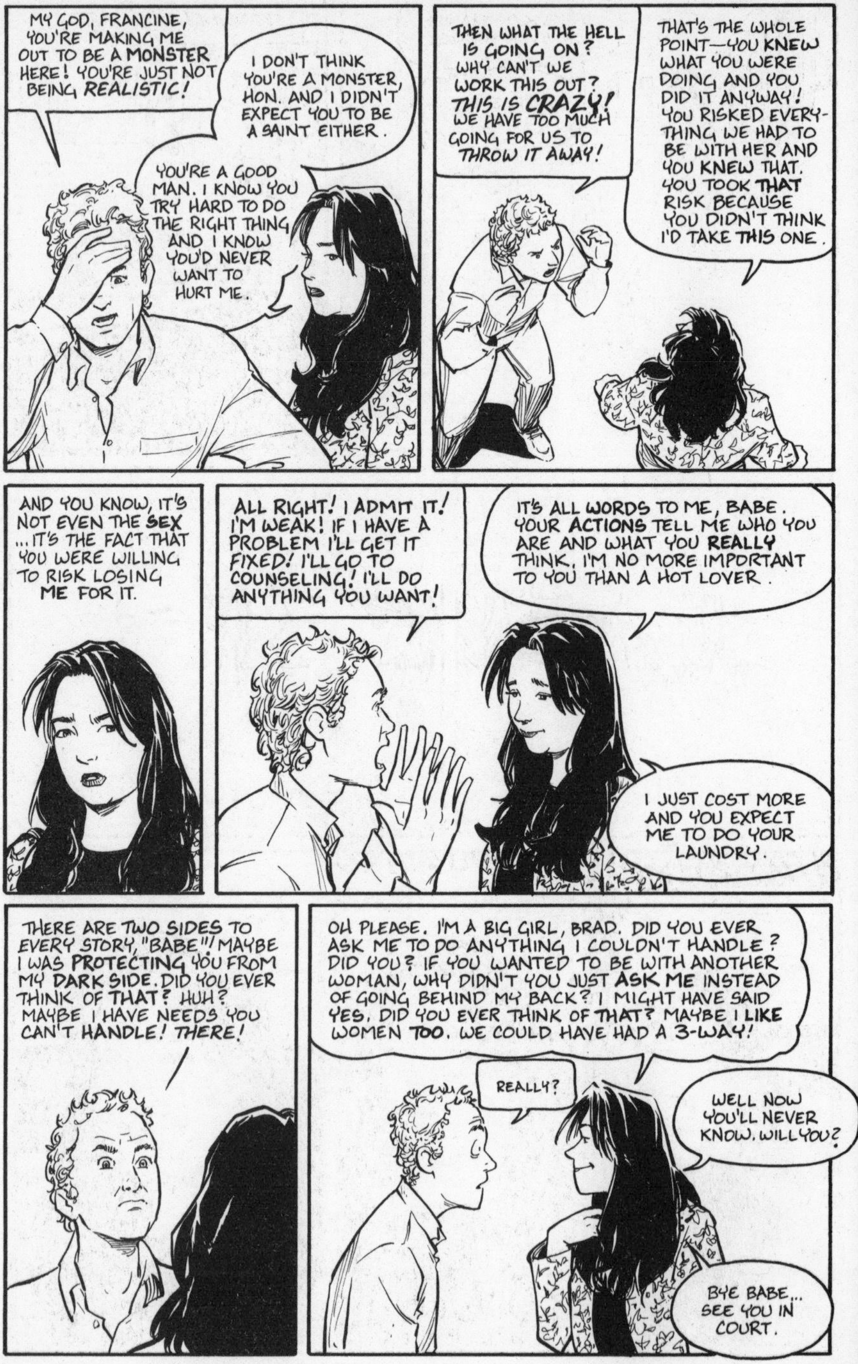

MY GOD, FRANCINE, YOU'RE MAKING ME OUT TO BE A MONSTER HERE! YOU'RE JUST NOT BEING REALISTIC!
I DON'T THINK YOU'RE A MONSTER, HON. AND I DIDN'T EXPECT YOU TO BE A SAINT EITHER.
YOU'RE A GOOD MAN. I KNOW YOU TRY HARD TO DO THE RIGHT THING AND I KNOW YOU'D NEVER WANT TO HURT ME.
THEN WHAT THE HELL IS GOING ON? WHY CAN'T WE WORK THIS OUT? THIS IS CRAZY! WE HAVE TOO MUCH GOING FOR US TO THROW IT AWAY!
THAT'S THE WHOLE POINT—YOU KNEW WHAT YOU WERE DOING AND YOU DID IT ANYWAY! YOU RISKED EVERYTHING WE HAD TO BE WITH HER AND YOU KNEW THAT. YOU TOOK THAT RISK BECAUSE YOU DIDN'T THINK I'D TAKE THIS ONE.
AND YOU KNOW, IT'S NOT EVEN THE SEX ...IT'S THE FACT THAT YOU WERE WILLING TO RISK LOSING ME FOR IT.
ALL RIGHT! I ADMIT IT! I'M WEAK! IF I HAVE A PROBLEM I'LL GET IT FIXED! I'LL GO TO COUNSELING! I'LL DO ANYTHING YOU WANT!
IT'S ALL WORDS TO ME, BABE. YOUR ACTIONS TELL ME WHO YOU ARE AND WHAT YOU REALLY THINK. I'M NO MORE IMPORTANT TO YOU THAN A HOT LOVER.
I JUST COST MORE AND YOU EXPECT ME TO DO YOUR LAUNDRY.
THERE ARE TWO SIDES TO EVERY STORY, "BABE"! MAYBE I WAS PROTECTING YOU FROM MY DARK SIDE. DID YOU EVER THINK OF THAT? HUH? MAYBE I HAVE NEEDS YOU CAN'T HANDLE! THERE!
OH PLEASE. I'M A BIG GIRL, BRAD. DID YOU EVER ASK ME TO DO ANYTHING I COULDN'T HANDLE? DID YOU? IF YOU WANTED TO BE WITH ANOTHER WOMAN, WHY DIDN'T YOU JUST ASK ME INSTEAD OF GOING BEHIND MY BACK? I MIGHT HAVE SAID YES. DID YOU EVER THINK OF THAT? MAYBE I LIKE WOMEN TOO. WE COULD HAVE HAD A 3-WAY!
REALLY?
WELL NOW YOU'LL NEVER KNOW. WILL YOU?
BYE BABE... SEE YOU IN COURT.

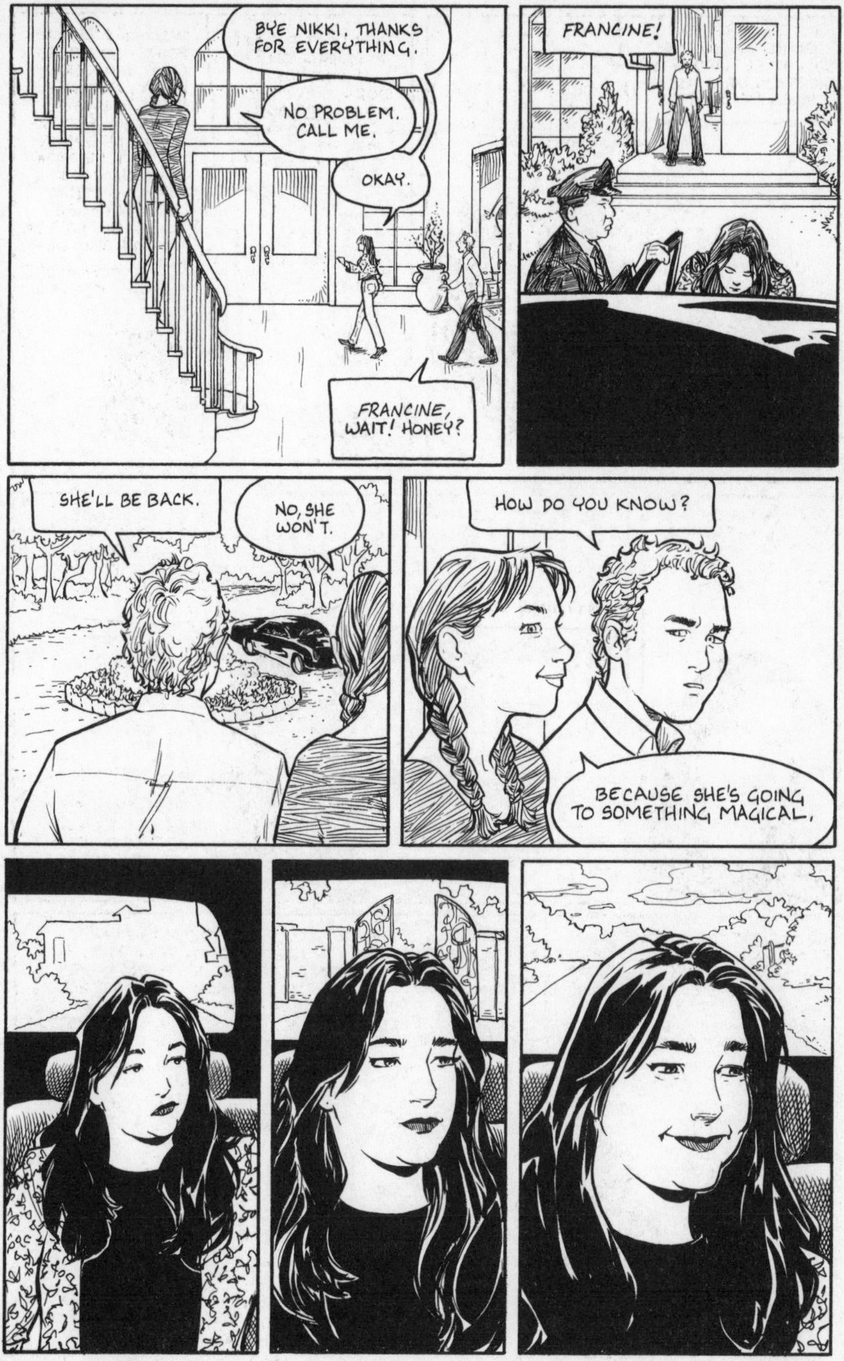
BYE NIKKI. THANKS FOR EVERYTHING.
NO PROBLEM. CALL ME.
OKAY.
FRANCINE, WAIT! HONEY?
FRANCINE!
SHE'LL BE BACK.
NO, SHE WON'T.
HOW DO YOU KNOW?
BECAUSE SHE'S GOING TO SOMETHING MAGICAL.

Fool me once, shame on you.
Fool me twice, shame on me.
Try it again and I'll kick your ass
and trash your car and spam your
email and post your phone
number on myspace and
write your unauthorized
biography and train your
dog to poop when the phone
rings then sign you up for
every call list in the country.
—Katchoo

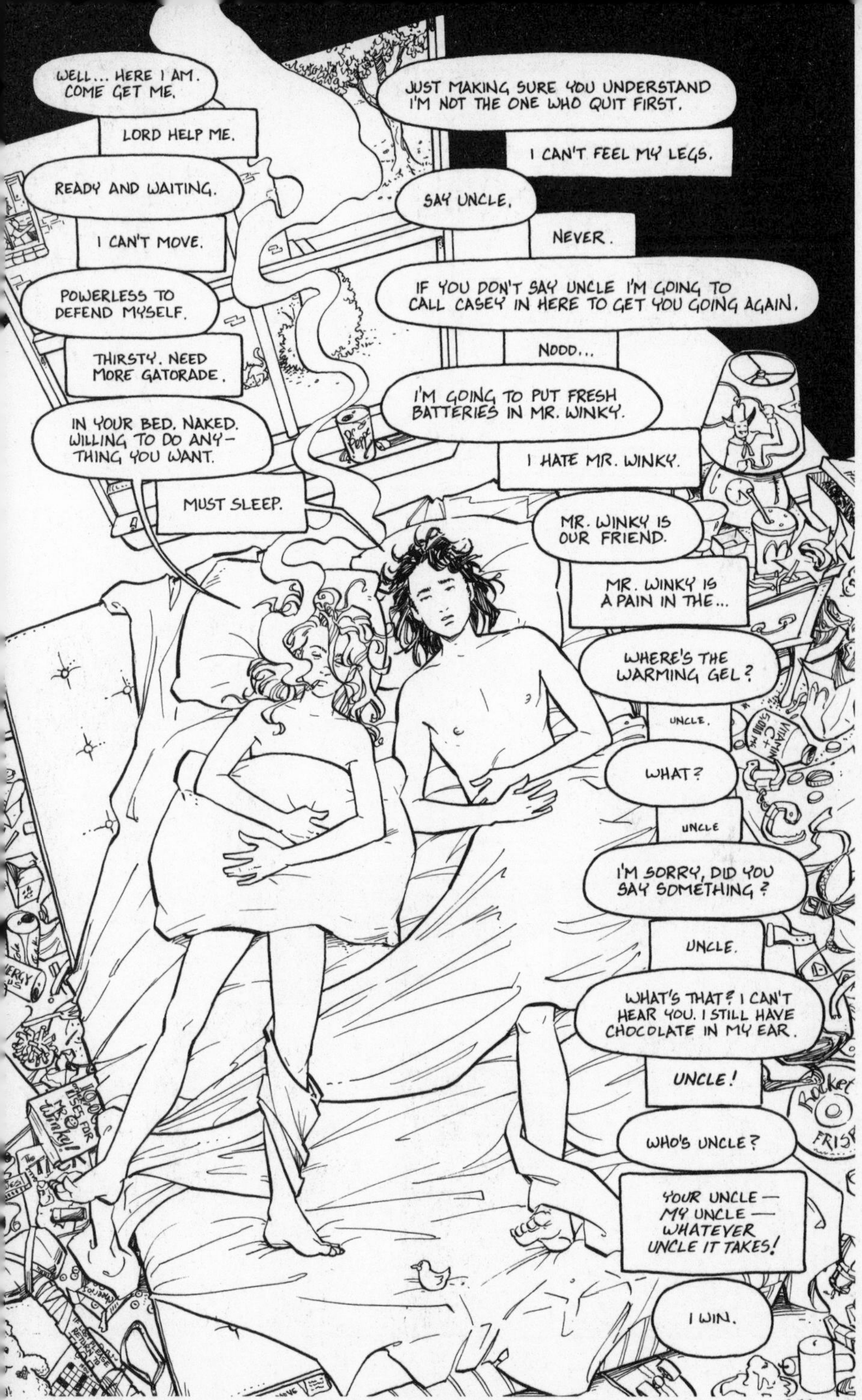
WELL... HERE I AM. COME GET ME.
LORD HELP ME.
READY AND WAITING.
I CAN'T MOVE.
POWERLESS TO DEFEND MYSELF.
THIRSTY. NEED MORE GATORADE.
IN YOUR BED. NAKED. WILLING TO DO ANY-THING YOU WANT.
MUST SLEEP.
JUST MAKING SURE YOU UNDERSTAND I'M NOT THE ONE WHO QUIT FIRST.
I CAN'T FEEL MY LEGS.
SAY UNCLE.
NEVER.
IF YOU DON'T SAY UNCLE I'M GOING TO CALL CASEY IN HERE TO GET YOU GOING AGAIN.
NOOO...
I'M GOING TO PUT FRESH BATTERIES IN MR. WINKY.
I HATE MR. WINKY.
MR. WINKY IS OUR FRIEND.
MR. WINKY IS A PAIN IN THE...
WHERE'S THE WARMING GEL?
UNCLE.
WHAT?
UNCLE
I'M SORRY, DID YOU SAY SOMETHING?
UNCLE.
WHAT'S THAT? I CAN'T HEAR YOU. I STILL HAVE CHOCOLATE IN MY EAR.
UNCLE!
WHO'S UNCLE?
YOUR UNCLE— MY UNCLE— WHATEVER UNCLE IT TAKES!
I WIN.

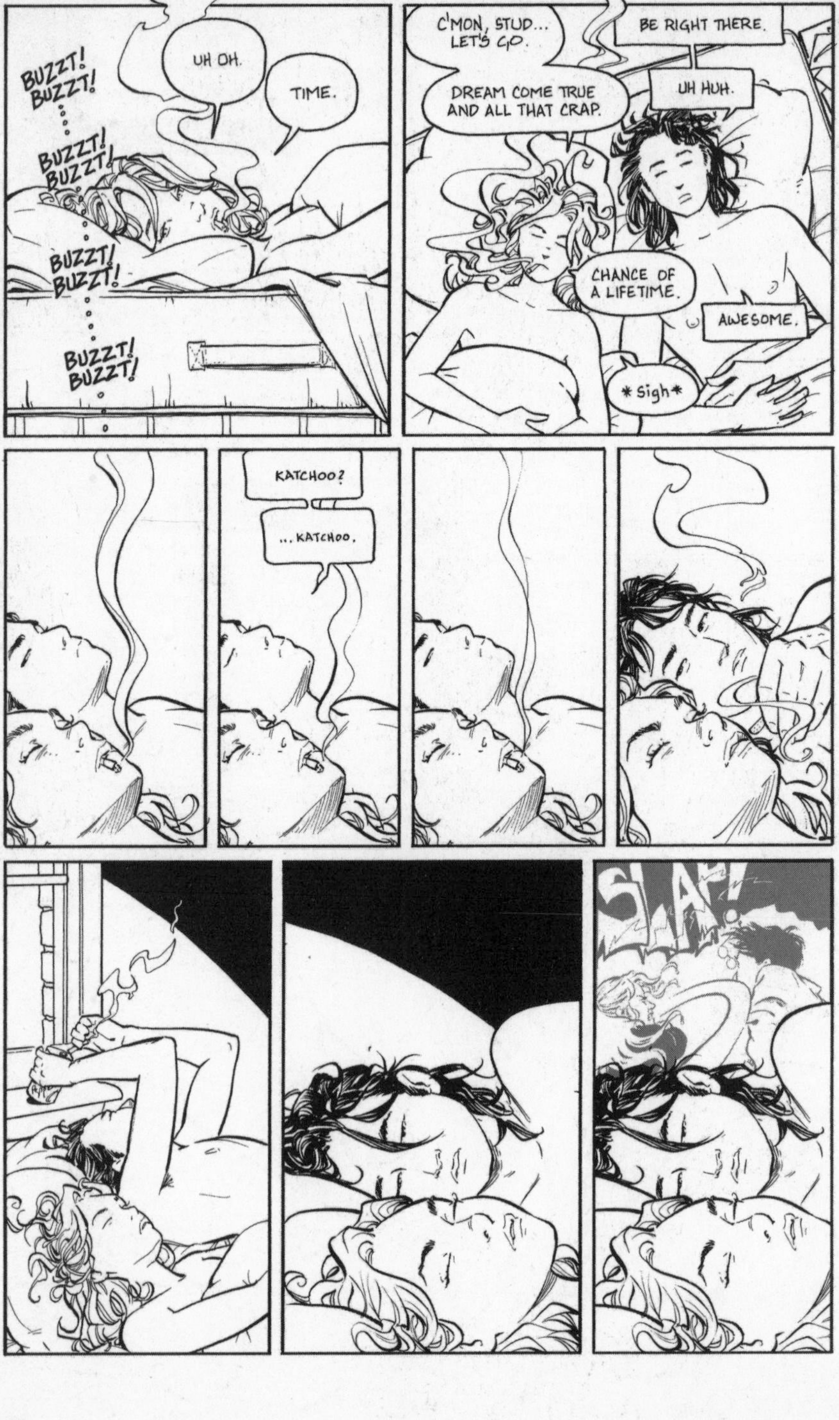
BUZZT! BUZZT!
BUZZT! BUZZT!
BUZZT! BUZZT!
BUZZT! BUZZT!
UH OH.
TIME.
C'MON, STUD... LET'S GO.
BE RIGHT THERE.
DREAM COME TRUE AND ALL THAT CRAP.
UH HUH.
CHANCE OF A LIFETIME.
AWESOME.
Sigh
KATCHOO?
...KATCHOO.

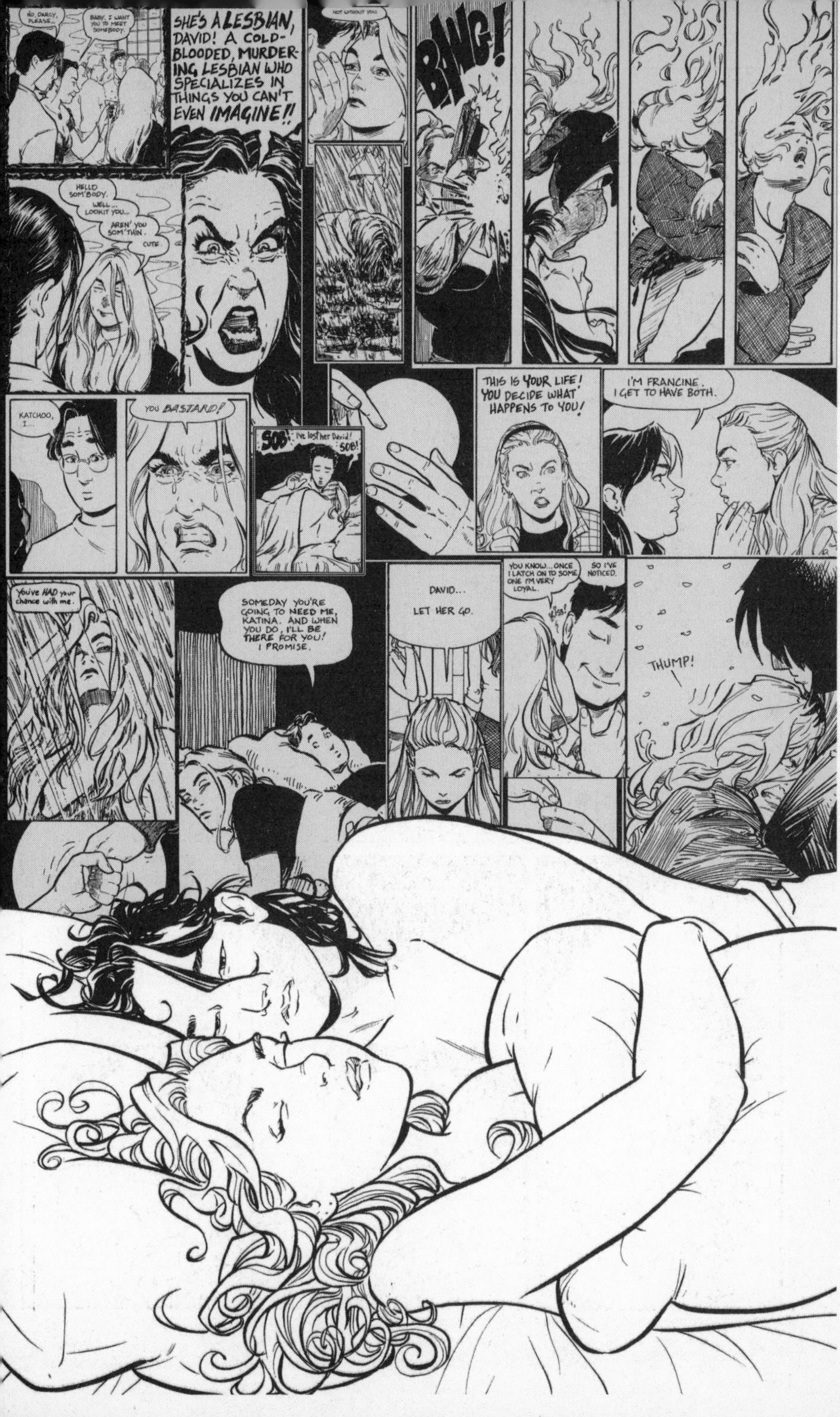

NO, DARCY, PLEASE...
BABY, I WANT YOU TO MEET SOMEBODY.
SHE'S A LESBIAN, DAVID! A COLD-BLOODED, MURDERING LESBIAN WHO SPECIALIZES IN THINGS YOU CAN'T EVEN IMAGINE!!
NOT WITHOUT YOU.
BANG!
HELLO SOM'BODY. WELL... LOOKIT YOU... AREN' YOU SOM'THIN. CUTE.
KATCHOO, I...
YOU BASTARD!
SOB! I've lost her David! SOB!
THIS IS YOUR LIFE! YOU DECIDE WHAT HAPPENS TO YOU!
I'M FRANCINE. I GET TO HAVE BOTH.
You've HAD your chance with me.
SOMEDAY YOU'RE GOING TO NEED ME, KATINA. AND WHEN YOU DO, I'LL BE THERE FOR YOU! I PROMISE.
DAVID... LET HER GO.
YOU KNOW... ONCE I LATCH ON TO SOME ONE I'M VERY LOYAL.
SO I'VE NOTICED.
THUMP!

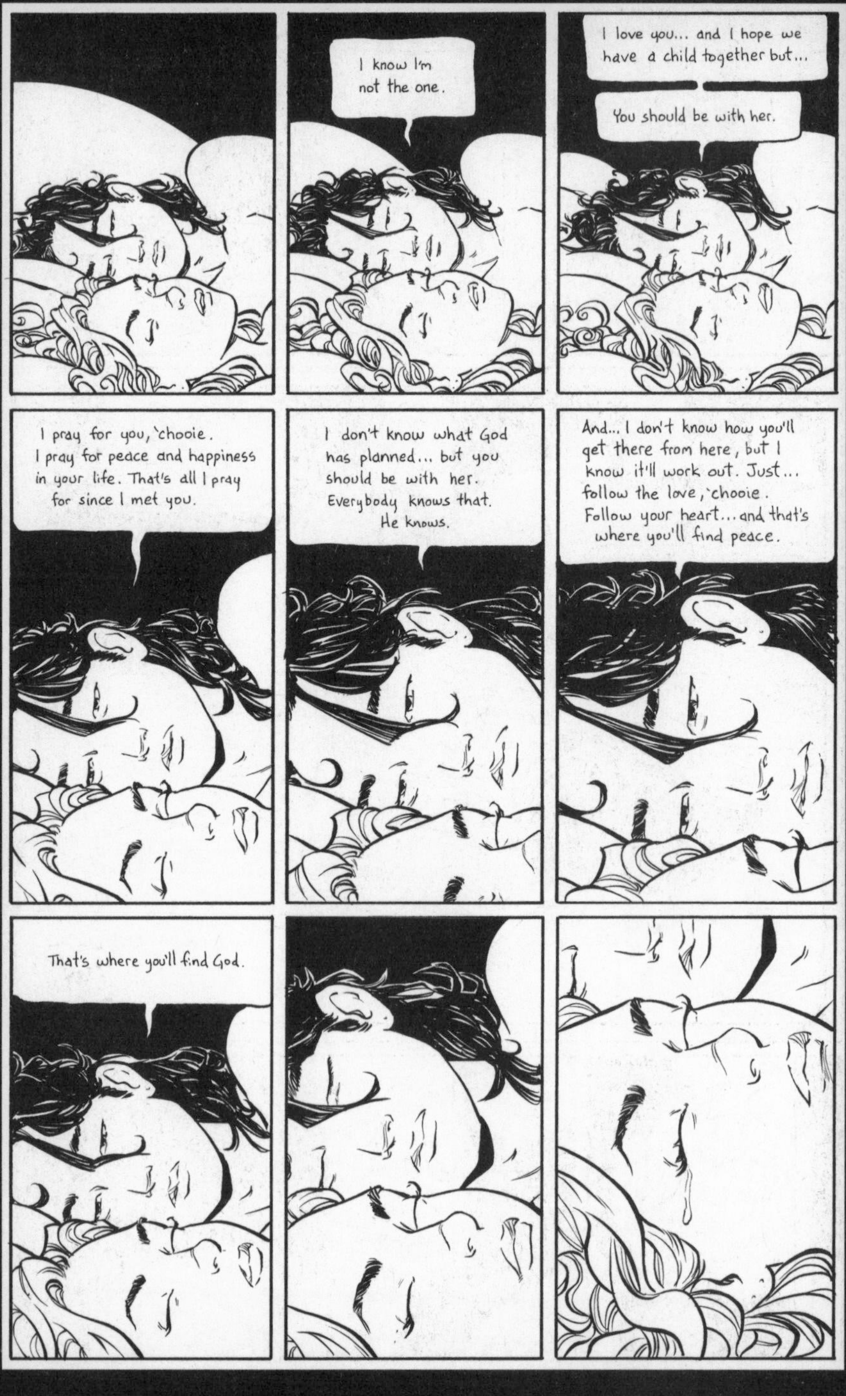
I know I'm not the one.
I love you... and I hope we have a child together but...
You should be with her.
I pray for you, 'chooie. I pray for peace and happiness in your life. That's all I pray for since I met you.
I don't know what God has planned... but you should be with her. Everybody knows that. He knows.
And... I don't know how you'll get there from here, but I know it'll work out. Just... follow the love, 'chooie. Follow your heart... and that's where you'll find peace.
That's where you'll find God.

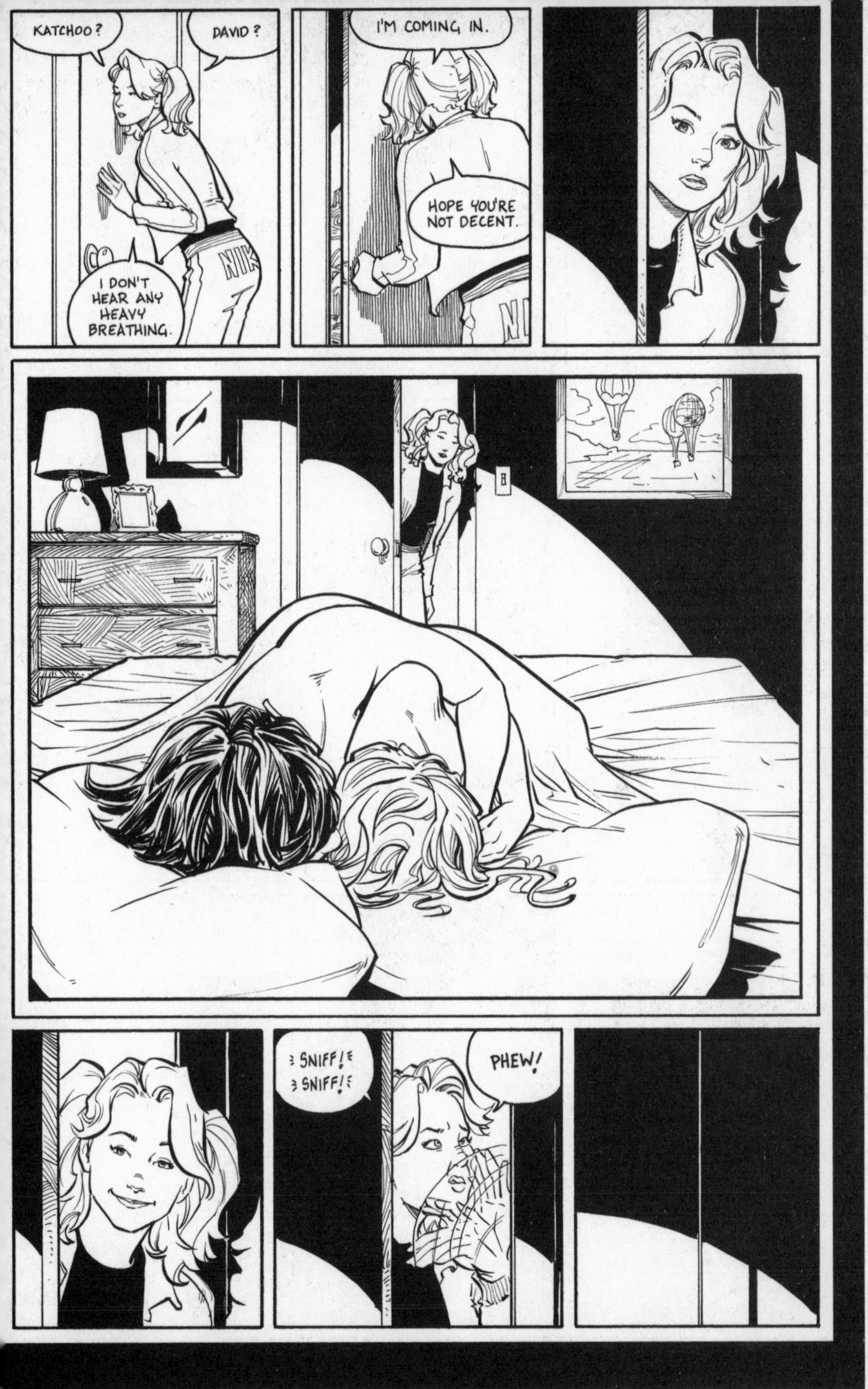
KATCHOO?
DAVID?
I DON'T HEAR ANY HEAVY BREATHING.
I'M COMING IN.
HOPE YOU'RE NOT DECENT.
SNIFF! SNIFF!
PHEW!

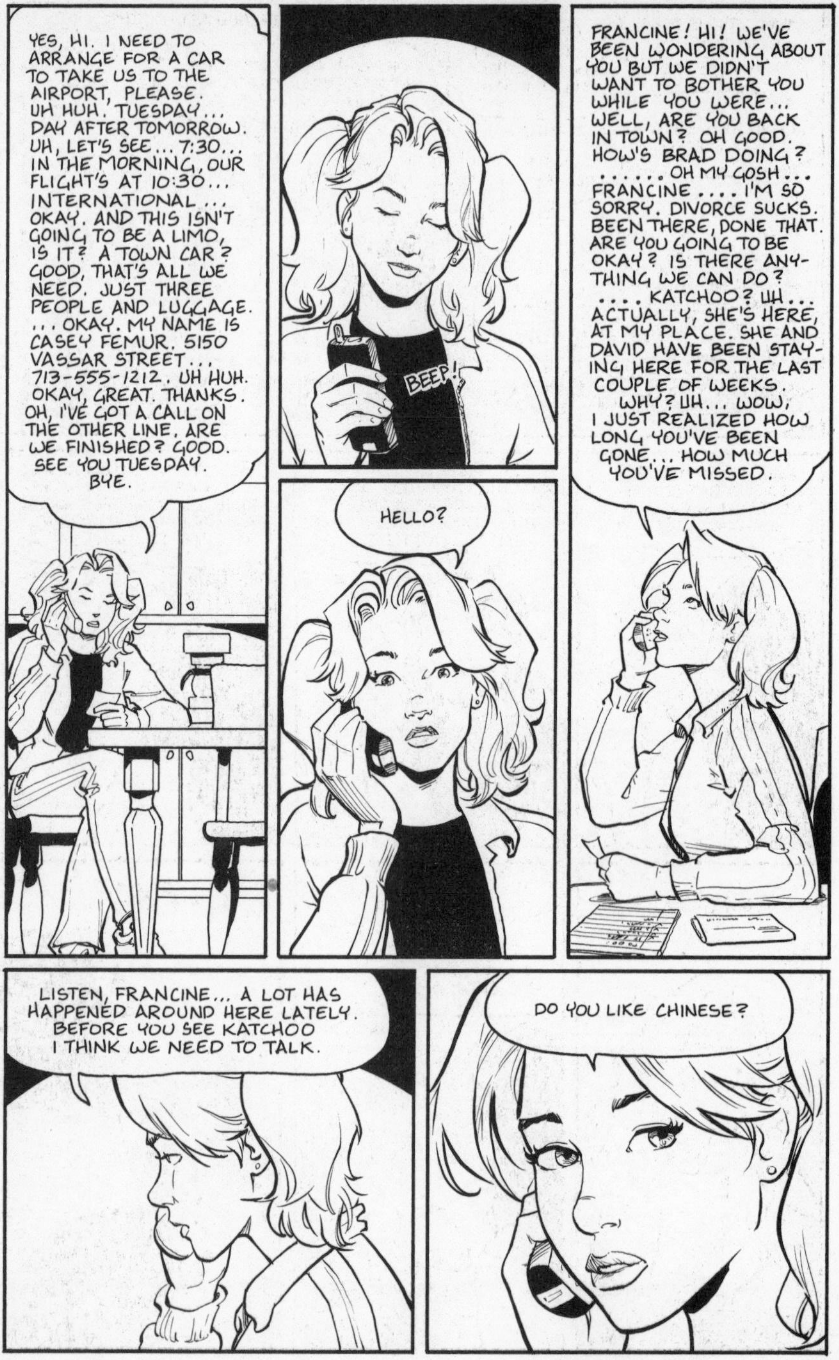
YES, HI. I NEED TO ARRANGE FOR A CAR TO TAKE US TO THE AIRPORT, PLEASE. UH HUH. TUESDAY... DAY AFTER TOMORROW. UH, LET'S SEE... 7:30... IN THE MORNING, OUR FLIGHT'S AT 10:30... INTERNATIONAL... OKAY. AND THIS ISN'T GOING TO BE A LIMO, IS IT? A TOWN CAR? GOOD, THAT'S ALL WE NEED. JUST THREE PEOPLE AND LUGGAGE. ... OKAY. MY NAME IS CASEY FEMUR. 5150 VASSAR STREET... 713-555-1212. UH HUH. OKAY, GREAT. THANKS. OH, I'VE GOT A CALL ON THE OTHER LINE, ARE WE FINISHED? GOOD. SEE YOU TUESDAY. BYE.
BEEP!
HELLO?
FRANCINE! HI! WE'VE BEEN WONDERING ABOUT YOU BUT WE DIDN'T WANT TO BOTHER YOU WHILE YOU WERE... WELL, ARE YOU BACK IN TOWN? OH GOOD. HOW'S BRAD DOING? ...... OH MY GOSH... FRANCINE.... I'M SO SORRY. DIVORCE SUCKS. BEEN THERE, DONE THAT. ARE YOU GOING TO BE OKAY? IS THERE ANYTHING WE CAN DO? .... KATCHOO? UH... ACTUALLY, SHE'S HERE, AT MY PLACE. SHE AND DAVID HAVE BEEN STAYING HERE FOR THE LAST COUPLE OF WEEKS. WHY? UH... WOW, I JUST REALIZED HOW LONG YOU'VE BEEN GONE... HOW MUCH YOU'VE MISSED.
LISTEN, FRANCINE... A LOT HAS HAPPENED AROUND HERE LATELY. BEFORE YOU SEE KATCHOO I THINK WE NEED TO TALK.
DO YOU LIKE CHINESE?

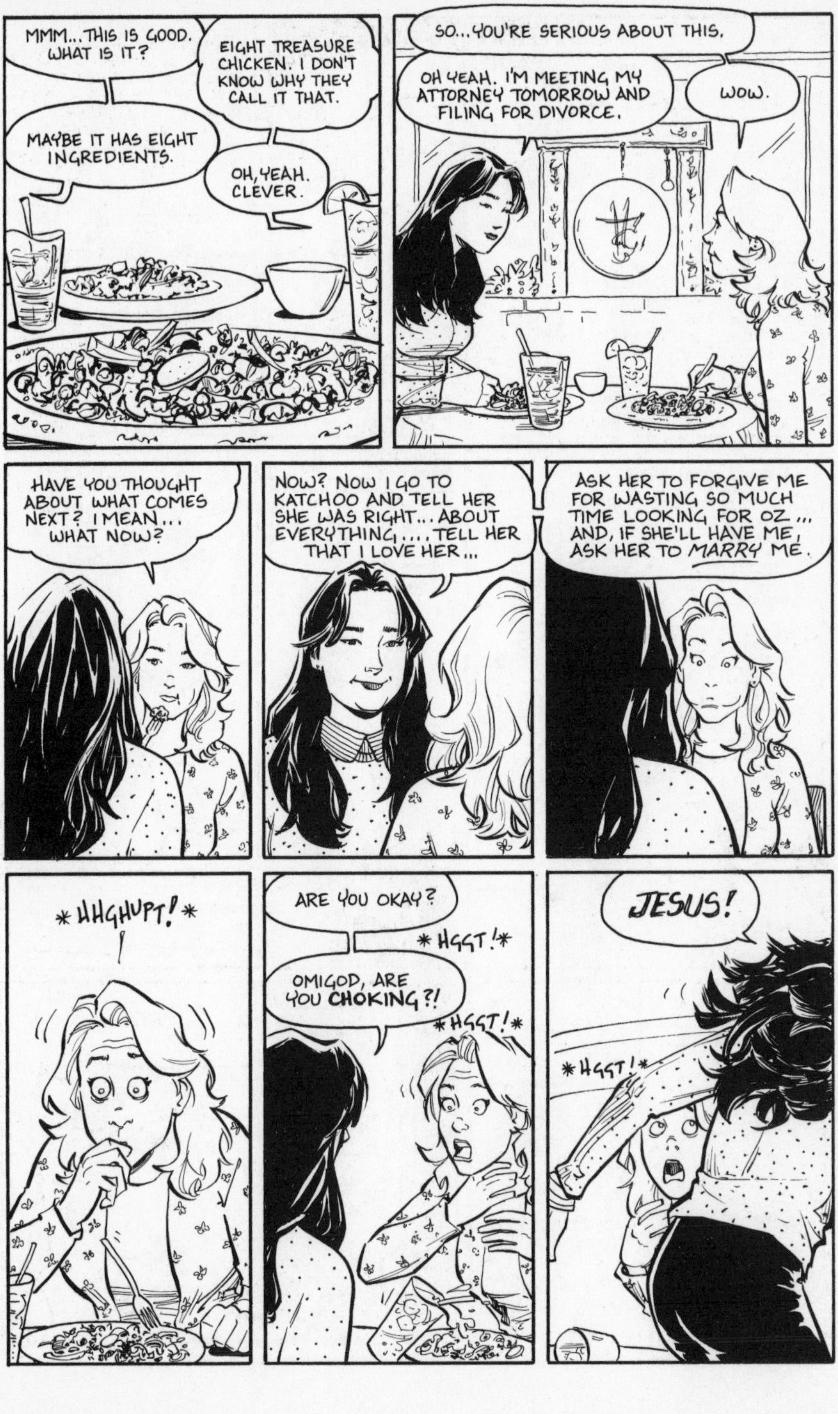
MMM... THIS IS GOOD. WHAT IS IT?
EIGHT TREASURE CHICKEN. I DON'T KNOW WHY THEY CALL IT THAT.
MAYBE IT HAS EIGHT INGREDIENTS.
OH, YEAH. CLEVER.
SO... YOU'RE SERIOUS ABOUT THIS.
OH YEAH. I'M MEETING MY ATTORNEY TOMORROW AND FILING FOR DIVORCE.
WOW.
HAVE YOU THOUGHT ABOUT WHAT COMES NEXT? I MEAN... WHAT NOW?
NOW? NOW I GO TO KATCHOO AND TELL HER SHE WAS RIGHT... ABOUT EVERYTHING.... TELL HER THAT I LOVE HER...
ASK HER TO FORGIVE ME FOR WASTING SO MUCH TIME LOOKING FOR OZ... AND, IF SHE'LL HAVE ME, ASK HER TO MARRY ME.
HHGHUPT!
!
ARE YOU OKAY?
HGGT!
OMIGOD, ARE YOU CHOKING?!
HGGT!
JESUS!
HGGT!

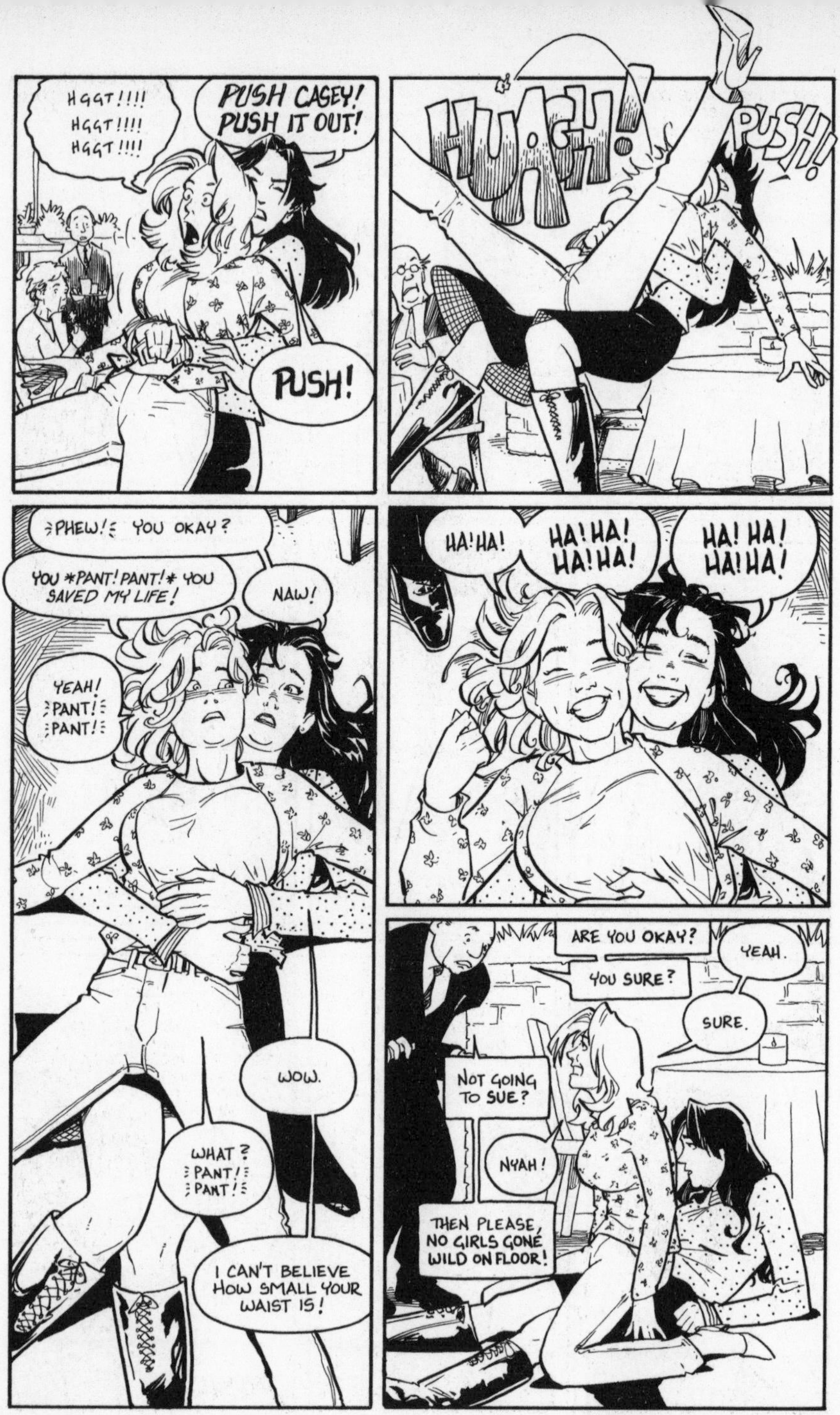
HGGT!!!!
HGGT!!!!
HGGT!!!!
PUSH CASEY! PUSH IT OUT!
PUSH!
HUAGH!
PUSH!
PHEW! YOU OKAY?
YOU *PANT! PANT!* YOU SAVED MY LIFE!
NAW!
YEAH! PANT! PANT!
WOW.
WHAT? PANT! PANT!
I CAN'T BELIEVE HOW SMALL YOUR WAIST IS!
HA! HA!
HA! HA! HA! HA!
HA! HA! HA! HA!
ARE YOU OKAY?
YEAH.
YOU SURE?
SURE.
NOT GOING TO SUE?
NYAH!
THEN PLEASE, NO GIRLS GONE WILD ON FLOOR!

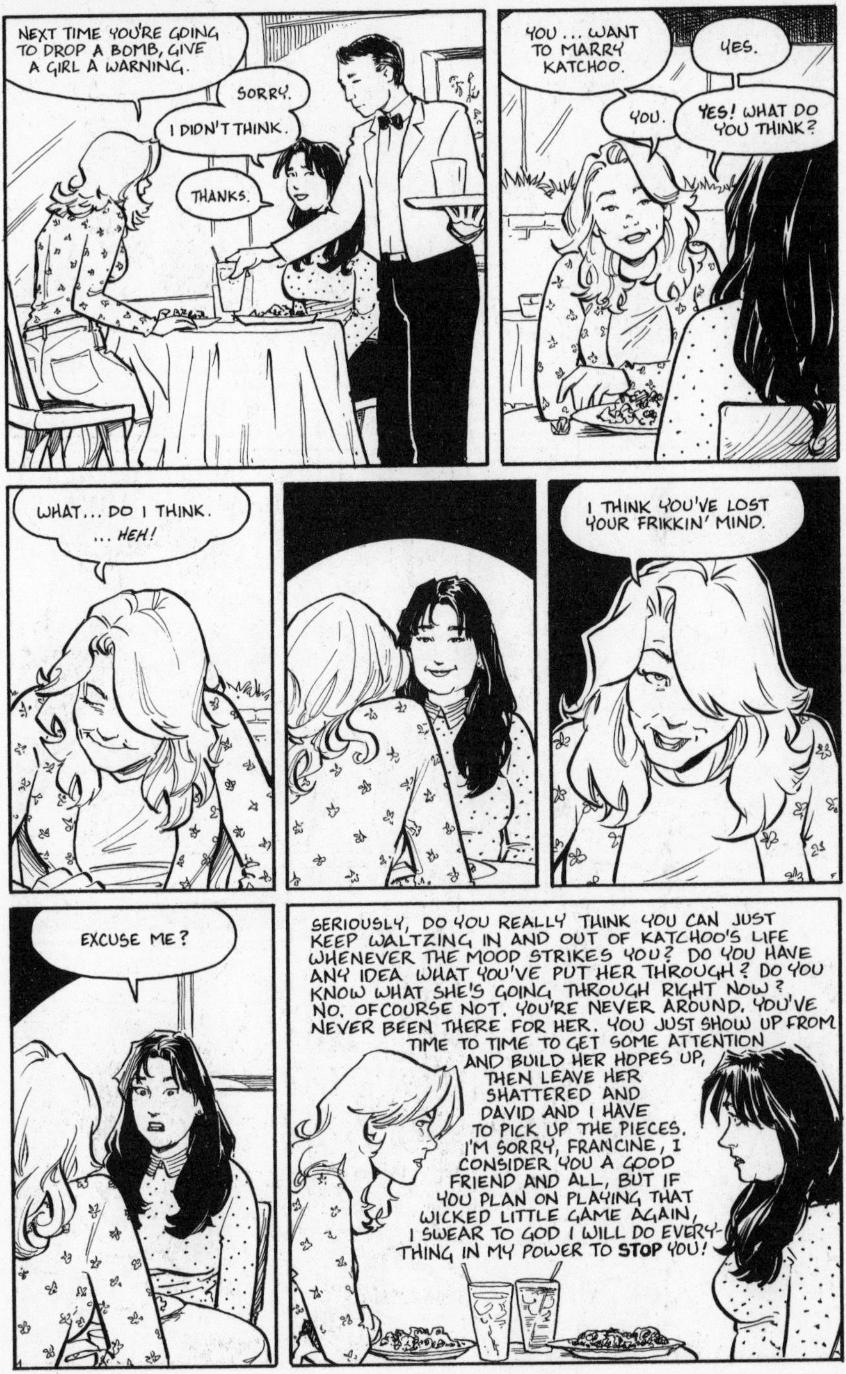
NEXT TIME YOU'RE GOING TO DROP A BOMB, GIVE A GIRL A WARNING.
SORRY.
I DIDN'T THINK.
THANKS.
YOU ... WANT TO MARRY KATCHOO.
YES.
YOU.
YES! WHAT DO YOU THINK?
WHAT... DO I THINK.
... HEH!
I THINK YOU'VE LOST YOUR FRIKKIN' MIND.
EXCUSE ME?
SERIOUSLY, DO YOU REALLY THINK YOU CAN JUST KEEP WALTZING IN AND OUT OF KATCHOO'S LIFE WHENEVER THE MOOD STRIKES YOU? DO YOU HAVE ANY IDEA WHAT YOU'VE PUT HER THROUGH? DO YOU KNOW WHAT SHE'S GOING THROUGH RIGHT NOW? NO. OFCOURSE NOT. YOU'RE NEVER AROUND. YOU'VE NEVER BEEN THERE FOR HER. YOU JUST SHOW UP FROM TIME TO TIME TO GET SOME ATTENTION AND BUILD HER HOPES UP, THEN LEAVE HER SHATTERED AND DAVID AND I HAVE TO PICK UP THE PIECES. I'M SORRY, FRANCINE, I CONSIDER YOU A GOOD FRIEND AND ALL, BUT IF YOU PLAN ON PLAYING THAT WICKED LITTLE GAME AGAIN, I SWEAR TO GOD I WILL DO EVERY-THING IN MY POWER TO STOP YOU!

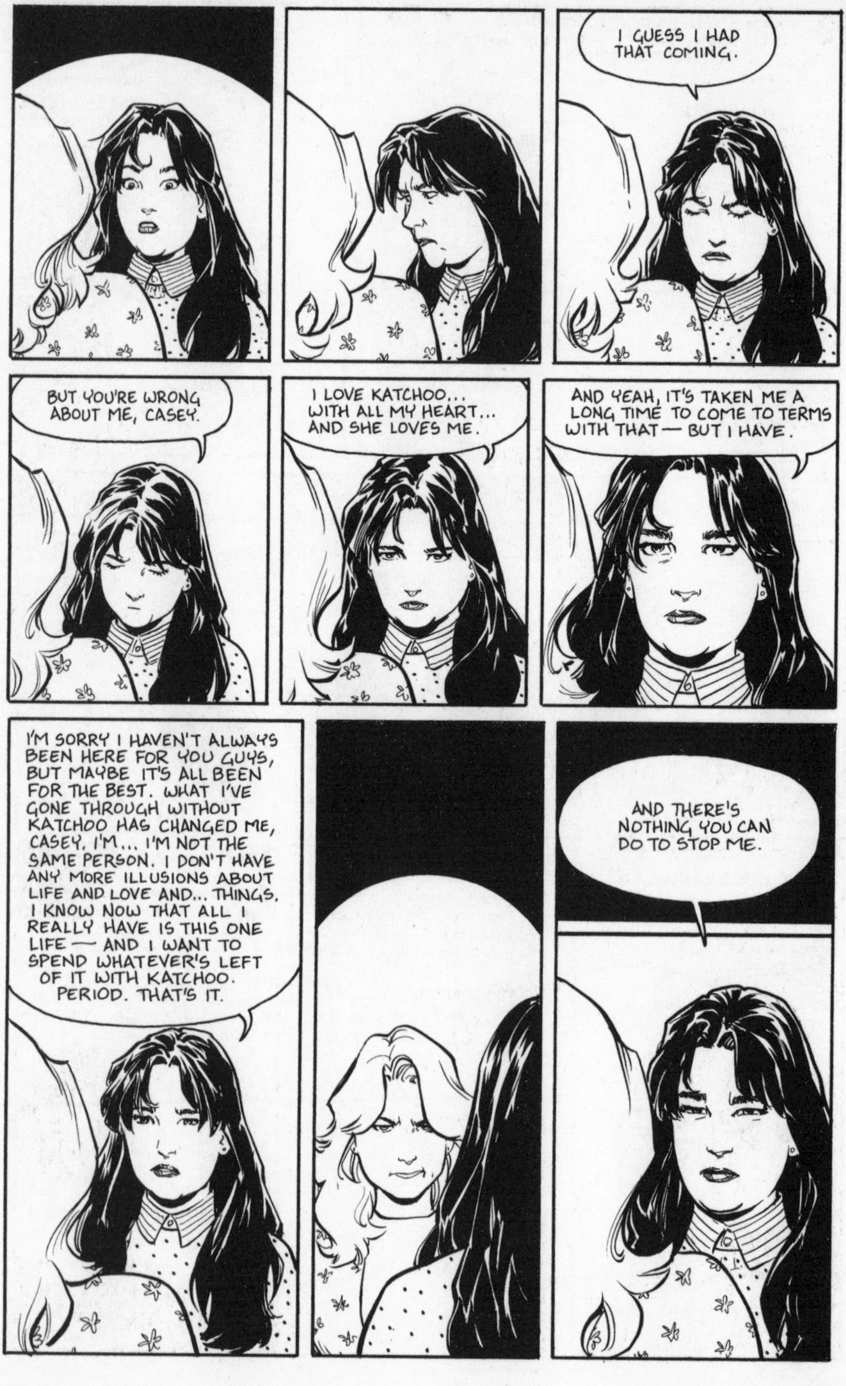
I GUESS I HAD THAT COMING.
BUT YOU'RE WRONG ABOUT ME, CASEY.
I LOVE KATCHOO... WITH ALL MY HEART... AND SHE LOVES ME.
AND YEAH, IT'S TAKEN ME A LONG TIME TO COME TO TERMS WITH THAT— BUT I HAVE.
I'M SORRY I HAVEN'T ALWAYS BEEN HERE FOR YOU GUYS, BUT MAYBE IT'S ALL BEEN FOR THE BEST. WHAT I'VE GONE THROUGH WITHOUT KATCHOO HAS CHANGED ME, CASEY. I'M... I'M NOT THE SAME PERSON. I DON'T HAVE ANY MORE ILLUSIONS ABOUT LIFE AND LOVE AND... THINGS. I KNOW NOW THAT ALL I REALLY HAVE IS THIS ONE LIFE — AND I WANT TO SPEND WHATEVER'S LEFT OF IT WITH KATCHOO. PERIOD. THAT'S IT.
AND THERE'S NOTHING YOU CAN DO TO STOP ME.

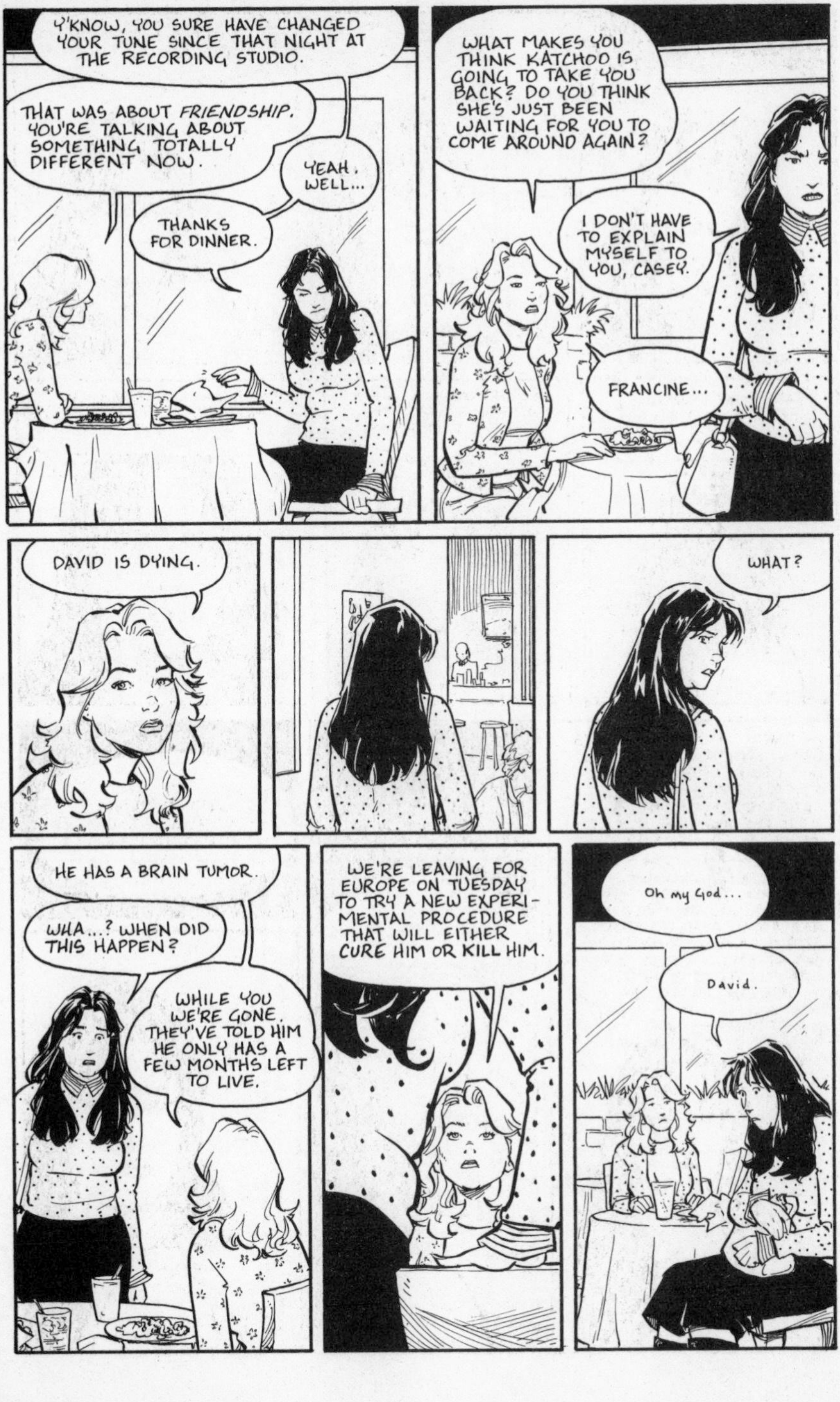
Y'KNOW, YOU SURE HAVE CHANGED YOUR TUNE SINCE THAT NIGHT AT THE RECORDING STUDIO.
THAT WAS ABOUT *FRIENDSHIP.* YOU'RE TALKING ABOUT SOMETHING TOTALLY DIFFERENT NOW.
YEAH. WELL...
THANKS FOR DINNER.
WHAT MAKES YOU THINK KATCHOO IS GOING TO TAKE YOU BACK? DO YOU THINK SHE'S JUST BEEN WAITING FOR YOU TO COME AROUND AGAIN?
I DON'T HAVE TO EXPLAIN MYSELF TO YOU, CASEY.
FRANCINE...
DAVID IS DYING.
WHAT?
HE HAS A BRAIN TUMOR.
WHA...? WHEN DID THIS HAPPEN?
WHILE YOU WE'RE GONE, THEY'VE TOLD HIM HE ONLY HAS A FEW MONTHS LEFT TO LIVE.
WE'RE LEAVING FOR EUROPE ON TUESDAY TO TRY A NEW EXPERI-MENTAL PROCEDURE THAT WILL EITHER **CURE** HIM OR **KILL** HIM.
Oh my God...
David.

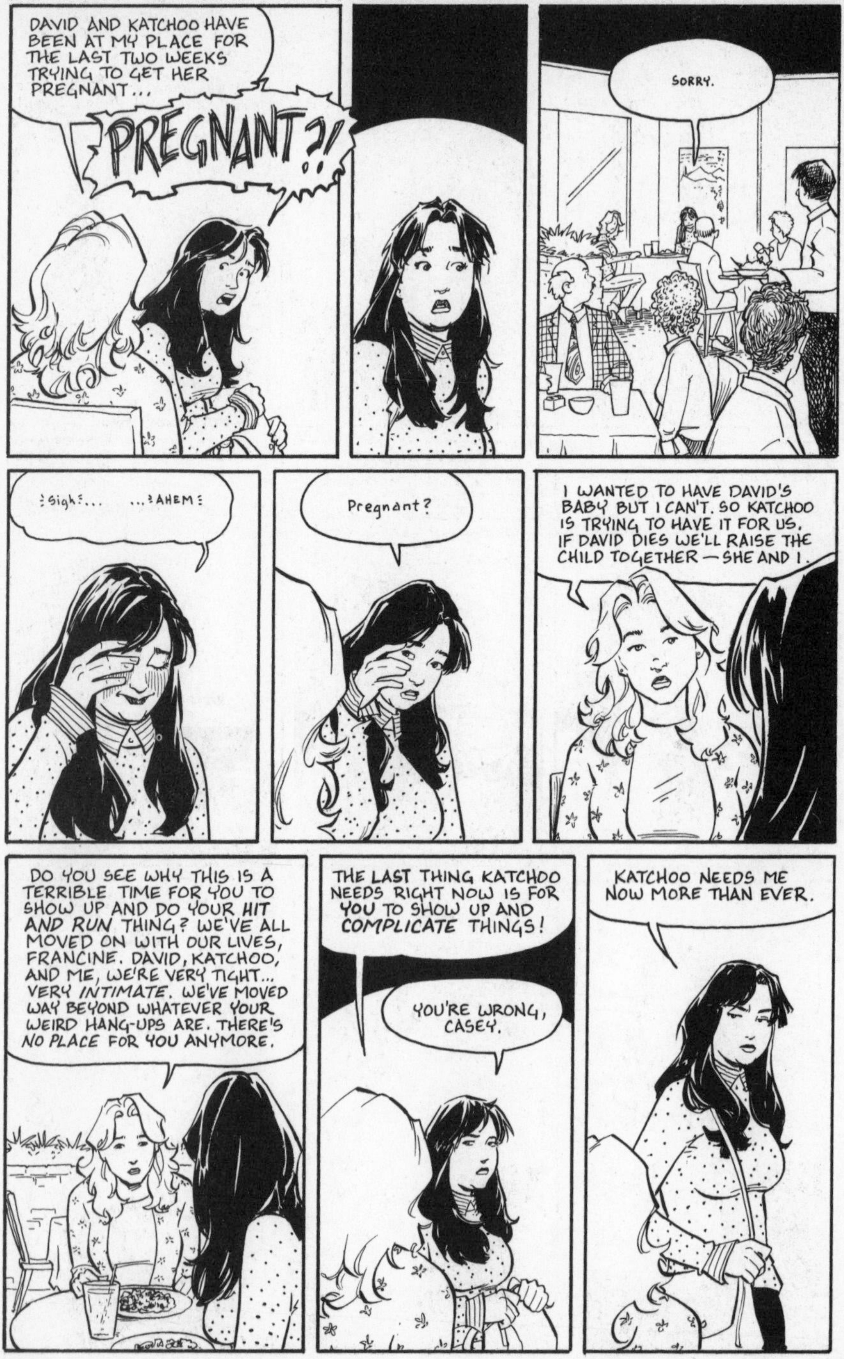

DAVID AND KATCHOO HAVE BEEN AT MY PLACE FOR THE LAST TWO WEEKS TRYING TO GET HER PREGNANT...
PREGNANT?!
SORRY.
Sigh... ...AHEM
Pregnant?
I WANTED TO HAVE DAVID'S BABY BUT I CAN'T. SO KATCHOO IS TRYING TO HAVE IT FOR US. IF DAVID DIES WE'LL RAISE THE CHILD TOGETHER — SHE AND I.
DO YOU SEE WHY THIS IS A TERRIBLE TIME FOR YOU TO SHOW UP AND DO YOUR HIT AND RUN THING? WE'VE ALL MOVED ON WITH OUR LIVES, FRANCINE. DAVID, KATCHOO, AND ME, WE'RE VERY TIGHT... VERY INTIMATE. WE'VE MOVED WAY BEYOND WHATEVER YOUR WEIRD HANG-UPS ARE. THERE'S NO PLACE FOR YOU ANYMORE.
THE LAST THING KATCHOO NEEDS RIGHT NOW IS FOR YOU TO SHOW UP AND COMPLICATE THINGS!
YOU'RE WRONG, CASEY.
KATCHOO NEEDS ME NOW MORE THAN EVER.

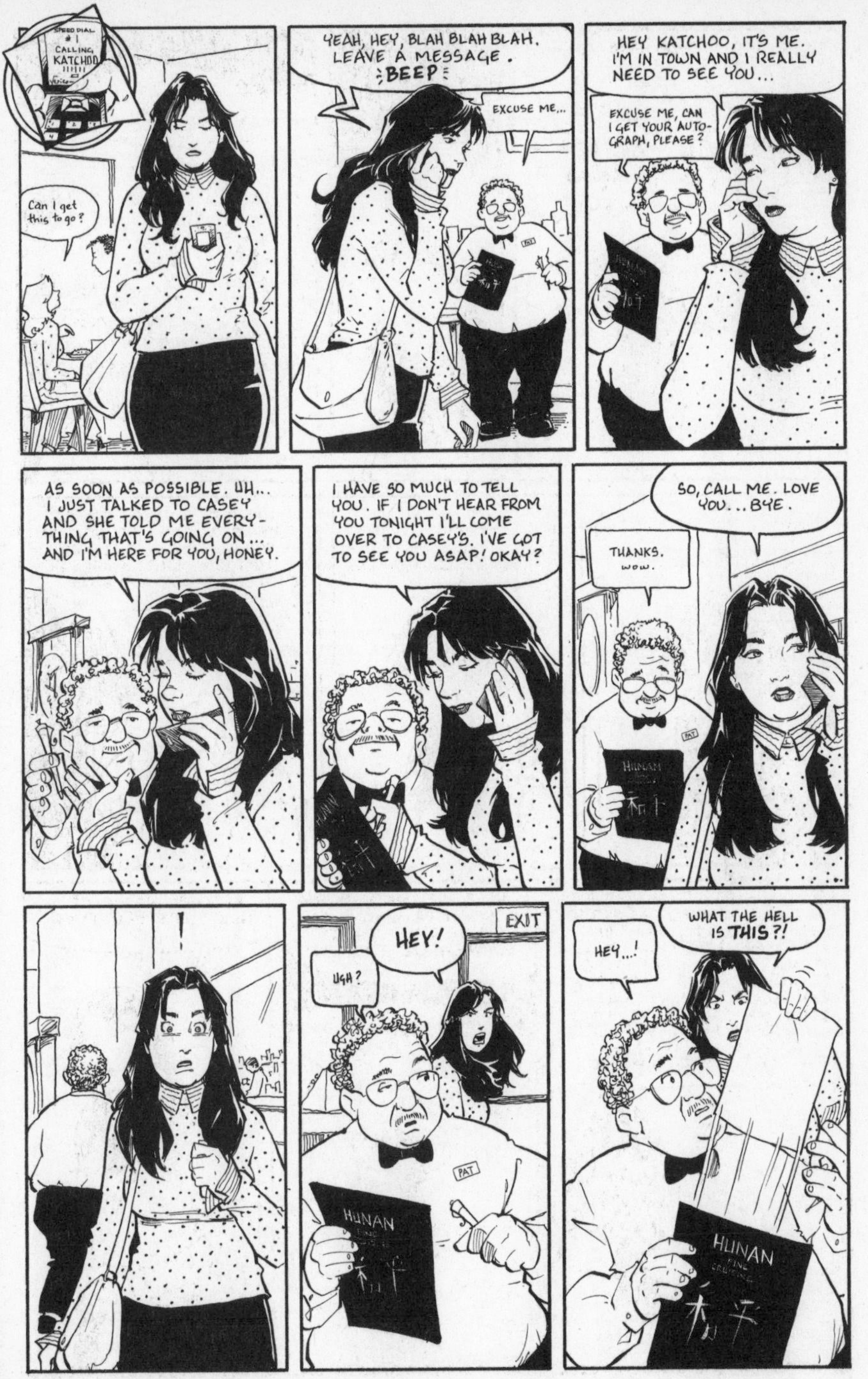
SPEED DIAL #1 CALLING KATCHOO
Can I get this to go?
YEAH, HEY, BLAH BLAH BLAH. LEAVE A MESSAGE. BEEP
EXCUSE ME...
HEY KATCHOO, IT'S ME. I'M IN TOWN AND I REALLY NEED TO SEE YOU...
EXCUSE ME, CAN I GET YOUR AUTOGRAPH, PLEASE?
AS SOON AS POSSIBLE. UH... I JUST TALKED TO CASEY AND SHE TOLD ME EVERYTHING THAT'S GOING ON... AND I'M HERE FOR YOU, HONEY.
I HAVE SO MUCH TO TELL YOU. IF I DON'T HEAR FROM YOU TONIGHT I'LL COME OVER TO CASEY'S. I'VE GOT TO SEE YOU ASAP! OKAY?
SO, CALL ME. LOVE YOU... BYE.
THANKS. WOW.
!
EXIT
HEY!
UGH?
PAT
HUNAN
HEY...!
WHAT THE HELL IS THIS?!
HUNAN

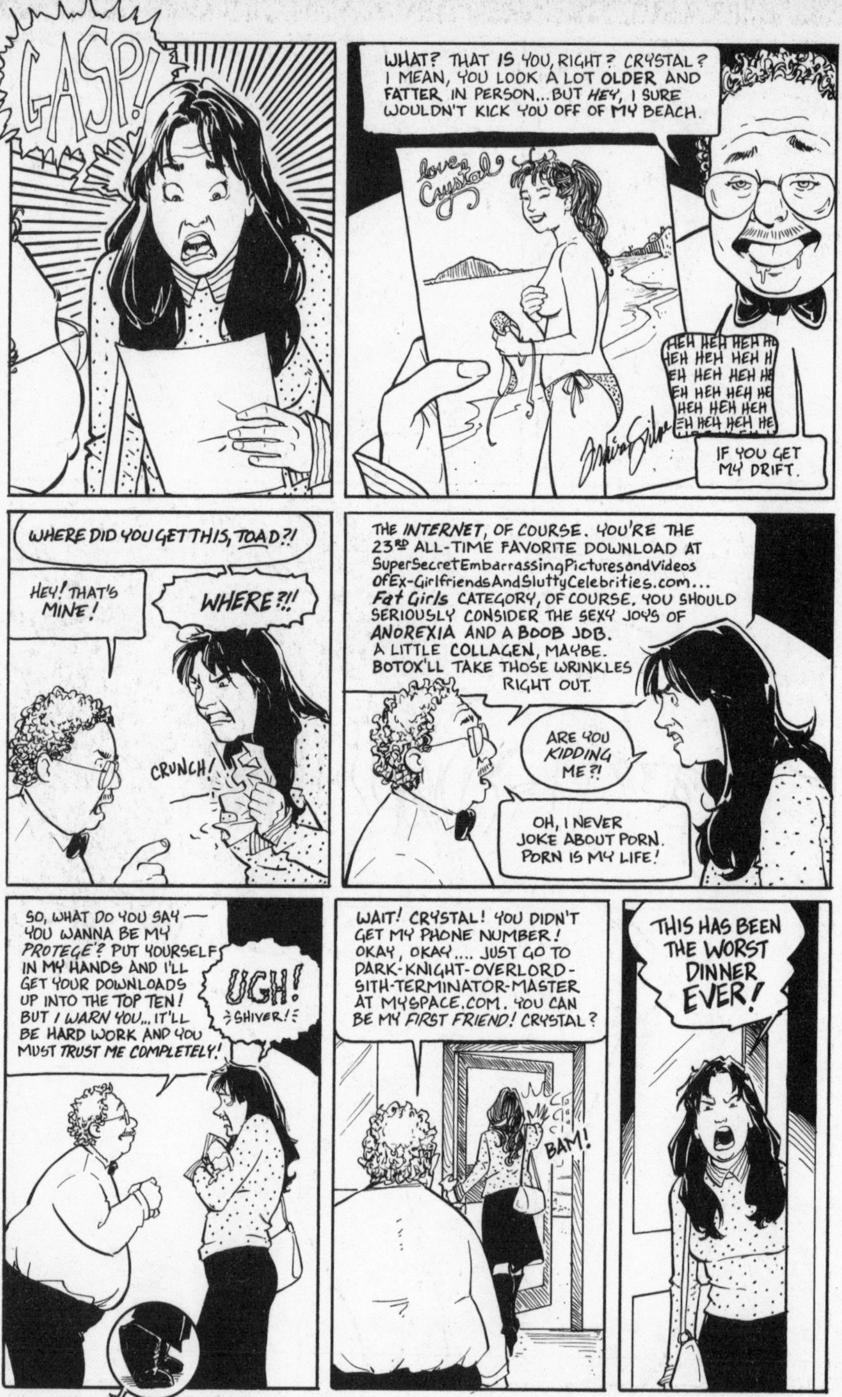
GASP!
WHAT? THAT IS YOU, RIGHT? CRYSTAL? I MEAN, YOU LOOK A LOT OLDER AND FATTER IN PERSON... BUT HEY, I SURE WOULDN'T KICK YOU OFF OF MY BEACH.
love, Crystal
HEH HEH HEH HEH HEH HEH HEH HEH HEH HEH HEH HEH HEH HEH HEH HEH HEH HEH HEH HEH HEH HEH HEH
IF YOU GET MY DRIFT.
WHERE DID YOU GET THIS, TOAD?!
HEY! THAT'S MINE!
WHERE?!!
CRUNCH!
THE INTERNET, OF COURSE. YOU'RE THE 23RD ALL-TIME FAVORITE DOWNLOAD AT SuperSecretEmbarrassingPicturesandVideosOfEx-GirlfriendsAndSluttyCelebrities.com... Fat Girls CATEGORY, OF COURSE. YOU SHOULD SERIOUSLY CONSIDER THE SEXY JOYS OF ANOREXIA AND A BOOB JOB. A LITTLE COLLAGEN, MAYBE. BOTOX'LL TAKE THOSE WRINKLES RIGHT OUT.
ARE YOU KIDDING ME?!
OH, I NEVER JOKE ABOUT PORN. PORN IS MY LIFE!
SO, WHAT DO YOU SAY — YOU WANNA BE MY PROTEGE? PUT YOURSELF IN MY HANDS AND I'LL GET YOUR DOWNLOADS UP INTO THE TOP TEN! BUT I WARN YOU... IT'LL BE HARD WORK AND YOU MUST TRUST ME COMPLETELY!
UGH!
SHIVER!
WAIT! CRYSTAL! YOU DIDN'T GET MY PHONE NUMBER! OKAY, OKAY.... JUST GO TO DARK-KNIGHT-OVERLORD-SITH-TERMINATOR-MASTER AT MYSPACE.COM. YOU CAN BE MY FIRST FRIEND! CRYSTAL?
BAM!
THIS HAS BEEN THE WORST DINNER EVER!

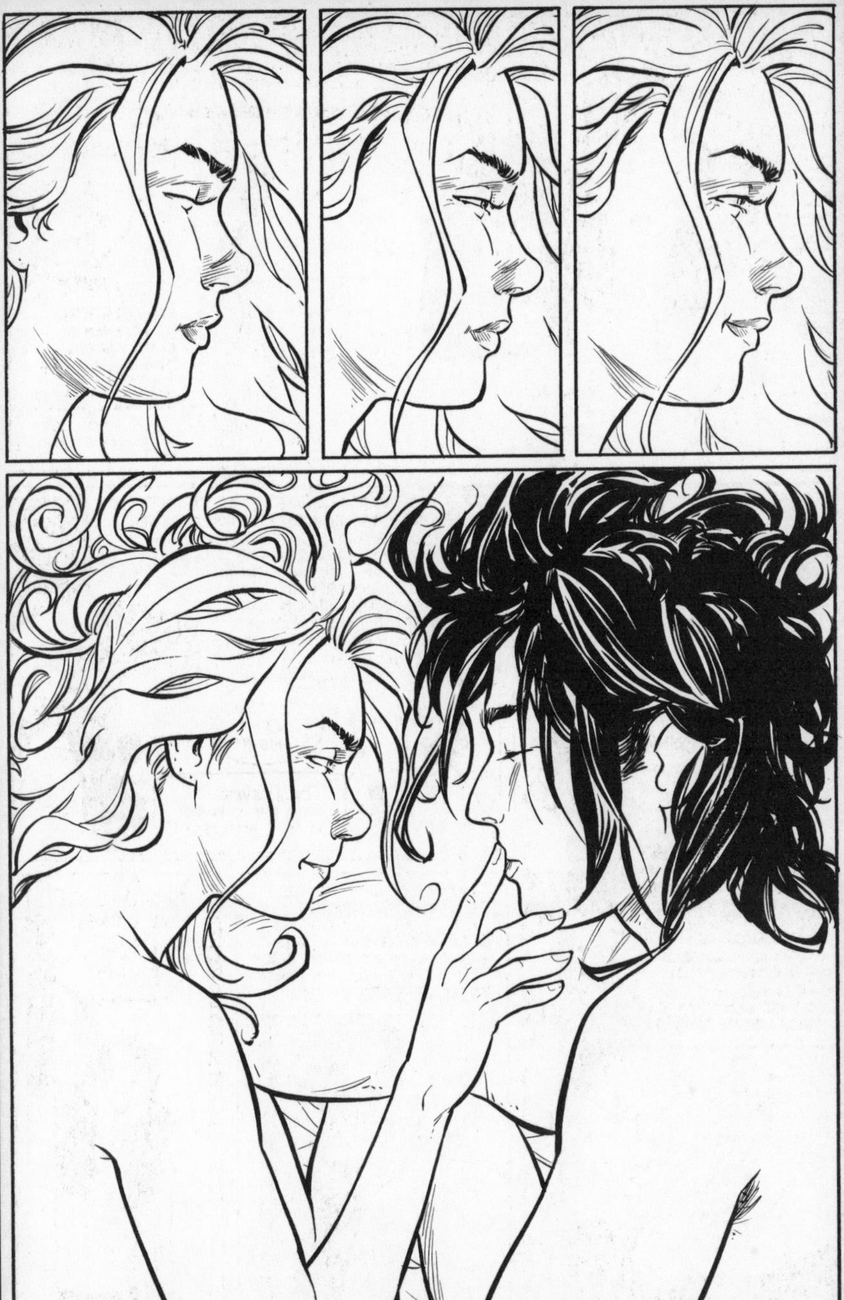

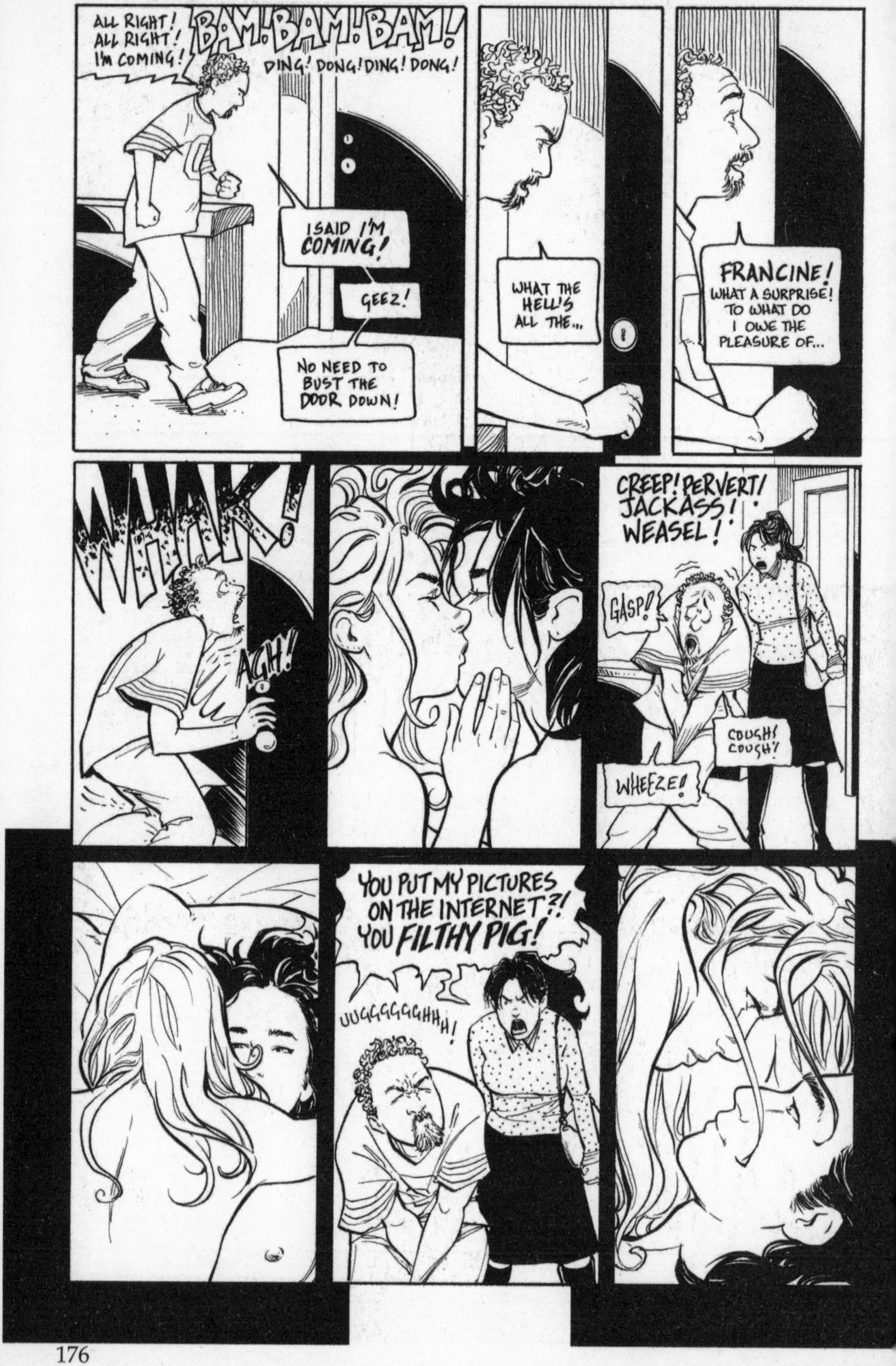

ALL RIGHT! ALL RIGHT! I'M COMING!
BAM! BAM! BAM!
DING! DONG! DING! DONG!
I SAID I'M COMING!
GEEZ!
NO NEED TO BUST THE DOOR DOWN!
WHAT THE HELL'S ALL THE...
FRANCINE! WHAT A SURPRISE! TO WHAT DO I OWE THE PLEASURE OF...
WHAK!
AGH!
CREEP! PERVERT! JACKASS! WEASEL!
GASP!
COUGH! COUGH!
WHEEZE!
YOU PUT MY PICTURES ON THE INTERNET?! YOU FILTHY PIG!
UUGGGGGGHHH!

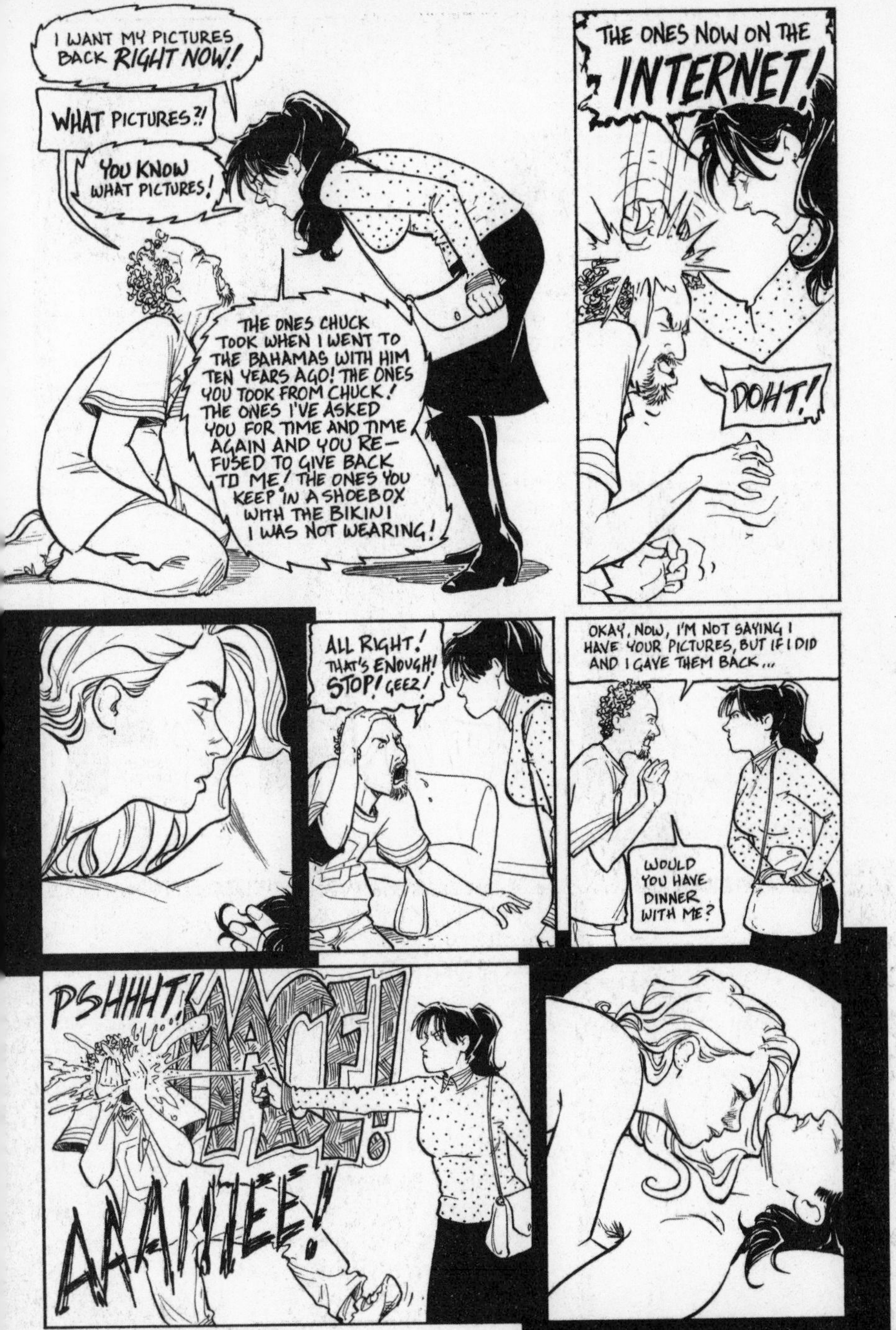
I WANT MY PICTURES BACK RIGHT NOW!
WHAT PICTURES?!
YOU KNOW WHAT PICTURES!
THE ONES CHUCK TOOK WHEN I WENT TO THE BAHAMAS WITH HIM TEN YEARS AGO! THE ONES YOU TOOK FROM CHUCK! THE ONES I'VE ASKED YOU FOR TIME AND TIME AGAIN AND YOU RE-FUSED TO GIVE BACK TO ME! THE ONES YOU KEEP IN A SHOEBOX WITH THE BIKINI I WAS NOT WEARING!
THE ONES NOW ON THE INTERNET!
DOHT!
ALL RIGHT! THAT'S ENOUGH! STOP! GEEZ!
OKAY, NOW, I'M NOT SAYING I HAVE YOUR PICTURES, BUT IF I DID AND I GAVE THEM BACK...
WOULD YOU HAVE DINNER WITH ME?
PSHHHT!
MACE!
AAAIIIEE!

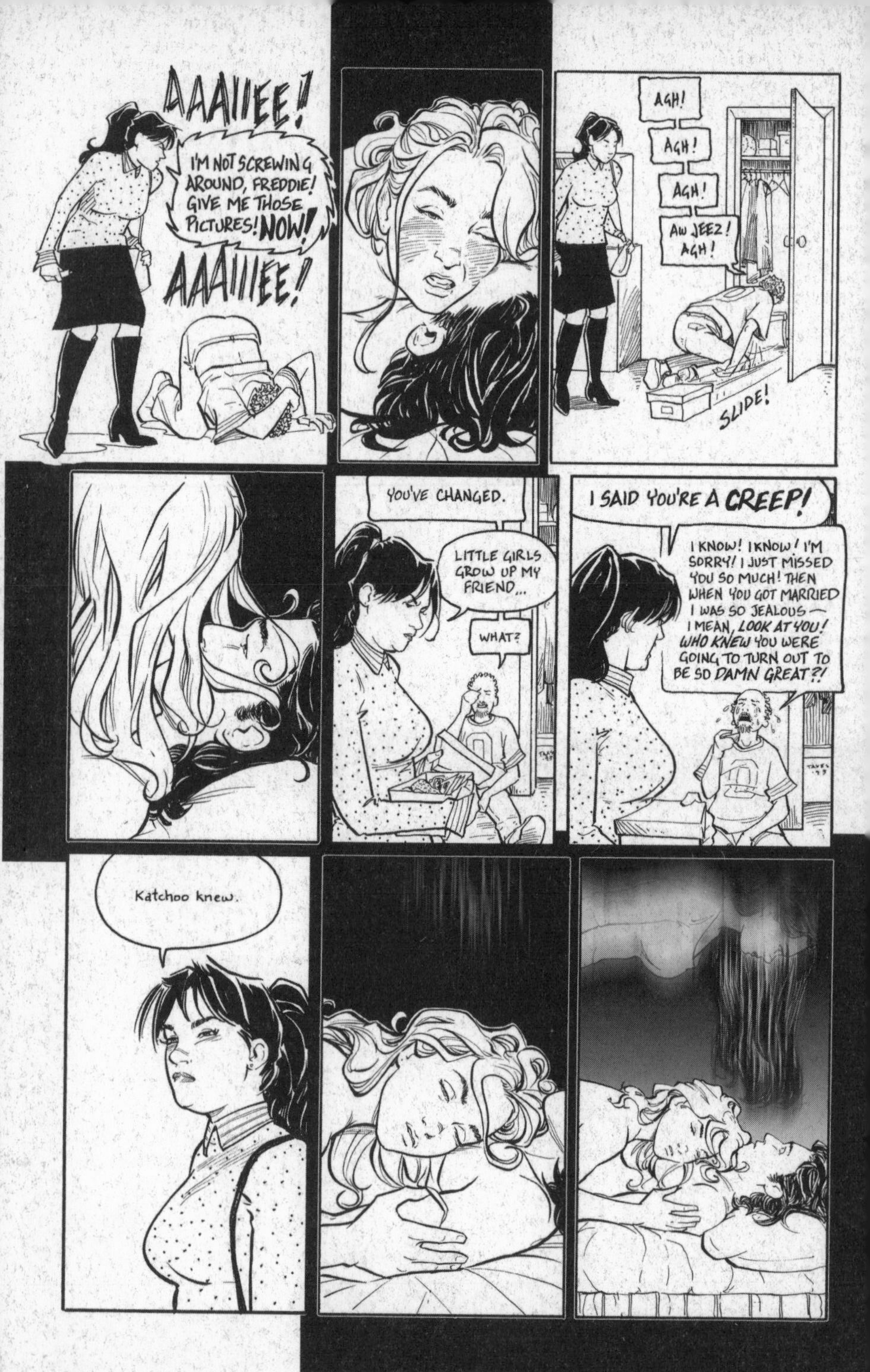
AAAIIIEE!
I'M NOT SCREWING AROUND, FREDDIE! GIVE ME THOSE PICTURES! NOW!
AAAIIIEE!
AGH!
AGH!
AGH!
AW JEEZ! AGH!
SLIDE!
YOU'VE CHANGED.
LITTLE GIRLS GROW UP MY FRIEND...
WHAT?
I SAID YOU'RE A CREEP!
I KNOW! I KNOW! I'M SORRY! I JUST MISSED YOU SO MUCH! THEN WHEN YOU GOT MARRIED I WAS SO JEALOUS— I MEAN, LOOK AT YOU! WHO KNEW YOU WERE GOING TO TURN OUT TO BE SO DAMN GREAT?!
Katchoo knew.

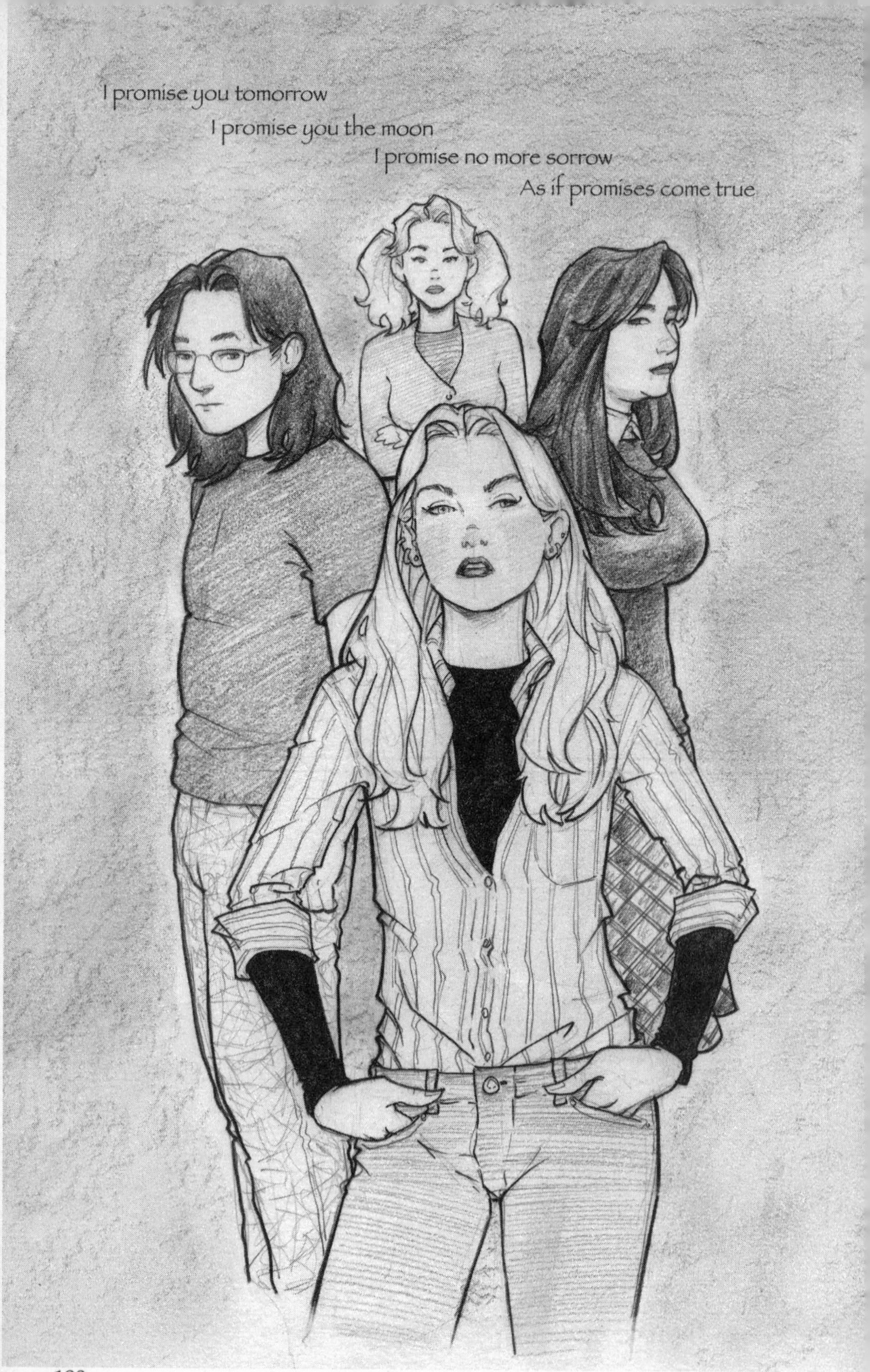
I promise you tomorrow
I promise you the moon
I promise no more sorrow
As if promises come true

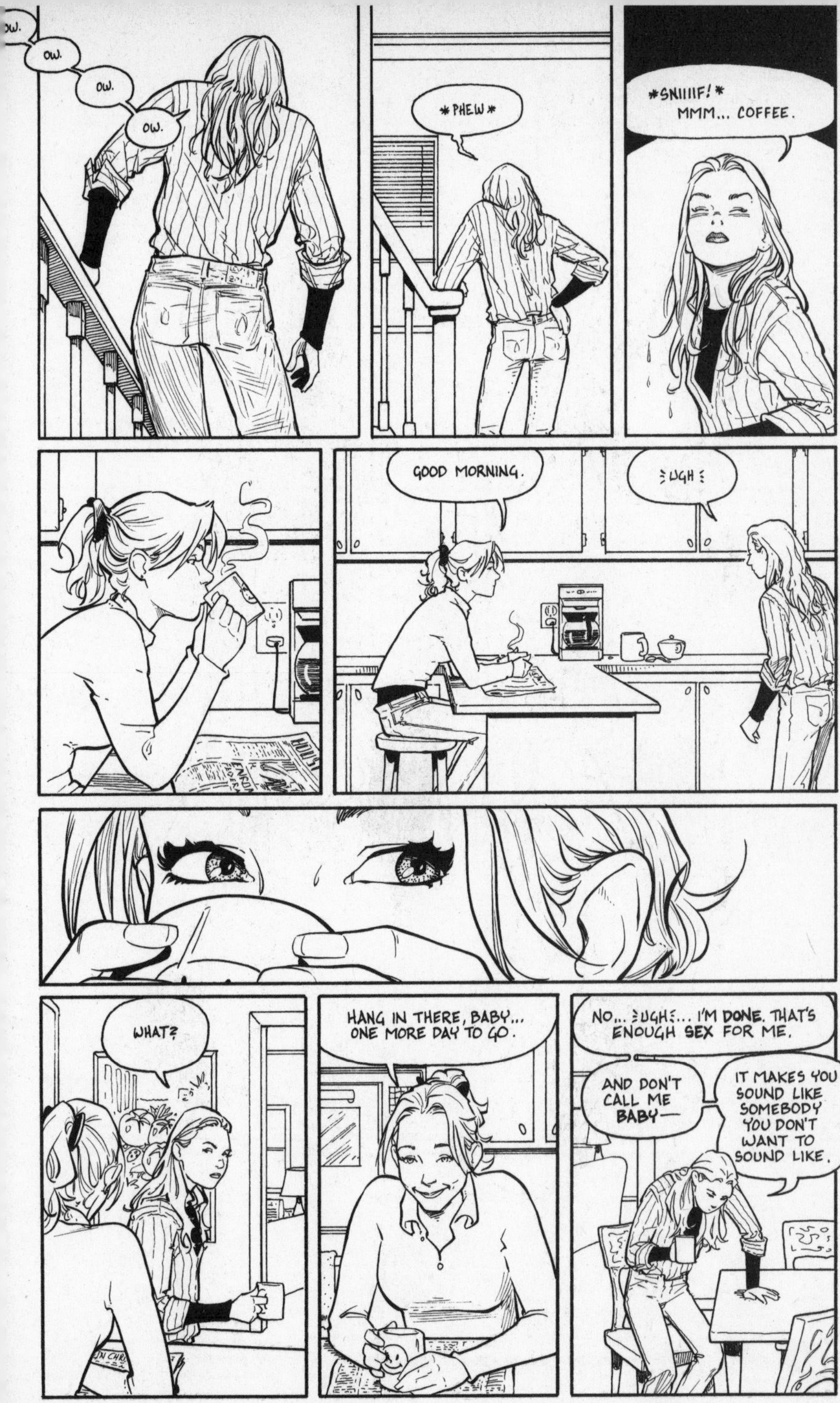
OW.
OW.
OW.
OW.
PHEW
SNIIIIF! MMM... COFFEE.
GOOD MORNING.
UGH
WHAT?
HANG IN THERE, BABY... ONE MORE DAY TO GO.
NO... UGH... I'M DONE. THAT'S ENOUGH SEX FOR ME.
AND DON'T CALL ME BABY—
IT MAKES YOU SOUND LIKE SOMEBODY YOU DON'T WANT TO SOUND LIKE.

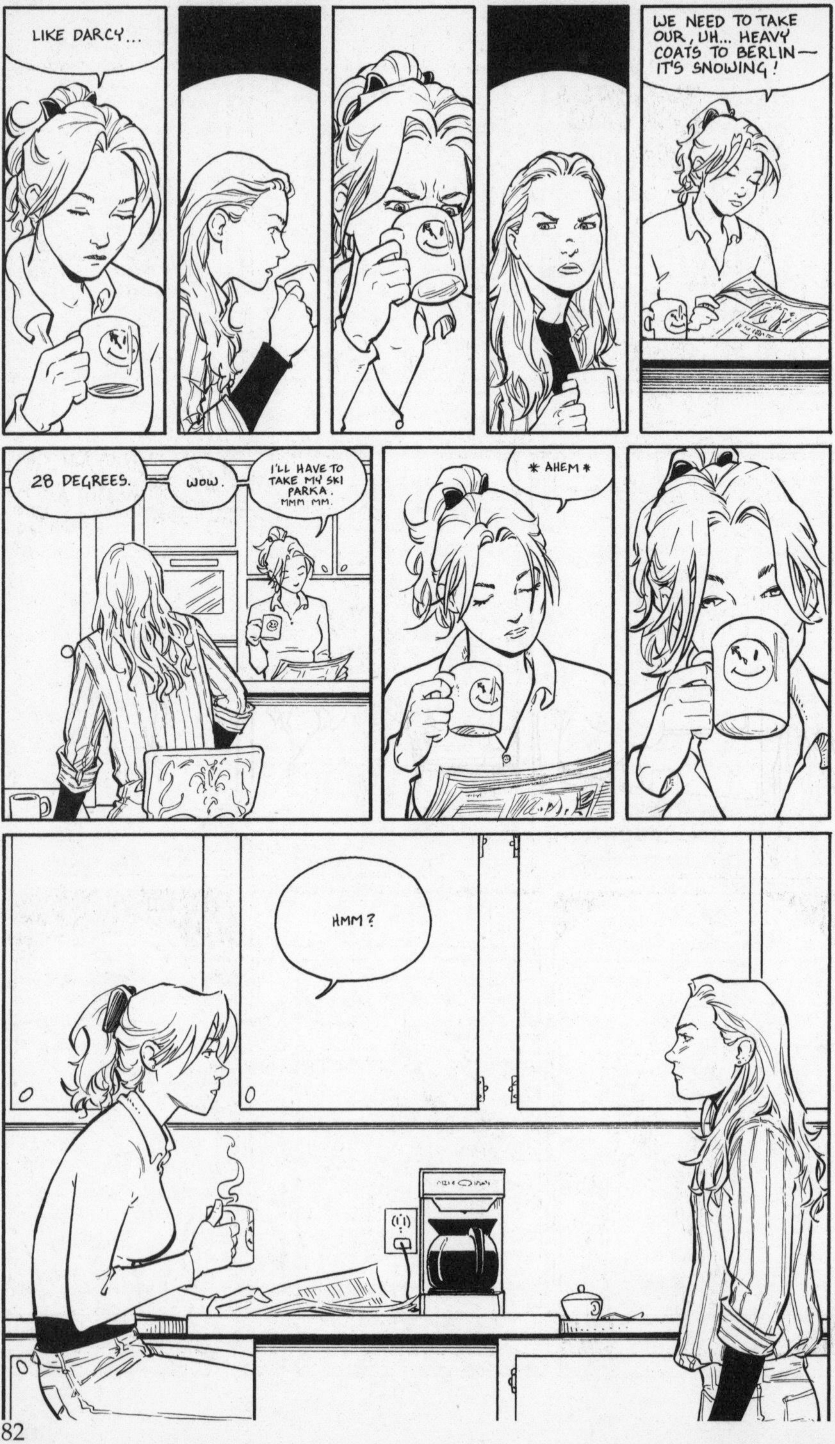
LIKE DARCY...
WE NEED TO TAKE OUR, UH... HEAVY COATS TO BERLIN— IT'S SNOWING!
28 DEGREES.
WOW.
I'LL HAVE TO TAKE MY SKI PARKA. MMM MM.
* AHEM *
HMM?

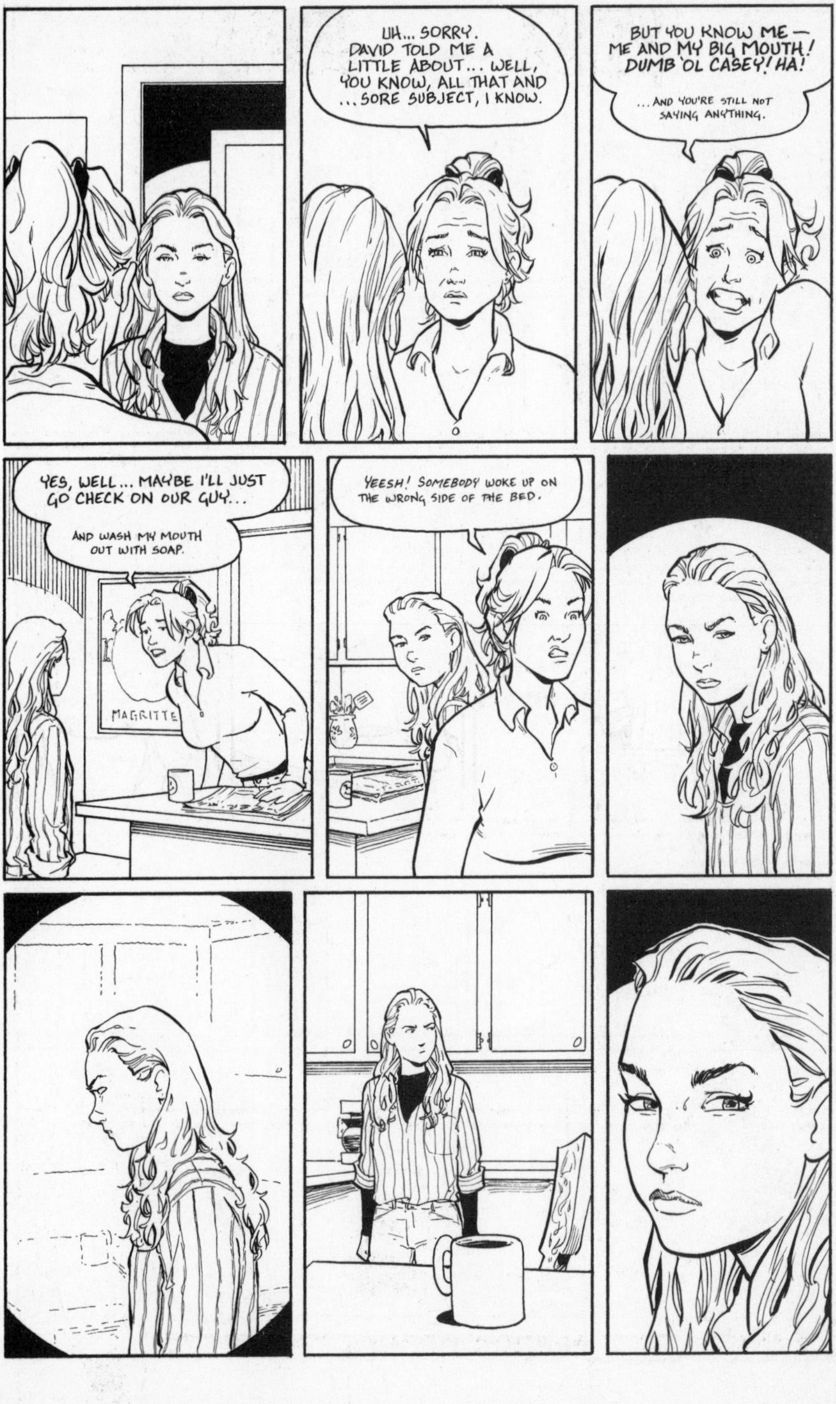
UH... SORRY. DAVID TOLD ME A LITTLE ABOUT... WELL, YOU KNOW, ALL THAT AND ...SORE SUBJECT, I KNOW.
BUT YOU KNOW ME — ME AND MY BIG MOUTH! DUMB 'OL CASEY! HA!
...AND YOU'RE STILL NOT SAYING ANYTHING.
YES, WELL... MAYBE I'LL JUST GO CHECK ON OUR GUY...
AND WASH MY MOUTH OUT WITH SOAP.
MAGRITTE
YEESH! SOMEBODY WOKE UP ON THE WRONG SIDE OF THE BED.

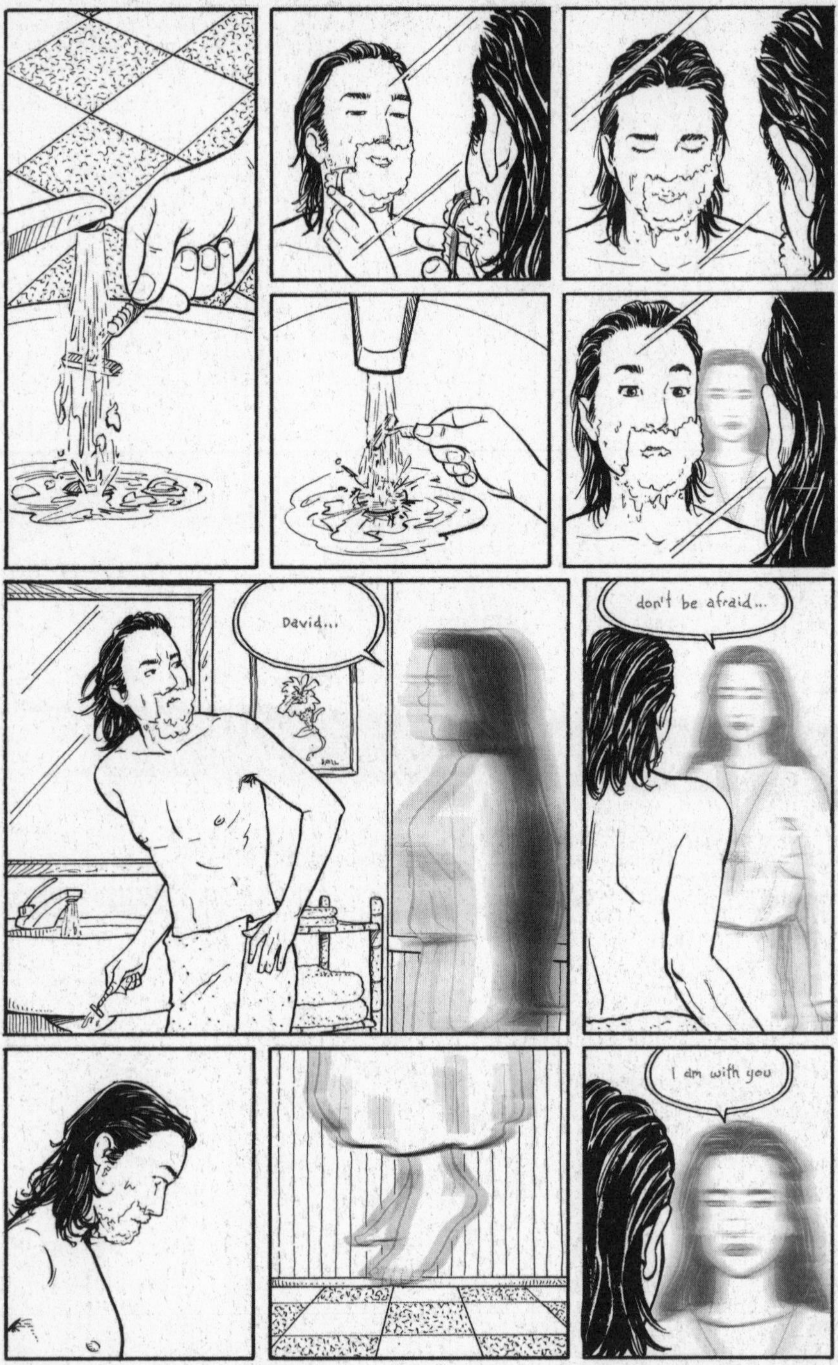
David...
don't be afraid...
I am with you

as if promises come true...

DAVID? ARE YOU ALMOST READY? WE NEED TO GET STARTED IF WE'RE GOING TO GET ALL THESE ERRANDS DONE TODAY.

DAVID?

HRGGGT!

HRGGGT!

HRRRGT!

HRGGGT!

DAVID?

HRGGT!

HRGGT!

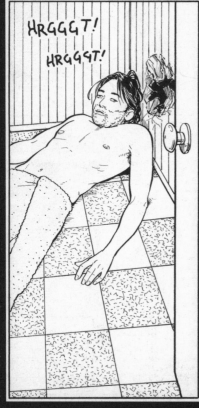

HRGGGT!

HRGGGT!

DAVID!

JESUS! KATCHOO!

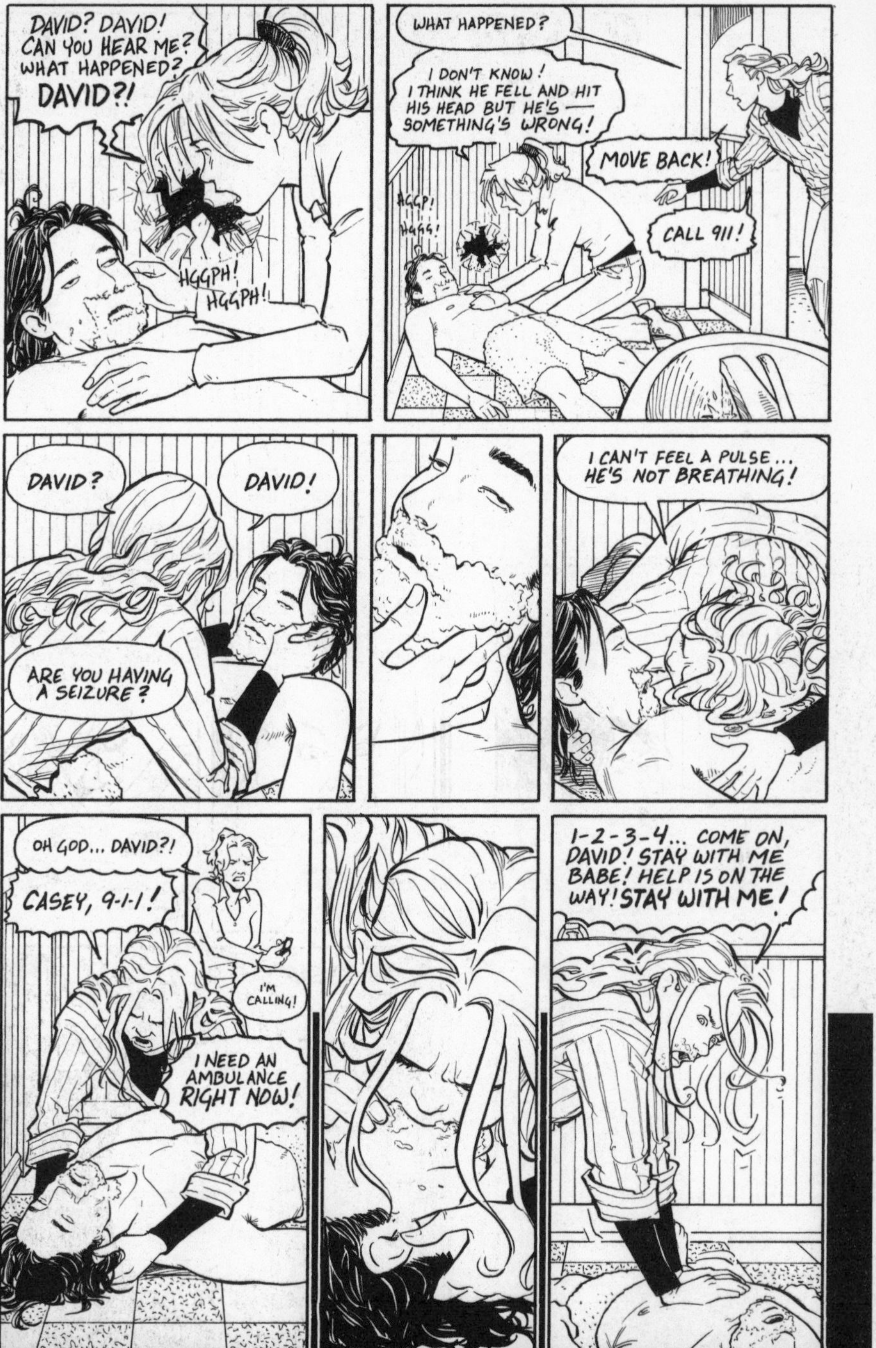
DAVID? DAVID! CAN YOU HEAR ME? WHAT HAPPENED? DAVID?!
HGGPH! HGGPH!
WHAT HAPPENED?
I DON'T KNOW! I THINK HE FELL AND HIT HIS HEAD BUT HE'S — SOMETHING'S WRONG!
MOVE BACK!
HGGP! HGGG!
CALL 911!
DAVID?
DAVID!
ARE YOU HAVING A SEIZURE?
I CAN'T FEEL A PULSE... HE'S NOT BREATHING!
OH GOD... DAVID?!
CASEY, 9-1-1!
I'M CALLING!
I NEED AN AMBULANCE RIGHT NOW!
1-2-3-4... COME ON, DAVID! STAY WITH ME BABE! HELP IS ON THE WAY! STAY WITH ME!

YES, I NEED AN AMBULANCE *RIGHT NOW* AT 5150 VASSAR STREET! MY BOYFRIEND IS UNCONSCIOUS—HE'S NOT BREATHING AND WE CAN'T FEEL A PULSE! 5150 VASSAR!

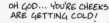

1-2-3-4... BREATHE, DAVID— BREATHE!

IT'S AN APARTMENT BUT MY FRONT DOOR OPENS TO THE STREET. YEAH. *PLEASE HURRY*—I NEED THEM *RIGHT NOW!* WHEN I FOUND HIM HIS FACE WAS PURPLE BUT NOW IT'S WHITE!

CASEY, WAIT FOR THEM OUTSIDE!

THE AMBULANCE IS ON THE WAY? OKAY—I'LL BE OUT FRONT TO FLAG THEM DOWN. CASEY... MY NAME IS CASEY FEMURS. OKAY, I'LL STAY ON THE LINE.

1-2-3-4!

OH GOD... YOU'RE CHEEKS ARE GETTING COLD!

DAVID! DON'T YOU *DARE* LEAVE ME LIKE THIS! *YOU HEAR ME?!*

1! 2! 3! 4! BREATHE, GODDAMMIT! BREATHE!

DAVID? DAVID!

DON'T LEAVE ME! ≥ SOB ≥ DON'T LEAVE ME!

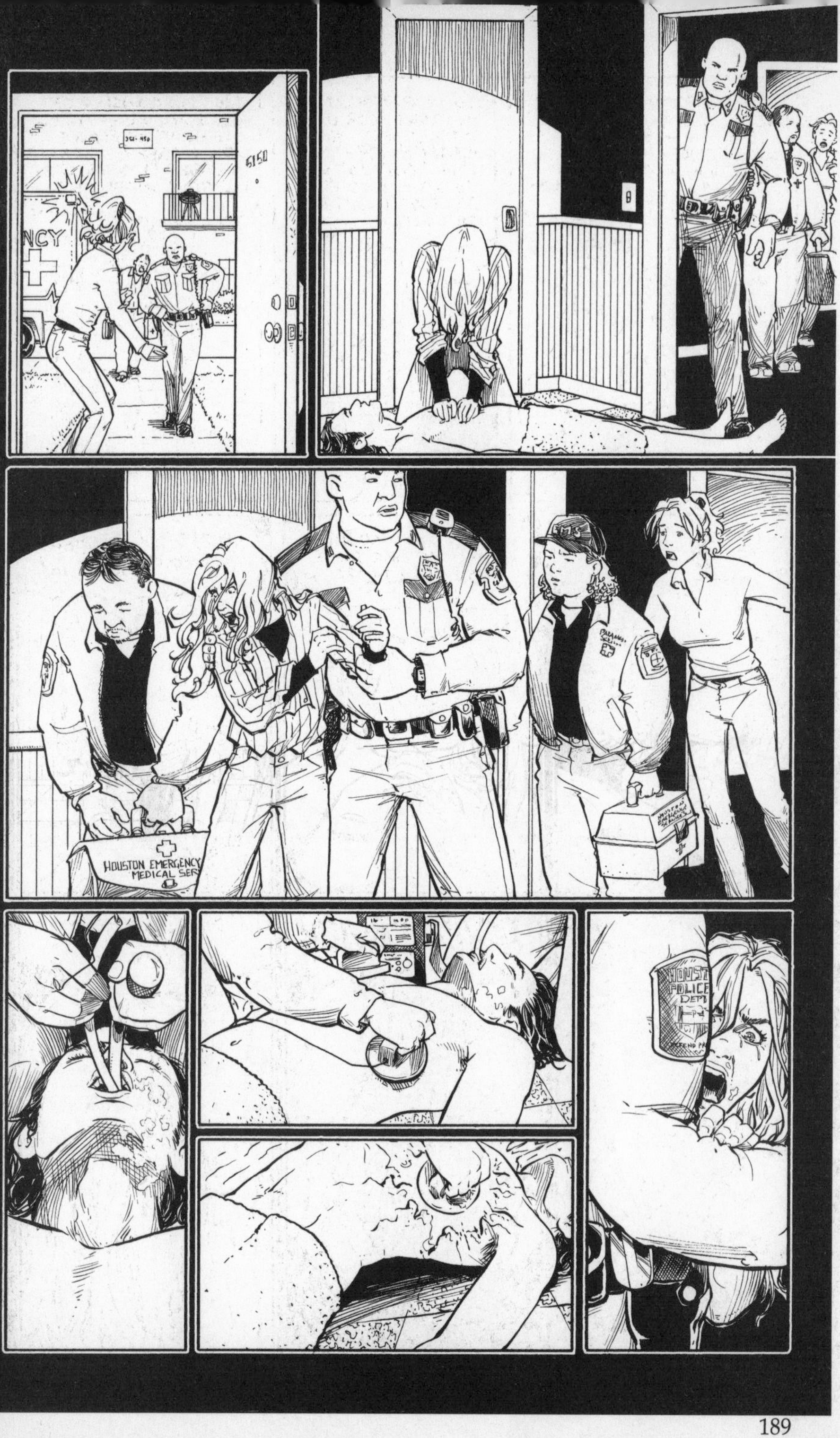
5150
NCY
HOUSTON EMERGENCY
MEDICAL SER
POLICE
DEPT

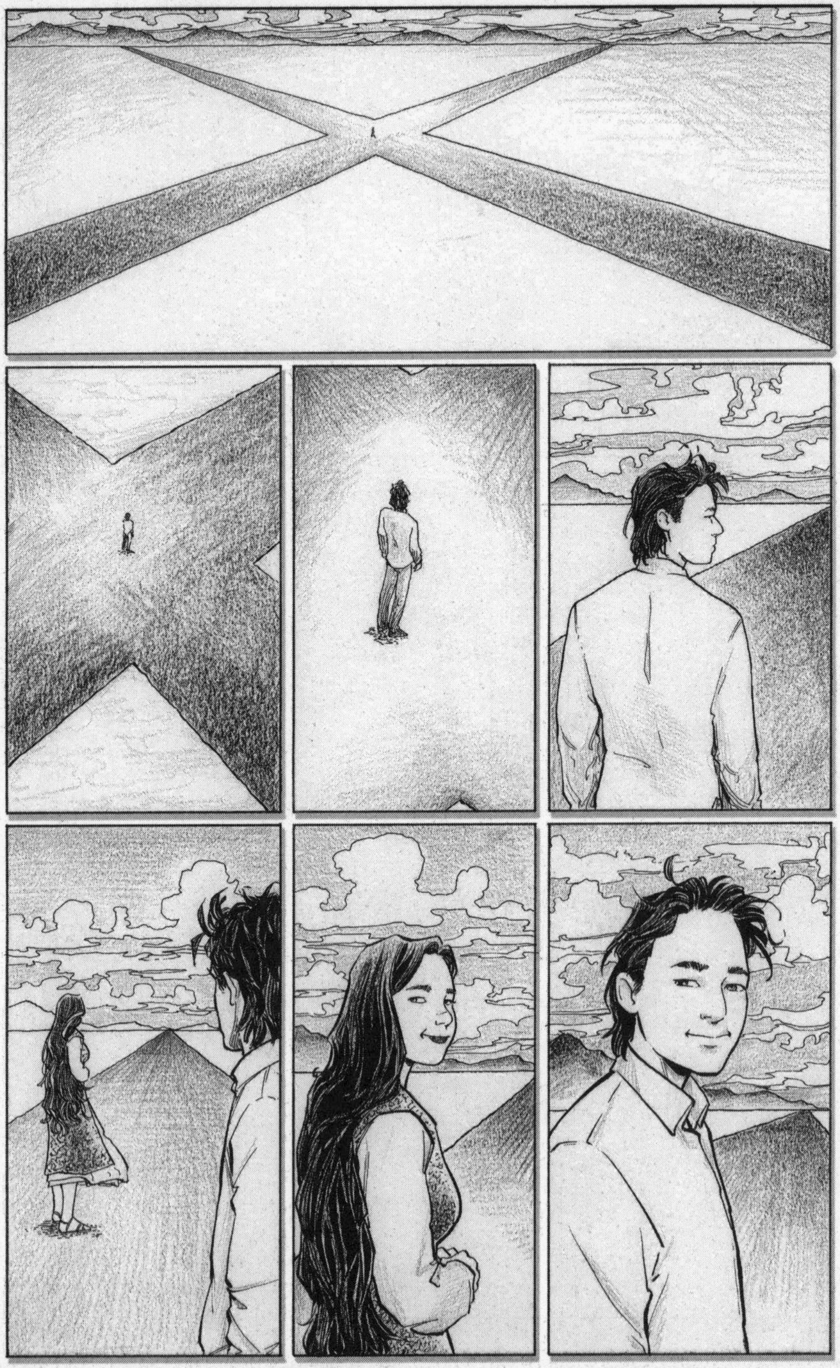

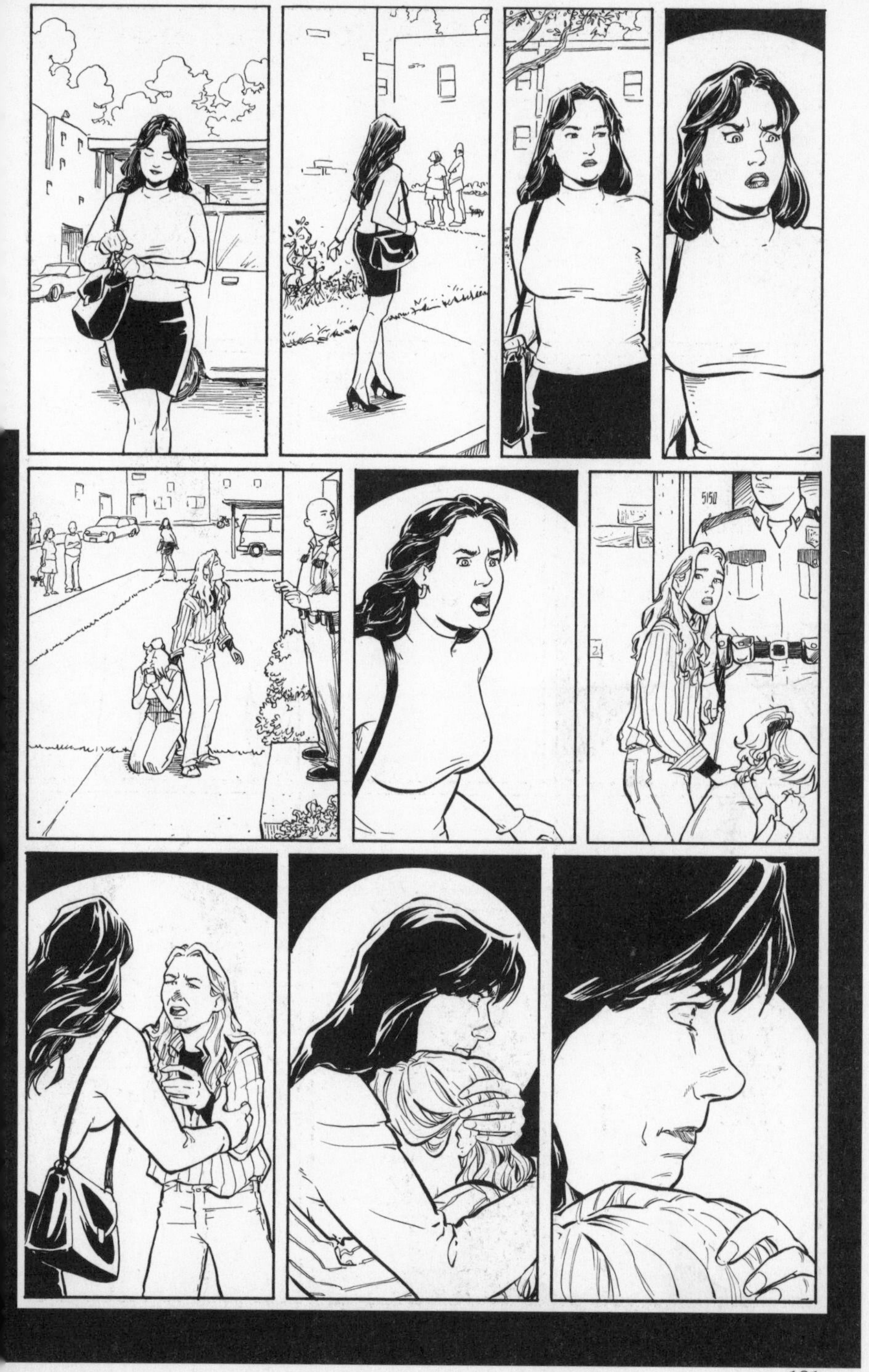
5150

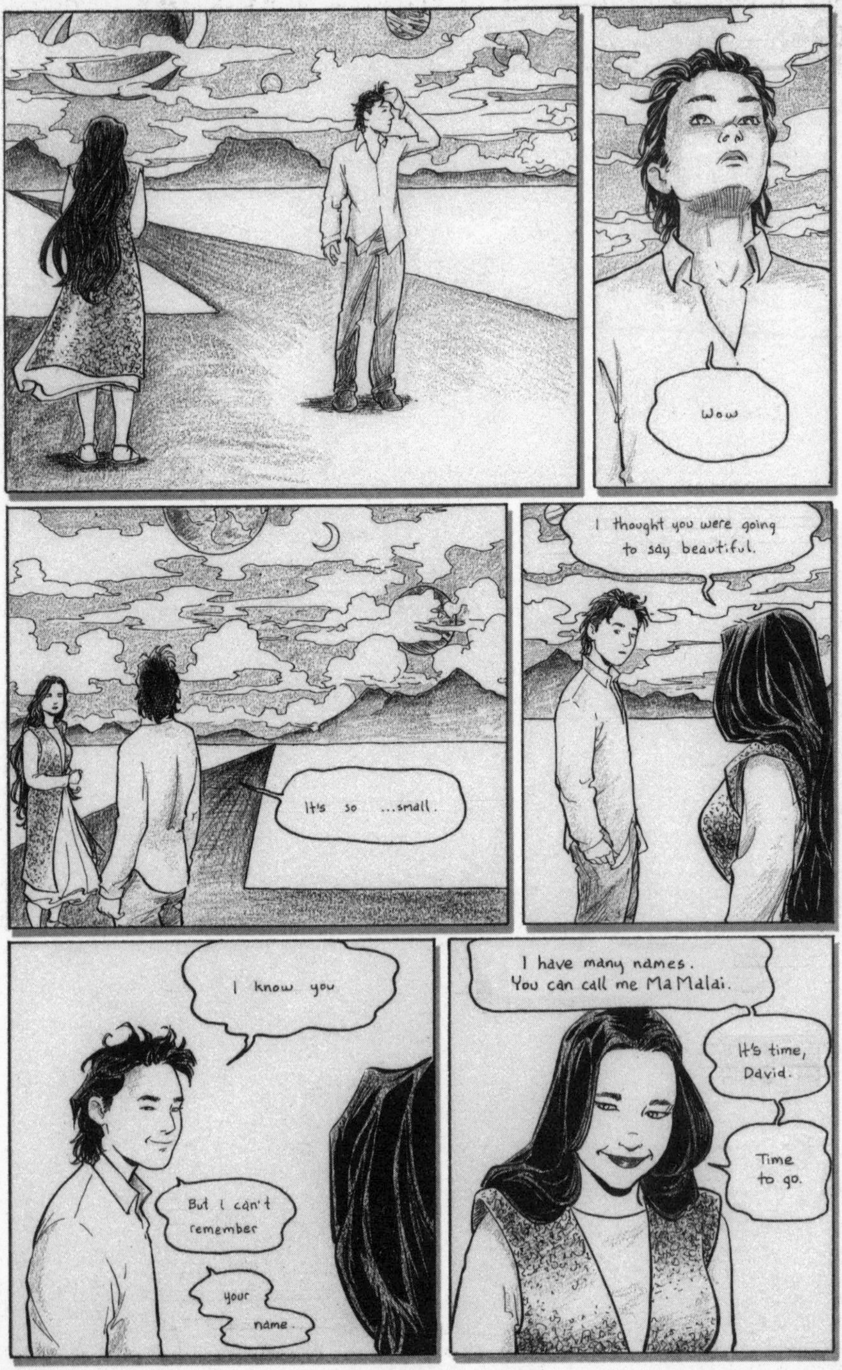
Wow
I thought you were going to say beautiful.
It's so ...small.
I know you
But I can't remember
your
name.
I have many names. You can call me Ma Malai.
It's time, David.
Time to go.

Text visible in images: EMERGENCY MEDICAL SERVICE

HERMANN EMERGENCY ENTRANCE

AMBULANCE

EMERGENC[Y]

[AUTH]ORIZED [PERS]ONNEL ONLY

EMERGENCY

PRIVATE CONSULTATION

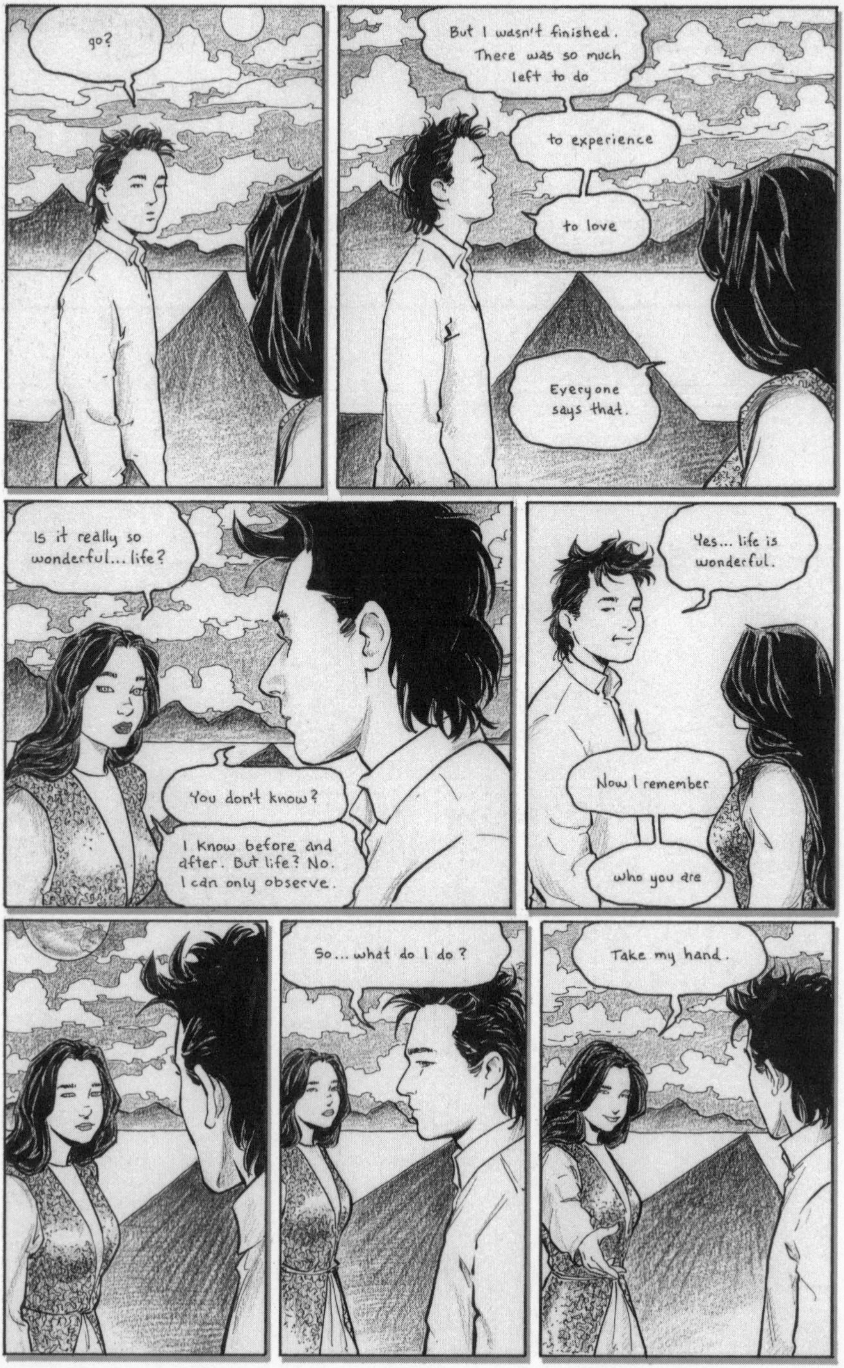
go?
But I wasn't finished. There was so much left to do
to experience
to love
Everyone says that.
Is it really so wonderful... life?
You don't know?
I know before and after. But life? No. I can only observe.
Yes... life is wonderful.
Now I remember
who you are
So... what do I do?
Take my hand.

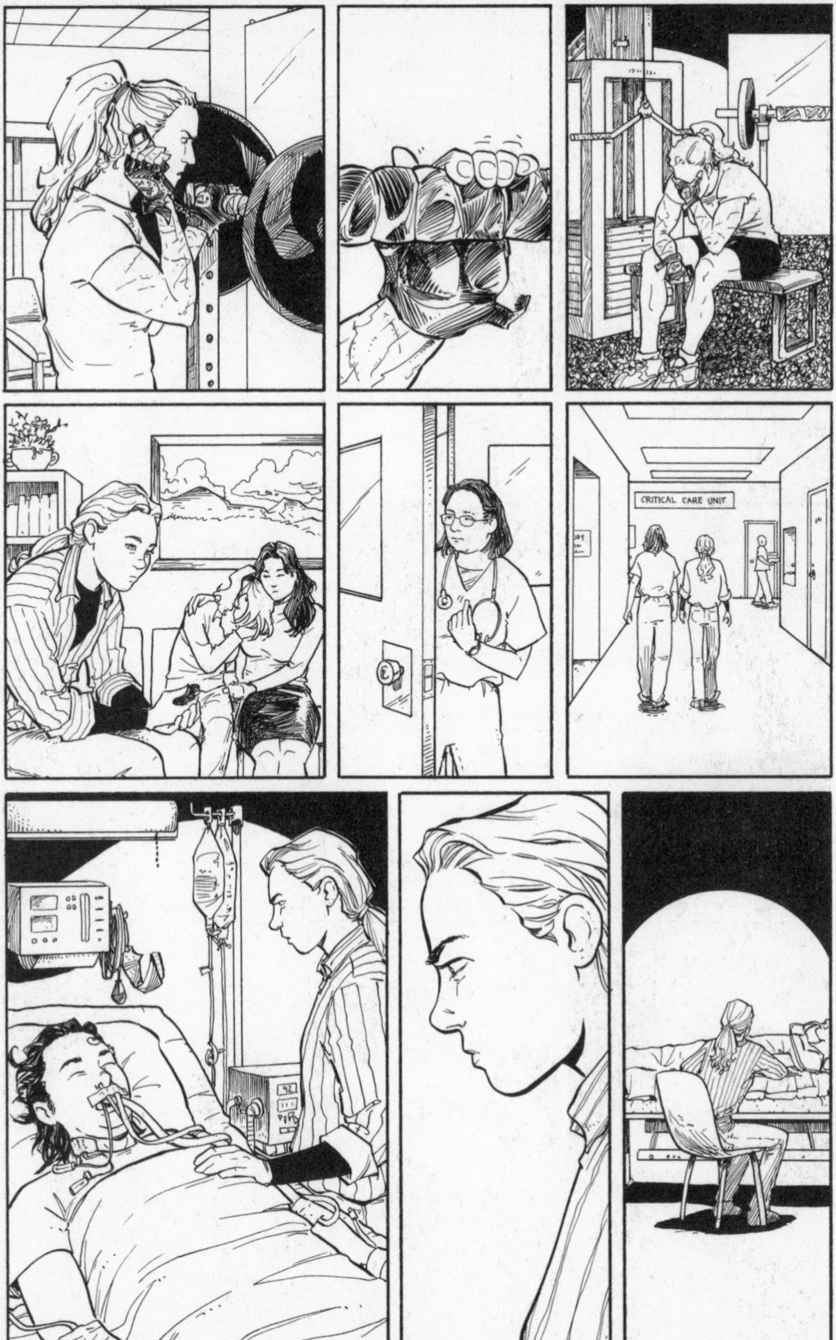
CRITICAL CARE UNIT

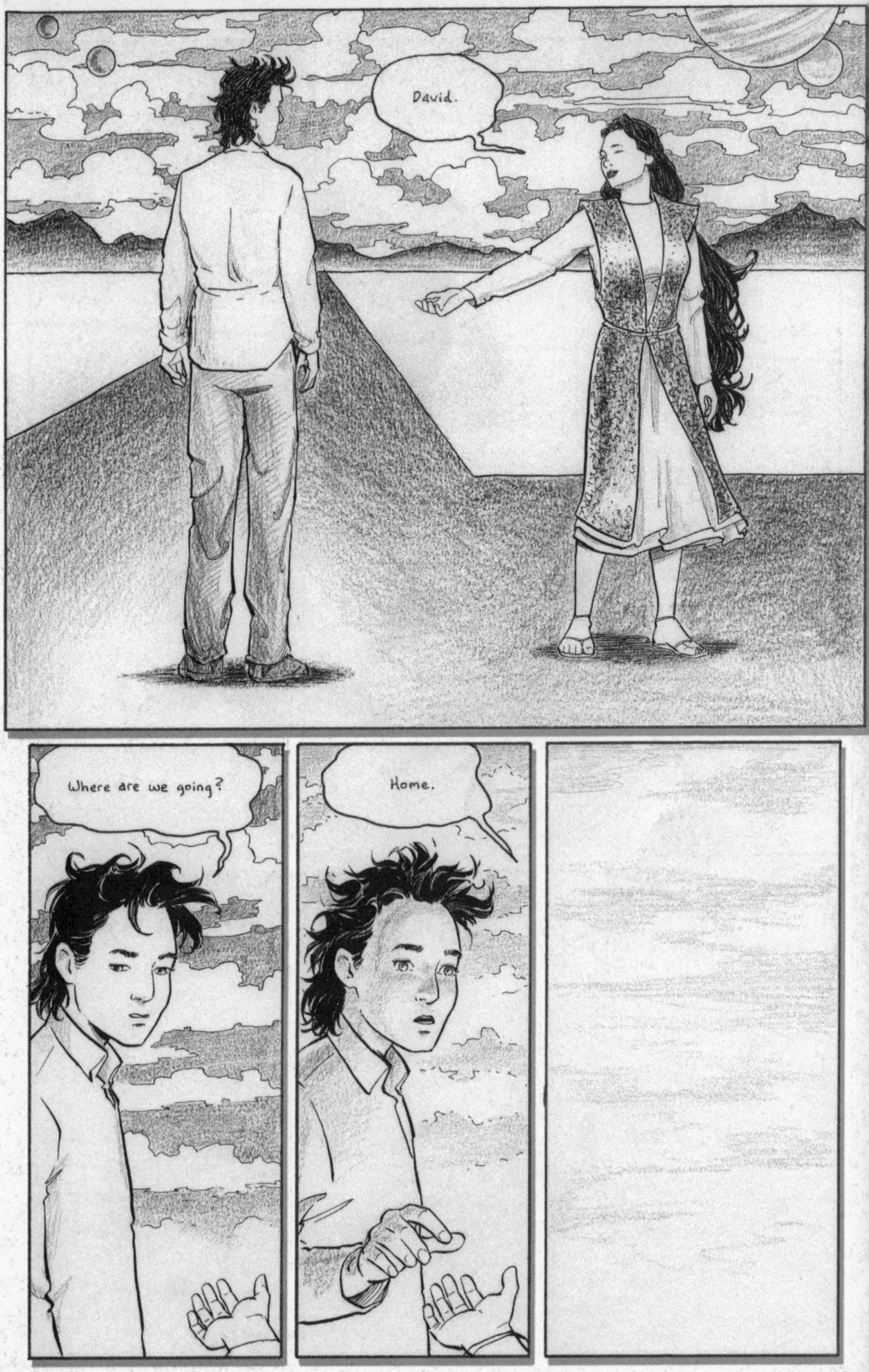
David.
Where are we going?
Home.

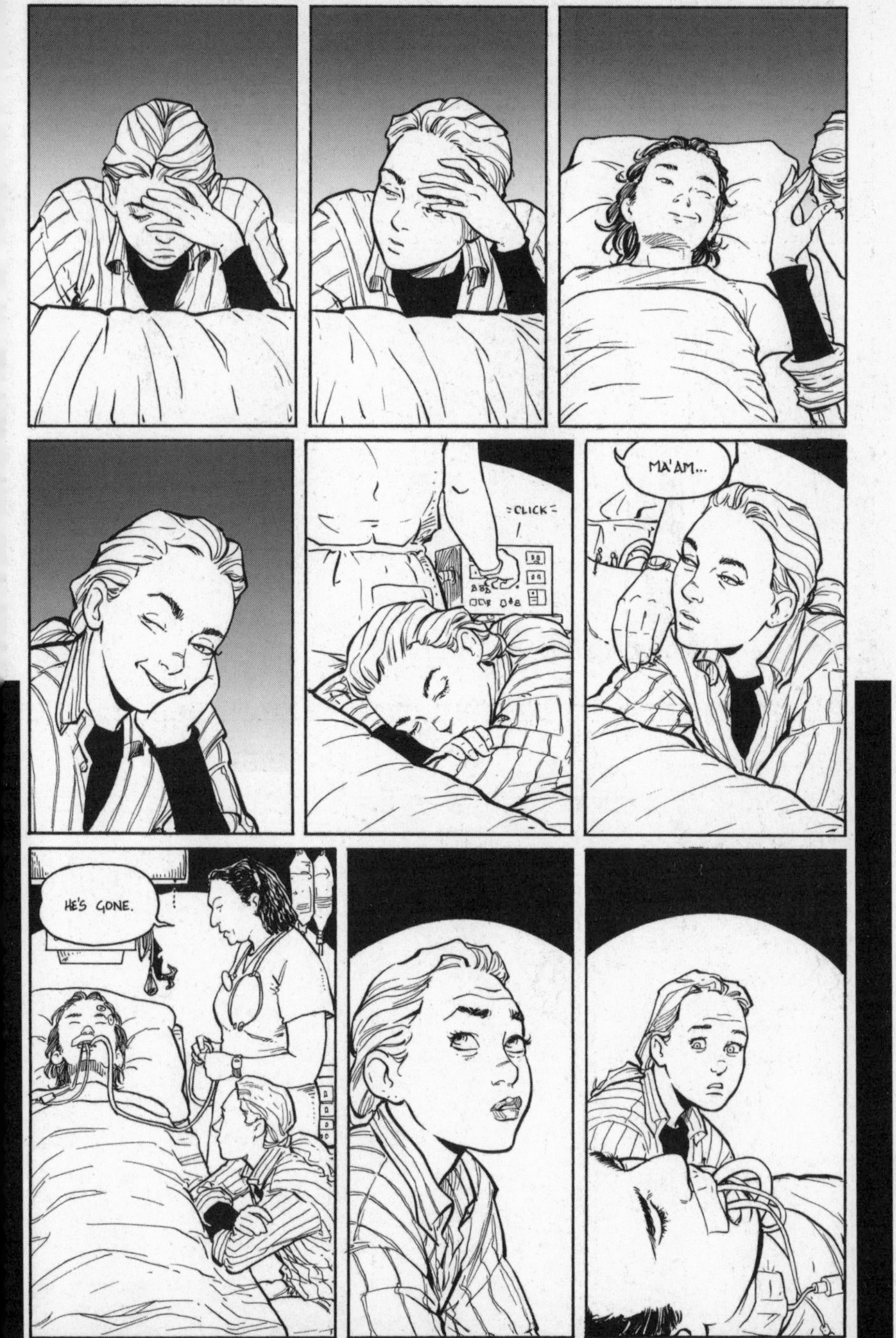
=CLICK=
MA'AM...
HE'S GONE.

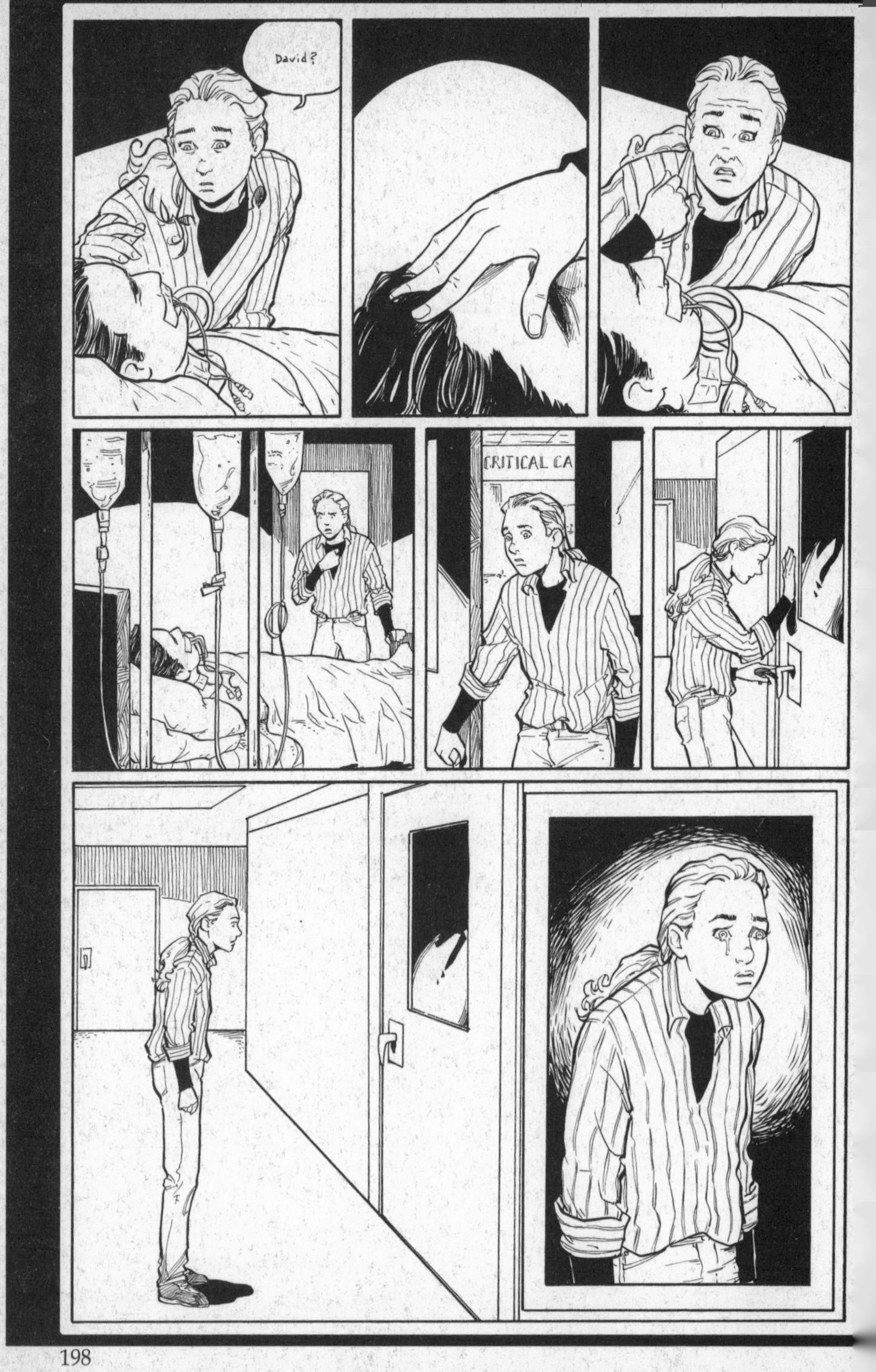
David?
CRITICAL CA

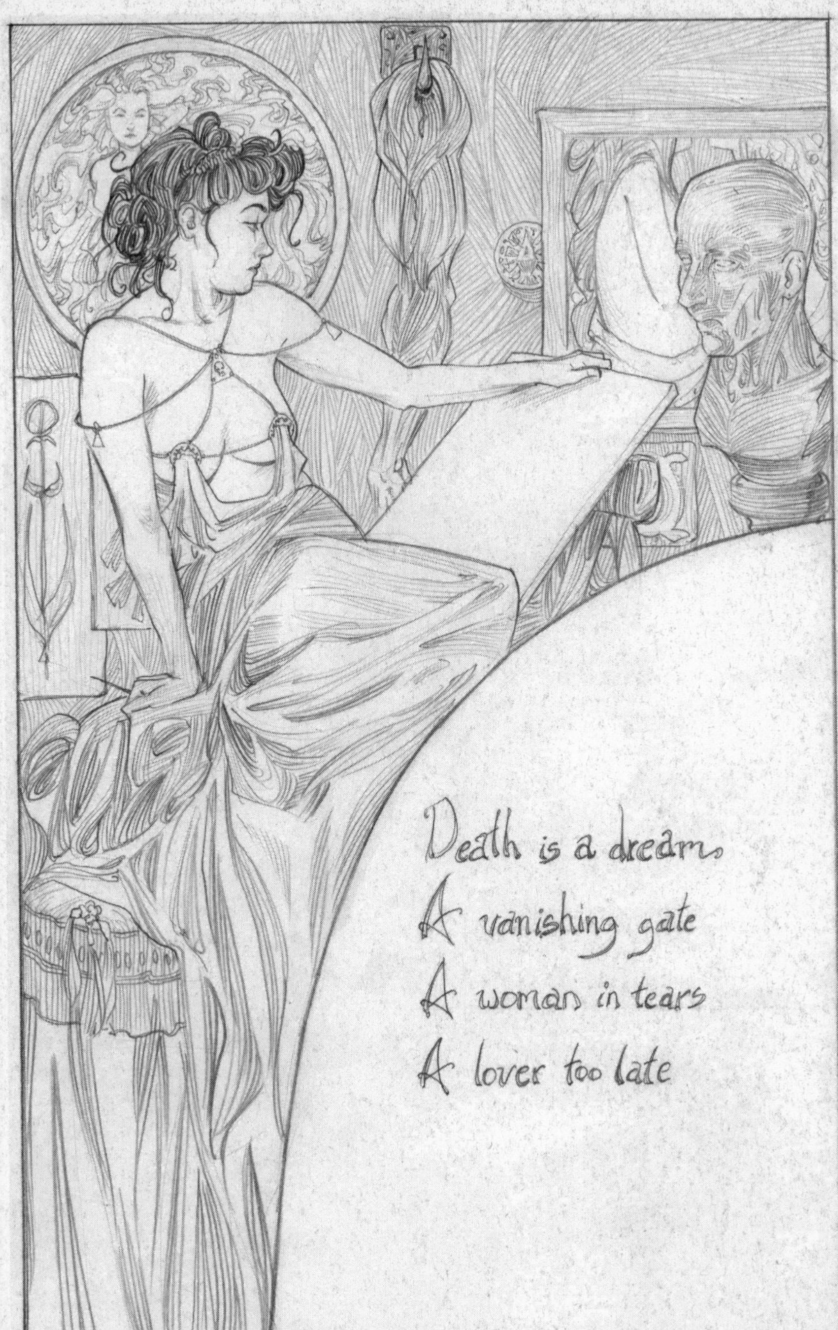
Death is a dream
A vanishing gate
A woman in tears
A lover too late

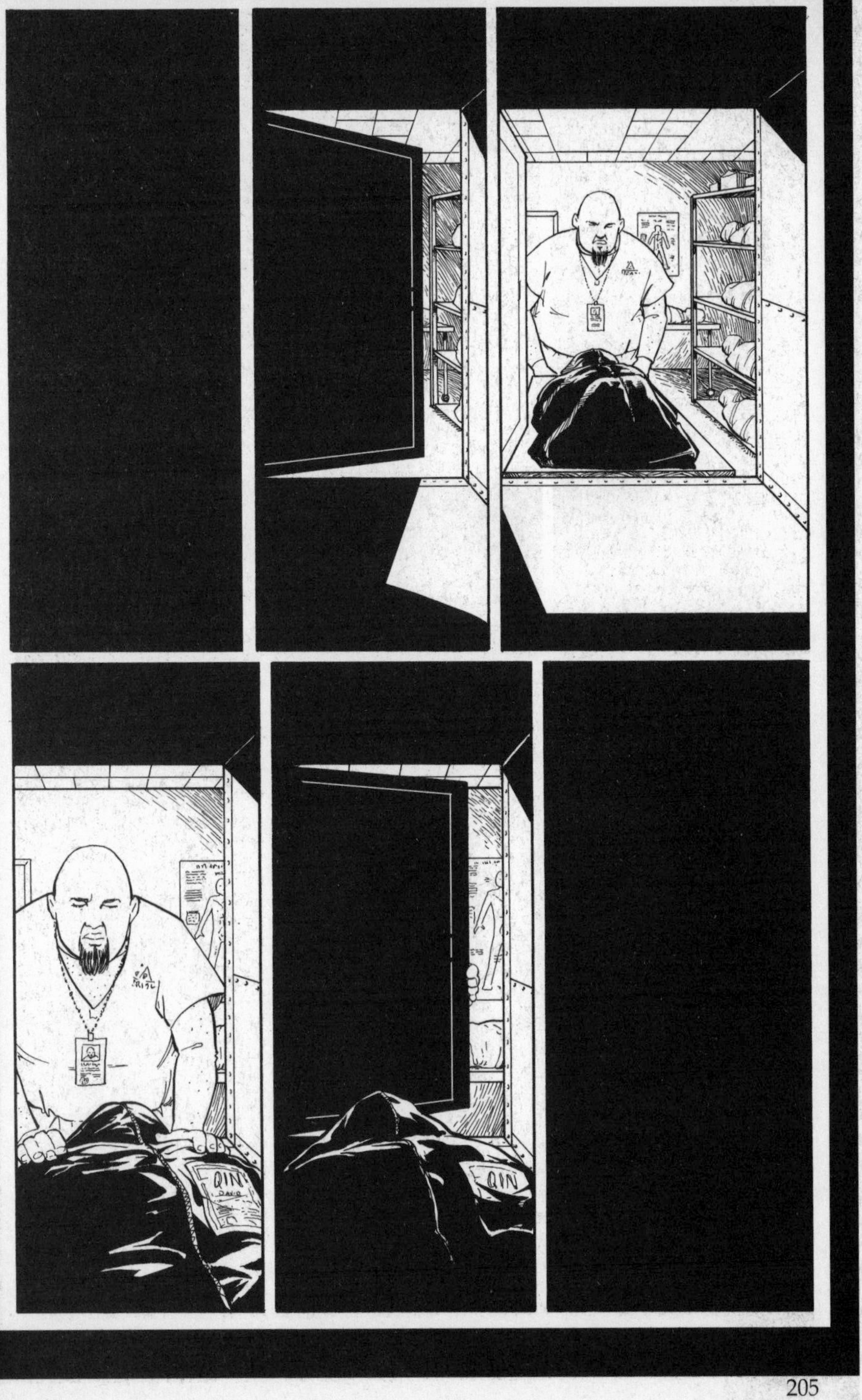
QIN
DAVID
QIN

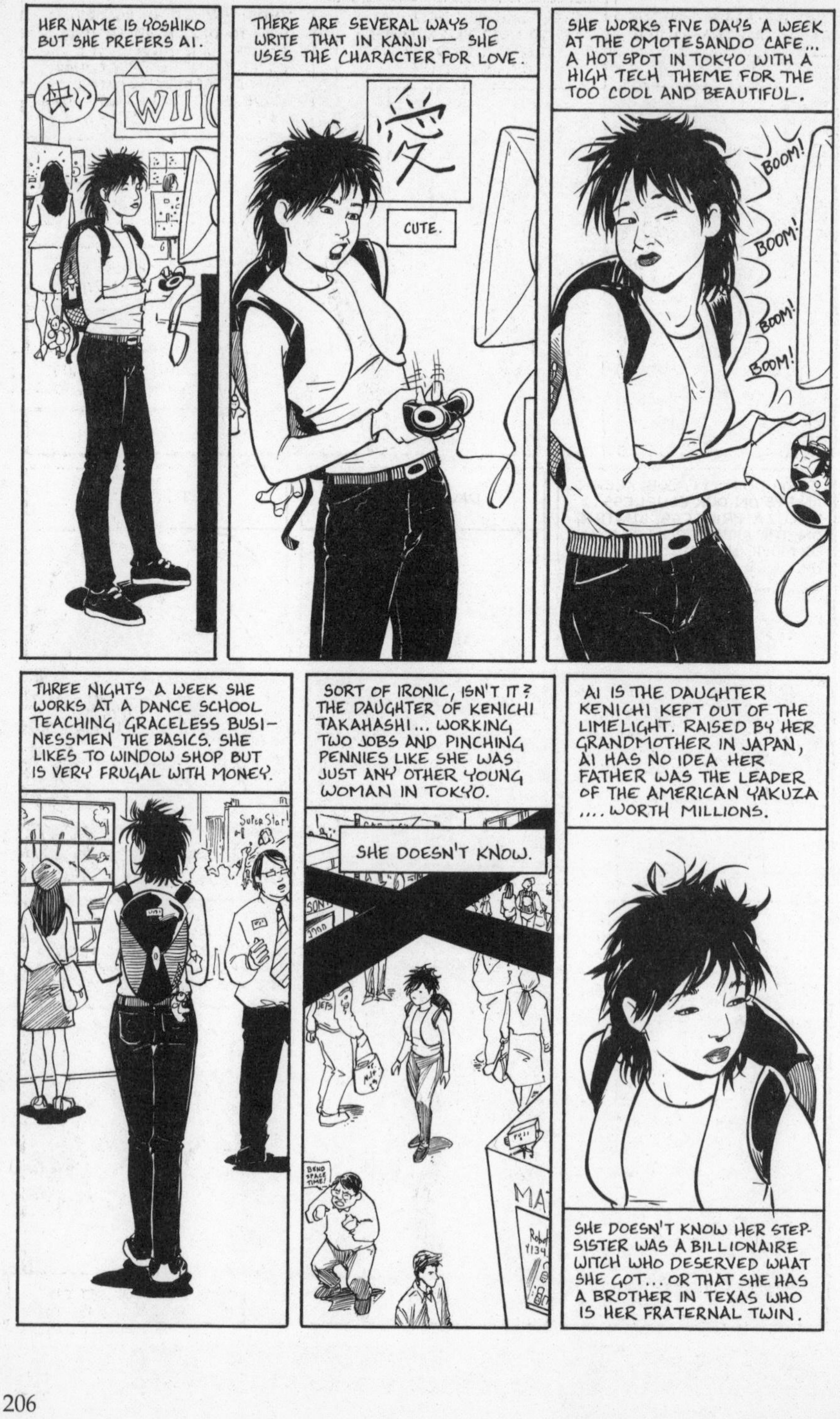
HER NAME IS YOSHIKO BUT SHE PREFERS AI.
WII
THERE ARE SEVERAL WAYS TO WRITE THAT IN KANJI — SHE USES THE CHARACTER FOR LOVE.
愛
CUTE.
SHE WORKS FIVE DAYS A WEEK AT THE OMOTESANDO CAFE... A HOT SPOT IN TOKYO WITH A HIGH TECH THEME FOR THE TOO COOL AND BEAUTIFUL.
BOOM!
BOOM!
BOOM!
BOOM!
THREE NIGHTS A WEEK SHE WORKS AT A DANCE SCHOOL TEACHING GRACELESS BUSINESSMEN THE BASICS. SHE LIKES TO WINDOW SHOP BUT IS VERY FRUGAL WITH MONEY.
Super Star!
SORT OF IRONIC, ISN'T IT? THE DAUGHTER OF KENICHI TAKAHASHI... WORKING TWO JOBS AND PINCHING PENNIES LIKE SHE WAS JUST ANY OTHER YOUNG WOMAN IN TOKYO.
SHE DOESN'T KNOW.
AI IS THE DAUGHTER KENICHI KEPT OUT OF THE LIMELIGHT. RAISED BY HER GRANDMOTHER IN JAPAN, AI HAS NO IDEA HER FATHER WAS THE LEADER OF THE AMERICAN YAKUZA .... WORTH MILLIONS.
SHE DOESN'T KNOW HER STEP-SISTER WAS A BILLIONAIRE WITCH WHO DESERVED WHAT SHE GOT... OR THAT SHE HAS A BROTHER IN TEXAS WHO IS HER FRATERNAL TWIN.

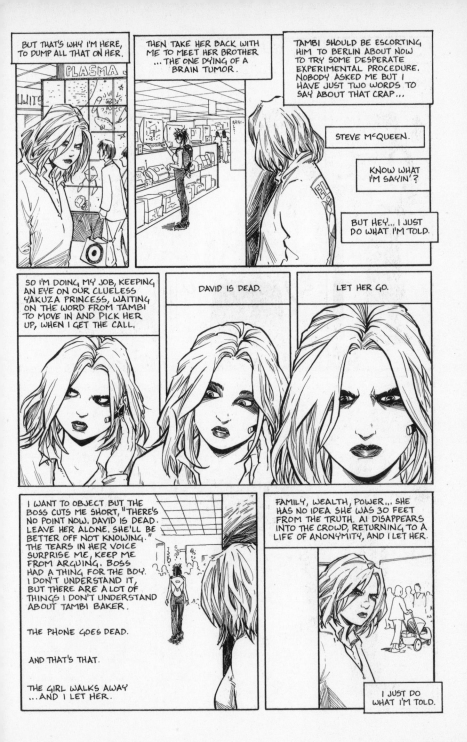

BUT THAT'S WHY I'M HERE, TO DUMP ALL THAT ON HER.

THEN TAKE HER BACK WITH ME TO MEET HER BROTHER ...THE ONE DYING OF A BRAIN TUMOR.

TAMBI SHOULD BE ESCORTING HIM TO BERLIN ABOUT NOW TO TRY SOME DESPERATE EXPERIMENTAL PROCEDURE. NOBODY ASKED ME BUT I HAVE JUST TWO WORDS TO SAY ABOUT THAT CRAP...

STEVE McQUEEN.

KNOW WHAT I'M SAYIN'?

BUT HEY... I JUST DO WHAT I'M TOLD.

SO I'M DOING MY JOB, KEEPING AN EYE ON OUR CLUELESS YAKUZA PRINCESS, WAITING ON THE WORD FROM TAMBI TO MOVE IN AND PICK HER UP, WHEN I GET THE CALL.

DAVID IS DEAD.

LET HER GO.

I WANT TO OBJECT BUT THE BOSS CUTS ME SHORT, "THERE'S NO POINT NOW. DAVID IS DEAD. LEAVE HER ALONE. SHE'LL BE BETTER OFF NOT KNOWING." THE TEARS IN HER VOICE SURPRISE ME, KEEP ME FROM ARGUING. BOSS HAD A THING FOR THE BOY. I DON'T UNDERSTAND IT, BUT THERE ARE A LOT OF THINGS I DON'T UNDERSTAND ABOUT TAMBI BAKER.

THE PHONE GOES DEAD.

AND THAT'S THAT.

THE GIRL WALKS AWAY ...AND I LET HER.

FAMILY, WEALTH, POWER... SHE HAS NO IDEA SHE WAS 30 FEET FROM THE TRUTH. AI DISAPPEARS INTO THE CROWD, RETURNING TO A LIFE OF ANONYMITY, AND I LET HER.

I JUST DO WHAT I'M TOLD.

207

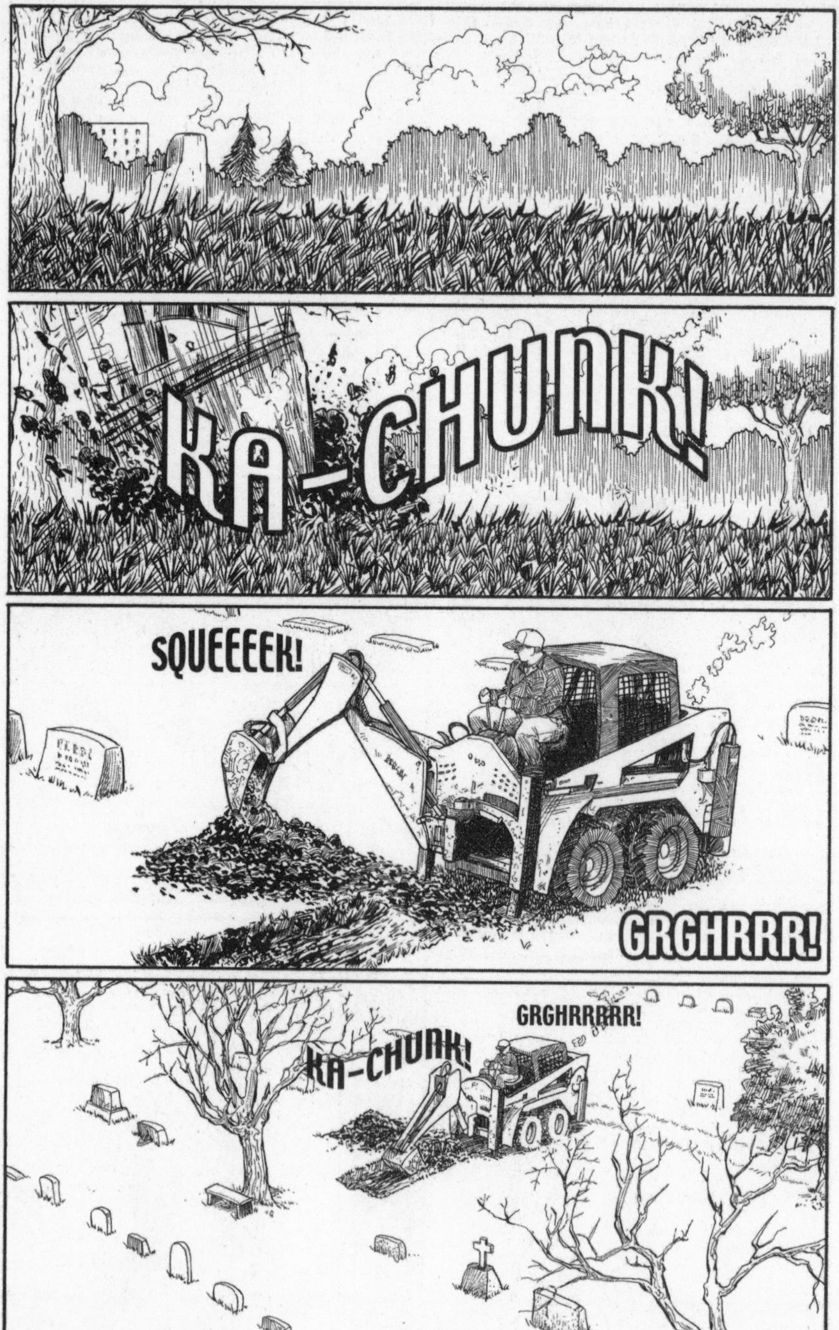
KA-CHUNK!
SQUEEEEK!
GRGHRRR!
GRGHRRRRR!
KA-CHUNK!

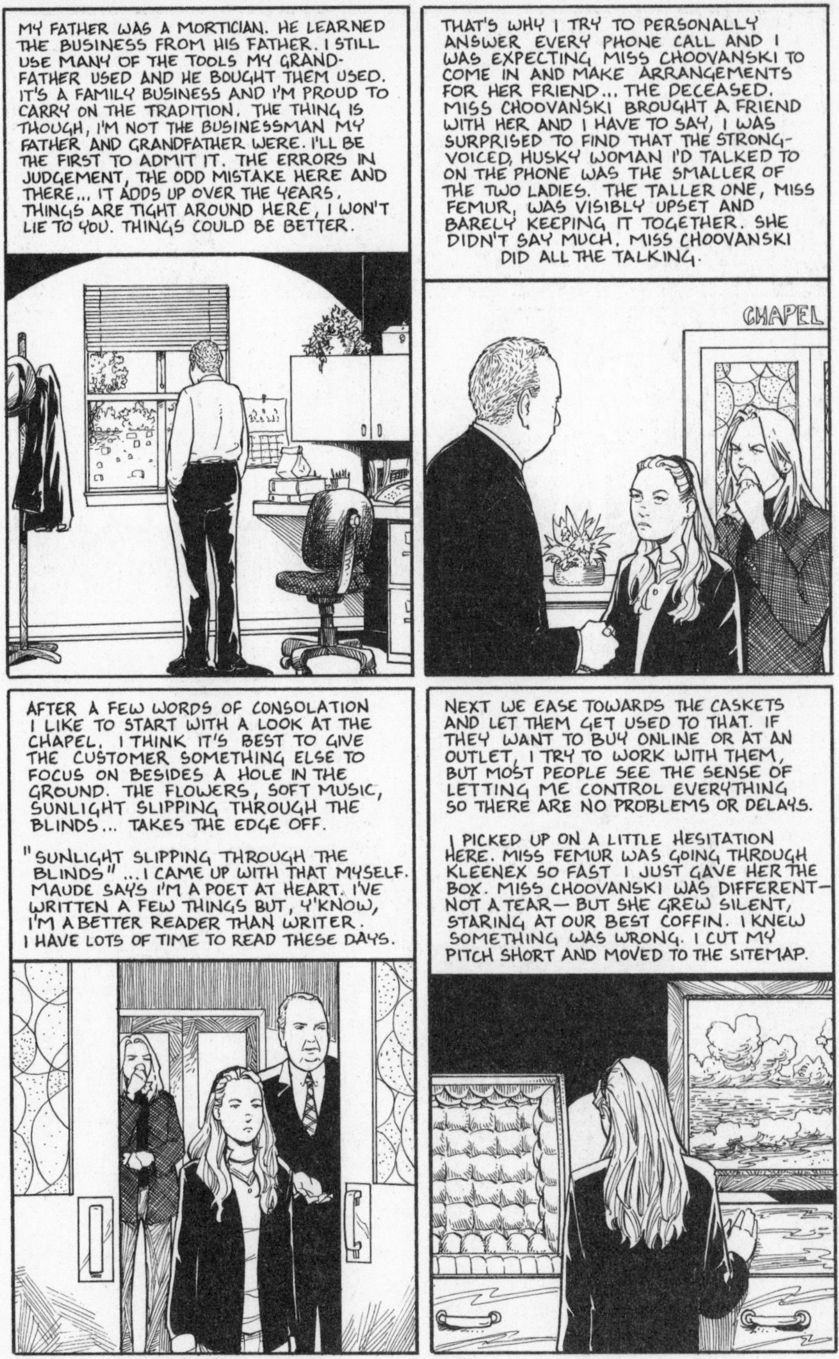
MY FATHER WAS A MORTICIAN. HE LEARNED THE BUSINESS FROM HIS FATHER. I STILL USE MANY OF THE TOOLS MY GRANDFATHER USED AND HE BOUGHT THEM USED. IT'S A FAMILY BUSINESS AND I'M PROUD TO CARRY ON THE TRADITION. THE THING IS THOUGH, I'M NOT THE BUSINESSMAN MY FATHER AND GRANDFATHER WERE. I'LL BE THE FIRST TO ADMIT IT. THE ERRORS IN JUDGEMENT, THE ODD MISTAKE HERE AND THERE... IT ADDS UP OVER THE YEARS. THINGS ARE TIGHT AROUND HERE, I WON'T LIE TO YOU. THINGS COULD BE BETTER.
THAT'S WHY I TRY TO PERSONALLY ANSWER EVERY PHONE CALL AND I WAS EXPECTING MISS CHOOVANSKI TO COME IN AND MAKE ARRANGEMENTS FOR HER FRIEND... THE DECEASED. MISS CHOOVANSKI BROUGHT A FRIEND WITH HER AND I HAVE TO SAY, I WAS SURPRISED TO FIND THAT THE STRONG-VOICED, HUSKY WOMAN I'D TALKED TO ON THE PHONE WAS THE SMALLER OF THE TWO LADIES. THE TALLER ONE, MISS FEMUR, WAS VISIBLY UPSET AND BARELY KEEPING IT TOGETHER. SHE DIDN'T SAY MUCH. MISS CHOOVANSKI DID ALL THE TALKING.
CHAPEL
AFTER A FEW WORDS OF CONSOLATION I LIKE TO START WITH A LOOK AT THE CHAPEL. I THINK IT'S BEST TO GIVE THE CUSTOMER SOMETHING ELSE TO FOCUS ON BESIDES A HOLE IN THE GROUND. THE FLOWERS, SOFT MUSIC, SUNLIGHT SLIPPING THROUGH THE BLINDS... TAKES THE EDGE OFF.
"SUNLIGHT SLIPPING THROUGH THE BLINDS" ...I CAME UP WITH THAT MYSELF. MAUDE SAYS I'M A POET AT HEART. I'VE WRITTEN A FEW THINGS BUT, Y'KNOW, I'M A BETTER READER THAN WRITER. I HAVE LOTS OF TIME TO READ THESE DAYS.
NEXT WE EASE TOWARDS THE CASKETS AND LET THEM GET USED TO THAT. IF THEY WANT TO BUY ONLINE OR AT AN OUTLET, I TRY TO WORK WITH THEM, BUT MOST PEOPLE SEE THE SENSE OF LETTING ME CONTROL EVERYTHING SO THERE ARE NO PROBLEMS OR DELAYS.
I PICKED UP ON A LITTLE HESITATION HERE. MISS FEMUR WAS GOING THROUGH KLEENEX SO FAST I JUST GAVE HER THE BOX. MISS CHOOVANSKI WAS DIFFERENT— NOT A TEAR— BUT SHE GREW SILENT, STARING AT OUR BEST COFFIN. I KNEW SOMETHING WAS WRONG. I CUT MY PITCH SHORT AND MOVED TO THE SITEMAP.

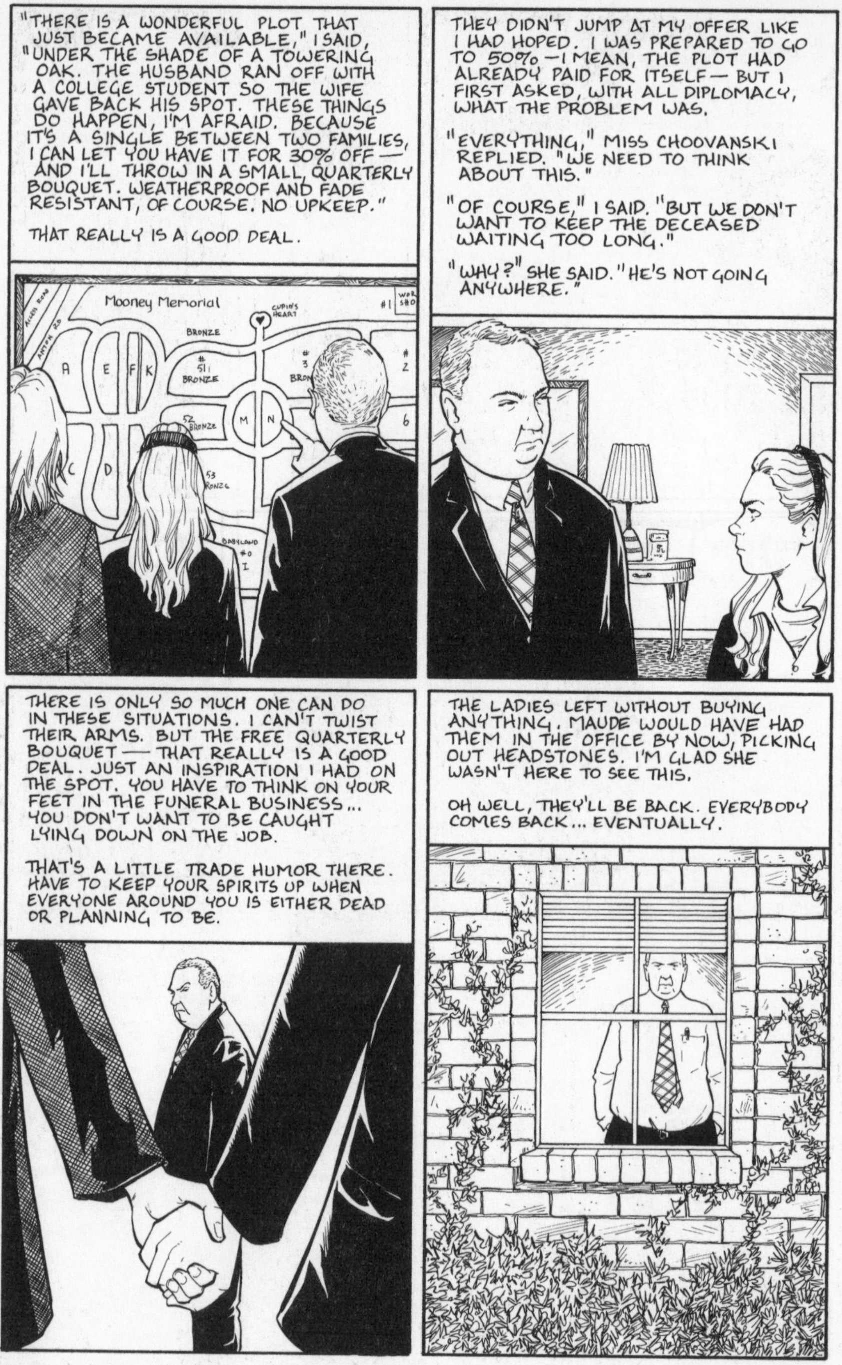
"THERE IS A WONDERFUL PLOT THAT JUST BECAME AVAILABLE," I SAID, "UNDER THE SHADE OF A TOWERING OAK. THE HUSBAND RAN OFF WITH A COLLEGE STUDENT SO THE WIFE GAVE BACK HIS SPOT. THESE THINGS DO HAPPEN, I'M AFRAID. BECAUSE IT'S A SINGLE BETWEEN TWO FAMILIES, I CAN LET YOU HAVE IT FOR 30% OFF — AND I'LL THROW IN A SMALL, QUARTERLY BOUQUET. WEATHERPROOF AND FADE RESISTANT, OF COURSE. NO UPKEEP."
THAT REALLY IS A GOOD DEAL.
Mooney Memorial
THEY DIDN'T JUMP AT MY OFFER LIKE I HAD HOPED. I WAS PREPARED TO GO TO 50% — I MEAN, THE PLOT HAD ALREADY PAID FOR ITSELF — BUT I FIRST ASKED, WITH ALL DIPLOMACY, WHAT THE PROBLEM WAS.
"EVERYTHING," MISS CHOOVANSKI REPLIED. "WE NEED TO THINK ABOUT THIS."
"OF COURSE," I SAID. "BUT WE DON'T WANT TO KEEP THE DECEASED WAITING TOO LONG."
"WHY?" SHE SAID. "HE'S NOT GOING ANYWHERE."
THERE IS ONLY SO MUCH ONE CAN DO IN THESE SITUATIONS. I CAN'T TWIST THEIR ARMS. BUT THE FREE QUARTERLY BOUQUET — THAT REALLY IS A GOOD DEAL. JUST AN INSPIRATION I HAD ON THE SPOT. YOU HAVE TO THINK ON YOUR FEET IN THE FUNERAL BUSINESS... YOU DON'T WANT TO BE CAUGHT LYING DOWN ON THE JOB.
THAT'S A LITTLE TRADE HUMOR THERE. HAVE TO KEEP YOUR SPIRITS UP WHEN EVERYONE AROUND YOU IS EITHER DEAD OR PLANNING TO BE.
THE LADIES LEFT WITHOUT BUYING ANYTHING. MAUDE WOULD HAVE HAD THEM IN THE OFFICE BY NOW, PICKING OUT HEADSTONES. I'M GLAD SHE WASN'T HERE TO SEE THIS.
OH WELL, THEY'LL BE BACK. EVERYBODY COMES BACK... EVENTUALLY.

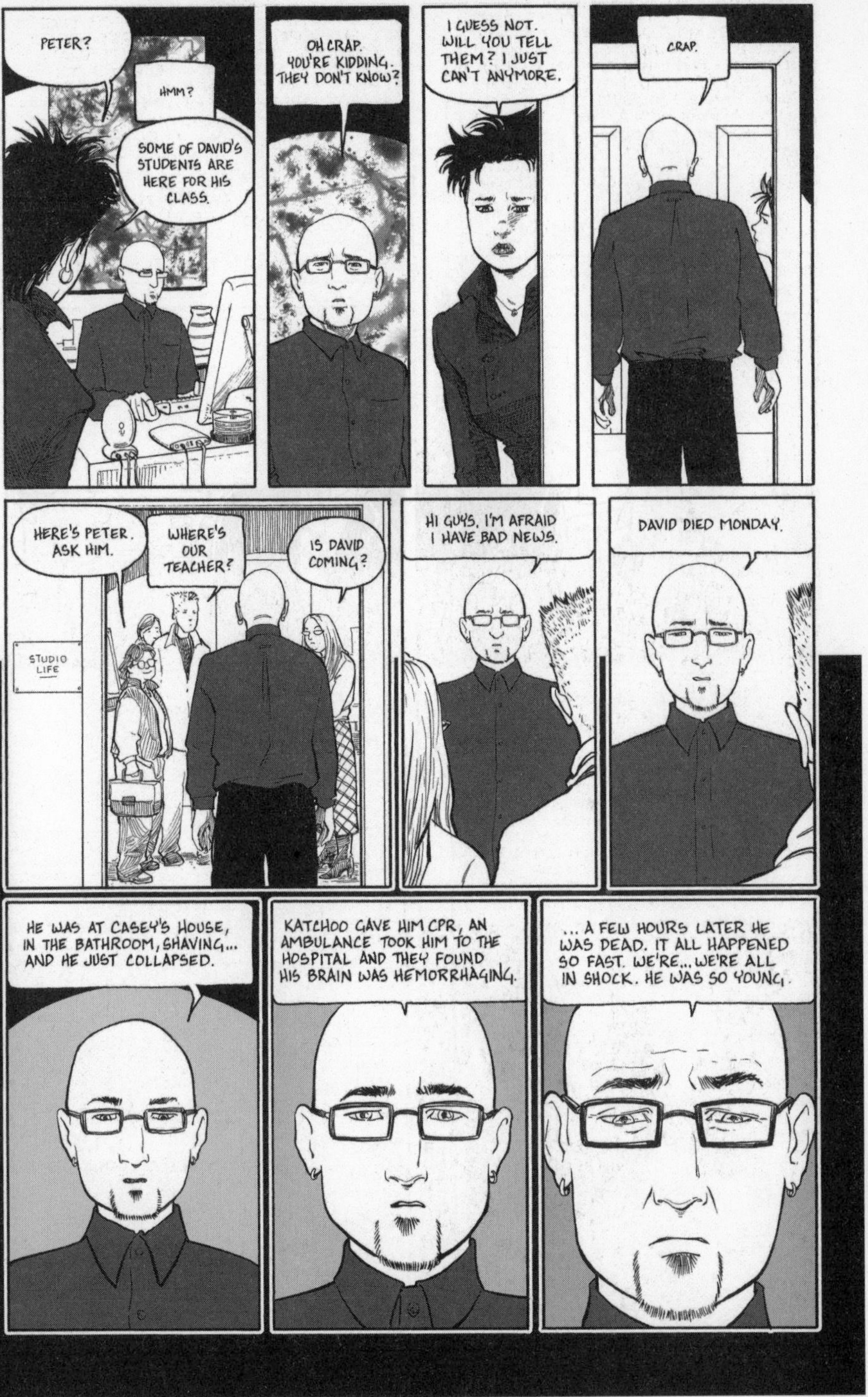
PETER?
HMM?
SOME OF DAVID'S STUDENTS ARE HERE FOR HIS CLASS.
OH CRAP. YOU'RE KIDDING. THEY DON'T KNOW?
I GUESS NOT. WILL YOU TELL THEM? I JUST CAN'T ANYMORE.
CRAP.
HERE'S PETER. ASK HIM.
WHERE'S OUR TEACHER?
IS DAVID COMING?
STUDIO LIFE
HI GUYS. I'M AFRAID I HAVE BAD NEWS.
DAVID DIED MONDAY.
HE WAS AT CASEY'S HOUSE, IN THE BATHROOM, SHAVING... AND HE JUST COLLAPSED.
KATCHOO GAVE HIM CPR, AN AMBULANCE TOOK HIM TO THE HOSPITAL AND THEY FOUND HIS BRAIN WAS HEMORRHAGING.
... A FEW HOURS LATER HE WAS DEAD. IT ALL HAPPENED SO FAST. WE'RE... WE'RE ALL IN SHOCK. HE WAS SO YOUNG.

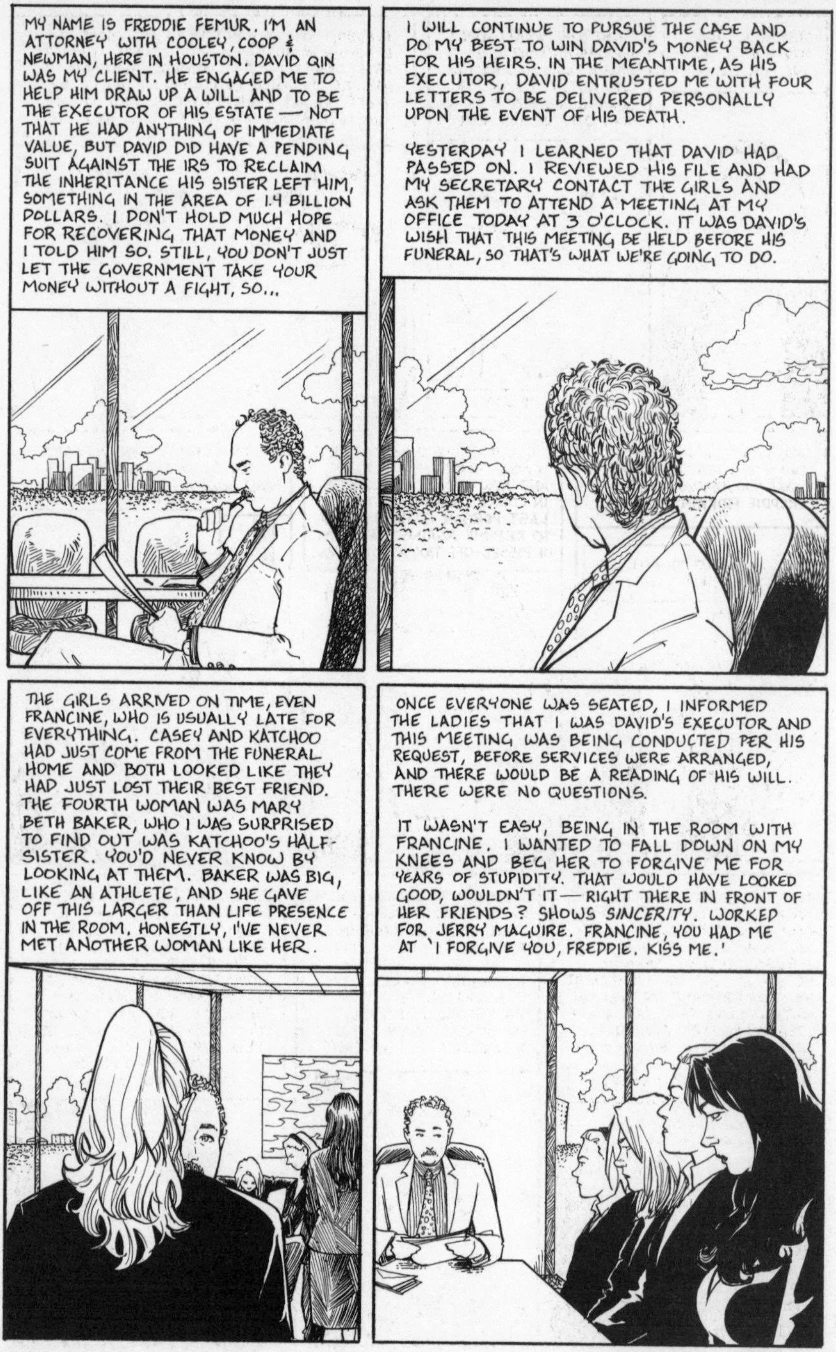
MY NAME IS FREDDIE FEMUR. I'M AN ATTORNEY WITH COOLEY, COOP & NEWMAN, HERE IN HOUSTON. DAVID QIN WAS MY CLIENT. HE ENGAGED ME TO HELP HIM DRAW UP A WILL AND TO BE THE EXECUTOR OF HIS ESTATE — NOT THAT HE HAD ANYTHING OF IMMEDIATE VALUE, BUT DAVID DID HAVE A PENDING SUIT AGAINST THE IRS TO RECLAIM THE INHERITANCE HIS SISTER LEFT HIM, SOMETHING IN THE AREA OF 1.4 BILLION DOLLARS. I DON'T HOLD MUCH HOPE FOR RECOVERING THAT MONEY AND I TOLD HIM SO. STILL, YOU DON'T JUST LET THE GOVERNMENT TAKE YOUR MONEY WITHOUT A FIGHT, SO...
I WILL CONTINUE TO PURSUE THE CASE AND DO MY BEST TO WIN DAVID'S MONEY BACK FOR HIS HEIRS. IN THE MEANTIME, AS HIS EXECUTOR, DAVID ENTRUSTED ME WITH FOUR LETTERS TO BE DELIVERED PERSONALLY UPON THE EVENT OF HIS DEATH.
YESTERDAY I LEARNED THAT DAVID HAD PASSED ON. I REVIEWED HIS FILE AND HAD MY SECRETARY CONTACT THE GIRLS AND ASK THEM TO ATTEND A MEETING AT MY OFFICE TODAY AT 3 O'CLOCK. IT WAS DAVID'S WISH THAT THIS MEETING BE HELD BEFORE HIS FUNERAL, SO THAT'S WHAT WE'RE GOING TO DO.
THE GIRLS ARRIVED ON TIME, EVEN FRANCINE, WHO IS USUALLY LATE FOR EVERYTHING. CASEY AND KATCHOO HAD JUST COME FROM THE FUNERAL HOME AND BOTH LOOKED LIKE THEY HAD JUST LOST THEIR BEST FRIEND. THE FOURTH WOMAN WAS MARY BETH BAKER, WHO I WAS SURPRISED TO FIND OUT WAS KATCHOO'S HALF-SISTER. YOU'D NEVER KNOW BY LOOKING AT THEM. BAKER WAS BIG, LIKE AN ATHLETE, AND SHE GAVE OFF THIS LARGER THAN LIFE PRESENCE IN THE ROOM. HONESTLY, I'VE NEVER MET ANOTHER WOMAN LIKE HER.
ONCE EVERYONE WAS SEATED, I INFORMED THE LADIES THAT I WAS DAVID'S EXECUTOR AND THIS MEETING WAS BEING CONDUCTED PER HIS REQUEST, BEFORE SERVICES WERE ARRANGED, AND THERE WOULD BE A READING OF HIS WILL. THERE WERE NO QUESTIONS.
IT WASN'T EASY, BEING IN THE ROOM WITH FRANCINE. I WANTED TO FALL DOWN ON MY KNEES AND BEG HER TO FORGIVE ME FOR YEARS OF STUPIDITY. THAT WOULD HAVE LOOKED GOOD, WOULDN'T IT — RIGHT THERE IN FRONT OF HER FRIENDS? SHOWS SINCERITY. WORKED FOR JERRY MAGUIRE. FRANCINE, YOU HAD ME AT 'I FORGIVE YOU, FREDDIE. KISS ME.'

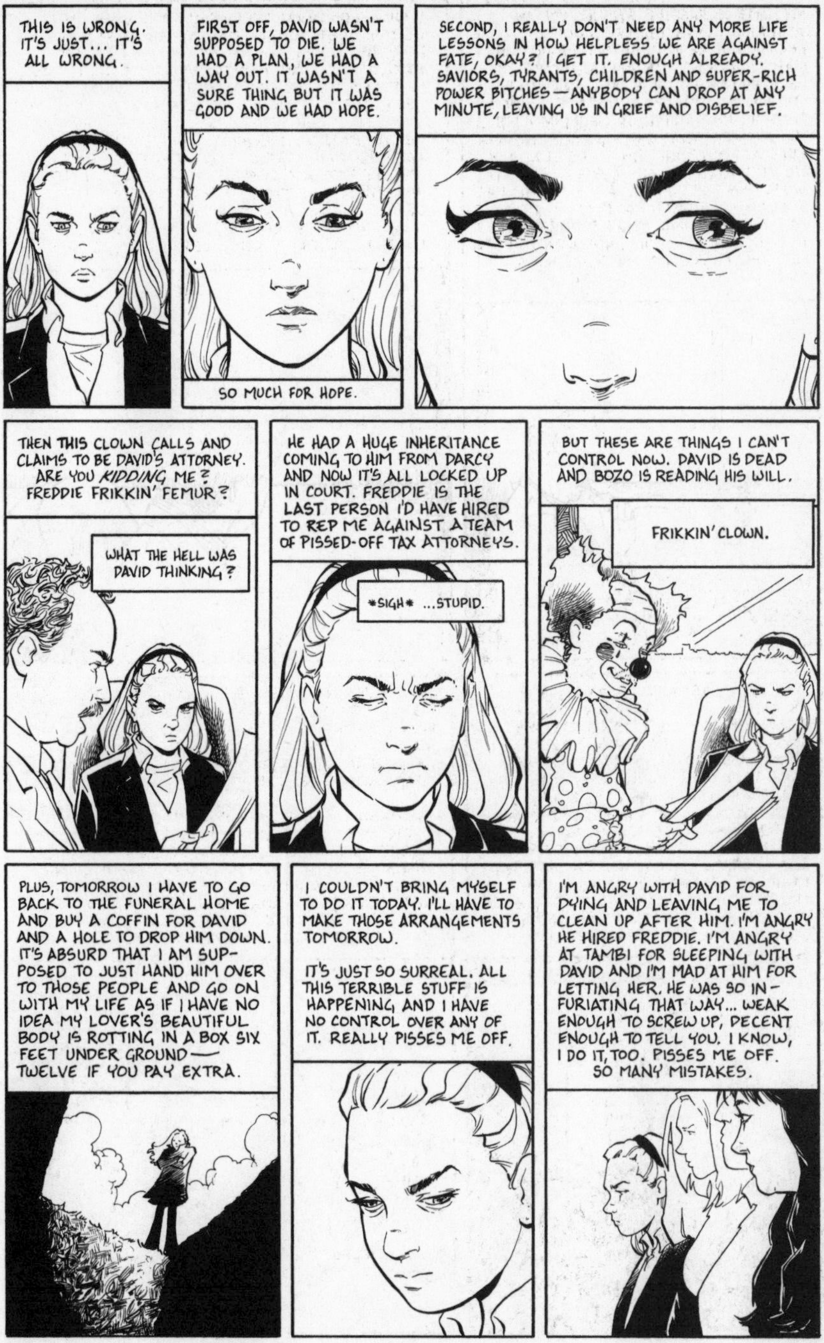
THIS IS WRONG. IT'S JUST... IT'S ALL WRONG.
FIRST OFF, DAVID WASN'T SUPPOSED TO DIE. WE HAD A PLAN, WE HAD A WAY OUT. IT WASN'T A SURE THING BUT IT WAS GOOD AND WE HAD HOPE.
SO MUCH FOR HOPE.
SECOND, I REALLY DON'T NEED ANY MORE LIFE LESSONS IN HOW HELPLESS WE ARE AGAINST FATE, OKAY? I GET IT. ENOUGH ALREADY. SAVIORS, TYRANTS, CHILDREN AND SUPER-RICH POWER BITCHES—ANYBODY CAN DROP AT ANY MINUTE, LEAVING US IN GRIEF AND DISBELIEF.
THEN THIS CLOWN CALLS AND CLAIMS TO BE DAVID'S ATTORNEY. ARE YOU *KIDDING* ME? FREDDIE FRIKKIN' FEMUR?
WHAT THE HELL WAS DAVID THINKING?
HE HAD A HUGE INHERITANCE COMING TO HIM FROM DARCY AND NOW IT'S ALL LOCKED UP IN COURT. FREDDIE IS THE LAST PERSON I'D HAVE HIRED TO REP ME AGAINST A TEAM OF PISSED-OFF TAX ATTORNEYS.
SIGH ...STUPID.
BUT THESE ARE THINGS I CAN'T CONTROL NOW. DAVID IS DEAD AND BOZO IS READING HIS WILL.
FRIKKIN' CLOWN.
PLUS, TOMORROW I HAVE TO GO BACK TO THE FUNERAL HOME AND BUY A COFFIN FOR DAVID AND A HOLE TO DROP HIM DOWN. IT'S ABSURD THAT I AM SUPPOSED TO JUST HAND HIM OVER TO THOSE PEOPLE AND GO ON WITH MY LIFE AS IF I HAVE NO IDEA MY LOVER'S BEAUTIFUL BODY IS ROTTING IN A BOX SIX FEET UNDER GROUND—TWELVE IF YOU PAY EXTRA.
I COULDN'T BRING MYSELF TO DO IT TODAY. I'LL HAVE TO MAKE THOSE ARRANGEMENTS TOMORROW.
IT'S JUST SO SURREAL. ALL THIS TERRIBLE STUFF IS HAPPENING AND I HAVE NO CONTROL OVER ANY OF IT. REALLY PISSES ME OFF.
I'M ANGRY WITH DAVID FOR DYING AND LEAVING ME TO CLEAN UP AFTER HIM. I'M ANGRY HE HIRED FREDDIE. I'M ANGRY AT TAMBI FOR SLEEPING WITH DAVID AND I'M MAD AT HIM FOR LETTING HER. HE WAS SO INFURIATING THAT WAY... WEAK ENOUGH TO SCREW UP, DECENT ENOUGH TO TELL YOU. I KNOW, I DO IT, TOO. PISSES ME OFF. SO MANY MISTAKES.

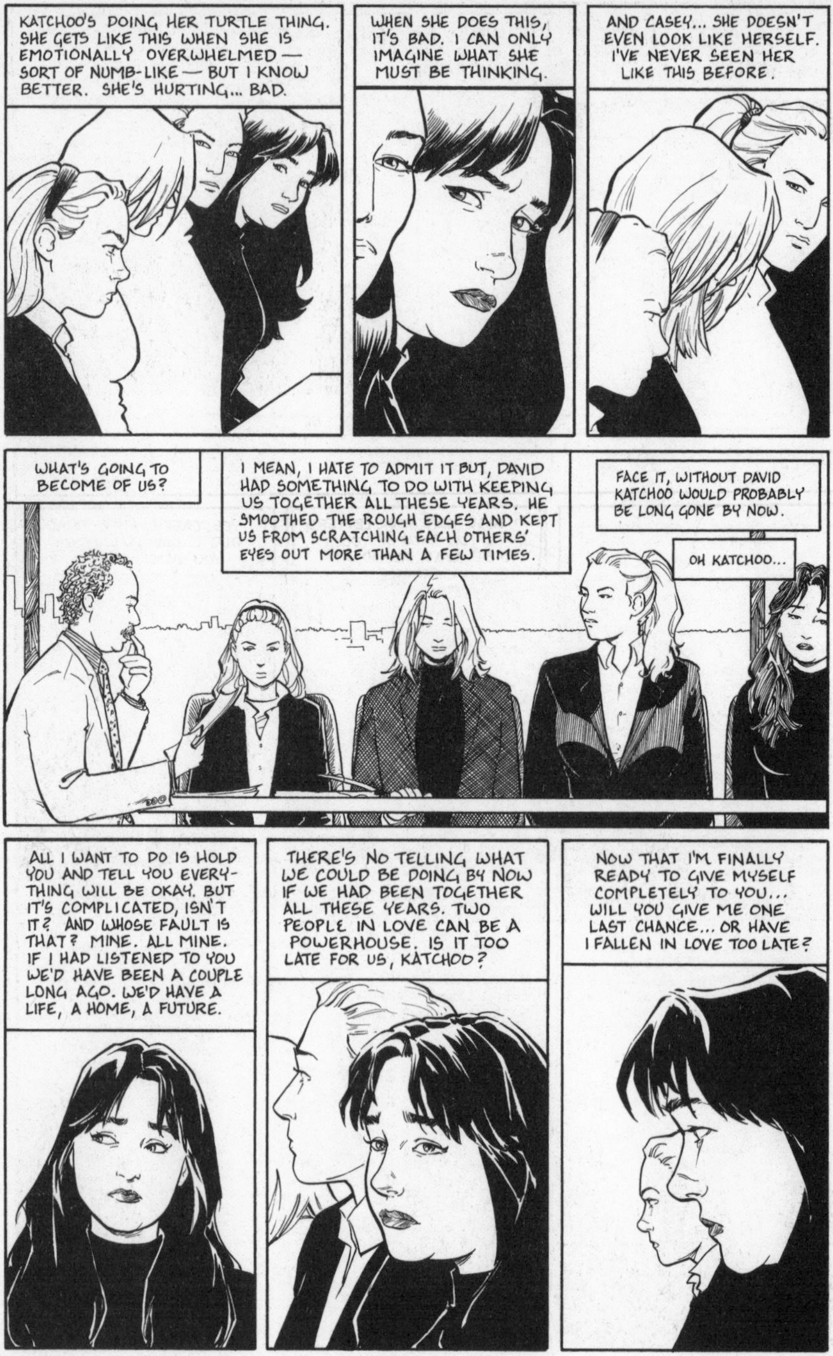
KATCHOO'S DOING HER TURTLE THING. SHE GETS LIKE THIS WHEN SHE IS EMOTIONALLY OVERWHELMED— SORT OF NUMB-LIKE— BUT I KNOW BETTER. SHE'S HURTING... BAD.
WHEN SHE DOES THIS, IT'S BAD. I CAN ONLY IMAGINE WHAT SHE MUST BE THINKING.
AND CASEY... SHE DOESN'T EVEN LOOK LIKE HERSELF. I'VE NEVER SEEN HER LIKE THIS BEFORE.
WHAT'S GOING TO BECOME OF US?
I MEAN, I HATE TO ADMIT IT BUT, DAVID HAD SOMETHING TO DO WITH KEEPING US TOGETHER ALL THESE YEARS. HE SMOOTHED THE ROUGH EDGES AND KEPT US FROM SCRATCHING EACH OTHERS' EYES OUT MORE THAN A FEW TIMES.
FACE IT, WITHOUT DAVID KATCHOO WOULD PROBABLY BE LONG GONE BY NOW.
OH KATCHOO...
ALL I WANT TO DO IS HOLD YOU AND TELL YOU EVERY-THING WILL BE OKAY. BUT IT'S COMPLICATED, ISN'T IT? AND WHOSE FAULT IS THAT? MINE. ALL MINE. IF I HAD LISTENED TO YOU WE'D HAVE BEEN A COUPLE LONG AGO. WE'D HAVE A LIFE, A HOME, A FUTURE.
THERE'S NO TELLING WHAT WE COULD BE DOING BY NOW IF WE HAD BEEN TOGETHER ALL THESE YEARS. TWO PEOPLE IN LOVE CAN BE A POWERHOUSE. IS IT TOO LATE FOR US, KATCHOO?
NOW THAT I'M FINALLY READY TO GIVE MYSELF COMPLETELY TO YOU... WILL YOU GIVE ME ONE LAST CHANCE... OR HAVE I FALLEN IN LOVE TOO LATE?

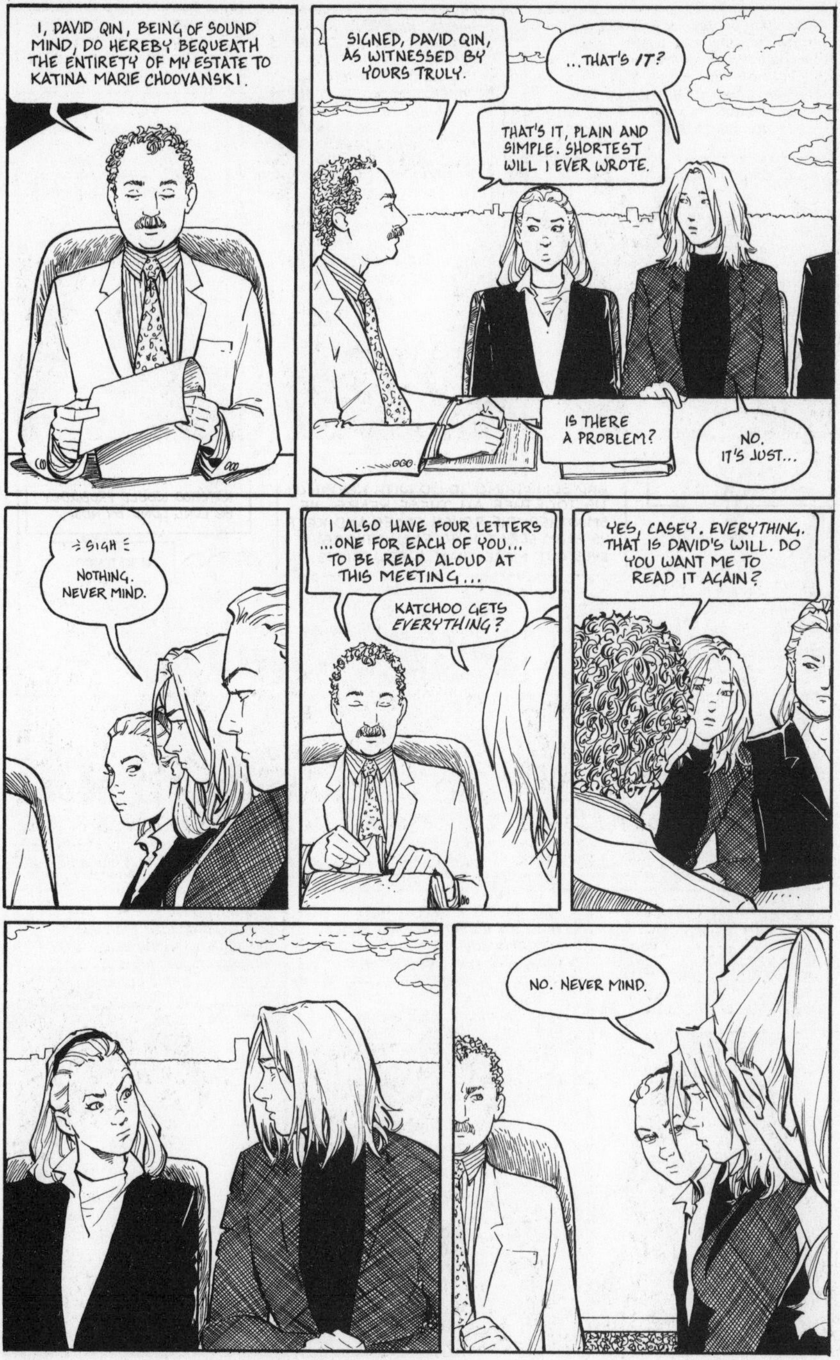
I, DAVID QIN, BEING OF SOUND MIND, DO HEREBY BEQUEATH THE ENTIRETY OF MY ESTATE TO KATINA MARIE CHOOVANSKI.
SIGNED, DAVID QIN, AS WITNESSED BY YOURS TRULY.
...THAT'S IT?
THAT'S IT, PLAIN AND SIMPLE. SHORTEST WILL I EVER WROTE.
IS THERE A PROBLEM?
NO. IT'S JUST...
SIGH
NOTHING. NEVER MIND.
I ALSO HAVE FOUR LETTERS ...ONE FOR EACH OF YOU... TO BE READ ALOUD AT THIS MEETING...
KATCHOO GETS EVERYTHING?
YES, CASEY. EVERYTHING. THAT IS DAVID'S WILL. DO YOU WANT ME TO READ IT AGAIN?
NO. NEVER MIND.

AS YOU CAN SEE, THESE LETTERS ARE SEALED. I DO NOT KNOW THEIR CONTENTS AND I AM OPENING THEM FOR THE FIRST TIME. DAVID HAS REQUESTED YOU LISTEN TO ALL FOUR LETTERS BEFORE COMMENTING. AGREED?

OKAY, FRANCINE... THE FIRST LETTER IS TO YOU.

* AHEM *

FRANCINE... WHEN I WAS AT MY LOWEST YOU WERE THERE FOR ME. YOU OPENED UP YOUR HEART AND HOME AND NURSED ME BACK TO HEALTH. FOR THAT I WILL BE ETERNALLY GRATEFUL. I TRIED TO PRESENT YOU WITH A MONETARY GIFT AFTERWARDS THAT BECAME LOST IN THE GOVERNMENT LAWSUIT. I HAVE LEFT INSTRUCTIONS TO INSURE YOU RECEIVE THAT GIFT, IN FULL AFTER TAXES, IF AND WHEN THE LAWSUIT CAN BE RESOLVED.

UNTIL THEN, ALL I CAN OFFER YOU IS MY LOVE AND SINCERE GRATITUDE. I PRAY THAT YOU WILL NOT GIVE UP ON YOUR LOVE FOR KATCHOO, BECAUSE I KNOW SHE'S NEVER GIVEN UP ON YOU. ONLY YOU KNOW WHAT'S IN YOUR HEART, BUT I KNOW YOU LOVE KATCHOO AND ALL LOVE IS FROM GOD. THE REST IS UP TO YOU. MAY GOD BLESS YOU ALWAYS. LOVE, DAVID.

≥ SNIFF ≤

OKAY... ≥ AHEM ≤ ...EXCUSE ME, THE NEXT LETTER IS TO MARY BETH... OR TAMBI, AS DAVID WRITES HERE. ≥ AHEM ≤

TAMBI... WHEN I FIRST MET YOU AND KATCHOO ALL THOSE YEARS AGO AT DARCY'S HOUSE, I NEVER IMAGINED OUR LIVES WOULD BRAID TOGETHER SO TIGHTLY. YOU ARE THE MOST POWERFUL PERSON I'VE EVER KNOWN BUT YOU SHOWED ME KINDNESS AND CONSIDERATION AT CRITICAL TIMES IN MY LIFE EVEN IF YOUR MANNER WAS SOMETIMES FRIGHTENING.

Tambi-
When I first met you and Katchoo all those years ago at Darcy's house I never imagined our lives would braid together so tightly. You are the most powerful person I've ever known but you showed me kindness consideration at critical times in my life, even if your manner was sometimes frightening.
I know you cared a lot for me to share so much of yourself with you

I KNOW YOU CARED A LOT FOR ME TO SHARE SO MUCH OF YOURSELF WITH ME... AND I FOUND MUCH ABOUT YOU TO LOVE. BUT I ALSO KNOW....

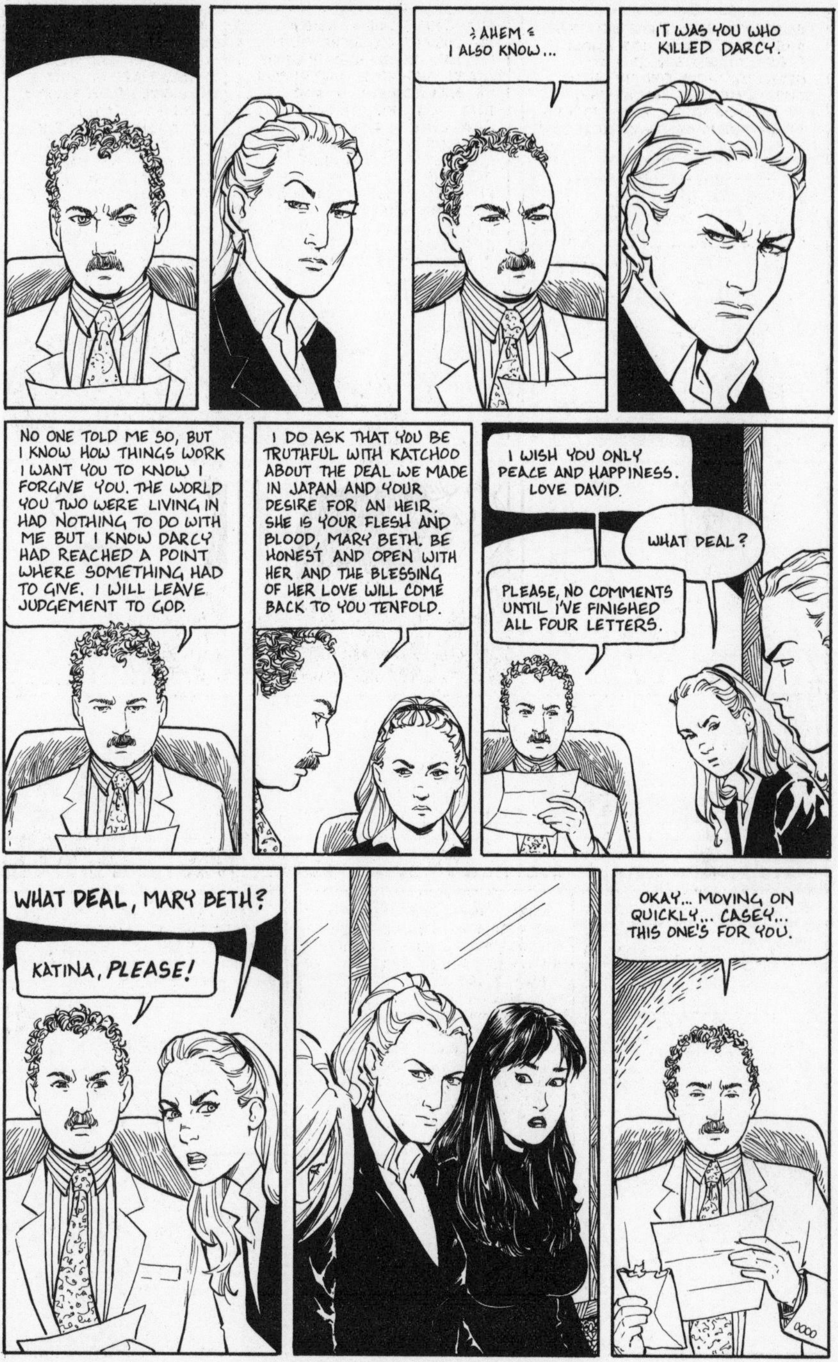

AHEM
I ALSO KNOW...
IT WAS YOU WHO KILLED DARCY.
NO ONE TOLD ME SO, BUT I KNOW HOW THINGS WORK I WANT YOU TO KNOW I FORGIVE YOU. THE WORLD YOU TWO WERE LIVING IN HAD NOTHING TO DO WITH ME BUT I KNOW DARCY HAD REACHED A POINT WHERE SOMETHING HAD TO GIVE. I WILL LEAVE JUDGEMENT TO GOD.
I DO ASK THAT YOU BE TRUTHFUL WITH KATCHOO ABOUT THE DEAL WE MADE IN JAPAN AND YOUR DESIRE FOR AN HEIR. SHE IS YOUR FLESH AND BLOOD, MARY BETH. BE HONEST AND OPEN WITH HER AND THE BLESSING OF HER LOVE WILL COME BACK TO YOU TENFOLD.
I WISH YOU ONLY PEACE AND HAPPINESS. LOVE DAVID.
WHAT DEAL?
PLEASE, NO COMMENTS UNTIL I'VE FINISHED ALL FOUR LETTERS.
WHAT DEAL, MARY BETH?
KATINA, PLEASE!
OKAY... MOVING ON QUICKLY... CASEY... THIS ONE'S FOR YOU.

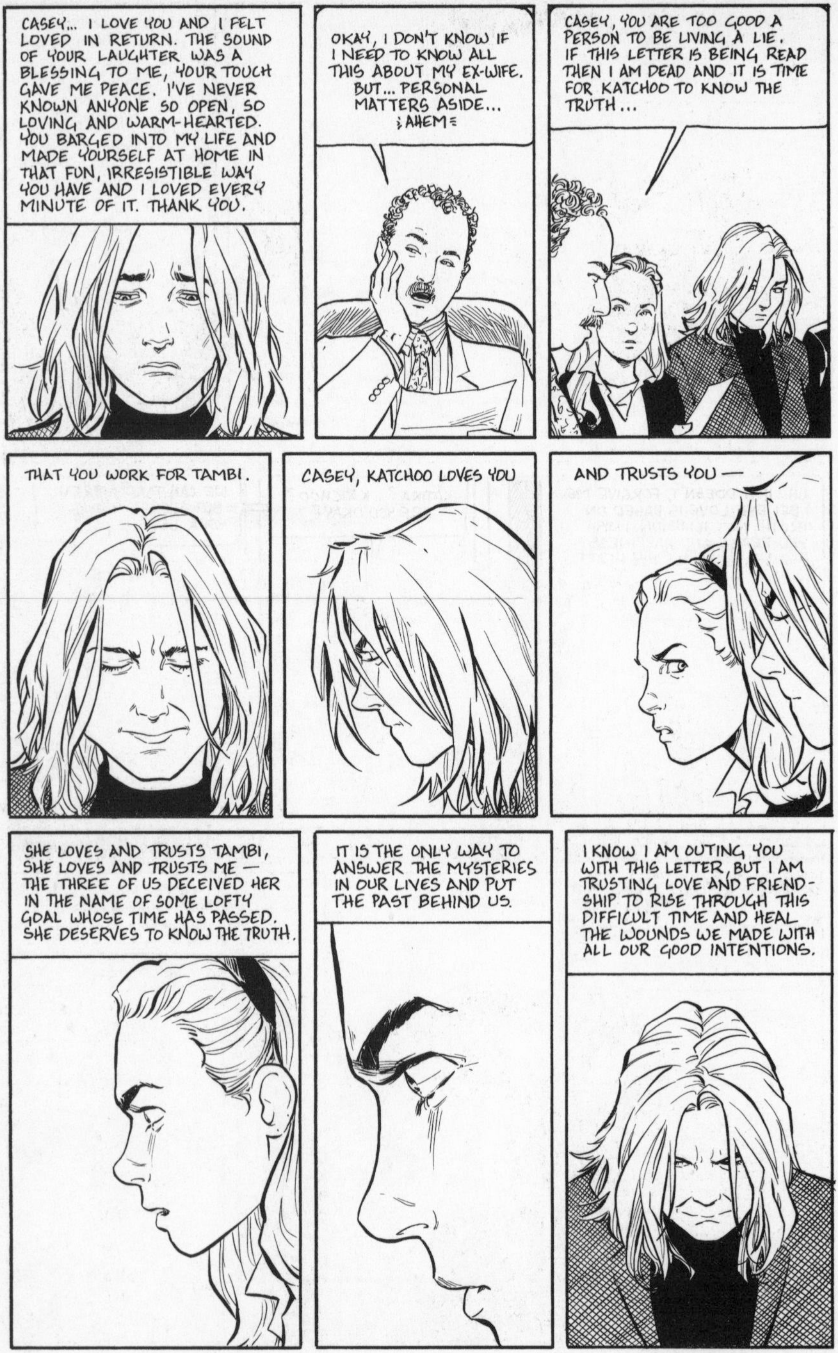
CASEY... I LOVE YOU AND I FELT LOVED IN RETURN. THE SOUND OF YOUR LAUGHTER WAS A BLESSING TO ME, YOUR TOUCH GAVE ME PEACE. I'VE NEVER KNOWN ANYONE SO OPEN, SO LOVING AND WARM-HEARTED. YOU BARGED INTO MY LIFE AND MADE YOURSELF AT HOME IN THAT FUN, IRRESISTIBLE WAY YOU HAVE AND I LOVED EVERY MINUTE OF IT. THANK YOU.
OKAY, I DON'T KNOW IF I NEED TO KNOW ALL THIS ABOUT MY EX-WIFE. BUT... PERSONAL MATTERS ASIDE... AHEM
CASEY, YOU ARE TOO GOOD A PERSON TO BE LIVING A LIE. IF THIS LETTER IS BEING READ THEN I AM DEAD AND IT IS TIME FOR KATCHOO TO KNOW THE TRUTH...
THAT YOU WORK FOR TAMBI.
CASEY, KATCHOO LOVES YOU
AND TRUSTS YOU —
SHE LOVES AND TRUSTS TAMBI, SHE LOVES AND TRUSTS ME — THE THREE OF US DECEIVED HER IN THE NAME OF SOME LOFTY GOAL WHOSE TIME HAS PASSED. SHE DESERVES TO KNOW THE TRUTH.
IT IS THE ONLY WAY TO ANSWER THE MYSTERIES IN OUR LIVES AND PUT THE PAST BEHIND US.
I KNOW I AM OUTING YOU WITH THIS LETTER, BUT I AM TRUSTING LOVE AND FRIENDSHIP TO RISE THROUGH THIS DIFFICULT TIME AND HEAL THE WOUNDS WE MADE WITH ALL OUR GOOD INTENTIONS.

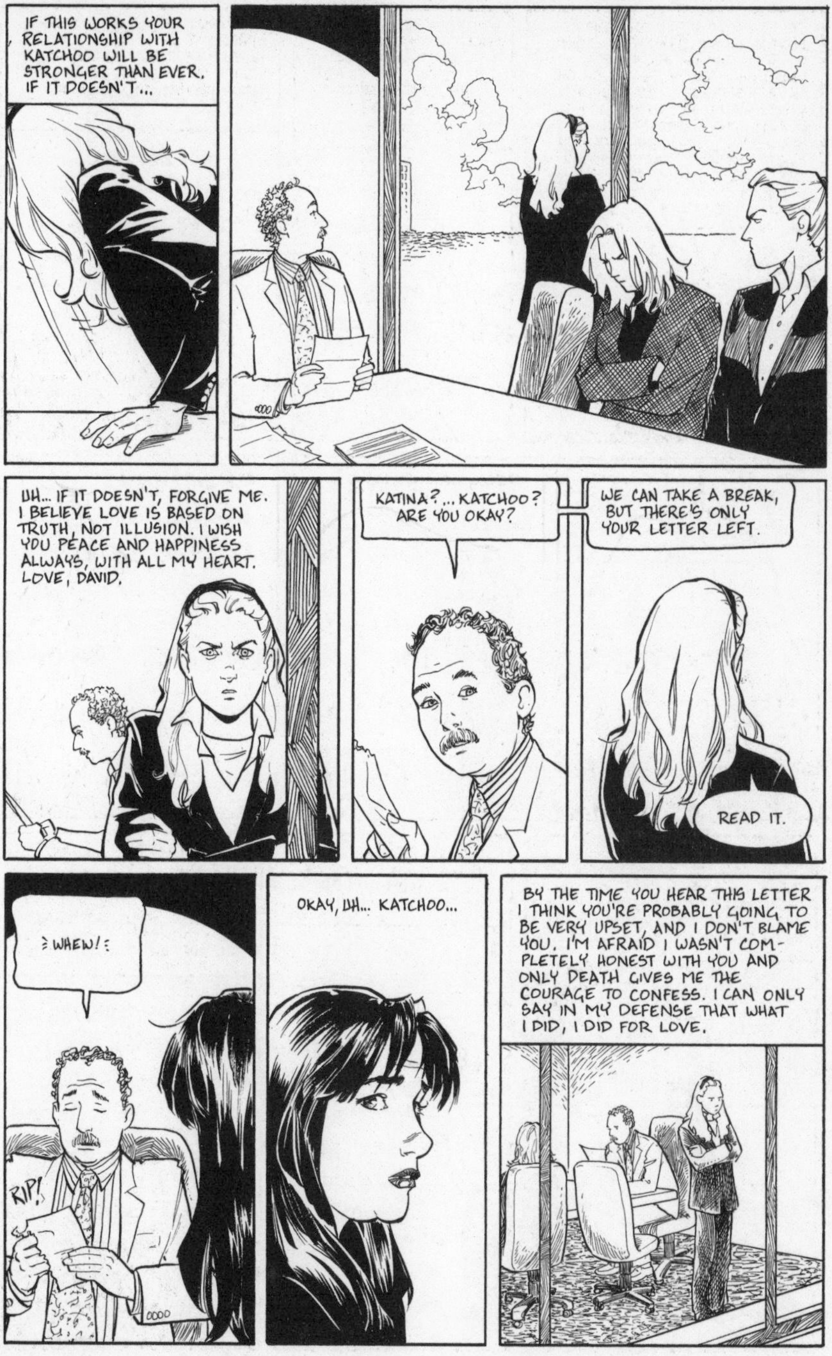
IF THIS WORKS YOUR RELATIONSHIP WITH KATCHOO WILL BE STRONGER THAN EVER. IF IT DOESN'T...
UH... IF IT DOESN'T, FORGIVE ME. I BELIEVE LOVE IS BASED ON TRUTH, NOT ILLUSION. I WISH YOU PEACE AND HAPPINESS ALWAYS, WITH ALL MY HEART. LOVE, DAVID.
KATINA? ... KATCHOO? ARE YOU OKAY?
WE CAN TAKE A BREAK, BUT THERE'S ONLY YOUR LETTER LEFT.
READ IT.
WHEW!
RIP!
OKAY, UH... KATCHOO...
BY THE TIME YOU HEAR THIS LETTER I THINK YOU'RE PROBABLY GOING TO BE VERY UPSET, AND I DON'T BLAME YOU. I'M AFRAID I WASN'T COMPLETELY HONEST WITH YOU AND ONLY DEATH GIVES ME THE COURAGE TO CONFESS. I CAN ONLY SAY IN MY DEFENSE THAT WHAT I DID, I DID FOR LOVE.

YOU LEFT HER.
SHE DOESN'T LOVE ME, TAMBI. SHE LOVES FRANCINE PETERS.
FRANCINE PETERS CANNOT IMPREGNATE HER!
I WAS COUNTING ON YOU, DAVID.
YOU'RE THE ONLY MAN KATINA WILL ALLOW NEAR HER.
YOU ARE OF NO FURTHER USE TO ME.
THERE IS... HUFF!HUFF!
ANOTHER...
WAY! HUFF!
I'M LISTENING.
KATINA IS NOT THE LAST BAKER.
THERE'S YOU!
IF YOU WANT AN HEIR THIS BAD— YOU HAVE IT!
AND I WILL HELP YOU!
HERE. FILL THIS.
ALL RIGHT DAMMIT! I'LL GIVE IT BACK TOMORROW.
NOW.

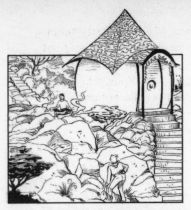

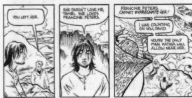

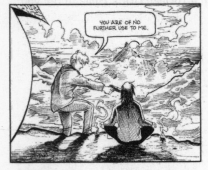

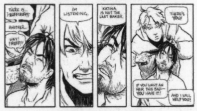

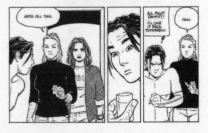

When I was in Japan, Tambi came to see me. She was angry because you and I had not produced a child that could be the heir to the Baker and Takahashi families. I realized this was the reason I had been allowed to live after Darcy's death, the reason I had been allowed to get near you, and most importantly, the reason you had been allowed to leave the family business to lead a private life.

Tambi loves you very much, Katchoo, but I think she's also dedicated to building some future vision she believes to be paramount to us all. We had failed her and I was no longer useful. At gunpoint I made a deal with her: leave you to your private life and I would return to America to try and resume our relationship and hopefully produce the heir Tambi believed was so vitally important.

In all honesty Katchoo, I also offered to try and make this heir directly with Tambi, in hopes of sparing you any more drama. It was a desperate act on my part, an offer I half-expected would get me killed. Who knows why things happen the way they do sometimes. I don't understand it. All I know is, believe it or not, we did have sex and I returned to Houston under false pretenses. I assume my night with Tambi failed because she never mentioned it again. She did visit me at my apartment recently and demanded a sperm sample from me to be stored for future use. I gave her what she wanted.

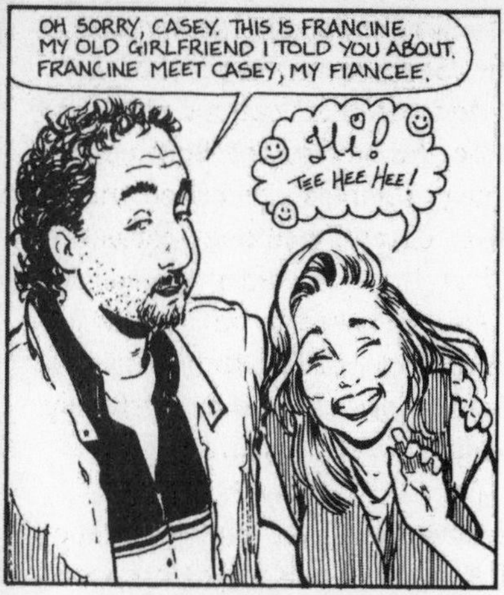
OH SORRY, CASEY. THIS IS FRANCINE MY OLD GIRLFRIEND I TOLD YOU ABOUT. FRANCINE MEET CASEY, MY FIANCEE.
Hi! TEE HEE HEE!

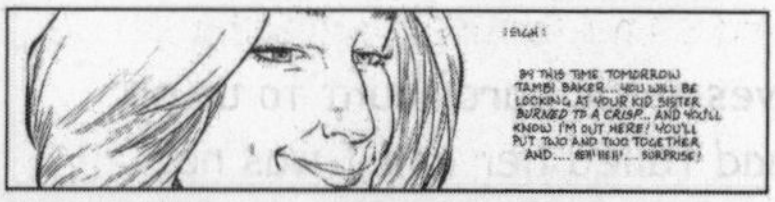
BY THIS TIME TOMORROW TAMBI BAKER... YOU WILL BE LOOKING AT YOUR KID SISTER BURNED TO A CRISP... AND YOU'LL KNOW I'M OUT HERE! YOU'LL PUT TWO AND TWO TOGETHER

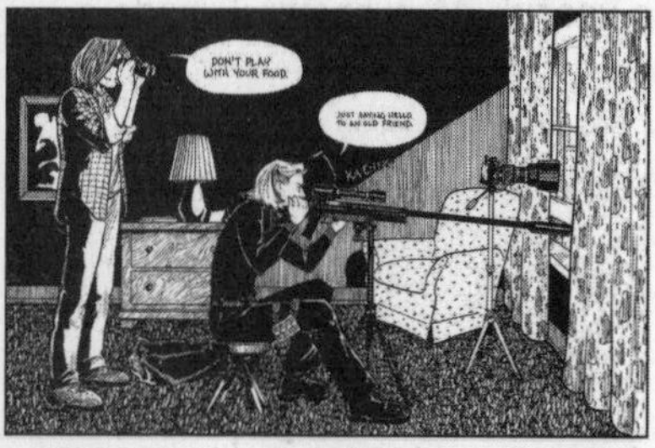
DON'T PLAY WITH YOUR FOOD.
JUST SAYING HELLO TO AN OLD FRIEND.

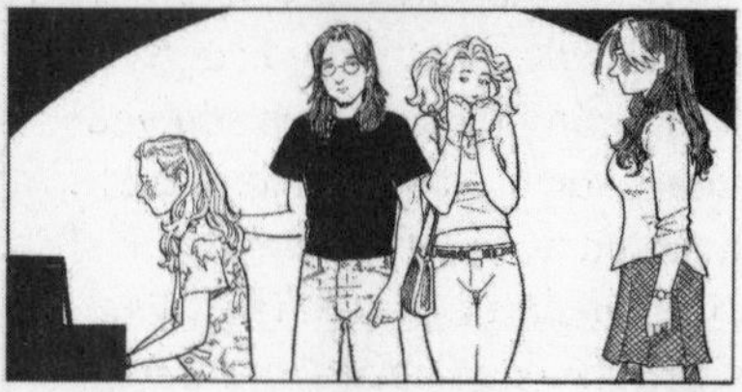

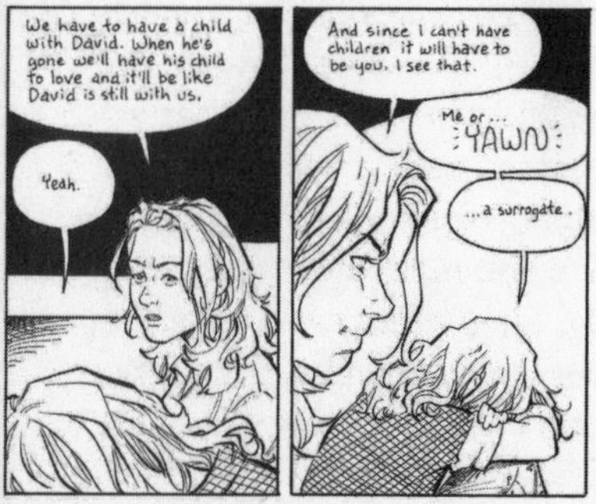
We have to have a child with David. When he's gone we'll have his child to love and it'll be like David is still with us.
Yeah.
And since I can't have children it will have to be you. I see that.
Me or... YAWN
...a surrogate.

Katchoo, in Japan Tambi told me Casey works for her. She's not a DUCk, she's a CPA who became bored as Tambi's accountant and asked for a field assignment. Tambi gave her us. This was back when Darcy was sending people after you, the Big Six were looking for you and everybody was worried about your safety. You might ask what good an accountant would be in a crisis, but Casey proved to be an incredibly brave person who kept your sister informed of anything suspicious that might be of danger to you. I'm sure Casey saved you from more trouble than you know. I know of one time when a former DUCk came after you and you never knew it. Casey alerted Tambi and the situation was handled by Cherry Hammer and Becky, who is Casey's sister. So don't be too hard on her, Katchoo. I think Casey was as honest with us as she could be and still do what she thought important, watch over you. I know she grew to love us and care for us and we felt the same for her. Don't forget that. You were never fully honest with Francine about your life, but you love her with all your heart, don't you? Remember that in the coming weeks as you guys talk and work things out. I would never have said anything if I didn't truly believe you would all be closer once the truth was known and put in the past. True peace and happiness can never come from a lie, and my only prayer for you now is peace and happiness.

DAVID...! WHY WOULDN'T YOU HAVE SURGERY IF IT COULD SAVE YOUR LIFE?
I'D RATHER GO TO MY GRAVE AS DAVID THAN LIVE ANOTHER FIVE YEARS AS SOMETHING LESS!
NOW HE TURNS STUPID.
THAT'S NOT STUPID... THAT'S FEAR.
HELLO?

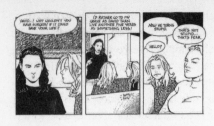

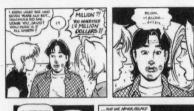

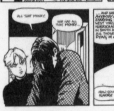

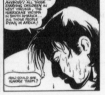

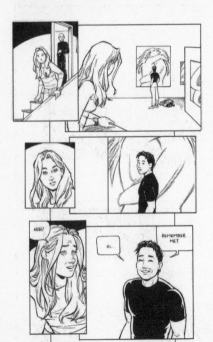

You know I love you with all my heart, Katchoo. Right or wrong, we've all done things out of love or faith that may have hurt others. I hope you can find it in your heart to forgive me, forgive Casey and Tambi. We meant well.

I KNOW WHAT SHE HAD SEVEN YEARS AGO BUT... HOW MUCH DID SHE LEAVE YOU, DAVID? HOW MUCH IS IT ALL WORTH?
1.4
MILLION ?! YOU INHERITED 1.4 MILLION DOLLARS ?!
BILLION. 1.4 BILLION... ...dollars...
ALL THAT MONEY.
SHE HAD ALL THAT MONEY...
...AND SHE NEVER HELPED ANYBODY! ALL THOSE STARVING CHILDREN IN WEST VIRGINIA, THE HURRICANE VICTIMS IN SOUTH AMERICA... ALL THOSE PEOPLE DYING IN AFRICA!
HOW COULD SHE IGNORE THEM?

As for now, I ask that you do what you can to win my inheritance back from the government for two reasons. One, it will provide financial security for you and you will be able to relax, enjoy your life and pursue your art. Two, I ask that you put half of the money towards humanitarian efforts in Africa. I'll leave it to you to decide the best route for that.

I've thought about it and decided I don't want a traditional burial. Please have my body cremated and take my ashes to a place of natural beauty and spread them there. Where this happens I leave to you. I think it will be a decision of the heart.

HUH!
HI..
REMEMBER ME?

I've left you a list of my holdings in Japan under my given name. These are yours as well. Don't forget them. These are assets I hid from Darcy and saved for security. They supported me and will provide a comfortable life for you until the inheritance is returned .

I love you Katchoo, with all my heart, all my mind and all my soul. I loved you the minute I saw you and I thank God for every day I've been lucky enough to spend with you. I don't regret a minute of it.

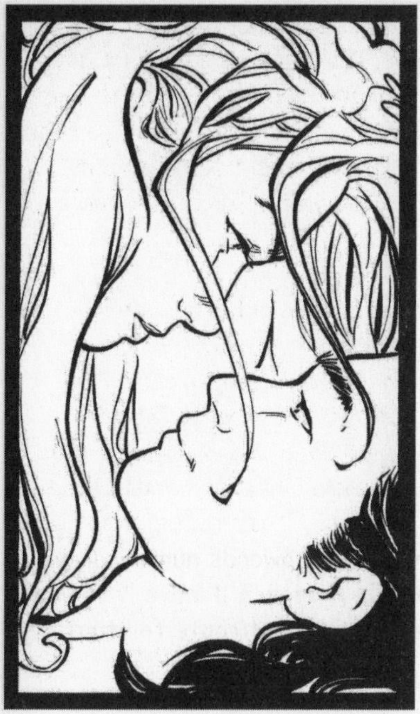

Thank you for sharing your life with me. Thank you for loving me. My faith compels me to believe there is a life beyond the grave, life with God, life with love, and we will be together again someday. Until then I hope you have a long life, peace, love and happiness. I love you.

Katchoo, you and Francine have something special. You know it, she knows it, we all know it. Francine is your future, Katchoo, because that's where the love is. Follow the love.

David

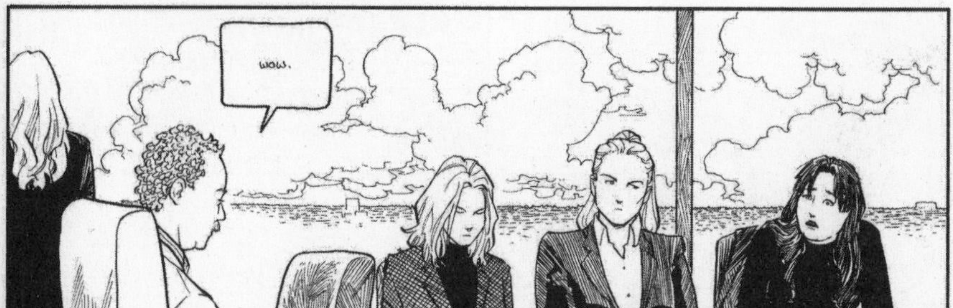
wow.

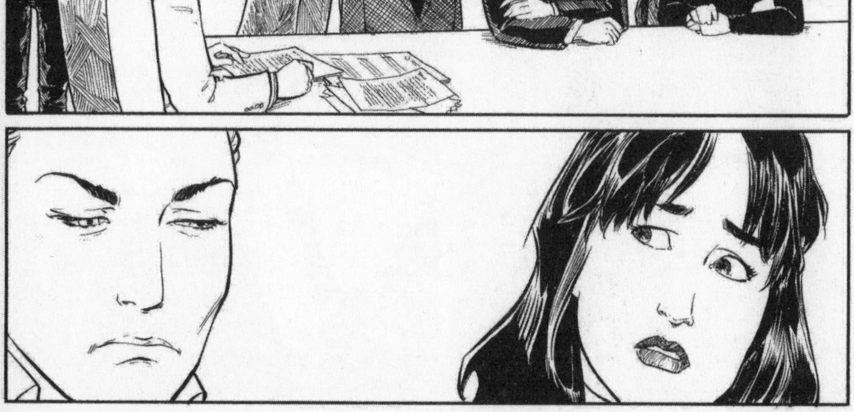

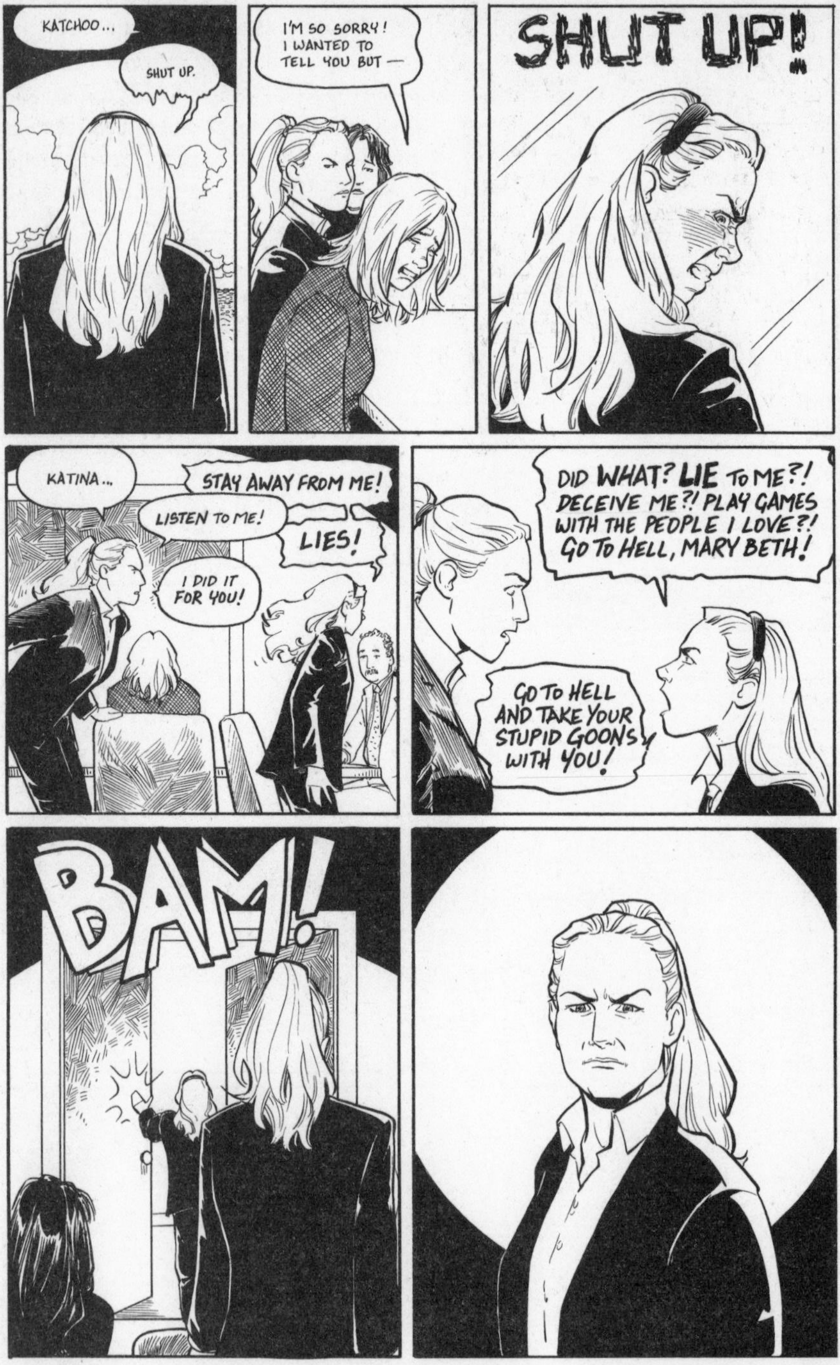
KATCHOO...
SHUT UP.
I'M SO SORRY! I WANTED TO TELL YOU BUT —
SHUT UP!
KATINA...
STAY AWAY FROM ME!
LISTEN TO ME!
LIES!
I DID IT FOR YOU!
DID WHAT? LIE TO ME?! DECEIVE ME?! PLAY GAMES WITH THE PEOPLE I LOVE?! GO TO HELL, MARY BETH!
GO TO HELL AND TAKE YOUR STUPID GOONS WITH YOU!
BAM!

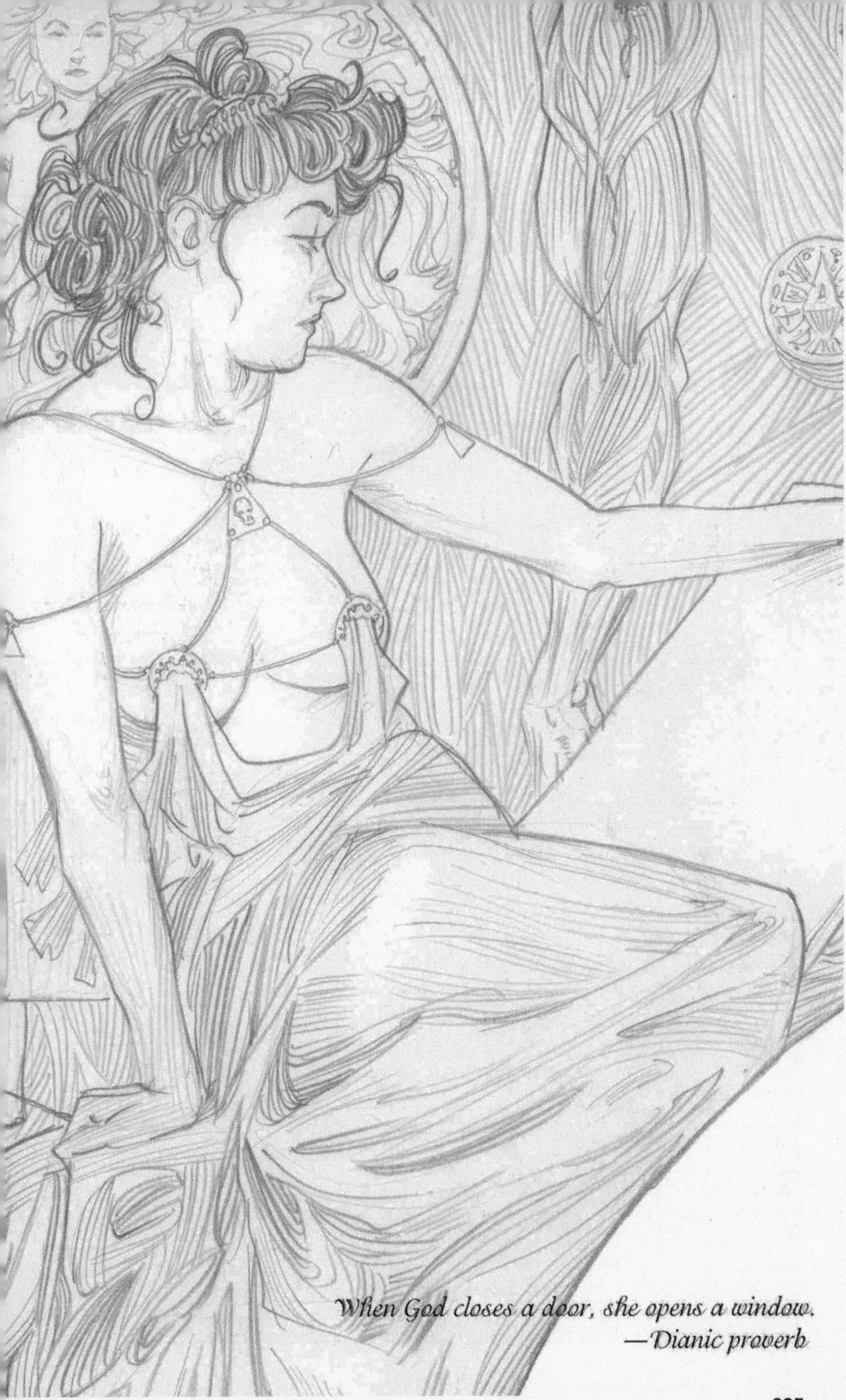

When God closes a door, she opens a window.
—Dianic proverb

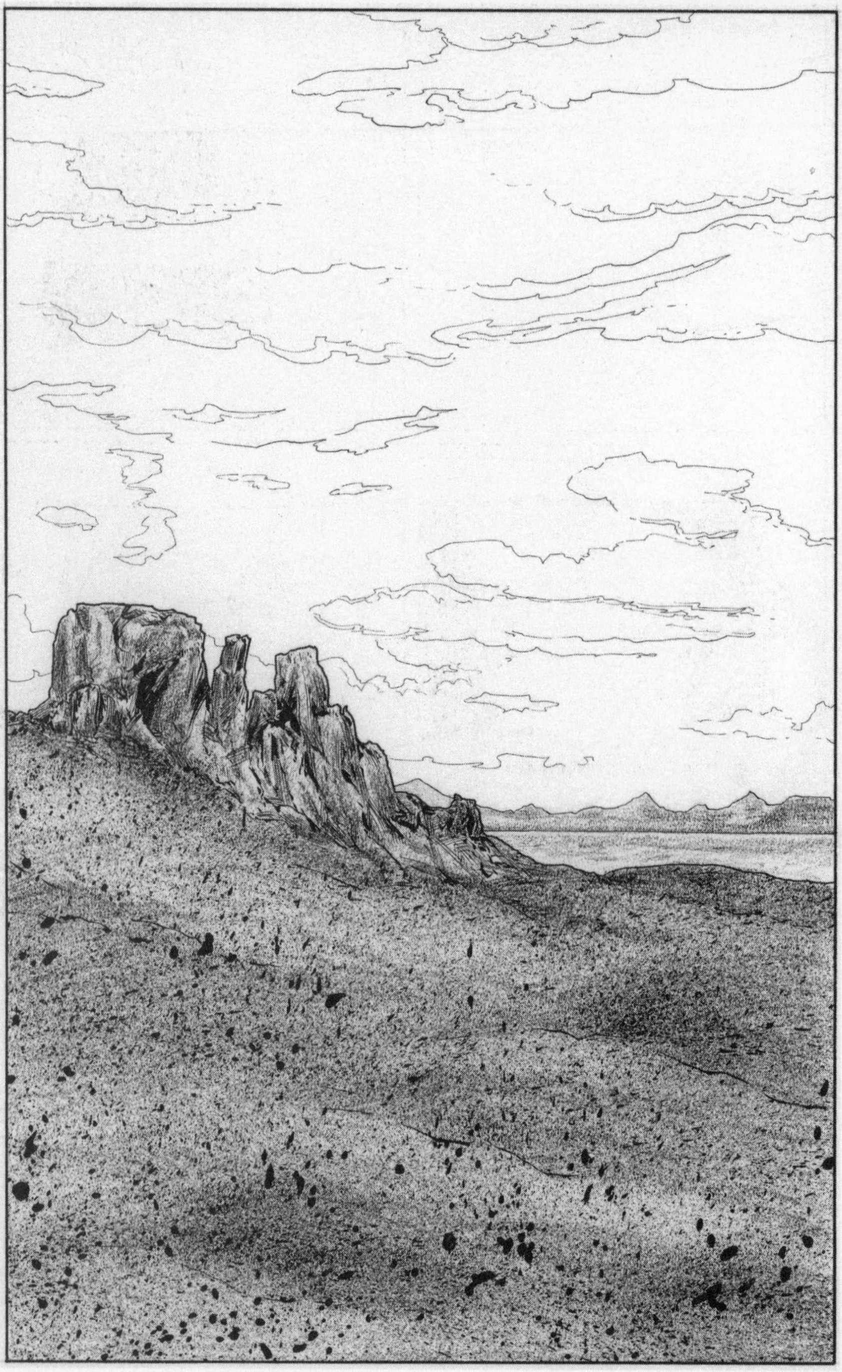

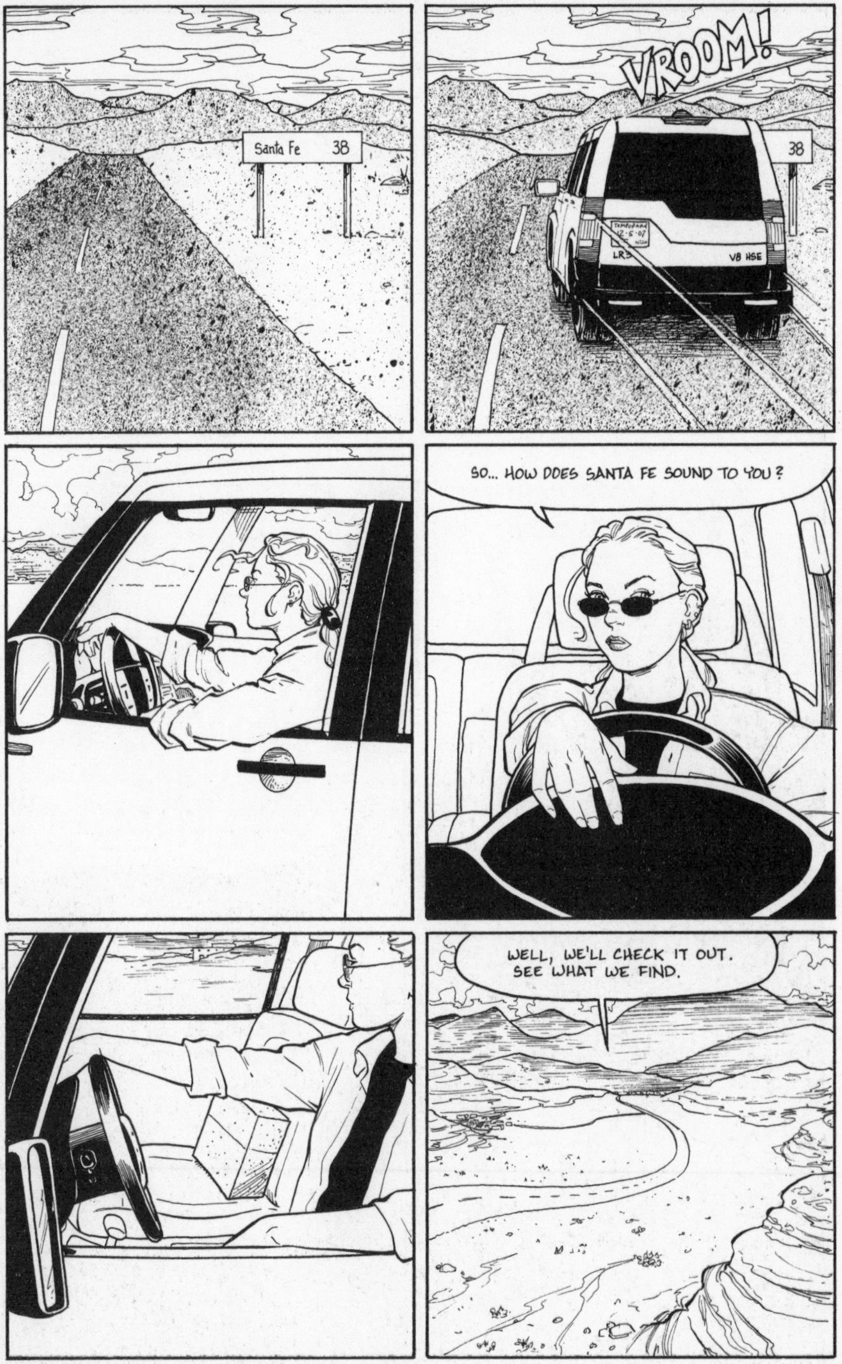
Santa Fe 38
VROOM!
38
V8 HSE
SO... HOW DOES SANTA FE SOUND TO YOU?
WELL, WE'LL CHECK IT OUT. SEE WHAT WE FIND.

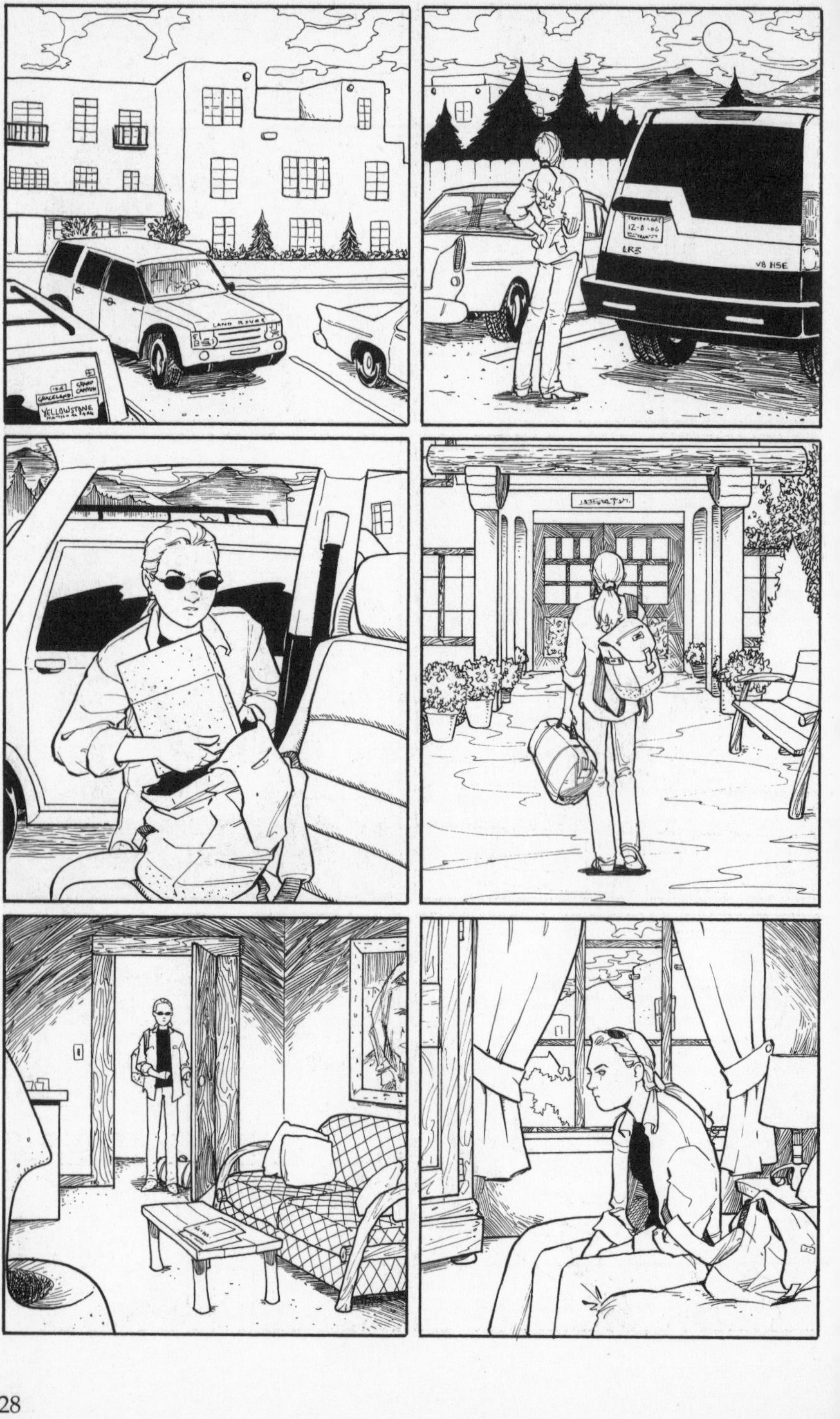
LAND ROVER
GRACELAND
GRAND CANYON
YELLOWSTONE
TEMPORARY
12-8-06
LR3
V8 HSE

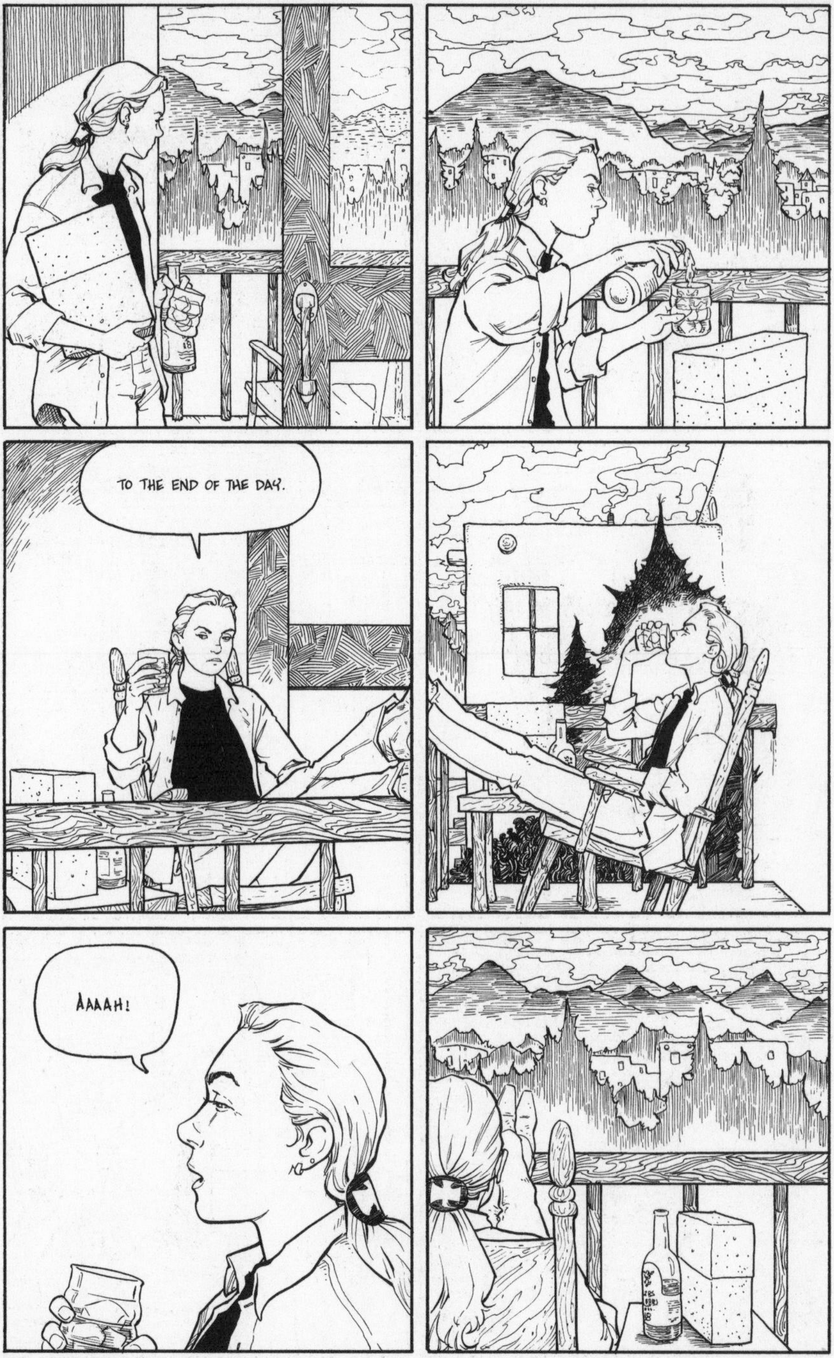
TO THE END OF THE DAY.
AAAAH!

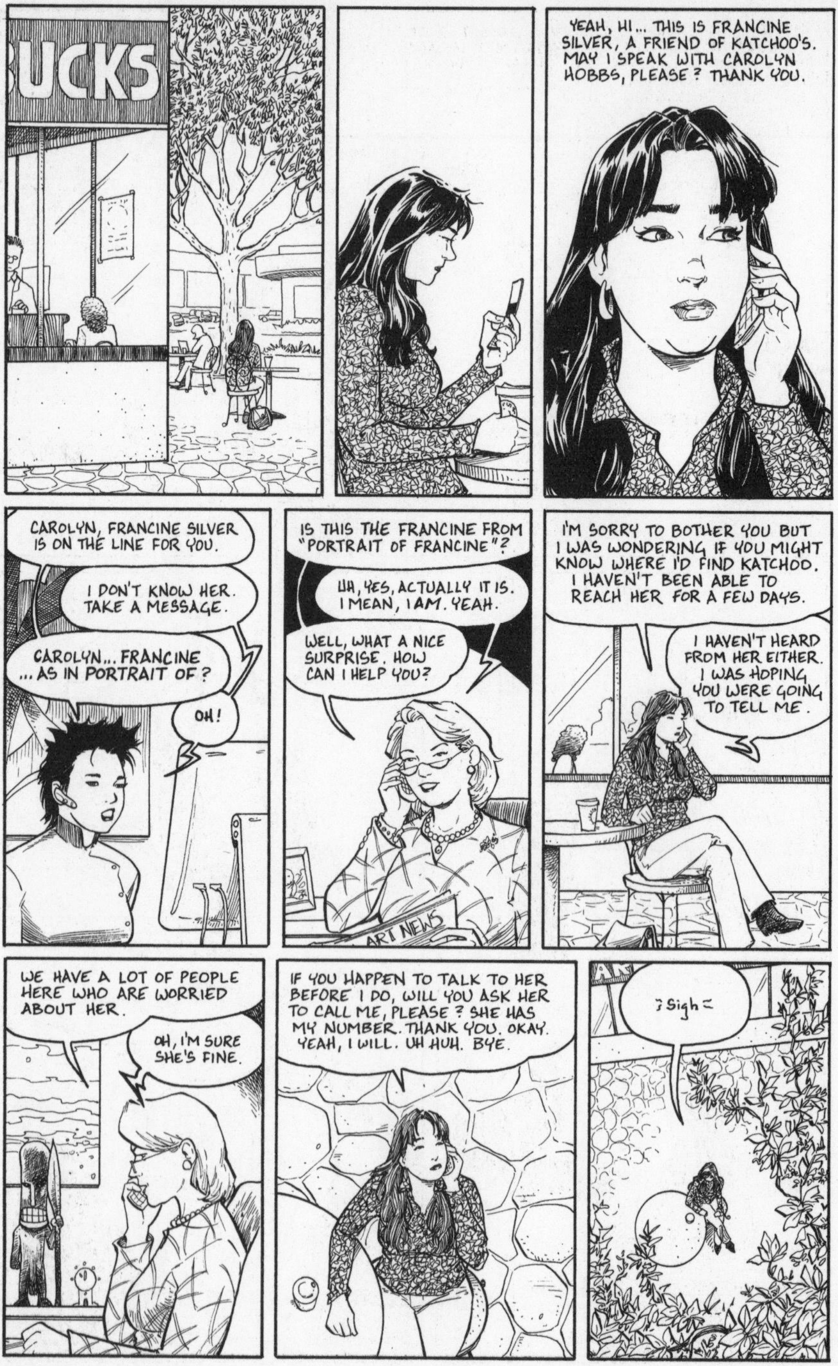
BUCKS
YEAH, HI... THIS IS FRANCINE SILVER, A FRIEND OF KATCHOO'S. MAY I SPEAK WITH CAROLYN HOBBS, PLEASE? THANK YOU.
CAROLYN, FRANCINE SILVER IS ON THE LINE FOR YOU.
I DON'T KNOW HER. TAKE A MESSAGE.
CAROLYN... FRANCINE ...AS IN PORTRAIT OF?
OH!
IS THIS THE FRANCINE FROM "PORTRAIT OF FRANCINE"?
UH, YES, ACTUALLY IT IS. I MEAN, I AM. YEAH.
WELL, WHAT A NICE SURPRISE. HOW CAN I HELP YOU?
ART NEWS
I'M SORRY TO BOTHER YOU BUT I WAS WONDERING IF YOU MIGHT KNOW WHERE I'D FIND KATCHOO. I HAVEN'T BEEN ABLE TO REACH HER FOR A FEW DAYS.
I HAVEN'T HEARD FROM HER EITHER. I WAS HOPING YOU WERE GOING TO TELL ME.
WE HAVE A LOT OF PEOPLE HERE WHO ARE WORRIED ABOUT HER.
OH, I'M SURE SHE'S FINE.
IF YOU HAPPEN TO TALK TO HER BEFORE I DO, WILL YOU ASK HER TO CALL ME, PLEASE? SHE HAS MY NUMBER. THANK YOU. OKAY. YEAH, I WILL. UH HUH. BYE.
Sigh

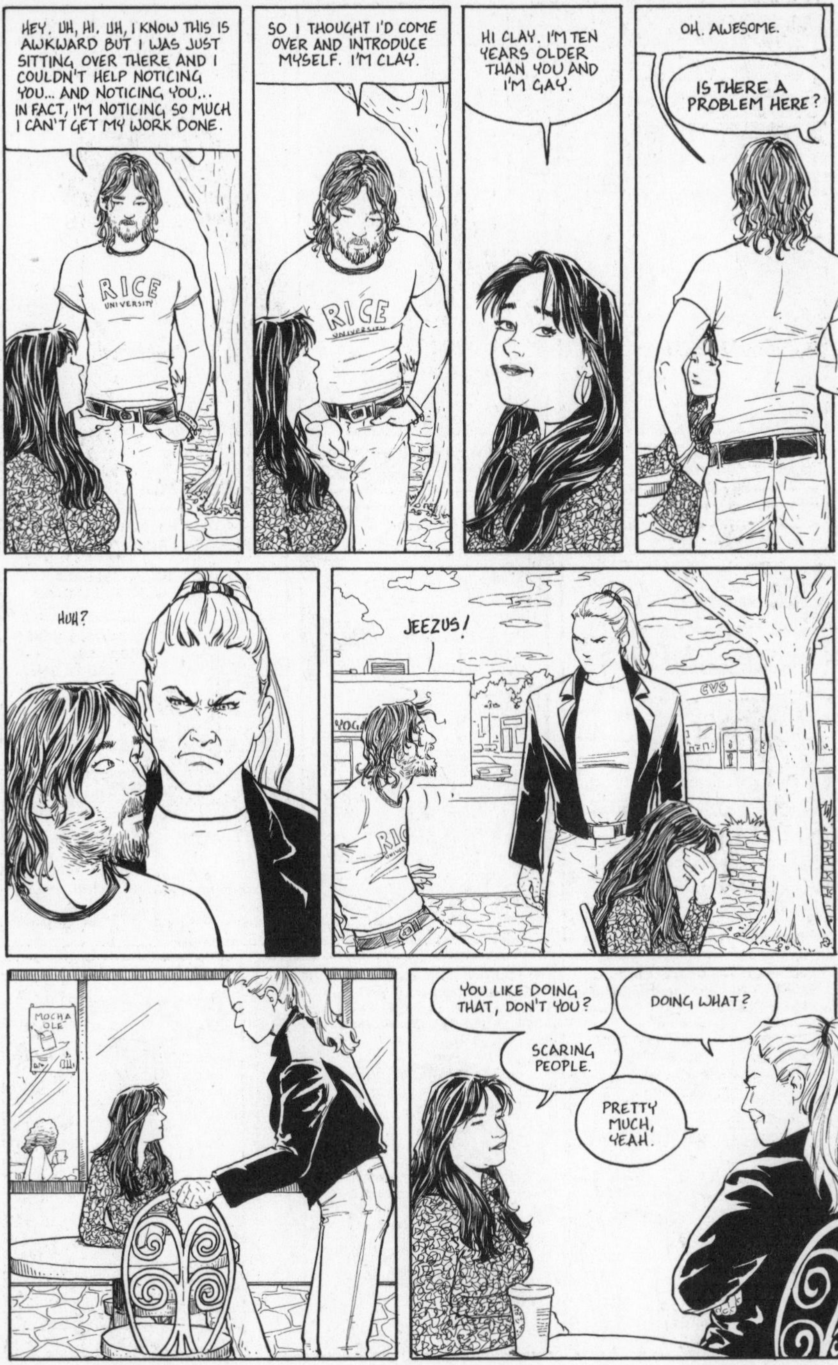
HEY. UH, HI. UH, I KNOW THIS IS AWKWARD BUT I WAS JUST SITTING OVER THERE AND I COULDN'T HELP NOTICING YOU... AND NOTICING YOU... IN FACT, I'M NOTICING SO MUCH I CAN'T GET MY WORK DONE.
RICE UNIVERSITY
SO I THOUGHT I'D COME OVER AND INTRODUCE MYSELF. I'M CLAY.
RICE UNIVERSITY
HI CLAY. I'M TEN YEARS OLDER THAN YOU AND I'M GAY.
OH. AWESOME.
IS THERE A PROBLEM HERE?
HUH?
JEEZUS!
CVS
MOCHA OLE
YOU LIKE DOING THAT, DON'T YOU?
DOING WHAT?
SCARING PEOPLE.
PRETTY MUCH, YEAH.

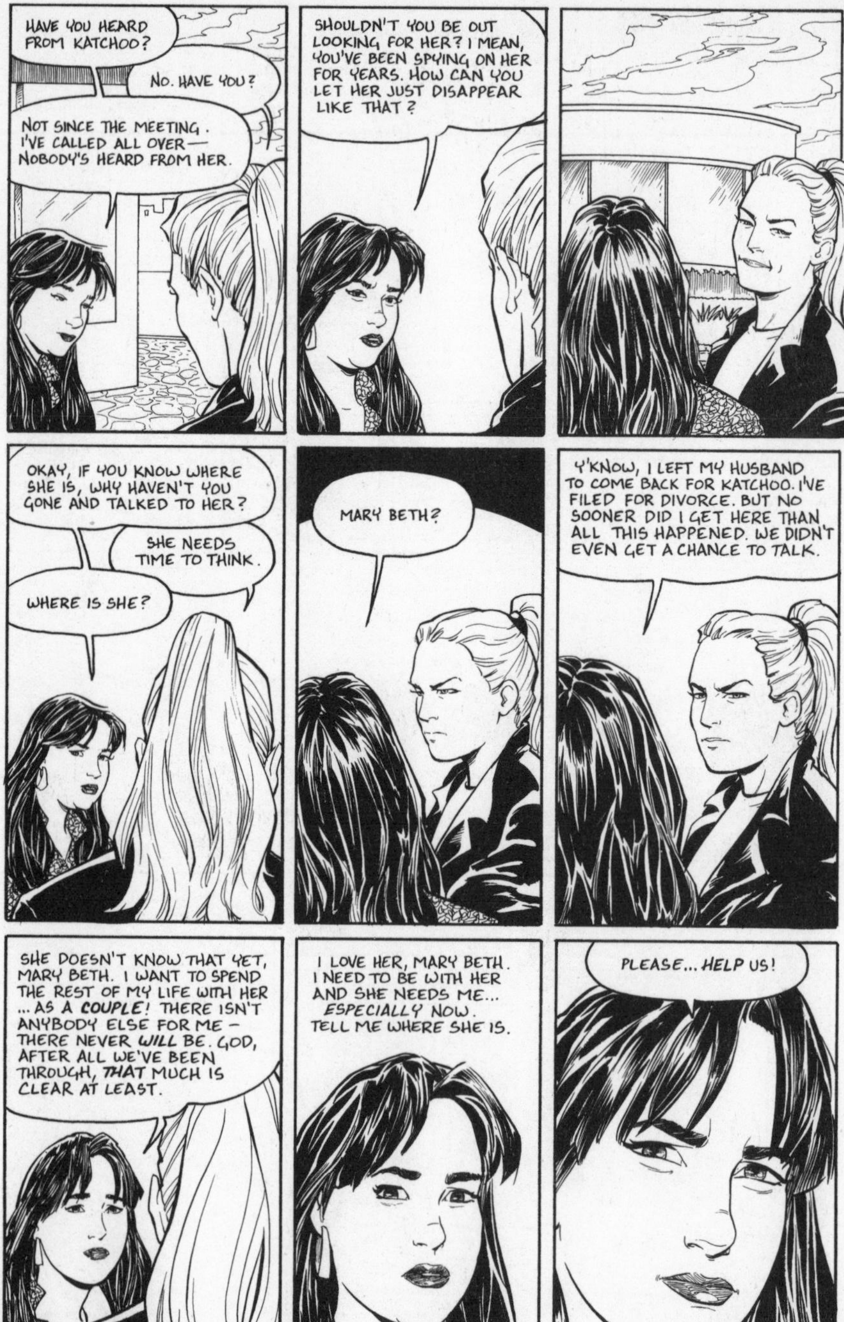
HAVE YOU HEARD FROM KATCHOO?
NO. HAVE YOU?
NOT SINCE THE MEETING. I'VE CALLED ALL OVER— NOBODY'S HEARD FROM HER.
SHOULDN'T YOU BE OUT LOOKING FOR HER? I MEAN, YOU'VE BEEN SPYING ON HER FOR YEARS. HOW CAN YOU LET HER JUST DISAPPEAR LIKE THAT?
OKAY, IF YOU KNOW WHERE SHE IS, WHY HAVEN'T YOU GONE AND TALKED TO HER?
SHE NEEDS TIME TO THINK.
WHERE IS SHE?
MARY BETH?
Y'KNOW, I LEFT MY HUSBAND TO COME BACK FOR KATCHOO. I'VE FILED FOR DIVORCE. BUT NO SOONER DID I GET HERE THAN ALL THIS HAPPENED. WE DIDN'T EVEN GET A CHANCE TO TALK.
SHE DOESN'T KNOW THAT YET, MARY BETH. I WANT TO SPEND THE REST OF MY LIFE WITH HER ...AS A COUPLE! THERE ISN'T ANYBODY ELSE FOR ME – THERE NEVER WILL BE. GOD, AFTER ALL WE'VE BEEN THROUGH, THAT MUCH IS CLEAR AT LEAST.
I LOVE HER, MARY BETH. I NEED TO BE WITH HER AND SHE NEEDS ME... ESPECIALLY NOW. TELL ME WHERE SHE IS.
PLEASE... HELP US!

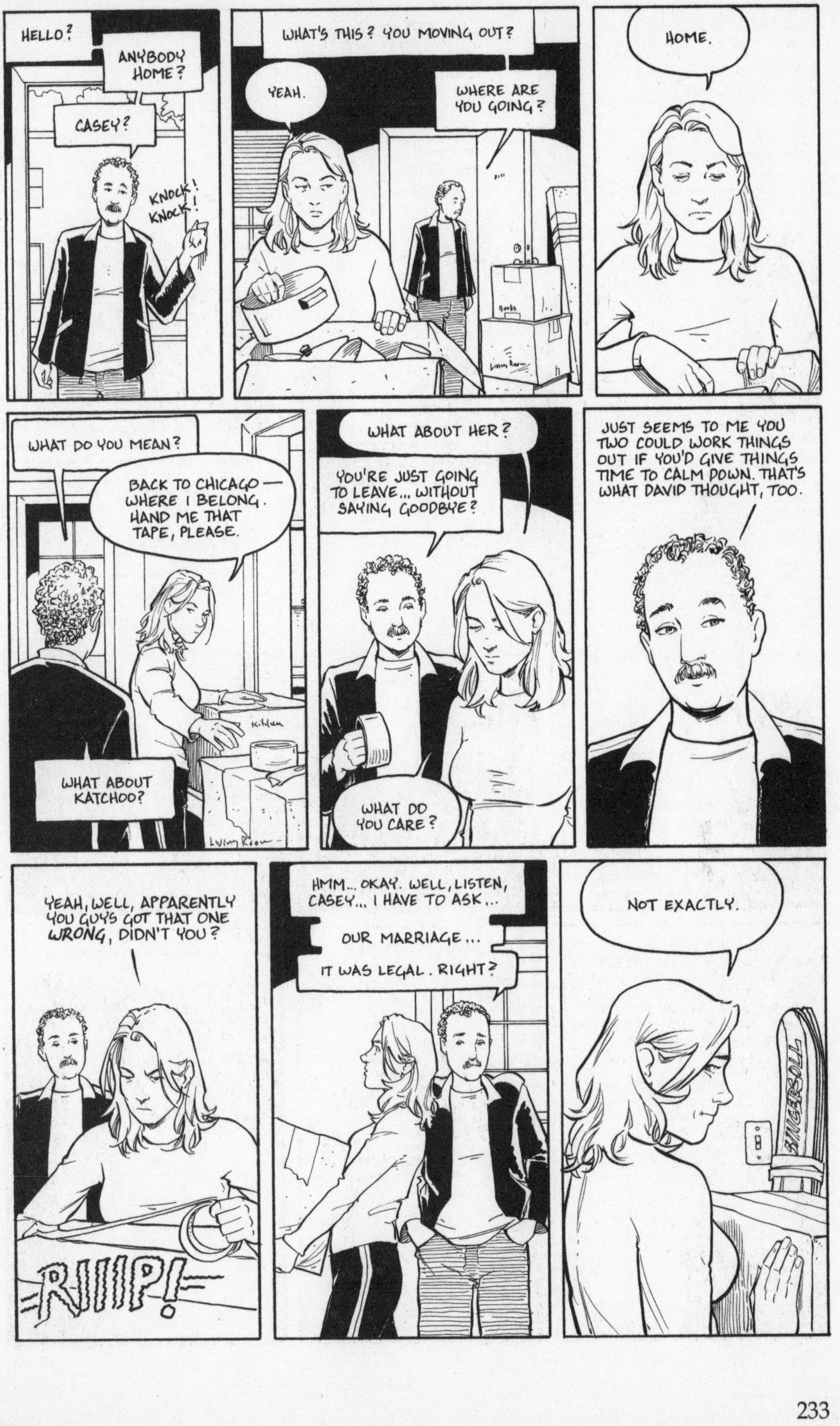
HELLO?
ANYBODY HOME?
CASEY?
KNOCK! KNOCK!
WHAT'S THIS? YOU MOVING OUT?
YEAH.
WHERE ARE YOU GOING?
...
HOME.
WHAT DO YOU MEAN?
BACK TO CHICAGO — WHERE I BELONG. HAND ME THAT TAPE, PLEASE.
WHAT ABOUT KATCHOO?
WHAT ABOUT HER?
YOU'RE JUST GOING TO LEAVE... WITHOUT SAYING GOODBYE?
WHAT DO YOU CARE?
JUST SEEMS TO ME YOU TWO COULD WORK THINGS OUT IF YOU'D GIVE THINGS TIME TO CALM DOWN. THAT'S WHAT DAVID THOUGHT, TOO.
YEAH, WELL, APPARENTLY YOU GUYS GOT THAT ONE WRONG, DIDN'T YOU?
RIIIP!
HMM... OKAY. WELL, LISTEN, CASEY... I HAVE TO ASK...
OUR MARRIAGE...
IT WAS LEGAL. RIGHT?
NOT EXACTLY.

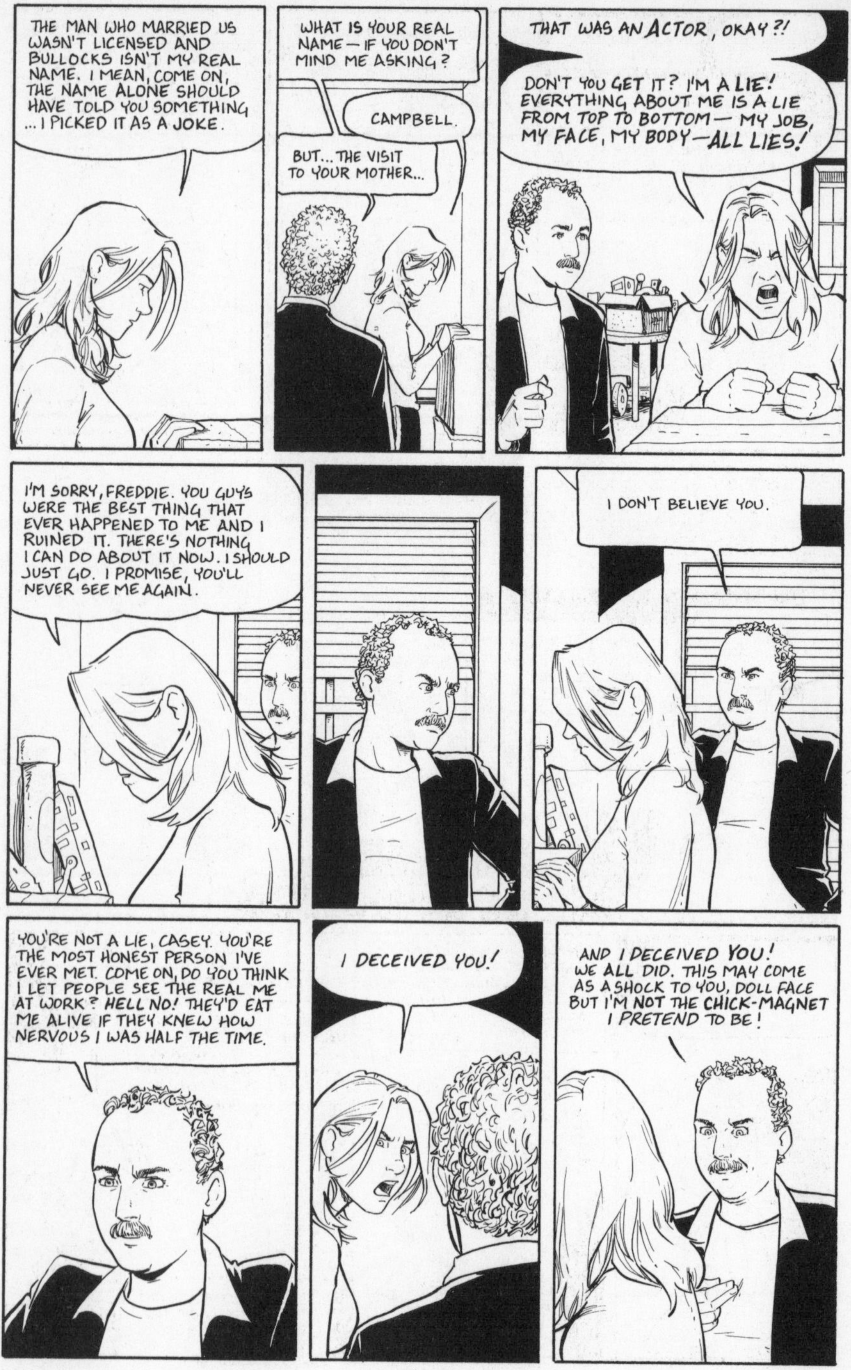
THE MAN WHO MARRIED US WASN'T LICENSED AND BULLOCKS ISN'T MY REAL NAME. I MEAN, COME ON, THE NAME ALONE SHOULD HAVE TOLD YOU SOMETHING ...I PICKED IT AS A JOKE.
WHAT IS YOUR REAL NAME—IF YOU DON'T MIND ME ASKING?
CAMPBELL.
BUT... THE VISIT TO YOUR MOTHER...
THAT WAS AN ACTOR, OKAY?!
DON'T YOU GET IT? I'M A LIE! EVERYTHING ABOUT ME IS A LIE FROM TOP TO BOTTOM— MY JOB, MY FACE, MY BODY—ALL LIES!
I'M SORRY, FREDDIE. YOU GUYS WERE THE BEST THING THAT EVER HAPPENED TO ME AND I RUINED IT. THERE'S NOTHING I CAN DO ABOUT IT NOW. I SHOULD JUST GO. I PROMISE, YOU'LL NEVER SEE ME AGAIN.
I DON'T BELIEVE YOU.
YOU'RE NOT A LIE, CASEY. YOU'RE THE MOST HONEST PERSON I'VE EVER MET. COME ON, DO YOU THINK I LET PEOPLE SEE THE REAL ME AT WORK? HELL NO! THEY'D EAT ME ALIVE IF THEY KNEW HOW NERVOUS I WAS HALF THE TIME.
I DECEIVED YOU!
AND I DECEIVED YOU! WE ALL DID. THIS MAY COME AS A SHOCK TO YOU, DOLL FACE BUT I'M NOT THE CHICK-MAGNET I PRETEND TO BE!

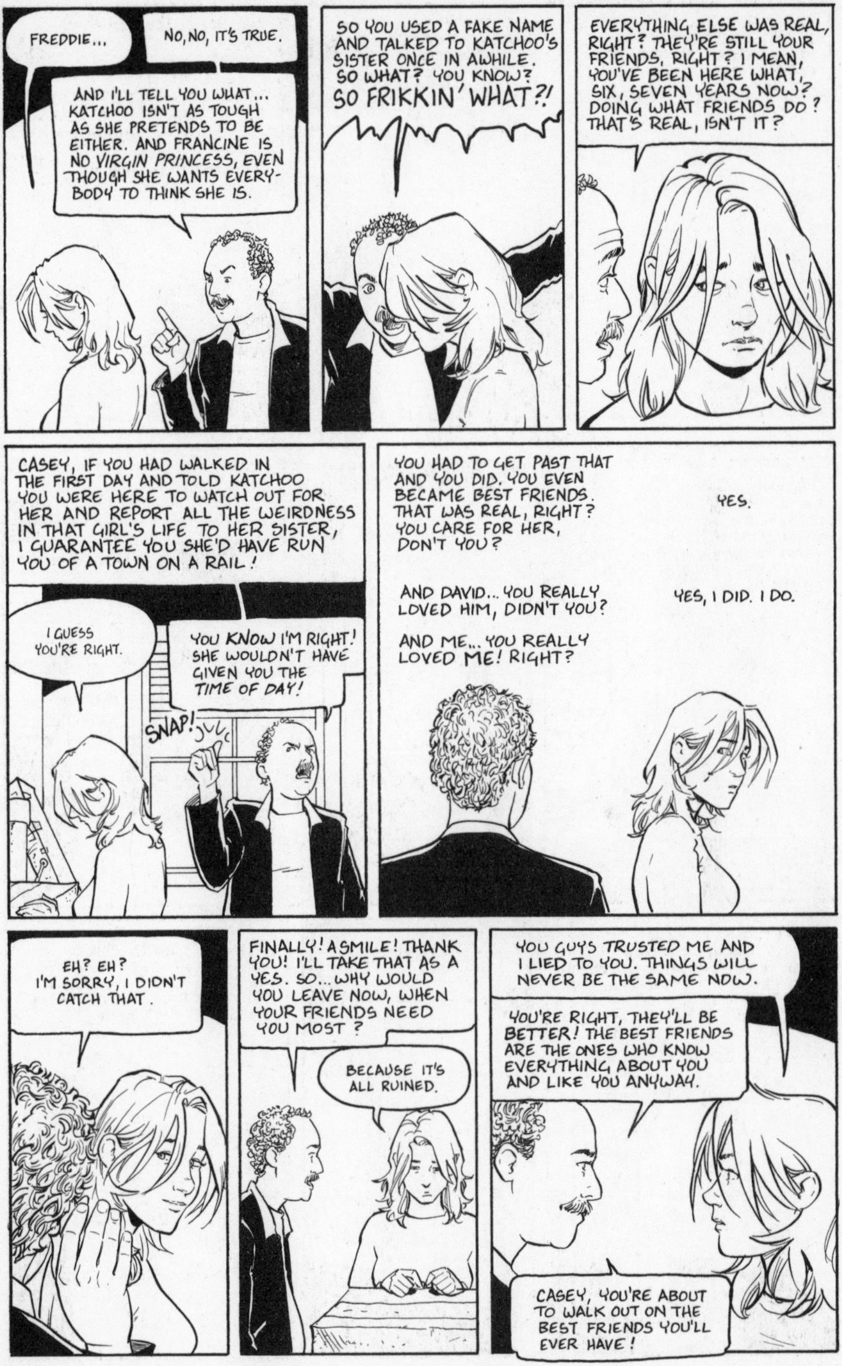
FREDDIE...
NO, NO, IT'S TRUE.
AND I'LL TELL YOU WHAT... KATCHOO ISN'T AS TOUGH AS SHE PRETENDS TO BE EITHER. AND FRANCINE IS NO *VIRGIN PRINCESS*, EVEN THOUGH SHE WANTS EVERY-BODY TO THINK SHE IS.
SO YOU USED A FAKE NAME AND TALKED TO KATCHOO'S SISTER ONCE IN AWHILE. SO WHAT? YOU KNOW? SO FRIKKIN' WHAT?!
EVERYTHING ELSE WAS REAL, RIGHT? THEY'RE STILL YOUR FRIENDS, RIGHT? I MEAN, YOU'VE BEEN HERE WHAT, SIX, SEVEN YEARS NOW? DOING WHAT FRIENDS DO? THAT'S REAL, ISN'T IT?
CASEY, IF YOU HAD WALKED IN THE FIRST DAY AND TOLD KATCHOO YOU WERE HERE TO WATCH OUT FOR HER AND REPORT ALL THE WEIRDNESS IN THAT GIRL'S LIFE TO HER SISTER, I GUARANTEE YOU SHE'D HAVE RUN YOU OF A TOWN ON A RAIL!
I GUESS YOU'RE RIGHT.
YOU KNOW I'M RIGHT! SHE WOULDN'T HAVE GIVEN YOU THE *TIME OF DAY!*
SNAP!
YOU HAD TO GET PAST THAT AND YOU DID. YOU EVEN BECAME BEST FRIENDS. THAT WAS REAL, RIGHT? YOU CARE FOR HER, DON'T YOU?
YES.
AND DAVID... YOU REALLY LOVED HIM, DIDN'T YOU?
YES, I DID. I DO.
AND ME... YOU REALLY LOVED ME! RIGHT?
EH? EH? I'M SORRY, I DIDN'T CATCH THAT.
FINALLY! A SMILE! THANK YOU! I'LL TAKE THAT AS A YES. SO... WHY WOULD YOU LEAVE NOW, WHEN YOUR FRIENDS NEED YOU MOST?
BECAUSE IT'S ALL RUINED.
YOU GUYS TRUSTED ME AND I LIED TO YOU. THINGS WILL NEVER BE THE SAME NOW.
YOU'RE RIGHT, THEY'LL BE BETTER! THE BEST FRIENDS ARE THE ONES WHO KNOW EVERYTHING ABOUT YOU AND LIKE YOU ANYWAY.
CASEY, YOU'RE ABOUT TO WALK OUT ON THE BEST FRIENDS YOU'LL EVER HAVE!

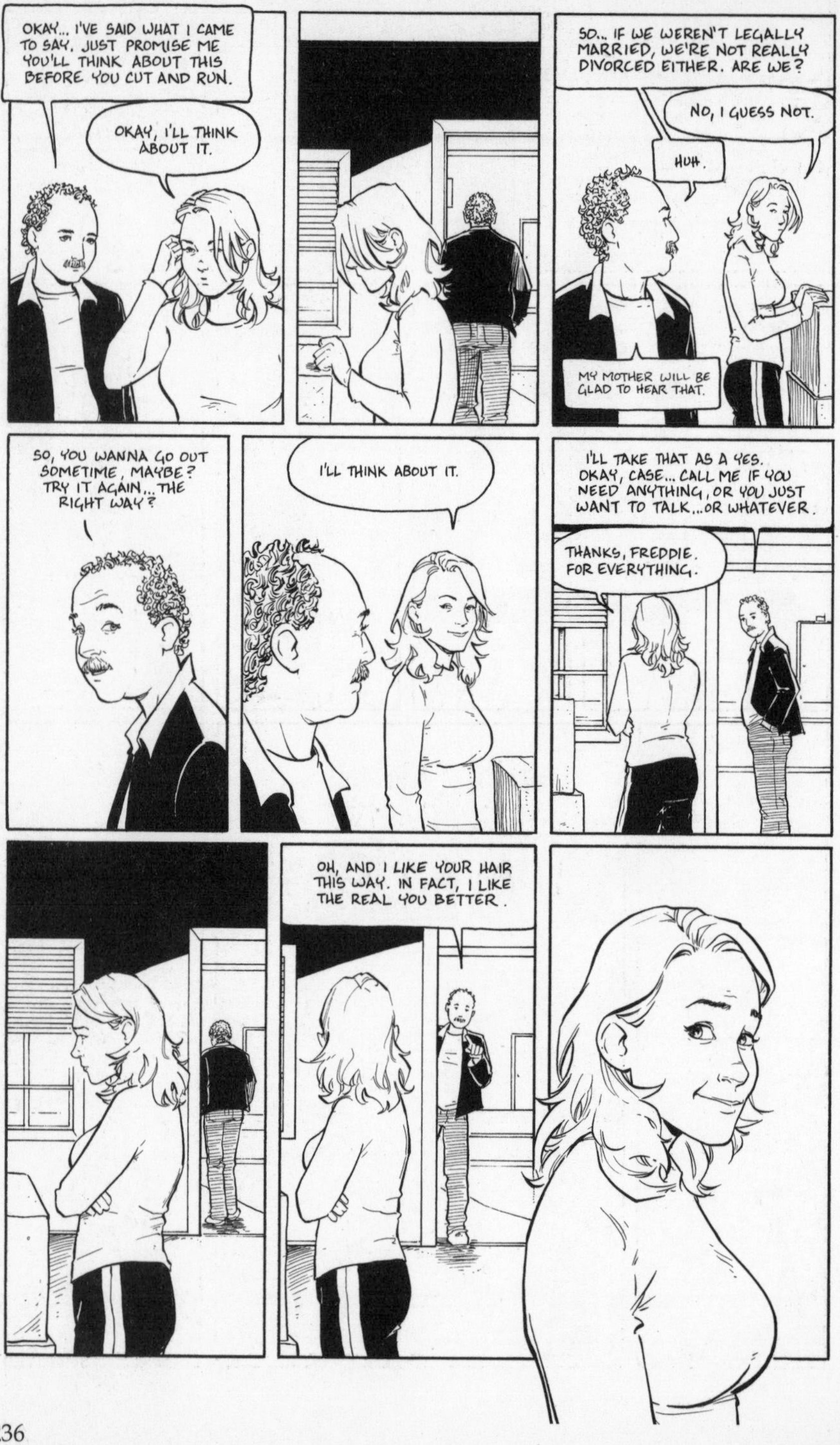
OKAY... I'VE SAID WHAT I CAME TO SAY. JUST PROMISE ME YOU'LL THINK ABOUT THIS BEFORE YOU CUT AND RUN.
OKAY, I'LL THINK ABOUT IT.
SO... IF WE WEREN'T LEGALLY MARRIED, WE'RE NOT REALLY DIVORCED EITHER. ARE WE?
NO, I GUESS NOT.
HUH.
MY MOTHER WILL BE GLAD TO HEAR THAT.
SO, YOU WANNA GO OUT SOMETIME, MAYBE? TRY IT AGAIN... THE RIGHT WAY?
I'LL THINK ABOUT IT.
I'LL TAKE THAT AS A YES. OKAY, CASE... CALL ME IF YOU NEED ANYTHING, OR YOU JUST WANT TO TALK... OR WHATEVER.
THANKS, FREDDIE. FOR EVERYTHING.
OH, AND I LIKE YOUR HAIR THIS WAY. IN FACT, I LIKE THE REAL YOU BETTER.

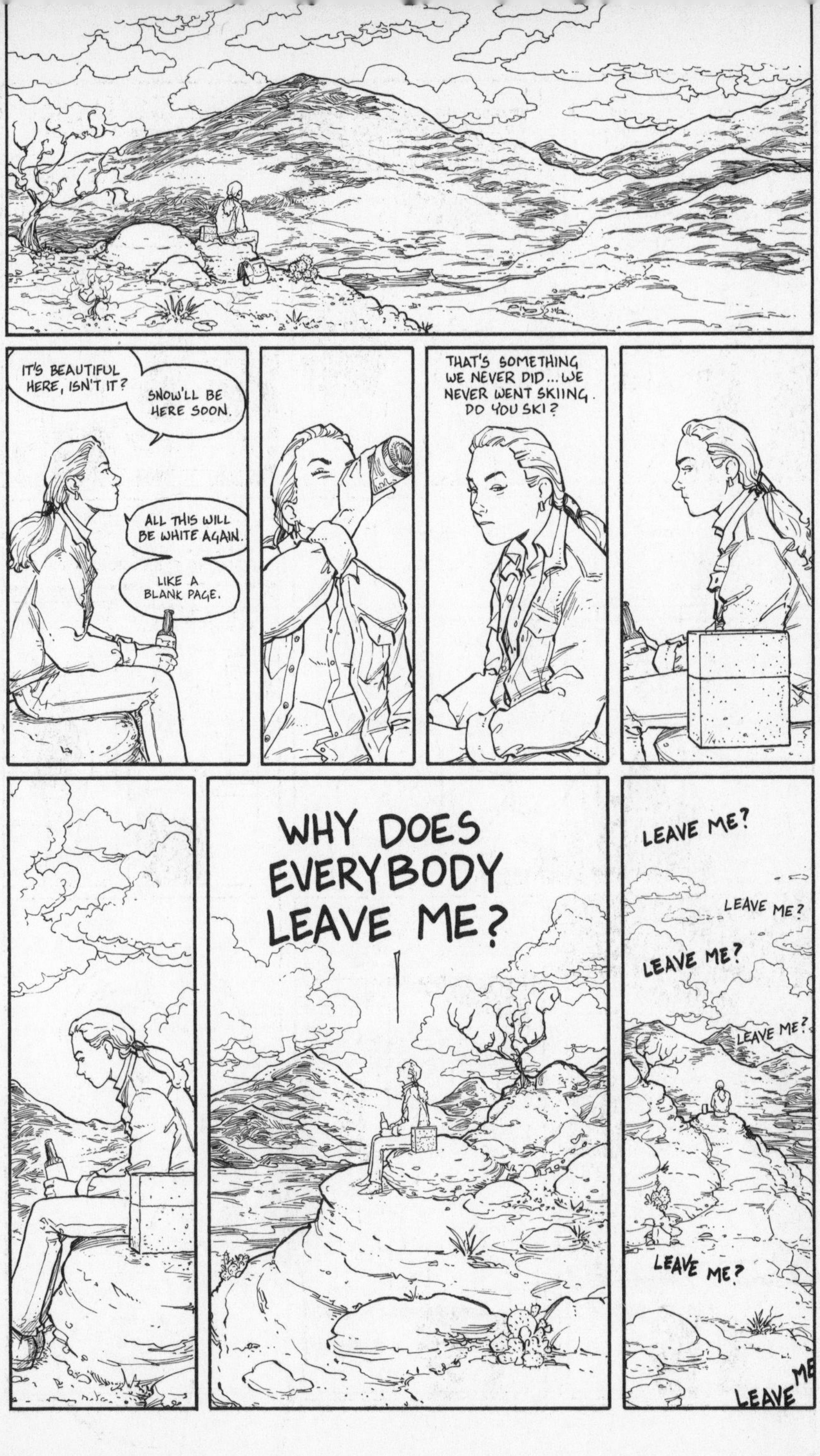

IT'S BEAUTIFUL HERE, ISN'T IT?
SNOW'LL BE HERE SOON.
ALL THIS WILL BE WHITE AGAIN.
LIKE A BLANK PAGE.
THAT'S SOMETHING WE NEVER DID... WE NEVER WENT SKIING. DO YOU SKI?
WHY DOES EVERYBODY LEAVE ME?
LEAVE ME?
LEAVE ME?
LEAVE ME?
LEAVE ME?
LEAVE ME?
LEAVE ME

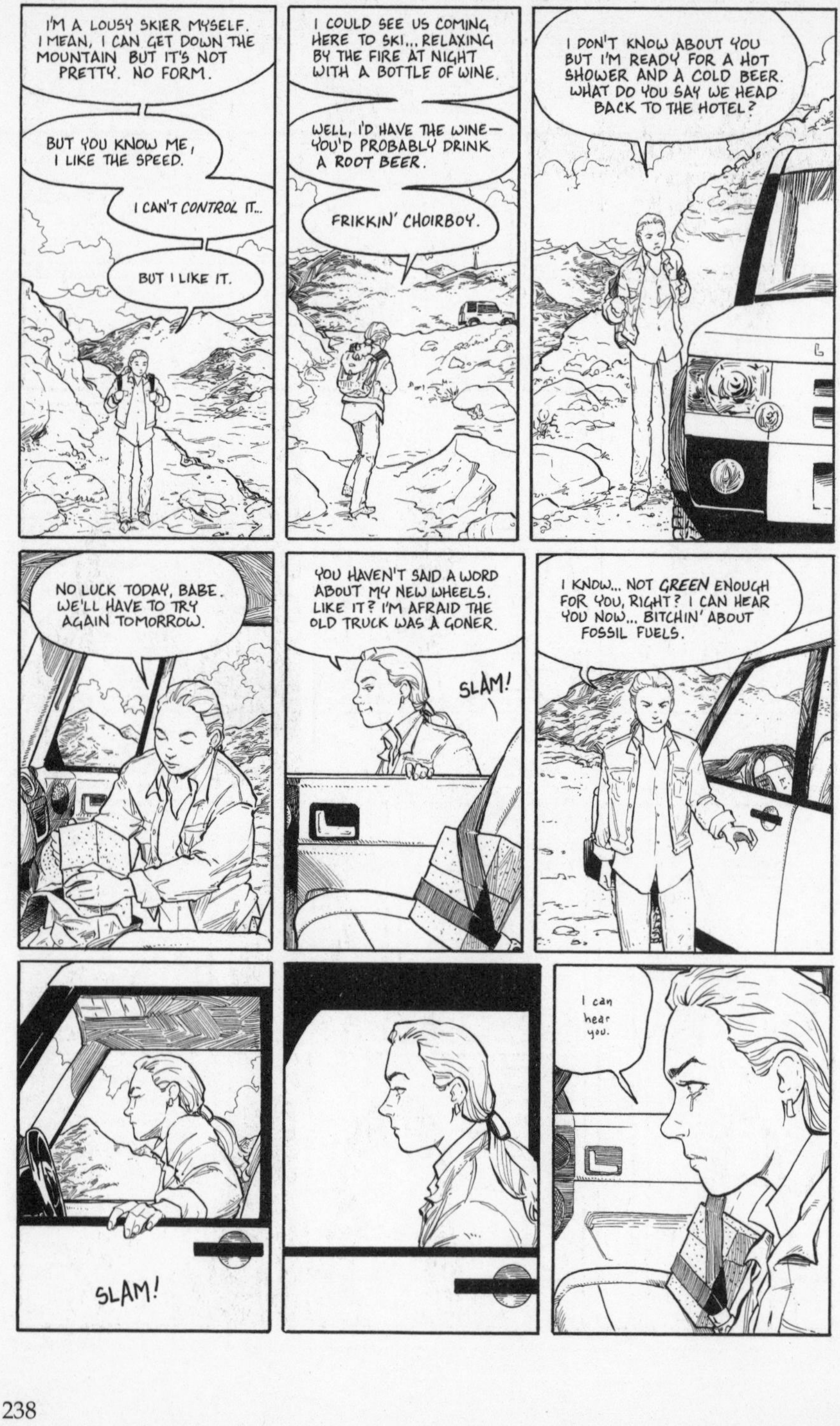
I'M A LOUSY SKIER MYSELF. I MEAN, I CAN GET DOWN THE MOUNTAIN BUT IT'S NOT PRETTY. NO FORM.
BUT YOU KNOW ME, I LIKE THE SPEED.
I CAN'T CONTROL IT...
BUT I LIKE IT.
I COULD SEE US COMING HERE TO SKI... RELAXING BY THE FIRE AT NIGHT WITH A BOTTLE OF WINE.
WELL, I'D HAVE THE WINE— YOU'D PROBABLY DRINK A ROOT BEER.
FRIKKIN' CHOIRBOY.
I DON'T KNOW ABOUT YOU BUT I'M READY FOR A HOT SHOWER AND A COLD BEER. WHAT DO YOU SAY WE HEAD BACK TO THE HOTEL?
NO LUCK TODAY, BABE. WE'LL HAVE TO TRY AGAIN TOMORROW.
YOU HAVEN'T SAID A WORD ABOUT MY NEW WHEELS. LIKE IT? I'M AFRAID THE OLD TRUCK WAS A GONER.
SLAM!
I KNOW... NOT GREEN ENOUGH FOR YOU, RIGHT? I CAN HEAR YOU NOW... BITCHIN' ABOUT FOSSIL FUELS.
SLAM!
I can hear you.

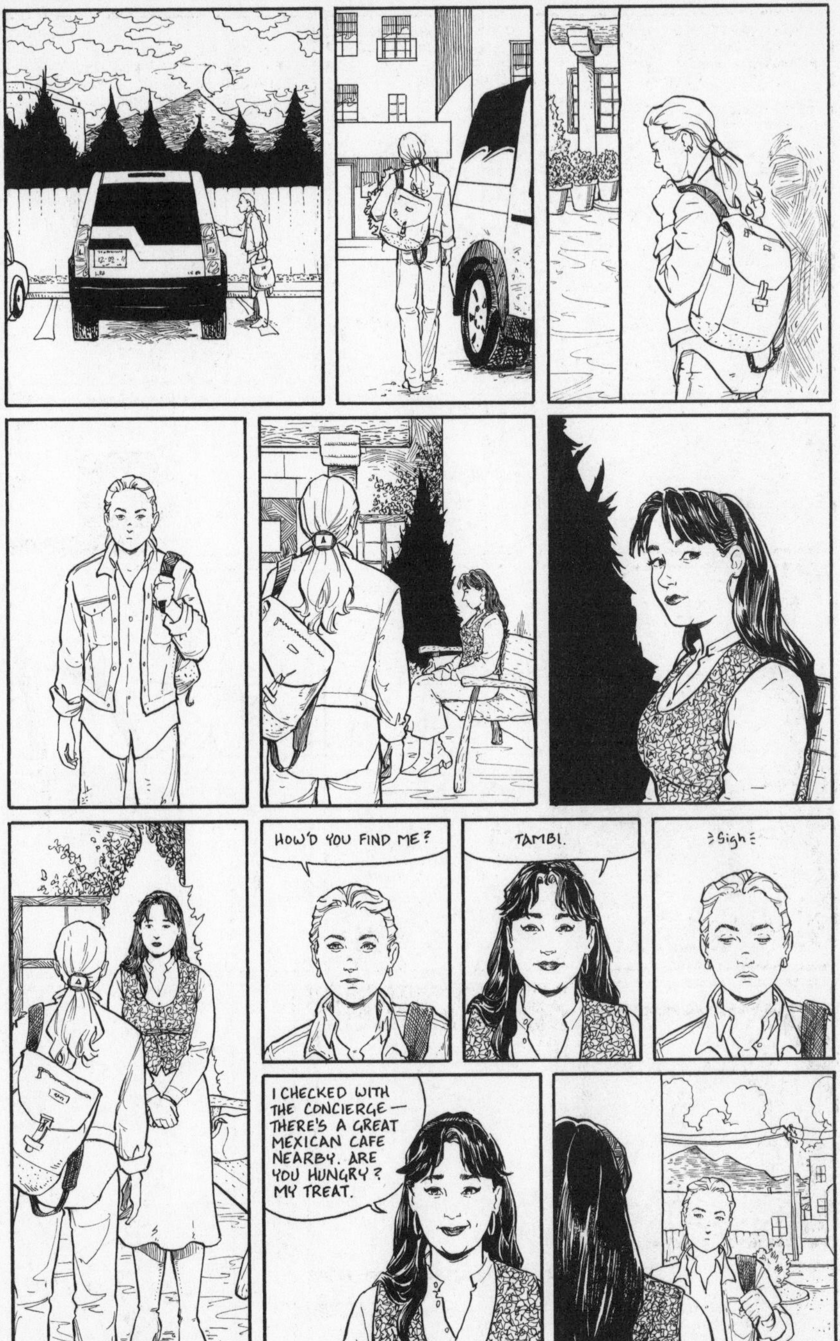
HOW'D YOU FIND ME?
TAMBI.
Sigh
I CHECKED WITH THE CONCIERGE— THERE'S A GREAT MEXICAN CAFE NEARBY. ARE YOU HUNGRY? MY TREAT.

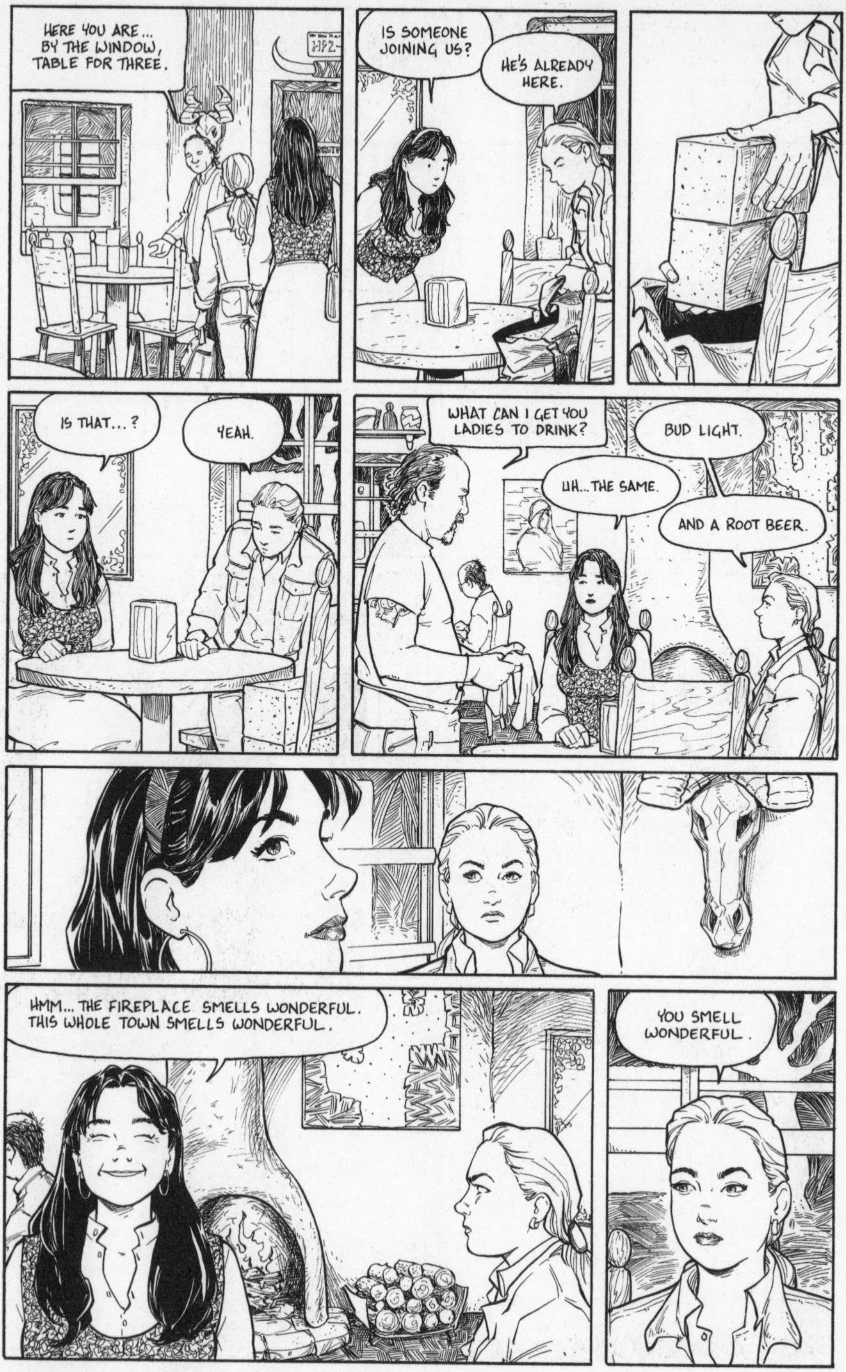

HERE YOU ARE... BY THE WINDOW, TABLE FOR THREE.
IS SOMEONE JOINING US?
HE'S ALREADY HERE.
IS THAT...?
YEAH.
WHAT CAN I GET YOU LADIES TO DRINK?
BUD LIGHT.
UH... THE SAME.
AND A ROOT BEER.
HMM... THE FIREPLACE SMELLS WONDERFUL. THIS WHOLE TOWN SMELLS WONDERFUL.
YOU SMELL WONDERFUL.

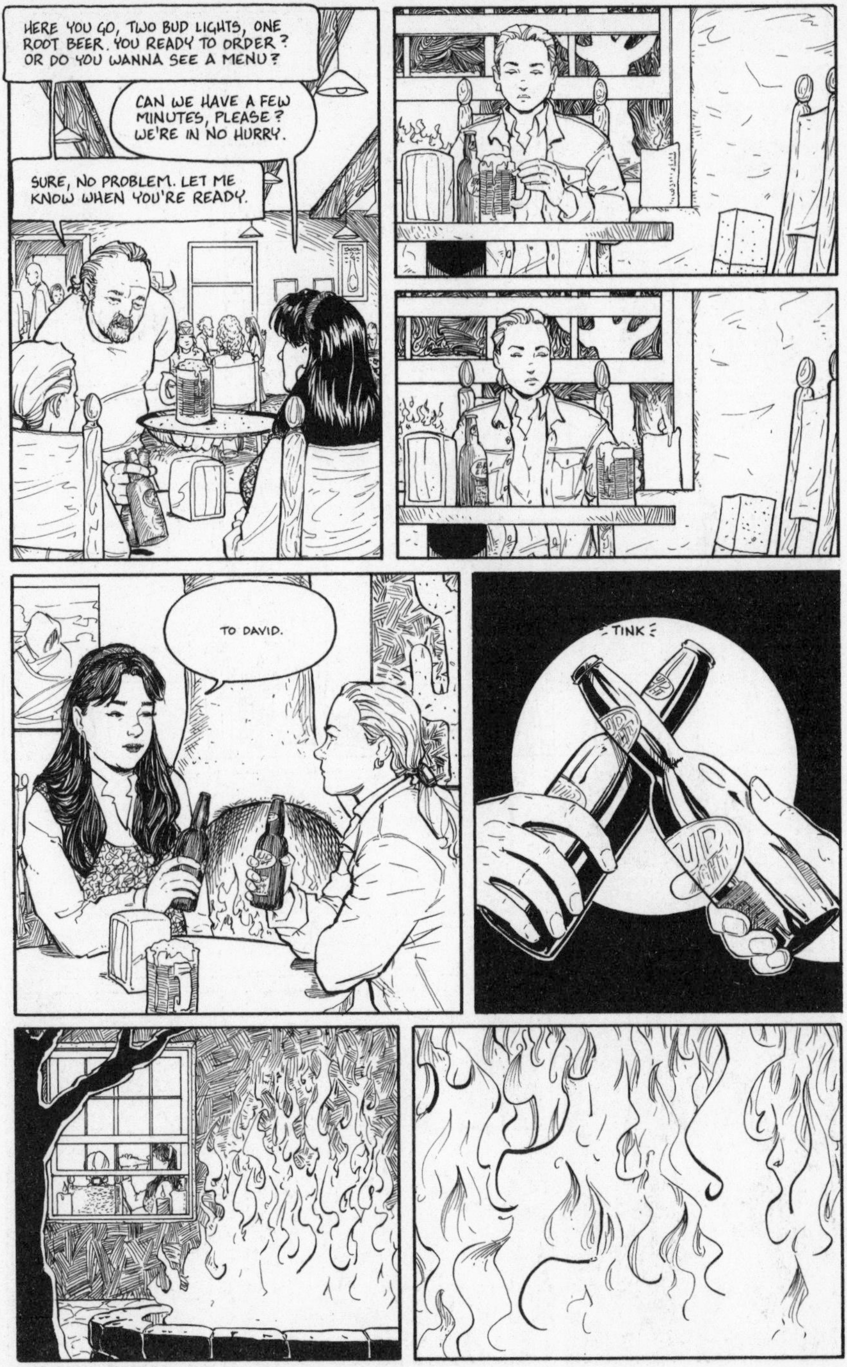
HERE YOU GO, TWO BUD LIGHTS, ONE ROOT BEER. YOU READY TO ORDER? OR DO YOU WANNA SEE A MENU?
CAN WE HAVE A FEW MINUTES, PLEASE? WE'RE IN NO HURRY.
SURE, NO PROBLEM. LET ME KNOW WHEN YOU'RE READY.
TO DAVID.
TINK

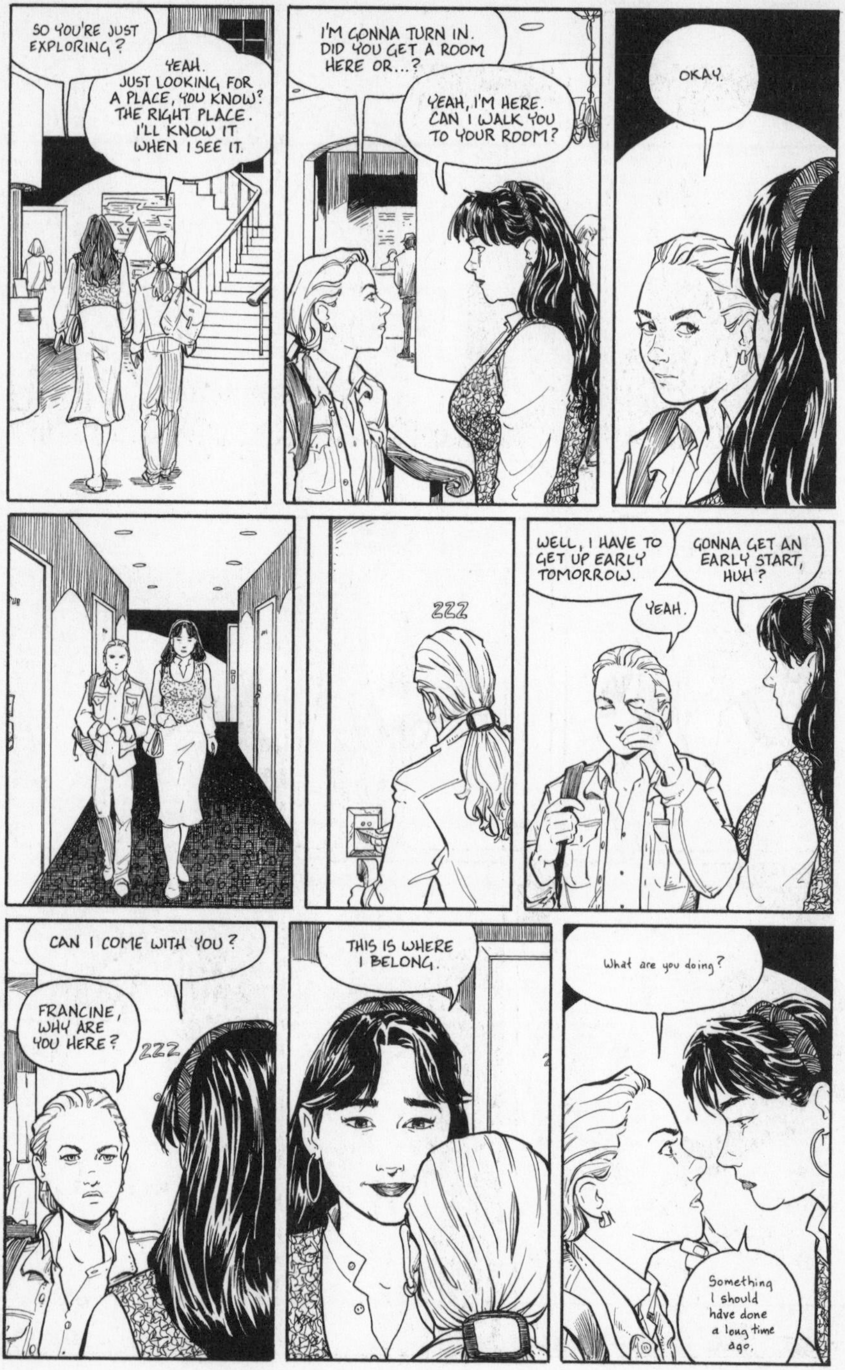
SO YOU'RE JUST EXPLORING?
YEAH. JUST LOOKING FOR A PLACE, YOU KNOW? THE RIGHT PLACE. I'LL KNOW IT WHEN I SEE IT.
I'M GONNA TURN IN. DID YOU GET A ROOM HERE OR...?
YEAH, I'M HERE. CAN I WALK YOU TO YOUR ROOM?
OKAY.
ZZZ
WELL, I HAVE TO GET UP EARLY TOMORROW.
GONNA GET AN EARLY START, HUH?
YEAH.
CAN I COME WITH YOU?
FRANCINE, WHY ARE YOU HERE?
ZZZ
THIS IS WHERE I BELONG.
What are you doing?
Something I should have done a long time ago.

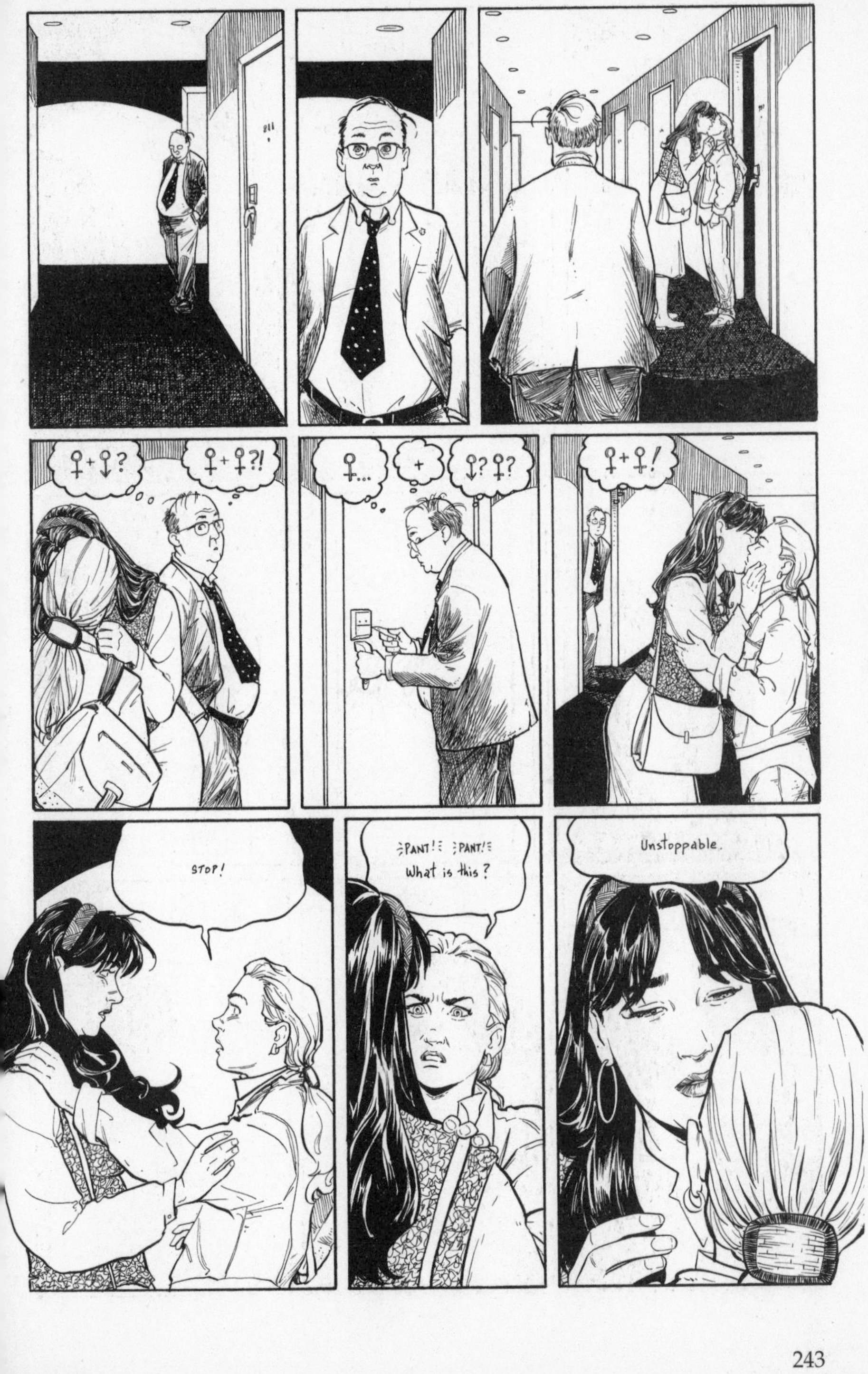
♀+♀!
STOP!
PANT! PANT!
What is this?
Unstoppable.

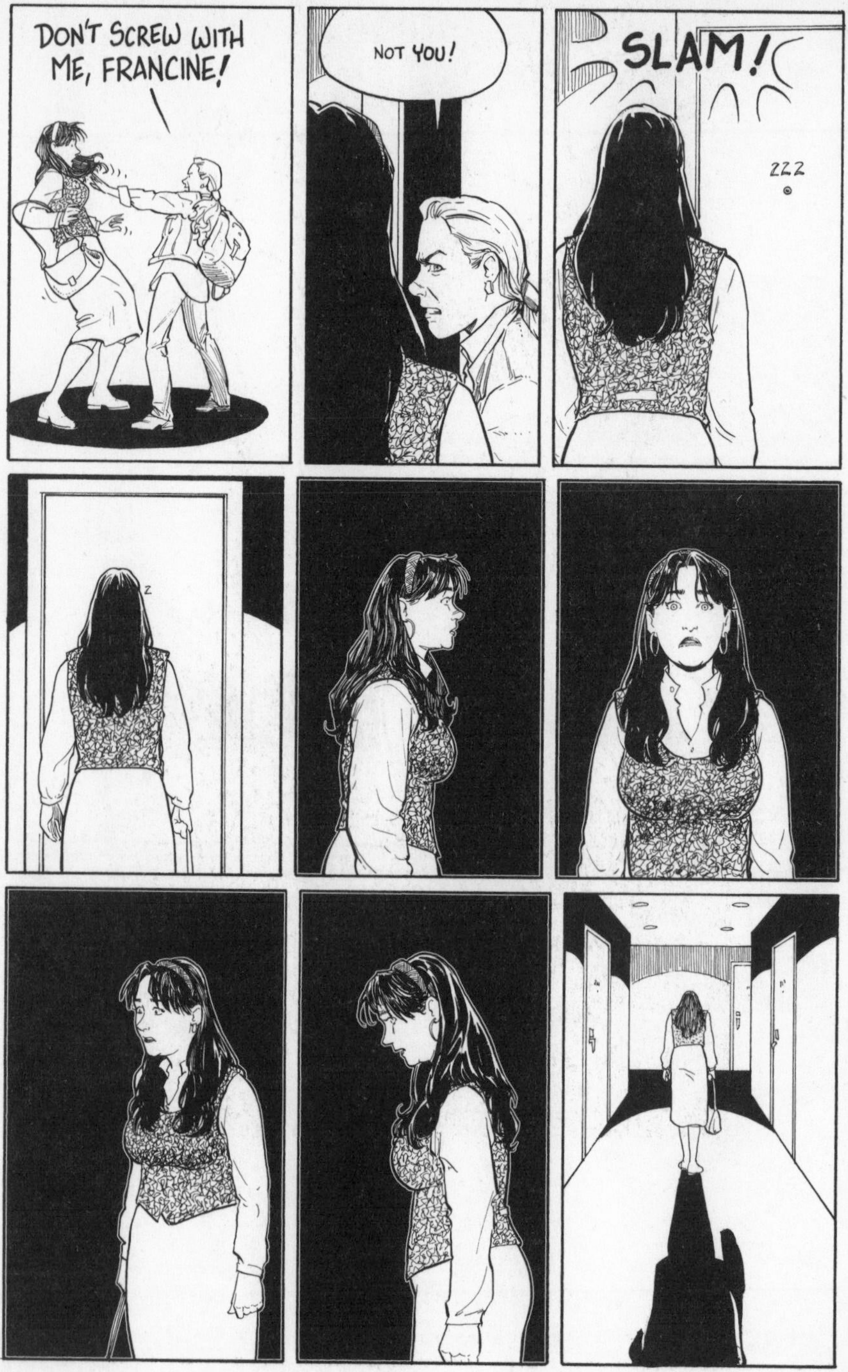
DON'T SCREW WITH ME, FRANCINE!
NOT YOU!
SLAM!
ZZZ
Z

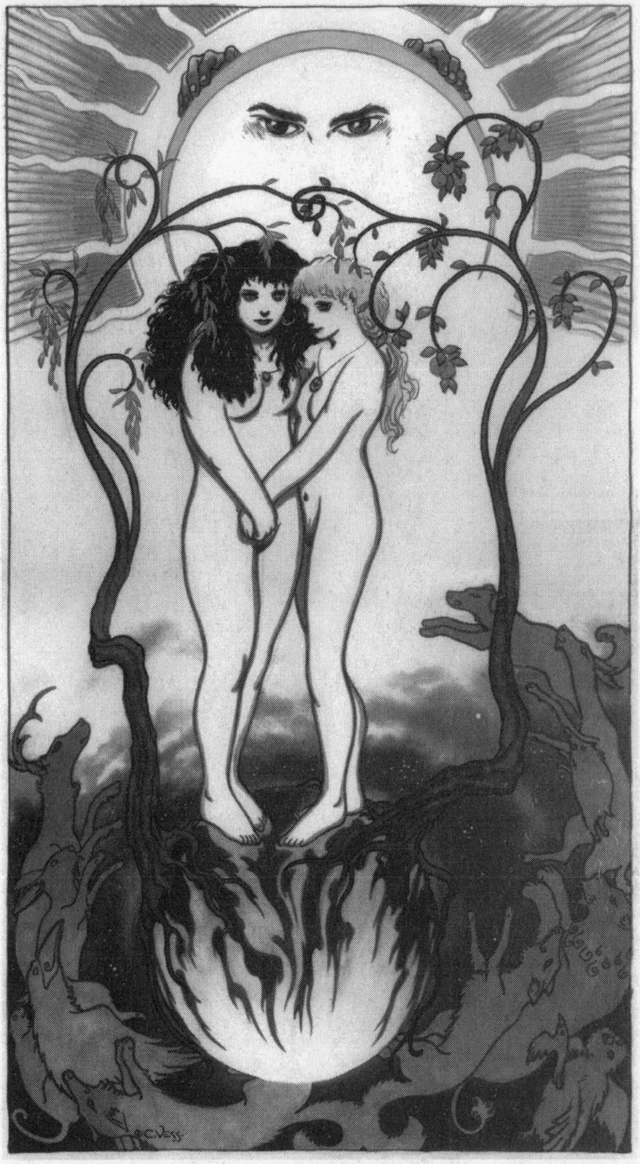

I've been without you
I've been so deep within you
And the feeling's still the same
When I'm holding you
I can't even remember my name

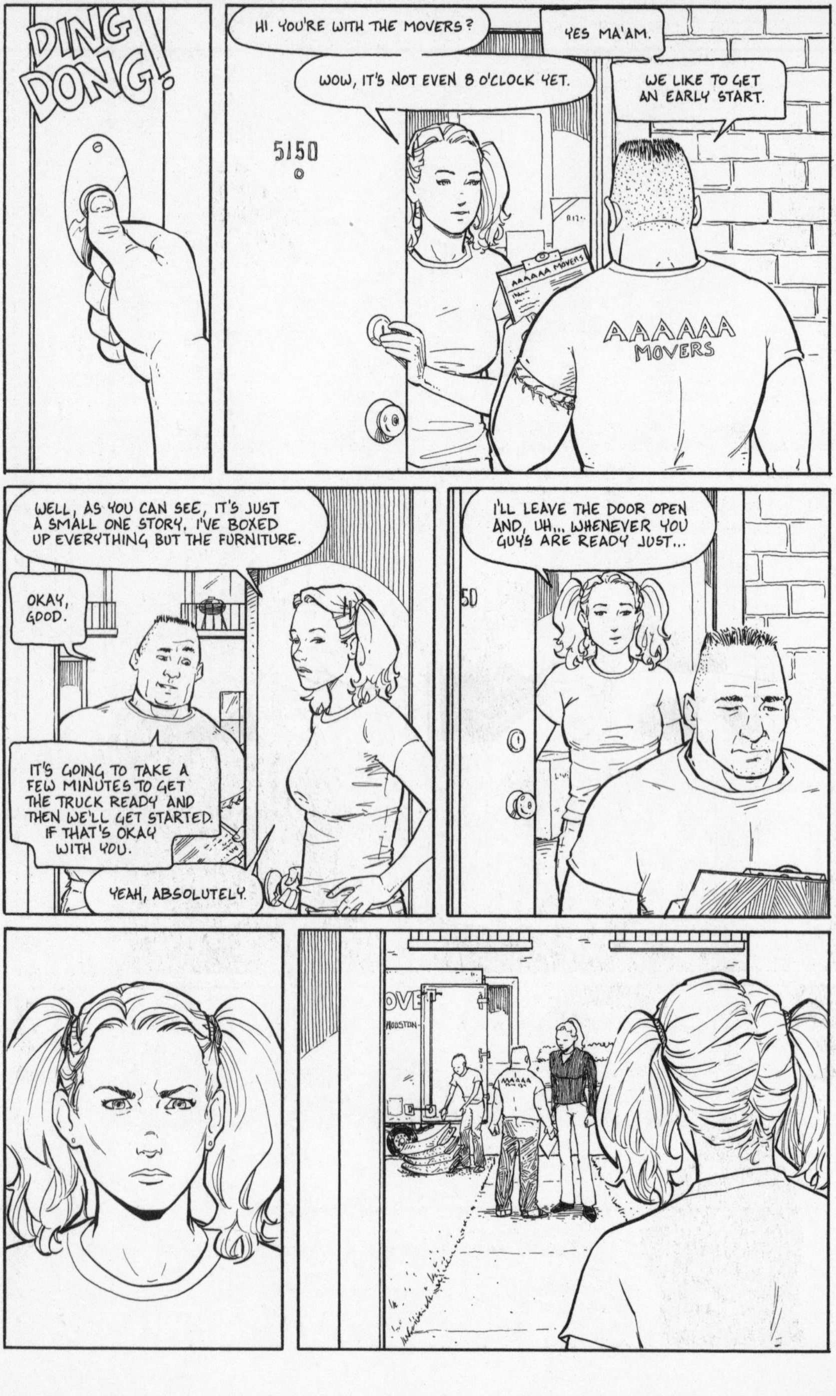
DING DONG!
HI. YOU'RE WITH THE MOVERS?
YES MA'AM.
WOW, IT'S NOT EVEN 8 O'CLOCK YET.
WE LIKE TO GET AN EARLY START.
5150
AAAAAA MOVERS
AAAAAA MOVERS
WELL, AS YOU CAN SEE, IT'S JUST A SMALL ONE STORY. I'VE BOXED UP EVERYTHING BUT THE FURNITURE.
OKAY, GOOD.
IT'S GOING TO TAKE A FEW MINUTES TO GET THE TRUCK READY AND THEN WE'LL GET STARTED. IF THAT'S OKAY WITH YOU.
YEAH, ABSOLUTELY.
I'LL LEAVE THE DOOR OPEN AND, UH... WHENEVER YOU GUYS ARE READY JUST...
50

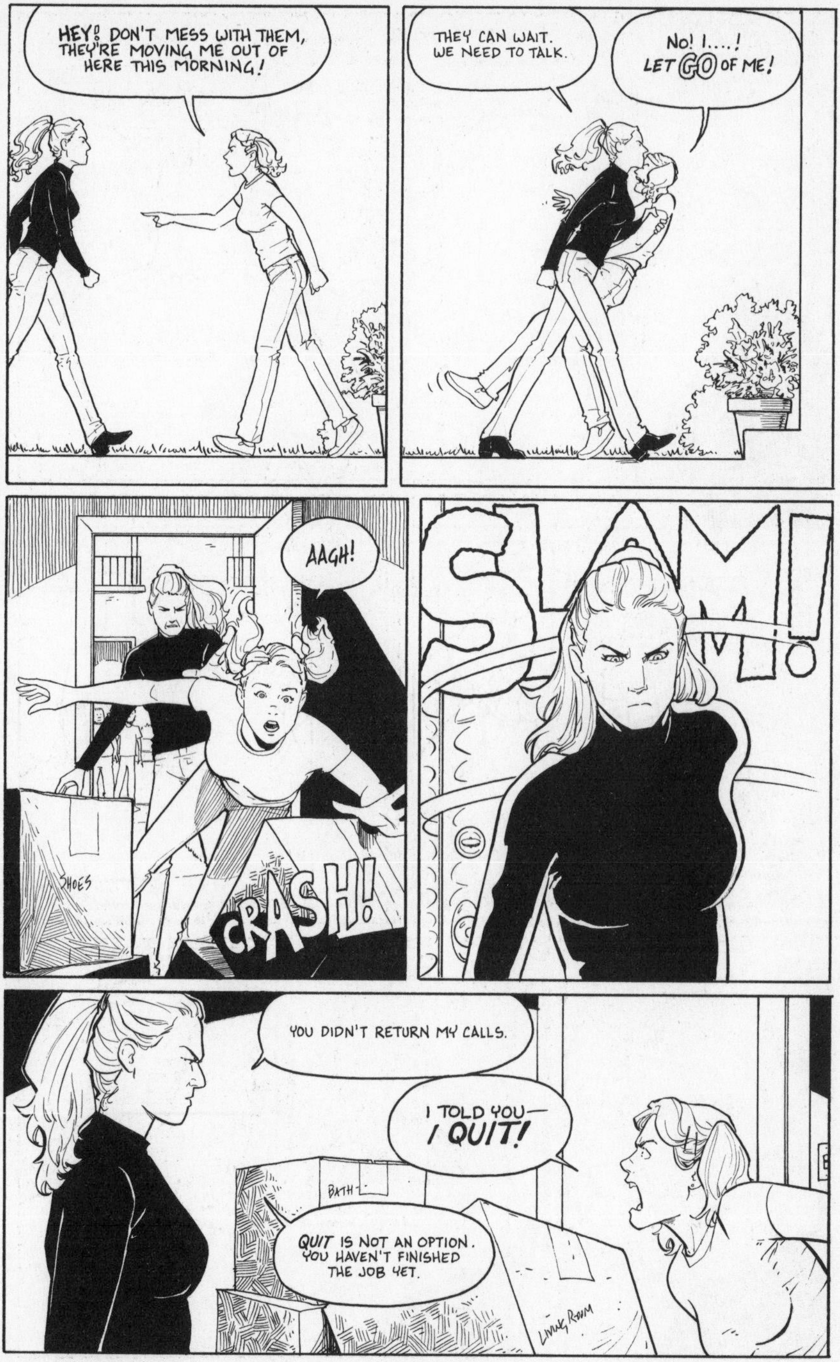
HEY! DON'T MESS WITH THEM, THEY'RE MOVING ME OUT OF HERE THIS MORNING!
THEY CAN WAIT. WE NEED TO TALK.
NO! I....! LET GO OF ME!
AAGH!
SHOES
CRASH!
SLAM!
YOU DIDN'T RETURN MY CALLS.
I TOLD YOU— I QUIT!
BATH
QUIT IS NOT AN OPTION. YOU HAVEN'T FINISHED THE JOB YET.
LIVING ROOM

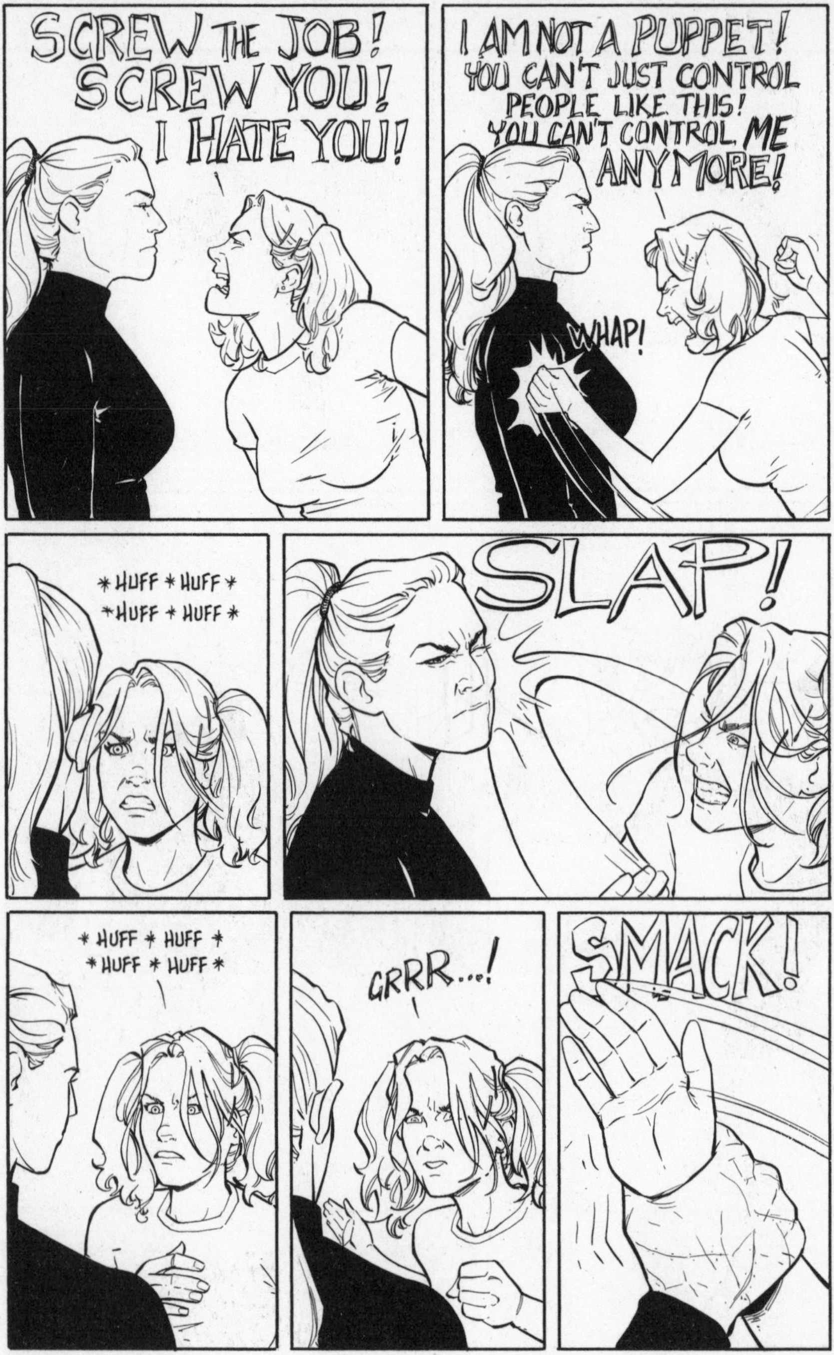
SCREW THE JOB! SCREW YOU! I HATE YOU!
I AM NOT A PUPPET! YOU CAN'T JUST CONTROL PEOPLE LIKE THIS! YOU CAN'T CONTROL ME ANYMORE!
WHAP!
* HUFF * HUFF * * HUFF * HUFF *
SLAP!
* HUFF * HUFF * * HUFF * HUFF *
GRRR...!
SMACK!

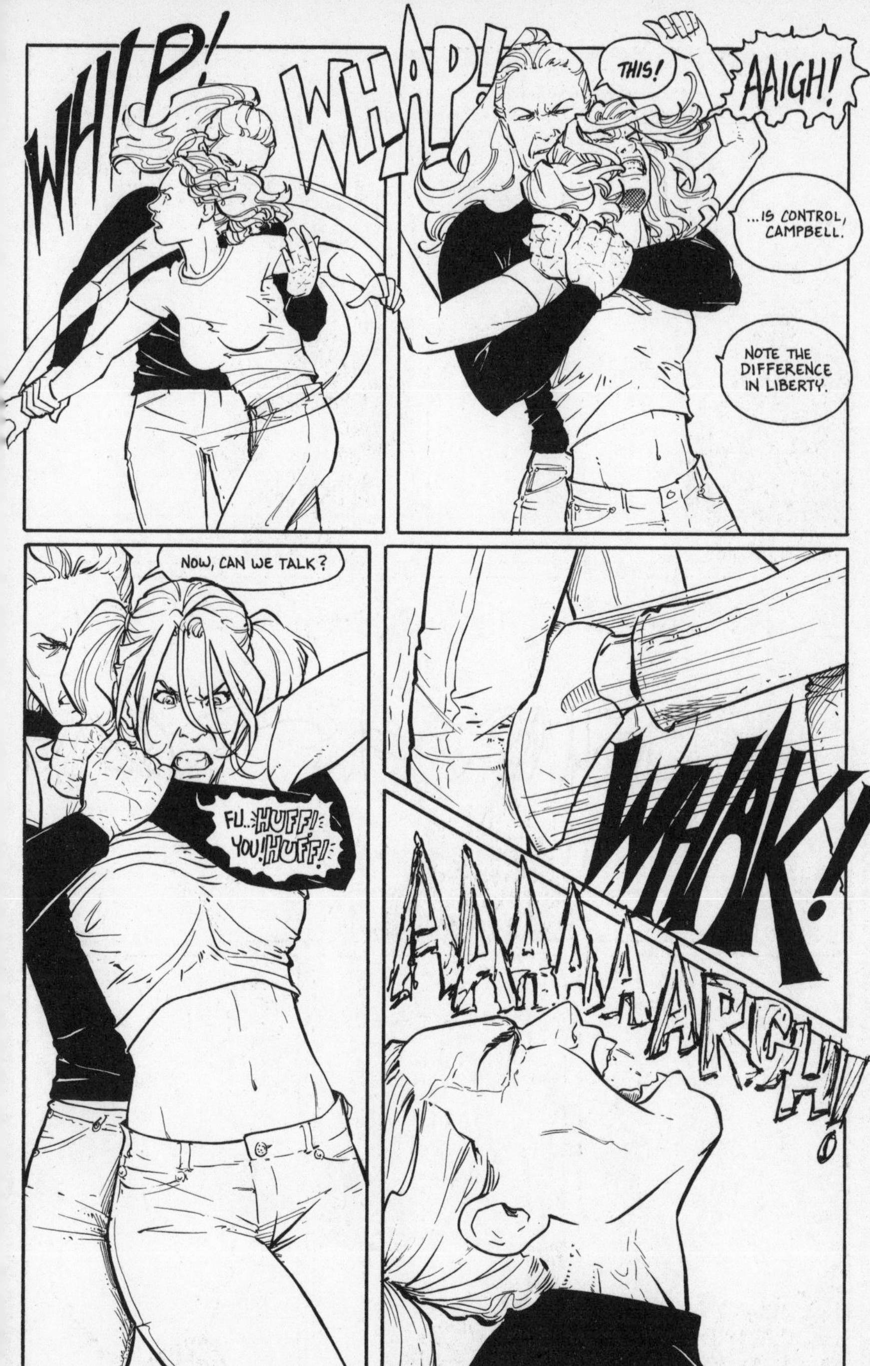
WHIP!
WHAP!
THIS!
AAIGH!
...IS CONTROL, CAMPBELL.
NOTE THE DIFFERENCE IN LIBERTY.
NOW, CAN WE TALK?
FU..HUFF! YOU!HUFF!
WHAK!
AAAAAARRGH!!

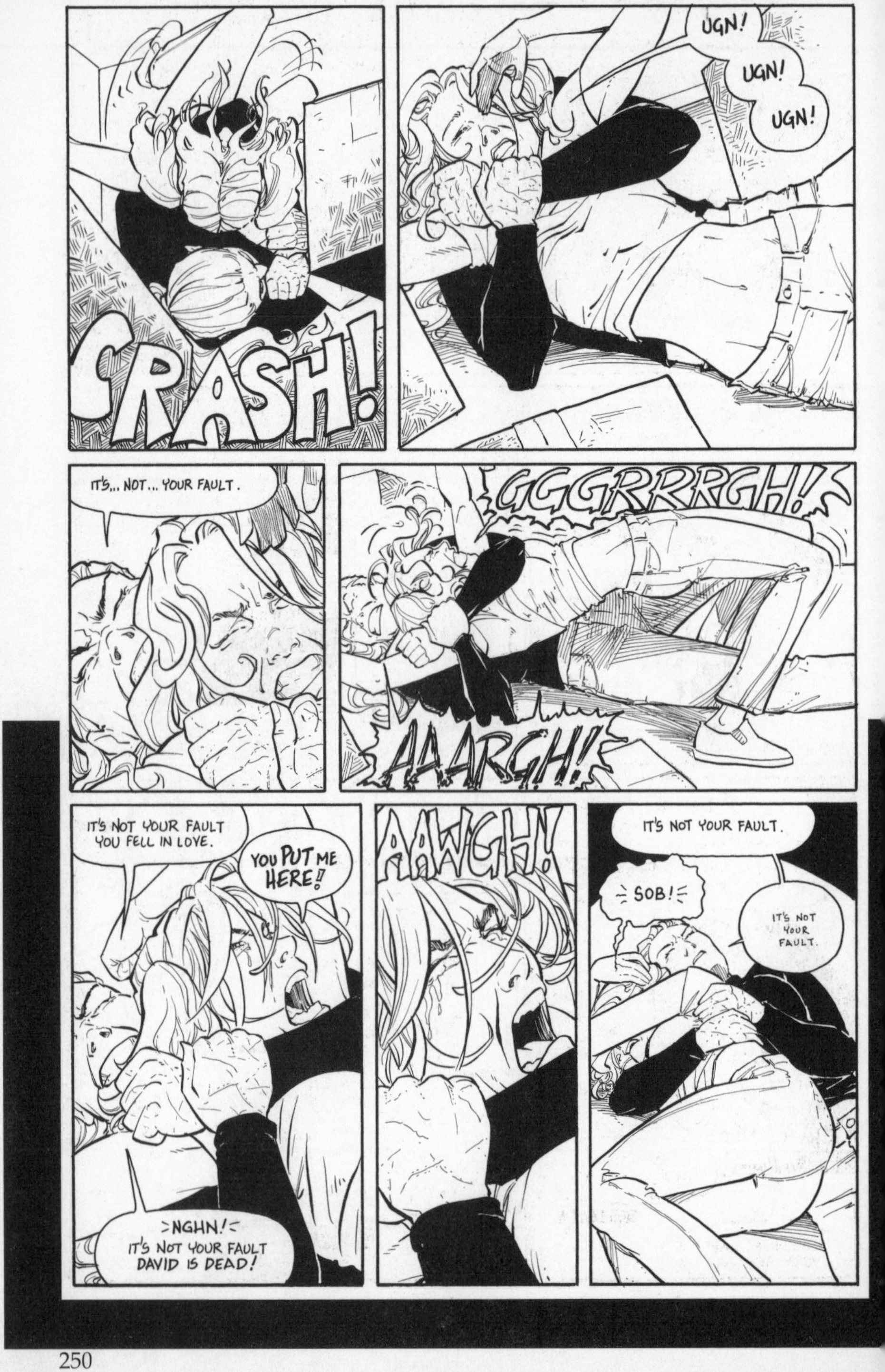
CRASH!
UGN!
UGN!
UGN!
IT'S... NOT... YOUR FAULT.
GGGRRRRGH!
AAARGH!
IT'S NOT YOUR FAULT
YOU FELL IN LOVE.
YOU PUT ME HERE!
NGHN!
IT'S NOT YOUR FAULT
DAVID IS DEAD!
AAWGH!
IT'S NOT YOUR FAULT.
SOB!
IT'S NOT YOUR FAULT.

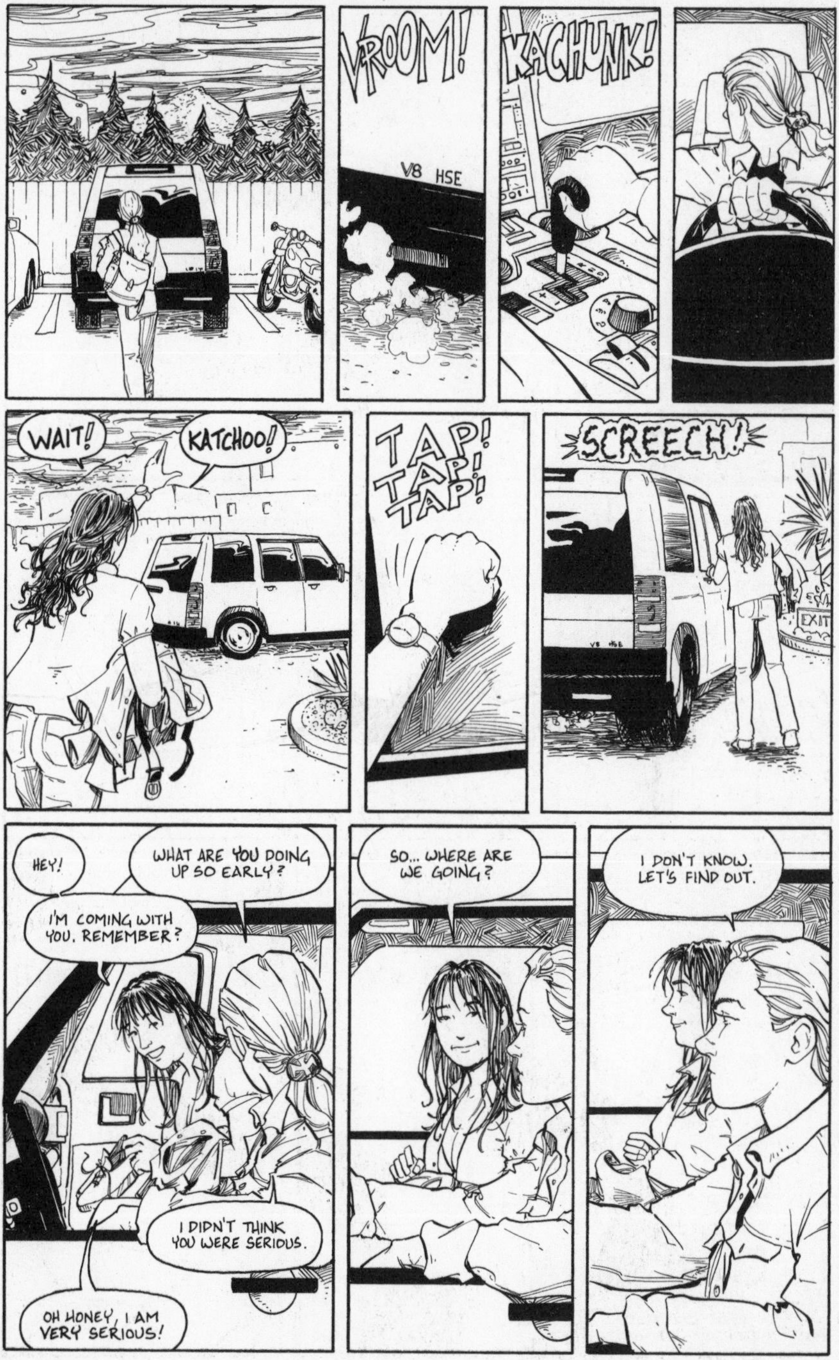
VROOM!
V8 HSE
KACHUNK!
WAIT!
KATCHOO!
TAP! TAP! TAP!
SCREECH!
V8 HSE
EXIT
HEY!
WHAT ARE YOU DOING UP SO EARLY?
I'M COMING WITH YOU. REMEMBER?
I DIDN'T THINK YOU WERE SERIOUS.
OH HONEY, I AM VERY SERIOUS!
SO... WHERE ARE WE GOING?
I DON'T KNOW. LET'S FIND OUT.

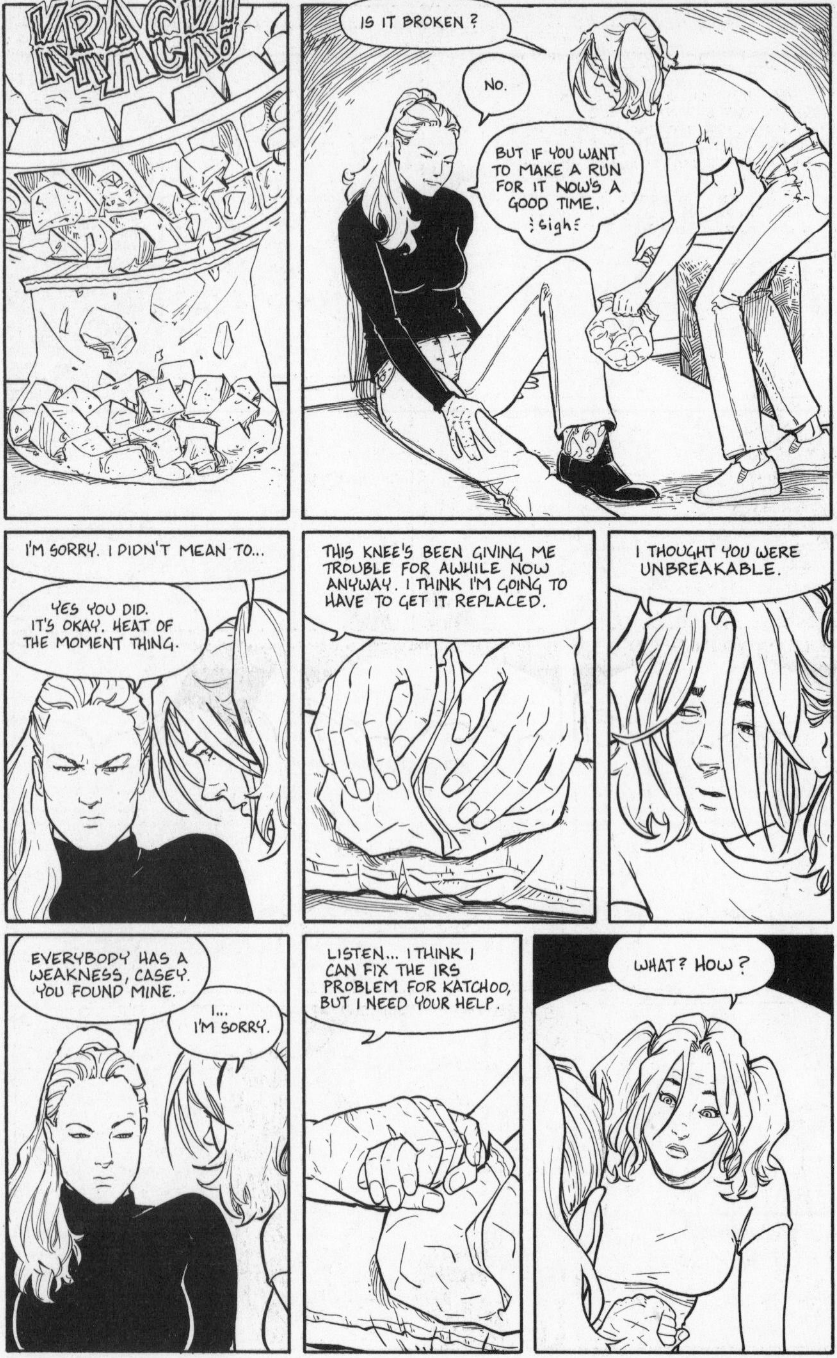
KRACK!
IS IT BROKEN ?
NO.
BUT IF YOU WANT TO MAKE A RUN FOR IT NOW'S A GOOD TIME.
sigh
I'M SORRY. I DIDN'T MEAN TO...
YES YOU DID. IT'S OKAY. HEAT OF THE MOMENT THING.
THIS KNEE'S BEEN GIVING ME TROUBLE FOR AWHILE NOW ANYWAY. I THINK I'M GOING TO HAVE TO GET IT REPLACED.
I THOUGHT YOU WERE UNBREAKABLE.
EVERYBODY HAS A WEAKNESS, CASEY. YOU FOUND MINE.
I... I'M SORRY.
LISTEN... I THINK I CAN FIX THE IRS PROBLEM FOR KATCHOO, BUT I NEED YOUR HELP.
WHAT? HOW?

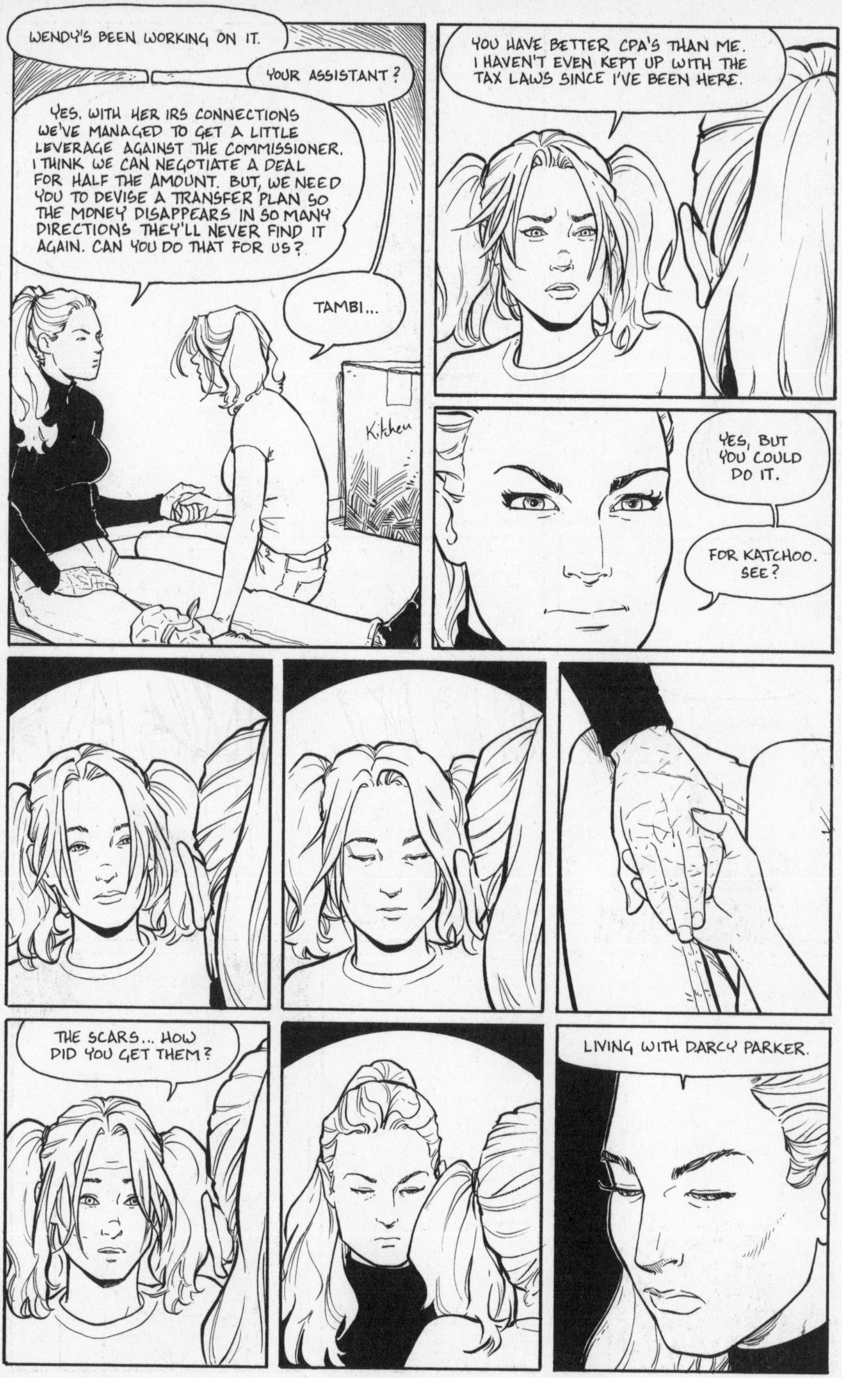
WENDY'S BEEN WORKING ON IT.
YOUR ASSISTANT?
YES. WITH HER IRS CONNECTIONS WE'VE MANAGED TO GET A LITTLE LEVERAGE AGAINST THE COMMISSIONER. I THINK WE CAN NEGOTIATE A DEAL FOR HALF THE AMOUNT. BUT, WE NEED YOU TO DEVISE A TRANSFER PLAN SO THE MONEY DISAPPEARS IN SO MANY DIRECTIONS THEY'LL NEVER FIND IT AGAIN. CAN YOU DO THAT FOR US?
TAMBI...
Kitchen
YOU HAVE BETTER CPA'S THAN ME. I HAVEN'T EVEN KEPT UP WITH THE TAX LAWS SINCE I'VE BEEN HERE.
YES, BUT YOU COULD DO IT.
FOR KATCHOO. SEE?
THE SCARS... HOW DID YOU GET THEM?
LIVING WITH DARCY PARKER.

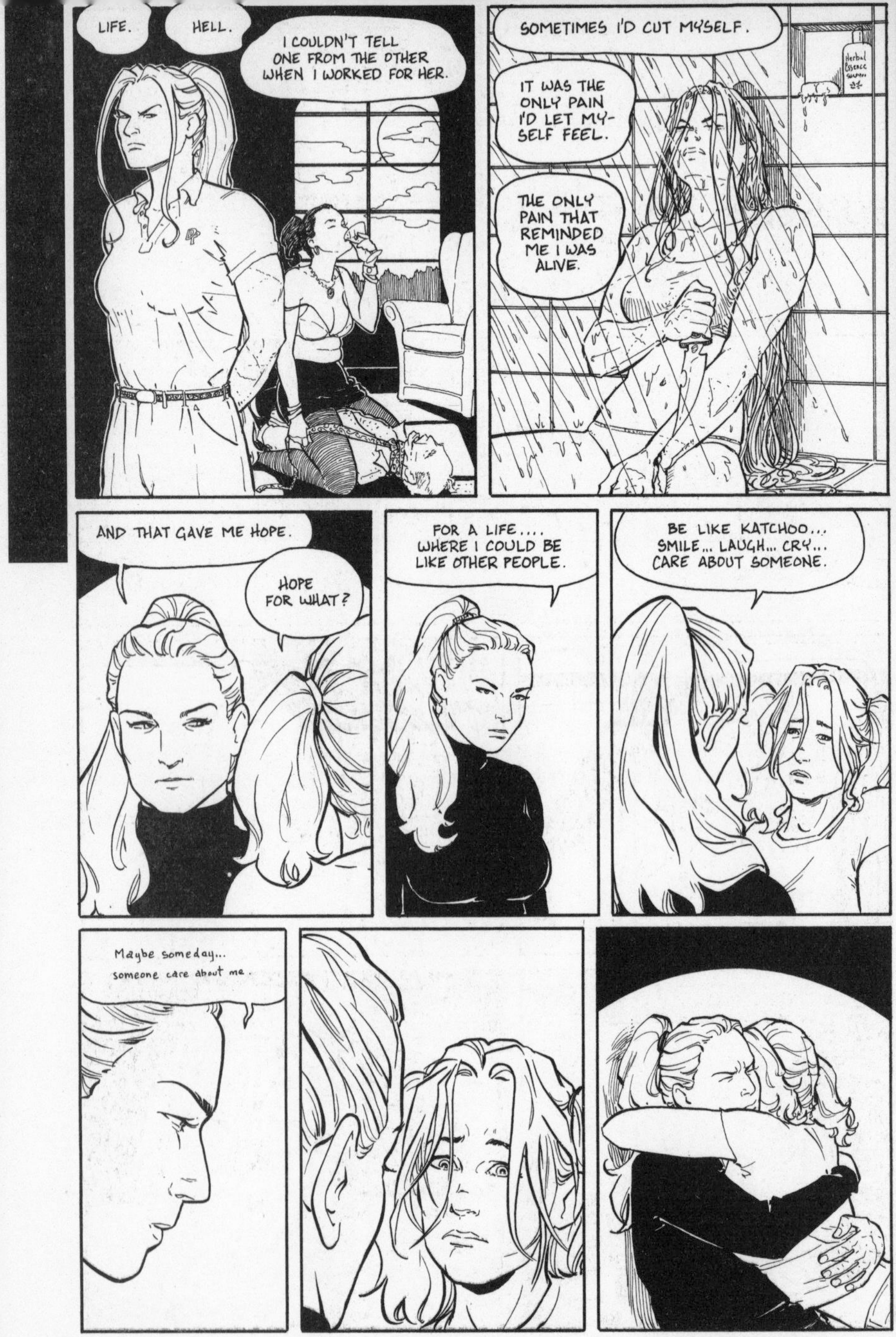
LIFE.
HELL.
I COULDN'T TELL ONE FROM THE OTHER WHEN I WORKED FOR HER.
SOMETIMES I'D CUT MYSELF.
IT WAS THE ONLY PAIN I'D LET MY-SELF FEEL.
THE ONLY PAIN THAT REMINDED ME I WAS ALIVE.
AND THAT GAVE ME HOPE.
HOPE FOR WHAT?
FOR A LIFE.... WHERE I COULD BE LIKE OTHER PEOPLE.
BE LIKE KATCHOO... SMILE... LAUGH... CRY... CARE ABOUT SOMEONE.
Maybe someday... someone care about me.

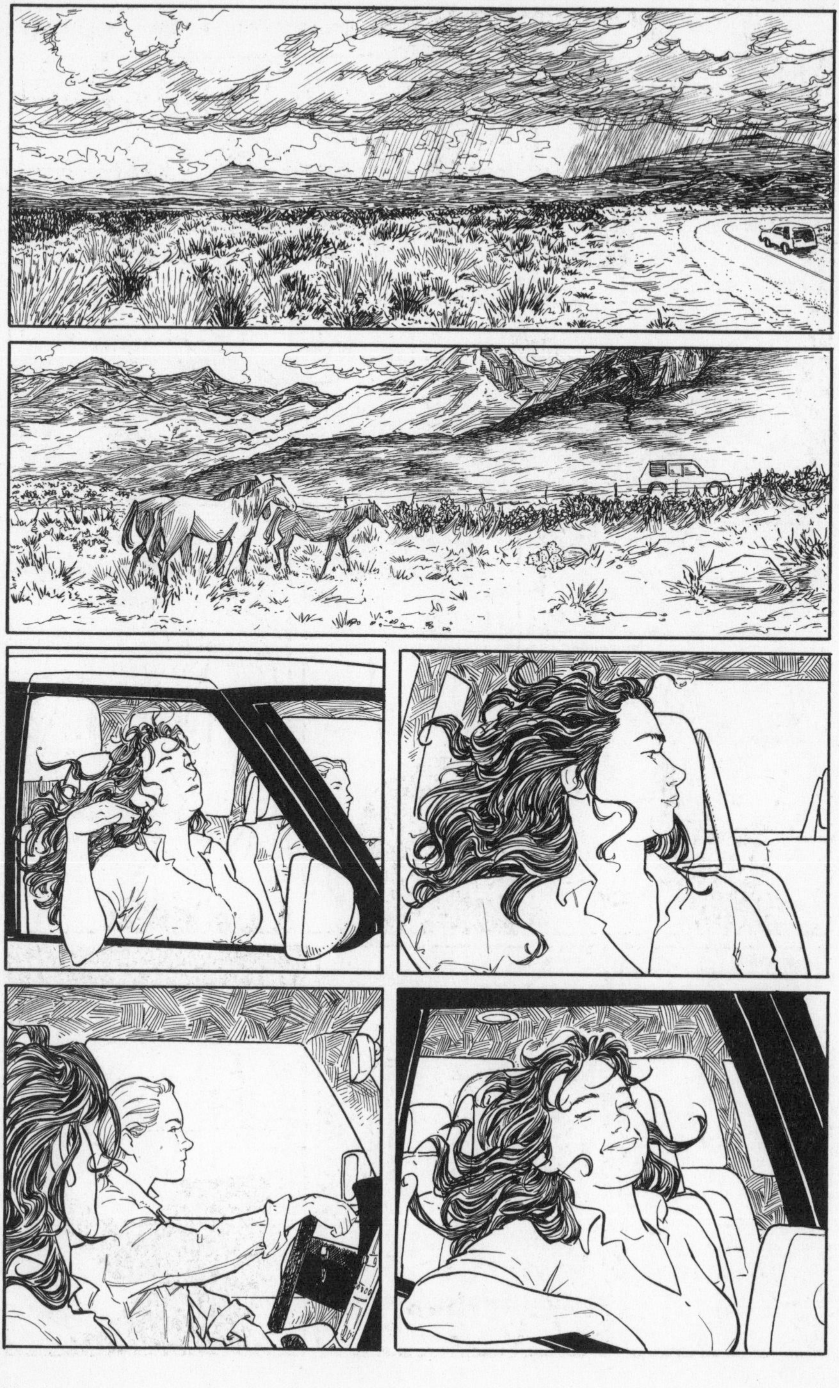

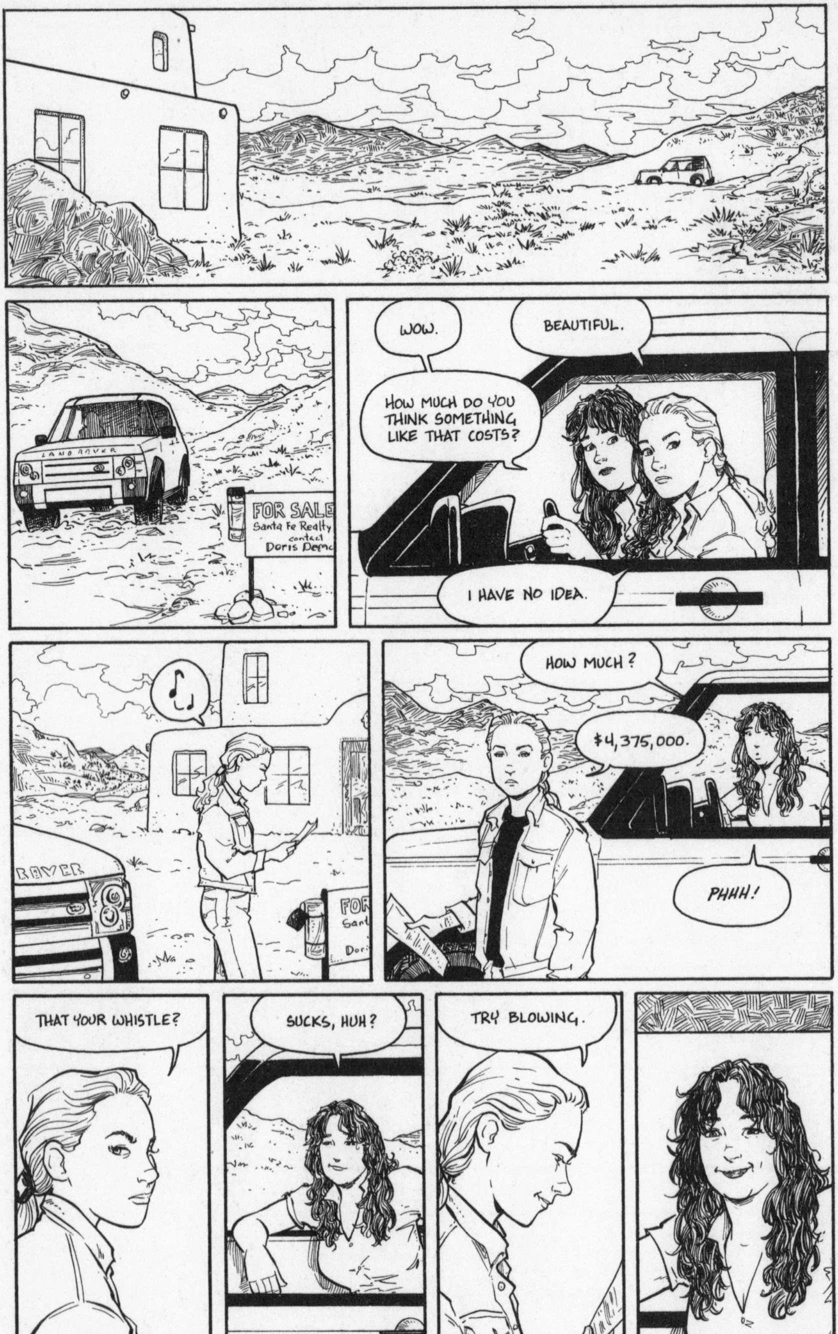
FOR SALE
Santa Fe Realty
contact
Doris Demo
WOW.
BEAUTIFUL.
HOW MUCH DO YOU THINK SOMETHING LIKE THAT COSTS?
I HAVE NO IDEA.
HOW MUCH?
$4,375,000.
PHHH!
THAT YOUR WHISTLE?
SUCKS, HUH?
TRY BLOWING.

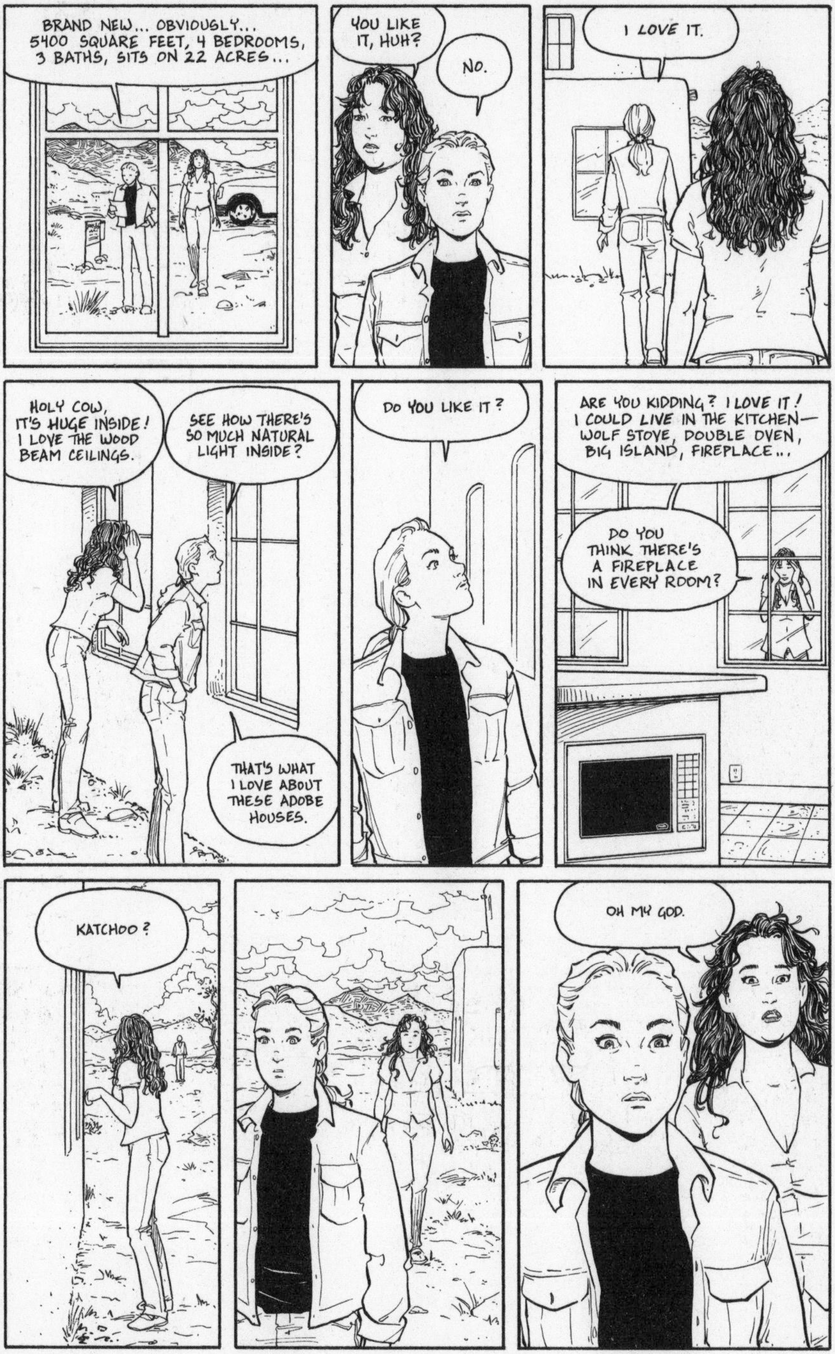

BRAND NEW... OBVIOUSLY... 5400 SQUARE FEET, 4 BEDROOMS, 3 BATHS, SITS ON 22 ACRES...
YOU LIKE IT, HUH?
NO.
I LOVE IT.
HOLY COW, IT'S HUGE INSIDE! I LOVE THE WOOD BEAM CEILINGS.
SEE HOW THERE'S SO MUCH NATURAL LIGHT INSIDE?
THAT'S WHAT I LOVE ABOUT THESE ADOBE HOUSES.
DO YOU LIKE IT?
ARE YOU KIDDING? I LOVE IT! I COULD LIVE IN THE KITCHEN— WOLF STOVE, DOUBLE OVEN, BIG ISLAND, FIREPLACE...
DO YOU THINK THERE'S A FIREPLACE IN EVERY ROOM?
KATCHOO?
OH MY GOD.

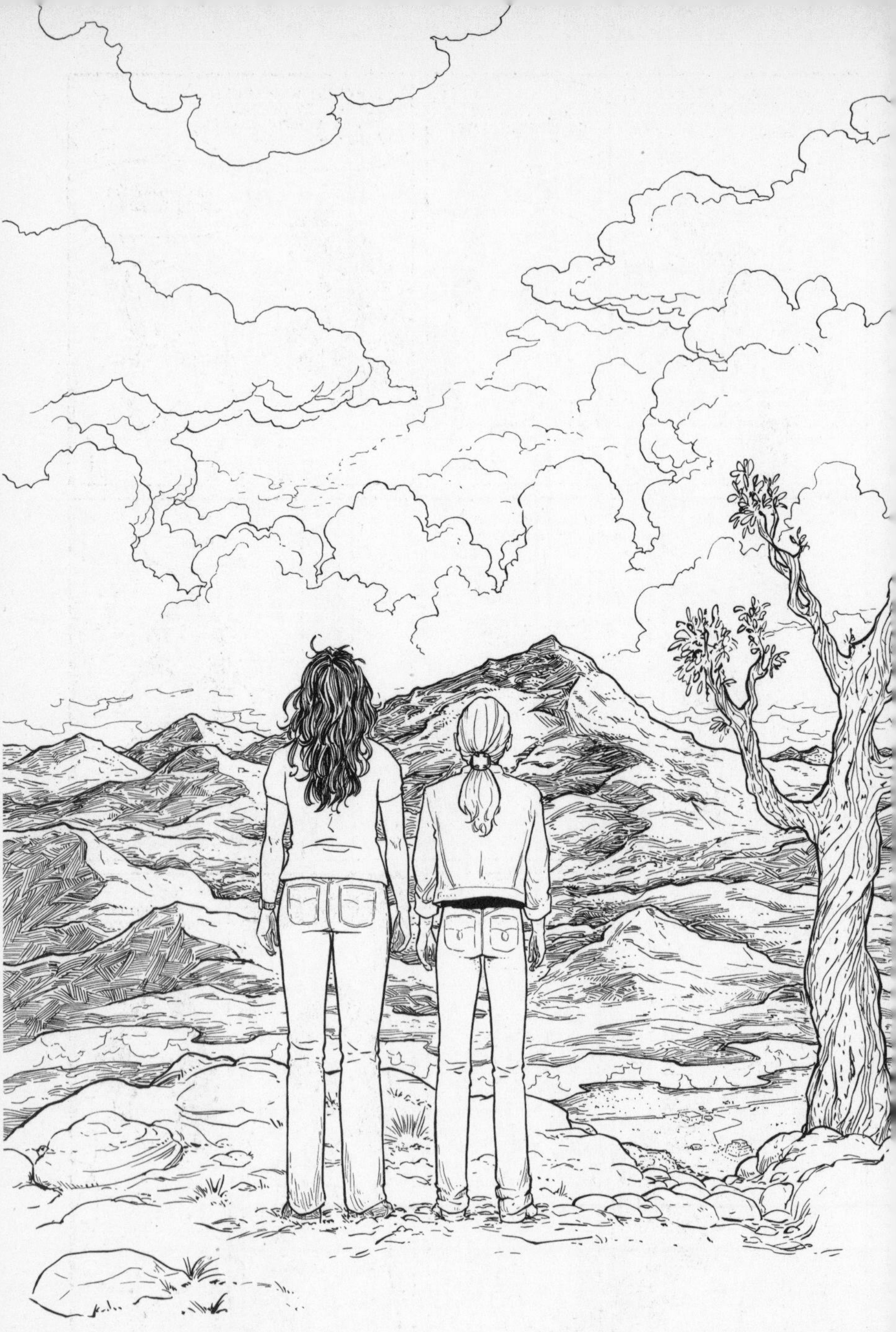

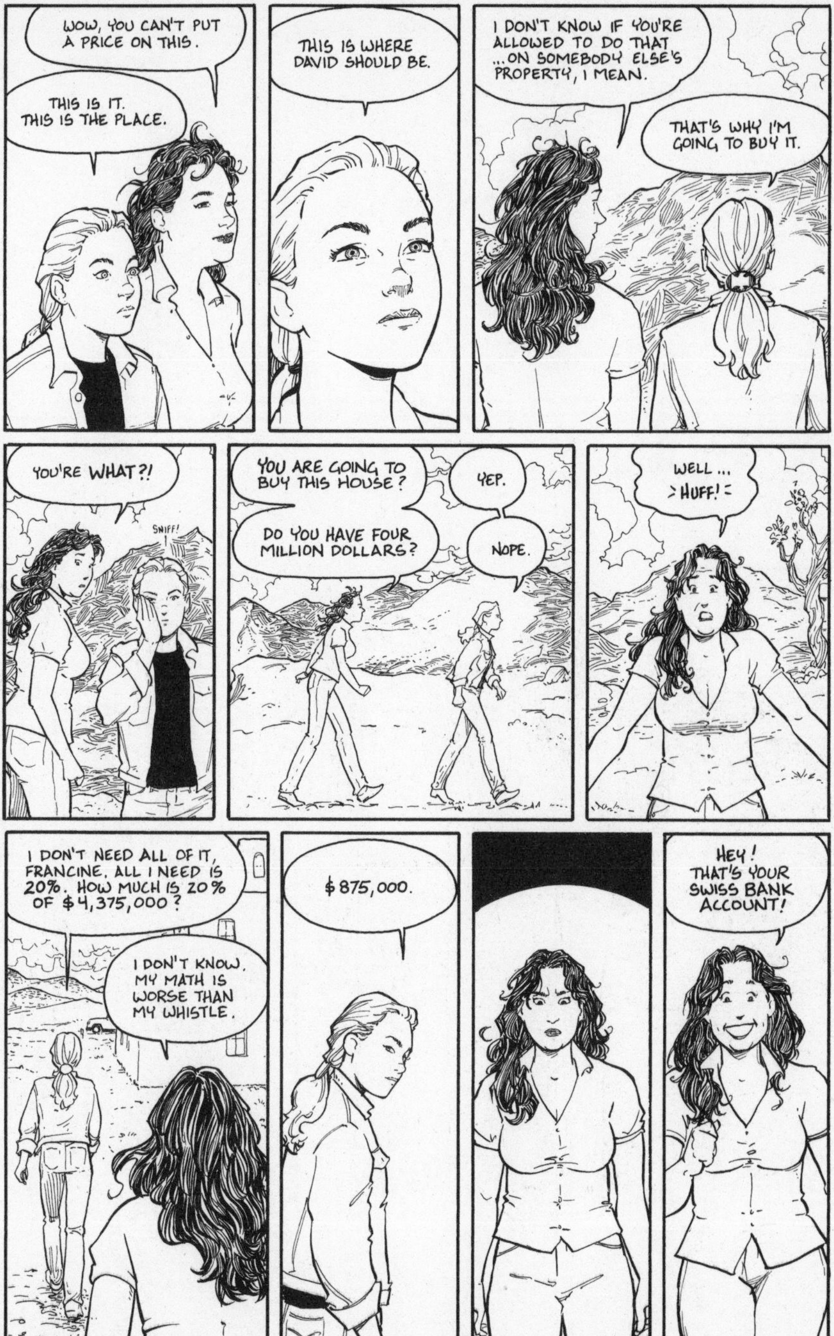

WOW, YOU CAN'T PUT A PRICE ON THIS.
THIS IS IT. THIS IS THE PLACE.
THIS IS WHERE DAVID SHOULD BE.
I DON'T KNOW IF YOU'RE ALLOWED TO DO THAT ...ON SOMEBODY ELSE'S PROPERTY, I MEAN.
THAT'S WHY I'M GOING TO BUY IT.
YOU'RE WHAT?!
SNIFF!
YOU ARE GOING TO BUY THIS HOUSE?
YEP.
DO YOU HAVE FOUR MILLION DOLLARS?
NOPE.
WELL ... HUFF!
I DON'T NEED ALL OF IT, FRANCINE. ALL I NEED IS 20%. HOW MUCH IS 20% OF $4,375,000?
I DON'T KNOW. MY MATH IS WORSE THAN MY WHISTLE.
$875,000.
HEY! THAT'S YOUR SWISS BANK ACCOUNT!

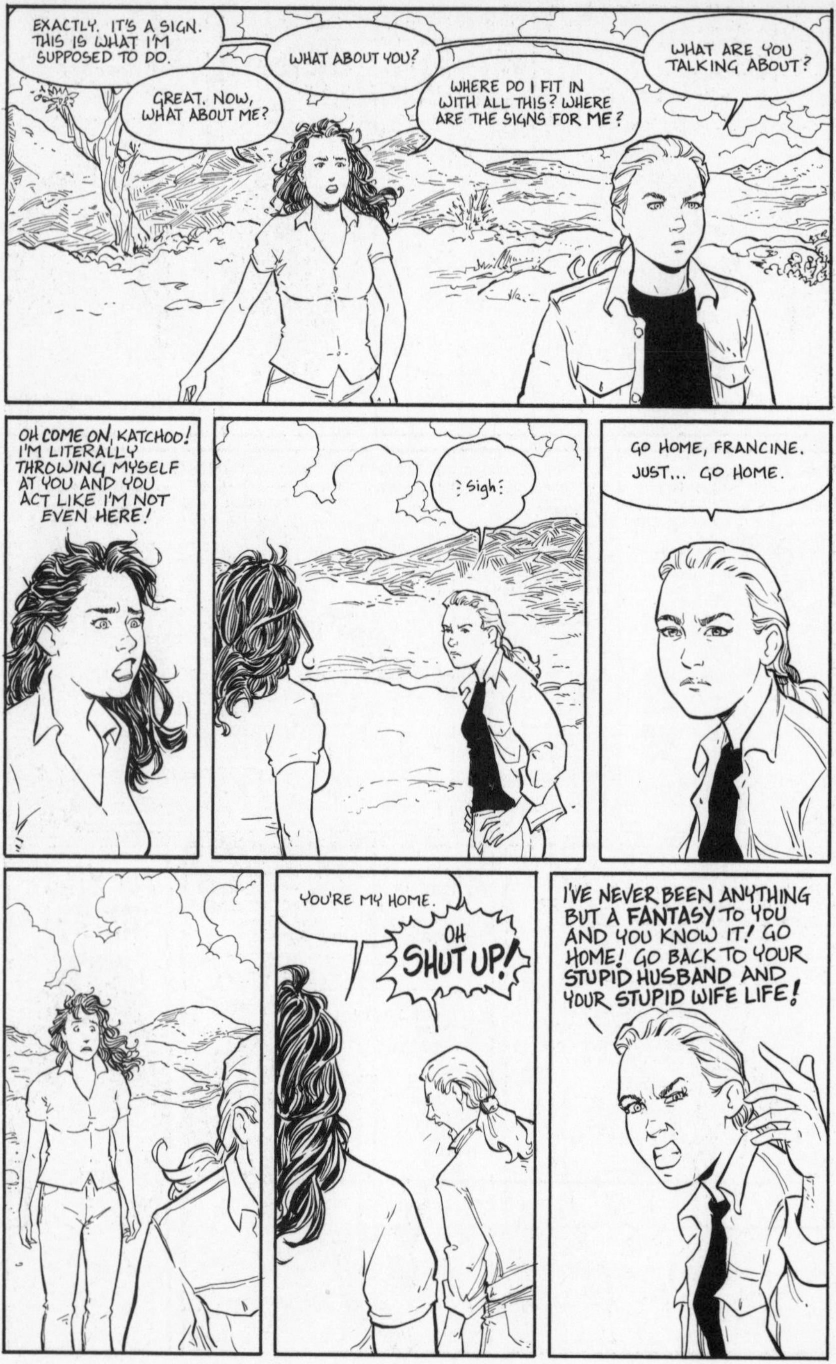

EXACTLY. IT'S A SIGN. THIS IS WHAT I'M SUPPOSED TO DO.
GREAT. NOW, WHAT ABOUT ME?
WHAT ABOUT YOU?
WHERE DO I FIT IN WITH ALL THIS? WHERE ARE THE SIGNS FOR ME?
WHAT ARE YOU TALKING ABOUT?
OH COME ON, KATCHOO! I'M LITERALLY THROWING MYSELF AT YOU AND YOU ACT LIKE I'M NOT EVEN HERE!
:Sigh:
GO HOME, FRANCINE. JUST... GO HOME.
YOU'RE MY HOME.
OH SHUT UP!
I'VE NEVER BEEN ANYTHING BUT A FANTASY TO YOU AND YOU KNOW IT! GO HOME! GO BACK TO YOUR STUPID HUSBAND AND YOUR STUPID WIFE LIFE!

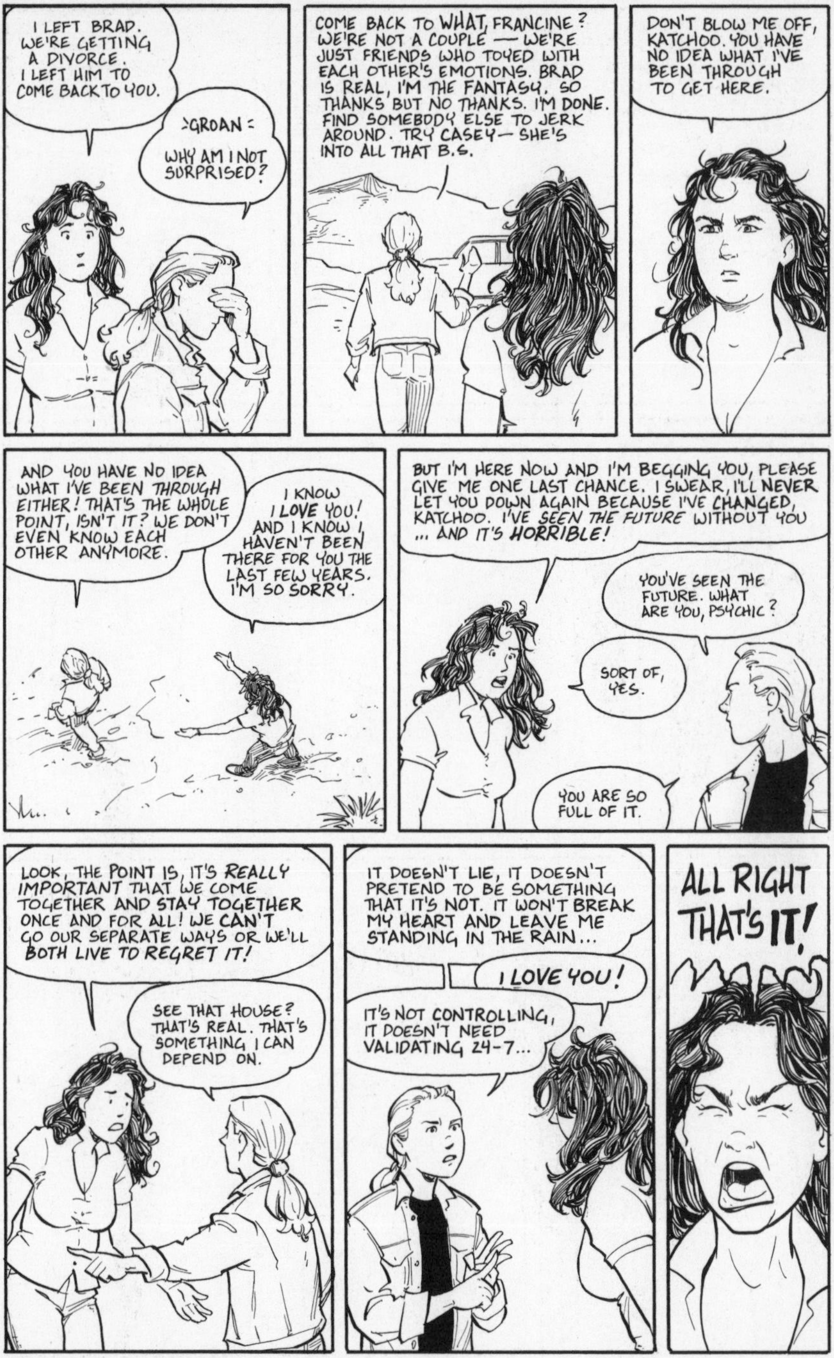
I LEFT BRAD. WE'RE GETTING A DIVORCE. I LEFT HIM TO COME BACK TO YOU.
:GROAN:
WHY AM I NOT SURPRISED?
COME BACK TO WHAT, FRANCINE? WE'RE NOT A COUPLE — WE'RE JUST FRIENDS WHO TOYED WITH EACH OTHER'S EMOTIONS. BRAD IS REAL, I'M THE FANTASY. SO THANKS BUT NO THANKS. I'M DONE. FIND SOMEBODY ELSE TO JERK AROUND. TRY CASEY— SHE'S INTO ALL THAT B.S.
DON'T BLOW ME OFF, KATCHOO. YOU HAVE NO IDEA WHAT I'VE BEEN THROUGH TO GET HERE.
AND YOU HAVE NO IDEA WHAT I'VE BEEN THROUGH EITHER! THAT'S THE WHOLE POINT, ISN'T IT? WE DON'T EVEN KNOW EACH OTHER ANYMORE.
I KNOW I LOVE YOU! AND I KNOW I HAVEN'T BEEN THERE FOR YOU THE LAST FEW YEARS. I'M SO SORRY.
BUT I'M HERE NOW AND I'M BEGGING YOU, PLEASE GIVE ME ONE LAST CHANCE. I SWEAR, I'LL NEVER LET YOU DOWN AGAIN BECAUSE I'VE CHANGED, KATCHOO. I'VE SEEN THE FUTURE WITHOUT YOU ... AND IT'S HORRIBLE!
YOU'VE SEEN THE FUTURE. WHAT ARE YOU, PSYCHIC?
SORT OF, YES.
YOU ARE SO FULL OF IT.
LOOK, THE POINT IS, IT'S REALLY IMPORTANT THAT WE COME TOGETHER AND STAY TOGETHER ONCE AND FOR ALL! WE CAN'T GO OUR SEPARATE WAYS OR WE'LL BOTH LIVE TO REGRET IT!
SEE THAT HOUSE? THAT'S REAL. THAT'S SOMETHING I CAN DEPEND ON.
IT DOESN'T LIE, IT DOESN'T PRETEND TO BE SOMETHING THAT IT'S NOT. IT WON'T BREAK MY HEART AND LEAVE ME STANDING IN THE RAIN...
I LOVE YOU!
IT'S NOT CONTROLLING, IT DOESN'T NEED VALIDATING 24-7...
ALL RIGHT THAT'S IT!

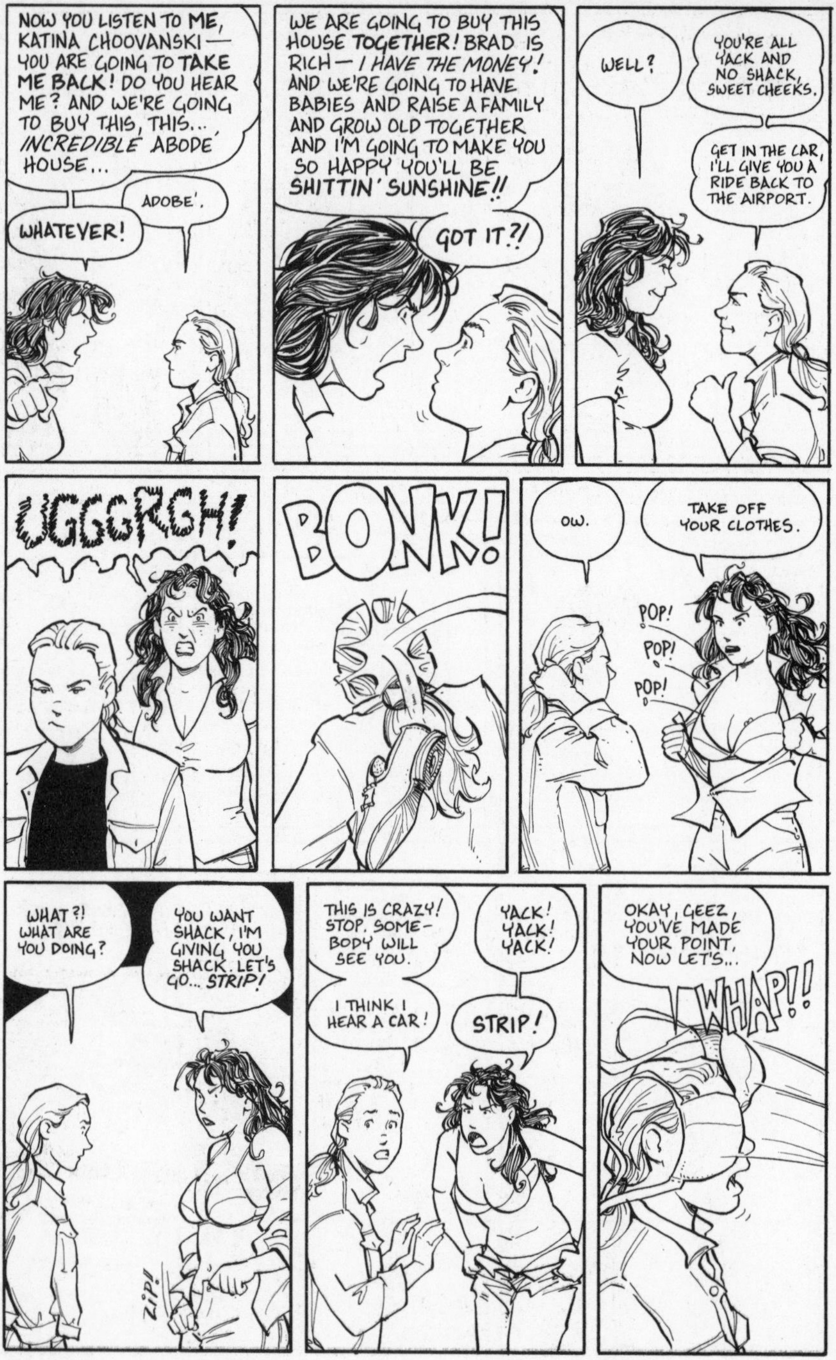
NOW YOU LISTEN TO ME, KATINA CHOOVANSKI — YOU ARE GOING TO TAKE ME BACK! DO YOU HEAR ME? AND WE'RE GOING TO BUY THIS, THIS... INCREDIBLE ABODE HOUSE...
ADOBE'.
WHATEVER!
WE ARE GOING TO BUY THIS HOUSE TOGETHER! BRAD IS RICH — I HAVE THE MONEY! AND WE'RE GOING TO HAVE BABIES AND RAISE A FAMILY AND GROW OLD TOGETHER AND I'M GOING TO MAKE YOU SO HAPPY YOU'LL BE SHITTIN' SUNSHINE!!
GOT IT?!
WELL?
YOU'RE ALL YACK AND NO SHACK, SWEET CHEEKS.
GET IN THE CAR, I'LL GIVE YOU A RIDE BACK TO THE AIRPORT.
UGGGRGH!
BONK!
OW.
TAKE OFF YOUR CLOTHES.
POP!
POP!
POP!
WHAT?! WHAT ARE YOU DOING?
YOU WANT SHACK, I'M GIVING YOU SHACK. LET'S GO... STRIP!
ZIP!
THIS IS CRAZY! STOP. SOMEBODY WILL SEE YOU.
I THINK I HEAR A CAR!
YACK! YACK! YACK!
STRIP!
OKAY, GEEZ, YOU'VE MADE YOUR POINT, NOW LET'S...
WHAP!!

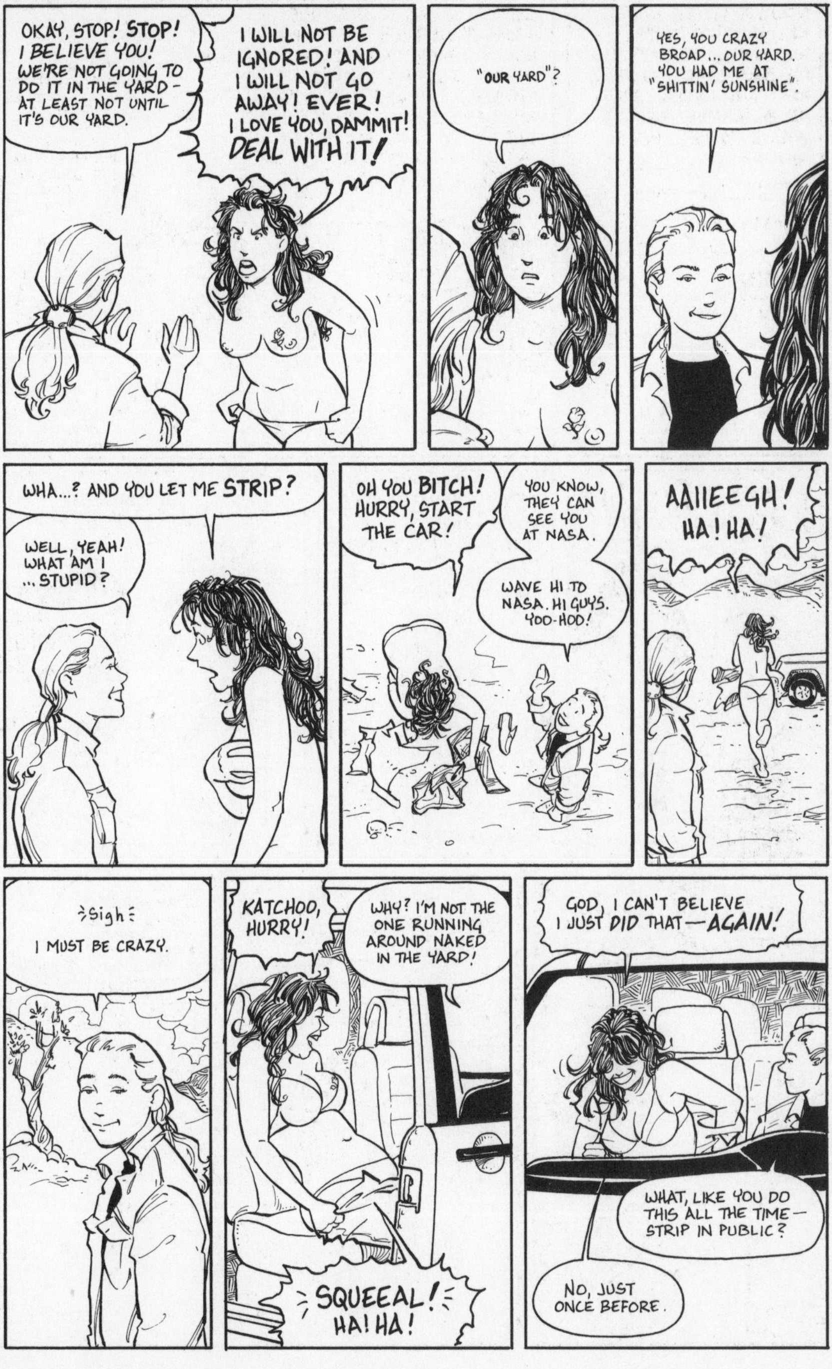
OKAY, STOP! STOP! I BELIEVE YOU! WE'RE NOT GOING TO DO IT IN THE YARD - AT LEAST NOT UNTIL IT'S OUR YARD.
I WILL NOT BE IGNORED! AND I WILL NOT GO AWAY! EVER! I LOVE YOU, DAMMIT! DEAL WITH IT!
"OUR YARD"?
YES, YOU CRAZY BROAD... OUR YARD. YOU HAD ME AT "SHITTIN' SUNSHINE".
WHA...? AND YOU LET ME STRIP?
WELL, YEAH! WHAT AM I ... STUPID?
OH YOU BITCH! HURRY, START THE CAR!
YOU KNOW, THEY CAN SEE YOU AT NASA.
WAVE HI TO NASA. HI GUYS. YOO-HOO!
AAIIEEGH! HA! HA!
Sigh
I MUST BE CRAZY.
KATCHOO, HURRY!
WHY? I'M NOT THE ONE RUNNING AROUND NAKED IN THE YARD!
SQUEEAL! HA! HA!
GOD, I CAN'T BELIEVE I JUST DID THAT—AGAIN!
WHAT, LIKE YOU DO THIS ALL THE TIME— STRIP IN PUBLIC?
NO, JUST ONCE BEFORE.

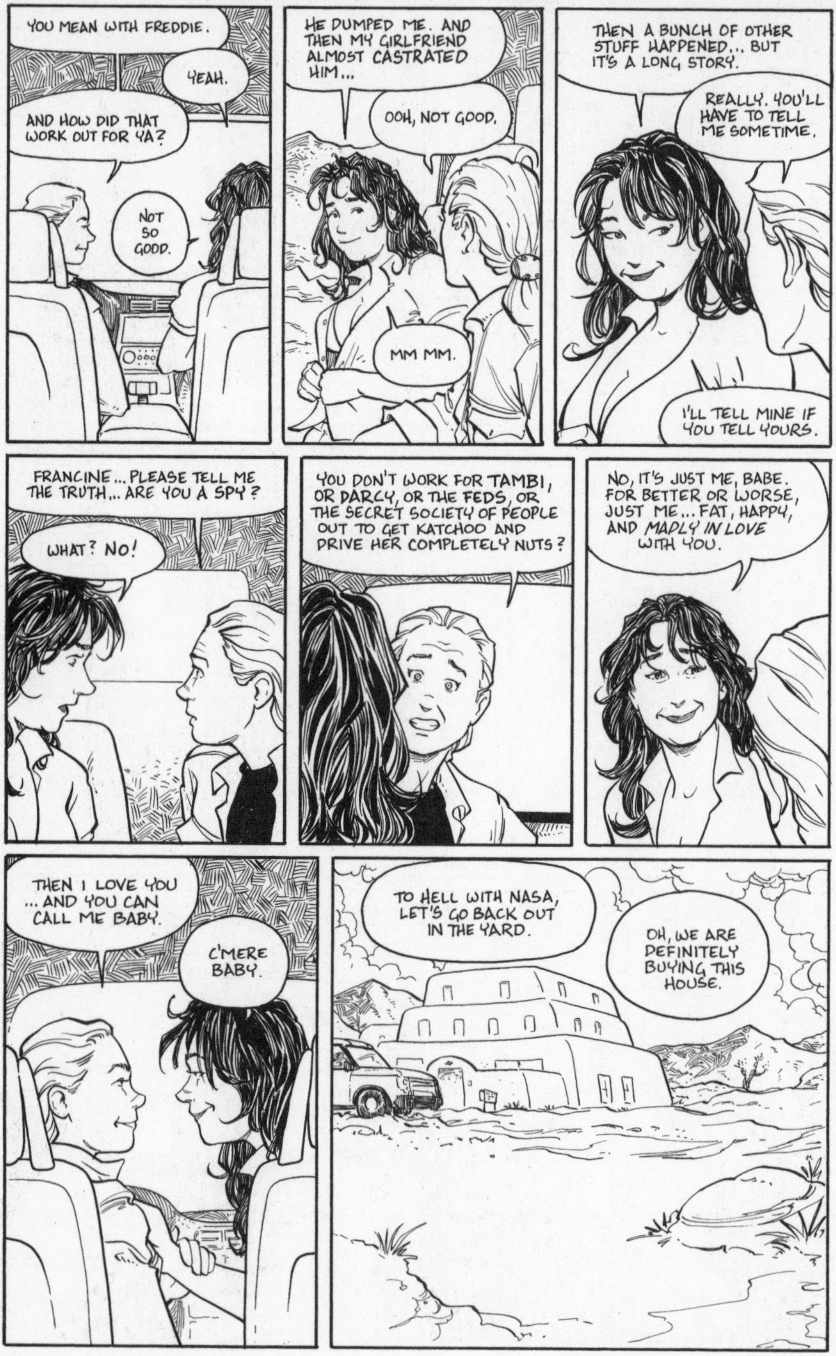

YOU MEAN WITH FREDDIE.
YEAH.
AND HOW DID THAT WORK OUT FOR YA?
NOT SO GOOD.
HE DUMPED ME. AND THEN MY GIRLFRIEND ALMOST CASTRATED HIM...
OOH, NOT GOOD.
MM MM.
THEN A BUNCH OF OTHER STUFF HAPPENED... BUT IT'S A LONG STORY.
REALLY. YOU'LL HAVE TO TELL ME SOMETIME.
I'LL TELL MINE IF YOU TELL YOURS.
FRANCINE... PLEASE TELL ME THE TRUTH... ARE YOU A SPY?
WHAT? NO!
YOU DON'T WORK FOR TAMBI, OR DARCY, OR THE FEDS, OR THE SECRET SOCIETY OF PEOPLE OUT TO GET KATCHOO AND DRIVE HER COMPLETELY NUTS?
NO, IT'S JUST ME, BABE. FOR BETTER OR WORSE, JUST ME... FAT, HAPPY, AND *MADLY IN LOVE* WITH YOU.
THEN I LOVE YOU ...AND YOU CAN CALL ME BABY.
C'MERE BABY.
TO HELL WITH NASA, LET'S GO BACK OUT IN THE YARD.
OH, WE ARE DEFINITELY BUYING THIS HOUSE.

INTERNAL
REVENUE
SERVICE

Internal Revenue Service
United States Department of the Treasury

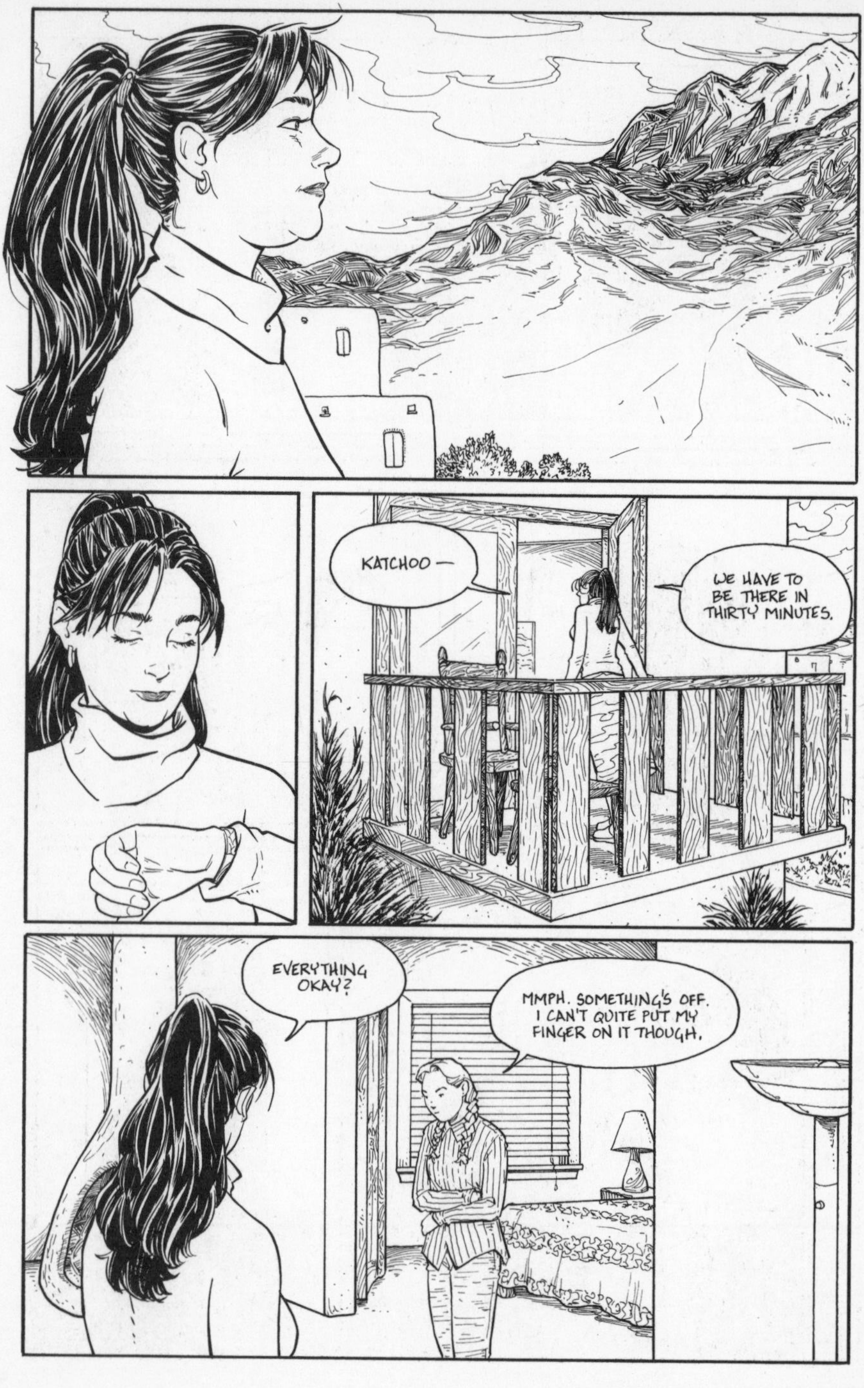
KATCHOO —
WE HAVE TO BE THERE IN THIRTY MINUTES.
EVERYTHING OKAY?
MMPH. SOMETHING'S OFF. I CAN'T QUITE PUT MY FINGER ON IT THOUGH.

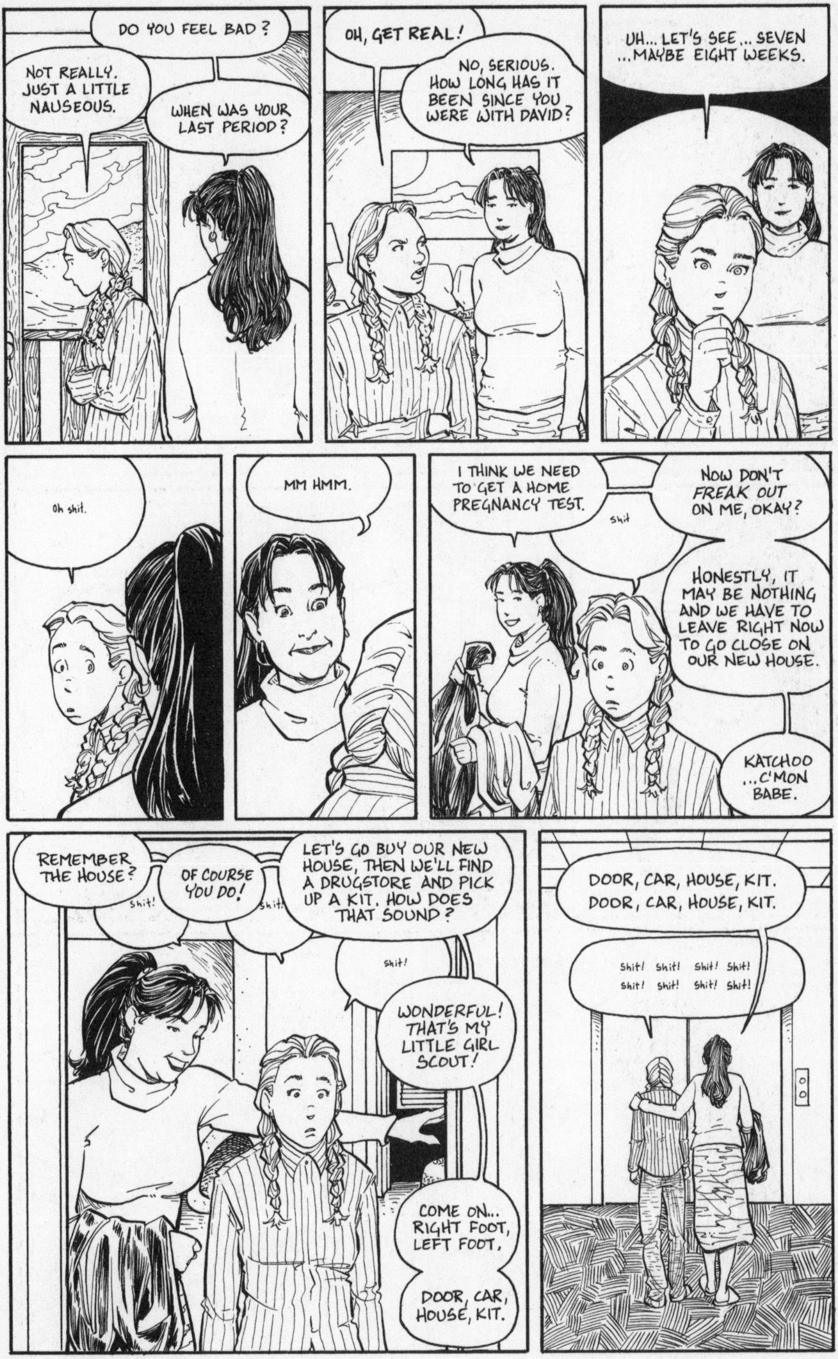

DO YOU FEEL BAD?
NOT REALLY. JUST A LITTLE NAUSEOUS.
WHEN WAS YOUR LAST PERIOD?
OH, GET REAL!
NO, SERIOUS. HOW LONG HAS IT BEEN SINCE YOU WERE WITH DAVID?
UH... LET'S SEE... SEVEN ...MAYBE EIGHT WEEKS.
Oh shit.
MM HMM.
I THINK WE NEED TO GET A HOME PREGNANCY TEST.
Shit
NOW DON'T FREAK OUT ON ME, OKAY?
HONESTLY, IT MAY BE NOTHING AND WE HAVE TO LEAVE RIGHT NOW TO GO CLOSE ON OUR NEW HOUSE.
KATCHOO ...C'MON BABE.
REMEMBER THE HOUSE?
Shit!
OF COURSE YOU DO!
Shit!
LET'S GO BUY OUR NEW HOUSE, THEN WE'LL FIND A DRUGSTORE AND PICK UP A KIT. HOW DOES THAT SOUND?
Shit!
WONDERFUL! THAT'S MY LITTLE GIRL SCOUT!
COME ON... RIGHT FOOT, LEFT FOOT.
DOOR, CAR, HOUSE, KIT.
DOOR, CAR, HOUSE, KIT. DOOR, CAR, HOUSE, KIT.
Shit! Shit! Shit! Shit! Shit! Shit! Shit! Shit!

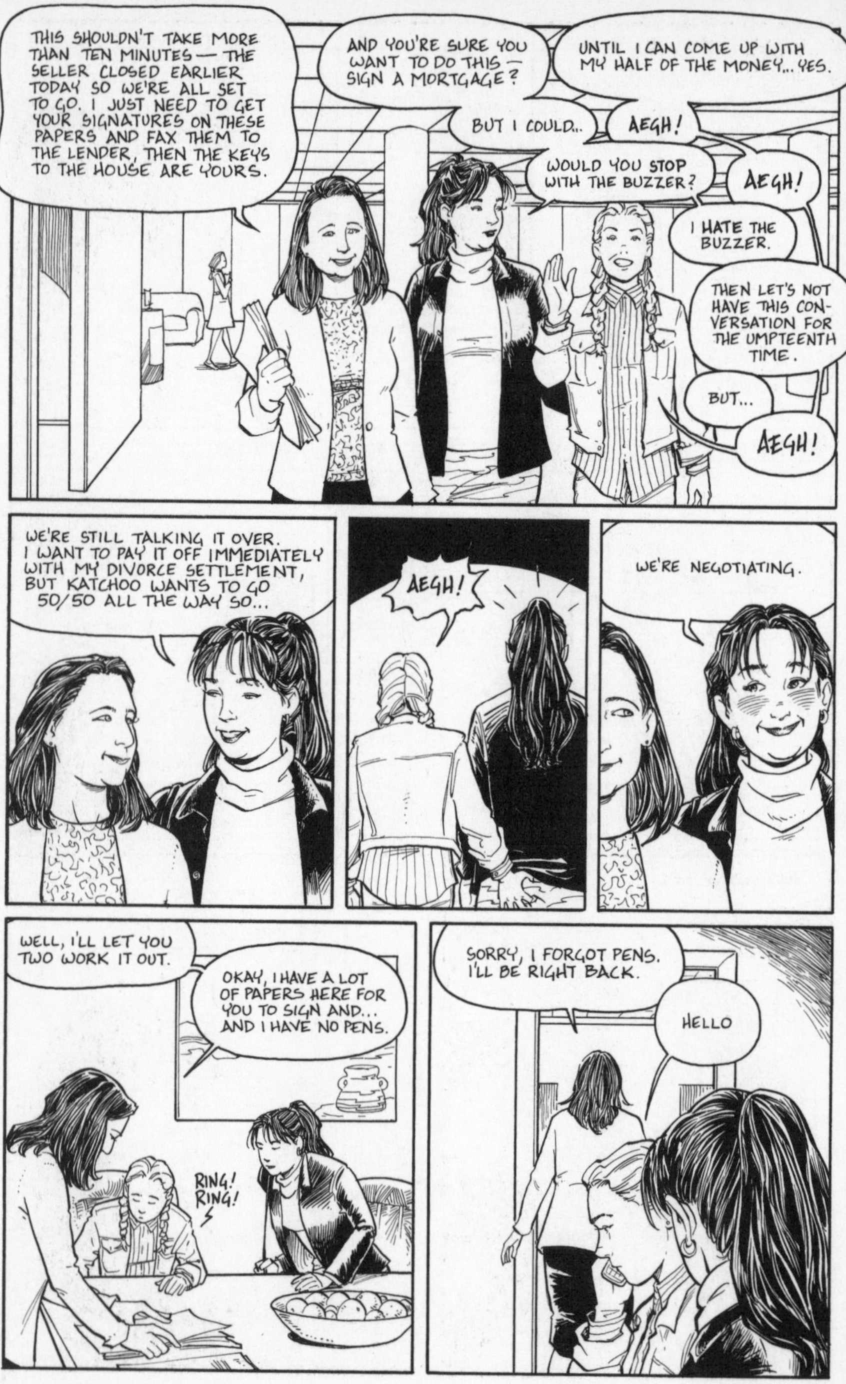
THIS SHOULDN'T TAKE MORE THAN TEN MINUTES — THE SELLER CLOSED EARLIER TODAY SO WE'RE ALL SET TO GO. I JUST NEED TO GET YOUR SIGNATURES ON THESE PAPERS AND FAX THEM TO THE LENDER, THEN THE KEYS TO THE HOUSE ARE YOURS.
AND YOU'RE SURE YOU WANT TO DO THIS — SIGN A MORTGAGE?
UNTIL I CAN COME UP WITH MY HALF OF THE MONEY... YES.
BUT I COULD..
AEGH!
WOULD YOU STOP WITH THE BUZZER?
AEGH!
I HATE THE BUZZER.
THEN LET'S NOT HAVE THIS CONVERSATION FOR THE UMPTEENTH TIME.
BUT...
AEGH!
WE'RE STILL TALKING IT OVER. I WANT TO PAY IT OFF IMMEDIATELY WITH MY DIVORCE SETTLEMENT, BUT KATCHOO WANTS TO GO 50/50 ALL THE WAY SO...
AEGH!
WE'RE NEGOTIATING.
WELL, I'LL LET YOU TWO WORK IT OUT.
OKAY, I HAVE A LOT OF PAPERS HERE FOR YOU TO SIGN AND... AND I HAVE NO PENS.
RING! RING!
SORRY, I FORGOT PENS. I'LL BE RIGHT BACK.
HELLO

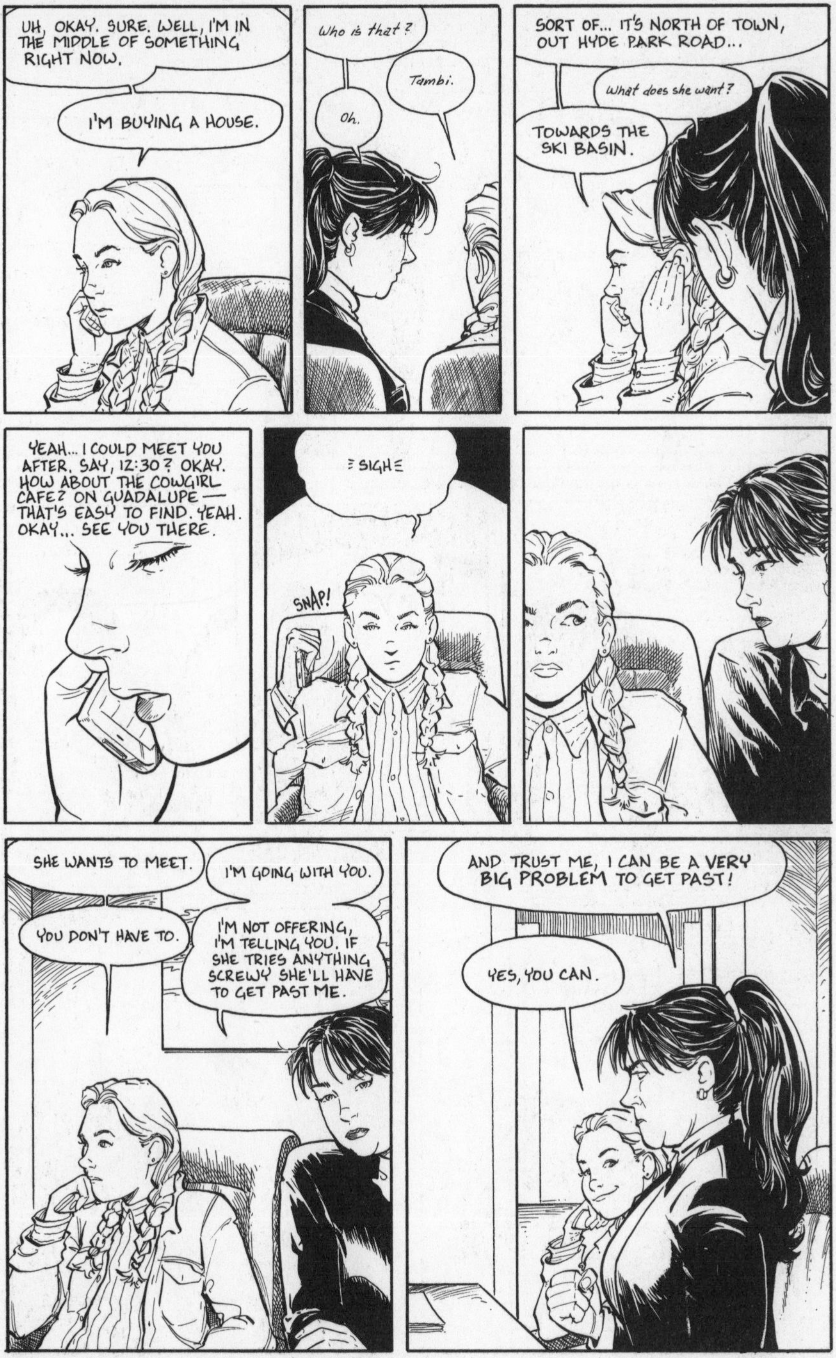
UH, OKAY. SURE. WELL, I'M IN THE MIDDLE OF SOMETHING RIGHT NOW.
I'M BUYING A HOUSE.
Who is that?
Tambi.
Oh.
SORT OF... IT'S NORTH OF TOWN, OUT HYDE PARK ROAD...
What does she want?
TOWARDS THE SKI BASIN.
YEAH... I COULD MEET YOU AFTER. SAY, 12:30? OKAY. HOW ABOUT THE COWGIRL CAFE? ON GUADALUPE — THAT'S EASY TO FIND. YEAH. OKAY... SEE YOU THERE.
SIGH
SNAP!
SHE WANTS TO MEET.
I'M GOING WITH YOU.
YOU DON'T HAVE TO.
I'M NOT OFFERING, I'M TELLING YOU. IF SHE TRIES ANYTHING SCREWY SHE'LL HAVE TO GET PAST ME.
AND TRUST ME, I CAN BE A VERY BIG PROBLEM TO GET PAST!
YES, YOU CAN.

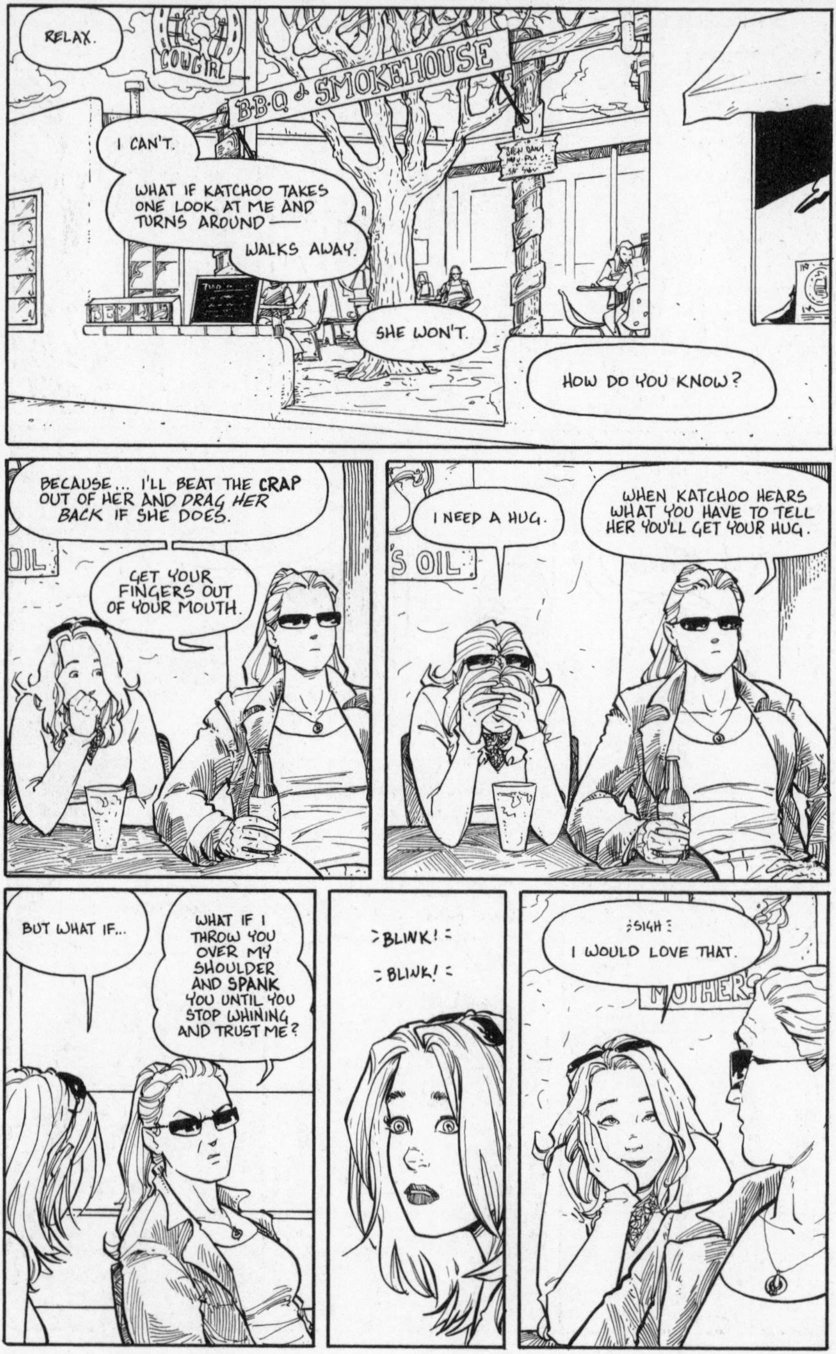
RELAX.
COWGIRL
BBQ & SMOKEHOUSE
I CAN'T.
WHAT IF KATCHOO TAKES ONE LOOK AT ME AND TURNS AROUND—
WALKS AWAY.
SHE WON'T.
HOW DO YOU KNOW?
BECAUSE... I'LL BEAT THE **CRAP** OUT OF HER AND *DRAG HER BACK* IF SHE DOES.
GET YOUR FINGERS OUT OF YOUR MOUTH.
I NEED A HUG.
WHEN KATCHOO HEARS WHAT YOU HAVE TO TELL HER YOU'LL GET YOUR HUG.
BUT WHAT IF...
WHAT IF I THROW YOU OVER MY SHOULDER AND **SPANK** YOU UNTIL YOU STOP WHINING AND TRUST ME?
BLINK!
BLINK!
SIGH
I WOULD LOVE THAT.

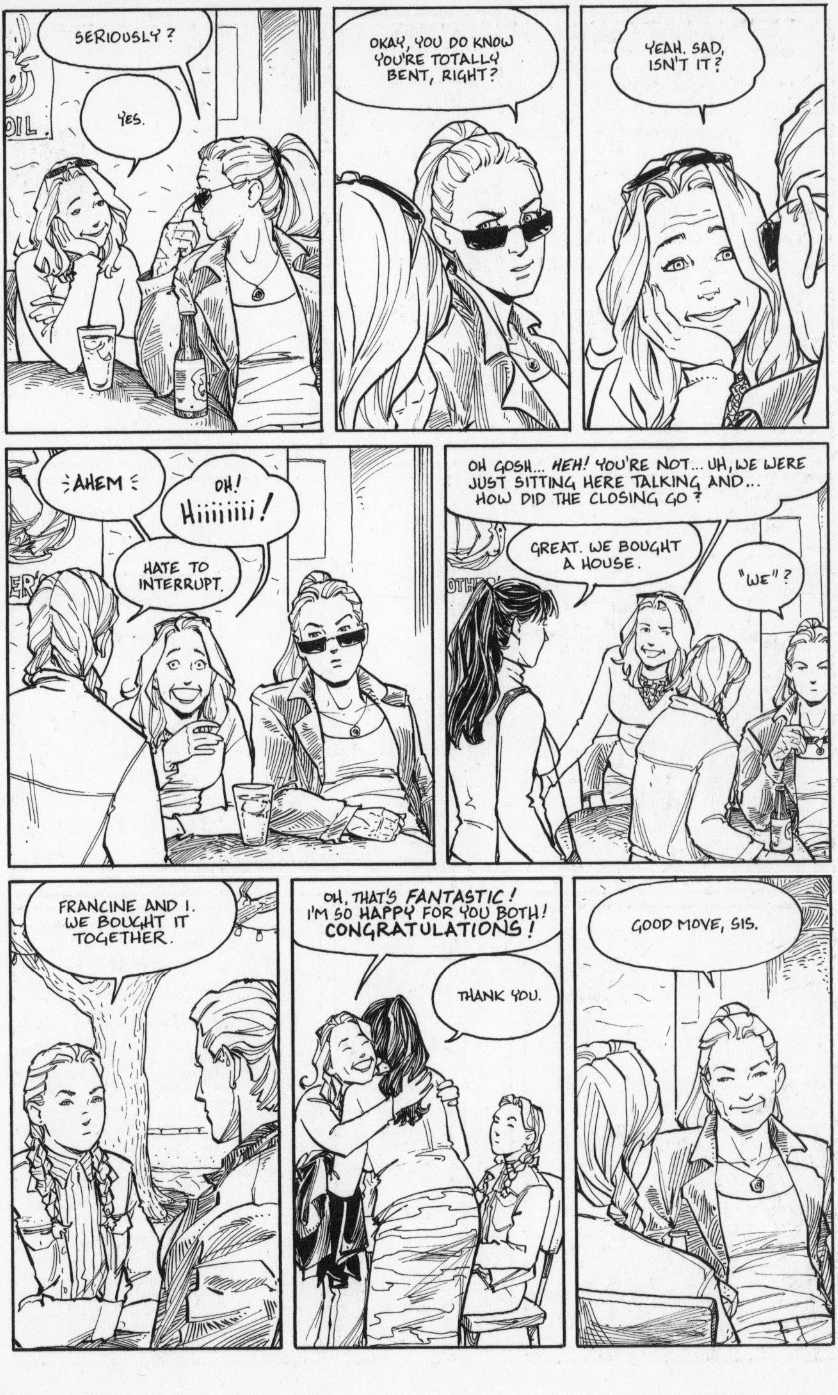
SERIOUSLY?
YES.
OKAY, YOU DO KNOW YOU'RE TOTALLY BENT, RIGHT?
YEAH. SAD, ISN'T IT?
AHEM
OH! Hiiiiiiii!
HATE TO INTERRUPT.
OH GOSH... HEH! YOU'RE NOT... UH, WE WERE JUST SITTING HERE TALKING AND... HOW DID THE CLOSING GO?
GREAT. WE BOUGHT A HOUSE.
"WE"?
FRANCINE AND I. WE BOUGHT IT TOGETHER.
OH, THAT'S FANTASTIC! I'M SO HAPPY FOR YOU BOTH! CONGRATULATIONS!
THANK YOU.
GOOD MOVE, SIS.

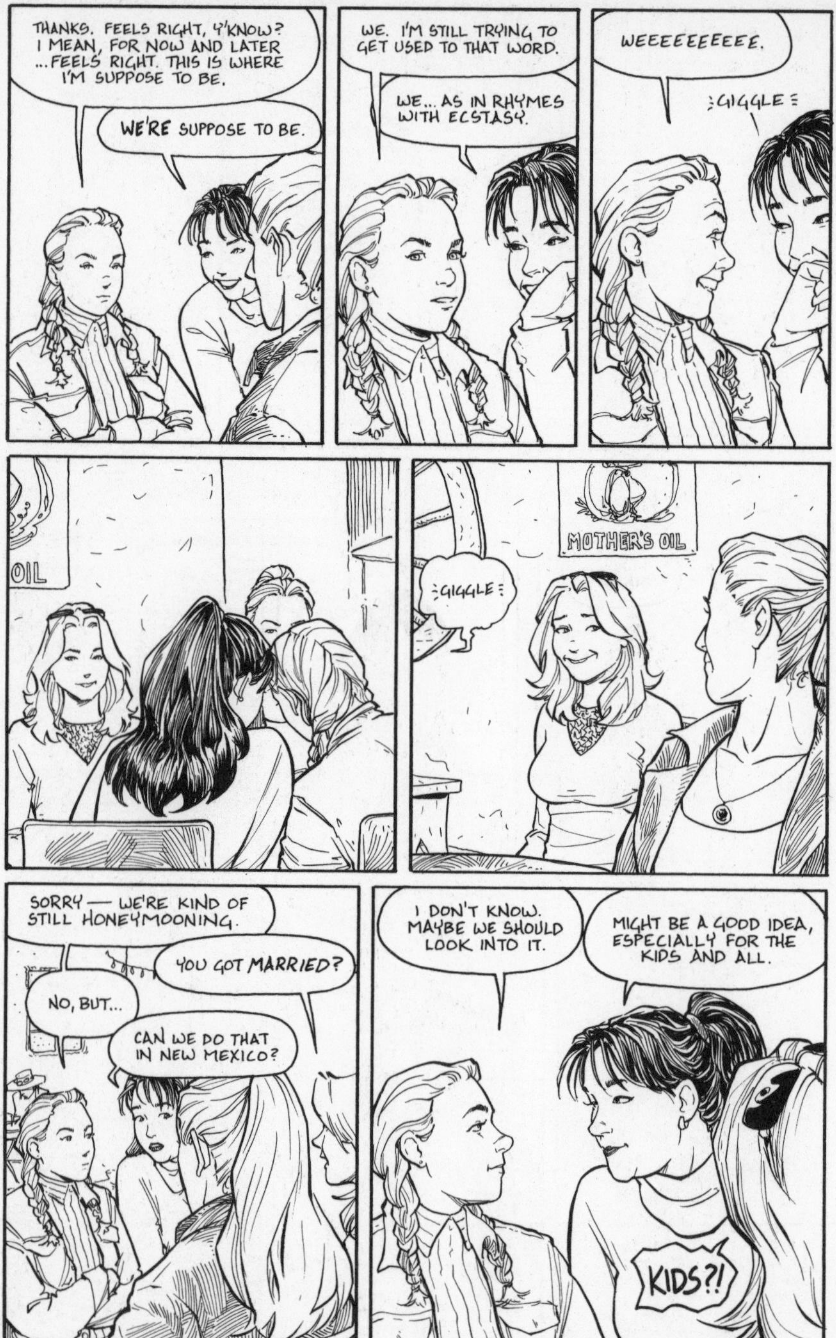
THANKS. FEELS RIGHT, Y'KNOW? I MEAN, FOR NOW AND LATER ...FEELS RIGHT. THIS IS WHERE I'M SUPPOSE TO BE.
WE'RE SUPPOSE TO BE.
WE. I'M STILL TRYING TO GET USED TO THAT WORD.
WE... AS IN RHYMES WITH ECSTASY.
WEEEEEEEEEE.
GIGGLE
MOTHER'S OIL
OIL
GIGGLE
SORRY — WE'RE KIND OF STILL HONEYMOONING.
YOU GOT MARRIED?
NO, BUT...
CAN WE DO THAT IN NEW MEXICO?
I DON'T KNOW. MAYBE WE SHOULD LOOK INTO IT.
MIGHT BE A GOOD IDEA, ESPECIALLY FOR THE KIDS AND ALL.
KIDS?!

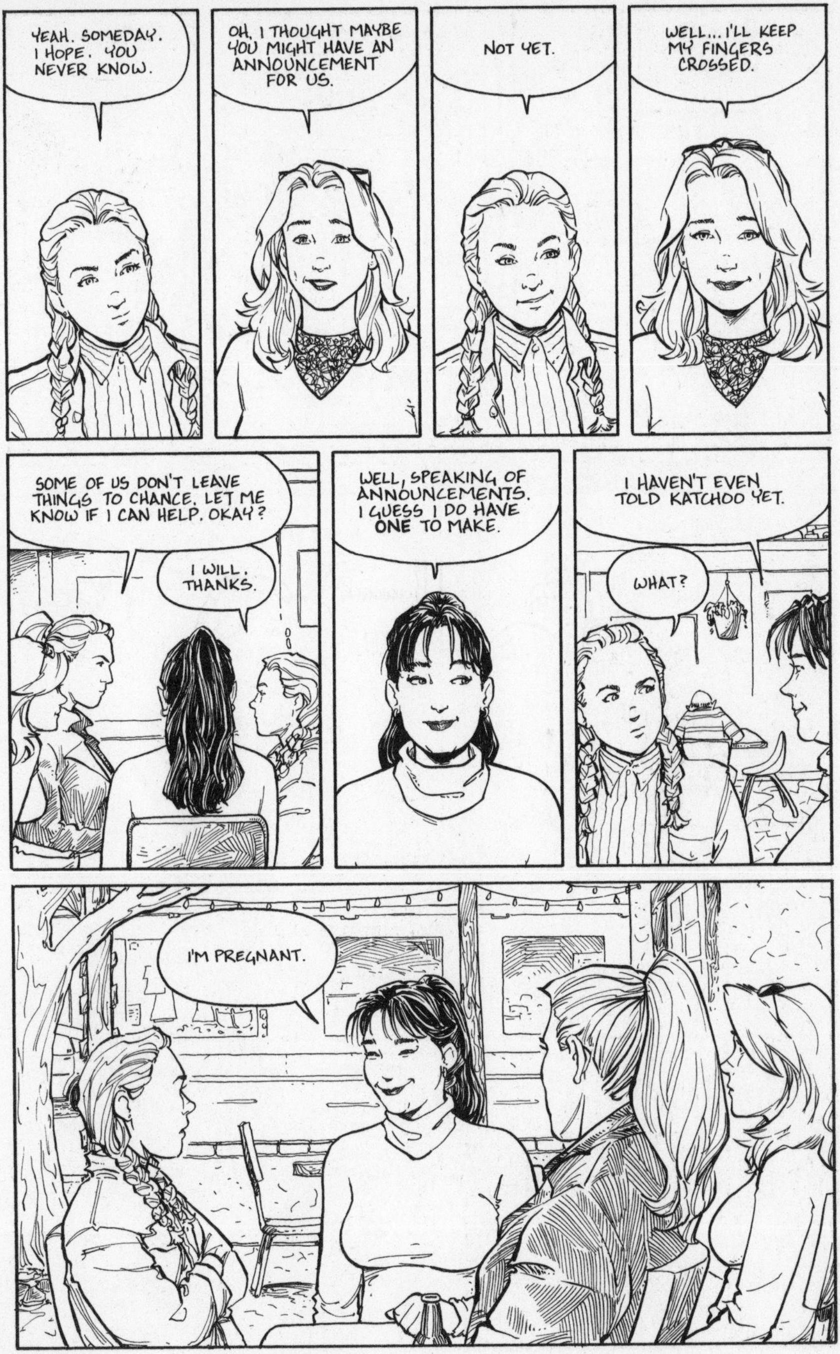
YEAH. SOMEDAY. I HOPE. YOU NEVER KNOW.
OH, I THOUGHT MAYBE YOU MIGHT HAVE AN ANNOUNCEMENT FOR US.
NOT YET.
WELL... I'LL KEEP MY FINGERS CROSSED.
SOME OF US DON'T LEAVE THINGS TO CHANCE. LET ME KNOW IF I CAN HELP. OKAY?
I WILL. THANKS.
WELL, SPEAKING OF ANNOUNCEMENTS. I GUESS I DO HAVE ONE TO MAKE.
I HAVEN'T EVEN TOLD KATCHOO YET.
WHAT?
I'M PREGNANT.

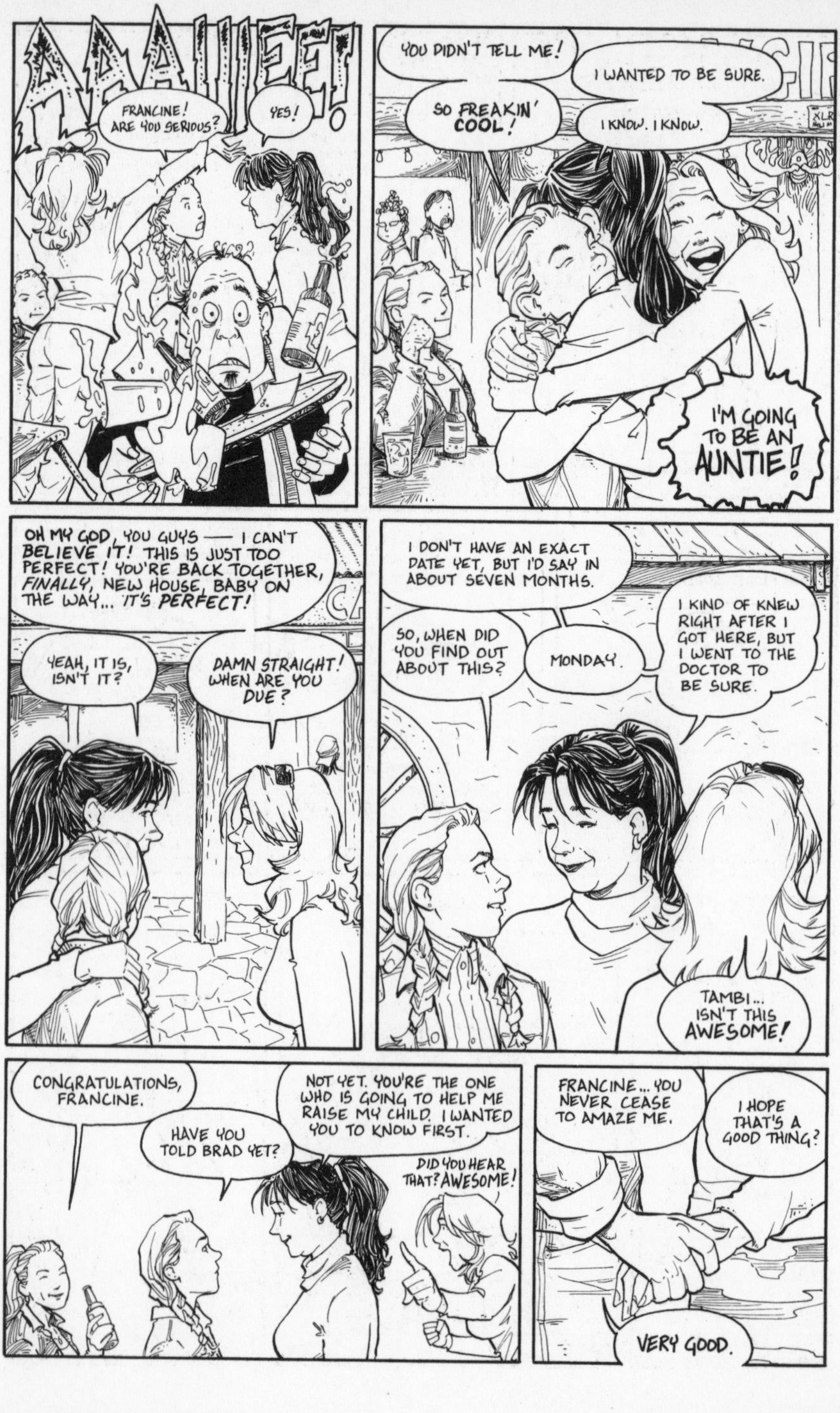
AAAIIIEE!
FRANCINE! ARE YOU SERIOUS?
YES!
YOU DIDN'T TELL ME!
I WANTED TO BE SURE.
SO FREAKIN' COOL!
I KNOW. I KNOW.
I'M GOING TO BE AN AUNTIE!
OH MY GOD, YOU GUYS — I CAN'T BELIEVE IT! THIS IS JUST TOO PERFECT! YOU'RE BACK TOGETHER, FINALLY, NEW HOUSE, BABY ON THE WAY... IT'S PERFECT!
YEAH, IT IS, ISN'T IT?
DAMN STRAIGHT! WHEN ARE YOU DUE?
I DON'T HAVE AN EXACT DATE YET, BUT I'D SAY IN ABOUT SEVEN MONTHS.
SO, WHEN DID YOU FIND OUT ABOUT THIS?
MONDAY.
I KIND OF KNEW RIGHT AFTER I GOT HERE, BUT I WENT TO THE DOCTOR TO BE SURE.
TAMBI... ISN'T THIS AWESOME!
CONGRATULATIONS, FRANCINE.
HAVE YOU TOLD BRAD YET?
NOT YET. YOU'RE THE ONE WHO IS GOING TO HELP ME RAISE MY CHILD. I WANTED YOU TO KNOW FIRST.
DID YOU HEAR THAT? AWESOME!
FRANCINE... YOU NEVER CEASE TO AMAZE ME.
I HOPE THAT'S A GOOD THING?
VERY GOOD.

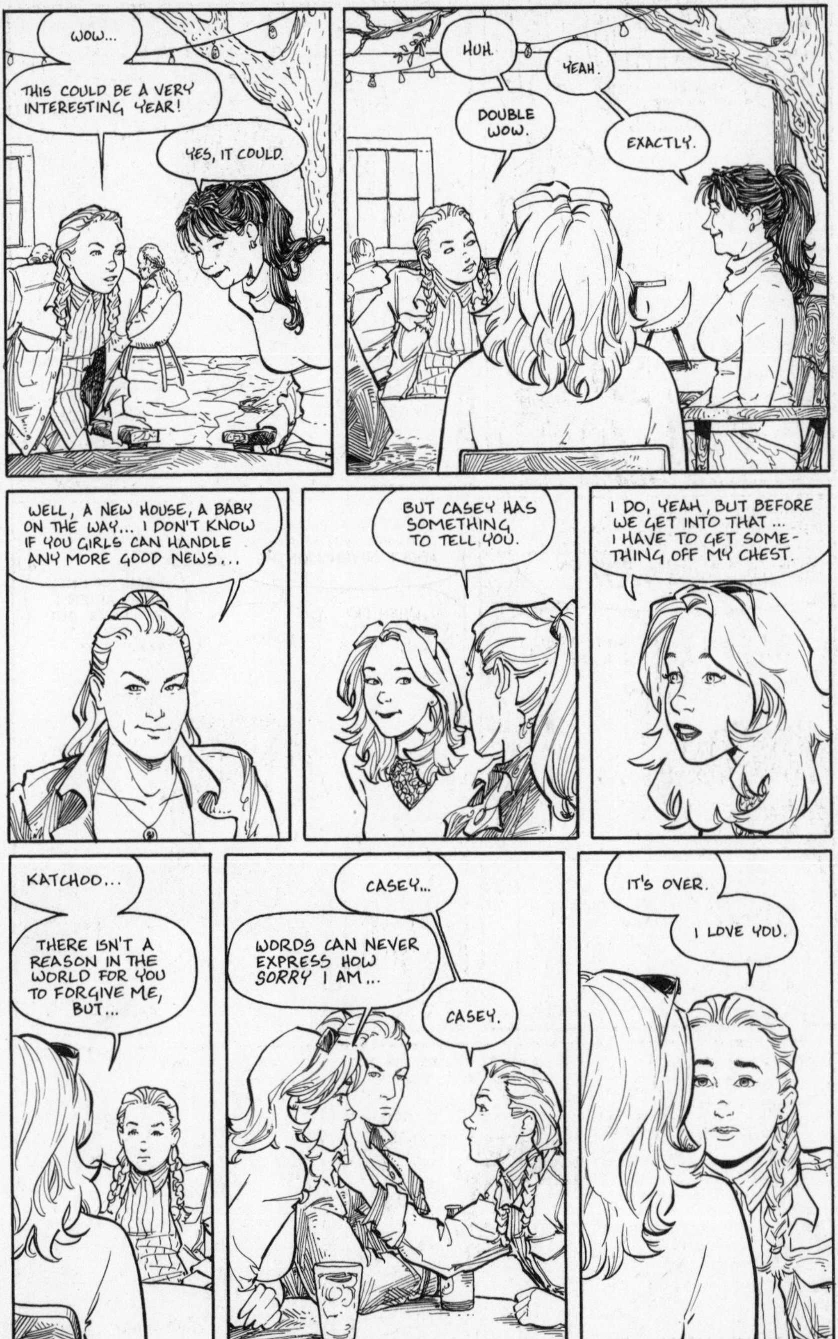
WOW...
THIS COULD BE A VERY INTERESTING YEAR!
YES, IT COULD.
HUH.
DOUBLE WOW.
YEAH.
EXACTLY.
WELL, A NEW HOUSE, A BABY ON THE WAY... I DON'T KNOW IF YOU GIRLS CAN HANDLE ANY MORE GOOD NEWS...
BUT CASEY HAS SOMETHING TO TELL YOU.
I DO, YEAH, BUT BEFORE WE GET INTO THAT... I HAVE TO GET SOMETHING OFF MY CHEST.
KATCHOO...
THERE ISN'T A REASON IN THE WORLD FOR YOU TO FORGIVE ME, BUT...
CASEY...
WORDS CAN NEVER EXPRESS HOW SORRY I AM...
CASEY.
IT'S OVER.
I LOVE YOU.

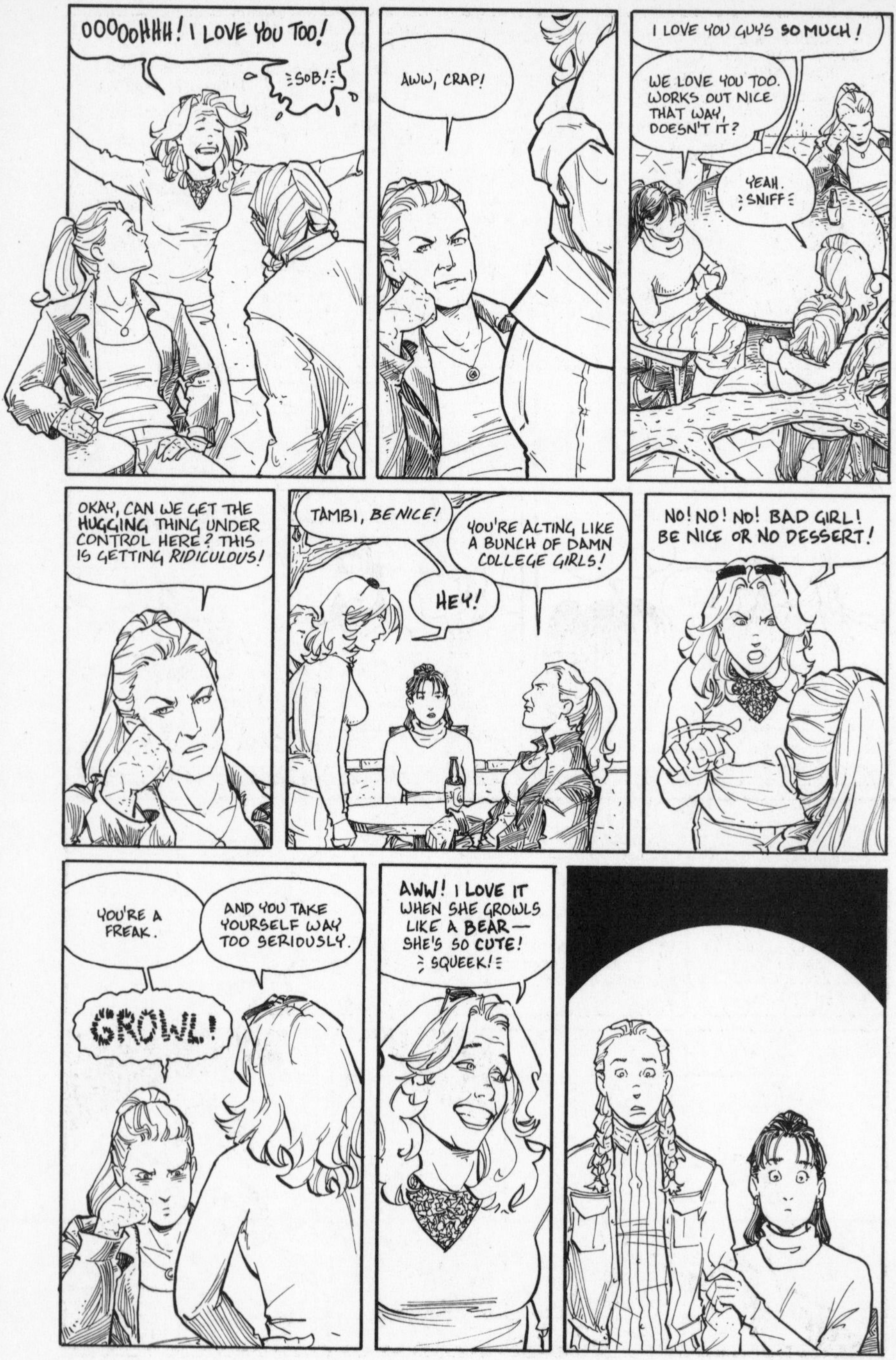
OOOOOHHH! I LOVE YOU TOO!
SOB!
AWW, CRAP!
I LOVE YOU GUYS SO MUCH!
WE LOVE YOU TOO. WORKS OUT NICE THAT WAY, DOESN'T IT?
YEAH. SNIFF
OKAY, CAN WE GET THE HUGGING THING UNDER CONTROL HERE? THIS IS GETTING RIDICULOUS!
TAMBI, BE NICE!
YOU'RE ACTING LIKE A BUNCH OF DAMN COLLEGE GIRLS!
HEY!
NO! NO! NO! BAD GIRL! BE NICE OR NO DESSERT!
YOU'RE A FREAK.
AND YOU TAKE YOURSELF WAY TOO SERIOUSLY.
GROWL!
AWW! I LOVE IT WHEN SHE GROWLS LIKE A BEAR— SHE'S SO CUTE!
SQUEEK!

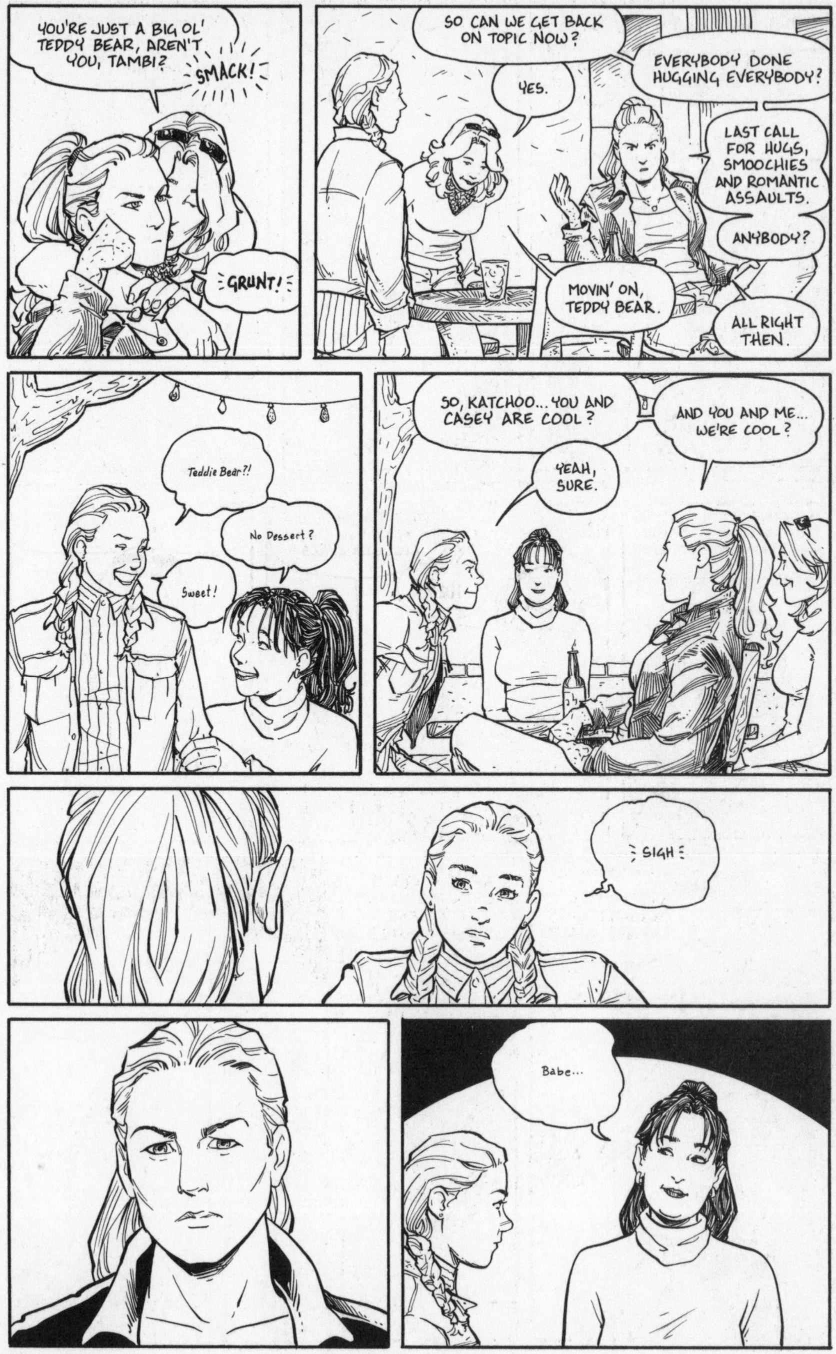
YOU'RE JUST A BIG OL' TEDDY BEAR, AREN'T YOU, TAMBI?
SMACK!
GRUNT!
SO CAN WE GET BACK ON TOPIC NOW?
YES.
EVERYBODY DONE HUGGING EVERYBODY?
LAST CALL FOR HUGS, SMOOCHIES AND ROMANTIC ASSAULTS.
ANYBODY?
MOVIN' ON, TEDDY BEAR.
ALL RIGHT THEN.
Teddie Bear?!
No Dessert?
Sweet!
SO, KATCHOO... YOU AND CASEY ARE COOL?
YEAH, SURE.
AND YOU AND ME... WE'RE COOL?
SIGH
Babe...

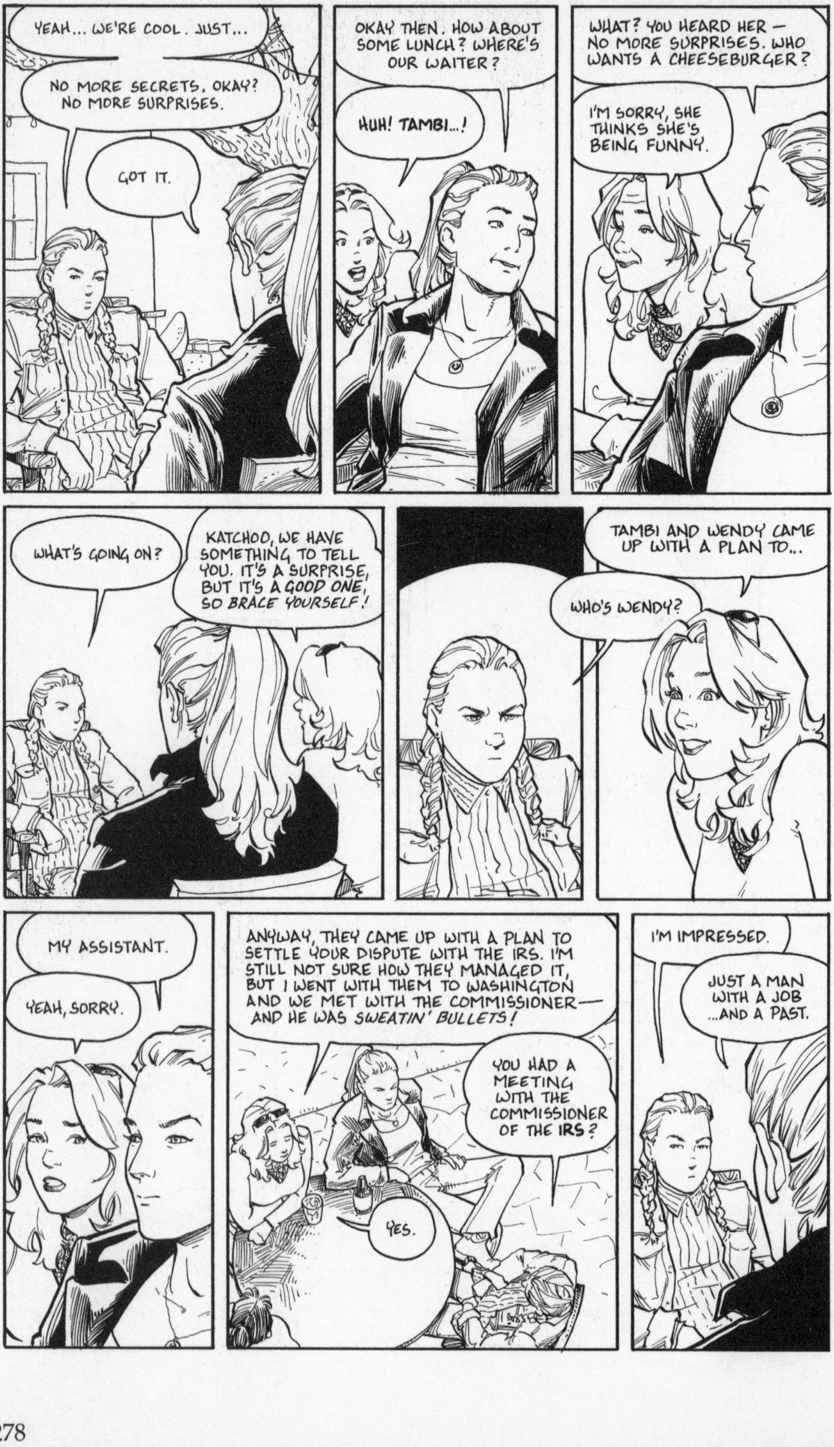
YEAH... WE'RE COOL. JUST...
NO MORE SECRETS, OKAY? NO MORE SURPRISES.
GOT IT.
OKAY THEN. HOW ABOUT SOME LUNCH? WHERE'S OUR WAITER?
HUH! TAMBI...!
WHAT? YOU HEARD HER — NO MORE SURPRISES. WHO WANTS A CHEESEBURGER?
I'M SORRY, SHE THINKS SHE'S BEING FUNNY.
WHAT'S GOING ON?
KATCHOO, WE HAVE SOMETHING TO TELL YOU. IT'S A SURPRISE, BUT IT'S A GOOD ONE, SO BRACE YOURSELF!
TAMBI AND WENDY CAME UP WITH A PLAN TO...
WHO'S WENDY?
MY ASSISTANT.
YEAH, SORRY.
ANYWAY, THEY CAME UP WITH A PLAN TO SETTLE YOUR DISPUTE WITH THE IRS. I'M STILL NOT SURE HOW THEY MANAGED IT, BUT I WENT WITH THEM TO WASHINGTON AND WE MET WITH THE COMMISSIONER— AND HE WAS SWEATIN' BULLETS!
YOU HAD A MEETING WITH THE COMMISSIONER OF THE IRS?
YES.
I'M IMPRESSED.
JUST A MAN WITH A JOB ...AND A PAST.

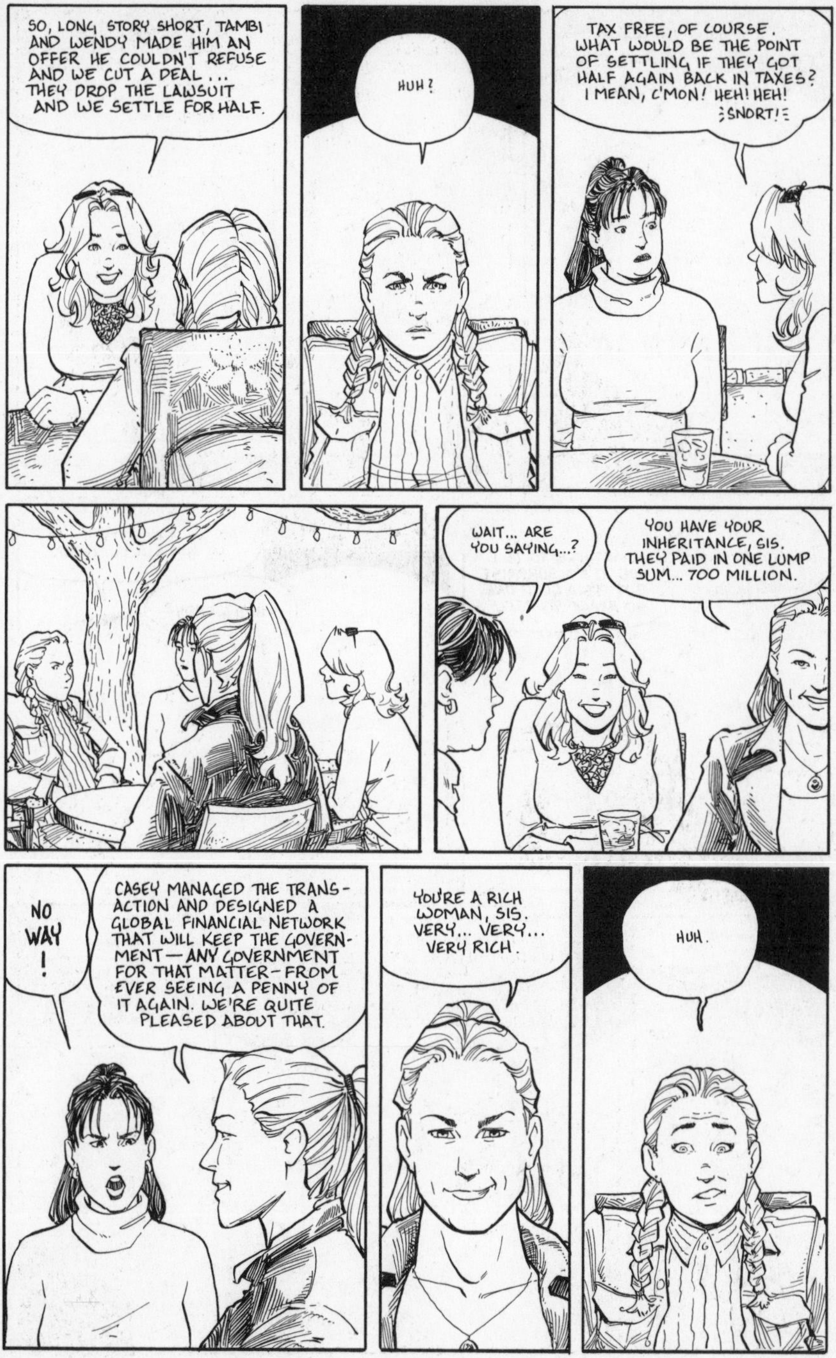
SO, LONG STORY SHORT, TAMBI AND WENDY MADE HIM AN OFFER HE COULDN'T REFUSE AND WE CUT A DEAL... THEY DROP THE LAWSUIT AND WE SETTLE FOR HALF.
HUH?
TAX FREE, OF COURSE. WHAT WOULD BE THE POINT OF SETTLING IF THEY GOT HALF AGAIN BACK IN TAXES? I MEAN, C'MON! HEH! HEH!
SNORT!
WAIT... ARE YOU SAYING...?
YOU HAVE YOUR INHERITANCE, SIS. THEY PAID IN ONE LUMP SUM... 700 MILLION.
NO WAY !
CASEY MANAGED THE TRANS-ACTION AND DESIGNED A GLOBAL FINANCIAL NETWORK THAT WILL KEEP THE GOVERN-MENT—ANY GOVERNMENT FOR THAT MATTER—FROM EVER SEEING A PENNY OF IT AGAIN. WE'RE QUITE PLEASED ABOUT THAT.
YOU'RE A RICH WOMAN, SIS. VERY... VERY... VERY RICH.
HUH.

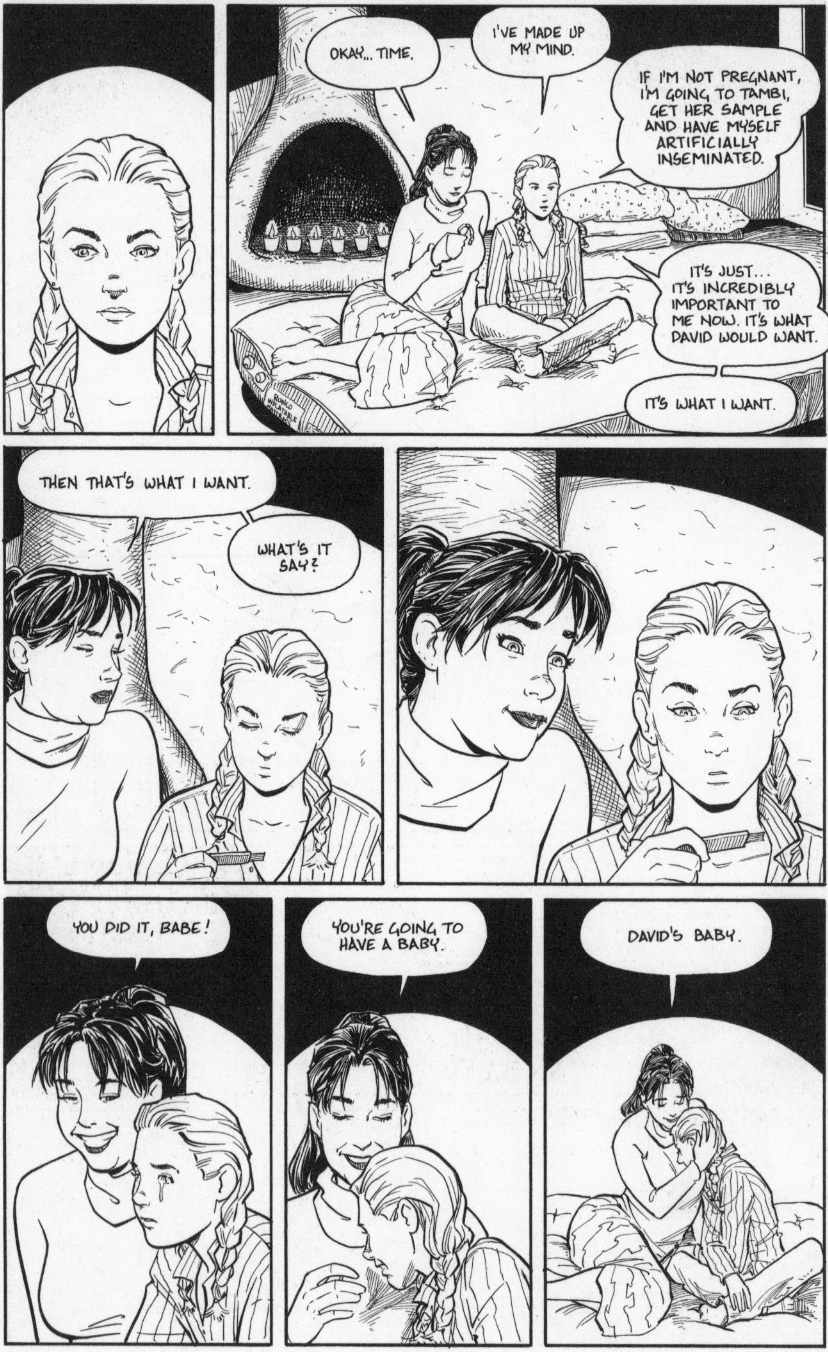
OKAY... TIME.
I'VE MADE UP MY MIND.
IF I'M NOT PREGNANT, I'M GOING TO TAMBI, GET HER SAMPLE AND HAVE MYSELF ARTIFICIALLY INSEMINATED.
IT'S JUST... IT'S INCREDIBLY IMPORTANT TO ME NOW. IT'S WHAT DAVID WOULD WANT.
IT'S WHAT I WANT.
THEN THAT'S WHAT I WANT.
WHAT'S IT SAY?
YOU DID IT, BABE!
YOU'RE GOING TO HAVE A BABY.
DAVID'S BABY.

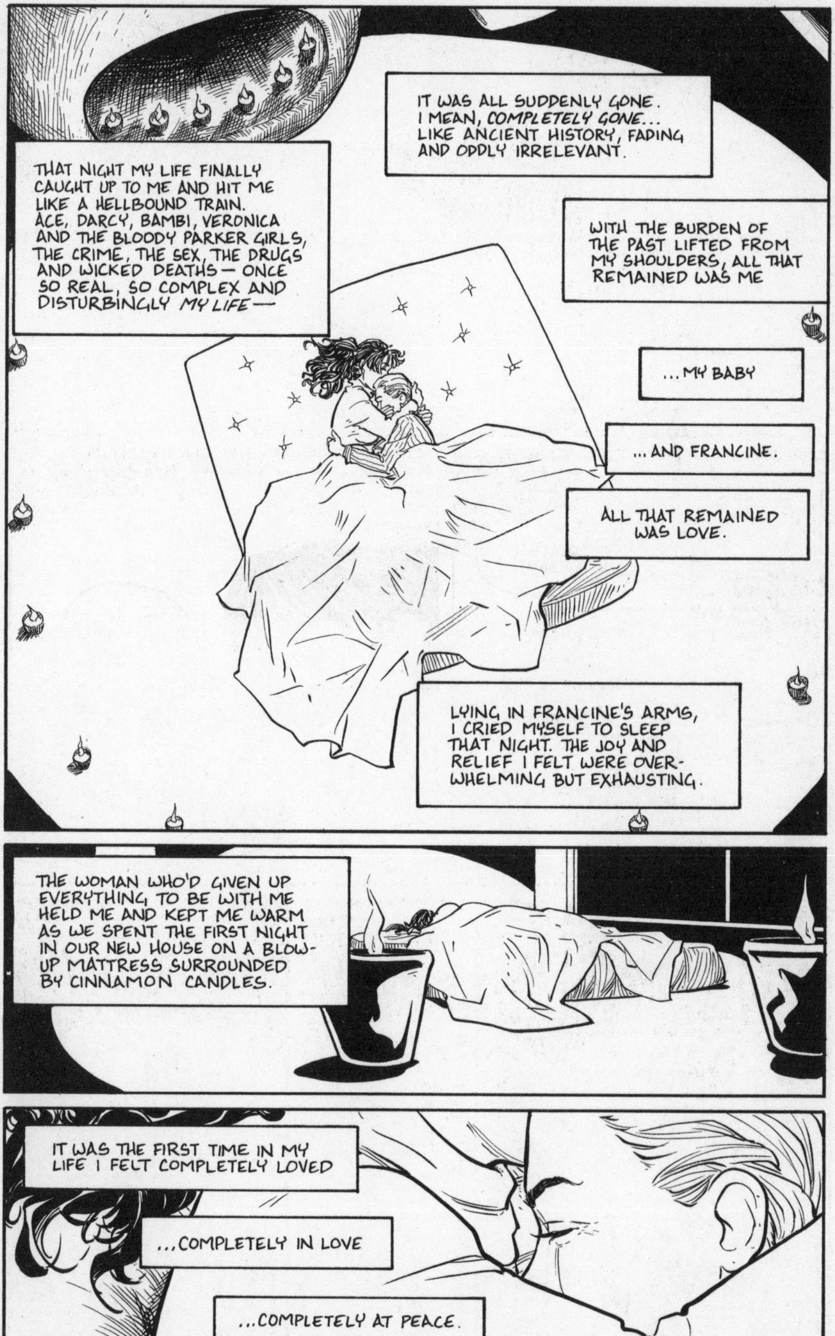
THAT NIGHT MY LIFE FINALLY CAUGHT UP TO ME AND HIT ME LIKE A HELLBOUND TRAIN. ACE, DARCY, BAMBI, VERONICA AND THE BLOODY PARKER GIRLS, THE CRIME, THE SEX, THE DRUGS AND WICKED DEATHS — ONCE SO REAL, SO COMPLEX AND DISTURBINGLY *MY LIFE* —
IT WAS ALL SUDDENLY GONE. I MEAN, *COMPLETELY GONE*... LIKE ANCIENT HISTORY, FADING AND ODDLY IRRELEVANT.
WITH THE BURDEN OF THE PAST LIFTED FROM MY SHOULDERS, ALL THAT REMAINED WAS ME
...MY BABY
...AND FRANCINE.
ALL THAT REMAINED WAS LOVE.
LYING IN FRANCINE'S ARMS, I CRIED MYSELF TO SLEEP THAT NIGHT. THE JOY AND RELIEF I FELT WERE OVER-WHELMING BUT EXHAUSTING.
THE WOMAN WHO'D GIVEN UP EVERYTHING TO BE WITH ME HELD ME AND KEPT ME WARM AS WE SPENT THE FIRST NIGHT IN OUR NEW HOUSE ON A BLOW-UP MATTRESS SURROUNDED BY CINNAMON CANDLES.
IT WAS THE FIRST TIME IN MY LIFE I FELT COMPLETELY LOVED
...COMPLETELY IN LOVE
...COMPLETELY AT PEACE.

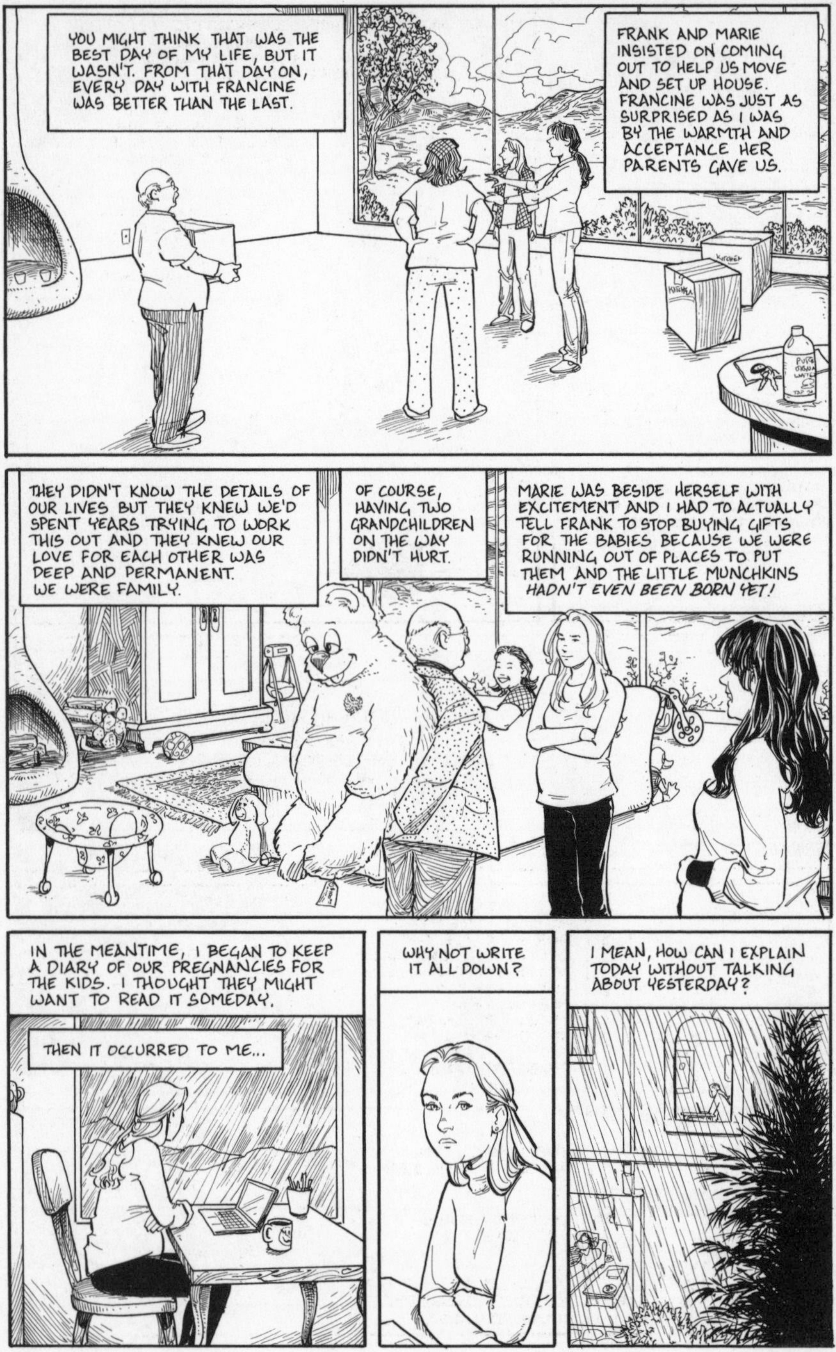
YOU MIGHT THINK THAT WAS THE BEST DAY OF MY LIFE, BUT IT WASN'T. FROM THAT DAY ON, EVERY DAY WITH FRANCINE WAS BETTER THAN THE LAST.
FRANK AND MARIE INSISTED ON COMING OUT TO HELP US MOVE AND SET UP HOUSE. FRANCINE WAS JUST AS SURPRISED AS I WAS BY THE WARMTH AND ACCEPTANCE HER PARENTS GAVE US.
THEY DIDN'T KNOW THE DETAILS OF OUR LIVES BUT THEY KNEW WE'D SPENT YEARS TRYING TO WORK THIS OUT AND THEY KNEW OUR LOVE FOR EACH OTHER WAS DEEP AND PERMANENT. WE WERE FAMILY.
OF COURSE, HAVING TWO GRANDCHILDREN ON THE WAY DIDN'T HURT.
MARIE WAS BESIDE HERSELF WITH EXCITEMENT AND I HAD TO ACTUALLY TELL FRANK TO STOP BUYING GIFTS FOR THE BABIES BECAUSE WE WERE RUNNING OUT OF PLACES TO PUT THEM AND THE LITTLE MUNCHKINS *HADN'T EVEN BEEN BORN YET!*
IN THE MEANTIME, I BEGAN TO KEEP A DIARY OF OUR PREGNANCIES FOR THE KIDS. I THOUGHT THEY MIGHT WANT TO READ IT SOMEDAY.
THEN IT OCCURRED TO ME...
WHY NOT WRITE IT ALL DOWN?
I MEAN, HOW CAN I EXPLAIN TODAY WITHOUT TALKING ABOUT YESTERDAY?

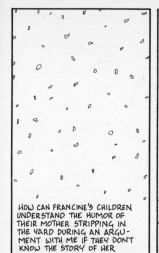

HOW CAN FRANCINE'S CHILDREN UNDERSTAND THE HUMOR OF THEIR MOTHER STRIPPING IN THE YARD DURING AN ARGUMENT WITH ME IF THEY DON'T KNOW THE STORY OF HER STRIPPING IN THE PARK YEARS BEFORE, OR LOSING HER TOGA DURING THE SCHOOL PLAY?

THERE'S A GOLDEN THREAD CONNECTING EVERYTHING WE DO — IT STRINGS THE DAYS TOGETHER AND IS EASILY SEEN WHEN WE LOOK BACK AT WHERE WE'VE BEEN.

I ALWAYS THOUGHT THE THREAD WAS PURPOSE — A SELF-DEFINING CORE — BUT I WAS WRONG.

WHEN I LOOK BACK NOW...

ALL I SEE IS LOVE.

FRANCINE...

TAMBI...

CASEY...

DAVID.

THEIR LOVE CARRIED ME THROUGH A LIFE OF PAIN THAT, IF NOT FOR THEM, WOULD HAVE CONSUMED ME. IF NOT FOR THEM I WOULD BE LYING IN DARCY'S GRAVE... I WOULD BE SCATTERED ACROSS VERONICA'S FIELD... I WOULD BE THE ASHES IN LINDSAY'S HOTEL ROOM.

THERE'S ONLY ONE REASON I'M STILL HERE —

I'M HERE BECAUSE I AM LOVED.

DAVID WOULD WANT OUR CHILD TO KNOW THAT. I WILL TELL HER.

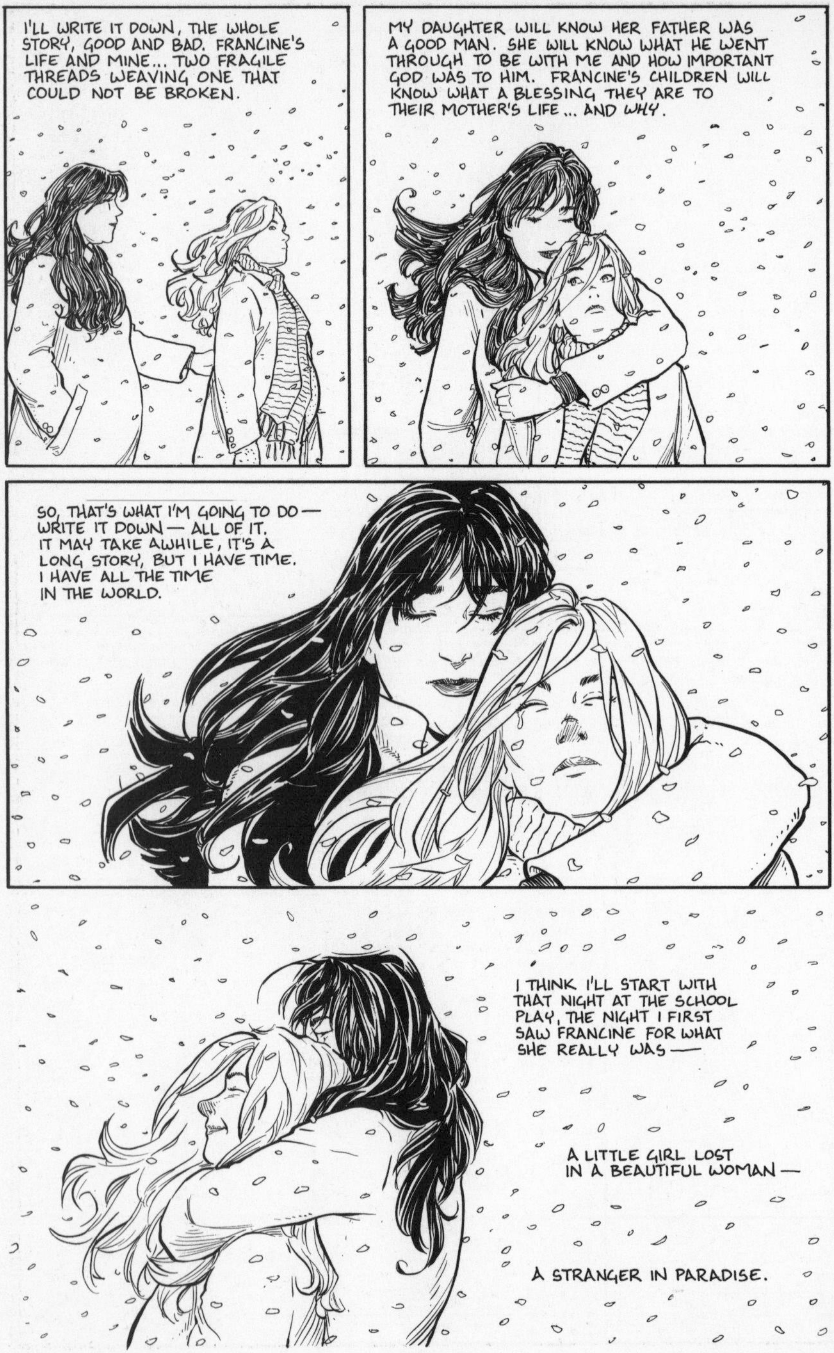
I'LL WRITE IT DOWN, THE WHOLE STORY, GOOD AND BAD. FRANCINE'S LIFE AND MINE... TWO FRAGILE THREADS WEAVING ONE THAT COULD NOT BE BROKEN.
MY DAUGHTER WILL KNOW HER FATHER WAS A GOOD MAN. SHE WILL KNOW WHAT HE WENT THROUGH TO BE WITH ME AND HOW IMPORTANT GOD WAS TO HIM. FRANCINE'S CHILDREN WILL KNOW WHAT A BLESSING THEY ARE TO THEIR MOTHER'S LIFE... AND WHY.
SO, THAT'S WHAT I'M GOING TO DO— WRITE IT DOWN— ALL OF IT. IT MAY TAKE AWHILE, IT'S A LONG STORY, BUT I HAVE TIME. I HAVE ALL THE TIME IN THE WORLD.
I THINK I'LL START WITH THAT NIGHT AT THE SCHOOL PLAY, THE NIGHT I FIRST SAW FRANCINE FOR WHAT SHE REALLY WAS—
A LITTLE GIRL LOST IN A BEAUTIFUL WOMAN—
A STRANGER IN PARADISE.

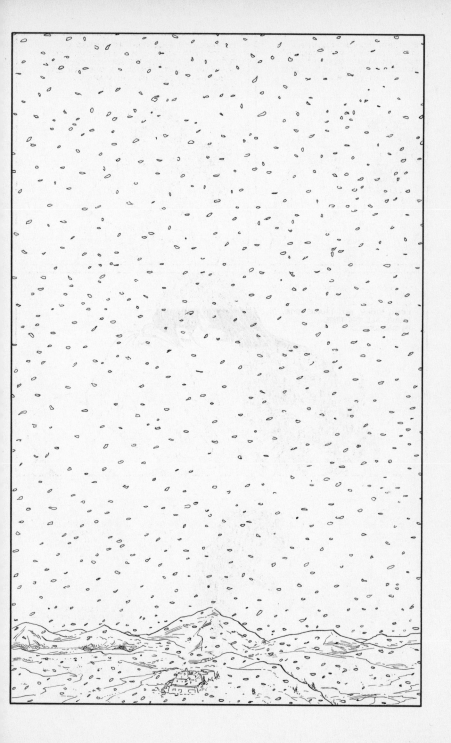

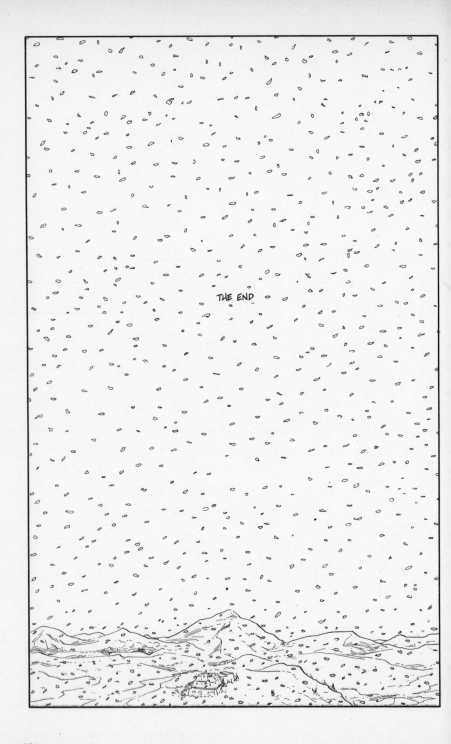

THE END